THE NATIONAL UNDERWRITER COMPANY

2018 TAX FACTS ON INDIVIDUALS & SMALL BUSINESS
Robert Bloink, J.D., LL.M., William H. Byrnes, Esq., LL.M, CWM®

2018 Tax Facts on Individuals & Small Business is the user-friendly, authoritative resource that completely clarifies the vital tax issues facing small businesses and individuals today.

The 2018 edition includes these key highlights:

- A new section on Family Limited Partnerships
- Additional questions on Professional Corporations
- A new section on Estate Planning and Blended Families
- A new section on Estate Planning and Digital Assets (with a 50 state Appendix))
- New questions and Planning Points
- 2018 inflation-adjusted numbers

AF880367

The ideal resource for those advising small business, *2018 Tax Facts on Individuals & Small Business* covers many vital topics, including:

- Healthcare, including new questions on the small employer mandate
- Home Office
- Contractor vs. Employee
- Business Deductions and Losses
- Business Life Insurance
- Small Business Valuation
- Small Business Entity Choices
- Accounting

And this book also delivers clear, concise, and highly practical guidance on:

- Income
- Deductions
- Exemptions
- Tax Credits

Related Titles Also Available:

- Tax Facts on Insurance & Employee Benefits
- Tax Facts on Investments

- Social Security & Medicare Facts
- Healthcare Reform Facts
- Field Guide: Retirement & Estate Planning, Business Planning & Employee Benefits

For customer service questions or to place additional orders, please call **1-800-543-0874**.

2018 TAX FACTS

ON INDIVIDUALS & SMALL BUSINESS

• Accounting • Business Deductions • Blended Families
• Business Life Insurance • Capital Gains and Losses
• Casualty and Theft Losses • Charitable Giving • Choice of Entity
• Digital Assets • Employer Sponsored Health Plans • Fringe Benefits
• Independent Contractors and Employees • Individual Income Taxation
• Net Investment Income and Medicare Tax
• Nontaxable Exchanges • Small Business Succession Planning
• Small Business Valuation • Tax Shelters

Robert Bloink, Esq., LL.M.
William H. Byrnes, Esq., LL.M., CWM®

2018 Edition

Tax Facts on Individuals & Small Business is published annually by the Practical Insights Division of The National Underwriter Company, a division of ALM Media, LLC. This edition reflects selected pertinent legislation, regulations, rulings and court decisions as of October 15, 2017. 2018 IRS inflation adjusted numbers, however are included in this edition.

ISBN: 978-1-945424-88-5

The National Underwriter Company
a division of ALM Media, LLC
4157 Olympic Blvd., Suite 225
Erlanger, KY 41018

Printed in U.S.A.

TABLE OF CONTENTS

TAX FACTS ON INSURANCE & EMPLOYEE BENEFITS – VOLUME 1

APPENDICES AND TABLES

TAX FACTS ON INSURANCE & EMPLOYEE BENEFITS – VOLUME 2

APPENDICES AND TABLES

TAX FACTS ON INVESTMENTS

APPENDICES AND TABLES

TAX FACTS ON INDIVIDUALS & SMALL BUSINESS

APPENDICES AND TABLES

The following Appendices and Tables are available for free download at: www.TaxFactsUpdates.com.

- Property That Can Be Given Under Uniform Gifts to Minors Act (by state)
- Donee's Age When Custodianship Established under UGMA or UTMA Ends
- States Authorizing Durable Power of Attorney; Ages of Majority in the Various States
- Tax Exempt Equivalents
- Numerical Finding List

ABOUT THE NATIONAL UNDERWRITER COMPANY

a division of ALM Media, LLC

For over 110 years, The National Underwriter Company, *a division of ALM Media, LLC* has been the first in line with the targeted tax, insurance, and financial planning information you need to make critical business decisions. Boasting nearly a century of expert experience, our reputable Editors are dedicated to putting accurate and relevant information right at your fingertips. With *Tax Facts*, *Tools & Techniques*, *Field Guide*, *FC&S®*, *FC&S Legal* and other resources available in print, eBook, CD, and online, you can be assured that as the industry evolves National Underwriter will be at the forefront with the thorough and easy-to-use resources you rely on for success.

Update Service Notification

This National Underwriter Company publication is regularly updated to include coverage of developments and changes that affect the content. If you did not purchase this publication directly from The National Underwriter Company, *a division of ALM Media, LLC* and you want to receive these important updates sent on a 30-day review basis and billed separately, please contact us at (800) 543-0874. Or you can mail your request with your name, company, address, and the title of the book to:

The National Underwriter Company
a division of ALM Media, LLC
4157 Olympic Boulevard
Suite 225
Erlanger, KY 41018

If you purchased this publication from The National Underwriter Company, *a division of ALM Media, LLC,* directly, you have already been registered for the update service.

Contact Information

To order any National Underwriter Company title, please

- call 1-800-543-0874, 8-6 ET Monday – Thursday and 8 to 5 ET Friday
- online bookstore at www.nationalunderwriter.com, or
- mail to Orders Department, The National Underwriter Company, *a division of ALM Media, LLC*, 4157 Olympic Blvd., Ste. 225, Erlanger, KY 41018

INTRODUCTION TO 2018 TAX FACTS ON SMALL BUSINESS & INDIVIDUAL INCOME TAXATION

Welcome to the 2018 edition of *Tax Facts on Small Business & Individual Income Taxation!* This year's edition of our newest addition to the *Tax Facts* series continues to offer a comprehensive guide to advising small business and individual clients. This publication enters its fifth year with greatly expanded coverage in a number of key areas as part of our continued commitment to the product and to addressing the most critical issues faced by individual and small business clients today.

Tax Facts on Small Business & Individual Income Taxation is presented in the same easy-to-use question and answer format that has made our earlier volumes (*Tax Facts on Insurance, Employment Benefits and Investments*) the research tools that financial professionals reach for first. We created this volume in 2013 in response to subscriber feedback indicating a need for a concise research tool to guide small business owner clients throughout the entirety of their small business endeavors—from choosing the appropriate business entity to succession planning and valuation guidelines.

This year, we introduced coverage on the important topic of digital assets with a new chapter that outlines the relevant laws governing digital assets and the importance of planning for digital assets in today's increasingly digital society. Second, we added the topic of tax planning for the modern, blended family with fifteen new questions designed to help the advisor with clients contemplating the need to plan for multiple spouses and children from both current and prior marriages. This chapter discusses the types of trust structures that may be useful, as well as basic issues surrounding Social Security planning and transfer taxes. This year's edition also expands our choice of entity chapter by including family limited partnerships (FLPs) as a potential structure. Our new materials on FLPs explain both the advantages and disadvantages of the FLP and its potential usefulness in your clients' tax planning. As always, readers can rely on our industry experts who have added "planning points" throughout the text that allow you to build on the expertise of these practitioners and the real life client scenarios they have encountered through years of practical experience.

In all cases we provide 2018 final inflation adjusted amounts released by the IRS so you have up-to-date information on tax bracket amounts, retirement contribution limits, etc.

Explanations of additional changes throughout the year—including revenue rulings, case law decisions, and legislative and regulatory activity—are available through subscription to our online tax service. Earlier this fall, we created *Tax Facts IntelligenceWeekly*, an electronic newsletter delivered to your email every week on recent rulings, regulations and cases affecting Tax Facts content—including analysis of tax reform issues that could most strongly impact your clients and business.

This edition of *Tax Facts* was developed with the assistance of authors Professor William H. Byrnes and Professor Robert Bloink. Prof. Byrnes is an Associate Dean and Professor at Texas

A&M School of Law l and is the author of numerous books, treatises and scholarly articles. Prof. Bloink is an insurance industry expert whose practice incorporates sophisticated wealth transfer techniques, as well as counseling institutions in the context of their insurance portfolios. He is also a Professor of Tax at Texas A&M School of Law.

ABOUT THE EDITORS

ABOUT THE AUTHORS

Robert Bloink, Esq., LL.M.

Robert Bloink worked to put in force in excess of $2B of longevity pegged portfolios for the insurance industry's producers in the past five years. His insurance practice incorporates sophisticated wealth transfer techniques, as well as counseling institutions in the context of their insurance portfolios and other mortality based exposures. Professor Bloink is working with William Byrnes, Associate Dean of Special Projects of Texas A&M School of Law, on development of executive programs for insurance underwriters, wealth managers and financial planners.

Previously, Mr. Bloink served as Senior Attorney in the IRS Office of Chief Counsel, Large and Mid-Sized Business Division, where he litigated many cases in the U.S. Tax Court, served as Liaison Counsel for the Offshore Compliance Technical Assistance Program, coordinated examination programs audit teams on the development of issues for large corporate taxpayers, and taught continuing education seminars to Senior Revenue Agents involved in Large Case Exams. In his governmental capacity, Mr. Bloink became recognized as an expert in the taxation of financial structured products and was responsible for the IRS' first FSA addressing variable forward contracts. Mr. Bloink's core competencies led to his involvement in prosecuting some of the biggest corporate tax shelters in the history of our country

William H. Byrnes, Esq., LL.M.

William Byrnes is the leader of National Underwriter's Financial Advisory Publications, having been appointed in 2010. He is a professor and an associate dean of Texas A&M University School of Law. He is one of the leading authors and best-selling authors in the professional markets with 30 books that have sold in excess of 100,000 copies in print and online, with thousands of online database subscribers. His National Underwriter publications include Tax Facts, Advanced Markets, and Sales Essentials.

Mr. Byrnes held senior positions of international tax for Coopers & Lybrand and has been commissioned and consulted by a number of governments on their tax and fiscal policy. He has served as an operational board member for companies in several industries including fashion, durable medical equipment, office furniture and technology.

He pioneered online legal education in 1994. In 1998 he developed the first online program to achieve American Bar Association acquiescence. His Master, LL.M. and doctoral programs are leveraged by wealth managers, financial planners and life insurance underwriters.

LEAD CONTRIBUTING EDITOR

Alexis Long, J.D.

Alexis Long formerly practiced corporate law as an associate with the business transactions group at Schulte Roth & Zabel in New York City. She was a corporate, securities and finance editor for the Practical Law Company before moving to Thomas Jefferson School of Law as publications director. Alexis is currently publications director at the Texas A&M School of Law. She holds a J.D. from the University of Michigan Law School.

THE TAX FACTS EDITORIAL ADVISORY BOARD

Jonathan H. Ellis, J.D., LL.M. (Taxation)

Mr. Ellis is currently a Shareholder in the law firm of Plotnick & Ellis, P.C., where his practice focuses primarily on estate planning, estate administration, elder law, and the representation of closely held businesses.

He has a B.S. in Accounting from Pennsylvania State University, J.D. from Widener University, and LL.M. (Taxation) from Temple University. In addition, Mr. Ellis is Executive Editor and Co-author, and along with Stephen Leimberg, et.al., of *Tools and Techniques of Estate Planning*, 16th Edition, The National Underwriter Company, as well as a Co-Author of the 15th Edition. Also, Mr. Ellis is the author of the book "Drafting Wills and Trusts in Pennsylvania", 2010 Edition for PBI Press. Mr. Ellis is also a member of the Editorial Advisory Board for Tax Facts 2012 through 2015, The National Underwriter Company. In addition, he is the author of 30 articles for Pennsylvania Tax Service Insights (LexisNexis Matthew Bender). Finally, he is a former member of the Adjunct Faculty at Villanova Law School where he taught Family Wealth Planning.

Mr. Ellis frequently speaks to a variety of groups, including attorneys, accountants and financial planners throughout Pennsylvania, New Jersey, Delaware and Maryland. Mr. Ellis is also the Course Planner for the PBI Courses "Drafting Wills and Trusts in Pennsylvania", "Wills v. Trusts: A Primer on the Right Tool for Your Clients", "Use of Trusts", and "Post-Mortem Estate Planning", and a participant in a variety of additional courses for PBI. He is also an annual participant in the Villanova University's annual tax conference, cosponsored with the Internal Revenue Service.

He is a member of the Pennsylvania, New Jersey and Florida Bars; the Montgomery County Bar Association; and the Philadelphia Estate Planning Council. Mr. Ellis is also a Fellow of the American College of Trust and Estate Counsel.

Stephen D. Forman, CLTC

Stephen Forman is senior vice president and co-founder of Long Term Care Associates, Inc. (LTCA), a national marketing firm focused exclusively on long-term care solutions. LTCA helped pioneer this field, with roots stretching back to 1972, pre-dating the LTC entry of many of today's carriers.

Mr. Forman has authored more than 50 articles on the topics of long-term care insurance, sales, marketing and regulation, and was chosen by National Underwriter to revise the latest edition of its popular franchise, "The Advisor's Guide to Long-Term Care." He has advised several major carriers in the design phase of their products, helped re-design Washington State's LTC Training requirement, and speaks frequently with the media, including Kiplinger's and Consumer Reports. His columns have been honored as as one of "7 Health Insurance Blogs You Should Know About," and he was recently named one of the "Top 20 Most Creative People in the Insurance Industry."

Mr. Forman graduated magna cum laude from UCLA and has been an active member of American MENSA since 2012.

Karl Frank, CFP®, MSF, MBA, MA

Karl Frank is the President of A&I Financial Services LLC, a Colorado company that helps a small number of successful businesses and families grow and protect their investments and choose how they want to be taxed. Karl and his team provide an array of small business advisory services in the Denver area.

Karl is a leader and a giver in the Denver community. He launched Denver Financial Planning Day in 2009, bringing together the best CFPs in Colorado and providing advice to everyone, whether they are homeless or have millions in their checking accounts. He is the 2014 President of the Financial Planning Association (FPA) of Colorado and has held numerous Director level roles for this, and other, nonprofit organizations. Karl was nominated by his peers as a "Leader in the Profession" and is profiled in the June 2012 edition of the Journal of Financial Planning for "Going the Extra Mile."

He is a Top of the Table member of the Million Dollar Roundtable (MDRT). MDRT membership is recognized internationally as the standard of excellence in the life insurance and financial services business. He was one of less than ten advisors in Colorado to achieve Top of the Table status every year since 2008. Additionally, he is among the top representatives at his broker dealer, Geneos, and a four-time winner of broker dealer of the year.

Karl is also the author of *Go Tax Free* and has written numerous articles that appear in publications such as the *Denver Business Journal* and *Denver Post*. His exit planning work for business owners was featured in *Financial Advisor Magazine* and *Investment Advisor Magazine*.

An accomplished public speaker, Karl spoke at the MDRT annual convention in 2013 about tax planning and retirement strategies to a group of more than 1,000 financial professionals. He frequently appears on local television stations and is also actively involved with the Metro Denver Chamber of Commerce as a member of the CEO Exchange.

Karl's education includes a Certified Financial Planner® designation and three Masters Degrees. He earned a Master of Business Administration and Masters of Science in Finance from the University of Denver, Daniels College and Reimann School of Finance. He also has a Master of Arts in English from the University of Colorado at Boulder. He holds FINRA securities licenses 7, 24, 52, 63, and 65, as well as a life insurance license.

Johni Hays, J.D.

Johni Hays is Vice-President of Thompson and Associates. With almost 20 years' experience as a practicing attorney in charitable and estate planning, Johni Hays is a recognized expert on the subject of charitable gift planning. Johni is the author of the book, *Essentials of Annuities* and co-author of the book, *The Tools and Techniques of Charitable Planning*. Johni serves on the Editorial Advisory Board for the books *Tax Facts on Investments* and *Tax Facts on Insurance and Employee Benefits*. She serves as a charitable planning author of Steve Leimberg's electronic newsletter service, LISI, found at www.leimbergservices.com. Johni has been quoted in the Wall Street Journal and has published charitable planning articles in Estate Planning Magazine, Planned Giving Today, Fundraising Success, Life Insurance Selling and the National Underwriter magazines.

Johni is in demand as a national lecturer on estate and charitable planning, probate, living wills, annuities, life insurance, retirement planning and IRAs, as well as income, estate and gift taxation. Johni has been engaged in the practice of law with an emphasis in charitable and estate planning since 1993.

Prior to joining Thompson & Associates, Johni served as the Senior Gift Planning Consultant for The Stelter Company. Prior to that Johni was the Executive Director of the Greater Des Moines Community Foundation Planned Giving Institute. In addition, Johni practiced estate planning with Myers Krause and Stevens, Chartered law firm in Naples Florida, where she specialized in estate planning.

Johni graduated cum laude with a Juris Doctor degree from Drake University in Des Moines, Iowa, in 1993. She also holds a Bachelor of Science degree in Business Administration from Drake University and graduated magna cum laude in 1988.

Johni is the president of the Charitable Estate Planning Institute and she also serves on the national board of the Partnership for Philanthropic Planning (PPP) formerly the National Committee on Planned Giving. Johni serves on the Technical Advisory Board for the Stelter Company and is a charter member of PPP's Leadership Institute. She is also a member of the Mid-Iowa Planned Giving Council and the Mid-Iowa Estate and Financial Planners Council (president 2007-2008). Johni has been a member of both the Iowa Bar and the Florida Bar since 1993. She resides in Johnston, Iowa, with her husband, Dave Schlindwein.

Jay Katz, J.D., LL.M.

Jay Katz is a tax attorney in Delaware with more than a decade of experience in private practice litigating tax cases and handling audits, collection matters, and offers in compromise for corporate and individual clients. He has earned LLMs in taxation from both the NYU and University of Florida graduate tax programs. During twelve years as a professor at Widener University Law School and Beasley School of Law at Temple University, Jay has taught virtually every tax and estate planning course on the curriculum and was the director of the Widener tax clinic.

In addition to being a coauthor of the 4th Edition of *The Tools & Techniques of Income Tax Planning*, Jay has penned seven published tax articles, including "An Offer in Compromise You Can't Confuse: It is not the Opening Bid of a Delinquent Taxpayer to Play Let's Make a Tax Deal with the Internal Revenue Service," 81 *Miss. L. J.* 1673 (2012) (lead article); "The William O. Douglas Tax Factor: Where Did the Spin Stop and Who Was He Looking Out For?" 3 *Charlotte Law Review* 133 (2012) (lead article); and "The Untold Story of Crane v. Commissioner Reveals an Inconvenient Tax Truth: Useless Depreciation Deductions Cause Global Basis Erosion to Bait A Hazardous Tax Trap For Unwitting Taxpayers," 30 *Va. Tax Rev.* 559 (2011).

Caroline B. McKay, J.D.

Caroline B. McKay is an Associate Counsel of the Advanced Markets department for John Hancock Insurance (USA). In her current position, Caroline provides estate and business planning support to home office employees, field personnel, and producers. Caroline is also a recurring host on John Hancock's weekly JHAM Radio program and a regular speaker at industry meetings around the country.

Caroline is a contributing author of the 16th edition of The Tools & Techniques of Estate Planning by Stephan Leimberg and previously has been published on Wealth Management.com.

Prior to joining John Hancock, Caroline was in private practice in the Boston area where she concentrated her practice on estate planning, probate, business succession planning, and charitable planning for moderate and high net worth individuals and companies.

Caroline received her Bachelor of Arts degree, *magna cum laude*, in History from Colby College in Waterville, Maine, and her Juris Doctor degree *cum laude* from Suffolk University Law School, Boston, Massachusetts. While at Suffolk Law, she was a member of the Law Review and was published in the Suffolk University Law Review. Upon receiving her J.D., Caroline spent one year clerking for the Honorable Chief Justice Paul Suttell of the Rhode Island Supreme Court.

Jayne Elizabeth Zanglein

Jayne Elizabeth Zanglein is a prolific writer on employee benefits. She contributes regularly to journals such as the *ABA Supreme Court Preview*, the *Journal of Taxation of Employee Benefits*, and the *NYU Review of Employee Benefits and Executive Compensation*. Her treatise, *ERISA Litigation*, was published in 2003 and is now in its fourth edition. She serves as an employee benefits expert and neutral in class action cases.

She is the cochair of the Fiduciary Duties Committee of the ABA Section on Labor and Employment Law's subcommittee on Employee Benefits. She has served on various task forces including Governor Cuomo's Task Force on Pension Fund Investments. She has worked on pension fund reform in Ontario and South Africa. She currently teaches law and dispute resolution at Western Carolina University.

OTHER CONTRIBUTORS

Publisher

Kelly B. Maheu, J.D., is Vice President of the Practical Insights Division of The National Underwriter Company, an ALM Media company. Kelly has been with The National Underwriter Company since 2006, serving in editorial, content acquisition, and product development roles prior to being named Vice President.

Prior to joining The National Underwriter Company, Kelly worked in the legal and insurance fields for LexisNexis®, Progressive Insurance, and a Cincinnati insurance defense litigation firm.

Kelly has edited and contributed to numerous books and publications including the *Personal Auto Insurance Policy Coverage Guide*, *Cyberliability and Insurance*, *The National Underwriter Sales Essentials Series*, and *The Tools and Techniques of Risk Management for Financial Planners*.

Kelly earned her law degree from The University of Cincinnati College of Law and holds a BA from Miami University, Ohio, with a double major in English/Journalism and Psychology.

Managing Editor

Richard H. Cline, J.D., is the Manager, Tax and Insurance Content for the Practical Insights Division of the National Underwriter Company, an ALM Media company. He is responsible for both the print and online versions of Tax Facts as well as developing new tax products for our customers.

Richard joined the company in 2013 but has over twenty-five years of tax editing and publishing experience. Prior to joining our team, Richard worked for Lexis-Nexis, CCH, Inc., and PricewaterhouseCoopers.

He has a B.S. degree from Franklin and Marshall College in Lancaster, Pennsylvania, and earned his law degree from Tulane University in New Orleans, Louisiana.

Editorial Services

Connie L. Jump, Sr. Manager, Editorial Operations

Patti O'Leary, Sr. Editorial Assistant

Emily Brunner, Editorial Assistant

ABBREVIATIONS

AAA	Accumulated Adjustments Account
ACA	Affordable Care Act
ACE	Adjusted Current Earnings
Acq. (Nonacq.)	Commissioner's acquiescence (nonacquiescence) in decision
AFR	Applicable Federal Rate
AFTR	American Federal Tax Reports (Research Institute of America, early decisions)
AFTR2d	American Federal Tax Reports (Research Institute of America, second series)
AGI	Adjusted Gross Income
AJCA 2004	American Jobs Creation Act of 2004
AMT	Alternative Minimum Tax
AMTI	Alternative Minimum Taxable Income
ARRA 2009	American Recovery and Reinvestment Act of 2009
ATRA 2012	American Taxpayer Relief Act of 2012
BTA	Board of Tax Appeals decisions (now Tax Court)
BTA Memo	Board of Tax Appeals memorandum decisions
CA or -- Cir.	United States Court of Appeals
CB	Cumulative Bulletin of Internal Revenue Service
CCA	Chief Counsel Advice
Cl. Ct.	U.S. Claims Court (designated U.S. Court of Federal Claims in 1992)
CLASS Act	Community Living Assistance Services and Support Act
COBRA	Consolidated Omnibus Budget Reconciliation Act of 1985
CRTRA 2000	Community Renewal Tax Relief Act of 2000
Ct. Cl.	Court of Claims (designated U.S. Claims Court in 1982)
DOL Adv. Op.	Department of Labor Advisory Opinion
EAP	Employee Assistance Program
EGTRRA 2001	Economic Growth and Tax Relief Reconciliation Act of 2001
EIEA 2008	Energy Improvement and Extension Act of 2008
EOLI	Employer-Owned Life Insurance
ERISA	Employee Retirement Income Security Act of 1974
ERTA	Economic Recovery Tax Act of 1981
ESBT	Electing Small Business Trust
F.2d	Federal Reporter, second series (later decisions of U.S. Court of Appeals to Mid-1993)
F.3rd	Federal Reporter, third series (decisions of U.S. Court of Appeals since Mid-1993)
F.Supp.	Federal Supplement (decisions of U.S. District Courts)
Fed.	Federal Reporter (early decisions)
Fed. Cl.	U.S. Court of Federal Claims
Fed. Reg.	Federal Register
FICA	Federal Insurance Contributions Act

FIFO	First-in first-out
FSA	Field Service Advice
FSA	Flexible spending account
FTE	Full-time equivalent employee
GCM	General Counsel Memorandum (IRS)
GRAT	Grantor Retained Annuity Trust
HCE	Highly compensated employee
HDMP	High deductible medical plan
HIPAA '96	Health Insurance Portability and Accountability Act
HHS	The Department of Health and Human Services
HRA	Health Reimbursement Account
HSA	Health Savings Account
HIREA (2010)	Hiring Incentives to Restore Employment Act
IDGT	Intentionally Defective Grantor Trust
IFRS	International Financial Reporting Standards Accounting Board
IR	Internal Revenue News Release
IRB	Internal Revenue Bulletin of Internal Revenue Service
IRC	Internal Revenue Code
IRS	Internal Revenue Service
IRSRRA '98	IRS Restructuring and Reform Act of 1998
IT	Income Tax Ruling Series (IRS)
ITCA	Installment Tax Correction Act of 2000
JCWAA	Job Creation and Worker Assistance Act of 2002
JGTRRA 2003	Jobs and Growth Tax Relief Reconciliation Act of 2003
KETRA 2005	Katrina Emergency Tax Relief Act of 2005
Let. Rul.	Letter Ruling (issued by IRS)
LIFO	Last-in first-out
LLC	Limited liability company
LLLP	Limited liability limited partnership
LLP	Limited liability partnership
MAGI	Modified Adjusted Gross Income
MERP	Medical Expense Reimbursement Plan
MFDRA 2007	Mortgage Forgiveness Debt Relief Act of 2007
MHPAEA	Mental Health Parity and Addiction Equity Act
MSA	Archer medical savings account
NHCE	Non highly compensated employee
NMHPA	Newborns' and Mothers' Health Protection Act
OASDI	Old age survivor and disability insurance
OBRA	Omnibus Budget Reconciliation Act of (year of enactment)
P.L.	Public Law
PLR	Private Letter Ruling
P&PS Rept.	Pension and Profit Sharing Report (Prentice-Hall)
PBGC	Pension Benefit Guaranty Corporation
PFEA 2004	Pension Funding Equity Act of 2004

PHC	Personal holding company
PHSA	Public Health Service Act
PPA 2006	Pension Protection Act of 2006
PPACA	Patient Protection and Affordable Care Act
Prop. Reg.	Proposed Regulation
PSC	Professional service corporation
PTE	Prohibited Transaction Exemption
QSSS	Qualified Subschapter S Subsidiary
QSST	Qualified Subschapter S Trust
REA '84	Retirement Equity Act of 1984
REIT	Real Estate Investment Trust
Rev. Proc.	Revenue Procedure (issued by IRS)
Rev. Rul.	Revenue Ruling (issued by IRS)
SBJPA '96	Small Business Job Protection Act of 1996
SBWOTA 2007	Small Business and Work Opportunity Tax Act of 2007
SCA	IRS Service Center Advice
SCIN	Self-cancelling installment note
SSBIC	Specialized small business investment company
TAM	Technical Advice Memorandum (IRS)
TAMRA '88	Technical and Miscellaneous Revenue Act of 1988
TC	Tax Court (official reports)
TC Memo	Tax Court memorandum decisions (official reports)
TC Summary Opinion	Tax Court Summary Opinion
TD	Treasury Decision
TEAMTRA 2008	Tax Extenders and Alternative Minimum Tax Relief Act of 2008
TEFRA	Tax Equity and Fiscal Responsibility Act of 1982
Temp. Reg.	Temporary Regulation
TIPA 2007	Tax Increase Prevention Act of 2007
TIPRA 2005	Tax Increase Prevention and Reconciliation Act of 2005
TIR	Technical Information Release (from the IRS)
TRA	Tax Reform Act of (year of enactment)
TRA '97	Taxpayer Relief Act of 1997
TRA 2010	Tax Relief Act of 2010
TRHCA 2006	Tax Relief and Health Care Act of 2006
TTCA 2007	Tax Technical Corrections Act of 2007
URAA '94	Uruguay Round Agreements Act of 1994
US	United States Supreme Court decisions
USERRA '94	Uniformed Services Employment and Reemployment Rights Act of 1994
USTC	United States Tax Cases (Commerce Clearing House)
VTTRA 2001	Victims of Terrorism Tax Relief Act of 2001
WFTRA 2004	Working Families Tax Relief Act of 2004
WHBAA 2009	Worker, Homeownership, and Business Assistance Act of 2009
WHCRA	Women's Health and Cancer Rights Act
WRERA 2008	Worker, Retiree, and Employer Recovery Act of 2008

COMPLETE LIST OF QUESTIONS 2018 TAX FACTS ON INDIVIDUALS & SMALL BUSINESS

PART I: FEDERAL INCOME TAX FOR INDIVIDUALS AND SMALL BUSINESSES

What Is Income?

Exemptions

Deductions

Credits

Social Security

Estimated Tax and Self-Employment Tax

Alternative Minimum Tax

Minors

PART II: CAPITAL GAINS AND LOSSES

PART III: INVESTMENT INCOME TAX AND ADDITIONAL MEDICARE TAX

PART IV: NONTAXABLE EXCHANGES

8631. How does an offsetting short position impact a taxpayer's eligibility to exclude 50 percent of the gain on the sale of qualified small business stock?

8632. Under what circumstances may a noncorporate taxpayer roll over gain from the sale or exchange of qualified small business stock that is held for six months or more?

8633. Under what circumstances can a taxpayer roll over the gain from a sale of stock in a specialized small business investment company?

PART V: INVESTOR LOSSES

8634. What is a tax shelter?

8635. What is an abusive tax shelter?

8636. What are the "at risk" rules with respect to investor losses?

8637. To what types of investment activities do the "at risk" rules apply?

8638. Who is subject to the at risk rules? Do the at risk rules apply to partnerships and S corporations?

8639. How does a taxpayer who is subject to the at risk rules determine how much is "at risk" in an investment?

8640. What rules apply in determining a taxpayer's amount "at risk" when the taxpayer has borrowed the funds that have contributed to the activity?

8641. What rules apply for determining whether a taxpayer has amounts "at risk" when the taxpayer receives qualified nonrecourse financing with respect to the purchase of real property?

8642. What are the passive loss rules?

8643. To which taxpayers do the passive rules apply?

8644. What is a passive activity for purposes of the passive loss rules?

8645. When is a taxpayer treated as materially participating in an activity for purposes of determining whether the activity is active or passive?

8646. What happens if a taxpayer's passive losses for a tax year are disallowed?

8647. What special passive activity rules apply to taxpayers who invest in rental real estate?

8648. How are the passive activities of publicly-traded partnerships treated under the passive loss rules?

8649. Do the passive loss rules apply to casualty losses?

8650. How do the passive loss rules interact with the at-risk rules?

8651. What are the tax results when a taxpayer disposes of interests in a passive activity?

8652. Can a taxpayer deduct interest expenses incurred in relation to property the taxpayer holds for investment?

8653. What is the result if a taxpayer has interest expenses that exceed net investment income for the tax year?

PART VI: CASUALTY AND THEFT LOSSES

PART VII: EMPLOYEES VS. INDEPENDENT CONTRACTORS

PART VIII: BUSINESS EXPENSE DEDUCTIONS

PART IX: BAD DEBT AND WORTHLESS SECURITIES

PART X: BUSINESS LIFE INSURANCE

PART XI: EMPLOYER-SPONSORED ACCIDENT & HEALTH INSURANCE BENEFITS

8752. What ordering rules for reimbursement apply if a taxpayer maintains both an HRA and a health FSA?

8753. Can HRA contributions be made via salary reduction or through a cafeteria plan?

8754. Under the ACA, can a health reimbursement arrangement (HRA) be integrated with health insurance coverage without violating the prohibition on plans that place annual dollar limits on available benefits?

8755. What is a qualified small employer health reimbursement arrangement (QSEHRA)? Can a QSEHRA be used by employers to reimburse employees for the cost of individual health insurance premiums?

8756. What is a health savings account (HSA) and how is it taxed?

8757. Who is an eligible individual for purposes of maintaining an HSA?

8758. Can an individual participate in both an HSA and a health FSA?

8759. What is a high deductible health plan for purposes of an HSA?

8760. What are the contribution limits on an HSA?

8761. What rules govern employer contributions to employee HSAs? Must an employer who offers HSAs to its employees contribute the same amount for each employee?

8762. What are the contribution rules for employers who establish HSAs for employees when an employee has not established an HSA at the time the employer makes contributions or is not eligible to participate for the entire year?

8763. Are there any exceptions to the comparability rules that govern employer contributions to employee HSAs?

8764. Is there a penalty if an employer fails to meet the HSA comparability requirements with respect to contributions to employee HSAs?

8765. Can employers allow employees to roll funds into their HSAs from HRAs or FSAs? What is a qualified HSA distribution?

8766. What is the penalty for making excess contributions to an HSA? How does an excess contribution impact the taxation of distributions from the HSA?

8767. How are funds accumulated in an HSA taxed prior to distribution?

8768. How are amounts distributed from HSAs taxed?

8769. What is the Affordable Care Act? When did its provisions become effective?

8770. What kinds of health plans are governed by the Affordable Care Act?

8771. What tax credit is available for employers who purchase health insurance? When does the credit become available?

8772. What employers are eligible for the new tax credit for health insurance under the Affordable Care Act?

8773. How does the Affordable Care Act impact the use of health savings accounts (HSAs)?

8774. What penalties are imposed by the Affordable Care Act for employers who violate the health insurance nondiscrimination rules?

8775. What is the penalty if an employer fails to provide the required health insurance under the Affordable Care Act?

8776. What is the penalty if an individual fails to obtain the required health insurance under the Affordable Care Act?

8777. When may a taxpayer be exempt from the rule that every taxpayer must obtain a certain level of health coverage or pay a penalty?

8778. How does a taxpayer who may be exempt from the Affordable Care Act requirements obtain the exemption?

8779. What are the requirements to claim the premium assistance tax credit under the Affordable Care Act?

8780. What is "household income" and how does it determine whether an individual is eligible for a premium assistance tax credit?

8781. If a taxpayer is eligible for the premium assistance tax credit, what happens if the household income level or family size changes during the tax year?

8782. Can a taxpayer still qualify for a premium assistance tax credit if exempt from the shared responsibility penalty under the Affordable Care Act?

8783. Is a taxpayer eligible for a premium assistance tax credit if he or she is eligible for, or enrolled in, an insurance plan offered through an employer?

8784. How does an eligible taxpayer obtain the premium assistance tax credit?

8785. How does an employer sponsored opt out arrangement impact a taxpayer's eligibility for the premium assistance tax credit?

8786. If a taxpayer changes health coverage during a year and has a gap in coverage will the taxpayer be subject to the shared responsibility penalty?

8787. Are U.S. citizens who are not U.S. residents subject to the shared responsibility penalty?

Employer Mandate

8788. How does an employer determine whether it is an applicable large employer and subject to the ACA employer shared responsibility provision?

8789. How does an employer that has been in existence for less than one year determine whether it is subject to the ACA shared responsibility provisions?

8790. How does an employer that has a common owner with another employer determine whether it is subject to the ACA shared responsibility provisions?

8791. Will an employer be subject to the ACA shared responsibility provisions if it offers employees and their dependents coverage that is both affordable and provides minimum value, but some of its employees, their spouses and/or dependents obtain coverage through the health insurance marketplace, Medicaid or Medicare?

8792. If an employer offers health coverage to fewer than 95 percent of its full-time employees, how is the employer shared responsibility payment amount calculated?

8793. If an employer offers health coverage to 95 percent or more of its full-time employees, but owes a shared responsibility penalty regardless, how is the amount of the payment owed calculated?

8794. When will employer-provided "wraparound" coverage constitute excepted benefits that are not subject to the ACA market reform provisions?

8795. How does an employer measure an employee's hours in determining whether that employee is a full-time employee for purposes of the ACA shared responsibility provisions?

8796. What constitutes an hour of service for purposes of determining whether an employee is a full-time employee in light of the ACA shared responsibility provisions?

8797. How does a small employer who hires additional employees throughout the year determine whether it is subject to the ACA shared responsibility provisions if some of those employees are part-time employees?

8798. How does a small employer that purchases another business during the year determine whether it is subject to the ACA shared responsibility provisions if the new business is a separate business entity?

8799. If an employer with fewer than fifty full-time employees offers health coverage that is generally affordable and provides minimum value to employees, but for certain employees the coverage is not affordable and so those employees purchase health insurance through the market and receive premium tax credits, is that employer subject to the ACA shared responsibility provisions?

8800. If an employer is subject to the shared responsibility provisions, but all of its employees obtain other health coverage, is that employer still required to offer health coverage?

8801. If an employer offers health coverage to all full-time employees, but not to their dependents, is that employer subject to the ACA shared responsibility provisions?

8802. If a taxpayer owns a business and the only employees are that taxpayer and his or her spouse, is that taxpayer still eligible for the self-employment health insurance tax deduction with respect to health coverage purchased through the health insurance marketplace?

8803. Does a retiree-only health reimbursement arrangement (HRA) provide minimum essential coverage under the ACA market reform provisions?

8804. Can an employer offer high-risk employees a choice between enrollment in a group health plan or cash without violating the Affordable Care Act market reform provisions?

8805. Will an employer receive a notification if it owes a shared responsibility penalty under the ACA?

8806. How does an employer who owes a shared responsibility penalty make a payment?

8807. Are non-profit employers subject to the ACA shared responsibility provisions?

8808. How are employees who work for two separate employers that are under common control treated in determining whether an employer is subject to the ACA shared responsibility provisions?

PART XII: FRINGE BENEFITS

PART XIII: CHOICE OF ENTITY AND THE SMALL BUSINESS

PART XIV: BUSINESS SUCCESSION PLANNING

8920. What tax considerations make the liquidation of an S corporation different than the liquidation of a C corporation?

8921. What gift tax concerns apply in the family business context when planning for business succession?

8922. How can a grantor retained annuity trust be used in family business succession planning?

8923. How can an intentionally defective grantor trust be used in family business succession planning?

8924. What are self-cancelling installment notes (SCINs)? How can SCINs be used in family business succession planning?

8925. Are there any special provisions available to allow the estate of a small business owner to defer payment of estate taxes?

8926. What issues arise when a family partnership is considering its small business succession strategy?

8927. How can a buy-sell agreement be useful in transitioning a family partnership?

8928. What special considerations arise when developing a business succession plan for a family partnership that is formed between a parent and adult children?

8929. How can the existence of preferred stock complicate business succession planning in the context of a family-owned business?

8930. How can the existence of voting stock create adverse estate tax consequences in the context of a transfer of stock in a controlled corporation?

8931. Can a qualified terminable interest property (QTIP) trust be useful in reducing the estate tax burden in a family business' succession plan?

8932. Can a qualified terminable interest property (QTIP) trust be used in a family business succession plan if the business interests at issue are subject to a buy-sell agreement?

8933. Should the transfer of stock to a successor generation pursuant to a family business succession plan be structured as gifts or compensation?

8934. How can a three-year grantor retained income trust (GRIT) be used in family business succession planning?

PART XV: SMALL BUSINESS VALUATION

8935. How is the value of a small business determined? Why is valuing a small business different from valuation in other business contexts?

8936. What general principles govern small business valuation for estate and gift tax purposes?

8937. How does the existence of a buy-sell agreement impact small business valuation?

8938. How are shares of stock valued in a closely-held corporation?

8939. What is the market valuation approach used in valuing closely-held business interests?

8940. What is the income valuation approach that is used in valuing closely-held business interests?

PART XVI: ACCOUNTING

PART XVII: CHARITABLE GIVING

PART XVIII: ASSET PROTECTION TRUSTS

PART XIX: MARRIAGE AND DIVORCE

PART XX: BLENDED FAMILIES

PART XXI: DIGITAL ASSET PLANNING

PART I: FEDERAL INCOME TAX FOR INDIVIDUALS AND SMALL BUSINESSES

8501. Who must file a federal income tax return?

Taxpayers with annual income that equals or exceeds certain threshold amounts are required to file a federal income tax return for the year. The threshold amounts are indexed annually for inflation. In 2018, based on filing status, every taxpayer whose gross income equals or exceeds the following amounts must file a tax return:[1]

(1) Married persons filing jointly–$21,300 (if one spouse is blind or sixty-five or older–$22,600; if both spouses are blind or sixty-five or older–$23,900).

(2) Surviving spouse–$17,150 (if blind or sixty-five or older–$18,450).

(3) Head-of-household–$13,700 (if blind or sixty-five or older–$15,000).

(4) Single persons–$10,650 (if blind or sixty-five or older–$12,250).

(5) Married filing separately–if neither spouse itemizes, a return must be filed if gross income equals or exceeds $4,150 in 2018, regardless of age.

(6) Dependents–every individual who may be claimed as a dependent of another must file a return for 2018 if he has either (x) unearned income in excess of $1,050 (plus any additional standard deduction if the individual is blind or sixty-five or older) or (y) total gross income that exceeds the sum of any additional standard deduction if the individual is blind or sixty-five or older plus the greater of (a) $1,050 or (b) the lesser of (i) $350 plus earned income, or (ii) $6,350.

Taxpayers claiming the additional deduction for blindness may need to attach additional documents to a tax return to verify entitlement to the additional standard deduction.

Certain parents whose children are required to file a return may be permitted to include the child's income over $2,100 on their own return, thus avoiding the necessity of the child filing a return (see Q 8562).

A taxpayer with self-employment income must file a return if *net* self-employment income is $400 or more.

An individual who was subject to wage withholding but did not have gross income in excess of the threshold amounts described above may desire to file a return in order to receive a refund of the withheld taxes. Similarly, an individual not required to file a return may desire to file a return in order to receive a refund resulting from a refundable credit (a tax credit or refund payable to the taxpayer even if he or she had paid no tax), such as the earned income credit.

---

1. IRC Secs. 6012(a), 63(c), 151; Rev. Proc. 2017-58.

8502. Who is allowed to file a joint federal income tax return? Who is eligible to file as a qualifying widow(er) with a dependent child?

Only legally married spouses may file joint returns. As a result of the Supreme Court's decision in the *Windsor* case, the federal government now recognizes same-sex marriages that were legally executed in any U.S. state. As a result, the IRS must apply the tax laws to same-sex spouses in the same way as they are applied to all spouses.

Although the income and deductions of both spouses are reported, a joint return may be filed even if only one spouse has income. If one spouse dies during the tax year, the spouses are considered married for the entire year, and, thus, may file a joint return.

Qualifying Widow(er)

For two years following the death of a spouse, the surviving spouse may file as a "qualifying widow(er)" with a dependent (using the joint filer tax brackets), if he or she satisfies the following requirements:

- The surviving spouse was entitled to file a joint return with the deceased spouse in the year of death, even if a joint return was not filed;
- The surviving spouse has a child or stepchild (excludes a foster child) for whom an exemption can be claimed;
- The child lived with the surviving spouse all year; and
- The surviving spouse paid more than half of the cost of keeping up the home.[1]

Finally, if the surviving spouse remarries, he or she can no longer file as a qualifying widow(er,), and instead must elect to file as either married filing separately or married filing jointly.

8503. Who is eligible to file a federal income tax return as head of household?

An individual who meets the following requirements may file a tax return as head of household:

- Taxpayer is not married or considered married (excluding a qualifying widow(er) with dependent child,[2] see Q 8502);
- Taxpayer paid more than half the cost of maintaining a home for the tax year;
- A "qualifying person" (see Q 8504) lived with the individual for more than half the year (except for temporary absences); and
- Taxpayer is not a nonresident alien.[3]

1. IRC Sec. 2.
2. IRC Sec. 2(b)(1).
3. IRC Secs. 2(b), 2(d).

8504. Who is a "qualifying person" for purposes of determining head of household filing status?

As discussed in Q 8503, in order to claim head of household filing status, an individual must maintain a home for a "qualifying person." A "qualifying person" is a:

1. "Qualifying child" (i.e., son, daughter, or grandchild) who is either:
   (a) Single (even if an exemption cannot be claimed for the person); or
   (b) Married and can be claimed as an exemption.
2. "Qualifying relative" who is the individual's father or mother and for whom an exemption can be claimed.
3. "Qualifying relative" other than a parent (i.e., grandparent, brother, or sister) for whom an exemption can be claimed.[1]

8505. What does it mean to be considered unmarried for purposes of determining filing status?

An individual who is legally married may nonetheless be considered unmarried if the individual meets all of the following requirements:

- Taxpayer filed a separate return;
- Taxpayer paid more than half the cost of maintaining the home for the tax year;
- The other spouse did not live in the home during the last six months of the tax year;
- The home was the main abode of the individual's child, stepchild, or foster child for more than half the year (except for temporary absences);
- Taxpayer can claim the child as an exemption or cannot claim the exemption because the exemption was transferred to the non-custodial spouse.[2]

8506. What are the tax advantages of filing as head of household?

Filing as head of household is much more tax advantageous than filing separately. The main advantages are a higher standard deduction ($9,550 for 2018) and lower tax rates.[3]

8507. What is a taxable year for individual income tax purposes?

The basic period for computing income tax liability is one year, known as the *taxable year*. The taxable year may be either (a) the calendar year or (b) a fiscal year. A "calendar year" is a

1. IRS Publication 17.
2. IRS Publication 17.
3. Rev. Proc. 2017-58.

period of twelve months ending on December 31. A "fiscal year" is a period of twelve months ending on the last day of a month other than December.[1]

Although most individuals report tax liability using a calendar year, it is possible to use a fiscal year. In any event, the year used for reporting tax liability must generally correspond to the taxpayer's accounting period.[2] Thus, if the taxpayer keeps books on a fiscal year basis the taxpayer cannot determine tax liability on a calendar year basis. If the taxpayer keeps no books, however, reporting on a calendar year basis is required.[3] Once the taxpayer has chosen a tax year, it cannot be changed without the permission of the IRS.[4] A principal partner cannot change to a taxable year other than that of the partnership unless the principal partner establishes, to the satisfaction of the IRS, a business purpose for doing so.[5]

A personal service corporation is required to use the calendar year for computing tax liability unless it can establish a valid business purpose for using a different period. The code specifically provides that deferral of income to shareholders does not constitute a valid business purpose.[6]

Under certain circumstances, partnerships and S corporations are required to use the calendar year for computing income tax liability.[7]

A short period (one that is less than twelve months) return is required where (1) the taxpayer changes the taxpayer's annual accounting period, and (2) a taxpayer has been in existence for only part of a taxable year.[8] A short period is treated in the law as a "taxable year."[9]

> *Example:* On June 1, 2018, ASK, Inc., a C corporation reporting its tax liability based on a calendar year, began doing business. Since ASK was not operating for the entire calendar year, a short period return (June 1 through December 31) is required.

If the short period return is made because of a change in accounting period, the income during the short period must be annualized, and deductions and exemptions prorated.[10] However, income for the short period is not required to be annualized if the taxpayer was not in existence for the entire taxable year.[11] For a discussion of the considerations applicable in determining a taxpayer's accounting period, see Q 8947 to Q 8953.

For the final regulations affecting taxpayers who want to adopt an annual accounting period (under IRC Section 441), or who must receive approval to adopt, change, or retain their annual accounting periods (under IRC Section 442), see Treasury Regulation Sections 1.441-0 to 1.441-4.[12]

1. IRC Secs. 441(a), 441(b), 441(d), 441(e).
2. IRC Sec. 441(f)(1).
3. IRC Sec. 441(g).
4. IRC Sec. 442.
5. IRC Sec. 706(b)(2).
6. IRC Sec. 441(i).
7. See IRC Secs. 706(b), 1378.
8. IRC Sec. 443(a).
9. IRC Sec. 441(b)(3).
10. IRC Secs. 443(b), 443(c).
11. Treas. Reg. §1.443-1(a)(2).
12. See Treas. Reg. §§1.441-0 to 1.441-4.

For the general procedures for establishing a business purpose and obtaining approval to adopt, change, or retain an annual accounting period, see Revenue Procedure 2002-39.[1]

In Revenue Procedure 2003-62, the IRS has set forth the procedure under which IRC Section 442 allows individuals (e.g., sole proprietors) filing tax returns on a fiscal year basis to obtain automatic approval to change their annual accounting period to a calendar year.[2]

The exclusive procedures for (1) certain partnerships, (2) S corporations, (3) electing S corporations, (4) personal service corporations, and (5) trusts to obtain automatic approval to adopt, change, or retain their annual accounting period are set forth in Revenue Procedure 2006-46.[3]

8508. How does a taxpayer compute annual tax liability?

A taxpayer computes the amount of tax owed using the following basic steps:

1. Gross income for the taxable year is determined (see Q 8512);
2. Certain deductions are subtracted from gross income (above the line deductions) to arrive at adjusted gross income (see Q 8519 to Q 8521);
3. The deduction for personal and dependency exemptions is determined (see Q 8515 to Q 8518);
4. Itemized deductions are totaled (see Q 8522), compared to the standard deduction and the additional standard deduction, if applicable (see Q 8519), and (generally) the greater amount, along with the deduction for exemptions, is deducted from adjusted gross income to arrive at taxable income;
5. The proper tax rate is applied to taxable income to determine the tax (see Q 8509);
6. The following amounts are subtracted from the tax to determine the net tax payable or overpayment refundable: (1) credits (see Q 8545 and Q 8546), and (2) prepayments toward the tax (e.g., overpayments or credits from a prior tax year carried over, tax withheld by an employer or estimated tax payments).

In some cases, there may be an alternative minimum tax liability. The steps in calculating the alternative minimum tax are explained in Q 8556.

8509. What are the current income tax rates for individuals?

Based on a taxpayer's filing status, the following individual income tax rates are applicable in 2018:[4]

1. 2002-1 CB 1046, *as modified by*, Notice 2002-72, 2002-2 CB 843, *and further modified by*, Rev. Proc. 2003-79, 2003-2 CB 1036.
2. 2003-2 CB 299, *modifying, amplifying, and superseding*, Rev. Proc. 66-50, 1966-2 CB 1260, and *modifying and superseding*, Rev. Proc. 81-40, 1981-2 CB 604. See also Ann. 2003-49, 2003-2 CB 339.
3. 2006-45 IRB 859.
4. Rev. Proc. 2017-58.

Taxable Income				
Tax Rate	Single	Married Filing Jointly Including Qualifying Widow(er) with Dependent Child	Married Filing Separately	Head of Household
10%	$0 to $9,525	$0 to $19,050	$0 to $9,525	$0 to $13,600
15%	$9,525-$38,700	$19,050-$77,400	$9,525-$38,700	$13,600-$51,850
25%	$38,700-$93,700	$77,400-$156,150	$38,700-$78,075	$51,850-$133,850
28%	$93,700-$195,450	$156,150-$237,950	$78,075-$118,975	$133,850-$216,700
33%	$195,450-$424,950	$237,950-$424,950	$118,975-$212,475	$216,700-$424,950
35%	$424,950-$426,700	$424,950-$480,050	$212,475-$240,025	$424,950-$453,350
39.6%	Over $426,700	Over $480,050	Over $240,025	Over $453,350

Based on a taxpayer's filing status, the following individual income tax rates were applicable in 2017:[1]

Taxable Income				
Tax Rate	Single	Married Filing Jointly Including Qualifying Widow(er) with Dependent Child	Married Filing Separately	Head of Household
10%	$0 to $9,325	$0 to $18,650	$0 to $9,325	$0 to $13,350
15%	$9,325-$37,950	$18,650-$75,900	$9,325-$37,950	$13,350-$50,800
25%	$37,950-$91,900	$75,900-$153,100	$37,950-$76,550	$50,800-$131,200
28%	$91,900-$191,650	$153,100-$233,350	$76,550-$116,675	$131,200-$212,500
33%	$191,650-$416,700	$233,350-$416,700	$116,675-$208,350	$212,500-$416,700
35%	$416,700-$418,400	$416,700-$470,700	$208,350-$235,350	$416,700-$444,550
39.6%	Over $418,400	Over $470,700	Over $235,350	Over $444,550

8510. Why are many tax provisions indexed for inflation each year?

Many tax provisions are indexed annually for inflation so that increases in a taxpayer's income that result solely from inflation do not push them into a higher tax bracket or over thresholds that would reduce or eliminate certain tax benefits.

Example: Asher, who is a single taxpayer, earns $92,750 as the manager of a computer superstore. Assume at that income level, Asher is at the very end of the 25 percent tax bracket. At the end of the year, he receives a cost of living adjustment (another term for an adjustment

1. Rev. Proc. 2016-55, 2016-45 IRB 707.

for inflation) that increases his salary to $93,500. If tax brackets were not indexed for inflation, Asher's cost of living raise of $750 would be taxed at 28 percent. Yet, based on inflation, $93,500 of today's dollars is the equivalent of $92,750 of yesterday's dollars. Thus, without indexing, Asher would experience a tax hike. However, by adjusting the tax brackets by inflation, i.e., increasing the 25 percent bracket to $93,700, Asher's tax liability essentially remains unchanged.

The following are examples of tax sensitive items that are indexed for inflation:

- Individual income tax brackets
- Basic standard deduction
- Additional standard deduction (taxpayers sixty-five or older)
- Exemptions
- Alternative minimum tax exemption amount
- Maximum earned income credit
- Overall limitation on itemized deductions
- Education credits (Hope Scholarship, American Opportunity and Lifetime Learning Credits)
- Adoption credit
- Child tax credit
- Low income housing credit
- Phase out of exemptions
- Deductibility of interest on education loans[1]

8511. What indexing factor does the IRS use to make the adjustments for inflation?

The indexing factor (referred to in the IRC as the cost-of-living adjustment) is the percentage by which the Consumer Price Index (CPI) for the prior calendar year exceeds the CPI for a year designated as a reference point in each respective IRC Section. In all cases, the CPI is the average Consumer Price Index as of the close of the twelve-month period ending on August 31 of the calendar year.[2] Thus, for example, in calculating the new tax rate schedules, the minimum and maximum dollar amounts for each rate bracket (except as described below) are increased by the applicable cost-of-living adjustment. The rates (percentages) themselves are not adjusted

1. Rev. Proc. 2014-61, 2014-47 IRB 860, Rev. Proc. 2015-53, 2015-44 IRB 615.
2. IRC Secs. 1(f)(3), 1(f)(4).

automatically for inflation. This method of increase explained above, however, does not apply to the phase out of the marriage penalty in the 15 percent bracket.[1]

The Secretary of the Treasury has until December 15 of each calendar year to publish new tax rate schedules (for joint returns, separate returns, single returns, head of household returns and for returns by estates and trusts) that will be effective for taxable years beginning in the subsequent calendar year.[2] As a practical matter the new numbers for the following tax year are often available as early as October of the preceding year. For a schedule of current tax rates, see Q 8509.

What Is Income?

8512. What is gross income?

Gross income is the starting point in computing the taxable income upon which individuals are subject to income tax. Gross income is a broad concept that includes all income (whether derived from labor or capital) *excluding* those items that are specifically identified by statute, and, thus, not taxable. For example, gross income includes salary, fees, commissions, business profits, interest and dividends, rents, alimony received, and gains from the sale of property – but not the mere return of capital expended by the taxpayer to purchase or improve the property.[3]

The following is a non-exhaustive list of items that are *excluded* from gross income and received income tax-free by an individual taxpayer:

1. Gifts and inheritances[4]
2. Gain (within limits) from the sale of a personal residence (see Q 8593)
3. 50 percent of gain (within limits) from the sale of certain qualified small business stock held for more than five years (see Q 8568)
4. Interest on many bonds issued by a state, city or other political subdivision
5. Social Security and railroad retirement benefits (within limits – see Q 8550 to Q 8553); veterans' benefits (but retirement pay is taxable)[5]
6. Workers' Compensation Act payments (within limits)[6]
7. Death proceeds of life insurance and, as to death proceeds of insurance on the life of an insured who died before October 23, 1986, up to $1,000 annually of interest received under a life income or installment option by a surviving spouse[7]

1. IRC Sec. 1(f)(2).
2. IRC Sec. 1(f)(1).
3. IRC Sec. 61(a).
4. IRC Sec. 102.
5. IRC Sec. 104(a)(4).
6. IRC Sec. 104(a)(1).
7. IRC Secs. 101(a), 101(d).

8. Amounts paid or expenses incurred by an employer for qualified adoption expenses in connection with the adoption of a child by an employee if the amounts are furnished pursuant to an adoption assistance program[1]

9. Contributions to a "Medicare Advantage MSA" by the Department of Health and Human Services[2]

10. Exempt-interest dividends from mutual funds

11. Interest on certain U.S. savings bonds purchased after 1989 and used to pay higher education expenses (within limits)[3]

12. Contributions paid by an employer to Health Savings Accounts (HSAs)[4]

13. Distributions from HSAs used to pay qualified medical expenses[5]

14. Federal subsidies for prescription drug plans[6]

8513. What is adjusted gross income?

Adjusted gross income is broadly defined as gross income minus certain specifically deductible items allowed by the Code. Deductions from gross income, also referred to as above the line deductions, are the most tax beneficial type of deductions because they tend to be taken dollar-per-dollar with fewer limitations than what are known as below-the-line or itemized deductions. Additionally, as a measuring tool, adjusted gross income is important because many thresholds upon which tax benefits phase out or taxes phase in are directly tied to adjusted gross income (for example, subject to the taxpayer being able to itemize, medical expenses are deductible only to the extent that they exceed 10 percent of adjusted gross income for the tax year).

The Code specifically designates which deductions are subtracted from adjusted gross income as above the line deductions. The following is a list of deductions permitted by the Code:

1. Expenses directly incurred in carrying on a trade, business or profession (not as an employee – see Q 8522)

2. The deduction allowed for contributions made by a self-employed individual to a qualified pension, annuity, or profit sharing plan, or a simplified employee pension or SIMPLE IRA plan

3. Certain reimbursed expenses of an employee in connection with employment, provided the reimbursement is included in gross income (if the employee accounts

1. IRC Sec. 137.
2. IRC Sec. 138.
3. See IRC Sec. 135.
4. IRC Sec. 106(d).
5. IRC Sec. 223(f)(1).
6. IRC Sec. 139A.

to his employer and reimbursement does not exceed expenses, reporting is not required)

4. Deductions related to property held for the production of rents and royalties (within limits)

5. Deductions for depreciation and depletion by a life tenant, an income beneficiary of property held in trust, or an heir, legatee or devisee of an estate

6. Deductions for losses from the sale or exchange of property

7. The deduction allowed for amounts paid in cash by an eligible individual to a traditional individual retirement account (IRA), or individual retirement annuity

8. The deduction allowed for amounts forfeited as penalties because of premature withdrawal of funds from time savings accounts

9. Alimony payments made to the taxpayer's spouse

10. Certain reforestation expenses

11. Certain jury duty pay remitted to the taxpayer's employer

12. Moving expenses permitted by IRC Section 217

13. The deduction for Archer Medical Savings Accounts under IRC Section 220(i)

14. The deduction for interest on education loans

15. The deduction for qualified tuition and related expenses

16. The deduction for contributions (within limits) to Health Savings Accounts

17. The deduction for attorneys' fees involving discrimination suits

18. The deduction for certain expenses of elementary and secondary school teachers up to $250 (this provision has been made permanent by the Protecting Americans from Tax Hikes Act of 2015 (PATH)). PATH also provided that the $250 dollar limit will now be adjusted annually for inflation (the 2018 amount remains at $250)

8514. Is a taxpayer's discharge of indebtedness taxable?

Editor's Note: Late in 2015, the Protecting Americans from Tax Hikes Act of 2015 (PATH) was passed to extend the treatment of qualified principal residence indebtedness, discussed below, for the 2016 tax year. The exclusion will also apply to qualified principal residence indebtedness discharged in 2017, if the discharge was pursuant to a contract entered into in 2016. However, as of the date of this revision, Congress has not indicated whether it will extend this treatment for tax years beyond 2017.

If a creditor of a taxpayer discharges all or part of a debt for no consideration, the amount of debt discharged is potentially taxable to the taxpayer.[1] However, such debt discharge is excluded from gross income; and, thus not taxable, if the discharge: (1) occurs in a bankruptcy; (2) occurs when the taxpayer is insolvent and the discharge does not render the taxpayer solvent; (3) the indebtedness discharged is "qualified farm indebtedness;"[2] (4) in the case of a taxpayer other than a C corporation, the indebtedness discharged is "qualified real property business indebtedness;" or (5) the indebtedness discharged is "qualified principal residence indebtedness" (see "Mortgage Forgiveness Debt Relief Act of 2007," below) that is discharged before January 1, 2017 (but see editor's note, above).[3]

Importantly, as stated above, "discharge of debt income" is triggered when a debt is forgiven for no consideration. So, if any consideration is involved, it would not be considered discharge of indebtedness income. Significantly, under those circumstances, the so-called discharge is completely taxable as none of the above exclusions would apply.

> *Example:* Asher borrows $10,000 from his employer. Instead of repaying the loan, his employer forgives the debt after Asher works 200 hours of overtime. In other words, it is as if the employer paid Asher $10,000 for his services; which, Asher, in turn used to repay the loan. Thus, the discharge of the loan is essentially compensation for services, or taxable wage income (not discharge of debt income).

In some cases, even though consideration is involved, the discharge of debt may not necessarily be taxable. For example, suppose a shareholder of a corporation loans $10,000 to the corporation. Subsequently, the shareholder forgives the loan for no consideration. Because the loan comes from someone with shareholder status, the proceeds of the forgiven loan that remain in the corporation are essentially a capital contribution to the corporation. It is as if the corporation repaid the loan to the shareholder, who, in turn, made a capital contribution to the corporation. Contributions to a corporation are not taxable to the corporation. So in this case, discharge of debt that is the equivalent of a capital contribution does not trigger taxable income.[4]

Exemptions

8515. What is the personal exemption?

A personal exemption is essentially a fixed tax deduction adjusted for inflation each year. For tax year 2018, the exemption amount is $4,150.[5] With an exception discussed below, regardless of filing status, each individual taxpayer who files a return is entitled to claim a personal exemption.

Married couples filing joint returns are entitled to claim two personal exemptions (one for each spouse). In addition to a personal exemption, an additional exemption in the same amount (sometimes referred to as a "dependency exemption") is available for each individual a taxpayer may claim as a dependent.

1. IRC Sec. 61(a)(12).
2. See IRC Sec. 108(g)(2), as amended by ATRA and PATH.
3. IRC Secs. 108(c)(3), 108(a)(1)(A), 108(a)(1)(B), 108(a)(1)(C), 108(a)(1)(D), 108(a)(1)(E).
4. Treas. Reg. §1.61-12(a).
5. IRC Sec. 151; Rev. Proc. 2017=58.

There are several special rules that apply to claiming exemptions. A married spouse filing a separate return may claim an exemption for the spouse provided the other spouse has no gross income and is not claimed as a dependent by another taxpayer.[1] A child or other dependent (such as a parent) who files his or her own return may not claim a personal exemption.[2] Generally, the exemption will not be allowed unless the Social Security number of the individual for whom the personal or dependency exemption is being claimed is provided.[3]

8516. Are personal and dependency exemptions for high-income taxpayers subject to being phased out?

Yes. Beginning in 2013, the personal and dependency exemptions of taxpayers with income over certain defined threshold levels are subject to being reduced and potentially phased out completely. The dollar amount of personal and dependency exemptions of taxpayers with adjusted gross income above the threshold levels (adjusted annually for inflation[4]) is reduced by 2 percent for every $2,500 (or fraction thereof; $1,250 in the case of a married individual filing separately) by which income exceeds the threshold levels. Depending upon filing status, at certain adjusted gross income levels, the exemptions are phased out to zero.

For 2018, the following chart illustrates the range of adjusted gross income in which the exemptions are gradually reduced until they are totally phased out:

Filing Status	AGI Threshold At Which Phase Out Begins	AGI Amount At Which Exemptions are Completely Phased Out
Married Joint and Surviving Spouse	$320,000	$442,500
Head of Household	$293,350	$415,850
Unmarried Individuals	$266,700	$389,200
Married Separate	$160,000	$221,250[5]

For 2017, the following chart illustrates the range of adjusted gross income in which the exemptions were gradually reduced until they are totally phased out:

Filing Status	AGI Threshold At Which Phase Out Begins	AGI Amount At Which Exemptions are Completely Phased Out
Married Joint and Surviving Spouse	$313,800	$436,300
Head of Household	$287,650	$410,150
Unmarried Individuals	$261,500	$384,000
Married Separate	$156,900	$218,150[6]

1. IRC Sec. 151.
2. IRC Sec. 151(d)(2).
3. IRC Sec. 151(e).
4. IRC Secs. 151(d)(3), 151(d)(4); Rev. Proc. 2015-53, 2015-44 IRB 615.
5. Rev. Proc. 2016-55.
6. Rev. Proc. 2016-55.

8517. When can a taxpayer claim a dependency exemption for a qualifying child or a qualifying relative?

In addition to the personal exemption, a taxpayer is entitled to an additional exemption (referred to as a dependency exemption) for each individual a taxpayer may claim as a dependent.[1] Under certain circumstances, the taxpayer may claim the exemption even though the dependent files a return. The taxpayer must include the Social Security number of any dependent claimed on the tax return.[2]

There are two categories of dependents: 1) a "qualifying child" and 2) a "qualifying relative."[3]

Qualifying child. The term "qualifying child" means an individual who:

(1) is the taxpayer's "child" (see below) or a descendant of such a child, *or* the taxpayer's brother, sister, stepbrother, stepsister or a descendant of any such relative;

(2) has the same principal place of abode as the taxpayer for more than one-half of the taxable year;

(3) is younger than the taxpayer claiming the exemption and (i) has not turned age nineteen as of the close of the calendar year in which the taxpayer's taxable year begins, *or* (ii) is a student who has not turned age twenty-four as of the close of such calendar year;

(4) has not provided over one-half of his or her own support for the calendar year in which the claiming taxpayer's taxable year begins; and

(5) who has not filed a joint tax return (other than to claim a refund) for the taxable year.[4]

A "child" (including an adopted child) is an individual who is: (1) a son, daughter, stepson, or stepdaughter of the taxpayer; or (2) an "eligible foster child" of the taxpayer.[5] An "eligible foster child" means an individual who is placed with the taxpayer by an authorized placement agency or by judgment decree, or other order of any court of competent jurisdiction.[6]

Qualifying relative. The term "qualifying relative" means an individual:

(1) who is the taxpayer's:

(i) child (who is not otherwise a "qualifying child") or a descendant of a child;

(ii) brother, sister, stepbrother, or stepsister;

(iii) father or mother or an ancestor of either, or stepfather or stepmother;

1. IRC Secs. 151, 152.
2. IRC Sec. 151(e).
3. IRC Sec. 152(a).
4. IRC Sec. 152(c).
5. IRC Sec. 152(f).
6. IRC Sec. 152(f)(3).

(iv) son or daughter of a brother or sister of the taxpayer;

(v) brother or sister of the father or mother of the taxpayer;

(vi) son-in-law, daughter-in-law, father-in-law, mother-in-law, brother-in-law, or sister-in-law; or

(vii) an individual (other than a spouse) who, for the taxpayer's taxable year, has the same principal place of abode as the taxpayer and is a member of the taxpayer's household.

(2) whose gross income for the calendar year in which the taxable year begins is less than the exemption amount;

(3) for whom the taxpayer provides over one-half of the individual's support for the calendar year in which the taxable year begins; and

(4) who is not a qualifying child of the taxpayer or of any other taxpayer for any taxable year beginning in the calendar year in which the taxable year begins.[1]

8518. Who is entitled to the dependency exemption for qualifying children when the parents are divorced or have never been married?

For purposes of determining if a parent is entitled to the dependency exemption for qualifying children, it makes no difference whether the parents were divorced or had never been married.[2] As a general rule, the custodial parent is entitled to claim the dependency exemption. According to the Code, the parent having custody for the greater portion of the year is considered to be the "custodial parent."[3] However, if both parents have custody for equal amounts of time during the taxable year, the parent with the highest adjusted gross income is entitled to claim the exemption.[4]

On the other hand, the custodial parent may release the claim for exemption to allow the noncustodial parent to claim the exemption. In order to claim the exemption, the custodial spouse executes a Form 8332 that the noncustodial parent must attach to the tax return. As explained below, it is also possible for the custodial spouse to revoke the release of the exemption in order to claim it for himself or herself.

Post 2008 Rules for Release and Revocation of Release of Claim to Exemption

For tax years beginning after July 2, 2008, there are prescribed procedures that allow a custodial parent to release his or her claim to a dependency exemption to the noncustodial parent, as well as to revoke the release of the claim to the exemption from the

1. IRC Sec. 152(d).
2. *King v. Comm.*, 121 TC 245 (2003). See also Preamble, REG-149856-03, 72 Fed. Reg. 24192, 24194 (5-2-2007).
3. IRC Sec. 152(e)(1)(B).
4. IRC Sec. 152(c)(4)(B).

noncustodial parent (effectively returning the right to claim the dependency exemption to the custodial parent).

- ***Releasing the Exemption to Noncustodial Spouse***

As mentioned above, the custodial spouse may release the claim to the exemption by executing a Form 8332 (Release/Revocation of Claim to Exemption for Child by Custodial Parent). Form 8332 provides the custodial parent with the option of releasing the right to claim the exemption for a single tax year or for multiple tax years. In the alternative, the custodial spouse may execute a conforming written document that includes the same information as it appears on a Form 8332. However, such written declaration must have been executed for the *sole purpose* of releasing the exemption to the noncustodial spouse for one or more tax years. Importantly, this means that attaching a court document such as a decree, or a divorce or separation agreement, would not be an acceptable written instrument even if it contains all of the required information.[1] Also, in order to claim the exemption, the noncustodial parent must attach the Form 8332 or written declaration to his or her tax return.

- ***Revoking the Release of the Exemption to Noncustodial Spouse***

According to the regulations, the custodial parent has the unilateral right to revoke the release of the exemption from the noncustodial spouse in order to claim it for himself or herself. To do so, the custodial parent is required to provide a noncustodial parent with written notice of the intent to revoke and make reasonable efforts to deliver such notice to the noncustodial parent. The revocation is effective no earlier than the tax year *following* the calendar year in which the custodial parent delivered or made reasonable efforts to deliver the notice to the noncustodial spouse.[2]

> *Example:* Ashley and Asher are divorced parents with one child. Prior to tax year 2017, Ashley had executed a Form 8332 releasing the claim to the dependency exemption to Asher through tax year 2019. In February 2018, Ashley provides Asher written notice of her intent to revoke the release. Even though Asher received written notice of Ashley's intent to revoke the release, it would not be effective earlier than tax year 2018. Thus, for tax year 2017, Asher remains entitled to claim the dependency exemption.

Similar to the release, the revocation is made on Form 8332 or a separate conforming written document containing the same information contained on Form 8332. If a separate written document is used, it must be executed for the sole purpose of revoking the release. Similar to the release, the revocation must specify the year or years in which it is to be in effect. To re-claim the exemption, the custodial spouse must attach the Form 8832 or conforming document to his or her return.[3]

1. Treas. Reg. §1.152-4(e).
2. Treas. Reg. §1.152-4(e)(3).
3. Treas. Reg. §1.152-4(e)(3).

Deductions

8519. What is the standard deduction?

The standard deduction is one of two "below-the-line" deduction options available to taxpayers. In other words, once a taxpayer determines adjusted gross income (gross income minus above the line deductions), the taxpayer may also deduct the sum of their exemptions and the greater of 1) the standard deduction; or 2) the sum of their itemized deductions (see Q 8522).[1]

The standard deduction for the 2018 tax year is $13,000 for married taxpayers filing jointly and surviving spouses, $9,550 for heads of households, and $6,500 for single taxpayers and married taxpayers filing separately.[2] The standard deduction for the 2017 tax year was $12,700 for married taxpayers filing jointly and surviving spouses, $9,350 for heads of households, and $6,350 for single taxpayers and married taxpayers filing separately.[3] The standard deduction is adjusted annually for inflation.[4]

Taxpayers who do not itemize and who are age 65 or older or blind are entitled to increase their standard deduction. In 2018, taxpayers who are married or are surviving spouses are each entitled to an additional deduction of $1,300, if age 65 or older, as well as an additional $1,300 deduction if blind. The additional standard deduction is $1,600 for unmarried taxpayers age 65 or older as well as $1,600 for unmarried blind taxpayers.[5] The additional amounts for elderly and blind taxpayers are indexed for inflation.[6]

8520. What taxpayers are ineligible to use the standard deduction?

The following taxpayers are ineligible for the standard deduction and unless they have itemized deductions, have no available "below-the-line" deductions:

(1) married taxpayers filing separately, if either spouse itemizes,[7]

(2) non-resident aliens,

(3) taxpayers filing a short year (less than 12 months) return because of a change in their annual accounting period, and

(4) estates or trusts, common trust funds, or partnerships.[8]

If a taxpayer dies within the tax year, the standard deduction is unaffected.

1. IRC Sec. 63.
2. IRC Sec. 63(c); Rev. Proc. 2016-55; Rev. Proc. 2017-58.
3. IRC Sec. 63(c); Rev. Proc. 2016-55.
4. IRC Sec. 63(c)(4).
5. IRC Sec. 63(f); IR-2015-119.
6. IRC Sec. 63(c)(4).
7. See, e.g., Legal Memorandum 200030023.
8. IRC Sec. 63(c)(6).

Example: Ashley, an unmarried individual, dies on February 1, 2018. As a result, her final tax year is only 32 days. However, even though Ashley died early in the tax year, in filing Ashley's final Form 1040, the executor or administrator of Ashley's estate would deduct the entire standard deduction for a single filer.

8521. What is the standard deduction for a taxpayer who may be claimed as a dependent by another taxpayer?

For taxable years beginning in 2017 and 2018, the standard deduction for an individual who may be claimed as a dependent by another taxpayer is the greater of $1,050 or the sum of $350 and the dependent's earned income.[1] These dollar amounts are adjusted for inflation.[2]

Planning Point: Self-employed and small business owners may be able to shift income taxable at their higher tax brackets to their lower tax bracket children by employing them in the business. This way the children's wage income would be taxed at their lower rates. The work must be legitimate and the pay must be reasonable, although it can be at the higher end of the reasonable scale.

8522. What are itemized deductions and how are they deducted?

As discussed in Q 8519, taxpayers are entitled to a "below-the-line" deduction, i.e., a deduction from adjusted gross income in arriving at taxable income, of the greater of 1) the applicable standard deduction (including the additional standard deduction for taxpayers who are blind and/or age 65 or older based on filing status); or 2) the sum of their itemized deductions. So, in order to make a determination as to which amount to deduct, the taxpayer must total all deductible items that qualify as itemized deductions. If the total amount of itemized deductions exceeds the standard deduction, the taxpayer deducts that larger sum.

The following is a non-exhaustive list of the itemized deductions:

...Interest (including mortgage interest on a principal residence), within limits (see Q 8526);

...Personal expenses for the production or collection of taxable income, within limits, or in conjunction with the determination, collection or refund of any tax (but some of these expenses may be considered "miscellaneous itemized deductions" (see Q 8525)). However, certain business expenses and expenses for the production of rents and royalties are above the line deductions rather than itemized deductions;

...Personal taxes of the following types: state, local and foreign real property taxes; state and local personal property taxes; state, local and foreign income, war profits and excess profits taxes, and the generation-skipping tax imposed on income distributions. If taxes other than these are incurred in connection with the acquisition or disposition of property, they must be treated as part of the cost of such property (included in basis) or as a reduction in the amount realized on the disposition;[3]

1. IRC Sec. 63(c)(5); Rev. Proc. 2016-55.
2. IRC Sec. 63(c)(4).
3. IRC Sec. 164(a).

...Uncompensated personal casualty and theft losses. These are deductible only to the extent that the aggregate amount of uncompensated losses in excess of $100 (for each casualty or theft) exceeds 10 percent of adjusted gross income. The taxpayer must file a timely insurance claim for damage to property that is not business or investment property or else the deduction is disallowed to the extent that insurance would have provided compensation.[1] Uncompensated casualty and theft losses in connection with a taxpayer's business or in connection with the production of income are deductible in full. For more on casualty losses, see Q 8656 to Q 8667;

...Contributions to charitable organizations, within certain limitations (see Q 8534 to Q 8539);

...Unreimbursed medical and dental expenses, and expenses for the purchase of prescribed drugs or insulin incurred by the taxpayer for himself and his spouse and dependents, to the extent that such expenses exceed 10 percent of adjusted gross income (7.5 percent of adjusted gross income for taxpayers sixty-five or older through 2016) (see Q 8540);

...Unreimbursed expenses of an employee connected with his employment. Generally, such expenses are "miscellaneous itemized deductions" (see Q 8525);

...Federal estate taxes and generation-skipping transfer taxes paid on "income in respect of a decedent."

8523. Are state and local sales taxes deductible?

Under AJCA 2004, taxpayers could elect to deduct state and local general sales taxes instead of state and local income taxes when they itemized deductions.[2] This option was available for tax years 2004 through 2011.[3] ATRA extended this option through 2013, with retroactive application to the 2012 tax year. This provision was made permanent by the Protecting Americans against Tax Hikes Act of 2015 (PATH).

8524. What are miscellaneous itemized deductions? To what extent are they deductible?

Editor's Note: The GOP tax reform framework calls for eliminating all miscellaneous itemized deductions, with the exception of the mortgage interest deduction and the charitable contributions deduction.

"Miscellaneous itemized deductions" are a subset of itemized deductions *other than* the regular itemized deductions for (1) interest, (2) taxes, (3) non-business casualty losses and gambling losses, (4) charitable contributions, (5) medical and dental expenses, (6) impairment-related work expenses for handicapped employees, (7) estate taxes on income in respect of a decedent,

1. IRC Sec. 165(h)(5)(E).
2. IRC Sec. 164(b)(5)(A).
3. IRC Sec. 164(b)(5)(I), as amended by TEAMTRA 2008, ATRA and PATH.

(8) certain short sale expenses, (9) certain adjustments under the IRC claim of right provisions, (10) unrecovered investment in an annuity contract, (11) amortizable bond premium, and (12) certain expenses of cooperative housing corporations.[1]

Examples of miscellaneous itemized deductions include unreimbursed employee business expenses, such as professional society dues or job hunting expenses, and expenses for the production of income, such as investment advisory fees or the cost for storage of taxable securities in a safe deposit box.[2]

"Miscellaneous itemized deductions" are included in the itemized deduction pool only to the extent that the aggregate of all miscellaneous itemized deductions for the tax year exceeds 2 percent of adjusted gross income.[3] Expenses that relate to both a trade or business activity (an above-the-line deduction) and a production of income or tax preparation activity must be allocated between the activities on a reasonable basis.[4]

> *Example:* In 2017, Henry, a single taxpayer, has adjusted gross income of $100,000. His deductible mortgage interest and property taxes (regular itemized deductions) total $4,050. In addition, Henry has unreimbursed employee business expenses of $2,500. Because unreimbursed employee business expenses are miscellaneous itemized deductions, they are deductible and added to the total of Henry's other regular itemized deductions only to extent they exceed 2 percent of his adjusted gross income. In this case, Henry's miscellaneous itemized deductions of $2,500 exceed $2,000 (2 percent of adjusted gross income) by $500. As a result, Henry's total itemized deductions would be $4,550 ($4,050 plus $500). However, because the standard deduction for a single filer is $6,350, Henry would deduct the higher standard deduction amount.

A taxpayer may not avoid the treatment of an item that would be a miscellaneous itemized deduction by virtue of it passing through to him or her through an entity such as a partnership or S corporation.[5]

> *Example:* Ashley is a 50 percent partner in a partnership engaging in an activity for the production of income. In 2017, Ashley's allocable share of Section 212 production of income deductible expenses is $200. Even though Ashley did not directly incur that expense, she must treat the $200 deductible items as a miscellaneous itemized deduction. Thus, she must add the $200 to all her other miscellaneous deductions to determine whether the aggregate amount of those items exceeds 2 percent of her adjusted gross income.[6]

8525. Are the itemized deductions of high-income taxpayers subject to phase-out?

Yes. The aggregate of most itemized deductions is reduced dollar-for-dollar by the lesser of (1) 3 percent of the individual's adjusted gross income that exceeds $266,700 for a single filer in 2018 ($320,000 in the case of a married taxpayer filing jointly, $293,350 for heads of household, and $160,000 for married taxpayers filing separately) or (2) 80 percent of the amount of such itemized deductions otherwise allowable for the taxable year.[7] In 2017, the threshold levels were

1. IRC Sec. 67(b).
2. Temp. Treas. Reg. §1.67-1T(a)(1).
3. IRC Sec. 67(a).
4. Temp. Treas. Reg. §1.67-1T(c).
5. IRC Sec. 67(c)(1); Temp. Treas. Reg. §1.67-2T.
6. Temp. Treas. Reg. §1.67-2T(b)(2).
7. IRC Sec. 68(a).

$261,500 for a single filer ($313,800 in the case of a married taxpayer filing jointly, $287,650 for heads of household, and $156,900 for married taxpayers filing separately).[1] The threshold income levels for determining the phaseout are adjusted annually for inflation.[2]

The phase-out of the value of itemized deductions is not applicable to medical expenses deductible under IRC Section 213, investment interest deductible under IRC Section 163(d), or certain casualty loss deductions.[3] The limitation also is not applicable to estates and trusts.[4] For purposes of certain other calculations, such as the limits on deduction of charitable contributions or the 2 percent floor on miscellaneous itemized deductions, the limitations on each separate category of deductions are applied *before* the overall ceiling on itemized deductions is applied.[5] The deduction limitation is not taken into account in the calculation of the alternative minimum tax.[6]

8526. What types of interest are deductible?

Whether or not interest is deductible depends on its classification as one of the following types of interest: (1) investment interest, (2) trade or business interest, (3) qualified residence interest, (4) interest relating to passive activities, (5) interest incurred on extended payment of estate tax, (6) interest on education loans or (7) personal interest. The deductibility of these seven types of interest is discussed in detail in Q 8527 to Q 8533.

The proper allocation of interest generally depends on the use to which the loan proceeds are put, except in the case of certain qualified residence interest. Detailed rules for classifying interest by tracing the use of loan proceeds are contained in temporary regulations.[7]

In some cases, the Code may specifically disallow the deductibility of interest. For example, no deduction is allowed for interest paid on a loan used to buy or carry tax-exempt securities.[8] The rationale for the disallowance is to prevent the taxpayer from receiving an unwarranted double tax benefit (first, the exclusion of the interest from gross income; and, second, a deduction for the interest on a loan used to purchase the underlying tax-exempt security).

Interest expense that is deductible under the rules outlined in Q 8527 to Q 8533 may also be subject to the additional limitations on itemized deductions (unless it is investment interest, which is not subject to that provision). See Q 8524 for a discussion of the limits on itemized deductions.

1. Rev. Proc. 2016-55.
2. IRC Sec. 68(b); as amended by ATRA, Sec. 101(2)(b); Rev. Proc. 2017-58.
3. IRC Sec. 68(c).
4. IRC Sec. 68(e).
5. IRC Sec. 68(d).
6. IRC Sec. 56(b)(1)(F).
7. See Temp. Treas. Reg. §1.163-8T.
8. IRC Sec. 265.

8527. What is investment interest and can individual taxpayers deduct investment interest?

Any interest expense on indebtedness properly allocable to property held for investment is classified as investment interest.[1] However, the investment interest deduction is limited, as investment interest is deductible only to the extent of net investment income. Any excess is carried forward to subsequent tax years subject to the same terms and conditions. Net investment income is investment income less investment expenses (other than interest). Investment income is income from property held for investment such as interest, dividends, annuity income and royalties.[2]

Example: In 2018, Asher has net investment income of $7,500 and investment interest of $10,000. Because the deductibility of investment interest is limited to net investment income, only $7,500 of the $10,000 of investment interest is deductible. The excess disallowed investment interest of $2,500 is carried forward to subsequent years.[3]

Net long-term capital gain and "qualified dividend" income are excluded from the definition of net investment income. These types of income are taxed at a maximum rate of 15 percent or 20 percent depending on the taxpayer's overall income (i.e., the 20 percent rate applies to high income taxpayers). On the other hand, other types of investment income such as non-qualified dividends, interest income, etc. are taxed at ordinary income rates (up to 39.6 percent). However, if a taxpayer elects to treat long-term capital gains or qualified dividends as ordinary income (waives the application of the 15 percent and 20 percent maximum rates), that income does count as investment income.

Example: Assume the same facts as the example above, except that Asher has a combined $2,500 of qualified dividends and net long-term capital gain. If Asher makes an election waiving the 15 percent and 20 percent maximum rates with respect to that income (meaning it could be taxed at a rate as high as 39.6 percent), he may include it as investment income. If he does, Asher can deduct the full $10,000 of investment interest expense because adding the $2,500 of qualified dividends and net long-term capital gain to the $7,500 of other net investment income creates a total offset.[4]

8528. What is deductible trade or business interest?

Trade or business interest, as the name suggests, includes any interest incurred in the conduct of a trade or business. So, for example, if a taxpayer borrows funds for working capital in a trade or business, the interest payments would be deductible.

8529. What is deductible qualified residence interest?

Qualified residence interest is interest paid or accrued during the taxable year on debt that is secured by the taxpayer's qualified residence and that is either (a) "acquisition indebtedness" (that is, debt incurred to acquire, construct or substantially improve the qualified residence, or any refinancing of such debt), or (b) "home equity indebtedness" (any other indebtedness secured by the qualified residence).

1. IRC Sec. 163(d)(3).
2. IRS Publication 550 (20162016).
3. IRC Sec. 163(d).
4. IRC Sec. 1(h)(11)(D)(i).

A "qualified residence" is the taxpayer's principal residence and one other residence that is essentially a second home.[1] A taxpayer may only treat an aggregate of $1,000,000 as acquisition indebtedness (spread over the two residences), *but* the amount of refinanced debt that may be treated as acquisition indebtedness is limited to the amount of debt being refinanced. The aggregate amount that may be treated as "home equity indebtedness" (that is, borrowing against the fair market value of the home, less the acquisition indebtedness to borrow against the "equity" in the home) is $100,000,[2] or a combined maximum of $1,100,000 of indebtedness.

> *Example*: In 2016, Ashley and Asher, a married couple, purchase a principal residence for $400,000 financed in part by a $300,000 home acquisition loan. In 2018, pursuant to a refinancing, they borrow $350,000 to pay off the initial $300,000 loan and the other $50,000 to purchase two cars. Of the amount borrowed, only $300,000 (the amount necessary to pay off the initial acquisition loan) is treated as acquisition debt. The other $50,000 does not qualify as acquisition indebtedness. However, assuming the residence is worth $400,000 (meaning there is $100,000 of equity), the $50,000 additional indebtedness would qualify as home equity indebtedness. As a result, the interest on the total indebtedness would be deductible as qualified residence interest.

8530. To what extent is the deductibility of interest limited by the application of the passive activity loss rules?

A passive activity is generally an activity that involves the conduct of a trade or business in which the taxpayer does not materially participate, or any rental activity.[3] Generally, the deductibility of passive expenses is limited to the amount of the taxpayer's passive income for the year. The excess, passive loss, is not deductible. Instead, it is carried over to subsequent tax years for potential deductibility against passive income generated in those years. The same rules apply to the deductibility of interest related to a passive activity. As a result, to the extent that otherwise deductible interest is related to a passive activity, some or all of the interest deductions that are allocated to those passive activities may be disallowed.[4] See Q 8642 to Q 8651 for a detailed discussion of the passive loss rules.

8531. Is the interest on extended payments of estate tax deductible?

If an extension to pay federal estate tax over a period of time is in effect, the interest portion of the payment is deductible.[5]

8532. Is the interest on education loans deductible?

An above-the-line deduction is available to certain taxpayers for interest paid on a "qualified education loan."[6] In 2018, the deduction is limited to $2,500 of such interest. However, the deduction is phased out for taxpayers with modified AGI between $65,000 and $80,000 ($135,000 and $165,000 for joint returns). Certain other requirements must be met for the deduction to be available.[7]

1. IRC Sec. 164(h)(4)(A).
2. IRC Sec. 164(h)(3).
3. IRC Sec. 469.
4. IRC Sec. 469, Treas. Reg. §1.163-8T.
5. IRC Sec. 163(h)(2).
6. IRC Secs. 163(h)(2)(F), 221.
7. See IRC Sec. 221; Treas. Reg. §1.221-1.

The individual claiming the deduction must be legally obligated to make the interest payments under the terms of the loan. If a third party who is not legally obligated to make a payment of interest on a qualified education loan makes an interest payment on behalf of a taxpayer who is legally obligated to make the payment, then the taxpayer is treated as receiving the payment from the third party and, in turn, paying the interest.[1]

The deduction may not be taken: (1) by an individual who may be claimed as a dependent on another's tax return; (2) if the expense can be claimed as a deduction elsewhere on the return; or (3) by married taxpayers filing separate returns.[2]

8533. Is personal interest deductible?

Generally, personal interest is not deductible. However, in defining personal interest, all of the types of interest described Q 8527 through Q 8532 are not considered personal interest, and, thus, are deductible subject to the limitations discussed therein. Generally, non-deductible personal interest includes, but is not limited to, consumer credit card interest, car loans and interest on tax deficiencies.

8534. How much of a charitable contribution is deductible?

An individual who itemizes may take a deduction for certain contributions "to" or "for the use of" charitable organizations. A gift is made "to" a charitable organization if it is a direct gift of property to the charitable organization. An indirect contribution of an interest in property to a charity that does not result in a complete gift of the property itself is considered to be a contribution "for the use of" the charity. For example, a gift of an income interest in property, but not the underlying property itself, to charity is considered to be a gift "for the use of" the charity.[3] The term "for the use of" does not refer to a gift of the right to use property such as office space. Such a gift would generally be a nondeductible gift.

The amount that may be deducted by the taxpayer in any tax year is subject to the income percentage ceilings explained in Q 8535 and Q 8536. The amount of the contribution depends on whether it is a gift of money or property; and, if the latter, the type of property. Also, for any charitable gift, the type of charity is relevant. These rules are explained in Q 8537 and Q 8538.

Charitable giving is discussed in detail in Q 8968 to Q 8982.

8535. What are the income percentage ceilings that limit the income tax deduction for charitable contributions?

50 percent ceiling. For a charitable contribution of money, an individual is allowed a charitable deduction of up to 50 percent of his or her adjusted gross income if made to the following types of organizations: churches, schools, hospitals or medical research organizations, organizations that normally receive a substantial part of their support from federal, state, or local governments or from the general public and that aid any of the above organizations, and federal, state, and

1. See, e.g., Treas. Reg. §1.221-1(b)(4)(ii), Example 1 (payment by employer) and Example 2 (payment by parent).
2. IRC Secs. 221(e), 221(c); Treas. Reg. §§1.221-1(b)(2), 1.221-1(b)(3); 1.221-1(g)(2).
3. See Treas. Reg. §1.170A-8(a)(2).

local governments. Also included in this list is a limited category of private foundations (private operating foundations and conduit foundations[1]) that generally direct their support to public charities.[2] The above organizations are often referred to as "public charities" or "50-percent-type charitable organizations."

Thus, a monetary contribution to a public charity is limited to 50 percent of adjusted gross income. The excess amount is carried over for a period of five years subject to the same limitations. Any amount of a charitable contribution not deducted within that time period is lost.[3]

> *Example*: In 2018, Asher made a monetary charitable contribution of $30,000 to a public charity. Asher's adjusted gross income is $50,000. Due to the 50 percent ceiling, Asher's contribution is limited to $25,000 (50 percent of $50,000). The remaining $5,000 is carried over to the next year subject to the same limitations for up to five years.

30 percent limit. The deduction for contributions of most long-term capital gain property to the above organizations, contributions *for the use of* any of the above organizations, as well as contributions (other than long-term capital gain property) *to* or *for the use of* any other types of charitable organizations (i.e., most private foundations, see Q 8538) is limited to the lesser of (a) 30 percent of the taxpayer's adjusted gross income, or (b) 50 percent of adjusted gross income minus the amount of charitable contributions allowed for contributions to the 50 percent -type charities.[4]

20 percent limit. The deduction for contributions of long-term capital gain property to most private foundations (see Q 8046) is limited to the lesser of (a) 20 percent of the taxpayer's adjusted gross income, or (b) 30 percent of adjusted gross income minus the amount of charitable contributions allowed for contributions to the 30 percent -type charities.[5] Deductions denied because of the 50 percent, 30 percent, or 20 percent limits may be carried over and deducted over the next five years, retaining their character as 50 percent, 30 percent, or 20 percent type deductions.[6]

Gifts are "to" a charitable organization if made directly to the organization. Even though the gift may be intended to be used by the charity, and the charity may use it, if it is given *directly* to the charity, it is a gift to the charity and not "for the use of" the charity, for purposes of the deduction limits. Unreimbursed out-of-pocket expenses incurred on behalf of an organization (e.g., unreimbursed travel expenses of volunteers) are deductible as contributions "to" the organization if they are directly related to performing services for the organization (and, in the case of travel expenses, there is no significant element of personal pleasure, recreation, or vacation in such travel).[7]

1. See IRC Sec. 170(b)(1)(E).
2. IRC Sec. 170(b)(1)(A).
3. IRC Sec. 170(d).
4. IRC Secs. 170(b)(1)(B), 170(b)(1)(C).
5. IRC Sec. 170(b)(1)(D).
6. IRC Secs. 170(d)(1), 170(b)(1)(D)(ii); Treas. Reg. §1.170A-10(b).
7. IRC Sec. 170(j); *Rockefeller v. Comm.*, 676 F.2d 35 (2nd Cir. 1982), aff'g 76 TC 178 (1981), acq. in part 1984-2 CB 2; Rev. Rul. 84-61, 1984-1 CB 39. See Rev. Rul. 58-279, 1958-1 CB 145.

"For the use of" applies to indirect contributions to a charitable organization.[1] The term "for the use of" does not refer to a gift of the right to use property. Such a gift would generally be a nondeductible gift of less than the donor's entire interest.

8536. How are the income percentage ceilings calculated if charitable contributions of money are made to both public charities and private foundations in the same tax year?

The combined amount of a taxpayer's monetary contributions to public charities and private foundations can never exceed 50 percent of adjusted gross income. Within the 50 percent ceiling, the deductible charitable contribution to a private foundation cannot exceed 30 percent. The application of this rule is illustrated by the following example:

> *Example*: In 2018, Asher contributes $70,000 to a public charity and $50,000 to a private foundation. His adjusted gross income is $180,000.
>
> Step 1 – Compute the limitation on the charitable deduction to the public charity.
>
> If the charitable contribution to the public charity was equal to or greater than 50 percent of adjusted gross income, this would be the end of the computation, as the amount of the charitable contribution to the public charity in excess of 50 percent of adjusted gross income, plus the full amount of the charitable contribution to the private foundation, would not be deductible. Instead, those amounts would be carried forward into subsequent tax years.
>
> In this case, Asher's $70,000 charitable contribution to the public charity is less than $90,000, or 50 percent of his $180,000 of adjusted gross income. Thus, the entire $70,000 charitable contribution is deductible.
>
> Step 2 – Compute the charitable contribution deduction to the private foundation.
>
> Since the maximum amount deductible is 50 percent of adjusted gross income, after the Step 1 public charity deduction of $70,000, there remains only $20,000 of potentially deductible charitable contributions to the private foundation. Therefore, in computing how much of Asher's $50,000 contribution to a private foundation is deductible, the result can be no greater than the lesser of (1) $20,000 or (2) 30 percent of his adjusted gross income. Since $20,000 is the lesser amount, $20,000 of Asher's $50,000 private foundation charitable contribution is deductible. The remaining $30,000 is not currently deductible and must be carried over into the next tax year subject to the same rules for up to five subsequent tax years.[2]

8537. How does the character of property donated to charity (long-term capital gain property, tangible personal property, S corporation stock, partial interests in property) impact the income tax deduction allowed to the taxpayer?

If an individual makes a charitable contribution to a public charity (see Q 8534) of property that, if sold, would have resulted in long-term capital gain (other than certain tangible personal property, see below), the taxpayer is generally entitled to deduct the full fair market value of the property, but the deduction will be limited to 30 percent of adjusted gross income.[3]

1. See Treas. Reg. §1.170A-8(a)(2). See *Davis v. United States*, 495 U.S. 472 (1990).
2. IRC Sec. 170(b)(1)(B)(i).
3. IRC Sec. 170(b)(1)(C).

Long-term capital gain property. "Long-term capital gain" means "gain from the sale or exchange of a capital asset held for more than one year, if and to the extent such gain is taken into account in computing gross income."[1]

> *Example:* Asher owns raw land he purchased five years ago for $100,000. The fair market value of the land is $500,000. If Asher were to sell the land, he would recognize $400,000 long-term capital gain. Because the land is long-term capital gain property, if Asher contributes the land to a public charity, he would be entitled to a $500,000 charitable deduction. However, the amount deductible would be limited to 30 percent of his adjusted gross income.

If any portion of a gift of long-term capital gain property to a public charity is disallowed as a result of the adjusted gross income ceiling, the taxpayer may carry the deduction over for five years subject to the same 30 percent ceiling.[2]

In lieu of a full fair market value contribution of property subject to the 30 percent ceiling, a taxpayer may elect to take a lesser contribution of the property's basis subject to the 50 percent ceiling. Once made, such an election applies to all contributions of capital gain property during the taxable year (except unrelated use gifts of appreciated tangible personal property, as explained below). The election is generally irrevocable for the year in which it is made.[3]

> *Example:* Asher owns raw land he purchased five years ago for $100,000. The fair market value of the land is $500,000. If Asher were to sell the land, he would recognize $400,000 long-term capital gain. Because the land is long-term capital gain property, if Asher contributes the land to a public charity, he would be entitled to a $500,000 charitable deduction. However, if Asher elects to limit his charitable deduction to $100,000 (the land's basis), the amount deductible would be 50 percent of his adjusted gross income.

See Q 8538 for the rules regarding contribution of property to private foundations.

Tangible Personal Property. The treatment of a contribution of appreciated tangible personal property (i.e., property which, if sold, would generate long-term capital gain) depends on whether the use of the property is related or unrelated to the purpose or function of the (public or governmental) organization. If the property is related use property (e.g., a contribution of a painting to a museum), generally the full fair market value is deductible, subject to the 30 percent ceiling. However, if the property is unrelated to the purpose or function of the charity, the deduction is generally limited to the donor's adjusted basis.[4]

Other Gifts of Property. The deduction for any charitable contribution of property is reduced by the amount of gain that would *not* be long-term capital gain if the property were sold at its fair market value at the time of the contribution.[5] In other words, the amount of such gifts are limited to the basis in the property.

In the case of a gift of S corporation stock, special rules (similar to those relating to the treatment of unrealized receivables and inventory items under IRC Section 751) apply in determining

1. IRC Sec. 1222(3).
2. IRC Sec. 170(b)(1)(C)(ii).
3. IRC Sec. 170(b)(1)(C)(iii); *Woodbury v. Comm.*, TC Memo 1988-272, *aff'd*, 90-1 USTC ¶50,199 (10th Cir. 1990).
4. IRC Secs. 170(e)(1)(B), 170(b)(1)(C); Treas. Reg. §1.170A-4(b).
5. IRC Sec. 170(e)(1)(A).

whether gain on such stock is long-term capital gain for purposes of determining the amount of a charitable contribution.[1]

8538. What income tax deduction may a taxpayer take for making a charitable donation to an organization classified as a private foundation?

Most private foundations are family foundations subject to restricted contribution limits. Certain other private foundations (i.e., conduit foundations and private *operating* foundations), which operate much like public charities, are treated as public charities (see Q 8534).[2] A private foundation is a charitable organization other than an organization described in IRC Sections 509(a)(1) through 509(a)(4). More specifically, a private foundation is usually a charitable organization that is 1) funded from a limited group such as an individual, family or company; 2) its expenses tend to be paid from investment earnings rather than regular charitable contributions; and 3) under certain circumstances it makes contributions to other charitable organizations. The term "private foundations" as used under this heading refers to standard private (e.g., family) foundations.

The amount of the deduction for a contribution of appreciated property (tangible or intangible) contributed *to* or *for the use of* private foundations generally is limited to the donor's adjusted basis. However, certain gifts of qualified appreciated stock made to a private foundation are deductible at their full fair market value.[3]

Qualified appreciated stock is generally publicly traded stock which, if sold on the date of contribution at its fair market value, would result in a long-term capital gain.[4] Such a contribution will not constitute qualified appreciated stock to the extent that it exceeds 10 percent of the value of all outstanding stock of the corporation. Family attribution rules apply in reaching the 10 percent level.[5] The IRS has determined that shares in a mutual fund can constitute qualified appreciated stock.[6]

Planning Point: Donor advised funds are an increasingly popular way for a donor to obtain more choice and control over how and when taxation occurs. A donor can wait to make a charitable contribution until the end of the calendar year, after the donor knows how much the donor wants (and is able) to deduct, make a gift to a public charity, and then decide the recipients of the donation at a future date.

Planning Point: From a tax perspective, it is not advisable to donate an investment expected to generate a tax loss. This is because the transfer of loss property to a charity does not allow for the taxpayer to claim the loss. In this situation, the taxpayer should consider selling the investment in order to claim the loss; and, then make a deductible charitable contribution of the proceeds from the sale.

1. IRC Sec. 170(e)(1).
2. See IRC Secs. 170(b)(1)(E), 170(b)(1)(A)(vii).
3. IRC Sec. 170(e)(5).
4. IRC Sec. 170(e)(5).
5. IRC Sec. 170(e)(5)(C).
6. Let. Rul. 199925029. See also Let. Rul. 200322005 (ADRs are qualified appreciated stock); Instructions for Form 8283 (Rev. December 2014).

8539. What substantiation requirements must a taxpayer satisfy in order to claim an income tax deduction for a charitable donation?

A taxpayer-donor is not entitled to a charitable deduction for a contribution of cash, check, or other monetary gift unless the donor maintains a contemporaneous written record, generally in the form of either a bank record or a written communication from the donee showing the name of the organization and the date and the amount of the contribution.[1]

A taxpayer must substantiate a charitable contribution of $250 or more (whether in cash or property) by a contemporaneous written acknowledgment of the contribution supplied by the charitable organization. The taxpayer is not required to provide substantiation if certain information is reported on a return filed by the charitable organization.[2] (An organization can provide the acknowledgement electronically, such as in an e-mail addressed to the donor.)[3] Special rules apply to the substantiation and disclosure of quid pro quo contributions and contributions made by payroll deduction.[4] A taxpayer must generally obtain a qualified appraisal for contributions of property that is difficult to value if the taxpayer claims a deduction of more than $5,000 for the donation.[5]

A taxpayer is not entitled to a deduction for a contribution of clothing or household items unless the property is in new or good used condition. A deduction for a contribution of clothing or household items may be denied if the property has minimal monetary value. These rules do not apply to a contribution of a single item if the taxpayer claims a deduction of more than $500 and includes a qualified appraisal with the return. Household items include furniture, furnishings, electronics, linens, appliances, and similar items; but not food, art, jewelry, and collections.[6]

Special rules apply to certain types of gifts, including charitable donations of patents and intellectual property, and for donations of used motor vehicles, boats, and airplanes.[7]

8540. When is an individual taxpayer entitled to a deduction for medical expenses?

A taxpayer who itemizes deductions can deduct unreimbursed expenses for "medical care" (the term "medical care" includes dental care) and expenses for *prescribed* drugs or insulin for himself, a spouse and dependents. The deduction is only allowed to the extent that such expenses exceed 10 percent of adjusted gross income for the tax year. (On a joint return, the 10 percent floor amount is based on the combined adjusted gross income of the two spouses.)

To determine whether the taxpayer is entitled to a deduction, the taxpayer first determines net unreimbursed expenses by subtracting all reimbursements received during the year from total expenses for medical care paid during the year. The taxpayer must then subtract 10 percent

1. IRC Sec. 170(f)(17).
2. IRC Sec. 170(f)(8).
3. IRS Pub. 1771 (March, 2016), p. 33.
4. Treas. Reg. §§1.170A-13(f), 1.6115-1.
5. IRC Sec. 170(f)(11).
6. IRC Sec. 170(f)(16).
7. See IRC Secs. 170(e)(1)(B), 170(f)(11), 170(f)(12), 170(m); Notice 2005-44, 2005-25 IRB 1287.

of the taxpayer's adjusted gross income from net unreimbursed medical expenses. Only the balance, if any, is deductible.[1] The deduction for medical expenses is not subject to the phase-out in itemized deductions for certain upper income taxpayers. (See Q 8524.)

Though the 7.5 percent threshold increased to 10 percent in 2013, taxpayers could continue to use the 7.5 percent threshold through 2016 if the taxpayer or the taxpayer's spouse had attained age sixty-five before the end of the taxable year.

"Medical care" is defined as amounts paid: (a) for the diagnosis, cure, mitigation, treatment, or prevention of disease, or for the purpose of affecting any structure or function of the body; (b) for transportation primarily for and essential to such medical care; (c) for qualified long-term care services; or (d) for insurance covering such care or for any qualified long-term care insurance contract.[2]

The IRS has ruled that amounts paid for diagnostic and certain similar procedures and devices are deductible medical care expenses, provided that they are not compensated by insurance or otherwise, even though the individuals had no symptoms of illness prior to incurring the expense. According to the IRS, this includes an annual physical examination, a full-body electronic scan and a pregnancy test.[3]

The term "medical care" does not include cosmetic surgery or other similar procedures unless necessary to correct a deformity resulting from a congenital abnormality, a personal injury resulting from accident or trauma, or a disfiguring disease.[4] Despite this general rule, in *Al-Murshidi v. Comm.*,[5] the surgical removal of excess skin from a formerly obese individual was not found to be "cosmetic surgery" for purposes of IRC Section 213(d)(9)(A) because the procedures meaningfully promoted the proper function of the individual's body and treated her disease. Therefore, the costs of the surgical procedures were deductible despite the "cosmetic surgery" classification given to the procedures by the surgeon.

The Social Security hospital tax that an individual pays as an employee or self-employed person cannot be deducted as a medical expense.[6] Conversely, a sixty-five-year-old who has signed up for the supplementary medical plan under Medicare can treat monthly premiums as amounts paid for insurance covering medical care.[7] Premiums paid for Medicare Part D, the voluntary prescription drug insurance program that went into effect on January 1, 2006, are included in the definition of medical expenses.[8]

The unreimbursed portion of an entrance fee for life care in a residential retirement facility that is allocable to future medical care is also deductible as a medical expense in the year paid (but, if the resident leaves the facility and receives a refund, the refund is includable in

1. IRC Sec. 213.
2. IRC Sec. 213(d)(1).
3. Rev. Rul. 2007-72, 2007-50 IRB 1154.
4. IRC Sec. 213(d)(9); see, e.g., Let. Rul. 200344010.
5. TC Summary Opinion 2001-185.
6. See IRC Sec. 213(d).
7. Rev. Rul. 66-216, 1966-2 CB 100.
8. See IRS Pub. 502, Medical and Dental Expenses.

gross income to the extent it is attributable to the deduction previously allowed).[1] Either the percentage method or the actuarial method may be used to calculate the portions of monthly service fees (paid for lifetime residence in a continuing care retirement community) allocable to medical care.[2] Despite this, a federal district court held that none of the entrance fee paid by married taxpayers to an assisted living facility was properly deductible as a medical expense because: (1) no portion of the entrance fee was attributable to the couple's medical care; and (2) the entrance fee was structured as a loan, which cannot serve as the basis for a deduction (the court cited *Comm. v. Tufts* in reaching this conclusion[3]).[4]

Amounts paid by an individual for medicines and drugs that can be purchased over-the-counter (without a doctor's prescription) are not deductible unless the individual has obtained a prescription.[5] However, amounts paid by an individual for equipment (e.g., crutches), supplies (e.g., bandages), or diagnostic devices (e.g., blood sugar test kits) may qualify as amounts paid for medical care and may be deductible under IRC Section 213. The IRS has ruled privately that crutches used to mitigate the effect of the taxpayer's injured leg and blood sugar test kits used to monitor and assist in treating the taxpayer's diabetes were amounts paid for medical care and were deductible.[6]

The costs of nutritional supplements, vitamins, herbal supplements, and "natural medicines" cannot be included in medical expenses unless they are recommended by a doctor as treatment for a specific medical condition diagnosed by a doctor.[7] Certain expenses for smoking cessation programs and products are deductible as a medical expense.[8]

Amounts paid by individuals for breast reconstruction surgery following a mastectomy for cancer and for vision correction surgery are medical care expenses and are deductible. Amounts paid by individuals to whiten teeth discolored as a result of age are not medical care expenses and are not deductible.[9]

Costs paid by individuals for participation in a weight-loss program as treatment for a specific disease or diseases (e.g., obesity, hypertension, or heart disease) diagnosed by a physician are deductible as medical expenses. Conversely, the costs of diet food are not deductible.[10] According to IRS Publication 502, this includes fees paid by a taxpayer for membership in a weight reduction group and attendance at periodic meetings. Membership dues for a gym, health club, or spa cannot be included in medical expenses, but separate fees charged for weight loss activities can be included as medical expenses. In informational guidance, the IRS has also stated that taxpayers may deduct exercise expenses, including the cost of equipment to use in the home, if required to treat an illness (including obesity) diagnosed by a physician. For an

1. Rev. Rul. 76-481, 1976-2 CB 82, *as clarified by* Rev. Rul. 93-72, 1993-2 CB 77; Let. Rul. 8641037.
2. *Baker v. Comm.*, 122 TC 143 (2004).
3. 461 U.S. 300, 307 (1983).
4. *Finzer v. United States*, 496 F. Supp. 2d 954 (N.D. Ill. 2007).
5. Rev. Rul. 2003-58, 2003-22 IRB 959.
6. Rev. Rul. 2003-58, above; see also IRS Information Letter INFO-2003-169 (6-13-2003).
7. IRS Pub. 502, Medical and Dental Expenses.
8. See Rev. Rul. 99-28, 1999-25 IRB 6.
9. Rev. Rul. 2003-57, 2003-22 IRB 959.
10. Rev. Rul. 2002-19, 2002-16 IRB 778.

exercise expense to be deductible, the taxpayer must establish the purpose of the expense is to treat a disease rather than to promote general health, and that the taxpayer would not have paid the expense but for this purpose.[1]

Expenses for childbirth classes were deductible as a medical expense to the extent that the class prepared the taxpayer for an active role in the process of childbirth.[2] Egg donor fees and expenses incurred in the process of obtaining a willing egg donor count as medical care expenses that are deductible.[3]

Finally, the cost of prescribed drugs brought in or shipped from another country is deductible only if imported legally. Additionally, the cost of prescribed drugs purchased and consumed in another country are also deductible provided the drug is legal in both the other country and the United States.[4]

8541. When is an individual taxpayer entitled to a deduction for a dependent's medical expenses?

A taxpayer can deduct the medical expenses paid for a dependent (within the specified limits, see Q 8540) even though the taxpayer is not entitled to a dependency exemption. The fact that the dependent's income for the year exceeds the annual personal exemption amount is immaterial so long as the taxpayer has furnished over one-half of his support during that tax year. A child of parents who are divorced (or in some situations, separated) *and* who between them provide more than one-half of the child's support for the calendar year and have custody of the child for more than one-half of the calendar year will be treated as a dependent of both parents for purposes of this deduction.[5] In the case of a multiple support agreement, however, only the person designated to take the dependency exemption may deduct the dependent's medical expenses, and then only to the extent that the designated person actually paid the expenses.[6] See Q 8518 for a discussion of which parent is entitled to take the dependency exemption.

IRS has privately ruled that taxpayers could deduct special education tuition for their children as a medical care expense where the children attended a school primarily to receive medical care in the form of special education and each child had been diagnosed as having a medical condition that handicapped the child's ability to learn in the years in which tuition was paid.[7]

8542. Can lodging expenses that are incurred in relation to the medical treatment of a taxpayer be deducted as medical expenses?

Deductible medical expenses include amounts paid for lodging, up to $50 per individual per night, when being away from home is *primarily for and essential to* medical care if such care is provided by a physician in a licensed hospital (or similar medical care facility) and there is no

1. Information Letter INFO 2003-0202.
2. Let. Rul. 8919009.
3. Let. Rul. 200318017; see also Information Letter INFO 2005-0102 (3-29-2005).
4. IRS Pub. 502.
5. IRC Sec. 213(d)(5).
6. Treas. Reg. §1.213-1(a)(3)(i).
7. See Let. Rul. 200521003. See also Let. Rul. 200729019.

element of personal pleasure, recreation or vacation in the travel away from home. No deduction is allowed if the lodgings are "lavish or extravagant."[1] A mother was permitted to deduct lodging expenses incurred when her child was receiving medical care away from home and her presence was essential to such care.[2] A parent's costs of attending a medical conference (i.e., registration fee, transportation costs) to obtain information about a chronic disease affecting the parent's child were deductible so long as the costs were primarily for and essential to the medical care of the dependent. However, the costs of meals and lodging incurred by the parent while attending the conference were not deductible.[3]

8543. In what year are medical expenses incurred by a taxpayer deductible?

Generally, medical expenses are deductible only in the year they are paid, regardless of when the expenses are incurred. Despite this, in *Zipkin v. U.S.*, expenses incurred by a taxpayer to build a home to meet his wife's special health needs were properly deducted in the year the home became habitable, even though the costs had been paid in earlier years.[4] Costs paid by parents to modify a van used to transport their handicapped child were deductible in the year those costs were paid; however, the court held that depreciation was not a deductible medical expense.[5]

8544. Can a decedent's medical expenses that are paid out of the estate be deducted?

Medical expenses of a decedent paid out of the estate within one year from the date of death are considered paid by the decedent at the time the expenses were incurred.[6] A decedent's medical expenses cannot be taken as an income tax deduction unless a statement is filed waiving the right to deduct them for estate tax purposes. Amounts that are not deductible under IRC Section 213 may not be treated as deductible medical expenses for estate tax purposes. Thus, expenses that do not exceed the 10 percent floor are not deductible.[7]

Credits

8545. What is a refundable tax credit and what are some examples?

On Form 1040, after the amount of tax owed is computed, the taxpayer is entitled to subtract certain payments and credits from the tax to arrive at the amount of tax that is actually payable.

A *refundable credit* is a tax credit that can result in a refund or credit even if the taxpayer owes no tax or the credit exceeds the amount of tax owing. The refundable credits include:

...Taxes withheld from salaries and wages.[8]

1. IRC Sec. 213(d)(2).
2. Let. Rul. 8516025.
3. Rev. Rul. 2000-24, 2000-19 IRB 963.
4. 2000-2 USTC ¶50,863 (D. Minn. 2000).
5. *Henderson v. Comm.*, TC Memo 2000-321.
6. IRC Sec. 213(c).
7. Rev. Rul. 77-357, 1977-2 CB 328.
8. IRC Sec. 31(a).

...Overpayments of tax.[1]

...The excess of Social Security withheld (which could occur, for example, if an individual has two or more employers).[2]

...The earned income credit.[3]

...The 72.5 percent health care tax credit for uninsured workers displaced by trade competition.[4]

...The unused long-term minimum tax credit.

Example: In 2018, Ashley, a single mother, is entitled to an earned income tax credit of $3,500. Her income tax liability before the application of the credit is $1,000. Other than the earned income tax credit, Ashley has no other credits. Because the earned income credit is a refundable credit, Ashley is entitled to a refund of $2,500 ($3,500 credit minus $1,000 tax liability).

8546. How does a nonrefundable tax credit work and what are some examples?

Editor's Note: Many of the credits listed below contain sunset provisions so that they apply only so long as Congress chooses to renew them from year to year. Late in 2015, Congress enacted the Protecting Americans from Tax Hikes Act of 2015 (PATH) to extend the following credits (discussed below): the nonbusiness energy property credit (extended through 2016), the work opportunity credit (extended through 2019), the research credit (made permanent), the empowerment zone employment credit (extended through 2016), the Indian employment credit (extended through 2016), the new markets tax credit (extended through 2019), the railroad track maintenance credit (extended through 2016), the biodiesel fuels credit (extended through 2016), the energy efficient home credit (extended through 2016), the portion of the alternative fuel vehicle refueling property credit to which IRC Section 30C(d)(1) applies (extended through 2016) and the credit for certain plug-in electric cars (extended through 2016). However, as of the date of this revision and with respect to provisions that were not made permanent, Congress has not indicated whether it will extend this treatment for future years.

A nonrefundable credit is a credit that is limited by the amount of the taxpayer's tax liability for the year. A taxpayer is only entitled to claim nonrefundable tax credits to the extent that the combined amount of the credits does not exceed total income tax liability for the tax year. So unlike refundable credits (Q 8545), a nonrefundable credit can never result in a refund or credit.

However, because certain nonrefundable credits in excess of a taxpayer's tax liability for a tax year may be carried forward into future tax years (and others cannot be carried over), it is important to consider the order in which a taxpayer claims the nonrefundable credits.[5]

1. IRC Sec. 35.
2. Treas. Reg. §1.31-2.
3. IRC Sec. 32.
4. IRC Sec. 35.
5. See, for example, IRC Secs. 23 (adoption expense credit), 25 (mortgage interest credit) and 25D (residential energy efficient property credit) for examples of nonrefundable credits that may be carried over to succeeding tax years.

The American Taxpayer Relief Act of 2012 (ATRA) and Protecting Americans from Tax Hikes Act of 2015 (PATH) extended or made permanent many expiring credits (as indicated below).

The following tax credits are classified as *nonrefundable credits*:

> ...Personal credits which consist of the child and dependent care credit;[1] the credit for the elderly and the permanently and totally disabled,[2] the qualified adoption credit,[3] the nonrefundable portion of the child tax credit,[4] the American Opportunity (the increased limits were made permanent by PATH), Hope Scholarship, and Lifetime Learning credits,[5] the credit for elective deferrals and IRA contributions (the "saver's credit," which became permanent under PPA 2006);[6]
>
> ...The nonbusiness energy property credit (extended through 2016)[7]; and the residential energy efficient property credit;[8]
>
> ...Other nonbusiness credits;[9]
>
> ...The general business credit is the sum of the following credits determined for the taxable year:

(1) the investment credit determined under IRC Section 46 (including the rehabilitation credit);

(2) the work opportunity credit determined under IRC Section 51(a) (extended through 2019 by PATH);

(3) the alcohol fuels credit determined under IRC Section 40(a);

(4) the research credit determined under IRC Section 41(a) (made permanent by PATH);

(5) the low-income housing credit determined under IRC Section 42(a);

(6) the enhanced oil recovery credit under IRC Section 43(a);

(7) in the case of an eligible small business, the disabled access credit determined under IRC Section 44(a);

(8) the renewable electricity production credit under IRC Section 45(a) (extended only through 2009 under EIEA 2008);

1. IRC Sec. 21.
2. IRC Sec. 22.
3. IRC Sec. 23.
4. See IRC Sec. 24.
5. IRC Sec. 25A, as amended by ATRA, Sec. 103 and PATH, Sec. 102.
6. IRC Sec. 25B.
7. IRC Sec. 25C, as amended by ATRA, Sec. 401 and PATH, Sec. 181.
8. IRC Sec. 25D.
9. See e.g., IRC Secs. 53, 901.

(9) the empowerment zone employment credit determined under IRC Section 1396(a) (extended through 2016 by PATH);

(10) the Indian employment credit as determined under IRC Section 45A(a) (extended through 2016 by PATH);

(11) the employer Social Security credit determined under IRC Section 45B(a);

(12) the orphan drug credit determined under IRC Section 45C(a);

(13) the new markets tax credit determined under IRC Section 45D(a) (extended through 2019 by PATH);

(14) in the case of an eligible employer (as defined in IRC Section 45E(c)); the small employer pension plan startup cost credit determined under IRC Section 45E(a);

(15) the employer-provided child care credit determined under IRC Section 45F(a);

(16) the railroad track maintenance credit determined under IRC Section 45G(a) (extended through 2016 by PATH);

(17) the biodiesel fuels credit determined under IRC Section 40A(a) (extended through 2016 by PATH);

(18) the low sulfur diesel fuel production credit determined under IRC Section 45H(a);

(19) the marginal oil and gas well production credit determined under IRC Section 45I(a);

(20) for tax years beginning after September 20, 2005, the distilled spirits credit determined under IRC Section 5011(a);

(21) for tax year beginning after August 8, 2005, the advanced nuclear power facility production credit determined under IRC Section 45J(a);

(22) for property placed in service after December 31, 2005, the nonconventional source production credit determined under IRC Section 45K(a);

(23) the energy efficient home credit determined under IRC Section 45L(a) (extended through 2016 by PATH);

(24) the energy efficient appliance credit determined under IRC Section 45M(a) (extended through 2014);

(25) the portion of the alternative motor vehicle credit to which IRC Section 30B(g)(1) applies; and

(26) the portion of the alternative fuel vehicle refueling property credit to which IRC Section 30C(d)(1) applies (extended through 2016 by PATH).[1]

1. IRC Sec. 38(b).

A credit was also available for new qualified plug-in electric drive motor vehicles acquired and placed in service after 2009. The amount of the credit can vary from $2,500 to $7,500 depending on battery capacity (and subject to phase-out based on number of vehicles sold by the manufacturer). The portion of the credit attributable to property of a character subject to an allowance for depreciation is treated as part of the general business credit. The balance of the credit is generally treated as a nonrefundable personal credit.[1] An alternative credit is available for certain plug-in electric cars placed in service after February 17, 2009 and before 2016. This credit is equal to 10 percent of cost, up to $2,500.[2]

8547. What tax credit is available for small business retirement plan start-up costs?

A tax credit for qualified retirement plan start-up costs is available to small business owners. A small business employer is eligible if, during the preceding tax year, it employed 100 or fewer employees who received at least $5,000 in annual compensation from the employer (the same definition that generally applies for SIMPLE retirement plans).[3] The plan must be available to at least one employee who is a non-highly compensated employee (for 2018, a highly compensated employee is one who owns 5 percent of the business or who has earned more than $120,000).[4]

Importantly, the small business employer is only eligible for the credit if its employees were not able to participate in another retirement plan sponsored by the employer, a member of a controlled group or a predecessor of either within three years of establishing the new plan (essentially, this requirement ensures that the plan truly is a newly-established retirement plan).[5]

The credit is equal to 50 percent of the ordinary and necessary costs of starting up the retirement plan, including both the costs of setting up and administering the plan and costs related to educating employees about the plan, up to a maximum credit of $500 per year.[6] The credit is available for three years, with the option of first claiming the credit in the year before the year in which the plan becomes effective.[7]

If the entire value of the plan cannot be maximized in a single year, the small business employer has the option of carrying it back or forward to another tax year, so long as that tax year does not begin prior to January 1, 2002. In order to claim the credit, the taxpayer must file Form 8881 with the IRS.[8]

1. IRC Sec. 30D, as amended by ARRA 2009.
2. IRC Sec. 30, as amended by ARRA 2009 and ATRA.
3. IRS Pub. 560 (20162016).
4. IRC Sec. 45E(d)(1), IR-2014-99 (Oct. 23, 2014), Notice 2017-64.
5. IRC Sec. 45E(c).
6. IRC Secs. 38, 45E (a), 45E(b).
7. IRC Sec. 45E(b).
8. IRS Pub. 560 (20162016).

8548. When does a taxpayer qualify for the tax credit for the elderly and the permanently and totally disabled and how is the credit computed?

The tax credit for the elderly and the permanently and totally disabled is a nonrefundable credit, meaning that it is available only to the extent that it does not exceed the taxpayer's tax liability (see Q 8546). The credit is available to (1) taxpayers age sixty-five or older, or (2) those who are under age sixty-five, retired on disability, and were considered permanently and totally disabled when they retired.[1]

> "An individual is permanently and totally disabled if he is unable to engage in any substantial gainful activity by reason of any medically determinable physical or mental impairment which can be expected to result in death or which has lasted or can be expected to last for a continuous period of not less than twelve months. An individual shall not be considered to be permanently and totally disabled unless he furnishes proof of the existence thereof in such form and manner, and at such times, as the Secretary may require."[2]

The credit equals 15 percent of an individual's IRC Section 22 amount for the taxable year, but may not exceed the amount of tax. This IRC Section 22 base amount is $5,000 for a single taxpayer or married taxpayers filing jointly if only one spouse qualifies for the credit; $7,500 for married taxpayers filing jointly if both qualify; and $3,750 for a married taxpayer filing separately.[3] Married taxpayers must file a joint return to claim the credit, unless they lived apart for the entire taxable year.[4]

For individuals under age sixty-five, this base figure is limited to the amount of the disability income (taxable amount an individual receives under an employer plan as wages or payments in lieu of wages for the period the individual is absent from work on account of permanent and total disability) received during the taxable year.[5] (The taxpayer may be required to provide proof of continuing permanent and total disability.)[6] For married taxpayers who are both qualified and who file jointly, the base figure cannot exceed the total of both spouses' disability income if both are under age 65. If only one spouse is under age sixty-five, the base figure cannot exceed the sum of $5,000 plus the disability income of the spouse who is under sixty-five.[7]

The base figure (or the amount of disability income in the case of individuals under age sixty-five, if lower) is reduced dollar-for-dollar by one-half of adjusted gross income in excess of $7,500 (single taxpayers), $10,000 (joint return), or $5,000 (married filing separately).[8] A reduction is also made for Social Security and railroad retirement benefits that are excluded from gross income, and certain other tax-exempt income.[9]

1. IRC Sec. 22(b).
2. IRC Sec. 22(e)(3).
3. IRC Sec. 22(c).
4. IRC Sec. 22(e)(1).
5. IRC Sec. 22(c)(2)(B)(i).
6. GCM 39269 (8-2-84).
7. IRC Sec. 22(c)(2)(B)(ii).
8. IRC Sec. 22(d).
9. IRC Sec. 22(c)(3).

8549. When is a taxpayer entitled to claim the child tax credit?

The child tax credit is generally a nonrefundable tax credit that is available for each "qualifying child" (defined below) of eligible taxpayers who meet certain income requirements. The child tax credit may be refundable to the extent that the taxpayer has three or more qualifying children or for a certain portion of the taxpayer's earned income (see below). The child tax credit is $1,000 per child.[1]

The term *qualifying child* means a "qualifying child" of the taxpayer (as defined under IRC Section 152(c) – see below) who has not attained the age of seventeen;[2] and

(1) who is the taxpayer's "child" (see below) or a descendant of such a child, *or* the taxpayer's brother, sister, stepbrother, or stepsister or a descendant of any such relative;

(2) who has the same principal place of abode as the taxpayer for more than one-half of the taxable year; and

(3) who has not provided over one-half of his or her own support for the calendar year in which the taxpayer's taxable year begins.[3]

Additionally, a qualifying child must be either a citizen or a resident of the United States.[4]

The term "child" means an individual who is: (1) a son, daughter, stepson, or stepdaughter of the taxpayer; or (2) an "eligible foster child" of the taxpayer.[5] An "eligible foster child" means an individual who is placed with the taxpayer by an authorized placement agency or by judgment decree, or other order of any court of competent jurisdiction.[6] Any adopted children of the taxpayer are treated the same as natural born children.[7]

The amount of the credit is reduced for taxpayers whose modified adjusted gross income (MAGI) exceeds certain levels. A taxpayer's MAGI is adjusted gross income without regard to the exclusions for income derived from certain foreign sources or sources within United States possessions. The credit amount is reduced by $50 for every $1,000, or fraction thereof, by which the taxpayer's MAGI exceeds the following threshold amounts: $110,000 for married taxpayers filing jointly, $75,000 for unmarried individuals, and $55,000 for married taxpayers filing separately.[8]

The child tax credit is also refundable. If the child tax credit exceeds the taxpayer's tax liability, a taxpayer with one or two children can receive a refund of the lesser of the unused

1. IRC Sec. 24(a).
2. IRC Sec. 24(c)(1).
3. IRC Sec. 152(c).
4. IRC Sec. 24(c)(2).
5. IRC Sec. 152(f)(1).
6. IRC Sec. 152(f)(1)(C).
7. IRC Sec. 152(f)(1)(B).
8. IRC Sec. 24(b)(2).

amount of the credit or 15 percent of earned income in excess of $3,000.[1] For families with three or more qualifying children, the amount of the refundable credit is the greater of (1) 15 percent of earned income over $3,000 or (2) the sum of Social Security and Medicare taxes paid minus the earned income credit.

The nonrefundable child tax credit can be claimed against the individual's regular income tax *and* alternative minimum tax (see Q 8556 and Q 8558). The tax credit cannot exceed the excess of (i) the sum of the taxpayer's regular tax plus the alternative minimum tax over (ii) the sum of the taxpayer's nonrefundable personal credits (other than the child tax credit, adoption credit, and saver's credit) and the foreign tax credit for the taxable year.[2] Finally, the refundable child tax credit is not required to be reduced by the amount of the taxpayer's alternative minimum tax.[3]

Some additional restrictions applying to the child tax credit include: (1) an individual's tax return must identify the name and taxpayer identification number (Social Security number) of the child for whom the credit is claimed; and (2) the credit may be claimed only for a full taxable year, unless the taxable year is cut short by the death of the taxpayer.[4]

For purposes of applying a uniform method of determining when a child attains a specific age, the IRS has ruled that a child attains a given age on the anniversary of the date that the child was born (e.g., a child born on January 1, 1987, attains the age of seventeen on January 1, 2004).[5]

Social Security

8550. Are Social Security and railroad retirement benefits taxable?

A taxpayer must include a portion of benefits in gross income if the taxpayer's modified adjusted gross income (in most cases the taxpayer's adjusted gross income) plus one-half of the Social Security benefits (including tier I railroad retirement benefits) received during the taxable year exceeds certain base amounts. The amounts that are required to be included in gross income are taxed as ordinary income. As the taxpayer's income in addition to Social Security benefits increases, so does the amount of those benefits that are taxable. However, the amount of benefits that are taxable can never exceed 85 percent of the total benefits received by the taxpayer.

To calculate the extent to which Social Security benefits are taxable, add one-half of Social Security benefits received during the tax year to all other income including wages, interest (including tax exempt interest), dividends, taxable pension distributions, etc. (modified adjusted gross income).[6] Next, compare that amount with the applicable base amounts, which are the following:

1. IRC Sec. 24(d). The $3,000 earned income threshold was made permanent by the Protecting Americans from Tax Hikes Act of 2015 (PATH).
2. IRC Sec. 24(b)(3).
3. IRC Sec. 24(d)(1).
4. IRC Secs. 24(e), 24(f).
5. Rev. Rul. 2003-72, 2003-2 CB 346.
6. IRC Sec. 86(b)(2).

- $25,000 for taxpayers filing as single, head of household or qualifying widow(er)s;
- $25,000 for married taxpayers who file separately and live apart from the other spouse for the entire tax year;
- $32,000 for married taxpayers filing jointly; or
- $0 for married taxpayers who file separately, but live with a spouse at any time during the tax year.[1]

If the modified adjusted gross income plus one-half of Social Security benefits is equal to or less than the base amount, no portion of the Social Security benefits are taxable.

On the other hand, if the sum of modified adjusted gross income plus one-half of Social Security benefits exceeds the base amount, then a portion of those benefits are potentially taxable. The computation, however, involves the "adjusted base amount" which is the following:

- $34,000 for all filers with the exception of joint filers and a married taxpayer that both files separately and lives with his or her spouse at any time during the tax year.
- $44,000 for joint filers.
- $0 for a married taxpayer who files separately and lives with his or her spouse at any time during the taxable year.[2]

If the sum of modified adjusted gross income plus one-half of Social Security benefits is *greater than* the base amount but *less than* the adjusted base amount, the amount included in gross income is the lesser of 1) one-half of the Social Security benefits received during the tax year; or 2) one-half of the excess of the sum of modified adjusted gross income plus one-half of the amount of Social Security benefits that exceeds the base amount (referred to as the "Section 86(a)(1) Amount").[3]

Example: A married couple files a joint return. During the taxable year, they received $12,000 in Social Security benefits and have a modified adjusted gross income of $35,000. Their modified adjusted gross income plus one-half of their Social Security benefits [$35,000 + (½ of $12,000) = $41,000] is greater than the *base amount* of $32,000 but less than the *adjusted base amount* of $44,000.

So in computing the taxable amount of Social Security benefits, consider the following: the taxpayers' Social Security benefits are $12,000 and the excess of (1) modified adjusted gross income plus one-half of their Social Security benefits over (2) the base amount is equal to $9,000 ($41,000 minus $32,000). However, referring back to the formula, the amount includible is one-half of the lesser amount. Therefore, the amount of Social Security benefits included in gross income is $4,500 (one-half of $9,000) because it is less than $6,000 (one-half of the $12,000 total Social Security benefits).

1. IRC Sec. 86(c)(1).
2. IRC Sec. 86(c)(2).
3. IRC Sec. 86(a)(1).

If the sum of modified adjusted gross income plus one-half of Social Security benefits is *greater than* the adjusted base amount, the amount included in gross income is the lesser of the sum of 1) 85 percent of the amount of modified adjusted gross income over the adjusted base amount plus the lesser of (a) the Section 86(a)(1) Amount or (b) one-half of the difference between the adjusted base amount and the base amount or 2) 85 percent of the Social Security benefits received during the tax year.

Example: During the taxable year, a single individual had a modified adjusted gross income of $33,000 and received $8,000 in Social Security benefits. His modified adjusted gross income plus one-half of his Social Security benefits [$33,000 + (½ of $8,000) = $37,000] is greater than the applicable *adjusted base amount* of $34,000.

So tracking the formula above: the lesser of

1) 85 percent of the amount of modified adjusted gross income over the adjusted base amount of $3,000 ($37,000 (modified adjusted gross income) minus the $34,000 adjusted base amount), or $2,550, plus the lesser of a) the Section 86(a)(1) amount of $6,500 (which is one-half of $13,000, i.e., the excess of $37,000 (modified adjusted gross income) over the base amount of $24,000) or b) $4,500 (which is one-half of $9,000, the difference between the $34,000 adjusted base amount and the $25,000 base amount); or

2) 85 percent of total Social Security benefits of $8,000, or $6,800.

So consolidating the above formula, 85 percent of $3,000, or $2,550 plus $4,500, equals $6,550 which is less than 85 percent of $8,000, or $6,800. Therefore, the amount included in gross income is $6550.

8551. What other issues relate to the taxation of Social Security and railroad retirement benefits?

Railroad retirement benefits (other than Tier I benefits) are taxed like benefits received under a qualified pension or profit sharing plan. For this purpose, the Tier II portion of the taxes imposed on employees and employee representatives is treated as an employee contribution, while the Tier II portion of the taxes imposed on employers is treated as an employer contribution.[1]

As mentioned in Q 8550, the base amount and adjusted base amount of a married taxpayer filing separately who lives with his or her spouse at any time during the tax year is zero. This means it is much more likely that 85 percent of his or her Social Security benefits will be taxable even if the other income is relatively low. As a result, the issue of whether separated taxpayers are living apart is significant.

To address this point, the Tax Court has held that the term "live apart" means living in separate residences for purposes of IRC Section 86(c)(1)(C)(ii). Thus, where the taxpayer lived in the same residence as his spouse for at least thirty days during the tax year in question (even though maintaining separate bedrooms), the Tax Court ruled that he did not "live apart" from his spouse at all times during the year; therefore, the taxpayer's base amount was zero.[2]

A taxpayer may elect to treat a lump sum payment of benefits as received in the year in which the benefits are attributable.[3]

1. See IRC Sec. 72(r)(1).
2. *McAdams v. Comm.*, 118 TC 373 (2002).
3. IRC Sec. 86(e).

Any workers' compensation pay that reduced the amount of Social Security received and any amounts withheld to pay Medicare insurance premiums are included in the figure for Social Security benefits.[1]

Another issue that has arisen is whether Social Security disability payments should be lumped in with regular Social Security benefits in determining whether the benefits are taxable. In *Green v. Comm.*,[2] the taxpayer argued that his Social Security disability benefits were excludable from gross income[3] because they had been paid in lieu of workers' compensation. The Tax Court determined, however, that Title II of the Social Security Act is *not* comparable to workers' compensation, which provides benefits based on a taxpayer's employment. Instead, the Act allows for disability payments to individuals regardless of employment. Consequently, the taxpayer's Social Security disability benefits were includable in gross income.

In a case of first impression, the Tax Court held that a taxpayer's Social Security disability insurance benefits (payable as a result of the taxpayer's disability due to lung cancer that resulted from exposure to Agent Orange during his Vietnam combat service) were includable in gross income under IRC Section 86 and were not excludable under IRC Section 104(a)(4). The court reasoned that Social Security disability insurance benefits do not take into consideration the nature or cause of the individual's disability. Furthermore, the Social Security Act does not consider whether the disability arose from service in the Armed Forces or was attributable to combat-related injuries. Eligibility for purposes of Social Security disability benefits is determined on the basis of the individual's prior work record, not on the cause of disability. Moreover, the amount of Social Security disability payments is computed under a formula that does not consider the nature or extent of the injury. Consequently, because the taxpayer's Social Security disability insurance benefits were not paid for personal injury or sickness in military service within the meaning of IRC Section 104(a)(4), the benefits were not eligible for exclusion under IRC Section 104(a)(4).[4]

8552. What are the Social Security tax and Medicare rates for self-employed taxpayers?

Similar to the FICA tax imposed on wage income, Social Security and Medicare taxes are imposed on self-employment income pursuant to the Self-Employment Contributions Act of 1954 (collectively, the two taxes are more formally referred to as the "SECA tax").[5]

Unlike a wage earner whose liability is limited to one-half of the FICA tax, a self-employed individual is obligated to pay the entire amount of the 15.3 percent SECA tax, or 12.4 percent Social Security tax and 2.9 percent Medicare tax in 2018. Similar to FICA, the Social Security

1. Rev. Rul. 84-173, 1984-2 CB 16.
2. TC Memo 2006-39.
3. Under IRC Sec. 104(a)(1).
4. *Reimels v. Comm.*, 123 TC 245 (2004), aff'd, 436 F.3d 344 (2d Cir. 2006); *Haar v. Comm.*, 78 TC 864, 866 (1982), aff'd, 709 F.2d 1206 (8th Cir. 1983), followed.
5. SECA is codified as Chapter 2 of the Internal Revenue Code.

tax cap for self-employment income is the same dollar amount as the Social Security wage cap. Indexed for inflation, for 2018, the Social Security cap for self-employment income is $128,700.[1]

On the other hand, there is no cap on the amount of self-employment income subject to the Medicare tax. Moreover, effective for tax years beginning after December 31, 2012, subject to filing status thresholds, there is an additional Medicare surtax of 0.9 percent added to the 2.9 percent Medicare tax rate (see Q 8604).

8553. What are the Social Security and Medicare tax rates for traditional employees and employers?

The Social Security tax and Medicare tax rates that apply to the wage income of a wage earner are the same as those applicable to the self-employment income of a self-employed individual. However, the operative statute for the imposition of payroll taxes on wage earners is the Federal Insurance Contributions Act (the "FICA tax").[2] Unlike the self-employed, the liability for FICA tax imposed on the wages of a wage earner is split equally between the employee and the employer. In other words, the employee and the employer are each responsible for 6.2 percent of the 12.4 percent of Social Security tax and for 1.45 percent of the 2.9 percent of Medicare tax.[3]

Although the Social Security tax rate is much higher than the Medicare tax rate, it only applies to wages that do not exceed the earnings cap (as adjusted annually for inflation). Therefore, wages in excess of the cap amount are not subject to Social Security tax. For 2018, the Social Security tax does not apply to wages in excess of $128,700.[4] Thus, the maximum amount of Social Security tax liability for the combined employee and employer share is $15,958 (12.4 % × $128,700), or $7,979 each.

On the other hand, there is no cap on the Medicare tax. This means the combined employer/employee 2.9 percent tax rate will be imposed on all wages without limit. Therefore, for 2018, although the imposition of Social Security tax ceases to apply to wages in excess of $128,700, the Medicare tax continues to be imposed on all wages. Moreover, effective for tax years beginning after December 31, 2012, there is an additional Medicare surtax of 0.9 percent added to the 1.45 percent rate on the employee portion of the Medicare tax for certain high-income taxpayers (see Q 8604).

Estimated Tax and Self-Employment Tax

8554. Who must pay the estimated tax and are penalties imposed for underpayment of the tax?

Subject to the potential imposition of penalties, any taxpayer who expects to owe tax of $1,000 or more is required to make estimated tax payments.[5] In other words, a taxpayer should project the current year's taxable income, tax and credits based on expected income,

1. www.socialsecurity.gov
2. Codified as Chapter 21 of the Internal Revenue Code, IRC Secs. 3101-3128.
3. IRC Secs. 3101(a), 3111(a), 3101(b) and 3111(b).
4. www.socialsecurity.gov.
5. http://www.irs.gov/Businesses/Small-Businesses-&-Self-Employed/Estimated-Taxes.

deductions, etc. Based on "a pay as you go" method, estimated tax payments are payable periodically throughout the year. For this purpose, tax liability includes regular income tax, alternative minimum tax and self-employment tax (Social Security and Medicare tax).[1]

For self-employed taxpayers, the requirement to make estimated payments is more problematic than for employees. Unlike employees, no part of a self-employed individual's compensation is withheld by the payor and paid over to the IRS for taxes. Moreover, in addition to regular income tax, these taxpayers are required to pay the full 15.3 percent of the Social Security and Medicare tax. For this reason, a self-employed individual with even a modest amount of income who may owe little or no income tax, may, nonetheless have a significant Social Security and Medicare tax liability.

However, even employed individuals who are subject to withholding should consider making estimated payments under the following circumstances:

- The amount being withheld by the employer is insufficient.
- The taxpayer has a significant amount of other income such as dividends, interest, alimony, rent, etc. that is not subject to withholding.

On the other hand, an individual need not make estimated payments if all three of the following conditions are met:

- The individual had no tax liability for the prior tax year.
- The individual was a U.S. citizen for the entire tax year.
- The prior tax year was a twelve month period.[2]

Although estimated payments can be made at any time during the tax year, there is a "required annual payment" that is payable in "required installments" with specific due dates. For that purpose, the tax year is divided into four unequal quarters with the following due dates:

First Quarter: January through March	April 15th
Second Quarter: April through June	June 15th
Third Quarter: June through August	September 15th
Fourth Quarter: September through December	January 15th of following tax year[3]

The "required annual payment" is a) 90 percent of the taxpayer's expected tax liability for the tax year or b) 100 percent of the tax owing for the prior tax year (assuming the prior tax year spanned twelve months).[4] However, if the taxpayer's adjusted gross income

1. IRC Sec. 6654(a).
2. http://www.irs.gov/Businesses/Small-Businesses-&-Self-Employed/Estimated-Taxes.
3. IRC Sec. 6654(c).
4. IRC Sec. 6654(d)(1)(A).

exceeded $150,000 ($75,000 for filing married filing separately), the percentage in b), above, is increased to 110 percent.[1]

If the taxpayer fails to make timely estimated installment payments, the taxpayer is subject to penalties. Although the taxpayer can compute the penalty on Form 2210, the IRS will compute the penalty if the taxpayer does not complete the form.

8555. Who must pay the self-employment tax?

An individual who has annual net earnings from self-employment of $400 or more is subject to self-employment tax.[2] Generally, sole proprietors, single member LLCs treated as a disregarded entity and general partners are considered to be self-employed. Self-employment tax is reported on Schedule SE attached to Form 1040. However, a self-employed taxpayer is entitled to an above-the-line deduction equal to one-half of the self-employment tax paid.[3]

In essence, self-employment tax is the combination of Social Security tax and Medicare tax. The Social Security tax rate is 12.4 percent and the Medicare tax rate is 2.9 percent.[4] For 2018, Social Security taxes apply only to the first $128,700 of self-employment income. If the taxpayer has both wages and self-employment income, the amount of self-employment income subject to the Social Security tax is the difference between the cap amount and the amount of the taxpayer's wages.

> *Example:* In 2018, Asher has wages of $90,000. In addition, Asher has self-employment income of $50,000. Since the Social Security wage base is $128,700, only $38,700 of Asher's $40,000 of self-employment ($128,700 minus $90,000) is subject to Social Security tax.

On the other hand, in regard to Medicare tax, there is no cap on the amount of self-employment income that is subject to the tax. Also, for self-employment individuals with income that exceeds certain threshold amounts, an additional Medicare tax of 0.9 percent may be added to the base 2.9 percent Medicare rate, for a total tax of 3.8 percent. The additional tax applies for self-employed individuals with income in excess of $250,000 for joint filers, $125,000 for married taxpayers filing separately and $200,000 for all other taxpayers.[5]

Alternative Minimum Tax

8556. What is the alternative minimum tax and how is it calculated?

In addition to regular income tax, the *alternative minimum tax* (AMT) is an additional tax that certain taxpayers must pay. In theory, the purpose of AMT is to prevent high income taxpayers from taking advantage of tax benefits (such as exclusions, deductions and credits) to substantially reduce or even eliminate their tax liability. However, in reality, due to complex rules, many relatively low income taxpayers may become subject to AMT.

1. IRC Sec. 6654(d)(1)(C).
2. IRC Sec. 6017.
3. IRC Sec. 164(f).
4. IRC Sec. 1401.
5. IRC Sec. 1401(b)(2).

The AMT is calculated as follows:

(1) compute alternative minimum taxable income (AMTI, see Q 8558);

(2) subtract the exemption amount from AMTI; and

(3) multiply the remaining AMTI (step (2), above), by the applicable AMT rate.

For purposes of sheltering lower income taxpayers from being subject to AMT, the Code exempts certain amounts of income. Only AMTI in excess of the exemption amount is subject to AMT. The 2018 exemption amounts are as follows:[1]

Filing Status	AMT Exemption
Married filing jointly or qualifying widow(er)	$86,200
Single or Head of Household	$55,400
Married filing separately	$43,100

A 28 percent AMT rate applies to excess taxable income. In 2018, the 28 percent rate applies to excess taxable income above $95,750 for married taxpayers filing separately and $191,500 for joint returns, individual returns and estates and trusts.

For purposes of computing AMT, the taxpayer is allowed to take the foreign tax credit and certain other credits (see Q 8557).[2] After computing AMT, the AMT amount is compared with the taxpayer's regular income tax liability. If the regular tax is lower than AMT, the difference is AMT that is owing in addition to the tax. Stated differently, the taxpayer must pay the higher of the AMT or the regular tax.[3]

Example; For 2018, Asher's regular income tax liability is $75,000 but his AMT tax liability is $95,000, or $20,000 more than his regular income tax liability. Asher's liability is $95,000 ($75,000 regular income tax and $20,000 AMT).

8557. Are personal tax credits allowed to offset AMT liability?

Several refundable tax credits, such as the earned income credit and the refundable portion of the child tax credit, are allowed as an offset against AMT liability. Other personal nonrefundable credits also allowed as an offset include:

- Adoption tax credit
- Child and dependent care credit
- Nonrefundable portion of the child tax credit
- Certain learning credits

1. IRC Sec. 55(d)(1), Rev. Proc. 2017-58.
2. IRC Sec. 55(b)(1)(A), Rev. Proc. 2017-58.
3. IRC Sec. 55(a).

- Tax credit for IRAs and retirement plans
- Energy saving credits[1]

8558. How is alternative minimum taxable income (AMTI) computed?

Alternative minimum taxable income (AMTI) is taxable income, with adjustments made in the way certain items are treated for AMT purposes, increased by tax preference items.[2]

Except as otherwise provided below and in Q 8559 and Q 8560, the provisions that apply in determining the regular taxable income of a taxpayer also generally apply in determining the AMTI of the taxpayer.[3] In addition, references to a non-corporate taxpayer's adjusted gross income (AGI) or modified AGI in determining the amount of items of income, exclusion, or deduction must be treated as references to the taxpayer's AGI or modified AGI as determined for regular tax purposes.[4]

The following chart is a non-exclusive comparison of the different treatment of certain items in the computation of regular income tax as compared to the computation of AMT:[5]

Item	Regular Income Tax Computation	AMT Computation
Standard deduction (taxpayer does not itemize)	Allowed	Not allowed
Phase out of itemized deductions	Phased out if AGI exceeds applicable thresholds	No phase out
Medical Expenses	Allowed as itemized deductions to the extent they exceed 10% of AGI	Same
Taxes	State income taxes, property taxes, etc. allowed as itemized deductions	Not allowed
Home Mortgage Interest	Allowed	Allows only acquisition indebtedness including loans taken to improve principal residence or second home. Interest attributed to refinanced amounts in excess of original loan not allowed.

1. IRC Sec. 26(a)(2).
2. IRC Sec. 55(b)(2).
3. Treas. Reg. §1.55-1(a).
4. Treas. Reg. §1.55-1(b).
5. IRC Secs. 56, 58.

Item	Regular Income Tax Computation	AMT Computation
State Tax Refund	Included in gross income if previously deducted as itemized deduction	Since state taxes are not allowed as a deduction, refunds are not included in income. Amount of regular income entered as a negative amount.
Interest expense related to tax-exempt interest income	Not allowed	Allowed if interest expense is related to tax-exempt private activity bonds
Miscellaneous itemized deductions	Allowed to the extent they exceed 2% of AGI assuming the taxpayer itemizes	Not allowed
Qualified stock options	Exercise of a qualified stock option not taxable	Difference between amount paid to acquire the stock and the FMV of the stock is included as AMTI income
Tax-exempt income	Not included in gross income	Included in AMTI income

8559. Is there an alternative minimum tax (AMT) credit for an AMT liability incurred in a prior tax year?

Yes. There are two factors that contribute to the imposition of AMT. There are "exclusion items" and "deferral items." Examples of an exclusion item include miscellaneous itemized deductions and state or local taxes that are deductible for regular income tax purposes, but never for AMT purposes. For this reason, there is never a credit for an exclusion item.

For AMT purposes, a deferral item is simply a matter of a timing difference. For example, certain property depreciated using the accelerated depreciation method must be depreciated under the straight line method for AMT purposes. Thus, for regular income tax purposes, depreciation amounts in the early years of property depreciated under the accelerated method will be higher than under the straight line method. For that reason, it will cause AMTI to be higher than regular taxable income. However, in later years, depreciation amounts for property depreciated under the accelerated method will be lower than depreciation amounts calculated using straight line depreciation.

Therefore, in the absence of an AMT credit for a deferral item, the taxpayer would be subject to double negative tax consequences with respect to one item.

Example: In 2017, Asher is subject to AMT. Although for regular income tax purposes, based on the accelerated depreciation method, Asher is entitled to a $2,500 depreciation deduction, for AMT purposes the straight line depreciate deduction is $1,750. As a result, Asher's depreciation deduction is the lesser $1,750 amount.

In 2018, Asher is not subject to AMT. However, based on the accelerated depreciation method, his regular income tax depreciation deduction is $1,500 (it would have been $1,750 if depreciated under the straight line method)

So, in the AMT year, Asher was not allowed to take the higher accelerated depreciation deduction. Later, in the non-AMT year, Asher was compelled to take the lower accelerated depreciation deduction.

Fortunately, there is an AMT credit to allow an adjustment in the non-AMT year. Using Form 8801, the AMT from the prior year is recalculated based on what it would have been but for the deferral item.[1] So in the above example, Asher's AMT would be refigured using the accelerated depreciation deduction. The difference between the actual AMT tax and the recomputed AMT tax is called the AMT credit. Although the AMT credit is nonrefundable, it is cumulative, so it can be carried forward to subsequent tax years until it is fully used.[2]

8560. What is the alternative minimum tax (AMT) exemption? Is there a phase out of the AMT exemption?

The purpose of the AMT exemption is to prevent its imposition on lower income taxpayers. The exemption amounts are: $55,400 for single and head of household filers, $86,200 for joint filers and $43,100 for married taxpayers filing separately.

However, the AMT exemption does phase out when AMTI reaches certain threshold levels.[3] The phase out is a reduction of the exemption by 25 percent of each dollar over the applicable threshold. The following chart sets forth the applicable 2018 AMTI thresholds as well as the total phase out amount.[4]

Filing Status	AMTI Exemption Phase Out Threshold Amount	AMTI Total Phase Out Amount
Married filing jointly or qualifying widow(er)	$164,100	$508,900
Single or Head of Household	$123,100	$344,700
Married filing separately	$82,050	$254,450

Example: In 2018, Asher and Ashley, a married couple, have AMTI of $200,000. Their AMT exemption without considering the phase out is $86,200. However, the couple's AMTI is $200,000 and the AMTI exemption phase out threshold amount is $164,100. As a result, their AMT exceeds the threshold amount by $35,900. Applying the phase out, the couple's 2018 exemption amount is reduced from $86,200 to $77,225 (a reduction of $8,975, or 25 percent * $35,900).

8561. Are there special AMT exemption rules that apply to a child who is subject to the kiddie tax?

If a child is subject to the kiddie tax (see Q 8562), it is possible that he or she may be subject to AMT. Under special rules, the AMT exemption of a child subject to the kiddie tax in 2018 is the lesser of the AMT exemption for a single taxpayer ($55,400) or the total of the child's earned income plus $7,650.[5]

1. IRC Sec. 53(d).
2. IRC Sec. 53(b).
3. IRC Sec. 55(d)(3).
4. Rev. Proc. 2017-58.
5. IRC Sec. 59(j); Rev. Proc. 2017-58.

Minors

8562. What is the "kiddie tax"?

The so-called "kiddie tax" is designed to prevent parents from shifting unearned income that would otherwise be taxed at their higher rates to their children to be taxed at lower rates. To prevent this type of income shifting, the kiddie tax subjects a child's unearned income in excess of $2,100 (in 2018)[1] to taxation at the parents' highest marginal tax rate.

For the kiddie tax to apply, at least one parent must be alive at the close of the taxable year. The parent whose taxable income is taken into account is (a) in the case of parents who are not married, the custodial parent of the child (determined by using the support test for the dependency exemption, see Q 8518) and (b) in the case of married individuals filing separately, the individual with the greater taxable income.[2] If the custodial parent files a joint return with a spouse who is not a parent of the child, the total joint income is applicable in determining the child's rate.

If there is an adjustment to the parent's tax, the child's resulting liability must also be recomputed. In the event of an underpayment, interest, but not penalties, will be assessed against the child.[3]

The kiddie tax applies only to "net unearned income." "Net unearned income" is defined as adjusted gross income that is not attributable to earned income, and that exceeds (1) the $1,050 standard deduction for a dependent child in 2018 *plus* (2) the greater of $1,050 or (if the child itemizes) the amount of allowable itemized deductions that are directly connected with the production of his unearned income.[4] The source of the assets that produce unearned income need not be the child's parents.[5]

"Earned income" means all compensation for personal services actually rendered.[6] A child is therefore taxed at his own rate on reasonable compensation for services that he or she performs.

Regulations specify that "unearned income" includes any Social Security or pension payments received by the child, income resulting from a gift under the Uniform Gifts to Minors Act, and interest on both earned and unearned income.[7]

The kiddie tax applies to:

(1) a child under age eighteen; *or*

(2) a child age who has reached age eighteen, but whose earned income does not exceed one-half of his or her support; *or*

1. Rev. Proc. 2017-58.
2. Temp. Treas. Reg. §1.1(i)-1T, A-11, A-12.
3. Temp. Treas. Reg. §1.1(i)-1T, A-17, A-19.
4. IRC Sec. 1(g)(4); Rev. Proc. 2017-58.
5. Temp. Treas. Reg. §1.1(i)-1T, A-8.
6. IRC Secs. 911(d)(2), 1(g)(4)(A)(i).
7. Temp. Treas. Reg. §1.1(i)-1T, A-8, A-9, A-15.

(3) a child age nineteen to twenty-three who is a full time student with earned income that does not exceed one-half of his or her support.[1]

Whether a child's age is below the threshold ages listed above is determined at the end of the tax year. "Child," for purposes of the kiddie tax, includes children who are adopted, related by half-blood, or from a prior marriage of either spouse.[2] The kiddie tax applies without regard to whether the child is considered a dependent for tax purposes.

Example: In 2018, Pete is sixteen and both of his parents are alive. During 2018, Pete has $1,400 of interest income from a bank savings account and $1,700 of income that he earned from a paper route. Some of the interest income is attributable to Pete's paper route earnings that were deposited in the account. The balance of the interest was generated from cash gifts Pete received from his parents and grandparents. Pete has no itemized deductions and can be claimed as a dependent on his parent's return.

Therefore, for the taxable year 2018, Pete's standard deduction is $2,050, the amount of Pete's earned income, $1,700 from the paper route, plus $350. Of this standard deduction amount, $1,000 is allocated against unearned income, and $1,050 is allocated against earned income.

Although some of Pete's $1,400 of interest income is attributable to some of his paper route income deposited into his bank account, it is all treated as unearned income. Of that amount, $1,000 is taxed at Pete's own tax rate (10 percent). The remaining taxable unearned income of $400 will be taxed at his parents' highest marginal tax rate.

8563. Can parents include the amount of their child's unearned income subject to the kiddie tax on their own income tax return?

Under certain circumstances, parents may elect to include their child's unearned income subject to the kiddie tax on their own income tax return, thus avoiding the necessity of the child filing a return. The election is available to parents whose child has gross income of more than $1,050 and less than $10,500 (in 2018),[3] all of which is from interest and dividends.[4] However, by doing so, the parents increase their adjusted gross income and may become subject to potential phase outs or other reductions in tax benefits that decrease as AGI exceeds certain threshold levels.

The election is unavailable if there has been backup withholding under the child's Social Security number or if estimated tax payments have been made in the name and Social Security number of the child.

8564. Who is taxed on the income from property that is transferred to a minor under a uniform "Gifts to Minors" act?

As a general rule, the income is taxable to the minor. However, as discussed in Q 8562, unearned income of children (even potentially up to age twenty-three), may be subject to the kiddie tax.

1. IRC Sec. 1(g)(2).
2. Temp. Treas. Reg. §1.1(i)-1T, A-13, A-14.
3. Rev. Proc. 2017-58.
4. IRC Sec. 1(g)(7); Rev. Proc. 2008-66, 2008-45 IRB 107, as modified and superseded by Rev. Proc. 2009-21, 2009-1 CB 860.

To the extent that income from the transferred property is used for the minor's support, it may be taxed to the person who is legally obligated to support the minor.[1] State laws differ as to a parent's obligation to support. The income will be taxable to the parent only to the extent that it is actually used to discharge or satisfy the parent's obligation under state law.[2]

1. Rev. Rul. 56-484, 1956-2 CB 23; Rev. Rul. 59-357, 1959-2 CB 212.
2. IRC Sec. 677(b).

PART II: CAPITAL GAINS AND LOSSES

8565. What is a "capital asset"?

Generally, any property held as an investment is a capital asset, except that rental real estate is typically not a capital asset because it is treated as a trade or business asset.[1]

The Code defines a "capital asset" by exclusion. So for purposes of determining whether a certain type of property is a capital asset, the following types of property are excluded:

(1) property (including inventory and stock in trade) held primarily for sale to customers;

(2) real or depreciable property used in the taxpayer's trade or business;

(3) copyrights and literary, musical, or artistic compositions (or similar properties) created by the taxpayer, or merely owned by him, if the taxpayer's basis in the property is determined (other than by reason of IRC Section 1022, which governs the basis determination of inherited property) by reference to the creator's tax basis;

(4) letters, memoranda, and similar properties produced by or for the taxpayer, or owned by him if the taxpayer's basis is determined by reference to the tax basis of the producer or recipient;

(5) accounts or notes receivable acquired in the taxpayer's trade or business for services rendered or sales of property described in (1), above;

(6) certain publications of the United States government;

(7) any commodities derivative financial instrument held by a commodities derivatives dealer;

(8) any hedging instrument clearly identified as such by the required time; or

(9) supplies of a type regularly used or consumed by the taxpayer in the ordinary course of the taxpayer's trade or business.[2]

8566. What are the current long-term capital gains tax rates?

For long-term capital gain, adjusted net capital gain (see Q 8567) is generally subject to the following tax rates:

(1) 0 percent for taxpayers in the 10 and 15 percent tax brackets;

(2) 15 percent for taxpayers in the 25 percent, 28 percent, 33 percent and 35 percent tax brackets; and

(3) 20 percent for taxpayers in the 39.6 percent tax bracket.

1. See IRS Pub. 544.
2. IRC Sec. 1221; Treas. Reg. §1.1221-1.

However, detailed rules as to the exact calculation of the capital gains tax result in some exceptions. See Q 8567 (determining amount of capital gain), Q 8568 (Section 1250, Section 1202 and collectibles property) and Q 8572 (holding period requirement for determining whether gain is subject to long-term or short-term rates).[1]

See Q 8578 for an outline of the netting process used in determining capital gains and losses when multiple asset classes are involved.

Beginning in 2013, taxpayers with adjusted gross income in excess of certain thresholds may be subject to the 3.8 percent net investment income tax pursuant to IRC Section 1411 (see Q 8584 to Q 8594). This 3.8 percent is a surtax added to the taxpayer's otherwise applicable tax rate.

8567. How is net capital gain taxed?

Net capital gain is the excess of net long-term capital gain for the taxable year over net short-term capital loss for such year.[2] However, net capital gain for any taxable year is reduced (but not below zero) by any amount the taxpayer takes into account under the investment income exception to the investment interest deduction.[3]

If a taxpayer has net capital gain for any tax year, the IRC provides that the tax will not exceed the *sum* of the following six items:

(A) the tax computed at regular rates (without regard to the rules for capital gain) on the *greater* of (i) taxable income reduced by the net capital gain, or (ii) the *lesser* of (I) the amount of taxable income taxed at a rate below 25 percent, *or* (II) taxable income reduced by the adjusted net capital gain;

(B) 0 percent of the taxpayer's adjusted net capital gain (or, if less, taxable income) that does not exceed the *excess* (if any) of (i) the amount of taxable income that would (without regard to this paragraph) be taxed at a rate below 25 percent *over* (ii) the taxable income reduced by the adjusted net capital gain;

(C) 15 percent of the lesser of (i) so much of the taxpayer's adjusted net capital gain (or, if less, taxable income) as *exceeds* the amount on which a tax is determined under (B), above, or (ii) the *excess* of (I) the amount of taxable income which would be taxed at below 39.6 percent *over* (II) the sum of the amounts on which a tax is determined under (A) and (B), above;

(D) 20 percent of the taxpayer's adjusted net capital gain (or, if less, taxable income) in *excess* of the sum of the amounts on which tax is determined under (B) and (C), above;

(E) 25 percent of the *excess* (if any) of (i) the unrecaptured IRC Section 1250 gain (or, if less, the net capital gain (determined without regard to qualified dividend income)), *over* (ii) the *excess* (if any) of (I) the sum of the amount on which tax is

1. IRC Sec. 1(h), as amended by ATRA.
2. IRC Sec. 1222(11).
3. IRC Secs. 163(d)(4)(B)(iii), 1(h)(2).

determined under (A) above, *plus* the net capital gain, *over* (II) taxable income (see Q 8568 for a discussion of unrecaptured IRC Section 1250 gain); *and*

(F) 28 percent of the amount of taxable income in *excess* of the sum of the amounts on which tax is determined under (A) through (D) above. See Q 8568 for a discussion of 28 percent gain.

For most long-term capital gains, this complicated formula generally results in a maximum capital gains rate on adjusted net capital gain equal to: (i) 20 percent for individuals taxed at the 39.6 percent income tax rate, (ii) 15 percent for individuals taxed at the 25, 28, 33 or 35 percent income tax rates, and (iii) 0 percent for individuals taxed at the 15 percent or 10 percent income tax rates.

8568. What rates apply to gain attributable to the sale or exchange of capital gains property classified as Section 1250 property, Section 1202 stock or collectibles?

Gain attributable to the sale or exchange of collectibles, IRC Section 1202 gain (i.e., qualified small business stock), and unrecaptured IRC Section 1250 gain are subject to different tax rates. Gain on the sale or exchange of collectibles and IRC Section 1202 property is taxed at 28 percent, and unrecaptured gain on IRC Section 1250 property is taxed at 25 percent.[1]

"Collectibles gain" is taxable gain on the sale or exchange of a collectible that is a capital asset held for more than one year.[2] Examples of collectibles include artwork, gems and coins.[3]

"Section 1202 gain" is the gain on the sale or exchange of Section 1202 stock. Pursuant to IRC Section 1202, an individual may exclude 50 percent of the taxable gain on the sale or exchange of "qualified small business stock" that is held for more than 5 years.

"Unrecaptured Section 1250 gain" is the portion of the gain on the sale or exchange of real property attributable to depreciation. Nonresidential real property (such as commercial buildings) and residential rental property (such as apartment buildings) are Section 1250 property and are depreciated under the straight line method (i.e., the same amount of depreciation is taken every tax year).[4] Each year's depreciation reduces the basis of the real property by a like amount.[5] So when such real property is sold, the gain attributable to the basis reduction is considered unrecaptured Section 1250 gain.

Example: Asher owns a commercial building with an original basis in the building of $500,000. After several years, when the basis of the building had been reduced to $350,000, Asher sells the building for $500,000. Even though the building did not appreciate, Asher has a gain of $150,000 ($500,000 minus $350,000), all of which is attributable to the depreciation reduction of basis. Such gain is considered to be unrecaptured Section 1250 gain.

1. IRC Sec. 1(h).
2. IRC Sec. 1(h)(5).
3. See IRC Sec. 408(m)(2).
4. IRC Sec. 168(b)(3)(A) and (B).
5. IRC Sec. 1016(a)(2).

8569. What new rules have been developed in recent years to change the tax rates applicable to long-term capital gain?

Congress has taken steps in recent years to reduce the rates applicable to long-term capital gains. As such, long-term capital gains recognized on or after May 6, 2003 are subject to lower tax rates today than has historically been the case. For taxpayers in the 25, 28, 33 and 35 percent ordinary income tax brackets, the rate on long-term capital gains was reduced from 20 percent to 15 percent in 2003 through 2012. For taxpayers in the 10 and 15 percent brackets, the rate on long-term capital gains was reduced from 10 percent to 5 percent in 2003 through 2007, and then to 0 percent in 2008 through 2012. As discussed below, these lower capital gain rates have been made permanent for tax years beginning after 2012.[1]

The American Taxpayer Relief Act of 2012 ("ATRA") extended the 0 percent and 15 percent capital gain rates for most taxpayers and increased the rates for taxpayers in the highest income tax bracket.

ATRA permanently increased the rate on long-term capital gains to 20 percent for taxpayers with taxable income exceeding an annual applicable threshold amount. For 2018, the threshold amount is $426,700 for single taxpayers, $480,050 for married taxpayers filing jointly, $453,350 for heads of households and $240,025 for married taxpayers filing separately.[2] The applicable threshold amounts are adjusted annually for inflation.[3]

For taxpayers in the 10 or 15 percent income tax brackets, the rate on long-term capital gains is now permanently set at 0 percent. Taxpayers in the 25, 28, 33 and 35 percent tax brackets will continue to be taxed at 15 percent on long-term capital gains.[4]

In addition, beginning January 1, 2013, a new investment income tax of 3.8 percent applies to certain investment-type income (including income received from capital gains). The investment income tax applies for taxpayers whose annual adjusted gross income exceeds the investment income threshold amount ($250,000 for married taxpayers filing jointly, $125,000 for married taxpayers filing separately and $200,000 for all other taxpayers).[5] See Q 8584 to Q 8594 for a detailed discussion of the investment income tax.

The rates applicable for collectibles gain, IRC Section 1202 gain (i.e., qualified small business stock), and unrecaptured IRC Section 1250 gain remained unchanged. See Q 8568.[6]

Repeal of qualified 5-year gain. For tax years beginning after December 31, 2000, if certain requirements were met, the maximum rates on "qualified 5-year gain" could be reduced to 8 percent and 18 percent (in place of 10 percent and 20 percent, respectively). Furthermore, a noncorporate taxpayer in the 25 percent bracket (or higher) who held a capital asset on January 1, 2001 could elect to treat the asset as if it had been sold and repurchased for its fair

1. IRC Sec. 1(h)(1), as amended by ATRA; TIPRA 2005 Sec. 102, *amending* JGTRRA 2003 Sec. 303.
2. Rev. Proc. 2017-58.
3. IRC Secs. 1(i), 1(h), as amended by ATRA, Secs. 101(b)(3)(C) and 102(b).
4. IRC Sec. 1(h), as amended by ATRA, Sec. 102.
5. IRC Sec. 1411.
6. IRC Sec. 1(h).

market value on January 1, 2001 (or on January 2, 2001 in the case of publicly traded stock). If a noncorporate taxpayer made this election, the holding period for the elected assets began after December 31, 2000, thereby making the asset eligible for the 18 percent rate if it was later sold after having been held by the taxpayer for more than five years from the date of the deemed sale and deemed reacquisition.[1] Under JGTRRA 2003, the 5-year holding period requirement, and the 18 percent and 8 percent tax rates for qualified 5-year gain, were repealed. Though this repeal was scheduled to sunset along with the reduced rates on long-term capital gains, it was made permanent under ATRA.

8570. What is "tax basis" and how is it used in determining the amount of a taxpayer's capital gain or loss?

"Tax basis" is a taxpayer's after-tax investment in property. In other words, when a taxpayer acquires property for money, the purchase price is presumed to be his or her after tax investment in such property.[2] When property is sold or exchanged, for purposes of computing gain, the difference between the amount received less the taxpayer's basis in the property is the taxable gain.[3] Similarly, for purposes of computing a loss (meaning the taxpayer received less than the original cost of the property), the difference between the taxpayer's basis in the property and the amount received is the taxable loss.[4]

> *Example:* In 2016, Asher purchased Apple stock for $1,000. In 2018, Asher sold the stock for $1,500. Asher's taxable gain is $500, or the difference between the amount received and his basis in the stock ($1,500 minus $1,000). No tax applies to the $1,000 received because that amount represents the recovery of Asher's initial after-tax investment in the property, i.e., his basis.
>
> In the alternative, if Asher sold the Apple stock for $500, his taxable loss would be $500, or the difference between his basis in the stock (what he paid for it) and what he received in the sale ($1,000 minus $500). In this case, Asher would recognize a loss because the amount he received is less than what he originally paid.

If the taxpayer acquires property other than by purchase, basis is determined pursuant to different rules. For example, if the taxpayer acquires property from a decedent by inheritance or bequest, the basis in the property is its fair market value as of the date of the decedent's death.[5]

New rules regarding consistent basis reporting provide, generally, that the basis of property acquired from a decedent cannot exceed the final value of such property that has been used for estate tax purposes.[6]

With respect to a gift of property, the general rule is the donee taxpayer takes the donor's basis in the property.[7]

1. IRC Secs. 1(h)(2), 1(h)(9), prior to amendment by JGTRRA 2003; JCWAA 2002 Sec. 414(a) and CRTRA 2000 Sec. 314(c), amending TRA '97 Sec. 311(e).
2. IRC Sec. 1012.
3. IRC Sec. 1001(a).
4. IRC Sec. 1001(a).
5. IRC Sec. 1014.
6. IRC Sec. 1014(f).
7. IRC Sec. 1015(a).

Example: Asher gifts Apple stock he purchased for $1,000 to his friend Ashley. At the time of the gift, the stock had a fair market value of $1,500. Ashley's basis in the stock is $1,000, the same as Asher's. So if she sold the stock for $1500, she would recognize a $500 gain.

On the other hand, there is an exception to the rule that the donee taxpayer takes the donor's basis in the property. This occurs when, at the time of the gift, the donor's basis is greater than the fair market value of the gifted property. In that case, the donee taxpayer's basis is the fair market value of the property.[1]

Example: Asher gifts Apple stock he purchased for $1,000 to his friend Ashley. At the time of the gift, the stock had a fair market value of $500. Because Asher's basis of $1,000 is greater than the $500 fair market value, Ashley's basis in the stock is $500. As a result, if she sold the stock for $500, she would recognize no gain or loss. The reason for this rule is to prevent one taxpayer from shifting a taxable loss to the other taxpayer. If Ashley had taken Asher's $1,000 basis, she would have reported a $500 loss rather than Asher.

8571. How is tax basis adjusted and what affect does it have in the computation of capital gain or loss?

As discussed in Q 8570, gain or loss is measured by determining whether the amount received in a sale or exchange of property was more or less than the taxpayer's "basis." If the amount received is more than basis, there is a taxable gain. Conversely, if basis is greater than the amount received there is a loss. However, during the period of a taxpayer's ownership of property, certain adjustments to the original tax basis are required. Thus, tax basis, as adjusted, is referred to as "adjusted basis."

In the course of a taxpayer's ownership of property, basis can be increased or it can be decreased.

Capital Improvement

Example: Asher purchases a ten story office building for $500,000. Subsequently, Asher decides to add an eleventh story to the building at a cost of $100,000. As a capital improvement, Asher's original $500,000 basis is adjusted upward to $600,000[2] and becomes the adjusted basis in the building.

Depreciation

Generally, depreciation is a means of deducting the cost of an asset over its useful life. For example, the cost of a commercial building (excluding land, which is nondepreciable) is depreciated over a useful life of 39 years.[3] Based on a tax fiction, at the end of the 39 year depreciation period, the building will be completely "used up" and worth nothing. Therefore, every year, the basis of the building is adjusted downward by the amount of that year's depreciation deduction.[4]

Example: Asher purchases a ten story office building for $390,000.[5] Because the building is depreciable over thirty-nine years, Asher claims a $10,000 depreciation deduction each year. After nine years, Asher's

1. IRC Sec. 1015(a).
2. IRC Sec. 1016(a)(1).
3. IRC Sec. 168(c).
4. IRC Sec. 1016(a)(2).
5. For purposes of this example, the amount of the purchase price attributable to the land is ignored.

original basis is adjusted downward to $300,000 ($390,000 minus $90,000). At that time, if Asher were to sell the building for $400,000, he would have a taxable gain of $100,000 ($400,000 minus $300,000).

8572. What is the "holding period" for long-term and short-term capital gain, and how is the holding period calculated?

Whether a capital gain or loss is long-term or short-term is determined by how long the taxpayer owned the property in question. Generally, a capital gain or loss is long-term if the property giving rise to the gain or loss was owned *for more than one year* and short-term if the property was owned for *one year or less*.[1]

To determine how long a taxpayer has owned property (i.e., the "holding period"), the taxpayer must begin counting on the day *after* the property is acquired. For these purposes, the same date in each successive month is considered to be the first day of a new month. The date on which the property is disposed of is included (i.e., counted) in the holding period.[2]

If property is acquired on the last day of the month, the holding period begins on the first day of the following month. Therefore, if it is sold prior to the first day of the 13th month following the acquisition, the gain or loss will be short-term.[3] According to IRS Publication 544 (published in November 1982), if property is acquired *near* the end of the month and the holding period begins on a date that does not occur in every month (e.g., the 29th, 30th, or 31st), the last day of each month that lacks that date is considered to begin a new month (however, later editions of Publication 544 have omitted this statement).

Example 1: Mrs. Murphy bought a capital asset on January 1, 2018. She would begin counting on January 2, 2018. The 2nd day of each successive month would begin a new month. If Mrs. Murphy sold the asset on January 1, 2019, her holding period would not be more than one year. To have a long-term capital gain or loss she would have to sell the asset on or after January 2, 2019.

Example 2: Mrs. Tate bought a capital asset on January 30, 2018. She would begin counting on January 31, 2018. Since February does not have thirty-one days, Mrs. Tate will start a new month on February 28. In months that have only thirty days, the thirtieth will begin a new month.

In some cases, such as when property is received as a gift or in a like-kind exchange, the IRC allows for the "tacking" of a holding period meaning that the holding period of a previous owner of the property carries over to the new owner or the holding period of an asset exchanged for another carries over to the exchanged property.[4]

Example: Abe buys 500 shares of XYZ Corp. stock for $7,500, on December 4, 2017. On September 20, 2018, Abe transfers the stock to his daughter, Diana, as a gift. On December 20, 2018, Diana sells the stock for $9,000. Even though Diana actually owned the stock for more than a year, by application of the "tacking" rule, the holding period begins on December 4, 2017, the date the stock was purchased by Abe. Additionally, Diana assumes Abe's $7,500 basis in the stock. So upon the sale, Diana has a $1,500 long-term capital gain ($9,000 minus $7,500).

1. IRC Sec. 1222.
2. Rev. Rul. 70-598, 1970-2 CB 168.
3. Rev. Rul. 66-7, 1966-1 CB 188.
4. IRC Sec. 1223.

8573. Are there any special rules applicable in determining whether a gain or loss is long-term or short-term when a short sale is involved?

Whether capital gain or loss on a short sale is long-term or short-term will ordinarily be determined by the seller's holding period in the stock used to close the sale.[1] For most purposes, the capital gain or loss is long-term if the holding period is more than one year. If the holding period is one year or less, the gain is short-term. (See Q 8572 for a detailed discussion of the holding period requirement.)

In a "short sale," a seller agrees to sell stock to another at a fixed price on a future date. If the future date is more than a year from the date the taxpayer acquired the stock, he or she would be able to convert short-term capital gain (taxed at ordinary tax rates, i.e., up to 39.6 percent) to long-term capital gain (i.e., with rates of 0 percent, 15 percent or 20 percent). IRC Sections 1233 and 1259 are designed to prevent such abuse.

> *Example:* On March 1, 2017, Asher acquires stock for $200. On September 1, the fair market value of the stock is $300. To lock in the appreciation, Asher enters a short sale to close on April 1, 2018. Without IRC Sections 1233 and 1259, Asher would effectively convert a short-term holding period into a long-term holding period; and, thus, recognize long-term capital gain.

To prevent individuals from using short sales to convert short-term gains to long-term gains or long-term losses to short-term losses, and to prevent the creation of artificial losses, the IRC and regulations provide special rules as follows:

(1) If on the date the short sale is closed (see below), any "substantially identical property" has been held by the seller for a period of one year or less, any *gain* realized on property used to close the sale will, to the extent of the quantity of such substantially identical property, be *short-term* capital gain.[2] This is true even though the stock actually used to close the short sale has been held by the seller for more than one year. This rule does not apply to *losses* realized on the property used to close the sale;

(2) If *any* substantially identical property is acquired by the seller after the short sale and on or before the date the sale is closed, any *gain* realized on property used to close the sale will, to the extent of the quantity of such substantially identical property, be *short-term* capital gain.[3] This is true regardless of how long the substantially identical property has been held, how long the stock used to close the short sale has been held, and how much time has elapsed between the short sale and the date the sale is closed. This rule does not apply to *losses* realized on the property used to close the sale;

(3) The holding period of any substantially identical property held one year or less, or acquired after the short sale and on or before the date the short sale is closed will, to the extent of the quantity of stock sold short, be deemed to have begun on the

1. Treas. Reg. §1.1233-1(a)(3). See *Bingham*, 27 BTA 186 (1932), *acq.* 1933-1 CB 2.
2. IRC Sec. 1233(b)(1); Treas. Reg. §1.1233-1(c).
3. IRC Sec. 1233(b)(1); Treas. Reg. §1.1233-1(c).

date the sale is closed or the date such property is sold or otherwise disposed of, whichever is earlier. If the quantity of such substantially identical property held for one year or less or so acquired exceeds the quantity of stock sold short, the "renewed" holding period will normally be applied to individual units of such property in the order in which they were acquired (beginning with earliest acquisition), but only to so much of the property as does not exceed the quantity sold short. Any excess retains its original holding period.[1] Where the short sale is entered into as part of an *arbitrage operation* in stocks or securities, this order of application is altered so that the "renewed" holding period will be applied first to substantially identical property acquired for arbitrage operations and held at the close of business on the day of the short sale and then in the order of acquisition as described in the previous sentence. The holding period of substantially identical property *not* acquired for arbitrage operations will be affected only to the extent that the quantity sold short exceeds the amount of substantially identical property acquired for arbitrage operations;[2]

(4) If on the date of a short sale *any* substantially identical property has been held by the seller for more than one year, any *loss* realized on property used to close the sale will, to the extent of the quantity of such substantially identical property, be *long-term* capital loss.[3] This is true even though the stock actually used to close the short sale has been held by the seller for a year or less. This rule does not apply to *gains* realized on the property used to close the sale.

8574. How is a loss realized on a sale between related persons treated for tax purposes?

If an individual sells property at a loss to a related person (as defined below), that loss is disallowed and may *not* be used to offset capital gains for income tax purposes.[4] It makes no difference that the sale was a bona fide, arm's-length transaction.[5] Neither does it matter that the sale was made indirectly through an unrelated middleman.[6] The loss on the sale of stock will be disallowed even though the sale and purchase are made separately on a stock exchange and the stock certificates received are not the certificates sold.[7] However, these rules will not apply to any loss of the distributing corporation (or the distributee) in the case of a distribution in complete liquidation.[8]

A loss realized on the exchange of properties between related persons will also be disallowed under these rules.[9]

1. IRC Sec. 1233(b)(2); Treas. Reg. §1.1233-1(c)(2).
2. IRC Sec. 1233(f); Treas. Reg. §1.1233-1(f).
3. IRC Sec. 1233(d); Treas. Reg. §1.1233-1(c)(4).
4. IRC Sec. 267(a); Treas. Reg. §1.267(a)-1 and Rev. Rul. 2008-5, 2008-3 IRB 271.
5. Treas. Reg. §1.267(a)-1(c).
6. See *Hassen v. Comm.*, 599 F.2d 305 (9th Cir. 1979).
7. *McWilliams v. Comm.*, 331 U.S. 694 (1947).
8. IRC Sec. 267(a)(1).
9. IRC Sec. 267(a)(1).

"Related persons" for this purpose includes the following:

(1) members of the same family (i.e., brothers, sisters, spouses, ancestors, and lineal descendants (but not if they are in-laws));[1]

(2) an individual and a corporation of which the individual actually or constructively owns more than 50 percent of the stock;

Example: Amy owns a parcel of land with a fair market value of $50,000. Amy's basis in the land is $100,000. Amy sells the land to a corporation wholly owned by her brother, Asher. Although Asher owns no stock of the corporation, through the attribution rules, a taxpayer is deemed to constructively own all the stock owned by his brother.[2] For that reason, the $50,000 loss would be disallowed.

(3) a grantor and a fiduciary of a trust. The relationship between a grantor and fiduciary did not prevent recognition of loss on a sale of stock between them where the fiduciary purchased the stock in his individual capacity and where the sale was unrelated to the grantor-fiduciary relationship;[3]

(4) fiduciaries of two trusts if the same person is the grantor of both;

(5) a fiduciary and a beneficiary of the same trust;

(6) a fiduciary of a trust and a beneficiary of another trust set up by the same grantor;

(7) a fiduciary of a trust and a corporation of which the trust or the grantor of the trust actually or constructively owns more than 50 percent of the stock;

(8) a person and an IRC Section 501 tax-exempt organization controlled by the person or members of his family (as described in (1) above);

(9) a corporation and a partnership if the same person actually or constructively owns more than 50 percent of the stock of the corporation, and has more than a 50 percent interest in the partnership;

(10) two S corporations if the same persons actually or constructively own more than 50 percent of the stock of each;

(11) an S corporation and a C corporation, if the same persons actually or constructively own more than 50 percent of the stock of each;

(12) generally, an executor and a beneficiary of an estate; or

(13) possibly an individual and an individual retirement account (IRA).[4]

1. See Let. Rul. 9017008.
2. IRC Sec. 267(c)(4).
3. Let. Rul. 9017008.
4. IRC Sec. 267(b).

Special rules apply for purposes of determining constructive ownership of stock.[1]

Generally, loss will be disallowed on a sale between a partnership and a partner who owns more than a 50 percent interest, or between two partnerships if the same persons own more than a 50 percent interest in each.[2] Furthermore, with respect to transactions between two partnerships having one or more common partners *or* in which one or more of the partners in each partnership are related, a portion of the loss will be disallowed according to the relative interests of the partners.[3] If the transaction is between a partnership and an individual who is related to one of the partners, any deductions for losses will be denied with respect to the related partner's distributive share, but not with respect to the relative shares of each unrelated partner.[4] Loss on a sale or exchange (other than of inventory) between two corporations that are members of the same controlled group (using a 50 percent test instead of 80 percent) is generally not denied but is deferred until the property is transferred outside the controlled group.[5]

If the related person to whom property was originally sold (or exchanged), sells or exchanges the same property (or property whose tax basis is determined by reference to such property) at a gain, the gain will be recognized only to the extent it exceeds the loss originally denied by reason of the related parties rules.[6]

Planning Point: If one family member is considering selling a closely held business to another at a loss, there are probably better ways to achieve tax savings than for the seller to give up a tax loss. A related party buyer might pay a little more for a business than a non-related party. The goodwill may be justifiably higher because of the relationship, the customer base or the reputation, among other reasons. The seller can realize tax savings through the deal structure; the buyer can realize savings by depreciation and amortization.

8575. Can the redemption of a debt obligation result in capital gains treatment?

Redemption of a debt obligation can result in recognition of gain or loss in situations where the obligation was acquired at a premium or discount. The relevant issue for determining whether the retirement or satisfaction of the debt can result in a capital gain or loss is whether a sale or exchange has taken place. Historically, cases dealing with the subject have found that no sale or exchange takes place when the maker of a debt satisfies the obligations under the debt instrument.[7] IRC Section 1271 was enacted to change this result in many situations involving the redemption of debt obligations.

Under Section 1271, amounts received by the holder when the debt instrument is redeemed are treated as having been received in an exchange.[8] Because of this, gain or loss realized upon redemption can qualify for capital gains treatment.

1. See IRC Sec. 267(c).
2. IRC Sec. 707(b).
3. Temp. Treas. Reg. §1.267(a)-2T(c), A-2.
4. Treas. Reg. §1.267(b)-1(b).
5. IRC Sec. 267(f).
6. IRC Sec. 267(d); Treas. Reg. §1.267(d)-1.
7. See, for example, *Wood v. Comm.*, 25 TC 468 (1955).
8. IRC Sec. 1271(a)(1).

However, some debt instruments contain "original issue discount" which is a type of interest. These include debt instruments in which the maturity price exceeds the purchase price. The difference is the interest component.

> *Example:* Asher purchases an original issue discount debt for $1,000 that matures two years later for $1,250. The difference between the maturity amount and the purchase amount, $250, is essentially interest.

Original issue discount interest is reportable as ordinary income. Such ordinary income may be realized, however, in some transactions where there was an intention to call the obligation before maturity at the time the obligation was originally issued.[1] If this is the case, any gain realized in the transaction must be treated as ordinary income to the extent that the amount of gain does not exceed the sum of (a) the original issue discount, reduced by (b) the portion of original issue discount previously included in the gross income of any holder of the obligation.[2]

The requirement that ordinary income be recognized does not apply to certain tax-exempt obligations and to holders who purchased the debt instrument at a premium.[3]

8576. When is the gain or loss from sale or exchange of an option to purchase property treated as a capital gain or capital loss?

The sale or exchange of an option to purchase property may result in capital gain if the underlying property subject to the option is a capital asset. Similarly, losses arising from the taxpayer's failure to exercise the option may be treated as capital losses if the underlying property is a capital asset.[4]

> *Example:* Brenda is considering an investment in real property, but, because the purchase price is high, she purchases an option to buy the property for $5,000 within the next two years. The option is a capital asset because if Brenda had purchased the property outright it would have been a capital asset. Eleven months later, Brenda sells the option for $6,000. The $1,000 gain ($6,000 selling price minus $5,000 basis) is a short-term capital gain because Brenda held the option for less than one year.

Similarly, if the taxpayer fails to exercise the option, the option is treated as though it was sold or exchanged on the day the option expired for no consideration. Based on the taxpayer's holding period, the loss will be either long-term or short-term capital loss.[5]

In a recent Tax Court decision, the Tax Court held that a taxpayer was entitled to an ordinary loss deduction, rather than recognition of a capital loss, when the taxpayer abandoned an option to purchase certain real property. Because the taxpayer was in the business of purchasing and developing real property, the underlying real property was not a "capital asset." For that reason, the loss realized by the taxpayer when he abandoned his option was treated as an ordinary loss rather than a capital loss.[6]

1. IRC Sec. 1271(a)(2)(A).
2. IRC Sec. 1271(a)(2).
3. IRC Sec. 1271(a)(2)(B).
4. IRC Sec. 1234(a)(1).
5. IRC Sec. 1234(a)(2).
6. *Sutton v. Comm.*, TC Summ. Op. 20136, IRC Sec. 1221(a).

IRC Section 1234 provides special rules with regard to options to buy or sell stock, securities or commodities. Specifically, IRC Section 1234(b) provides short-term capital gain or loss treatment for the grantor of an option as follows:

- The option lapses or is terminated in a closing transaction.
- The underlying property is stock, securities, commodities or commodities futures.
- The option is not issued in the ordinary course of the grantors trade or business.

A "closing transaction" is defined as any transaction that terminates the taxpayer's obligations under the option other than an exercise or lapse of the option.[1]

See Q 8565 for a discussion of what constitutes a capital asset for purposes of capital gains treatment.

8577. Are there any special rules that apply in determining whether the sale of a patent gives rise to capital gains treatment?

Unlike typical asset sales, if the sale or exchange of a patent meets certain requirements, the sale will automatically qualify for long-term capital gains treatment regardless of the transferor's holding period and whether or not the patent would have been classified as a capital asset in the hands of the holder who transfers the patent.[2]

Sale of a patent will qualify for long-term capital gains treatment if the holder of the patent transfers either "all substantial rights" in the patent or an undivided interest in the patent.

The phrase "all substantial rights" is defined in the regulations to mean all rights in the patent that have value at the time the rights to the patent are transferred, whether or not the holder of the patent is the owner of those rights.[3] The holder does *not* transfer all substantial rights in the patent if the rights to the patent are:

(1) limited geographically within the country;

(2) confined to a period of time that is less than the entire remaining life of the patent;

(3) limited to a grant of rights, in fields of use within trades or industries, which are less than all the rights covered by the patent that exist and have value at the time of the transfer; or

(4) limited to a grant of rights that does not give the transferee rights to all the claims and inventions covered by the patent that exist and have value at the time of sale.[4]

1. IRC Sec. 1234(b)(2).
2. IRC Sec. 1235(a).
3. Treas. Reg. §1.1235-2(b)(1).
4. Treas. Reg. §1.1235-2(b)(2).

Conversely, the holder does not lose long-term capital gain treatment by retaining rights that are not considered substantial. The regulations provide that, depending upon all of the facts and circumstances of the transaction as a whole, the holder may retain the right to prohibit sub-licensing or sub-assignment by the transferee and may also fail to convey the right to use or sell the property that is the *subject* of the patent.[1]

The holder transfers an "undivided interest" in a patent when the holder transfers the same fractional share of every substantial right in the patent. A sale of the right to income from a patent, for example, does not constitute the sale of an undivided interest in the patent.[2]

This treatment is not available to all patent holders, however. The term "holder" is defined in IRC Section 1235 to include only (1) the original inventor of the property subject to the patent and (2) an individual who obtained his rights in the patent in exchange for money or other property *before* the property subject to the patent was actually put to use *if* that individual is neither (i) the inventor's employer or (ii) related to the inventor.[3]

Planning Point: Due to the limited definition of "holder" under the patent laws, if an employer maintains the rights to patents on property invented by its employees, the employer will not be eligible for this special capital gains treatment upon sale of the patent.

8578. What is the netting process used to determine whether the taxpayer has a capital gain or loss?

The complex rules applicable to capital gains taxation essentially establish four different types of capital assets. These groups of capital assets are:

(1) short-term capital assets, with no special tax rate;

(2) 28 percent capital assets, generally consisting of collectibles gain or loss, and IRC Section 1202 gain;

(3) 25 percent capital assets, consisting of assets that generate unrecaptured IRC Section 1250 gain; and

(4) all other long-term capital assets, which are taxed according to the taxpayer's income tax bracket: 20 percent (39.6 percent income tax bracket), 15 percent (25, 28, 33, or 35 percent income tax brackets), and 0 percent capital assets for taxpayers in the 15 and 10 percent tax brackets.

Within each group, gains and losses must be netted. Generally, if, as a result of this process, there is a net loss from asset-group "(1)," it is applied to reduce any net gain from groups "(2)," "(3)," or "(4)," in that order. If there is a net loss from group "(2)," it is applied to reduce any net

1. Treas. Reg. §1.1235-2(b)(3).
2. Treas. Reg. §1.1235-2(c).
3. IRC Sec. 1235(b).

gain from groups "(3)" or "(4)," in that order. If there is a net loss from group "(4)," it is applied to reduce any net gain from groups "(2)" or "(3)," in that order.[1]

If net capital losses result from the netting process described above, up to $3,000 ($1,500 in the case of married individuals filing separately) of losses can be deducted against ordinary income.[2] Any losses that are deducted would be treated as reducing net loss from groups "(1)," "(2)," or "(4)," in that order.

If there are net gains, such gains would generally be taxed as described above and discussed in Q 8566 and Q 8567.

If the taxpayer has capital gains and capital losses from investment property as well as gains and losses from Section 1231 business property (depreciable property used in a trade or business and held for more than one year), the latter gains and losses are netted against each other. If the netting results in a net gain, the gain is treated as if it were a long-term capital gain and included in the netting process for capital gains in group (4). On the other hand, if the netting results in a net loss from Section 1231 assets, this net loss is fully deductible as an ordinary loss and not subject to capital gain and loss netting.

Example: Claire, an attorney, sold 500 shares of stock, recognizing a $1,500 long-term capital gain and 200 shares of stock recognizing a $300 short-term capital gain. In the same year she sold an oriental rug used in her home for the past 5 years at a loss of $700 and a rental property, owned for nine months, for a short-term capital loss of $5,000. From her office she sold a computer system (a Section 1231 asset) at a loss of $1,200 and a set of law books (a Section 1231 asset) at a gain of $200. Both of these had been used in her practice for more than one year.

Claire's various gains and losses ("G/L") must first be grouped according to the following column headings and a net total computed for each group:

	Long-Term Capital G/L	**Short-Term Capital G/L**	**IRC 1231 Business Assets**
500 shares of stock	1,500		
200 shares of stock		300	
oriental rug *	—	—	—
rental property		(5,000)	
computer			(1,200)
law books			200
Net totals	1,500	(4,700)	(1,000)
* No loss deduction is allowed for the oriental rug since it was held for personal use.[3]			

Because the netting of the Section 1231 assets resulted in a net $1,000 loss, it is treated as a fully deductible ordinary loss and not subject to further netting. Netting short-term capital gain against short-term capital loss results in a net short-term capital loss of $4,700.

1. IRC Sec. 1(h)(1), as amended by ATRA; Notice 97-59, 1997-2 CB 309.
2. IRC Sec. 1211(b).
3. IRC Sec. 165.

That amount is netted against Claire's net long-term gain of $1,500, resulting in a net short-term loss of $3,200. Only $3,000 worth of capital losses in excess of capital gains are deductible in any single tax year. The remaining $200 capital loss is carried forward to subsequent tax years subject to the same rules.

8579. What is the tax significance of short-term capital gain?

Although as discussed in Q 8578 above, like long-term capital gain, short-term capital gain is netted against capital losses, net short-term capital gain is *not* subject to the preferential capital gains rates. Instead, such gain is taxed as ordinary income (up to 39.6 percent).

8580. Is there a limitation to the amount of capital losses a taxpayer may deduct in a tax year? How are disallowed capital losses treated?

Unlike ordinary losses that are deductible against any type of income (ordinary or capital), capital losses are deductible against capital gains (long and short-term). However, a noncorporate taxpayer who has capital losses in excess of capital gains is entitled to deduct from ordinary income the lesser of (a) $3,000 ($1,500 for married taxpayers filing separately) or (b) the excess of the taxpayer's net capital losses over gains.[1] Any nondeductible losses may be carried forward indefinitely to subsequent tax years. Losses that are carried forward retain their character as either short-term or long-term in future years.

Conversely, corporations are only permitted to recognize capital losses to the extent of capital gains with no exception.[2] However, unlike noncorporate taxpayers who must carry forward nondeductible losses to subsequent tax years, corporations may carry disallowed capital losses *back* for three tax years (beginning with the earliest of the three) with any remaining nondeductible capital losses to be carried forward for five successive tax years (beginning with the earliest of the five).[3]

8581. What are the reporting requirements for capital gains and losses?

New boxes have been added to Form 1099-DIV to allow for the reporting of qualified dividends (Box 1b) and post-May 5, 2003 capital gain distributions (Box 2b). Likewise, new boxes have also been added to Form 1099-B for reporting post-May 5, 2003 profits or losses from regulated futures or currency contracts.[4] Payments made in lieu of dividends ("substitute payments") are *not* eligible for the lower rates applicable to qualified dividends.

1. IRC Sec. 1211(b).
2. IRC Sec. 1211(a).
3. IRC Sec. 1212(a).
4. See Ann. 2003-55, 2003-38 IRB 597.

PART III: INVESTMENT INCOME TAX AND ADDITIONAL MEDICARE TAX

8582. What is the net investment income tax?

The investment income tax is a surtax of 3.8 percent in addition to the regular income tax that certain high income taxpayers would otherwise owe on the income in question. The tax is imposed on the *lesser* of the following amounts:

(1) Net investment income (see Q 8584 for an explanation of what amounts are included in net investment income); or

(2) The excess (if any) of (i) the taxpayer's modified adjusted gross income (MAGI) (as explained in Q 8583, below. For most taxpayers, MAGI is actually AGI) for the year over (ii) the applicable threshold amount.[1]

The applicable threshold amount for single taxpayers is $200,000. For married taxpayers filing a joint return, the applicable threshold amount is $250,000 (see Q 8585 for a detailed discussion of who is liable for the investment income tax). These amounts are not adjusted annually for inflation.

Example: In 2018, Erica and Mickey, a married couple filing jointly, have an AGI of $400,000 including net investment income of $125,000. The applicable threshold amount for a married couple filing jointly is $250,000.

Applying the formula, the 3.8 percent net investment tax is imposed on the lesser of:

1. Net investment income of $125,000; or

2. The excess of (i) AGI of $400,000 over (ii) the applicable threshold amount of $250,000, or $150,000.

Because the lesser of the two amounts is the $125,000 of net investment income, the 3.8 percent net investment income tax is imposed on the entire amount of net investment income.

Example: Assume in 2018, Erica and Mickey have AGI of $300,000 including net investment income of $125,000.

Applying the formula, the 3.8 percent net investment income tax is imposed on the lesser of:

1. Net investment income of $125,000; or

2. The excess of (i) AGI of $300,000 over (ii) the applicable threshold amount of $250,000, or $50,000.

In this case, the lesser of the two amounts is the excess of AGI over the applicable threshold amount. Thus, in spite of having net investment income of $125,000, only $50,000 is subject to the 3.8 percent net investment income tax.

Finally, certain trusts and estates are also subject to the net investment income tax (see Q 8601).

1. IRC Sec. 1411(a)(1).

8583. What is modified adjusted gross income for purposes of the investment income tax?

For most taxpayers, MAGI is the same as their AGI. This is because the only adjustments made to AGI in arriving at MAGI relate to foreign earned income. Specifically, in arriving at MAGI, AGI is increased by the excess of (1) any amounts excluded under IRC 911(a)(1) (foreign earned income) over (2) the amount of deductions and exclusions disallowed under IRC 911(d)(6) (which disallows certain deductions and exclusions that would otherwise be properly allocable to an amount excluded from gross income because it is foreign earned income).[1] Thus, absent any foreign earned income, AGI and MAGI are the same amount.

8584. What is net investment income?

Net investment income is the tax base for the 3.8 percent net investment income tax (see Q 8582 for a discussion of the computation of the tax). In general, net investment income potentially includes any income other than "earned" income that is subject to Social Security tax and Medicare tax. There are three general categories of net investment income. Pursuant to IRC Section 1411(c)(1), subject to exceptions discussed in Q 8594, the three categories of investment income are:

(a) income commonly considered to be traditional investment type income, such as interest, dividends, annuities, rents and royalties;

(b) gross income derived from a trade or business; and

(c) net gain attributable to the disposition of property.[2]

8585. Who is liable for paying the net investment income tax?

Any taxpayer who has net investment income (in any amount) and modified adjusted gross income (MAGI) in excess of the applicable threshold amount is subject to the 3.8 percent net investment income tax. The applicable thresholds are MAGI in excess of $200,000 for single taxpayers, $125,000 for married taxpayers filing separately and $250,000 for married couples filing jointly. Unlike many other income threshold amounts, these thresholds are not indexed annually for inflation.[3]

In addition to individuals, the net investment income tax applies to certain trusts and estates (see Q 8601).[4] Nonresident aliens are not subject to the tax.[5]

8586. Are distributions from retirement accounts and qualified plans included in net investment income?

No. Although distributions from qualified plans often include earnings generated by traditional investment income, i.e., dividends and interests, distributions from

1. IRC Sec. 1411(d).
2. IRC Sec. 1411(c)(1)(A).
3. See Preamble to notice of proposed rulemaking, REG-130507-11, 77 Fed. Reg. 72611, 72615.
4. IRC Sec. 1411(a).
5. IRC Sec. 1411(e).

qualified retirement plans are not included in net investment income and thus are not directly subject to the net investment income tax (however, see Q 8588).[1] This includes distributions from qualified plans pursuant to:

(1) IRC Section 401(a) (qualified pension, stock bonus or profit-sharing plans);

(2) IRC Section 403(a) (qualified annuity plans);

(3) IRC Section 403(b) (tax-sheltered annuities);

(4) IRC Section 408 (individual retirement accounts);

(5) IRC Section 408A (Roth IRAs); and

(6) IRC Section 457(b) (deferred compensation plans of state and local governments or tax-exempt organizations).

Deemed distributions under IRC Section 72(p) (loans from a qualified employer plan) are also excluded under this rule.[2] Additionally, amounts distributed from a qualified plan to purchase life insurance by the plan participant are not included in net investment income.[3]

8587. If a taxpayer converts a traditional IRA to a Roth IRA, does a taxable distribution take place that would subject the converted funds to the investment income tax?

In addition to actual retirement plan distributions (see Q 8586) that are excluded from net investment income, the final regulations also make it clear that deemed distributions from retirement plans are excluded. For example, a rollover of funds from a traditional IRA into a Roth IRA, where the funds are never actually received by the taxpayer, is nonetheless treated as a distribution for income tax purposes. Similar to actual retirement distributions, the IRA/Roth conversion deemed distribution is excluded from net investment income; and, thus, is not subject to the net investment income tax.[4]

8588. Can conversions from a traditional IRA to a Roth IRA cause an individual to indirectly become subject to the net investment income tax?

Officially, distributions from traditional retirement accounts (IRAs, 401(k)s) are excluded from the net investment income tax (NIIT). Similarly, amounts that are rolled over into Roth accounts from these traditional accounts are technically excluded.[5] While retirement account distributions (and Roth conversions)[6] are excluded from the definition of *net investment income* (see Q 8584), these amounts still count in determining an individual's AGI—and can cause the individual to exceed the applicable threshold and become subject to the NIIT (see Q 8582).

1. IRC Sec. 1411(c)(5;); Treas. Reg. §1.1411-8(a).
2. Treas. Reg. §1.1411-8(b)(2).
3. Treas. Reg. §1.1411-8(b)(3).
4. Treas. Reg. §1.1411-8(b)(2).
5. IRC Sec. 1411(c)(5); Treas. Reg. §1.1411-8(a).
6. Treas. Reg. §1.1411-8(b)(2).

As a result, for some individuals, Roth conversions are best exercised in small steps over time—converting only a small portion of traditional retirement funds each year to avoid crossing the AGI threshold. For others, Roth conversions may no longer be the best option for generating tax-free income during retirement—especially if the individual cannot balance the added income by contributing additional pre-tax dollars to traditional accounts because he or she has already maxed out the annual contributions.

8589. How do the net investment income rules apply to amounts received under an annuity contract?

Income from annuities included in gross income pursuant to IRC Sections 72(a) and 72(b) are also included in net investment income pursuant to IRC Section 1411(c)(1)(A)(i). For regular income tax purposes, a portion of an annuity payment is allocated to the taxpayer's investment in the annuity. That amount is excluded from gross income,[1] and, thus, not treated as net investment income. The difference between the total payment and the excluded amount is included in gross income,[2] as well as net investment income.[3]

> *Example*: Amy received $12,000 in annuity payments of which $7,000 was allocated to her investment in the annuity. As a result, pursuant to IRC Section 72(b), Amy would exclude $7,000 of the payments from gross income and net investment income. The difference between the total annuity payment of $12,000 and her $7,000 basis, or $5,000, would be included in gross income and in net investment income, subject to the net investment income tax.

If the taxpayer *sells* the annuity contract for a gain, the entire gain would be treated as net investment income either under IRC Section 1411(c)(1)(A)(i) (as annuity income) or 1411(c)(1)(A)(iii) (net gain attributable to the sale of property). For example, if the sale price of the annuity does not exceed the annuity surrender value, the gain recognized (difference between the sale price and the taxpayer's investment or basis in the annuity) is treated as annuity income. If the sale price exceeds the annuity surrender value, the portion of the gain attributable to the difference between the surrender value and the taxpayer's investment or basis in the annuity is also treated as annuity income. However, the gain attributable to the difference between the sale price and the surrender value of the annuity would be treated as net gain attributable to the sale of the annuity.[4]

8590. What is "net gain" with respect to the disposition of property and net investment income?

Pursuant to IRC Section 1411(c)(1)(A)(iii), "net gain" attributable to the disposition of property is included in net investment income. Significantly, the term "net gain" means dispositions of property that trigger gain and are netted against "losses" generated in those same types of dispositions. Similar to regular income taxation, only taxable gains and non-deductible losses are considered. Thus, because the gain must be "recognized" for income tax purposes, dispositions

1. IRC Sec. 72(b).
2. IRC Sec. 72(a).
3. Treas. Reg. §1.1411-4(a)(1)(i). See also Preamble to Proposed Regulations, 77 Fed. Reg. 72618; Preamble to Final Regulations, 78 Fed. Reg. 72394.
4. IRC Sec. 1411(c)(1)(A)(iii).

of property that are income tax-free are also net investment income tax-free. Examples of such tax-free gains include but are not limited to like-kind exchanges under IRC Section 1031 (see Q 8611 to Q 8633) and involuntary conversions (see Q 8611 to Q 8620).[1]

Although the term "net gain" means that the gains and losses described above have been netted, as discussed in Q 8595, gain attributable to the disposition of property held by a trade or business in which the taxpayer materially participates, i.e., non-passive gains (except gains derived from a trade or business that involves trading in financial instruments and commodities) is excluded from net investment income. In other words, the following are true:

- Net gain recognized from the disposition of property held in a trade or business in which the taxpayer materially participates is not included in net investment income.
- Net gain recognized from the disposition of property held in a trade or business in which the taxpayer does not materially participate is included in net investment income.
- Net gain recognized from the disposition of investment property (where no trade or business is involved) is always included in net investment income.
- Net gain recognized from the disposition of any property held by a business engaged in trading financial instruments or commodities (regardless of the taxpayer's participation in the business) is always included in net investment income.

See Q 8591 for a discussion of how net investment income gains are netted against net investment income losses.

8591. How are gains from the disposition of property netted against losses in determining "net gain" included in net investment income?

As discussed in Q 8590, above, for purposes of IRC Section 1411(c)(1)(A)(iii), "net gain" means that gains are netted against "losses." For example, a disposition of property held by a trade or business in which the taxpayer does not materially participate (i.e, the activity is passive) that results in a recognized gain would be offset by a similar disposition of property that results in an allowed deductible loss. Examples of losses include those allowed under IRC Section 165, i.e., casualty losses (see Q 8656), theft losses (see Q 8659), and losses realized as a result of worthless securities (see Q 8706) involving property held by a trade or business in which the taxpayer does not materially participate.

Additionally, the same rules for the deductibility of regular income tax losses also apply to the netting of net investment income losses against gains. As a result, similarly to regular income tax rules, net investment income ordinary losses are netted against net investment income capital gain and net investment ordinary gain.

1. Treas. Reg. §§1.1411-4(a)(1)(iii), 1.1411-4(d) (see examples).

Further, the final regulations provide for the offset of capital losses and capital gains in arriving at "net gain" included in net investment income in the same way as they offset each other for regular income tax purposes. For regular income tax purposes, capital losses are deductible to the extent of capital gains plus $3,000 of any excess being deductible against other income. The unused excess loss is carried over to subsequent tax years subject to being netted against capital gains generated in such years.[1] Similarly, for net investment income purposes, a taxpayer may use the same netting rules to reduce "net gain" to zero, with $3,000 of any excess reducing other investment income. Any unused excess capital loss is carried over to subsequent years to be netted against capital gain in the same manner.[2]

Planning Point: Significantly, in the aggregate, net investment income losses are only deductible to the extent of net investment income gains, meaning that net gain cannot be reduced below zero.[3] In other words, there can never be a "net loss." However, as discussed in Q 8592, the final regulations do allow excess investment income losses to be used to reduce other net investment income.[4]

8592. Can excess net investment income losses be used to reduce other net investment income?

Yes. As discussed in Q 8591, the offsetting of net investment income losses against net investment income gains can never result in a "net loss." However, pursuant to the final regulations, excess losses may be used to reduce other net investment income provided those losses were deducted in the computation of regular income tax. In other words, the loss must be deductible for regular income tax purposes for it to be deducible in this context.[5]

Example: Iris, a single taxpayer, has $125,000 of interest and dividends, $60,000 of ordinary losses from a trade or business in which Iris does not materially participate and long-term capital gain from the sale of undeveloped land. For purposes of IRC Section 1411(c)(1)(A)(iii), the net long-term capital gain is net investment income gain because the property was held for investment and there is no trade or business involved. The $60,000 ordinary losses are net investment income losses because the underlying property was held by a trade or business in which Iris did not materially participate. As a result of netting the $60,000 of ordinary losses against the $50,000 of long-term capital gain, there is an excess loss of $10,000. Assuming the excess loss is deducted for regular income tax purposes, the final regulations allow that amount to be deducted against Iris' other net investment income, i.e., $125,000 of interest and dividend net investment income (includible under IRC Section 1411(c)(1)(A)(i)).[6]

So in the end, the entire amount of $60,000 of net investment income loss was fully deductible against some type of net investment income. First, $50,000 of the loss offset $50,000 of long-term capital gain. Second, the excess loss, $10,000, was deductible against the $125,000 of interest and dividends, resulting in $115,000 of net investment income.

1. IRC Sec. 1211(b).
2. Treas. Reg. §1.1411-4(d)(2).
3. Treas. Reg. §1.1411-4(d)(2).
4. Treas. Reg. §1.1411-4(f)(1).
5. Treas. Reg. §1.1411-4(f)(1).
6. Treas. Reg. §1.1411-4(h).

8593. How does gain on the sale of a taxpayer's principal residence impact the determination of whether the taxpayer is subject to the investment income tax?

The sale of a taxpayer's principal residence is potentially includible in net investment income as net gain from the sale of property.[1] However, for income tax purposes, a single taxpayer excludes the first $250,000 of capital gain realized from the sale of a principal residence from gross income ($500,000 for a married couple filing jointly).[2] Since only amounts included in gross income for regular income tax purposes are included in net investment income, the amount of gain that is excluded from gross income is similarly excluded from net investment income.[3] Consequently, the portion of the gain from the sale of a principal residence that is included in gross income is also included in net investment income.[4]

> *Example:* In 2000, Dave and Janice purchased a principal residence for $100,000. Years later, they sell that residence for $700,000 realizing a total gain of $600,000. Pursuant to IRC Section 121, $500,000 of the gain is excluded from gross income and from net investment income. However, $100,000 of the gain (the amount exceeding the $500,000 exclusion) is includible in gross income and in net investment income. In addition, Dave and Janice have dividend and interest income of $200,000. Their AGI is $425,000.
>
> Applying the formula (see Q 8582), the 3.8 percent net investment tax is imposed on the lesser of:
>
> 1. Net investment income of $200,000 (interest and dividends) plus $100,000 (taxable gain on sale of principal residence), a total of $300,000; or
> 2. The excess of (i) AGI of $425,000 over (ii) the applicable threshold amount of $250,000 (married couple filing jointly), or $175,000.

As illustrated in the example above, the taxpayers' net investment income includes the interest and dividend income of $200,000 plus only $100,000 of the $600,000 gain from the sale of their principal residence. The excluded gain of $500,000 pursuant to IRC Section 121 does not factor into the computation. In other words, the amount of gain included in gross income is also the amount of gain treated as net investment income. Thus, because the excess of AGI over the applicable threshold amount ($175,000) is less than the taxpayers' net investment income ($300,000), the 3.8 percent tax is imposed on the lesser amount.

8594. How does a taxpayer determine whether income is derived from the taxpayer's trade or business and, if so, excluded from net investment income?

The test for determining whether interest, dividends, annuities, royalties and rents which would otherwise be included as net investment income pursuant to IRC Section 1411(c)(1)(A)(i) (trade or business income) are excluded from net investment income is different from the test

1. IRC Sec. 1411(c)(1)(A)(iii). It is treated as investment income because it is not property held in a trade or business in which the taxpayer materially participates.
2. IRC Sec. 121(a).
3. Treas. Reg. §1.1411-1(d)(4)(i).
4. IRC Sec. 1411(c)(1)(A)(iii).

used to determine whether net investment income otherwise included pursuant to IRC Sections 1411(c)(1)(A)(ii) and (iii) are similarly excluded.

IRC Section 1411(c)(1)(A)(i) governs the traditional types of investment income. With respect to this income, the exclusion applies if such income is derived in the "ordinary course" of a trade or business within the meaning of Treasury Regulation Section 1.469–2T(c)(3)(ii). This means the income is the type of income that the trade or business is designed to generate. The following are examples of such income:

1. Interest income on loans and investments made in the ordinary course of a trade or business of lending money;

2. Interest on accounts receivable arising from the performance of services or the sale of property in the ordinary course of a trade or business of performing such services or selling such property, but only if credit is customarily offered to customers of the business;

3. Income from investments made in the ordinary course of a trade or business of furnishing insurance or annuity contracts or reinsuring risks underwritten by insurance companies;

4. Income or gain derived in the ordinary course of an activity of trading or dealing in any property if such activity constitutes a trade or business;

5. Royalties derived by the taxpayer in the ordinary course of a trade or business of licensing intangible property.[1]

The common denominator in these examples is the nexus between the trade or business and the income generated. For example, interest income on loans is the type of income a bank is designed to generate. Conversely, interest or dividend income derived from invested working capital for future use in the taxpayer's trade or business is not that type of income, and, thus is treated as net investment income.[2] Moreover, under no circumstances is any income derived from trading in financial instruments or commodities excludable from net investment income.[3]

With respect to income derived in a trade or business that is not treated as net investment income pursuant to IRC Sections 1411(c)(1)(A)(ii) or (iii), there is a much looser test for the application of the exclusion. That test is the same for both sections. As discussed in Q 8584, IRC Section 1411(c)(1)(A)(ii) governs the regular gross income of a trade or business. Conversely, IRC Section 1411(c)(1)(A)(iii) governs net gain attributable to the sale or exchange of property.

1. Treas. Reg. §§1.469-2T(c)(3)(ii); 1.1411-6.
2. IRC Sec. 1411(c)(3).
3. IRC Sec. 1411(c)(2).

Unlike the IRC Section 1411(c)(1)(A)(i) exclusion, there is no requirement that the income must be of the type that the trade or business is designed to generate. Instead, to qualify for the exception, the income must be derived from a trade or business in which the taxpayer materially participates (non-passive), so long as the income is not derived from trading in financial instruments or commodities.[1] Stated differently, pursuant to IRC Section 1411(c)(1)(A)(ii), net investment income includes all income derived from a trade or business that is passive with respect to the taxpayer. However, if the trade or business is non-passive with respect to the taxpayer, the income is excluded from net investment income. For a discussion regarding the determination of whether an activity is passive or non-passive, see Q 8595.

As mentioned above, the same test is used to determine whether net gain attributable to disposition of property (sale or exchange) otherwise included in net investment income pursuant to IRC Section 1411(c)(1)(A)(iii) is excluded from net investment income. In applying this test, the net gain is excluded only if the disposed of property is held in a trade or business which is non-passive with respect to the taxpayer and is not derived from a business trading in financial instruments or commodities. Thus, the net gain from the disposition of property held by a trade or business that is passive with respect to the taxpayer would be included in net investment income.

Net Investment Income Exclusion for Income Derived in the Taxpayer's Trade or Business		
	Included as Net Investment Income	**Excluded from Net Investment Income**
IRC Section 1411(c)(1)(A)(i) Interest, Dividends, Annuities, Rents and Royalties	Traditional Investment Income	The type of income the business was designed to generate, i.e., interest income earned by a bank.
IRC Section 1411(c)(1)(A)(ii) Gross Income from a Trade or Business	Income derived from a trade or business that is passive with respect to the taxpayer or derived from a business trading in financial instruments or commodities. Also includes income from an activity that does not rise to the level of a trade or business.	Income derived from a trade or business that is non-passive with respect to the taxpayer other than income derived from a business trading in financial instruments or commodities.
IRC Section 1411(c)(1)(A)(iii) Net Gain from the Disposition of Property Held in a Trade or Business	The underlying trade or business is passive with respect to the taxpayer or is a business trading in financial instruments or commodities.	The underlying trade or business is non-passive with respect to the taxpayer and is not a business trading in financial instruments or commodities.

1. IRC Sec. 1411(c)(2).

8595. For purposes of the net investment income tax, why is it important to determine whether trade or business activities are considered "passive ?

Prior to the enactment of the net investment income tax, the relevance of "passive" activities was to limit deductible passive expenses to passive income.[1] Now, as a result of the net investment income tax, the characterization of an activity as passive has new significance. As discussed in Q 8594, gross income derived from a trade or business and/or net gain attributable to the sale or exchange of property that is passive with respect to the taxpayer is included in net investment income subject to the 3.8 percent net investment income tax. To qualify for the exclusion, the taxpayer must "materially participate" in the business activity so as to make it a non-passive activity.

Section 1411 and the regulations reference the definition of passive activity set forth in IRC Section 469, indicating that the rules for determining whether an activity is active or passive apply in the context of determining whether the income is included in investment income.[2] Whether an activity is passive or non-passive depends on the level of the taxpayer's participation in the activity. A passive activity is any trade or business activity in which the taxpayer does not "materially participate."[3] Generally, a taxpayer is considered to *materially participate* in an activity if he or she is involved in the operations of the activity on a regular, continuous, and substantial basis. Many of the factors considered by the IRS involve the number of hours that the taxpayer devotes to the activity annually. The IRS may also compare the number of hours that a taxpayer devotes to the activity to the hours spent by others engaged in the same business. A traditional facts and circumstances test is typically applied in making a final determination. See Q 8645 for a discussion of the material participation requirement in the context of the passive activity rules.

So, if a taxpayer materially participates in a trade or business, it is considered non-passive; and, thus, the income described above would qualify for the exclusion. As an important caveat, even if the taxpayer participates in a trade or business, if the income from such business is considered to be self-employment income, it can never be considered net investment income. Instead, such income is subject to Medicare tax and potentially the additional Medicare tax (see Q 8604).[4]

For a detailed discussion of the passive activity rules in general, see Q 8642 to Q 8651.

8596. Can a taxpayer "group" multiple activities in order to meet the material participation test for purposes of the net investment income exclusion?

Yes. Another way to satisfy the material participation test is to "group" several activities into a single activity to demonstrate that the taxpayer has materially participated in the combined activities. Under Treasury Regulation Section 1.469-4,[5] one or more trade or business activities may be "grouped" and treated as one economic unit for purposes of determining whether the

1. IRC Sec. 469.
2. IRC Sec. 1411(c); Treas. Reg. §1.1411-5(b).
3. IRC Sec. 469(c).
4. IRC Sec. 1411(c)(6).
5. Treas. Reg. §1.469-4.

taxpayer materially participated. By doing so, the taxpayer's participation for all the activities is aggregated as if it was one activity. Whether or not the IRS will recognize grouped activities as a single economic unit is based on a facts and circumstances analysis. The following five factors are relevant in determining whether such activities qualify to be treated as a single economic unit:[1]

(1) similarities and differences in types of trades or businesses,

(2) the extent of common control,

(3) the extent of common ownership,

(4) geographical location, and

(5) interdependencies between or among the activities.

Once a taxpayer has grouped activities, the taxpayer is generally not permitted to regroup those activities in later tax years.[2] See Q 8597 for the limited exception to this rule.

8597. After an initial grouping of activities has taken place, can a taxpayer regroup activities for purposes of satisfying the material participation test in order to avoid application of the net investment income tax?

The grouping rules were the outgrowth of the passive activity income and loss rules that far predate the enactment of the net investment income tax. For this reason, allowing the taxpayer to regroup certain activities in view of net investment income tax considerations could potentially generate significant tax savings.

The final regulations provide a small window allowing such a regrouping. In order to regroup,

(1) the regrouping was required to occur only in the first taxable year beginning after December 31, 2012; and

(2) the regrouping taxpayer must be subject to net investment income tax during that year.

In other words, regrouping was allowed only in the one single tax year referenced above, and, only if a taxpayer is subject to the net investment income tax in that same year. Consequently, any taxpayer who is not subject to the net investment income tax in that taxable year, but may be subject to it in a subsequent year, is not entitled to a "fresh start" regrouping.[3]

Planning Point: In drafting the final regulations, the IRS refused to allow pass through entities such as S corporations and partnerships to regroup. In declining to do so, the final regulations noted that taxpayers not subject to the net investment income tax for the taxable year beginning after December 31, 2012, would get the benefit of regrouping indirectly (i.e., by virtue of the pass through of income from those entities), that they would not be entitled to receive directly.[4]

For additional discussion of the passive activity rules in general, see Q 8642 to Q 8651.

1. Treas. Reg. §§1.469-4(c)(1), 1.469-4(c)(2).
2. Treas. Reg. §1.469-4(e)(1).
3. Preamble to Final Regulations, 78 Fed. Reg. 72396.
4. Preamble to Final Regulations, 78 Fed. Reg. 72396.

8598. How does the investment income tax effectively increase the tax rate for capital gains and dividends?

The 3.8 percent net investment income tax is a surtax, which means it is imposed independently on net investment income that is also subject to any other applicable income tax. To illustrate, the capital gains and dividend tax rate for taxpayers in the 39.6 percent tax bracket is 20 percent. However, if the taxpayer is also subject to the net investment income tax, there is an additional 3.8 percent tax imposed on those same capital gains and dividends. Thus, adding the two tax rates together, the overall effective tax rate for capital gain and dividends for those taxpayers is 23.8 percent (20 percent plus 3.8 percent).

For taxpayers who are not in the 39.6 percent tax bracket, the capital gains and dividend tax rate is only 15 percent. However, it is possible that such taxpayers with modified adjusted gross income that exceeds the threshold levels for the net investment income tax (see Q 8585) may also be subject to the net investment income tax. Adding the 15 percent regular income tax capital gain and dividend rate to the 3.8 percent net investment income tax rate, the effective rate of such taxpayers would be 18.8 percent (15 percent plus 3.8 percent).

8599. Can federal income tax credits be used to offset net investment income tax liability?

Although federal income tax credits set forth in Subtitle A of the IRC can offset any tax liability, the final regulations state that income tax credits are allowed only against regular income tax (Chapter 1 of Subtitle A) and may not reduce net investment income tax.[1] Examples of this type of tax credit include the foreign income tax credit and the general business tax credit.[2]

The denial of tax credits as an offset of the net investment income tax is reflected by the sequence of reporting tax and tax credits on Form 1040. To this point, regular income tax is reported on line 46 of Form 1040. All tax credits reducing that regular income tax are taken lines 47-53. Beginning on line 56, "other taxes," including the net investment income tax (reported on line 60), are reported. So logistically, all tax credits that reduce regular income tax are taken *before* the entry for the net investment income tax. Moreover, none of those credits are refundable credits (meaning the credits can only reduce the regular tax to zero and not generate a refundable overpayment). Thus, they are of no consequence with regard to the net investment income tax reported on line 60.

8600. What form is used to report net investment income tax?

As discussed in Q 8599, net investment income tax is reported on line 60 of Form 1040. On Form 8960 (attached to Form 1040), the taxpayer computes the tax. In addition to reporting all the taxpayer's net investment income, amounts reported on Form 8814 (Parents' Election to Report Child's Interest and Dividends) are also included.

1. Treas. Reg. §1.1411-1(e).
2. See IRC Secs. 27, 901, 38.

Planning Point: Similar to regular income tax or self-employment tax, individuals who expect to be liable for the net investment income tax may either make estimated tax payments or request that their employer withhold additional amounts to avoid being subject to penalties for under-payment of taxes.[1]

8601. When is an estate or trust subject to the investment tax?

Certain trusts and estates may be subject to the 3.8 percent net investment income tax. Basically, the tax is imposed on any net investment income that remains in the estate or the trust and, thus, is not distributed to beneficiaries, otherwise referred to as "undistributed net investment income." Unlike individual taxpayers, the threshold amount is the amount at which the highest regular income tax bracket begins. Additionally, unlike the applicable threshold amount for individuals, the applicable threshold is adjusted for inflation.[2] For example, in 2018, the amount at which the highest income tax bracket begins is adjusted gross income in excess of $12,700.[3] Since this amount is relatively low, many estates and trusts should expect to be subject to the tax.

The following examples are used to demonstrate the computation of the net investment income tax for a trust.

> *Example*: In 2018, the Dinosaur trust has AGI of $16,000 and undistributed net investment income of $6,000.
>
> The net investment income tax is imposed on trusts and estates on the lesser of:
>
> 1) Undistributed Net Investment Income, $6,000; or
>
> 2) The excess of (i) AGI of $16,000, over (ii) $12,700, the amount at which the highest regular tax bracket begins, or $3,300.

Even though there is $6,000 of undistributed net investment income, because the lesser of the two amounts is $3,300, only that amount is subject to the 3.8 percent net investment income tax.

> *Example*: In 2018, the Dinosaur trust has AGI of $20,000 and undistributed net investment income of $6,000.
>
> The net investment income tax is imposed on trusts and estates on the lesser of:
>
> 1) Undistributed Net Investment Income, $6,000; or
>
> 2) The excess of (i) AGI of $20,000, over (ii) $12,700, the amount at which the highest regular tax bracket begins, or $7,300.

Because the lesser of the two amounts is the undistributed net investment income of $6,000, the entire amount of undistributed net investment income is subject to the 3.8 percent net investment income tax.

1. IRS Q&A on the Net Investment Income Tax, available at: http://www.irs.gov/uac/Newsroom/Net-Investment-Income-Tax-FAQs (last accessed May 26, 2017).
2. IRC Sec. 1411(a)(2)(B)(ii).
3. Rev. Proc. 2016-55.

8602. Which trusts are not subject to the net investment income tax?

Trusts not subject to the net investment income tax include charitable trusts exempt from tax under IRC Section 501[1] or IRC Section 664[2] (charitable remainder trusts) and trusts that are not classified as "trusts" for federal income tax purposes.[3] Moreover, if all of the remaining interests in a trust are designated for certain qualified purposes, the trust is not subject to the net investment income tax. These qualified purposes described in IRC Section 170(c)(2)(B) include religious, charitable, scientific, literary or educational purposes.[4]

Finally, grantor trusts such as revocable trusts are not subject to the net investment income tax. This is because the income of a grantor trust is taxed directly to the grantor. As a result, any net investment income generated by the trust is included in the grantor's net investment income – potentially subject to the 3.8 percent tax at the individual level.[5]

8603. What considerations are relevant in determining if a trade or business is non-passive with respect to a trust for purposes of treating the income derived therefrom as excluded from net investment income?

As discussed in Q 8595, whether a trade or business activity from which the taxpayer derives income is passive depends on the taxpayer's level of participation in the activity in question. In the case of a trust that owns interests in a pass-through entity, such as an S corporation or partnership, it is the trustee's participation in the business activities that is generally relevant in determining whether the investment is active or passive with respect to the trust.

In a 2013 technical advice memorandum, the IRS expressed a restrictive view of what participation in a business activity by a trustee is attributable to the trust. In that memorandum, the IRS declared that a trustee's participation in a business in which the trust owned interests was *not* material even though the trustee was also the president of the company through which the business activity was conducted.[6] The IRS reached this conclusion based on its view that the trustee's participation in the company as an *employee* was separate from his role as trustee; and, thus, it was not attributable to the trust. Further, although the IRS did count the trustee's time spent serving as *trustee* in dealing with the company's business, it determined that the trustee's activities were nonetheless not "regular, continuous and substantial" within the meaning of IRC Section 469 (governing passive activities generally).[7]

Although the technical advice memorandum did not address the issue of whether the trust income was net investment income, it reflects the IRS view that the participation of a trustee as an employee or officer of an entity is not attributed to his or her role as the trustee. Based on such a restrictive view of the role of the trustee, it may be virtually impossible for any trust to materially participate in a business activity.

---

1. Treas. Reg. §1.1411-3(b)(1)(ii).
2. Treas. Reg. §1.1411-3(b)(1)(iii).
3. Treas. Reg. §1.1411-3(b)(1)(iv).
4. Treas. Reg. §1.1411-3(b)(1); IRC Sec. 170(c)(2)(B).
5. Treas. Reg. §1.1411-3(b)(1)(v).
6. TAM 201317010.
7. IRC Sec. 469(h)(1).

However, in a recent decision, the Tax Court rejected the IRS' restrictive position.[1] In that case, a trust owned rental real estate properties and engaged in other real estate activities. Three of the five trustees worked full-time in the trust's wholly owned rental real estate LLC. The issue was whether the personal services of the trustees as employees of the LLC would be attributable to the trust.

Pursuant to IRC Section 469(c)(2), all rental activities are passive. In order to rebut that characterization, IRC Section 469(c)(7)(B) requires the taxpayer to meet the following two tests: (1) more than one-half of the personal services performed in the trades or businesses by the taxpayer during the taxable year is performed in real property trades or businesses in which the taxpayer materially participates; and, (2) the taxpayer performs more than 750 hours of services during the year in real property trades or businesses in which the taxpayer materially participates.

Consistent with the technical advice memorandum, the IRS argued that the personal services performed by the trustees as employees of the LLC were not attributable to the trust. The Tax Court, however, rejected the IRS' view as being too narrow and held that the participation of the trustees as employees were attributable to the trust. So, because the activities of those trustees/employees met the two IRC Section 469(b)(7)(B) tests, the trust was deemed to have materially participated in the rental real estate activities, and, for that reason, they were non-passive activities.

Planning Point: Although the Tax Court case also did not involve net investment income, based on the holding, the non-passive rental income would have most likely been excluded from net investment income. Additionally, the Tax Court case is significant because it was a regular opinion reviewed by the entire Tax Court bench rather than a Tax Court Memorandum decision that carries less authoritative weight. In any event, IRS has not yet indicated whether it will follow the decision or continue to apply the restrictive view of the technical advice memorandum. Because a low applicable threshold subjects many trusts to the net investment income tax (see Q 8601), trustees should pay attention to how the IRS will deal with this issue as it relates to treating rental real estate activities of a trust as passive or non-passive.

8604. What is the additional Medicare tax? Who is liable for paying the additional Medicare tax?

The additional Medicare tax is a tax of 0.9 percent that is tacked on to the "regular" Medicare tax on all wages and self-employment income (collectively referred to as "earned income") that exceed applicable threshold amounts. Thus, on earned income in excess of the applicable threshold amount, the total Medicare tax rate is 3.8 percent (the 2.9 percent regular Medicare tax rate plus the 0.9 percent additional Medicare tax rate).

In spite of its name, the tax revenue generated by the additional Medicare tax is not specifically earmarked for the Medicare fund. Similar to the regular Medicare tax, the additional Medicare tax is imposed only on individual taxpayers (see Q 8605 for a discussion of an employer's obligation to withhold the additional Medicare tax). Thus, entities such as C corporations, trusts and estates are not subject to the tax.[2]

1. *Frank Aragona Trust et. al. v. Comm.*, 142 TC 165 (March 27, 2014).
2. IRC Sec. 3101(b)(2).

The applicable thresholds for the additional Medicare tax (not adjusted for inflation) are the sum of the taxpayer's earned income (wages and/or self-employment income) in excess of the following amounts:

(1) $250,000 for married taxpayers filing jointly;

(2) $125,000 for married taxpayers filing separate returns; and

(3) $200,000 for single taxpayers and heads of households.[1]

Planning Point: The tax base of the additional Medicare tax and the net investment income are mutually exclusive. To this point, the additional Medicare surtax is imposed on earned income whereas the net investment income tax is imposed on investment income. This means that a taxpayer cannot be subject to both additional taxes on the same income.[2] If income could be included in both tax bases, it will be included in the Medicare tax base.

8605. If one spouse's wages exceed $200,000, triggering mandatory withholding by the employer of the additional Medicare tax, but the couple's wages, combined, are less than the $250,000 threshold for married taxpayers filing jointly (meaning there is no additional Medicare tax owing), can the first spouse request that the employer not withhold the additional Medicare tax?

No. Pursuant to IRC Section 3102(a), once an employee's wages exceed $200,000 (the mandatory wage withholding amount), the employer must withhold 0.9 percent of the excess amount even if the employee does not actually owe any additional Medicare tax. So for wages in excess of $200,000, the employer must withhold the additional Medicare tax even if those wages combined with his or her spouse's wages do *not* exceed the applicable threshold for a married couple filing jointly ($250,000).[3] To the extent the amount withheld exceeds the employee's liability, the employee's remedy is to apply it as a payment against other tax he or she may owe or receive a refund for the excessive withholding.

8606. What are the consequences of an employer's failure to withhold the additional Medicare tax that an employee is liable to pay?

There are several possible ways that an employer might fail to withhold the additional Medicare tax an employee is liable to pay. For example, this scenario might occur if each spouse individually earns wages under the mandatory $200,000 withholding amount. Therefore, if one spouse has wages of $100,000 and the other spouse has wages of $199,000, neither spouse's wages are subject to mandatory withholding. However, because the couple's combined wages of $299,000 exceed the $250,000 applicable threshold by $49,000, they must pay the additional

1. IRC Sec. 3101(b)(2).
2. IRS FAQ, *Questions and Answers for the Additional Medicare Tax*, available at http://www.irs.gov/Businesses/Small-Businesses-&-Self-Employed/Questions-and-Answers-for-the-Additional-Medicare-Tax (last accessed May26 2017).
3. IRS FAQ, *Questions and Answers for the Additional Medicare Tax*, available at http://www.irs.gov/Businesses/Small-Businesses-&-Self-Employed/Questions-and-Answers-for-the-Additional-Medicare-Tax (last accessed May 26 2017); Treas. Reg. §31.3102-4(a).

Medicare tax on that amount. Thus, on Form 8959, the couple would compute the additional Medicare tax of 0.9 percent on $49,000 – reporting it on line 60 of Form 1040.[1]

On the other hand, an employer obligated to withhold the additional Medicare tax on wages in excess of $200,000 may simply fail to do so. Under those circumstances, the employer remains obligated to pay the tax to the IRS unless and until the employer can prove that it was paid by the employee. However, even if the employee ultimately pays the tax, it does not relieve the employer of its liability for any interest or penalties assessed as a result of its failure to withhold the additional Medicare tax.[2]

8607. Can a taxpayer request additional withholding specifically earmarked to pay anticipated additional Medicare tax?

No, a taxpayer cannot make such a request. However, the taxpayer may modify Form W-4 to request that his or her employer withhold additional income tax. Even though the additional amount withheld is technically regular income tax (not additional Medicare tax), it is nonetheless credited as a payment to be applied to all Form 1040 tax liability owing including the additional Medicare tax.[3]

8608. Can a taxpayer make estimated tax payments to cover the additional Medicare tax liability?

Although the additional Medicare tax is a separate tax, the IRS considers it to be part of the taxpayer's overall tax liability. So, if the taxpayer's withholdings are not sufficient to cover the entire tax liability, there may be a penalty imposed on the failure to make an estimated tax payment. For that reason, it may benefit a taxpayer who does not increase the amount withheld by the employer to make estimated payments to cover any shortfall.[4]

8609. How does a taxpayer calculate additional Medicare tax liability if the taxpayer receives both wage income and self-employment income in the same tax year?

The taxpayer's combined wages and self-employment income is subject to the additional Medicare tax. This means the tax is imposed on the excess of the taxpayer's entire amount of earned income over the applicable threshold. The following fact pattern demonstrates the three-step procedure for calculating the tax owed:

> *Example*: Sam is a single taxpayer with $130,000 in wages and $145,000 in self-employment income, or total earned income of $275,000. The applicable threshold for a single taxpayer is $200,000.
>
> Step 1 – Calculate additional Medicare tax on wages in excess of the applicable threshold;

1. Treas. Reg. §31.3102-4(b), Example J.
2. Treas. Reg. §31.3102-4(c).
3. See IRS Q&A on the Additional Medicare Tax, available at: http://www.irs.gov/Businesses/Small-Businesses-&-Self-Employed/Questions-and-Answers-for-the-Additional-Medicare-Tax (last accessed May 26, 2017).
4. See IRS Q&A on the Additional Medicare Tax, available at: http://www.irs.gov/Businesses/Small-Businesses-&-Self-Employed/Questions-and-Answers-for-the-Additional-Medicare-Tax (last accessed May 26, 2017).

As mentioned above, the applicable threshold for a single taxpayer is $200,000. However, since Sam's wages of $130,000 do not exceed the applicable threshold, there is no additional Medicare tax on his wages.

Step 2 - Reduce the applicable threshold by the total amount of wages, but not below zero;

In this case, the applicable threshold of $200,000 minus Sam's $130,000 of wages equals a reduced threshold of $70,000.

Step 3 - Calculate the additional Medicare tax on any self-employment income received in excess of the reduced threshold.

In Step 1, $130,000 of the applicable threshold is absorbed by Sam's wages. Then, in Step 2, the applicable threshold minus Sam's wages is reduced to $70,000. Finally, in Step 3, Sam's self-employment income of $145,000 exceeds the reduced threshold of $70,000 by $75,000, the amount of Sam's self-employment income subject to the additional Medicare tax. The actual tax is $675 (0.9% * $75,000).

8610. Are noncash fringe benefits received by an employee subject to the additional Medicare tax?

Yes. The value of any taxable noncash employee fringe benefits is added to an employee's cash wages to determine whether the taxpayer's overall wage income exceeds the applicable threshold (see Q 8604). If so, the excess amount will be subject to the additional Medicare tax.[1] Moreover, similar to the payment of only cash wages, if the combined amount of cash wages and taxable noncash fringe benefits exceeds the mandatory wage withholding amount of $200,000 (see Q 8605), the employer must withhold the additional Medicare tax on the excess amount of combined wage income.[2]

See Q 8816 to Q 8842 for a discussion of the tax treatment of various noncash fringe benefits.

1. IRS FAQ, *Questions and Answers for the Additional Medicare Tax*, available at http://www.irs.gov/Businesses/Small-Businesses-&-Self-Employed/Questions-and-Answers-for-the-Additional-Medicare-Tax (last accessed May 26, 2017).
2. IRS FAQ, *Questions and Answers for the Additional Medicare Tax*, available at http://www.irs.gov/Businesses/Small-Businesses-&-Self-Employed/Questions-and-Answers-for-the-Additional-Medicare-Tax (last accessed May 26, 2017).

PART IV: NONTAXABLE EXCHANGES

8611. What is a nontaxable exchange? What is the difference between a nontaxable exchange and a tax-free transaction?

In certain circumstances, the IRC permits a taxpayer to obtain new property in order to replace previously held property without recognizing gain on the exchange. This nonrecognition treatment reflects Congress' acknowledgment that, while the taxpayer acquires a new asset in exchange for an existing asset, in substance the taxpayer has not changed economic positions.

In a nontaxable exchange, although gain or loss on the disposition of property is not recognized at the time of the exchange, the nonrecognition treatment is only temporary. Thus, when the taxpayer eventually sells the replacement property the taxpayer will then be required to recognize gain or loss.

A direct exchange is not always necessary in order for a transaction to qualify as a nontaxable exchange. For example, in an involuntary conversion, a taxpayer obtains an asset to replace property that was lost. See Q 8617 to Q 8620 for a discussion of the rules applicable in the context of an involuntary conversion.

On the other hand, in a tax-free transaction, the gain or loss is never recognized. For example, within certain limits the gain on the sale of a taxpayer's primary residence is excluded from gross income and, thus, never taxed.[1]

8612. What exchanges of property qualify as like-kind exchanges and are therefore eligible for nonrecognition treatment?

IRC Section 1031(a) provides that no gain or loss is recognized if property held for productive use in trade or business or for investment is exchanged solely for property of a "like-kind" to be held for productive use in trade or business or for investment.[2] IRC Section 1031 does not provide a permanent exclusion of gain or loss because the taxpayer's basis in the property exchanged transfers to the exchanged property, becoming the basis of that property.[3] So if the taxpayer subsequently sells the replacement property, the deferred gain or loss would be recognized.

The phrase "like-kind" refers to the nature or character of the property and not to its grade or quality.[4] So, whether real property is improved or unimproved is not relevant because virtually all types of real property are deemed to be of the same nature or character. Perhaps for this reason, the Section 1031 nonrecognition provision is frequently used in connection with exchanges of real property. Interestingly, the regulations provide that a leasehold interest with at least 30 years to run is equivalent to an ownership interest in real property.[5]

1. IRC Sec. 121.
2. IRC Sec. 1031(a)(1).
3. IRC Sec. 1031(d).
4. Treas. Reg. §1.1031(a)-1(b).
5. Treas. Reg. §1.1031(a)-1(c); *VIP Industries Inc. v. Comm.*, TC Memo 2013-157.

Only certain types of property are eligible for nonrecognition treatment under the rules applicable to like-kind exchanges. Exchanges of stock in trade (or other property held primarily for sale) and stocks, bonds, notes, and other securities or evidences of indebtedness or interest are specifically excluded under Section 1031, even though they might otherwise qualify as business or investment property.[1] Additionally, IRC Section 1031(h) specifically excludes exchanges in which at least one of the properties is real property located outside the United States. Similarly, an exchange involving a partnership interest in a real estate partnership is specifically excluded from like-kind exchange treatment.[2]

Though the like-kind exchange rules are well-settled in the area of real property, application of the "like-kind" standard is not so clear with respect to exchanges of personal property. In Revenue Ruling 82-166, the IRS ruled that an exchange of gold bullion (held for investment purposes) for silver bullion (which would also be held for investment purposes) did not qualify as a like-kind exchange, based on the finding that silver and gold are intrinsically different metals and are used in different ways; silver is essentially an industrial commodity while gold is primarily utilized as an investment in itself. Therefore, the IRS reasoned that an investment in one of the metals is fundamentally different from an investment in the other metal.[3] Conversely, the IRS has found that trades of major league player contracts, as well as the exchange of gold bullion for Canadian Maple Leaf gold coins, qualified for like-kind treatment.[4]

In one recent example, the IRS ruled upon the exchange of intangible property in the form of contract rights under two separate manufacturing and distribution contracts. The IRS found that a taxpayer could exchange rights to manufacture and distribute a certain set of products under one contract with those available to the taxpayer's subsidiary under a second contract in a like-kind exchange without recognition of gain or loss. Both contracts at issue in this case involved the manufacturing and distribution of a certain set of products, though the contracts covered different territories and had different terms and renewal periods. The IRS found that the contract rights were of a like-kind using a two part test that examined (1) the nature or character of the rights involved and (2) the nature or character of the underlying property to which the agreements relate. Both contracts were in the nature of manufacturing and distribution agreements. While the IRS found that manufacturing and distribution are distinct business activities, and that the rights to each would not be of a like kind, it also found that in the case of the particular products at issue, manufacturing and distribution are historically treated as two aspects of a single business activity, so that the first prong was satisfied. Each agreement covered a group of products that share substantially similar manufacturing and distribution processes. Though the products had different brand names, packaging and appearances, among other differences, these differences impacted the grade or quality of the products, not their nature or character. As a result, the second prong was satisfied and the IRS ruled that the contracts could be transferred in a like-kind exchange.[5]

1. IRC Sec. 1031(a)(2).
2. IRC Sec. 1031(a)(2)(D).
3. Rev. Rul. 82-166, 1982-2 CB 190.
4. Rev. Rul. 67-380, 1967-2 CB 291; Rev. Rul. 71-137, 1971-1 CB 104; Rev. Rul. 82-96, 1982-1 CB 113.
5. Let. Rul. 201531009.

8613. What is a taxpayer's basis in property received in a like-kind exchange?

In a transaction qualifying for nonrecognition treatment, the property received takes a carryover or transferred basis from the property given up. In this manner, the unrecognized gain or loss on the property disposed of is deferred by becoming the basis of the replacement property to be recognized later when the replacement property is disposed of in a taxable transaction.[1]

8614. What are the tax consequences if a taxpayer receives consideration other than like-kind property in an exchange that qualifies for nonrecognition treatment?

If a transaction otherwise qualifying for nonrecognition treatment under IRC Section 1031 involves the receipt of money or non-like-kind property ("boot") in addition to the like-kind property received in the exchange, any realized gain on the exchange must be recognized to the extent of the value of the boot received, and the carryover or transferred basis must be adjusted.

Example: Joanne owns a small business that has three delivery vans. A few years later, Joanne transfers one of the delivery vans, which had an adjusted basis of $2,500 and a fair market value of $2,800, to Calin, in exchange for a truck with a fair market value of $2,200, and $600 in cash.

Joanne's realized gain is $300 ($2,200 truck and $600 cash received, or $2,800 minus $2,500 basis). Because the cash is boot, Joanne must recognize gain to the extent of the boot. Joanne's overall gain is $300 and the boot is $600. As a result, Joanne must recognize the entire $300 gain.

Joanne's carryover basis is increased by the amount of any gain recognized and decreased by the amount of any money received.[2] As a result, in this case, Joanne's basis of $2,500 is increased to $2,800 as a result of the $300 gain. That $2,800 basis is decreased by the amount of money received, $600, to $2,200. As a result, Joanne's basis in the replacement truck is $2,200. Therefore, if Joanne were to sell the truck for $2,200 (its fair market value), she would have no gain or loss.[3]

Similarly, if the person who receives the like-kind property assumes a liability that secures the property, the transferor is treated as having received money to the extent of the assumed liability. If the property received in the exchange is also secured by a liability, then the boot deemed received is only the excess, if any, of the liability transferred with the original property over the liability assumed on the replacement property.[4]

Example: Al owns a warehouse with a basis of $160,000, a value of $200,000, and subject to a mortgage of $150,000. He transfers the warehouse to Asher in exchange for an office building with a value of $175,000, which is subject to a $125,000 mortgage.

From a strictly economic perspective, Al's amount realized is the fair market value of the office building, $175,000, plus a net assumption by Asher of $25,000 of liability (Al's property is subject to $150,000 mortgage and Asher's property is subject to a $125,000 mortgage.) Thus, Al's realized gain is $40,000 ($200,000 minus $160,000 basis).

1. IRC Sec. 1031(d).
2. IRC Sec. 1031(d).
3. Treas. Reg. §1.1031(d)-1(b).
4. Treas. Reg. §1.1031(b)-1(c).

Although the transaction is a like-kind exchange, Al must recognize the realized gain to the extent of the boot received. In this case, as a result of the transfer of mortgages, Al is deemed to have received $25,000 in cash ($150,000 minus $125,000).

Of the $40,000 realized gain, Al must recognize $25,000. The balance of the gain, $15,000, is not recognized.

Al's carryover basis is adjusted as follows: The $160,000 basis is increased to $185,000 by the $25,000 of recognized gain. It is then decreased by $25,000, the amount of money Al is deemed to receive. As a result, Al's basis in the office building is $160,000.

Therefore, if Al were to sell the office building for $175,000 (its fair market value), he would recognize $15,000 of gain. To recap, Al realized $40,000 of gain with respect to the exchange. Of that amount, $25,000 was immediately recognized and $15,000 was deferred.

Realized Gain Computation

Nonrecognized Portion of Gain	
Amount Realized	$200,000
Basis	$160,000
Total Gain Realized	$40,000
Recognized Gain (Mortgage Boot)	$25,000
Deferred Gain	$15,000
Recognized Portion Of Gain (Boot)	
Mortgage Given Up	$150,000
Mortgage Taken On	($125,000)
Boot	$25,000
Basis of Building Received	
Carryover Basis From Property Given Up	$160,000
Plus: Gain Recognized	$25,000
Less: Cash Boot Deemed Received	($25,000)
Basis of Building Received	$160,000

8615. Can a taxpayer defer recognition of gain under the like-kind exchange rules if the exchange is made between related parties?

If like-kind property is exchanged between persons who are "related" to each other (as defined in IRC Sections 267(b) or 707(b)(1)), the nonrecognition treatment provided under Section 1031 will not apply if either party disposes of the replacement property within two years after the exchange.[1]

If such a disposition is made by either party, then both parties must recognize gain on the exchange in the year of the subsequent disposition.[2] IRC Section 1031(f)(2) contains certain

1. IRC Sec. 1031(f).
2. IRC Sec. 1031(f)(1).

specific exceptions to this rule and a general exception for transactions that the IRS concludes did not have tax avoidance as one of the principal purposes.

As a result, nonrecognition treatment will be permitted if the property was disposed of within two years of the exchange as a result of:

(1) the death of the taxpayer or the related person; or

(2) an involuntary conversion (see Q 8611) if the exchange occurred before the threat of the conversion arose.[1]

IRC Section 1031(f)(4) provides that if an exchange is part of a transaction (or series of transactions) structured to avoid the related party rules of Section 1031, the section will not apply at all (except for subsection (f)(4)) and any gain will be recognized in the year of the original sale.

8616. When might a taxpayer want to avoid like-kind exchange treatment?

Like-kind exchange treatment is not elective. Despite this, there are situations where a taxpayer may wish to avoid nonrecognition treatment. If this is the case, in order to avoid application of the like-kind exchange rules, the taxpayer should seek to structure the transaction so that one or more of the requirements under IRC Section 1031 are not met.

There are many reasons why a taxpayer may wish to recognize gain in the current year rather than deferring it until some point in the future. For example, a taxpayer may wish to recognize gain in order to obtain a higher basis in the property for depreciation purposes.

> *Example:* Asher owns a warehouse with a fair market value of $200,000 and a basis of $40,000. A like-kind exchange of the warehouse for an office building of equal value will result in Asher having a carryover basis of $40,000 in the office building. If the exchange did not qualify as a like-kind exchange, Asher would recognize a gain of $160,000 ($200,000 minus $40,000). However, due to the recognition of gain, Asher's basis in the office building would increase to $200,000. Thus, with a higher basis, Asher would be entitled to greater depreciation deductions.

Additionally, if the taxpayer has a substantial amount of capital loss, a recognized gain would be offset by such loss (see Q 8580). Current recognition of gain can also be advantageous if the taxpayer's current income tax rate is expected to rise in the future. See Q 8566 for a discussion of the current capital gains rates and their interaction with a taxpayer's income tax rates.

Planning Point: For taxpayers who anticipate that their capital gains rate will increase (perhaps from the current low of 0 percent (for taxpayers in the 10 or 15 percent ordinary income tax brackets) to as much as 23.8 percent (when the investment income tax (see Q 8566 and Q 8575) is applied), deferring capital gains in a nontaxable exchange could actually cause their tax liability to increase. In 2013 and beyond, the long-term capital gains tax rate is 20 percent for high income taxpayers (but remains at 0 percent for taxpayers in the 10 and 15 percent tax brackets).

1. IRC Sec. 1031(f)(2).

8617. What are the tax consequences of an involuntary conversion?

IRC Section 1033 applies in cases where property is compulsorily or involuntarily converted. This provision recognizes that a taxpayer who has suffered an involuntary conversion has experienced an economic hardship and may not have the ability to pay taxes on any gain resulting from the conversion. This is because any proceeds in excess of the taxpayer's basis in the converted property would generate taxable gain. Thus, IRC Section 1033 postpones recognition of the gain to the extent the proceeds obtained in the conversion, whether through insurance or otherwise, are reinvested in replacement property (see Q 8618).[1]

An "involuntary conversion" may be the result of the destruction of property (whether in whole or in part, see Q 8620 for a discussion of partial conversions), the theft of property, the seizure of property, the requisition or condemnation of property, or the threat or imminence of requisition or condemnation.

On the other hand, the taxpayer is required to recognize any gain that exceeds the amounts reinvested in replacement property following the involuntary conversion.[2]

> *Example*: Patrick received $500,000 in insurance proceeds when his warehouse with an adjusted basis of $100,000 was destroyed in a hurricane. If Patrick decided to retire and keep the insurance proceeds, he would have a gain of $400,000 (it is as if he sold the warehouse to the insurance company for $500,000). However, in evaluating his financial situation, Patrick decides to downsize his business and purchase a new warehouse for $350,000. Because Patrick reinvested $150,000 *less* than he actually received, he must recognize $150,000 of the $400,000 gain.

Planning Point: All the details of an involuntary conversion of property at a gain (including information about the replacement of the converted property, a decision not to replace it, or the expiration of the period for replacement) must be reported in the return for the year or years in which any of the gain is realized.[3]

Section 1033 applies only with respect to gains. If a taxpayer experiences a loss as a result of an involuntary conversion, Section 1033 is inapplicable and the loss is recognized or not recognized in accordance with the general rules applicable to loss recognition. See, for example, Q 8656 to Q 8667, which explain the rules that apply when a taxpayer has experienced a casualty loss.

8618. How does the type of property into which lost or destroyed property is converted impact whether the taxpayer can claim nonrecognition treatment as the result of an involuntary conversion?

Conversion into Similar Property

Whether or not the taxpayer is required to recognize gain resulting from an involuntary conversion of property depends upon the type of property into which the lost or destroyed property is converted.[4] If, as explained below, the replacement property is similar or related in

1. IRC Sec. 1033(a).
2. IRC Sec. 1033(a)(2).
3. Treas. Reg. §1.1033(a)-2(c)(2).
4. IRC Sec. 1033(a).

service or use to the lost or destroyed property, no gain is recognized (losses are always recognized). For nonrecognition treatment to apply, no election is required.

The determination of whether property is similar for purposes of IRC Section 1033 differs from the rules used in determining whether property is "like-kind" property for purposes of IRC Section 1031. The taxpayer's *use* of the replacement property must be similar to the use of the converted property.[1] For example, if a taxpayer's principal residence is replaced by rental property, it would not be considered a similar use.

In the business context, the following factors are relevant in determining whether the taxpayer has replaced converted property with similar property:

(1) Whether the properties provide a similar service to the taxpayer;

(2) The nature of the business risks connected with the properties; and

(3) The demands of the properties upon the taxpayer, including management, required services or relations to tenants.[2]

Conversion into Money or Dissimilar Property

The result is different when the original property is converted into money or dissimilar property. In such cases the proceeds arising from the disposition of the converted property must (within the time limits specified, see Q 8619) be reinvested in similar property (as described above) in order to avoid recognition of any gain realized.[3] If the taxpayer reinvests the entire proceeds in replacement property, no gain will be recognized. However, if the taxpayer only invests part of the proceeds, the taxpayer can elect to recognize the gain only to the extent that the cost of the replacement property exceeds the reinvested proceeds. If the taxpayer fails to make the election the entire gain would be recognized.[4]

Example: A warehouse Asher used in his trade or business was totally destroyed by fire. At the time of the destruction of the warehouse, the warehouse had an adjusted basis of $100,000. The insurance company promptly paid Asher $500,000 for the loss. As a result, Asher realizes a gain of $400,000. Later that year, Asher purchases a new warehouse for $350,000. Thus, the insurance proceeds exceeded the cost of the replacement property by $150,000 ($500,000 minus $350,000). If Asher fails to make an election pursuant to IRC Section 1033(a)(2), the entire realized gain, $400,000, would be included in his gross income. On the other hand, if Asher makes the election, only $150,000 (the amount of the proceeds he did not reinvest) of the $400,000 gain would be included in gross income.

8619. Is a taxpayer whose property is involuntarily converted into money required to replace the lost or destroyed property within a certain amount of time to qualify for nonrecognition treatment?

In order to qualify for nonrecognition treatment under IRC Section 1033, the taxpayer must replace the property that has been involuntarily converted within a two-year period.

1. Rev. Rul. 70-466, 1970-2 CB 165.
2. Rev. Rul. 64-237, 1964-2 CB 319.
3. IRC Sec. 1033(a)(2)(A).
4. Treas. Reg. §1.1033(a)-2(c)(1).

The time period begins to run on the date of the disposition of the converted property or, if the conversion results from condemnation of the property, the date when the condemnation became imminent.[1]

If a taxpayer's principal residence is destroyed as a result of an involuntary conversion that takes place in a federally-declared disaster area, the time period for purchasing replacement property is extended to four years.[2]

8620. Must a taxpayer's property be completely destroyed to qualify for nonrecognition treatment under the rules governing involuntary conversions?

The involuntary conversion of a taxpayer's property need not occur as a result of one sudden event (e.g., a natural disaster) in order for the taxpayer to qualify for nonrecognition treatment under IRC Section 1033.[3] For example, the IRS ruled that the progressive pollution of a taxpayer's water supply with salt water constituted an involuntary conversion for purposes of IRC Section 1033.[4] Similarly, the IRS has ruled that chemical contamination of property, which did not destroy the property per se, but made it unsafe for its intended use, qualified as a Section 1033 "destruction."[5]

Despite this, if the taxpayer disposes of partially destroyed property that could have been repaired, nonrecognition treatment under IRC Section 1033 could be denied. This is because the decision not to repair is treated as "voluntary," as contrasted with a conversion that is purely involuntary. For example, the Tax Court denied nonrecognition treatment when the taxpayer sold a ship damaged in a collision and invested both the sale proceeds and insurance proceeds in another vessel. Because the taxpayer could have used the insurance proceeds to repair the ship, but instead *chose* to purchase a second ship, the conversion was not found to be involuntary. Although the court recognized that it may have been a sound business decision to replace rather than repair, having the choice negated the possibility that the conversion was involuntary. The taxpayer was, therefore, required to recognize all the gain realized in the transaction.[6]

Conversely, the IRS has ruled privately that when the cost of repairs exceeded the value of the property prior to its destruction, there was no practical alternative other than selling the property and purchasing replacement property. Under these circumstances, the taxpayer was entitled to nonrecognition treatment under IRC Section 1033 although, theoretically, the property *could* have been repaired.[7]

Based on these rulings, a taxpayer whose property is partially destroyed will generally qualify for nonrecognition treatment under IRC Section 1033 if the economics of selling the property outweigh the cost of repairing it.

1. IRC Sec. 1033(a)(2)(B).
2. IRC Sec. 1033(h).
3. Rev. Rul. 59-102, 1959-1 CB 200.
4. Rev. Rul. 66-334, 1966-2 CB 302.
5. Rev. Rul. 89-2, 1989-1 CB 259.
6. *Willis v. Comm.*, 41 TC 468 (1964).
7. Let. Rul. 8928011.

8621. Under what circumstances does all or part of the gain from the sale of a principal residence qualify for nonrecognition treatment?

As a general rule, taxpayers may exclude up to $250,000 ($500,000 for married taxpayers filing jointly) of gain on the sale of a principal residence.[1] In order to qualify for this exclusion, the taxpayer must have owned and used the residence as the taxpayer's principal residence for two of the preceding five years.[2]

Planning Point: Note that the Internal Revenue Code does not contain a definition of the term "principal residence." IRS guidance advises that, whether or not property is used by the taxpayer as his principal residence depends on all the facts and circumstances in each case, including the good faith of the taxpayer. Determinative factors include the taxpayer's place of employment, place of abode of family members, and the address listed on taxpayer's tax returns.[3]

The use does not need to be continuous in order to satisfy this requirement, and short absences are disregarded for purposes of making the calculation. Thus, for example, a taxpayer who owns his principal residence for two years and takes a two-month vacation each summer will qualify for the Section 121 exclusion despite the fact that he was not physically present in his principal residence for a full twenty-four months.[4]

The taxpayer may only take advantage of this exclusion once within each two-year period.[5]

Example: Shannon and Mike sell their home in January 2018, excluding $50,000 of gain under IRC Section 121. In the same month, they purchase a new primary residence. Less than two years later, in August 2019, they sell that primary residence. Any gain on the2019 sale cannot be excluded because they have already excluded gain from the sale of one principal residence under IRC Section 121 within a two-year period. The fact that their2018 exclusion was only $50,000 of a possible $500,000 total exclusion is irrelevant.

However, in some cases, taxpayers may qualify for a reduced exclusion (i.e., a proportionate amount of the potential exclusion) if they sell multiple principal residences during a two-year period because of (a) a change in place of employment; (b) health problems or (c) certain unforeseen circumstances (see Q 8616 for a discussion of these exceptions).[6]

8622. Are there circumstances in which a taxpayer can exclude the gain on the sale of a principal residence even though the taxpayer fails to meet the requirements otherwise required for exclusion treatment?

If a taxpayer fails to meet the ownership and use requirements, or sells multiple principal residences within the two-year period (see Q 8621), a portion of the exclusion (as discussed below) may still be available if the principal residence is sold for reasons that were *primarily* caused by a change in the taxpayer's place of employment, health, or, to the extent provided in

1. IRC Sec. 121(b).
2. IRC Sec. 121(a).
3. Treas. Reg. §1.121-1(b)(2); IRS Chief Counsel Memo No. 200947036 (11-20-2009).
4. See IRS Pub. 523.
5. IRC Sec. 121(b)(3).
6. See IRS Pub. 523, above.

regulations, unforeseen circumstances.[1] In determining a taxpayer's primary reason for selling a principal residence, the following factors are considered:

(1) Whether the sale and the circumstances giving rise to the sale are proximate in time;

(2) Material changes in the suitability of the property as the taxpayer's principal residence;

(3) Impairments to the taxpayer's financial ability to maintain the property;

(4) Whether the taxpayer has used the property as his residence during the period of ownership;

(5) Whether or not the circumstances giving rise to the sale are reasonably foreseeable at the time when the taxpayer began using the property as his or her principal residence; or

(6) Whether or not the circumstances giving rise to the sale occur during the period of the taxpayer's ownership and use of the property as his or her principal residence.[2]

For taxpayers claiming a Section 121 exclusion based on a change in place of employment, a safe harbor applies if the change in employment occurs during the period of the taxpayer's ownership and use of the property as a principal residence and the taxpayer's new place of employment is at least fifty miles from the residence that was sold.[3]

Similarly, for taxpayers claiming the exclusion based on health reasons, a safe harbor exists for taxpayers whose physician has recommended a change in residence for health reasons.[4]

The exception for a sale based on "unforeseen circumstances" may be met based on any of the following specific events:

(1) An involuntary conversion of the residence;

(2) Natural or man-made disasters, or acts of war or terrorism, resulting in a casualty to the residence;

(3) The death of the taxpayer;

(4) Loss of employment resulting in eligibility for unemployment compensation;

(5) Change in employment that results in the taxpayer's inability to pay housing costs and reasonable basic living expenses for the taxpayer's household;

1. IRC Sec. 121(c)(2).
2. Treas. Reg. §1.121-3(b).
3. Treas. Reg. §1.121-3(c)(2).
4. Treas. Reg. §1.121-3(d)(2).

(6) Divorce or legal separation; or

(7) Multiple births resulting from the same pregnancy.[1]

The taxpayer does *not* qualify for the exclusion based on unforeseen circumstances if the unforeseen circumstance is an *improvement* in the taxpayer's financial condition.[2]

Example: In April 2017 George buys a house that he uses as his principal residence. He sells it in October2018 because the house has greatly appreciated in value and mortgage rates have substantially decreased, making a bigger house affordable. The specific event safe harbors described above do not apply. In examining the facts and circumstances of the case, the primary reasons for the sale of the house—the changes in George's house value and in the mortgage rates—are an improvement in his financial circumstances. However, an improvement in financial circumstances, even if the result of unforeseen circumstances, does not qualify for the reduced maximum exclusion by reason of unforeseen circumstances under IRC Section 121(c)(2).[3]

For purposes of determining the reduced exclusion, the maximum amount of gain that would have been excluded but for the premature sale of the principal residence is multiplied by a fraction. The numerator of the fraction equals the shorter of (1) the aggregate periods during the five-year period ending on the date of the sale or exchange that the property has been owned or used by the taxpayer as a principal residence, or (2) the period between the date of the most recent prior sale or exchange by the taxpayer to which the two-year limitation applied and the date of the sale or exchange. The denominator equals two years.[4]

Example: On July 2, 2015, Ashley, a single taxpayer, purchased her first principal residence for $150,000. More than two years later, on August 15, 2017, Ashley sold the home for $200,000. Because she met all the requirements of IRC Section 121, Ashley excluded the entire amount of her gain. On September 15, 2017, Ashley purchased a new principal residence for $250,000. Nine months later, on June 15, 2018, Ashley sold the new principal residence for $275,000 because she lost her job and had to take a new job in a different state.

Although the sale of the new principal residence does not qualify for the full exclusion because Ashley used and owned the home for only nine months, the unforeseen circumstance of losing her job that necessitated her relocation qualifies her for the exclusion. Applying the partial exclusion formula, her $250,000 maximum exclusion (single taxpayer) is multiplied by 9/24, or $93,750. This is because, per the formula, the numerator is the lesser of the time between the date of the sale of the previous home (August 15 or ten months to the June 15 sale date) or the time she used and owned the latter residence as her principal residence and the date of the sale (September 15 or nine months until the June 15 sale date). For that reason, Ashley may exclude the entire amount of her gain ($25,000) because it was less than the reduced exclusion amount ($93,750).

If the taxpayer is mentally or physically incapable of caring for himself, and the taxpayer owned and used the property as a principal residence for an aggregate of one year during the five-year period ending on the date of the sale or exchange, an exception to the use requirement applies. Such a taxpayer will be *treated as using* the property during any time within the five-year period that the taxpayer *owns* the property and resides in a facility (including a nursing home) licensed by the state or a political subdivision to care for such an individual.[5]

1. Treas. Reg. §1.121-3(e)(2).
2. Treas. Reg. §1.121-3(e)(1).
3. Treas. Reg. §1.121-3(e)(4), Example 8.
4. IRC Sec. 121(c)(1).
5. IRC Sec. 121(d)(7).

8623. How much gain is a taxpayer permitted to exclude from income on the sale of a principal residence? How is the exclusion calculated?

Generally, an individual who sells a principal residence may elect to exclude up to $250,000 of gain from gross income.[1] However, married couples filing jointly may exclude up to $500,000 if they meet the following requirements:

(1) they must file a joint return for the taxable year of the sale or exchange;

(2) *either* spouse must meet the ownership requirements outlined in Q 8621;

(3) *both* spouses must meet the use requirements outlined in Q 8621; and

(4) *neither* spouse is ineligible to use the exclusion because he or she had used the exclusion in the two-year period ending on the date of the sale or exchange.[2]

8624. If a taxpayer has multiple residences, which residence qualifies as the principal residence in determining whether exclusion of gain upon sale is permissible?

Under IRC Section 121, an individual may elect to exclude up to $250,000 ($500,000 for married couples) on the sale of a principal residence (see Q 8621 and Q 8623). This exclusion is only available with respect to the taxpayer's principal residence. If a taxpayer has multiple residences, the taxpayer may still only exclude gain from the sale of the residence that is considered to be the principal residence.

Whether or not a residence is considered the taxpayer's principal residence for purposes of the Section 121 exclusion requires a traditional facts and circumstances analysis.[3] Assuming that the taxpayer alternates between two or more residences, the residence in which the taxpayer resides for the majority of the time generally will be considered the principal residence. Additionally, other factors are considered in making the determination, including the following nonexhaustive list:

(1) the taxpayer's place of employment;

(2) the principal place of residence of the taxpayer's family members;

(3) the address listed by the taxpayer on his or her driver's license, tax returns, car registration and voter registration card;

(4) the taxpayer's mailing address for bills and correspondence;

(5) the location of the taxpayer's bank; and

1. IRC Sec. 121(b).
2. IRC Sec. 121(b).
3. Treas. Reg. §1.121-1(b)(1).

(6) the location of religious organizations and recreational clubs with which the taxpayer is affiliated.[1]

In a case involving two different residences that were located in different states, the Tax Court held that the taxpayer's principal residence was the one in which the taxpayer spent a substantial amount of time (i.e., threw family parties and celebrated holidays) even though the second residence address appeared on the taxpayer's tax returns over the years. In addition, the Tax Court rejected the IRS' contention that the second residence was the taxpayer's principal residence because the taxpayer (1) owned a business in that state and (2) held a liquor license that required state residency.[2]

With respect to multiple residences, it is possible that over a five-year period, a taxpayer may not spend the majority of days in any one residence for the two required years. Thus, he or she would not be able to take advantage of the exclusion due to the failure to meet the two-year use requirement (see Q 8621).

Example: In the past five years, Jim and Nancy alternated between homes in Michigan, Florida and New York. During that five-year period, they spent more time in the Florida residence than in any other home. *However*, within that period, there was only one year in which they spent the majority of days in Florida. Therefore, even though their principal residence is in Florida, they will be unable to exclude gain on its sale under Section 121 because they will be unable to satisfy the two-year use requirement.[3]

Although not expressly addressed in the regulations, if the taxpayers were able to satisfy the two-year use requirement for more than one residence during the relevant five-year period, they should be able to exclude gain from the sale of *either* residence (but not both residences).

Example: During the previous five-year period, Jim and Nancy spend the majority of their days in Florida during years one and two. In years three and five, they spend the majority of their days in Michigan. If they choose to sell either of the Florida or Michigan residences, they will have satisfied the two-year use requirement for both residences and, assuming the other requirements are met, they should be able to exclude the gain on the sale of *either* residence as their principal residence.

8625. Is a taxpayer permitted to exclude gain on the sale of a principal residence used partially for business purposes if the business portion of the property is separate from the taxpayer's dwelling unit?

If a portion of a piece of property is used as the taxpayer's principal residence and another portion of that same property is used for business purposes, the taxpayer is required to allocate any gain on the sale of the property between the residential and business portions *if* the portion used for business is separate from the taxpayer's "dwelling unit."

"Dwelling unit," for this purpose, is defined in IRC Section 280A as a house, apartment, condominium, mobile home, boat or similar property, except appurtenant structures (such as

1. Treas. Reg. §1.121-1(b)(2).
2. *Wickersham v. Comm.*, TC Memo 2011-178.
3. See *Guinan v. U.S.*, 2003-1 USTC 50,475 (2003).

a detached garage, barn or stable located on the same land).[1] Only the gain from the portion of the property that is used as the taxpayer's principal residence (dwelling unit) may be excluded under Section 121.[2]

Example: Joe operates a dock installation business on a small lake. Rather than renting a separate office space, Joe uses a barn located one hundred feet from his home (the "dwelling unit") to store and repair any broken portions of the docks, as well as for general office space. During the past ten years, the barn has been his place of business and the home has been his principal residence. In year eleven, Joe sells the entire property for $360,000. Because the barn he used for his business is separate from his dwelling unit, he must allocate the basis of the property between the barn and the home.[3]

One way to allocate basis is based on physical size. To illustrate, when Joe acquired the property, the purchase price and basis for the entire property was $300,000. Physically, the home occupies 2/3 of the property and the barn occupies one-third of the property. Thus, based on size, the basis of home should be $200,000 and the basis of the barn should be $100,000. However, as a result of depreciation deductions Joe claimed on the barn, the basis had been decreased to $45,000.

As to the sale of the property in year eleven, Joe's overall economic gain is $60,000 ($360,000 selling price less $300,000 original purchase price). Based on the same allocation method described above, the gain should be allocated $40,000 to the home and $20,000 to the barn. As to the gain allocated to the home, since Joe meets the requirements of IRC Section 121, the entire amount of that gain is excluded from gross income.

On the other hand, $20,000 of the gain is attributable to the barn. None of the gain attributable to the barn is excludable pursuant to IRC Section 121. Thus, it is as if Joe sold the barn for $120,000 (allocating 2/3rd of the $360,000 sales price to the barn). In other words, Joe's gain would be computed in the same way as if he had simply sold the barn. Thus, because his basis in the barn is $45,000, Joe's taxable gain would be computed as follows:

Amount Realized	$120,000
Original Basis	$100,000
Capital Gain	$20,000 (amount of gain attributable to the appreciation of the barn from $100,000 to $120,000)
Adjusted Basis	$45,000 ($100,000 minus $55,000 depreciation deductions)
Unrecaptured Section 1250 gain	$55,000 ($100,000 original basis minus adjusted basis).

8626. Is a taxpayer permitted to exclude gain on the sale of a principal residence used partially for business purposes if the business portion of the property is not separate from the taxpayer's dwelling unit?

Allocation is only required if the property used for business purposes is separate from the taxpayer's principal residence. However, if a taxpayer uses a *non-separate* portion of the residence for business and claims a depreciation deduction as a result of such use, the taxpayer may be required to recognize unrecaptured gain under IRC Section 1250.[4]

1. Treas. Reg. §1.121-1(e)(1); IRC Sec. 280A(f)(1)(A).
2. Treas. Reg. §1.121-1(e)(1).
3. Treas. Reg. §1.121-1(e)(3).
4. Treas. Reg. §1.121-1(e)(1).

Example: Kacey is a lawyer and has used three rooms in her residence as her law office for a seven year period. Over this period, she claimed depreciation deductions totaling $10,000. Later, she sells the house for a $30,000 gain. She has no other capital gains or losses for the year. She must recognize $10,000 of the gain (an amount equal to her depreciation deductions) but may exclude the remaining $20,000 because she is not required to allocate gain between residential and business use property under Treasury Regulation Section 1.121-1(e)(1). If Kacey had not been entitled to claim depreciation deductions with respect to the business use of the house, the entire $30,000 of gain would be excluded from gross income.[1]

8627. Can a taxpayer exclude gain on the sale of vacant land under the same principles that apply to excluding gain on the sale of a principal residence?

A taxpayer may be able to exclude gain on a sale of vacant land made within two years of the sale of a residence if certain requirements are met. A sale of vacant land can "piggy back" onto the sale of a taxpayer's principal residence provided (a) the vacant land is adjacent to a dwelling unit used by the taxpayer as the taxpayer's principal residence; (b) the taxpayer owned and used the vacant land as part of the taxpayer's principal residence; (c) the taxpayer sells the dwelling unit in a sale that meets the requirements of IRC Section 121 within two years before or two years after the date of the sale of the vacant land; and (d) the requirements of IRC Section 121 are otherwise met with respect to the land.[2]

For purposes of excluding the gain on the sale of the vacant land, the sales of the land and the dwelling are treated as a single sale. Therefore, the taxpayer's $250,000 ($500,000 for married couples) exclusion applies to the combined sale. If the sales take place in different tax years, gain on the sale of the dwelling unit is taken into account and excluded first. After, if there is any exclusion amount remaining, it will be applied to the sale of the vacant land.[3]

Example: In 2018, Asher, a single taxpayer who owns a primary residence with adjacent land, sells the primary residence for $400,000 with respect to which there is a $100,000 gain. Assuming Asher meets all the requirements of IRC Section 121, the entire $100,000 gain is excluded from gross income. Because a single taxpayer can exclude up to $250,000 of gain, there is $150,000 of remaining available exclusion. Later in 2018, Asher sells the adjacent land for $300,000 and realizes a $200,000 gain. Again, assuming the requirements of IRC Section 121 are met, Asher can exclude $150,000 of the $200,000 gain. This is because the sale of the home and the vacant land are treated as a single transaction. Since the total gain was $300,000 ($100,000 on the home and $200,000 on the vacant land), the $100,000 gain on the sale of the home is excluded, $150,000 of the gain on the land is excluded and $50,000 of the gain in excess of $250,000 is included in gross income.

If the taxpayer sells the dwelling unit in a tax year that begins *after* the tax year in which the vacant land is sold, and *after* the due date for the tax return for that earlier year, the taxpayer must include in gross income any gain on the sale of the vacant land in the year it is sold. Then upon the later sale of the dwelling unit, the taxpayer is permitted to claim the appropriate IRC Section 121 exclusion with respect to the vacant land by filing an amended return.[4]

1. Treas. Reg. §1.121-1(e)(4), Ex.6.
2. Treas. Reg. §1.121-1(b)(3)(i).
3. Treas. Reg. §1.121-1(b)(3)(ii)(A).
4. Treas. Reg. §1.121-1(b)(3)(ii)(C).

8628. In the case of an involuntary conversion of a principal residence, how does the nonrecognition treatment under IRC Section 1033 interact with the exclusion of gain under IRC Section 121?

If a taxpayer's principal residence is destroyed and the proceeds from insurance are used to purchase a replacement residence, IRC Section 1033 and IRC Section 121 interact as follows:

1. For purposes of determining potential gain for purposes of IRC Section 1033, the amount realized is the fair market value of the relinquished property;

2. Next, the amount of gain that would have been excluded pursuant to IRC Section 121 is subtracted from that amount; and

3. Gain is recognized to the extent that the amount computed pursuant to 2), above, exceeds the cost of a replacement home.[1]

Example: Asher, a single taxpayer, has a principal residence with a fair market value of $600,000 and a basis of $250,000. In a storm, Asher's home is totally destroyed. Asher uses $300,000 of the $600,000 insurance proceeds to purchase a new principal residence. Asher's regular realized gain would be $350,000 ($600,000 minus $250,000). Of that gain, since Asher is a single taxpayer, he may exclude $250,000.

Step 1 and Step 2. $600,000 insurance proceeds minus the $250,000 gain Asher can exclude pursuant to IRC Section 121 equals $350,000.

Step 3. Asher used $300,000 of the insurance proceeds to purchase a replacement home. However, since $350,000 (Step 1 and Step 2 amount) exceeds that amount by $50,000, the latter amount is included in gross income.[2]

Asher's basis should be computed as follows:

1. Original basis in home – $250,000

2. Gain recognized – $50,000

3. Gain Excluded – $250,000

4. New Basis – $550,000 (1 plus 2 plus 3).

Thus, Asher's new home has a fair market value of $300,000 and a basis of $550,000. The difference between the fair market value of the home and the basis reflects the $250,000 of excluded IRC Section 121 gain. In essence, with this higher basis, Asher's exclusion is preserved. So, if Asher sells the home for up to $550,000, no gain is realized.

8629. Does an exchange of corporate stock for corporate stock qualify for nonrecognition treatment?

Pursuant to IRC Section 1036, common stock in a corporation may be exchanged for common stock in the same corporation tax-free. The nonrecognition rules of IRC Section 1036 apply to exchanges of common stock in the same corporation, even though the stocks are of a different class and have different voting, preemptive, or dividend rights.[3] Nonrecognition treatment also

1. IRC Sec. 121(d)(5)(B).
2. Rev. Proc. 2005-14, 2005-7 IRB 492.
3. Rev. Rul. 72-199, 1972-1 CB 228; Treas. Reg. §1.1036-1.

applies to an exchange of preferred stock for preferred stock in the same corporation. However, gain or loss may be recognized if cash or other property is also received. This treatment applies both to exchanges between an individual shareholder and the corporation and to exchanges between two shareholders. Such an exchange is treated in substantially the same manner as a "like-kind" exchange (see Q 8612 to Q 8616).

Finally, the exchange of stock in different corporations and exchanges of common stock for preferred stock do *not* qualify for nonrecognition treatment even if the shares of stock are similar in all other aspects.[1]

8630. What are the requirements to exclude 50, 75 or 100 percent of the gain on the sale of qualified small business stock?

If certain requirements are met, a noncorporate taxpayer (including certain partnerships and S corporations) may exclude from gross income 100 percent of any gain from the sale or exchange of qualified small business stock held for more than five years if the stock was purchased after September 27, 2010.[2] For stock purchased before February 18, 2009, the exclusion was limited to 50 percent, and for stock purchased between February 18, 2009 and September 27, 2010, the exclusion was limited to 75 percent.[3] With certain exceptions, a qualifying small business is:

- A domestic C corporation (not an S corporation) with aggregate gross assets that do not exceed $50 million between August 10, 1993 and the date the stock was issued (the aggregate gross assets also cannot exceed $50 million immediately after the stock was issued);[4]
- Any trade or business other than one involving the performance of legal, health, engineering, architecture, accounting, actuarial services, or any other trade or business in which the principal asset is the skill or reputation of its employees; and
- At least 80 percent of its assets by value must be used in the active conduct of a qualified trade or business.

The aggregate amount of eligible gain from the disposition of qualified small business stock issued by one corporation that may be taken into account in a tax year may not exceed the greater of the following amounts:

(a) $10 million ($5 million in the case of married taxpayers filing separately) reduced by the aggregate amount of such gain taken into account in prior years; *or*

(b) ten times the aggregate bases of qualified stock of the issuer disposed of during the tax year.

1. IRC Secs. 1036, 1031(a); Treas. Reg. §1.1036-1.
2. IRC Sec. 1202(a)(4), as amended by ARRA 2009, ATRA and PATH. See also IRC Sec. 1(h)(7).
3. IRC Sec. 1202(a)(3).
4. IRC Sec. 1202(d)(1)(A).

For purposes of the limitation in (b), above, the adjusted basis of any qualified stock will not include any additions to basis occurring after the stock was issued.[1]

Gain realized by a partner, shareholder, or other participant that is attributable to a disposition of qualified small business stock held by a pass-through entity (i.e., a partnership, S corporation, regulated investment company, or common trust fund) is eligible for the exclusion if the entity held the stock for more than five years, and if the taxpayer held an interest in the pass-through entity at the time of acquisition and at all times since the acquisition of the stock.[2]

Significantly, a taxpayer is not entitled to the Section 1202 exclusion as well as the reduced capital gains rates (0 percent, 15 percent or 20 percent). Instead, the tax rate is subject to a maximum rate of 28 percent. Coupled with the 50 percent exclusion, the actual maximum effective rate on the gain is 14 percent.

Any gain excluded under IRC Section 1202 by a married couple filing jointly must be allocated equally between the spouses for purposes of claiming the exclusion in subsequent tax years.[3]

Special rules apply to IRC Section 1202 stock for alternative minimum tax purposes (see Q 8556 to Q 8561 for a discussion of the AMT). In the case of stock eligible for the 50 percent or 75 percent exclusion, an amount equal to 7 percent of the amount excluded from gross income for the taxable year under IRC Section 1202 will be treated as a preference item.[4] If the stock is eligible for the 100 percent exclusion, no portion of the excluded gain will be treated as a preference item (this provision was made permanent by the PATH Act).

8631. How does an offsetting short position impact a taxpayer's eligibility to exclude 50 percent of the gain on the sale of qualified small business stock?

Under IRC Section 1202, if a taxpayer has an *offsetting short position* with respect to any qualified small business stock, the otherwise applicable 50 percent exclusion (see Q 8630) is unavailable unless:

(a) the stock was held for more than five years as of the date of entering into the short position; *and*

(b) the taxpayer elects to recognize gain as if the stock were sold at its fair market value on the first day the offsetting position was held.[5]

A taxpayer has an "offsetting short position" with respect to any qualified small business stock if the taxpayer (or a related party) has (a) made a short sale of substantially identical property, (b) acquired an option to sell substantially identical property at a fixed price, or

1. IRC Sec. 1202(b).
2. IRC Sec. 1202(g).
3. IRC Sec. 1202(b)(3)(B).
4. IRC Sec. 57(a)(7).
5. IRC Sec. 1202(j)(1).

(c) to the extent expected to be provided in future regulations, entered into any other transaction that substantially reduces the taxpayer's risk of loss from holding the qualified small business stock.[1]

Taxpayers should note that certain offsetting short positions (e.g., a short sale) may also result in constructive sale treatment under the rules of IRC Section 1259. While the IRC does not specifically address the impact of IRC Section 1259 on IRC Section 1202, it would appear that if the requirements of IRC Section 1202(j) are otherwise met, the exclusion provided under IRC Section 1202 would not be lost merely because the taxpayer may be required to immediately recognize gain under IRC Section 1259.

8632. Under what circumstances may a noncorporate taxpayer roll over gain from the sale or exchange of qualified small business stock that is held for six months or more?

Generally, a noncorporate taxpayer, including certain partnerships and S corporations, may elect to roll over gain from the sale or exchange of qualified small business stock held more than six months to the extent that the taxpayer purchases other qualifying small business stock within 60 days of the sale of the original stock.[2]

If the taxpayer elects to roll over gain on the sale of qualified small business stock, gain will be recognized only to the extent that the amount realized on the sale exceeds (1) the cost of any qualified small business stock purchased by the taxpayer during the 60-day period beginning on the date of the sale, reduced by (2) any portion of such cost previously taken into account under this rollover provision. The rollover provisions of IRC Section 1045 will not apply to any gain that is treated as ordinary income.[3]

Rules similar to those applicable to rollovers of gain by an individual from certain small business stock[4] will apply to the rollover of such gain by a partnership or S corporation.[5] Thus, for example, the benefit of a tax-free rollover with respect to the sale of small business stock by a partnership will flow through to an "eligible partner"—meaning a partner who is not a corporation and who held his partnership interest at all times during which the partnership held the small business stock.[6] (A similar rule applies to S corporations and their shareholders.)[7]

For the rules regarding (1) the deferral of gain on a partnership's sale of qualified small business stock followed by an eligible partner's acquisition of qualified replacement stock, and (2) the deferral of gain on a partner's sale of qualified small business stock distributed by a partnership, see Treasury Regulation Section 1.1045-1.[8]

1. IRC Sec. 1202(j)(2).
2. See IRC Sec. 1045(a).
3. IRC Sec. 1045(a).
4. IRC Sec. 1202.
5. IRC Sec. 1045(b)(5).
6. See Treas. Reg. §§1.1045-1(b)(1), 1.1045-1(g)(3)(i).
7. General Explanation of Tax Legislation Enacted in 1998 (JCS-6-98), p. 167 (the 1998 Blue Book).
8. See Treas. Reg. §1.1045-1. TD 9353, 2007-2 CB 721.

Any gain not recognized because of a rollover of qualified small business stock will be applied to reduce (in the order acquired) the basis for determining gain or loss of any qualified small business stock purchased by the taxpayer during the sixty-day rollover period.[1]

Ordinarily, the holding period of qualified small business stock purchased in a rollover transaction will include the holding period of the stock sold. However, for purposes of determining whether the nonrecognition of gain applies to the stock that is sold, the holding period for the replacement stock begins to run on the date of purchase. In addition, only the first six months of the taxpayer's holding period for the replacement stock will be taken into account for purposes of determining whether the active business requirement is met.[2]

Planning Point: The taxpayer must make an election under IRC Section 1045 by the due date (including extensions) for filing the income tax return for the taxable year in which the qualified small business stock is sold.[3] The election is made by (1) reporting the entire gain from the sale of qualified small business stock on Schedule D; (2) writing "IRC Section 1045 rollover" directly below the line on which the gain is reported; ***and*** (3) entering the amount of the gain deferred under IRC Section 1045 on the same line as (2), above, as a loss, in accordance with the instructions for Schedule D.[4]

If a taxpayer has more than one sale of qualified small business stock in a taxable year that qualifies for the IRC Section 1045 election, the election can be made for any one or more of those sales. An IRC Section 1045 election is revocable only with the Commissioner's consent.[5]

8633. Under what circumstances can a taxpayer roll over the gain from a sale of stock in a specialized small business investment company?

Individual taxpayers and C corporations that invest in a specialized small business investment company (SSBIC, see below) may elect to roll over capital gain (within limits) on publicly-traded securities sold within sixty days of the SSBIC purchase. In order to defer the taxation of gain from such a sale, the individual or corporation must use the proceeds from the sale to purchase common stock or a partnership interest in a SSBIC within sixty days of the date of sale.[6]

The amount of gain that may be rolled over for any taxable year by an individual is limited to the lesser of (a) $50,000 or (b) $500,000, reduced by any gain previously excluded under this rollover provision. Thus, the most an individual may roll over during his lifetime is $500,000.[7] (The limits are $25,000 and $250,000, respectively, for married taxpayers filing separately.)

In the case of C corporations, the gain that may be deferred may not exceed the lesser of (a) $250,000 or (b) $1,000,000, reduced by any gain excluded in previous taxable years.[8]

1. IRC Sec. 1045(b)(3).
2. IRC Secs. 1045(b)(4), 1223(15).
3. Rev. Proc. 98-48, 1998-2 CB 367.
4. Rev. Proc. 98-48, 1998-2 CB 367.
5. Rev. Proc. 98-48, 1998-2 CB 367.
6. IRC Sec. 1044.
7. IRC Sec. 1044(b)(1).
8. IRC Sec. 1044(b)(2).

To the extent that gain from the sale of publicly-traded securities exceeds the cost of the SSBIC common stock or partnership interest subsequently purchased, such gain will be taxed in the year of sale. Any gain that is characterized as ordinary income is not eligible for rollover treatment. In addition, gain previously rolled over under this provision may not be rolled over again.[1]

Basis in the SSBIC common stock or partnership interest is generally reduced by the amount of gain that is rolled over. Despite this, the basis of any SSBIC stock is not reduced for purposes of calculating the gain eligible for the 50 percent exclusion for qualified small business stock (see Q 8630).[2]

A "specialized small business investment company" is defined as any partnership or corporation that is licensed by the Small Business Administration under Section 301(d) of the Small Business Investment Act of 1958, as in effect on May 13, 1993.[3]

Estates, trusts, partnerships, and S corporations are not eligible to take advantage of this rollover provision.[4]

1. IRC Sec. 1044(a).
2. IRC Sec. 1044(d).
3. IRC Sec. 1044(c)(3).
4. IRC Sec. 1044(c)(4).

PART V: INVESTOR LOSSES

8634. What is a tax shelter?

In the traditional sense, a tax shelter is simply a method that a taxpayer uses to generate tax deductions and credits by participating in certain "investment activities" that often are not expected to generate any real profits. Historically, taxpayers specifically entered into these transactions with the anticipation of producing losses that could be used to offset a taxpayer's otherwise taxable gains.

The basic concept is presented in the example below, which illustrates the potential results of tax shelters that were available to investors before the enactment of legislation designed to curb the use of these shelters.

> *Example:* Simon has annual income of $450,000 and dividend income of $30,000. He invests $40,000 in a 10 percent interest in ABC partnership ("ABC"), which is in the business of breeding racehorses (Simon had no active role in ABC's business). ABC, through the use of $800,000 in nonrecourse financing and $200,000 in cash, purchased several horses as a part of this breeding program. After depreciation, interest and other deductions relating to the breeding program, ABC experiences a loss of $500,000. Simon's share of the loss is $50,000 (10 percent). Even though Simon only actually invested $40,000 in the partnership (and could have only lost $40,000 if the investment subsequently became completely worthless), he would have been entitled to deduct his entire $50,000 share in ABC's loss.

Although characteristics of a tax sheltered investment may vary depending on the form and type of vehicle employed, several common features are:

(1) *Leverage*. This refers to the maximization of investment return through the use of borrowed capital (see Q 8652 for a discussion of the current limitations imposed on the deductibility of investment interest expenses);

(2) *Depreciation and Depletion*. The tax shelter vehicle, such as an equipment leasing venture, may use the accelerated cost recovery system or accelerated depreciation with respect to the cost of the property. This is true even though all or part of the cost of the asset has been financed by other parties;

A depletion deduction may be available for an investment in natural resources such as oil, gas, timber and minerals. Although deductions for depreciation and depletion may create a loss from a tax standpoint, the investment's cash flow may still be positive. Thus, the investor may benefit from both a currently deductible loss and the receipt of cash flow for other investment or business endeavors;

(3) *Deferral*. If an investment is made in a venture which initially operates at a loss, the loss may be available to shield other income from current taxation. The tax liability is effectively deferred to later years when the investment is producing income.

Timing is important in this regard to avoid having deferred income taxed at a steeper rate in a later taxable year. Obviously, it is desirable that deductions are available in current high-income years while gain or investment income is realized in later low bracket years.

In recent years, the IRS has enacted legislation designed to prevent the use of tax shelters as vehicles that operate solely for the purpose of tax avoidance (see "abusive tax shelters," Q 8635), but one of the key elements of tax shelter partnerships prior to this legislative reform was the allocation of annual operating losses among the partners in such a manner that the investors seeking tax shelter were allocated losses that were disproportionately greater than their true relative economic interest in the partnership.

IRC Section 704(a) generally permits a partner's distributive share of income, gain, loss or deduction to be determined by the partnership agreement. IRC Section 704(b)(2), however, provides that a partnership agreement's allocation provisions that are different from the partners' "interests in the partnership" (taking into account all facts and circumstances) will be effective only in situations in which the allocations have "substantial economic effect."[1] The IRS has developed an extensive set of economic effect tests and a definition of "substantiality" in the final regulations interpreting Section 704.[2]

8635. What is an abusive tax shelter?

While Congress has recognized that the loss of revenue is an acceptable side effect of special tax provisions designed to encourage taxpayers to make certain types of "tax shelter" investments that yield tax benefits, losses from tax shelters often produce little or no benefit to society, or produce tax benefits that are exaggerated beyond those intended. These cases are called "abusive tax shelters," and are described by the IRS in Publication 550 as follows:

> "Abusive tax shelters are marketing schemes involving artificial transactions with little or no economic reality. They often make use of unrealistic allocations, inflated appraisals, losses in connection with nonrecourse loans, mismatching of income and deductions, financing techniques that do not conform to standard commercial business practices, or mischaracterization of the substance of the transaction. Despite appearances to the contrary, the taxpayer generally risks little.
>
> Abusive tax shelters commonly involve package deals designed from the start to generate losses, deductions, or credits that will be far more than present or future investment. Or, they may promise investors from the start that future inflated appraisals will enable them, for example, to reap charitable contribution deductions based on those appraisals. They are commonly marketed in terms of the ratio of tax deductions allegedly available to each dollar invested. This ratio (or "write-off") is frequently said to be several times greater than one-to-one."[3]

The IRS has taken steps to combat abusive tax shelters and transactions. A comprehensive strategy is in place to:

- Identify and deter promoters of abusive tax transactions through audits, summons enforcement and targeted litigation;

1. IRC Sec. 704(b)(2).
2. IRC Secs. 465, 704(d), 704(e)(2), 706(d). See also Treas. Reg. §1.704-1(b).
3. IRS Publication 550, Investment Income and Expenses (20162016).

- Keep the public advised by publishing guidance on transactions and shelters that are determined to be abusive;
- Promote disclosure by those who market and participate in abusive transactions; and
- Develop and implement alternative methods for resolving abusive transactions claimed by taxpayers.

Planning Point: An investment that is considered a tax shelter is subject to restrictions, including the requirement that it be disclosed and registered. The regulations require taxpayers to disclose certain reportable transactions involving abusive tax shelters in which they participate. These transactions include transactions that are the same as, or substantially similar to, a transaction specifically identified by the IRS or state tax agency as a tax avoidance transaction (a so-called "listed transaction").[1]

8636. What are the "at risk" rules with respect to investor losses?

The at risk rules are a group of provisions in the IRC and regulations that limit the current deductibility of "losses" generated by tax shelters (see Q 8634) and certain other activities to the amount that the taxpayer actually has "at risk" (i.e., in the economic sense) in the tax shelter. "Loss" for purposes of the at risk rules means the excess of allowable deductions for the tax year (including depreciation or amortization allowed or allowable and disregarding the at risk limits) over the taxpayer's income from the activity for the tax year.[2]

Historically, the primary targets of the at risk rules have been limited partners and the non-recourse financing of a limited partner's investment in the tax shelter (which was once common in tax shelters, see the example in Q 8634 for an illustration).

Despite this, the rules also apply to certain corporations and general partners in both limited and general partnerships and to non-leveraged risk-limiting devices (e.g., guaranteed repurchase agreements) designed to generate tax deductions in excess of the amount for which the investor actually bears a risk of loss in a shelter.[3]

Other at risk provisions of the IRC limit the availability of the investment tax credit with respect to property acquired for purposes of the tax shelters or other activities.[4]

8637. To what types of investment activities do the "at risk" rules apply?

The "at risk" rules apply to each of the following activities when engaged in by an individual (including partners and S corporation shareholders, see Q 8638) as a trade or business or for the production of income:

(1) holding, producing, or distributing motion picture films or video tapes;

1. IRC Secs. 6707A(c)(2) and 6664(d)(2)(A); Treas. Reg. §1.6011-4.
2. IRC Sec. 465(d); IRS Pub. 925, Passive Activity and At-Risk Rules (2016).
3. See Sen. Rep. 94-938, 1976-3 CB (vol. 3) 57 at 83.
4. IRC Secs. 49(a)(1), 49(a)(2).

(2) farming (including raising, shearing, feeding, caring for, training, or management of animals);

(3) leasing of depreciable personal property (and certain other "IRC Section 1245" property);

(4) exploring for, or exploiting, oil and gas reserves;

(5) exploring, or exploiting, geothermal deposits;

(6) holding real property.[1]

8638. Who is subject to the at risk rules? Do the at risk rules apply to partnerships and S corporations?

Generally, the at risk rules apply to individuals, estates, trusts, and certain closely-held C corporations.[2] A C corporation is considered to be closely-held, and thus subject to the at risk rules, if more than 50 percent of its stock is owned, directly or indirectly, by five or fewer individuals.[3]

In the case of pass-through entities (such as partnerships and S corporations), the at risk rules will apply at the individual taxpayer level (e.g., to the partner or S corporation shareholder), rather than directly to the entity itself.

8639. How does a taxpayer who is subject to the at risk rules determine how much is "at risk" in an investment?

In the most general terms, an individual has amounts "at risk" to the extent the individual is not protected against the loss of money or other property contributed to the activity. If the individual borrows the money that he or she contributes to the activity, the individual is "at risk" only to the extent the individual is not protected against the loss of the borrowed amount (i.e., to the extent of the individual's personal liability for repayment of such amount).[4] See Q 8640 for a discussion of when borrowed amounts will be considered "at risk."

A partner's "amount at risk" is not affected by a loan made to the partnership by any other partner.[5] Payment by a purchaser to the seller for an interest in an activity is treated by the purchaser as a "contribution" to the activity.[6]

More specifically, an individual has an amount "at risk" in an activity equal to the sum of the following:

(1) The amount of money and the adjusted basis of any property that the taxpayer contributes to the activity; and

1. IRC Secs. 465(c); 464(e).
2. IRC Sec. 465(a); IRS Pub. 925, supra.
3. IRC Sec. 465(a), 542(a)(2).
4. Prop. Treas. Reg. §1.465-6.
5. Prop. Treas. Reg. §1.465-7.
6. Prop. Treas. Reg. §1.465-22(d).

(2) Amounts that the taxpayer has borrowed with respect to the activity, to the extent the taxpayer (i) is personally liable for the repayment of the loan proceeds or (ii) has pledged property (other than property otherwise used in the activity) as security on the loan (to the extent of the fair market value of the taxpayer's interest in that property).[1] See Q 8640 and Q 8641 for a detailed discussion of the rules applicable when the taxpayer borrows the amounts contributed to the activity.

In the case of a partnership, amounts required to be contributed under the partnership agreement are not "at risk" until the partner actually makes the contribution. Similarly, a partner's amount at risk does not include the amount of a note that is payable to the partnership and on which the partner is personally liable until such time as the proceeds are actually applied to the activity.[2]

An individual is not considered "at risk" with respect to any amount that is protected against loss through guarantees, stop loss agreements, nonrecourse financing (other than qualified nonrecourse financing of real estate described in Q 8641), or other similar arrangements.[3] An investor is *not* at risk with respect to a note that may be satisfied by transferring to the creditor property that is derived from the activity if there is no obligation on the part of the investor-borrower to pay the difference should the value of the property transferred be less than the amount of the note.[4]

In any case, if a taxpayer engages in a pattern of conduct or utilizes a device that is not within normal business practice, or that has the effect of avoiding the "at risk" limitations, the taxpayer's amount at risk may be adjusted to more accurately reflect the amount that is actually at risk. For example, if considering all the facts and circumstances, it appears that an event that results in an increased amount at risk at the close of one year will be accompanied by an event that will decrease the amount at risk after the year ends, these amounts may be disregarded, unless the taxpayer can establish a valid business purpose for the events and establish that the resulting increases and decreases are not a device for avoiding the at risk limitations in the earlier year.[5] In effect, the increased amount of risk at the close of the year would be ignored under the proposed regulations except in limited circumstances.[6]

A partner's amount at risk is increased by the amount of the partner's share of undistributed partnership income and the partner's share of any tax-exempt proceeds.[7] It is reduced by distributions of taxable income and by losses deducted.[8] It is also reduced by nondeductible expenses relating to production of tax-exempt income of the activity.[9]

1. IRC Sec. 465(b).
2. Prop. Treas. Reg. §1.465-22(a).
3. IRC Sec. 465(b)(4). See Rev. Rul. 78-413, 1978-2 CB 167; Rev. Rul. 79-432, 1979-2 CB 289.
4. Rev. Rul. 85-113, 1985-2 CB 150.
5. Prop. Treas. Reg. §1.465-4.
6. Prop. Treas. Reg. §1.465-4(a).
7. Prop. Treas. Reg. §1.465-22(c)(1).
8. Prop. Treas. Reg. §§1.465-22(b), 1.465-22(c)(2).
9. Prop. Treas. Reg. §1.465-22(c)(2).

8640. What rules apply in determining a taxpayer's amount "at risk" when the taxpayer has borrowed the funds that have contributed to the activity?

In general, if an individual borrows the money contributed to an activity (or, in the case of a limited partnership, the money with which the interest is purchased), the individual is "at risk" only to the extent the individual is personally liable to repay such amounts, or to the extent property is pledged that is not otherwise used in the activity as security for the loan.[1]

If the individual borrowed funds to purchase the property contributed to the activity, the individual is "at risk" with respect to such property only to the extent that the individual would have been "at risk" had the borrowed funds themselves been contributed instead of the purchased property.[2]

If an individual is personally liable for amounts borrowed in the conduct of the activity, the individual is "at risk" to the extent of such amounts even if property used in the activity is also pledged as security for such amounts.[3] The fact that the partnership or other partners are in the chain of liability does not reduce the amount a partner is "at risk" if the partner bears ultimate responsibility.[4]

If the individual is initially personally liable for the borrowed amounts (i.e., as in recourse liabilities), but after the occurrence of some event or lapse of a period of time the liability will become nonrecourse, the individual is considered "at risk" during the period of recourse liability if both of the following are true:

(a) the borrowing arrangement was motivated primarily for business reasons and not tax avoidance; and

(b) the arrangement is consistent with the normal commercial practice of financing the activity for which the money was borrowed.[5]

If amounts are borrowed for use in the activity and the individual is not personally liable for repaying those amounts, but the individual pledges property that is not used in the activity as *security* for repayment, the individual is "at risk" only to the extent that the amount of the liability does not exceed the fair market value of the pledged property. If the fair market value of the security changes after the loan is made, the taxpayer must redetermine the amount at risk using the new fair market value.[6]

Property cannot be treated as security if such property itself is financed (directly or indirectly) by loans secured with property contributed to the activity.[7]

1. Treas. Reg. §1.465-20; Prop. Treas. Reg. §§1.465-6, 1.465-25.
2. See Prop. Treas. Reg. §1.465-23.
3. See Let. Rul. 7927007.
4. *Pritchett v. Comm.*, 87-2 USTC ¶9517 (9th Cir. 1987).
5. Prop. Treas. Reg. §1.465-5. See Rev. Rul. 82-123, 1982-1 CB 82; Rev. Rul. 81-283, 1981-2 CB 115.
6. Prop. Treas. Reg. §1.465-25(a).
7. IRC Sec. 465(b)(2).

Even if an individual is personally liable or has pledged security for borrowed funds, borrowed amounts cannot (unless it is eventually provided in future regulations) be considered at risk (1) if they are borrowed from a person who has an interest (other than as a creditor) in the activity, or (2) if they are borrowed from a person who is related to another person (other than the taxpayer) having an interest in the activity.[1]

For this purpose, a "related" person includes the following: (1) members of a family (i.e., an individual and brothers, sisters, spouse, ancestors, and lineal descendants); (2) a partnership and any partner owning, directly or indirectly, 10 percent of the capital or profits interests in such partnership; (3) two partnerships in which the same persons own, directly or indirectly, more than 10 percent of the capital or profits interest; (4) an individual and a corporation in which such individual owns, directly or indirectly, more than 10 percent in value of the outstanding stock; (5) two corporations that are members of the same controlled group; (6) a grantor and a fiduciary of the same trust; (7) fiduciaries of trusts that have a common grantor; (8) a fiduciary of a trust and the beneficiaries of that trust, or beneficiaries of another trust if both trusts have the same grantor; (9) a fiduciary of a trust and a corporation if more than 10 percent in value of outstanding stock is owned, directly or indirectly, by the trust or by the grantor of the trust; (10 a person and a tax-exempt organization controlled by such person or family of such person; (11) a corporation and a partnership in which the same person owns a more-than-10 percent interest (by value of stock in the case of the corporation and by capital or profits interest in the case of the partnership); (12) two or more S corporations if more than 10 percent of the stock (by value) of each is owned by the same person; (13) an S corporation and a C corporation if more than 10 percent of the stock (by value) is owned by the same person; and (14) an executor of an estate and a beneficiary of such estate (except in the case of a sale or exchange in satisfaction of a pecuniary bequest).[2]

Planning Point: Money borrowed to finance a contribution to an activity cannot increase the amount at risk by the contribution and by the amount borrowed to finance the contribution. The amount at risk may be increased only once.[3]

See Q 8641 for the rules that apply when a taxpayer has obtained "qualified" nonrecourse financing with respect to an activity involving real property.

8641. What rules apply for determining whether a taxpayer has amounts "at risk" when the taxpayer receives qualified nonrecourse financing with respect to the purchase of real property?

An investor in real estate (excluding mineral property) is considered at risk with respect to nonrecourse financing if:

(a) no person is personally liable for repayment (except to the extent provided in regulations);

(b) the financing is secured by real property used in the activity;

1. IRC Sec. 465(b)(3).
2. IRC Secs. 465(b)(3)(C), 267(b), 707(b)(1).
3. IRS Publication 925, Passive Activity and At-Risk Rules (20162016).

(c) the financing is borrowed with respect to the activity of holding real property;

(d) the financing is not convertible debt, and either (1) the financing is borrowed from a "qualified person" or represents a loan from any federal, state, or local government or instrumentality thereof, or is guaranteed by any federal, state, or local government, or (2) the financing is borrowed from a related person upon commercially reasonable terms that are substantially the same terms as loans involving unrelated persons.[1]

A "qualified person" is one who is actively and regularly engaged in the business of lending money and who is *not* (1) related in certain ways to the investor, (2) the one from whom the taxpayer acquired the property (or related to such a person), or (3) a person who receives a fee with respect to the lessor's investment in the real estate (or related to such a person).[2]

In the case of a partnership, a partner's share of qualified nonrecourse financing of the partnership is determined on the basis of the partner's share of such liabilities incurred in connection with the financing.[3]

8642. What are the passive loss rules?

The passive loss rules are a set of rules that are generally intended to prevent losses from passive activities from offsetting salaries, interest, dividends, and income from "active" businesses. They apply to individuals, estates, trusts, closely-held C corporations, and personal service corporations (see Q 8643).

Under the passive loss rules, aggregate losses from "passive" activities (see Q 8644) may generally be deducted in a tax year only to the extent they do not exceed aggregate income from passive activities in that year. Similarly, credits from passive activities may be taken against tax liability allocated only to passive activities.[4] (In the case of certain publicly traded partnerships, aggregation is not permitted. See Q 8648 for details.) The passive loss rules generally apply to losses incurred in tax years beginning after 1986.

An *individual* can also deduct a limited amount of losses (and the deduction-equivalent of credits) arising from certain rental real estate activities against nonpassive income. A *closely-held C corporation* (other than a personal service corporation) can deduct its passive activity losses against its net active income (other than its investment, or "portfolio," income) and its passive credits can be applied against tax liability attributable to its net active income.[5]

Generally, a corporation is considered to be closely-held if it has five or fewer shareholders who own more than 50 percent of the value of its stock.[6] A personal service corporation is a corporation the principal activity of which is the performance of personal services and these services are substantially performed by employee-owners.[7]

1. IRC Sec. 465(b)(6).
2. IRC Secs. 465(b)(6)(D)(i), 49(a)(1)(D)(iv).
3. IRC Sec. 465(b)(6)(C).
4. IRC Sec. 469.
5. IRC Sec. 469(e)(2).
6. IRC Sec. 469(j)(1).
7. IRC Sec. 469(j)(2).

A taxpayer may elect to treat investment interest (see Q 8652) as a passive activity deduction if the interest was carried over from a year prior to 1987 and is attributable to property used in a passive activity after 1986.[1] However, the interest deduction is not treated as being from a pre-enactment interest in a passive activity.[2]

8643. To which taxpayers do the passive rules apply?

IRC Section 469, which governs the treatment of passive losses, applies to individual taxpayers, estates and trusts. Closely-held C corporations and personal service corporations are also subject to the passive loss rules in an attempt to prevent taxpayers from creating these entities solely to avoid the passive loss rules (see Q 8642).[3]

Planning Point: Even though the passive activity rules do not apply to grantor trusts, partnerships, and S corporations directly, they do apply to the owners of these entities (i.e., they are applied at the individual level, rather than the entity level).[4]

The passive loss rules apply to S corporations and partnerships indirectly, because income and losses flow through the entity to apply at the individual taxpayer level (e.g., to the S corporation's shareholders or partnership's partners). See Q 8883 and Q 8848 for a detailed discussion of the pass-through rules applicable to S corporations and partnerships, respectively.

8644. What is a passive activity for purposes of the passive loss rules?

A passive activity is any activity that involves the conduct of a trade or business in which the taxpayer does not "materially participate," (see Q 8645) or is a rental activity, without regard to whether or to what extent the taxpayer participates in such activity.[5]

The IRC provides that regulations may define the term "trade or business" to include activities undertaken in connection with a trade or business or activities that are engaged in for the production of income under IRC Section 212.

The regulations provide that the IRS will treat real property held for the production of income under IRC Section 212 as a trade or business for purposes of the rental real estate with material participation exception (see Q 8647).

The term "passive activity" does not include a working interest in an oil or gas property that the taxpayer holds directly or through an entity that does not limit the liability of the taxpayer with respect to the interest.[6] It also does not include the activity of trading personal property (e.g., stocks or bonds) on behalf of the owners of interests in the activity.[7]

1. TAMRA '88, Sec. 1005(c)(11).
2. Notice 89-36, 1989-1 CB 677.
3. IRC Sec. 469(a)(2).
4. Temp. Treas. Reg. §1.469-1T(b); IRS Pub. 925.
5. Temp. Treas. Reg. §1.469-1T(e)(1).
6. IRC Sec. 469(c)(3).
7. Temp. Treas. Reg. §1.469-1T(e)(6).

Planning Point: However, if the taxpayer's interest in an oil and gas well would, but for the exception for wells drilled or operated pursuant to a working interest, be an interest in a passive activity for the year, and the well suffers a net loss for the year, then (1) the taxpayer's disqualified deductions (under IRC Section 469(e)(4)) from the well for the year will be treated as passive activity deductions; and (2) a ratable portion of the taxpayer's gross income from the well will be treated as passive activity gross income for the year.[1]

Whether an activity is passive or active with regard to a partner or an S corporation shareholder is determined at the level of the partner or shareholder, not at the level of the entity. This determination is made by considering the activities that took place during the entity's taxable year (not the partner's or shareholder's taxable year).[2]

However, if a publicly traded partnership is taxed as a corporation, the partnership is the taxpayer, and apparently the partnership is not subject to the passive loss rules.[3] In the case of a limited partnership interest in an electing large partnership, all passive loss limitation activities of the partnership are treated as a single passive activity.

8645. When is a taxpayer treated as materially participating in an activity for purposes of determining whether the activity is active or passive?

In general, a taxpayer is considered to materially participate in an activity if the taxpayer is involved in the operations of the activity on a regular, continuous, and substantial basis.[4] The material participation requirement is generally met by a taxpayer who is able to satisfy any one of the following five tests:

(1) the taxpayer does substantially all of the work required by the activity;

(2) the taxpayer participates in the activity for more than 500 hours during the year;

(3) the taxpayer participates in the activity for more than 100 hours during the year and meets certain other requirements;

(4) the activity is a significant participation activity for the taxable year, and the individual's total participation in all significant participation activities during such year exceeds 500 hours;

(5) the taxpayer has materially participated in the activity in five out of the ten preceding years (determined without regard to this test); or

(6) the taxpayer has materially participated in the activity, which involves the performance of personal services, in any three preceding years.

1. Temp. Treas. Reg. §1.469-1T(e)(4).
2. Temp. Treas. Reg. §1.469-2T(e)(1), 1.469-3T(b)(3).
3. IRC Sec. 469(a).
4. IRC Sec. 469(h)(1).

Planning Point: For purposes of (4) above, an activity is a significant participation activity if, and only if, the activity: (1) is a trade or business activity in which the individual significantly participates for the year; and (2) would be an activity in which the individual does not materially participate if material participation for the year were determined without regard to whether the individual's total participation in all significant participation activities during the year exceeded 500 hours.[1]

An individual who is a limited partner is treated as materially participating only if the individual also owns a general partnership interest, or can meet tests (2), (5) or (6), above.[2]

In determining whether an individual materially participates, the participation of the individual's spouse is considered.[3] Work done in the individual's capacity as an investor is not treated as participation unless the individual is involved in the day-to-day management or operations of the activity. The extent to which an individual participates may be shown by any reasonable means.[4]

A closely-held C corporation or a personal service corporation is considered to materially participate in an activity if either of the following are true:

(a) one or more stockholders who owns more than 50 percent (by value) of the outstanding stock of the corporation materially participates; *or*

(b) if the C corporation (other than a personal service corporation) has (1) an active full-time manager throughout the year, (2) at least three full-time non-owner employees whose services are directly related to the business of the corporation, and (3) certain deductions of the business exceed 15 percent of the income for the year.[5]

Whether a trust materially participates in an activity is determined by reference to the persons who conduct the business activity on the trust's behalf, in addition to whether the trustee materially participates in the activity.[6] (But see Q 8601 to Q 8603 with respect to the net investment income tax material participation requirements that apply to trusts.)

8646. What happens if a taxpayer's passive losses for a tax year are disallowed?

Losses and credits that are disallowed under the passive loss rules may be carried over to offset passive income and the tax attributable to this income in later years.[7] If passive losses (or credits) from a publicly traded partnership are carried forward, such losses (or credits) may only be offset by passive income (or tax attributable to passive income) from the same partnership.[8]

Suspended losses and credits of an activity may also offset the income and tax of that activity when the activity ceases to be passive or there is a change in status of a closely-held corporation

1. Temp. Treas. Reg. §1.469-5T(c).
2. Temp. Treas. Reg. §1.469-5T.
3. IRC Sec. 469(h)(5).
4. Temp. Treas. Reg. §1.469-5T(f).
5. IRC Sec. 469(h)(4).
6. *Carter Trust v. Comm.*, 2003-1 USTC 50,418 (N.D. Tex. 2003).
7. IRC Sec. 469(b).
8. IRC Sec. 469(k)(1).

or personal service corporation. For a discussion of the treatment of losses allowed upon disposition of an interest in a passive activity, see Q 8651.

The rules relating to the treatment of suspended losses and credits when the activity is disposed of require that losses and credits carried over from year to year be traceable to a particular activity. Because of this, where there are losses or credits from two or more activities which, in the aggregate, exceed passive gains from other passive activities, the amount disallowed and carried over must be allocated among the different activities and between capital and ordinary loss. Disallowed passive losses are allocated among activities in proportion to the loss from each activity. The disallowed loss allocated to an activity is then allocated ratably among deductions attributable to the activity. Disallowed credits are allocated ratably among all credits attributable to passive activities.

In identifying the deductions or credits that are disallowed, the taxpayer is only required to separately account for those items that, if separately taken into account by the taxpayer, would result in an income tax liability different from that which would result if such deduction were not taken into account separately. Deductions arising from a rental real estate activity, or in connection with a capital or IRC Section 1231 asset, must be accounted for separately. Credits (other than the low-income housing or rehabilitation credits) arising from a rental real estate activity must also be accounted for separately.[1]

If an activity ceases to be passive (e.g., because the taxpayer begins to participate materially), its unused losses (or credits) from prior years continue to be passive, but may be used against the income (and tax liability) of that activity. If there is a change in the status of a closely-held C corporation or personal service corporation, its suspended losses from prior years will continue to be treated as if the status of the corporation had not changed.[2]

8647. What special passive activity rules apply to taxpayers who invest in rental real estate?

Except as provided below, a passive activity includes any rental activity, without regard to whether the taxpayer materially participates in the activity.[3] A rental activity is any activity where rental payments are made principally for the use of tangible property.[4]

There are a number of exceptions to this rule. An activity is not treated as a rental activity if:

(1) the average rental period is less than eight days;

(2) the average rental period is less than 31 days and the owner of the property provides significant personal services in order to make it available for use by customers;

(3) the rental of the property is incidental to the receipt of personal services or to a nonrental activity;

1. Temp. Treas. Reg. §1.469-1T(f).
2. IRC Sec. 469(f).
3. IRC Sec. 469(c)(2).
4. IRC Sec. 469(j)(8).

(4) the taxpayer makes the property available on a nonexclusive basis during regular business hours;

(5) the taxpayer rents property to a pass-through entity engaged in a nonrental activity, in his capacity as an owner of that entity; or

(6) the personal use of a residence that is also rented out exceeds the greater of 14 days or 10 percent of the rental days.[1]

Planning Point: For purpose of (2) above, in determining if a property owner's rental services are significant, all relevant facts and services—including the frequency of the services, type and amount of labor needed to perform them, and their value relative to the amount charged for the property's use—are taken into account.[2]

If an individual actively participates in a rental real estate activity subject to the passive activity rules, the individual may use up to $25,000 of losses and the deduction-equivalent of credits to offset nonpassive income. An individual need not actively participate in a rental real estate activity to obtain the $25,000 rental real estate exemption with respect to taking the low-income housing credit or rehabilitation tax credit.

If the investment is in real estate which is not rental property, the real estate activity will generally be considered a passive activity subject to the passive loss rules unless the taxpayer materially participates in the activity. The $25,000 rental real estate exemption is not available with respect to nonrental property.

8648. How are the passive activities of publicly-traded partnerships treated under the passive loss rules?

Special restrictions apply to publicly traded partnerships under the passive loss rules. A publicly traded partnership is a partnership that is traded on an established securities market or is readily tradable on a secondary market (or the substantial equivalent thereof).[3]

The rules are applied separately to items attributable to a publicly traded partnership, meaning that income, losses, and credits attributable to the partnership may not be aggregated with other income, losses, and credits of the taxpayer-partner for purposes of the passive loss rules.[4] Net passive loss from a publicly traded partnership will be treated as passive, while net passive income from a publicly traded partnership is to be treated as investment income.[5]

Generally, net passive loss from a publicly traded partnership is carried forward until the partner has additional passive income from the partnership or the partner disposes of the partnership interest. Also, the $25,000 rental real estate exemption (see Q 8647) is available with respect to a publicly traded partnership only in connection with the low-income housing credit and the rehabilitation investment credit.

1. Treas. Reg. §1.469-1T(e)(3); IRC Sec. 469(j)(10).
2. Temp Treas. Reg. §1.469-1T(e)(3)(iv).
3. IRC Sec. 469(k).
4. IRC Sec. 469(k)(1).
5. Notice 88-75, 1988-2 CB 386.

Further, a taxpayer will not be treated as having disposed of the taxpayer's entire interest in an *activity* of a publicly-traded partnership until the taxpayer has disposed of the entire interest in the partnership. It would seem that if a publicly traded partnership is taxed as a corporation, the partnership is not a taxpayer subject to the passive loss rules.[1]

8649. Do the passive loss rules apply to casualty losses?

An exception to the passive loss restrictions is applied to certain casualty losses (see Q 8656 to Q 8667) resulting from unusual events (including fire, storm, shipwreck, and earthquake). Losses from such casualties are generally not subject to the passive loss rules.[2]

Likewise, passive activity income does not include reimbursements for such losses if both of the following are true:

(1) the reimbursement is includable in gross income under Treasury Regulation Section 1.165-1(d)(2)(iii) as an amount the taxpayer had deducted in a prior taxable year; and

(2) the deduction for the loss was not a passive activity deduction.

In other words, both the losses and the reimbursement should be taken into account in the calculation of the partnership's gross income, not its passive activity gross income.[3]

The exception does not apply to losses that occur regularly in the conduct of the activity, such as theft losses from shoplifting in a retail store, or accident losses sustained in the operation of a rental car business.[4]

8650. How do the passive loss rules interact with the at-risk rules?

When determining whether a loss deduction will be allowed, the taxpayer must first apply the at risk rules. If a deduction is disallowed in one year under the at risk rules (see Q 8636 to Q 8641), it generally cannot be deducted as a loss under the passive activity rules.[5] Therefore, the loss will be suspended under the at risk rules, and can be carried forward to the succeeding tax year if the taxpayer has sufficient amounts "at risk" in that later tax year.

8651. What are the tax results when a taxpayer disposes of interests in a passive activity?

If a taxpayer disposes of his interests in a passive activity in a fully taxable transaction, losses from the activity will receive *ordinary loss treatment* (i.e., they may generally be used to offset other income of the taxpayer) to the extent that they exceed net income or gain from all passive activities (determined without regard to the losses just discussed) for the year. This treatment applies both to current year losses as well as losses carried over from previous

1. See IRC Sec. 469(a).
2. Treas. Reg. §§1.469-2T(d)(2), 1.469-2(d)(2)(xi).
3. Treas. Reg. §§1.469-2T(c)(7), 1.469-2(c)(7)(vi).
4. TD 8290, 1990-1 CB 109.
5. Temp. Treas. Reg. §1.469-2T(d)(6)(i).

years, with respect to the activity disposed of. The IRS has been given the authority to issue regulations that will take income or gain from previous years into account to prevent the misuse of this rule.[1]

For the purpose of determining gain or loss from a disposition of property, the taxpayer may elect to increase the basis of the property immediately before disposition by an amount equal to the part of any unused credit that reduced the basis of the property for the year the credit arose.[2] If the passive interest disposed of is sold under the installment method, previously disallowed passive losses are allowed as a deduction in the same proportion as gain recognized for the year bears to gross profit from the sale.[3]

If the disposition of the passive interest is to a related person in an otherwise fully taxable transaction, suspended losses remain with the taxpayer and may continue to offset other passive income of the taxpayer. The taxpayer is considered to have disposed of an interest in a transaction described in the preceding sentence when the related party later disposes of the passive interest in a taxable transaction to a party unrelated to the taxpayer.[4]

If the disposition is by death, the carried over losses may be deducted only to the extent the losses exceed the step-up in basis of the interest in the passive activity.[5] If the disposition is by gift, the losses are not deductible. Instead, the donor's basis immediately prior to the transfer is increased by the amount of the disallowed losses allocable to the interest.[6] However, where a donor makes a gift of less than his or her entire interest in property, a portion of the carried over losses is allocated to the gift and increases the donor's basis. A portion of the losses will continue to be treated as passive losses attributable to the interest that the donor has retained.[7]

If a trust or estate distributes an interest in a passive activity, the basis of such interest immediately before the distribution is increased by the amount of passive losses allocable to the interest, and such losses are never deductible.[8]

A taxpayer is not treated as having disposed of the entire interest in an *activity* of a publicly-traded partnership until the taxpayer disposes of the entire interest in the partnership.[9]

Planning Point: IRS Publication 925 (Passive Activity and At-Risk Rules) contains a number of examples of, and various scenarios relating to, passive activities and losses, and includes worksheets and filing instructions necessary for the completed reporting of passive activities.

1. IRC Sec. 469(g)(1).
2. IRC Sec. 469(j)(9).
3. IRC Sec. 469(g)(3).
4. IRC Sec. 469(g)(1)(B).
5. IRC Sec. 469(g)(2).
6. IRC Sec. 469(j)(6).
7. Sen. Rep. 99-313, 1986-3 CB (vol. 3) 713, 726.
8. IRC Sec. 469(j)(12).
9. IRC Sec. 469(k)(3).

8652. Can a taxpayer deduct interest expenses incurred in relation to property the taxpayer holds for investment?

Yes, within limits. Because of the substantial tax benefits that can result when a taxpayer's interest expenses are large compared to the amount of income realized from the investments at issue, Congress has taken steps to limit the amount of investment interest that a taxpayer can deduct in any tax year.

Therefore, a noncorporate taxpayer is permitted to deduct interest expenses incurred in funding the purchase of investment assets, but only to the extent that the taxpayer's interest expenses exceed net investment income (see below) for the year.[1] Any other investment interest expense is considered excess interest and is disallowed.

"Net investment income" for purposes of the interest expense deduction means the excess of investment income over investment expenses.[2] "Investment income" means the sum of the following four items:

(1) Gross income derived from property held for investment *other than* gain derived from the disposition of that property (e.g., income from interest, dividends, annuities and royalties not derived in the ordinary course of the taxpayer's trade or business);

(2) The excess, if any, of (i) "net gain" attributable to the disposition of property held for investment over (ii) the "net capital gain" determined by taking into account gains and losses from dispositions of property held for investment;

(3) The taxpayer's net capital gain determined by only taking into account gains and losses derived from the disposition of investment property *or* the taxpayer's net gain attributable to disposition of property held for investment, whichever is lower, but only to the extent the taxpayer *elects* to treat such income as investment income for purposes of Section 163; and

(4) Qualified dividend income, to the extent the taxpayer elects to treat such income as investment income for purposes of Section 163.[3]

In other words, net investment income, for purposes of the interest expense deduction, generally does not include net capital gain from the disposition of investment property *unless* the taxpayer makes the election to do so (see Q 8654 for the tax consequences of this election).

The term "investment expenses" means deductions (other than the interest deduction) that are directly connected with the production of investment income.[4]

1. IRC Sec. 163(d).
2. IRC Sec. 163(d)(4)(A).
3. IRC Sec. 163(d)(4)(B).
4. IRC Sec. 163(d)(4)(C).

The Tax Court has held that net gain for purposes of IRC Section 163(d)(4)(B)(ii) means the excess (if any) of total gains over total losses, including capital loss carryovers, from the disposition of property held for investment. The Court further held that calculation of net gain required inclusion of the taxpayers' capital losses and capital loss carryovers for purposes of calculating the IRC Section 163(d)(1) limit on the investment interest expense deduction.[1]

The IRS has ruled privately that:

(1) The term "property" (under IRC Section 163(d)(5)(A)(i)) includes interest-free loans (which are deemed to yield gross income as a result of interest imputed under IRC Section 7872) to a tax-exempt foundation;

(2) Any imputed interest income that is deemed to be received by the taxpayer on the potential loan from the line of credit to the foundation is "investment income" (under IRC Section 163(d)(4)(B)(i)); and

(3) Any interest paid by the taxpayer on the line of credit used to make the potential loan to the foundation is "investment interest" (under IRC Section 163(d)(3)(A)).[2]

See Q 8653 for a discussion of the treatment of disallowed interest expenses and Q 8655 for a discussion of how the interest expense deduction is impacted by the passive loss rules.

8653. What is the result if a taxpayer has interest expenses that exceed net investment income for the tax year?

If a taxpayer has interest expenses that exceed his or her net investment income for the year, those expenses are considered excess interest and the deduction is disallowed. However, disallowed interest expenses from one year can be carried forward to the succeeding tax year.[3]

A taxpayer's investment interest expenses that are disallowed because of the investment income limitation in one year will be treated as investment interest paid or accrued in the succeeding tax year.[4] The IRS has issued guidance that provides it will not limit the carryover of a taxpayer's disallowed investment interest to a succeeding tax year to the taxpayer's taxable income for the tax year in which the interest is paid or accrued.[5] Prior to the issuance of this guidance, several federal courts had held that no taxable income limitation existed on the amount of disallowed investment interest that could be carried over.[6]

1. *Gorkes v. Comm.*, TC Summ. Op. 2003-160.
2. Let. Rul. 200503004.
3. IRC Sec. 163(d)(2).
4. IRC Sec. 163(d)(2).
5. Rev. Rul. 95-16, 1995-1 CB 9.
6. See, for example, *Sharp v. U.S.*, 94-1 USTC 50,001.

8654. In calculating the allowable investment interest deduction, what are the tax consequences when a taxpayer elects to treat all or a portion of capital gain or qualified dividend income as investment income?

Net investment income, for purposes of the interest expense deduction, generally does not include net capital gain from the disposition of investment property or qualified dividend income *unless* the taxpayer elects to treat this income as investment income. See Q 8652.

If the taxpayer makes this election, any net capital gain or qualified dividend income treated as investment income is not eligible to be taxed at the capital gains rates and will be subject to the taxpayer's ordinary income tax rate for that tax year, rather than the special lower tax rates that otherwise apply to these types of income (see Q 8566 for a discussion of the currently applicable tax rates for capital gains and qualified dividend income).[1]

The advantage of making the election is that a taxpayer may increase the amount of investment income against which investment interest is deducted, thus receiving the full benefit of the deduction.[2]

> *Example:* Shawn incurred $15,000 in interest expenses related to investment property in 2018. His investment income included $6,000 of interest income, $2,000 received as qualified dividends and a $5,000 net capital gain on the sale of securities held for investment. If Shawn does not elect to treat his income from net capital gains and dividends as investment income, his investment income is $6,000 (i.e., only the interest income he realized for the year). He would, therefore, have $9,000 of disallowed interest expenses for the year. While he could carry those expenses forward to 2019 (see Q 8653), if he does make the election, his investment income would equal $13,000 and he would only carry $2,000 forward.

The election to treat net capital gain and qualified dividend income as investment income must be made on or before the due date (including extensions) of the income tax return for the taxable year in which the net capital gain is recognized, or the qualified dividend income is received, respectively.[3] The IRS has, however, privately ruled that a taxpayer was permitted to make a late election to treat capital gains as investment income based on the IRS' conclusion that the taxpayer had acted reasonably and in good faith, and that granting the extension would not prejudice the interests of the government.[4]

The elections are made on Form 4952, "Investment Interest Expense Deduction" and may not be revoked for that year, except with IRS permission.[5] The IRS has ruled privately that certain taxpayers who were properly classified as securities traders were permitted to revoke their election because such gains should have been treated as investment interest anyway (based on their status as professional securities traders). Therefore, allowing them to revoke their election did not prejudice the government or cause undue administrative burdens.[6]

1. Treas. Reg. §1.163(d)-1(a).
2. See IRC Sec. 163(d)(4).
3. Treas. Reg. §1.163(d)-1(b).
4. Let. Rul. 200033020. See also Let. Rul. 200303013.
5. Treas. Reg. §§1.163(d)-1(b), 1.163(d)-1(c).
6. Let. Rul. 200146018.

A taxpayer can elect to treat capital gain or dividend income as investment income in one year without any obligation to make the election in any other tax year.[1]

8655. Is the determination of a taxpayer's allowable investment interest deduction coordinated with the passive loss rules?

The investment interest limitation is coordinated with the passive loss rules (see Q 8642 to Q 8651), so that interest and income subject to the passive loss rules are not taken into consideration under the investment interest limitation.[2] Interest expense incurred to purchase an interest in a passive activity is allocated to that passive activity and is not investment interest.[3]

However, portfolio income of a passive activity and expense (including interest expense) allocable to it is considered investment income and expense, not passive income and expense.[4]

Investment interest expense and investment income and expenses do not include items from a trade or business in which the taxpayer materially participates. The IRS has determined that interest on a loan incurred to purchase stock in a C corporation was investment interest (where the purchaser was not a dealer or trader in stock or securities), even though the purchaser acquired the stock to protect his employment with the C corporation.[5]

In a decision citing Revenue Ruling 93-68, the Tax Court held that interest on indebtedness incurred to purchase a taxpayer's share of stock in a family-owned mortuary business was subject to the investment interest limitation, despite the fact that the taxpayer purchased the stock to conduct business full time and the fact that no dividends had been paid on the stock.[6]

Temporary regulations provide that, for purposes of the investment interest and passive loss rules, interest expense is generally allocated on the basis of the use of the proceeds of the underlying debt.

1. Treas. Reg. §1.163(d)-1(c).
2. IRC Secs. 163(d), 469.
3. Temp. Treas. Reg. §1.163-8T(a)(4)(B).
4. IRC Sec. 469(e)(1).
5. Rev. Rul. 93-68, 1993-2 CB 72.
6. *Russon v. Comm.*, 107 TC 263 (1996).

PART VI: CASUALTY AND THEFT LOSSES

8656. What is a casualty loss?

A casualty loss is a loss that an individual taxpayer suffers as a direct result of an event that meets the following criteria:

(1) It is identifiable;

(2) It is damaging to property; and

(3) It is sudden, unexpected and unusual in nature.[1]

IRC Section 165 specifically permits a casualty loss deduction for fire, storm, shipwreck or "other casualty."[2] The term "other casualty" has been interpreted to include damage sustained as a result of, among other events, floods[3] and sudden freezing.[4] Other deductible casualty losses that are specifically allowed by the IRS include damage caused by fire, earthquake, government ordered demolition or relocation of a home rendered unsafe due to a disaster, mine cave-ins, shipwrecks, sonic booms, storms, terrorist attacks, vandalism and volcanic eruptions.[5]

The Tax Court allowed a taxpayer's casualty loss deduction for damage caused by blasting operations when the damage caused by the particular blast was unusual and heavier than the blasting that had occurred on a day-to-day basis in the area.[6] The Tax Court has also permitted a casualty loss deduction for damage sustained due to vandalism, because the vandalism in question was caused by persons outside of the taxpayers' control, was sudden in nature and destructive in effect.[7]

Damage to property created by termite infestation was *not* considered to be a casualty loss, because the damage was created by a progressive deterioration of property resulting from a steady cause operating over time—essentially, the casualty loss deduction was denied because the event that caused the destruction was not "sudden" in nature.[8]

A taxpayer was not entitled to claim a casualty deduction for losses sustained as a result of the worthlessness of currency held by the taxpayer. The Tax Court found that "other casualty" must be interpreted to mean an event similar to "fire, storm or shipwreck" and that a decrease in currency value was not a similar event. Further, the Court noted that the taxpayers actually still held the currency at issue—and thus, it was not technically damaged.[9]

Further, costs incurred by a taxpayer in order to *prevent* a potential casualty loss are not deductible under IRC Section 165 as casualty losses. According to the courts, such preventative

1. See *Fay v. Helvering*, 120 F.2d 253 (2nd Cir. 1941); *Torre v. Comm.*, TC Memo 2001-218; *Matheson v. Comm.*, 54 F.2d 537 (2nd Cir. 1931).
2. IRC Sec. 165(c)(3).
3. *Finkbohner v. United States*, 788 F.2d 723 (11th Cir. 1986).
4. *United States v. Barret*, 202 F.2d 804 (5th Cir. 1953).
5. IRS Pub. 547, Casualties, Disasters and Thefts (2016).
6. *Durden v. Comm.*, 3 TC 1 (1944).
7. *Davis v. Comm.*, 34 TC 586 (1960).
8. *Fay v. Helvering*, above.
9. *Billman v. Comm.*, 73 TC 139 (1979).

steps are not sudden and unexpected in nature, and thus do not qualify as events giving rise to casualty loss treatment.[1]

Special rules apply if a taxpayer suffers a casualty loss within a federally declared disaster area (see Q 8666.).

Generally, casualty losses are deductible during the taxable year that the loss occurred (see Q 8659).[2]

8657. What is a theft loss?

A theft loss is a loss sustained as a result of (among other things) larceny, embezzlement or robbery.[3] The taking of property must be illegal under the law of the state where it occurred and it must have been done with criminal intent. A conviction does not need to occur, however, to show a theft loss.[4]

The definition of "theft" is given a broad meaning and, therefore, a theft loss deduction may often be allowed in situations that do not involve the straightforward theft of property. For example, the IRS has allowed a theft loss deduction when a publicly-traded company misrepresented its financial condition in a business transaction in which the company traded its common stock in a tax-free reorganization and that stock subsequently became worthless. The IRS analogized the situation to "larceny by false pretenses" in that the company's officers knew that their representations were false.[5]

In Revenue Ruling 66-355, the IRS held that a theft occurred when a taxpayer's employee pledged shares of the taxpayer-employer's stock as collateral to secure a personal loan. When the bank later sold the stock, the taxpayer-employer was able to treat the property as stolen, and the proceeds obtained in the employer's settlement of the lawsuit against that employee were considered proceeds obtained as a result of an involuntary conversion (see Q 8658).[6]

The decline in the market value of stock is not deductible as a theft loss where the stock is acquired on the open market if the decline is caused by accounting fraud or other illegal misconduct by the officers or directors of the corporation that issued the stock. However, the loss sustained when stock is sold or exchanged, or becomes completely worthless, is deductible as a capital loss reportable on Schedule D of Form 1040.[7]

8658. How do the rules governing theft and casualty losses interact with the rules governing involuntary conversions of property?

The rules governing theft losses frequently intersect with the IRC Section 1033 provisions governing involuntary conversions (see Q 8617 to Q 8620). The rules on involuntary conversions

1. See *Austin v. Comm.*, 74 TC 1334 (1980).
2. IRS Pub. 547, above.
3. Treas. Reg. §1.165-8(d).
4. IRS Pub. 547, Casualties, Disasters and Thefts (2016).
5. Let. Rul. 8947032.
6. Rev. Rul. 66-355, 1966-2 CB 302.
7. IRS Pub. 547.

govern the treatment of any reimbursement that a taxpayer receives as a result of a loss, such as a casualty or theft loss.

Therefore, if a taxpayer receives insurance proceeds, for example, that exceed the amount lost as a result of a casualty or theft, the taxpayer would look to the rules on involuntary conversions for determining whether the gain must be recognized.[1] In these circumstances, the gain is characterized as stemming from an involuntary conversion because the casualty in effect causes the damaged property to suddenly be converted into cash from the insurance proceeds. The rules for determining what gain is or is not subject to taxation in involuntary conversions may differ for federally declared disasters.[2]

8659. When is a taxpayer entitled to take a deduction for a theft loss?

A taxpayer who sustains a theft loss may take the deduction for the tax year in which the taxpayer discovers the loss, rather than the year in which the loss was sustained (as is the general rule for casualty losses).[3]

The reasonable prospect of recovery doctrine (see Q 8663) applies in the case of theft losses, so that the taxpayer will not be entitled to take a deduction if there is a claim for reimbursement against a third party that may fully or partially compensate the taxpayer for the theft loss, and there is a reasonable prospect that the taxpayer will recover these amounts.[4] These rules do not apply to a theft loss discovered through a shortage in the inventories of a business.[5]

The amount of the taxpayer's theft loss deduction is determined using the same method applicable to casualty loss deductions (see Q 8660).

Example: Denise purchased a watch for $15,000 in 2014. In 2017, the watch, which now has a fair market value of $13,500, is stolen. Denise does not discover that the watch is missing until 2018. Though the watch was insured against theft, the insurance company challenges its liability for the loss. Despite this challenge, Denise has a reasonable prospect of recovering from the insurance company in 2018. In 2019, Denise settles with the insurance company and receives $12,000 in insurance proceeds to cover the theft loss. Denise is not permitted to take a deduction in 2017 or 2018, but in 2019, she is permitted a theft loss deduction for $1,500. The computation is made as follows:

Value of property immediately before theft	$13,500
Less: value of property immediately after theft	$0
Balance	$13,500
Loss to be taken into account for purposes of Section 165(a)	$13,500
Less: insurance received in 2019	$12,000
Deduction allowable for 2019	$1,500

1. See IRS Publication 225.
2. AICPA Casualty Loss Practice Guide (July 2012).
3. IRC Sec. 165(e); Treas. Reg. §1.165-8(a)(2).
4. Treas. Reg. §1.165-8(a)(2).
5. Treas. Reg. §1.165-8(e).

8660. How is the amount of a taxpayer's allowable casualty or theft loss deduction determined?

If a taxpayer has suffered a casualty (or theft) loss, regardless of whether the loss is personal in nature or is related to trade or business activities, the taxpayer may be entitled to deduct the lesser of the following amounts:

(1) The fair market value immediately before the casualty *minus* the fair market value of the property immediately after the casualty; or

(2) The adjusted basis of the property that would be used for determining the taxpayer's gain or loss if the property was sold or otherwise disposed of.[1]

Planning Point: Although the regulations use the term "immediately after" when referring to the post-casualty value, the IRS recognizes that taxpayers' ability to determine the decrease in the fair market values of their properties, as a result of a disaster, may be restricted by lack of access to the properties and the need to remove water from flooded properties. Under these circumstances, the decrease in fair market value would take into account additional damage sustained to the property as a result of delays due to legal and physical restrictions to taxpayers' access to their property and the need to remove standing water from the properties.[2]

The fair market value of the property must be ascertained by appraisal, and this appraisal must consider the impact of any general market decline affecting undamaged property (as well as damaged property) that may have occurred at the same time as the casualty, so that the casualty loss is limited to the actual loss caused by the casualty.[3]

The taxpayer claiming the casualty loss may use the actual cost of repairs to the property as evidence of the amount of loss if the following conditions are met:

(1) The repairs are necessary to restore the property to its condition immediately before the casualty;

(2) The cost of the repairs is not excessive;

(2) The repairs only fix the damage suffered as a result of the casualty; and

(4) The repairs do not cause the value of the property to exceed the value of the property immediately before the casualty.[4]

The cost of repairs may, in certain cases, be used to measure the decline in fair market value, but it cannot be used by itself to determine the amount of the loss. When the cost of repairs is determined to be a fair measure of the decline in fair market value, then the fair market value

1. Treas. Reg. §1.165-7(b)(1).
2. IRS FAQS for Disaster Victims-Casualty Loss (Valuations and Section 165(i), July 5, 2013).
3. Treas. Reg. §1.165-7(a)(2)(i).
4. Treas. Reg. §1.165-7(a)(2)(ii); http://www.irs.gov/Businesses/Small-Businesses-&-Self-Employed/FAQs-for-Disaster-Victims-Casualty-Loss-(Valuations-and-Sections-165-i).

of the property before the casualty is reduced by the cost of repairs to arrive at the fair market value after the casualty.[1]

If the property at issue was used in a trade or business (or otherwise held for the production of income) and was totally destroyed by the casualty, the taxpayer may use the adjusted basis to determine the amount of loss if the fair market value of the property immediately before the casualty is less than the adjusted basis.[2]

When property used in a taxpayer's trade or business (or otherwise held for profit) is destroyed, each single, identifiable piece of property must be considered separately in computing the amount of loss.[3]

> *Example:* Chase owns a marina comprised of a large storage building and a boat docking area. The marina is badly damaged in a hurricane. In determining the fair market value of the property for purposes of determining loss, Chase must measure the decrease in value by taking the building and the docks into account separately, rather than together as two integral pieces of the property as a whole. In other words, he must determine the losses separately for the building and the docks.

However, where separate property is considered to be an integral piece of the property as a whole (for example, ornamental trees and shrubs on residential property), no separate calculation is made.[4]

8661. What limitations apply to the amount a taxpayer is able to claim as a casualty or theft loss deduction?

Casualty and theft losses are deductible whether the loss relates to property held by the taxpayer (i) for use in a trade or business, (ii) for investment purposes or (iii) for use that is purely personal.[5] However, if the property involved is not held for a business or profit-generating purpose, the amount of the deduction is limited as follows:

(1) each loss is reduced by $100 and any insurance proceeds received (prior to 2010, the $100 limitation was $500);[6] and

(2) the aggregate of such adjusted losses is deductible only to the extent that it exceeds 10 percent of adjusted gross income.[7]

If the taxpayer sustains more than one loss from a single casualty event, only one $100 reduction is made. Conversely, a separate reduction of $100 is made for losses from *each* casualty or theft event. The 10 percent limit applies to the *total* of all of the taxpayer's losses from all casualty events occurring in the same tax year.[8]

1. IRS FAQS, above.
2. Treas. Reg. §1.165-7(b)(1) (flush language).
3. Treas. Reg. §1.165-7(b)(2).
4. See *Western Products Co. v. Comm.*, 28 TC 1196 (1957).
5. IRC Sec. 165.
6. IRC Sec. 165(h)(1).
7. IRC Sec. 165(h)(2).
8. See IRS Publication 547.

When casualty and theft losses exceed income for the tax year, the excess is considered a net operating loss and may be carried back to offset income in prior years and carried forward to offset income of future years under the net operating loss provisions. All casualty and theft losses qualify even though the property is personal.

As discussed in Q 8660, the amount of the loss which can be deducted above the $100 floor is limited to the lesser of (1) the difference between the fair market value of the property immediately before the casualty and the fair market value immediately after the casualty, or (2) the adjusted basis of the property.[1] (For a description of what the IRS considers to constitute "immediately after," see Q 8660.) This amount is further reduced by any insurance or other indemnification received. In addition, as discussed above, such loss is deductible only to the extent it exceeds 10 percent of adjusted gross income.

Example 1: In June, Pete and Karen discovered their house had been burglarized. Their loss after insurance reimbursement was $2,000. Their adjusted gross income for the tax year was $29,500. To determine their theft loss deduction, Pete and Karen must first apply the $100 rule and then the 10 percent rule. Their theft loss deduction is calculated as follows:

1. Amount of loss	$2,000
2. Subtract $100	(100)
3. Loss after $100 rule	1,900
4. Subtract 10 percent of $29,500 (AGI)	(2,950)
Theft loss deduction	-0-

Pete and Karen will not be allowed a theft loss deduction because their loss ($1,900) is less than 10 percent of their AGI.

Example 2: Cathy and Bernardo owned a group of apartment buildings that were damaged by flooding. Before the flood, the adjusted basis in the apartment buildings was $672,000. The fair market value of the property immediately prior to the flood was $2 million, and immediately after the flood was $750,000. Cathy and Bernardo received $767,000 from insurance coverage. Although the $1,250,000 decline in market value far exceeded the insurance recovery, no casualty loss deduction is allowable, since the insurance proceeds exceeded the adjusted basis in the property.[2]

8662. When will a taxpayer's otherwise allowable casualty loss deduction be disallowed? How does a taxpayer's eligibility to file an insurance claim with respect to the loss impact the availability of the deduction?

In general, a casualty loss deduction is only allowable to the extent that the taxpayer is not otherwise compensated for the loss by insurance or reimbursement from another third party.

However, if a taxpayer's casualty loss *would have* been covered by insurance, but the taxpayer fails to file a timely insurance claim with respect to the loss, the casualty loss deduction will be disallowed regardless of whether the taxpayer actually receives any insurance proceeds as

1. Treas. Reg. §1.165-7(b)(1).
2. See *Lafavre v. Comm.*, TC Memo 2000-297.

compensation for the loss.[1] Thus, if a taxpayer chooses not to file an insurance claim with respect to a loss, the casualty loss deduction will be limited to the portion of the loss that would *not* have been covered by insurance.

Further, a taxpayer is not entitled to deduct an otherwise allowable casualty loss if the loss has already been claimed for estate tax purposes on an estate tax return.[2]

8663. Can a casualty loss be spread over more than one tax year? What is the reasonable prospect of recovery doctrine?

Generally, a taxpayer is required to claim a casualty loss deduction for the tax year in which the loss was sustained. A taxpayer is considered to have sustained a casualty loss in the year in which the loss occurs as evidenced by closed and completed transactions and as fixed by identifiable events occurring in the year.[3]

The fact that a taxpayer is unable to determine the extent of the damage caused or the cost of repairing the damage is insufficient to allow the taxpayer to carry a casualty loss deduction into a succeeding tax year. The Tax Court has determined that an expert appraisal is sufficient to determine the level of damage sustained at the time the casualty loss occurred even if the extent of the damage was not immediately apparent.[4]

Despite this, the reasonable prospect of recovery doctrine will actually prohibit a taxpayer from claiming a casualty loss in the year the casualty occurs if the taxpayer has a claim for reimbursement with respect to which the taxpayer may reasonably be expected to recover all or a portion of the casualty loss.[5] The portion of the casualty loss to which the potential for reimbursement relates will be disallowed until it can be ascertained "with reasonable certainty" whether or not the reimbursement will be received.

> *Example*: Brent's cottage, which had an adjusted basis of $100,000, is completely destroyed by a fire in 2017. His only claim for reimbursement was an insurance claim for $80,000, which he settled in 2018. Brent sustained a loss of $20,000 for 2018. If the cottage was destroyed due to the negligence of a third party, and there is a reasonable prospect that the third party can be held liable for the entire amount of the damage, Brent cannot take a loss deduction until it is determined whether or not he can recover damages from that third party.[6]

Whether a "reasonable prospect of recovery" exists is a question of fact that is determined based on an examination of all of the facts and circumstances of the particular loss being claimed.[7]

If a taxpayer takes a casualty loss deduction for a loss sustained in one year, but receives reimbursement for that loss in a subsequent tax year, the taxpayer is not required to file an amended

1. IRC Sec. 165(h)(5)(E).
2. IRC Sec. 165(h)(5)(D).
3. Treas. Reg. §1.165-1(d)(1).
4. See *Allen v. Comm.*, 49 TCM 238 (1984).
5. Treas. Reg. §1.165-1(d)(2).
6. Treas. Reg. §1.165-1(d)(2)(ii).
7. Treas. Reg. §1.165-1(d)(2)(i).

return for the year in which the deduction was erroneously claimed. Instead, the taxpayer must include the reimbursed amount in gross income for the year it is received.[1]

A special rule applies in the case of casualty losses sustained in a federally declared disaster area. If the taxpayer's casualty loss was sustained in a disaster area, the taxpayer may elect to take the casualty loss deduction in the year immediately preceding the year in which the loss was sustained.[2] See Q 8666 for a detailed discussion of the treatment of casualty losses that occur in a disaster area.

The reasonable prospect of recovery doctrine also applies in the case of theft losses (see Q 8659).

8664. Is a business-related casualty loss treated differently than a personal casualty loss?

If a taxpayer sustains a casualty loss with respect to property used in the taxpayer's trade or business, the taxpayer will not be subject to the $100 floor or 10 percent of adjusted gross income limitations described in Q 8661. The taxpayer who sustains a casualty loss in connection with a trade or business can take the deduction as a business deduction.

A taxpayer who uses property and sustains a casualty or theft loss in performing services as an *employee* can deduct the casualty or theft loss as a miscellaneous itemized deduction subject to the 2 percent limit on these deductions (see Q 8525).[3] If the property subject to the loss was investment-type property held for profit, the deduction will not be subject to the 2 percent limit on miscellaneous itemized deductions.[4] This kind of investment-type property includes stocks, notes, bonds, gold, silver, vacant lots, and works of art.[5]

8665. What are the tax consequences to a taxpayer who has both personal (nonbusiness) casualty (or theft) gains and losses for the same tax year?

If a taxpayer has both personal casualty (or theft) gains and losses for the tax year, the taxpayer is required to offset (net) those casualty losses with any casualty gains for the year.

If a taxpayer has casualty or theft gains as well as losses to personal-use property, the taxpayer must compare total gains to his or her total losses after he or she has reduced each loss by any reimbursements and by $100, but before reducing the losses by 10 percent of adjusted gross income.

If the taxpayer's personal casualty losses for the year exceed personal casualty gains for the year, a deduction is allowable to the extent of the sum of the following:

1. Treas. Reg. §1.165-1(d)(2)(iii).
2. IRC Sec. 165(i); Treas. Reg. §1.165-1(d)(1).
3. See IRS Publication 529.
4. IRS Publication 529, above.
5. IRS Publication 529, above.

(1) The amount of personal casualty gains for the tax year; plus

(2) So much of the excess as exceeds 10 percent of the taxpayer's adjusted gross income for the tax year.[1]

If the taxpayer's casualty gains for the tax year exceed casualty losses, the gain or loss is treated as though it resulted from the sale or exchange of capital assets (see Q 8565).[2] As such, any gains will be taxed at the rates applicable to sales or exchanges of short-term or long-term capital assets, depending upon how long the taxpayer held the asset (see Q 8572).

If the taxpayer's casualty losses for the tax year exceed casualty gains, all gains and losses are treated as ordinary gains or losses.

These rules apply to both casualty losses and theft losses.[3]

8666. What special rules apply to taxpayers who suffer casualty losses within a federally-declared disaster area?

In recognition of the fact that taxpayers who sustain casualty losses as a result of disasters often have an immediate need for relief, the IRC contains provisions that accelerate the recognition of tax benefits to which disaster victims are entitled.

As such, disaster victims are entitled to claim casualty losses on their tax returns for the year *before* the disaster actually occurred.[4] This treatment is elective, so the taxpayer may choose to claim the casualty loss in the manner otherwise prescribed by IRC Section 165 (see Q 8663).

Planning Point: An election to claim a deduction for the preceding year must be made by filing a return, an amended return, or a claim for refund clearly showing that the election has been made. In general, the return or claim should specify the date or dates of the disaster which gave rise to the loss, and the city, town, county, and state in which the property which was damaged or destroyed was located at the time of the disaster. An election for a loss resulting from a particular disaster occurring after December 31, 1971, must be made by the later of (1) the due date for filing the income tax return (without regard to any filing extensions) for the year in which the disaster actually occurred, or (2) the due date for filing the return (determined with regard to any filing extension) for the taxable year immediately preceding the year in which the disaster actually occurred. The election is irrevocable 90 days after the date on which it's made.[5]

If the due date (including extensions) for filing the taxpayer's prior year tax return has not expired, the taxpayer can claim the deduction when the taxpayer files that return. If the due date has passed, the taxpayer can file an amended return to reflect the casualty loss deduction on the prior year's tax return.[6]

1. IRC Sec. 165(h)(2)(A).
2. IRC Sec. 165(h)(2)(B).
3. IRC Sec. 165(h)(4)(A).
4. IRC Sec. 165(i).
5. Temp. Treas. Reg. § 1.165-11T(e).
6. Temp. Treas. Reg. §1.165-11T(e).

The special treatment described in this question applies to taxpayers who have sustained a loss:

(1) Arising from a disaster in an area where the President of the United States determines that assistance is warranted by the federal government under the Robert T. Stafford Disaster Relief and Emergency Assistance Act (or a successor act);

(2) Occurring after December 31, 1971;

(3) That otherwise constitutes a loss allowable under IRC Section 165(a) and the regulations.[1]

A taxpayer is entitled to claim a loss under these provisions if the taxpayer's residence is located in a federally declared disaster area that has been declared unsafe for use as a residence because of the disaster, and the taxpayer is ordered to demolish or relocate the residence within 120 days after the area is declared to be a disaster area.[2]

The $100 floor and adjusted gross income limitations do not apply in the case of certain hurricanes and other natural disasters if specifically exempted. For example, victims of Hurricanes Katrina, Rita and Wilma (storms that caused extensive damage in 2005) were exempt from these limitations.[3]

8667. What is a qualified insolvent financial institution loss? Can a taxpayer treat such a loss as a casualty loss?

A taxpayer may choose to treat a qualified insolvent financial institution loss as a casualty loss if it can be ascertained with reasonable certainty that there is a loss on a qualified individual's deposit in a qualified financial institution and that the loss is caused by the bankruptcy or insolvency of that institution.[4] "Deposit" for this purpose means any deposit, withdrawable account or withdrawable or repurchasable share.[5]

The term "qualified individual" is defined by exclusion as any individual *other than* an individual who:

(1) owns at least 1 percent of the outstanding stock of the qualified institution;

(2) is an officer of the qualified institution; or

(3) is related to a person described in (1) or (2), above.[6]

A "qualified financial institution" is a bank, mutual savings bank, credit union (if its deposits are insured or protected under federal or state law) or any similar institution that is chartered and supervised under either federal or state law.[7]

1. Temp. Treas. Reg. §1.165-11T(b).
2. IRC Sec. 165(k).
3. IRC Sec. 1400S(b).
4. IRC Sec. 165(l)(1).
5. IRC Sec. 165(l)(4).
6. IRC Sec. 165(l)(2).
7. IRC Sec. 165(l)(3).

If the taxpayer elects to treat a qualified insolvent financial institution loss as a casualty loss, the election applies to all losses in that same financial institution for the tax year. The election can only be revoked with the consent of the Secretary.[1]

In the alternative, a taxpayer may elect to treat the loss as an ordinary loss in order to avoid the limits on the casualty loss deduction discussed in Q 8661. However, with respect to each financial institution, the taxpayer is only permitted to elect an ordinary loss deduction of up to $20,000 ($10,000 for married taxpayers filing separately). The taxpayer may *not* elect ordinary loss treatment if the deposit in question was federally insured.[2]

An election to treat a qualified insolvent financial institution loss as a casualty loss precludes treating the loss as a bad debt.[3]

1. IRC Sec. 165(l)(6).
2. IRC Sec. 165(l)(5).
3. IRC Sec. 165(l)(7).

PART VII: EMPLOYEES VS. INDEPENDENT CONTRACTORS

8668. Who is an "employee" for employment tax purposes?

Employers are often concerned with the classification of workers as employees or independent contractors because, among other reasons, the employer is responsible for paying one-half of an *employee's* employment taxes. Conversely, an independent contractor is liable for the entire sum of employment taxes (see Q 8670 for further discussion of the self-employment tax).

Generally, for employment tax purposes, the IRC defines "employee" to include the following taxpayers:

(1) Any officer of a corporation;

(2) Any individual who is an employee under the common law rules (see Q 8669); or

(3) Any individual who performs services as

a. A driver who distributes certain products (meat, vegetables, fruit, bakery products, beverages (other than milk), or laundry or dry cleaning services);

b. A full-time life insurance salesperson (but see below and Q 8678);

c. A home worker performing work pursuant to the specifications given by the person for whom the services are performed; or

d. A traveling salesperson who, on a full-time basis, solicits orders on behalf of a principal from wholesalers, retailers, contractors, or operators of hotels, restaurants or similar establishments for merchandise purchased for resale or supplies for use in their business.[1]

However, an individual will not be an "employee" for purposes of (3) above if the individual has a substantial investment in facilities used in connection with the performance of services (other than an investment in transportation facilities), or if the services are in the nature of a single transaction that is not part of a continuing relationship with the person for whom the services are performed.[2] For these purposes the term "substantial investment" refers to substantial facilities being furnished by the worker for conducting the business. All of the facts of each case must be considered to determine whether the facilities furnished by the worker are substantial. For factors considered in making these determinations, see Exhibit 4.23.5-3 (Statutory Employees) of the Internal Revenue Manual.

Despite this enumeration, the IRS has ruled that a full-time life insurance salesperson is not an "employee" for purposes of IRC Section 62 (deduction of trade or business expenses)

1. IRC Sec. 3121(d).
2. IRC Sec. 3121(d)(3).

and IRC Section 67 (2 percent floor on miscellaneous itemized deductions), even though he is treated as a "statutory employee" for Social Security tax purposes.[1]

See Q 8669 for a detailed discussion of the factors that are relevant in determining employment status. See Q 8678 to Q 8681 for a discussion of the tax treatment of life insurance salespersons.

8669. How is it determined whether a taxpayer is an independent contractor or a common law employee?

Generally speaking, an individual will be considered an employee under the common law rules if the person or organization for which the individual performs services has the right to control and direct the individual's work, not only as to the result to be accomplished, but also as to the details and means by which that result is accomplished.[2] In other words, an individual will be classified as an employee if the employer has the right to control not only *what* will be done, but also *how* that work will be accomplished. On the other hand, if the individual performing the work is only under the control of another to the extent of the end result that must be delivered, that individual will be classified as an independent contractor.

It is important to note that the employer does not actually have to direct and control the manner of an individual's work in order for that individual to be classified as an employee. The individual will be classified as an employee if an employer has the *right* to direct and control the manner in which that employee's work is accomplished even if the employer does not actually exercise this right.[3]

The parties' classification of the relationship as anything other than an employer-employee relationship is immaterial if the facts and circumstances show that the individual is performing services as an employee.[4] The IRS has developed three categories of control: behavioral control, financial control, and the type of relationship that exists between the parties.[5] Additionally, the IRS has developed a twenty factor test that is often applied in determining whether an individual is performing services as an employee or an independent contractor. These twenty factors include the following:

(1) *Instructions*. If the individual is required to comply with another person's instructions about when, where and how he or she works, that individual is usually an employee.

(2) *Training*. If an individual is trained alongside a more experienced employee or is required to attend training meetings, this indicates that the person for whom services are performed wants the individual to perform those services in a certain manner, making it more likely that an employer-employee relationship exists.

1. Rev. Rul. 90-93, 1990-2 CB 33.
2. Treas. Reg. §31.3121(d)-1(c)(2).
3. Treas. Reg. §31.3121(d)-1(c)(2).
4. Rev. Rul. 87-41, 1987-23 IRB 7.
5. IRS Pub 15-A, Employer's Supplemental Tax Guide (2017).

(3) *Integration*. When the success or failure of the business is significantly dependent upon the performance of services by the individual, the individual performing those services must necessarily be subject to a certain degree of control by the business owner, indicating that an employer-employee relationship exists.[1]

(4) *Services Rendered Personally*. If the services must be rendered personally, it is presumed that the person for whom the services are performed is interested in the methods used to accomplish the work, as well as the end results.

(5) *Hiring, Supervising and Paying Assistants*. If the person for whom the services are performed hires, supervises, and pays assistants, it can generally be shown that he or she exercises control over the workers on the job. However, if one worker hires, supervises, and pays the other assistants pursuant to a contract under which the worker agrees to provide materials and labor and under which the worker is responsible only for the attainment of a result, this factor indicates an independent contractor status exists.

(6) *Continuing Relationship*. A continuing relationship between the individual performing the services and the person for whom they are performed indicates an employer-employee relationship.

(7) *Set Hours of Work*. If the person for whom services are performed sets the individual's hours of work, this factor indicates an employer-employee relationship.

(8) *Full-Time Schedule Required*. If the individual must dedicate substantially all of the individual's time to the work, the person for whom the services are performed has control over the amount of time the worker spends working and *impliedly* restricts the individual from taking other work. An independent contractor, on the other hand, is free to work when and for whom he or she chooses.

(9) *Work on the Employer's Premises*. If work is performed on an employer's premises, control is suggested, especially if the work could be done elsewhere. Work done off premises indicates freedom from control, but is not sufficient, on its own, to show that the individual is not an employee.

(10) *Order or Sequence Set*. If the individual must complete the work in a certain order, this factor shows that it is likely that another is controlling his or her pattern of work.

(11) *Oral or Written Reports*. If oral or written reports must be submitted by the individual completing the work, it is likely that another is controlling his or her work.

(12) *Payment by Hour, Week or Month*. Payment by the hour, week, or month usually indicates an employer-employee relationship, provided that the payment method is not just a convenient way of paying a lump sum agreed upon as the cost of a job.

1. See, for example, *United States v. Silk*, 331 U.S. 704 (1947).

Payment made by the job or on a straight commission generally indicates that the worker is an independent contractor.

(13) *Payment of Business or Traveling Expenses*. If another pays the individual's business or traveling expenses, an employer-employee relationship is indicated because the employer, in order to control the individual's expenses, generally must have the right to direct the individual's business activities.

(14) *Furnishing Tools and Materials*. If the person for whom services are performed furnishes significant tools and materials, this tends to show an employer-employee relationship.

(15) *Significant Investment*. If the individual invests in facilities that are usually used by workers in performing services, but are not typically maintained by employees (such as office space), this factor indicates that the individual is an independent contractor. Special scrutiny is applied in the case of home offices.

(16) *Realization of Profit and Loss*. An individual who can realize profit or loss as a result of the services offered is generally an independent contractor. The IRS uses the example of an individual who has a risk of loss with respect to liability for expenses, such as payment to unrelated employees (indicating independent contractor status), and distinguishes this type of risk from the risk that the individual will not receive payment for services (which is common to both employees and independent contractors).

(17) *Working for more than One Firm at a Time*. If an individual performs more than de minimis services for more than one firm at a time, this factor indicates that the individual is an independent contractor.

(18) *Making Services Available to General Public*. If an individual makes services available to the general public on a regular and consistent basis, this factor indicates that the individual is an independent contractor.

(19) *Right to Discharge*. The right to discharge an individual suggests an employer-employee relationship is present. An independent contractor, on the other hand, cannot be fired so long as the individual produces the end result that meets the contract specifications.

(20) *Right to Terminate*. If the individual has the right to terminate the relationship without incurring liability, this indicates an employer-employee relationship is present.[1]

All of the facts and circumstances of the relationship must be considered in weighing these factors to determine whether the relationship is an employer-employee relationship or an independent contractor relationship. No one factor will be determinative in making the correct classification.

1. Rev. Rul. 87-41, 1987-23 IRB 7.

8670. What is the self-employment tax? Who is liable for paying it?

An individual whose net earnings from self-employment as an independent contractor equal $400 or more for the taxable year must pay the self-employment tax.[1]

In 2018, an individual who is liable for the self-employment tax must file a Schedule SE and pay Social Security taxes on up to $128,700 of self-employment income. The hospital insurance tax is imposed on all of a taxpayer's self-employment income.

Despite this, an above-the-line deduction is permitted for one-half of the self-employment tax paid by an individual and attributable to a trade or business carried on by the individual as an independent contractor (not as an employee).[2] If the individual also works in covered employment as an *employee*, his self-employment income (subject to the self-employment tax) is only the difference, if any, between his "wages" as an employee and the maximum Social Security earnings base.

See Q 8552 for a detailed discussion of the Social Security tax as it applies to self-employed individuals and Q 8554 for a discussion of estimated tax payments.

8671. How are employment expenses treated differently based on whether a taxpayer is an employee or an independent contractor?

An employer is entitled to deduct amounts paid as reasonable compensation to its employees.[3] Therefore, whether an individual is classified as an employee or as an independent contractor is important to an employer in determining whether or not that employer is entitled to deduct amounts paid to that individual as compensation.

If an individual is properly classified as an independent contractor, the individual is entitled to deduct business-related expenses without regard to the 2 percent floor on miscellaneous itemized deductions (see Q 8525) that would otherwise apply. Conversely, the business expense deductions of an employee are limited based on whether or not the employee is reimbursed for the expense.[4]

8672. Can a self-employed individual participate in a retirement savings plan?

While employers are often required to include all employees in fringe benefit plans and retirement plans, the same requirement does not apply with respect to independent contractors. If an employer includes non-employees (including independent contractors) in a qualified plan, that plan may lose its qualified status by violating the "exclusive benefit" rule of IRC Section 401(a). Therefore, most self-employed individuals who operate as independent contractors will be ineligible to participate in retirement savings plans maintained by another taxpayer-entity.

1. IRC Sec. 6017.
2. IRC Sec. 164(f).
3. IRC Sec. 162.
4. IRC Sec. 62(c); Treas. Reg. §§1.162-17(b)(2), 1.162-17(c).

For plan qualification purposes, a self-employed individual, as an owner-employee, is considered an "employee" for purposes of qualified plans established by that owner-employee.[1] An "owner-employee" is an employee who owns the entire interest in an unincorporated trade or business or, in the case of a partnership, owns more than 10 percent of either the capital interest or the profit interest in the partnership.[2]

Even if a partnership agreement does not specify that a "more than 10 percent interest in profits" exists for any partner, if the formula for dividing profits (e.g., based on a partner's earnings productivity during the year) in *operation* produced a distribution at the end of the year of more than 10 percent of profits to a partner, the Tax Court has ruled that the partner is an owner-employee for the year.[3]

An individual who owns the entire interest in an unincorporated trade or business is treated as the employer.[4] Thus, a proprietor or sole practitioner who has earned income (including "self-employment income") can establish a qualified plan under which the individual is both employer *and* employee.

A partnership is treated as the employer of each partner who is an employee.[5] Thus, partners individually cannot establish a qualified plan for a firm, but the partnership can establish a plan in which the partners can participate.

Individuals who are classified as independent contractors (see Q 8669) are able to set up their own retirement plans, including IRAs and Roth IRAs, so long as they have compensation (whether in the form of self-employment income, alimony or income earned as an employee in some capacity) and did not attain age 70½ during the year in which the account is established.[6] To establish a Roth IRA, the same income limitations apply to self-employed taxpayers as apply to employees, so that the self-employed taxpayer must not have adjusted gross income in excess of the annual income thresholds. For 2018, those thresholds are: (a) $199,000 or above in the case of a taxpayer filing a joint return; (b) $135,000 or above in the case of a taxpayer filing a single or head-of-household return; or (c) $10,000 or above in the case of a married individual filing separately.[7]

8673. If a self-employed owner-employee establishes a qualified retirement plan, is that plan entitled to ERISA protections that are normally granted to employees who participate in similar plans?

In some instances, a plan established by an owner-employee (see Q 8672) will be entitled to ERISA protections (such as rules regarding the vesting of benefits and ERISA's anti-alienation provisions), but in other cases, participants in such a plan will not be entitled to the same

1. IRC Sec. 401(c).
2. IRC Sec. 401(c)(3).
3. *Hill, Farrer & Burrill v. Commissioner*, 67 TC 411 (1976), *aff'd*, 594 F.2d 1282 (9th Cir. 1979).
4. IRC Sec. 401(c)(4).
5. IRC Sec. 401(c)(4).
6. IRC Secs. 219, 408A.
7. Notice 2017-64.

protections as are available to traditional employees. The answer turns on whether employees *other than* the self-employed individual and the individual's spouse also participate in the plan.

Regulations promulgated by the Department of Labor provide that an owner-employee and spouse are *not* considered employees of a business that is wholly owned by those individuals.[1] Therefore, if only the owner-employee and spouse participate, the plan will not be subject to ERISA. Accordingly, Section 514(a) of Title I of ERISA would not preempt state regulation of the arrangement.[2]

However, the Supreme Court has ruled that if the owner-employee and spouse allow additional employees to participate in the plan, that plan will be subject to ERISA and entitled to its protections. In this case, both the employees *and* the owner-employee and spouse are entitled to ERISA protection.[3]

Planning Point: In some instances, it may be desirable for a qualified plan to become subject to ERISA's rules and protections rather than the state law provisions that may be found to apply if ERISA does not preempt state law. In other instances, state law provisions that would otherwise govern may be preferable.

8674. Is a taxpayer who is classified as an independent contractor, and thus self-employed, entitled to deduct the cost of health insurance coverage?

A self-employed individual is generally entitled to deduct the cost of health insurance coverage. The IRS has ruled that a self-employed individual may deduct the medical care insurance costs for himself and his spouse and dependents under a health insurance plan established for his trade or business up to the net earnings of the specific trade or business with respect to which the plan is established.

In determining this deduction limit under IRC Section 162(l)(2)(A), a self-employed individual may not combine the net profits from all his trades and businesses. However, if a self-employed individual has more than one trade or business, the individual may deduct the medical care insurance costs of the self-employed individual and his spouse and dependents under *each* specific health insurance plan established under *each* specific business up to the net earnings of that specific trade or business.[4]

According to the IRS, a self-employed individual may not deduct the costs of health insurance on Schedule C. The deduction under IRC Section 162(l) must be claimed as an adjustment to gross income on the front of Form 1040.[5]

Partners and sole proprietors are self-employed individuals, not employees. However, the deduction is not available to a partner or sole proprietor for any calendar month in which the

1. DOL Reg. §2510.3-3(c)(1).
2. Labor Dept. Advisory Opinion 92-21A (10/19/1992).
3. *Raymond B. Yates Profit Sharing Plan v. Hendon*, 541 U.S. 1 (2004).
4. CCA 200524001.
5. CCA 200623001.

individual is eligible to participate in any subsidized health plan maintained by any employer of the self-employed individual or spouse.[1]

Beginning in 2003, a self-employed individual can deduct 100 percent of amounts paid during a taxable year for long-term care insurance up to the annual limits (see below) for an individual, spouse or dependents.[2] Sole proprietors, partners, and S corporation shareholders owning more than 2 percent of an S corporation's shares generally may take advantage of this deduction.

The deduction for eligible long-term care premiums that are paid during any taxable year for a qualified long-term care insurance contract[3] is subject to an annual dollar amount limit that increases with the age of the insured individual. In 2018, for taxpayers age forty or less, the limit is $420. For ages forty-one through fifty, the limit is $780. For ages fifty-one through sixty, the limit is $1,560. For ages sixty-one through seventy, the limit is $4,160. For those over age seventy, the limit is $5,200.[4] The age is the individual's attained age before the close of the taxable year. The limits are indexed annually for increases in the medical care cost component of the CPI (this is the so-called Medical Care Cost Adjustment) [5]

8675. What are the consequences if an employer wrongly characterizes an employee as an independent contractor?

The proper classification of individuals by an employer as either employees or independent contractors is important in many areas, and an employer who misclassifies its workers will be responsible for the consequences of the misclassification.

An employer who misclassifies an employee as an independent contractor may be liable for that employee's Social Security taxes because, in an employer-employee relationship, the employer is responsible for one-half of the tax owed, and the employer is responsible for deducting the employee's portion of the tax from wages.[6] Independent contractors, on the other hand, are liable for the entire amount of the tax, but are entitled to deduct one-half of the taxes paid (see Q 8670).

The IRS has ruled that if an employer wrongly classifies an individual as an independent contractor, the IRS can offset the refund of any self-employment taxes paid by that individual, but only with the employee portion of the employment taxes that would have been owed had the employee been properly classified.[7]

Therefore, if an employer hires an independent contractor who is later found to be an employee, the employee can claim a refund for the self-employment taxes paid while the employee was erroneously believed to be an independent contractor. The IRS, when processing

1. IRC Sec. 162(l).
2. IRC Sec. 162(l)(1)(B).
3. See IRC Sec. 7702B(b).
4. Rev. Proc. 2009-50, 2009-45 IRB 617, as modified by Rev Proc. 2010-24, 2010-25 IRB 764. Rev. Proc. 2017-58.
5. IRC Sec. 213(d)(10).
6. Treas. Reg. §31.3102-1(a).
7. See *Beane v. Commissioner*, TC Memo 2009-152 (2009) and IRS ECC 201315023.

the refund, can reduce the amount refundable to the employee by the employment taxes the *employee* would have paid with proper classification. The employer, however, remains liable for the remaining balance that was refunded to the employee.

The Tax Court has recently declined to apply a federal common law successor in interest standard in determining successor liability in the employment tax context. In this case, a taxpayer had been a partner in several partnerships that were later dissolved, with their assets (and certain operations) conveyed to a limited partnership in which that taxpayer became a limited partner. The IRS issued a notice of determination concerning worker classification, and attempted to collect employment taxes from the newly formed limited partnership as a successor in interest of the previously operating partnerships. While the Tax Court did agree with the IRS' worker classification, it held that the newly formed limited partnership was not liable for the resulting employment tax deficiency as a successor in interest because it had not expressly assumed the liabilities of the previously existing partnerships. The limited partnership was, however, liable for employment taxes owing since the date it assumed the operations that were carried on by the dissolved partnerships. The court did note that the IRS could have possibly succeeded had it used a transferee liability theory in attempting to collect the employment taxes from the newly formed partnership.[1]

Further, an employee who has been wrongly classified as an independent contractor may be entitled to claim benefits under the benefit plans that the employer has established for traditional employees. For example, the Ninth Circuit has held that certain "leased" employees that an employer leased from an employment agency, and sought to classify as independent contractors, could claim their rights to benefits under that employer's employee benefit plans (including health insurance coverage) if they qualified as employees under the 20-factor test laid out by the IRS in Revenue Ruling 87-41 (see Q 8669).[2]

Similarly, in *Vizcaino v. Microsoft Corp.*, the Ninth Circuit held that individuals whom the employer sought to characterize as independent contractors may have had rights under the employer's benefit plans after an IRS audit found that the individuals were common law employees, and the employer conceded that it had mischaracterized the individuals.[3]

In contrast, the Tenth and Eleventh Circuits have held that the contract language of the employer's benefit plans will control. In these circuits, "leased" employees that met the 20-factor test to qualify as employees were *not* permitted to claim benefits under the employer's benefit plans when the plan language specifically excluded temporary and leased employees.[4] This was the case even though the leased employees at issue performed substantially similar services as the employer's common law employees who qualified for plan benefits.

Until this split in the circuits is resolved, it seems that the question of whether an employee who is wrongly characterized as an independent contractor is entitled to employment related benefits under the employer's benefit plans will be answered based on where the question is litigated.

1. *TFT Galveston Portfolio Ltd. et al. v. Comm.*, 144 TC 9696 (2015).
2. *Burrey v. Pacific Gas and Electric Co.*, 159 F.3d 388 (1998).
3. 97 F.3d 1187 (9th Cir. 1996).
4. See *Bronk v. Mountain States Telephone & Telegraph*, 140 F.3d 1335 (10th Cir. 1998); *Wolf v. Coca-Cola Co.*, 200 F.3d 1337 (11th Cir. 2000).

Planning Point: Upon a request by a firm or worker, the IRS will determine whether a specific individual is an employee or independent contractor, provided the request is submitted for a tax year for which the statute of limitations on the tax return has not expired. A request is made by filing Form SS-8, **Determination of Worker Status for Purposes of Federal Employment Taxes and Income Tax Withholding**. Form SS-8 is filed to request a determination of the status of a worker for purposes of federal employment taxes and income tax withholding. A Form SS-8 determination may be requested only in order to resolve federal tax matters.[1]

8676. Are there any safe harbor provisions that an employer can use in order to ensure that its independent contractors are properly classified so that they will not retroactively be deemed employees?

Although it has not been incorporated into the Internal Revenue Code, Section 530 of the Revenue Act of 1978 provides a limited safe harbor for employers to prevent the IRS from retroactively reclassifying certain independent contractors as employees.[2] The purpose of the safe harbor rule is to prevent reclassification in situations where an employer has a reasonable basis for classifying an individual as an independent contractor.

An employer must satisfy three tests in order to qualify for relief under the Section 530 safe harbor:

(1) The employer must have a reasonable basis for treating the individual as an independent contractor (the "reasonable basis" requirement (see Q 8677));

(2) The employer must consistently treat all similarly-situated workers as independent contractors (the "substantive consistency" requirement); and

(3) All tax returns must have been filed on a basis consistent with independent contractor classification (the "reporting consistency" requirement).[3] The Tax Court has found that the untimely filing of a taxpayer's Forms 1099 would *not* preclude relief under Section 530.[4]

Whether the requirements of Section 530 have been satisfied is a question of fact to be decided by the courts. The employer has the burden of proof in showing that it is entitled to relief pursuant to the safe harbor provision.

8677. How can an employer show that it had a reasonable basis for classifying its workers as independent contractors, rather than employees, in order to qualify for the Section 530 safe harbor?

An employer can avoid IRS reclassification of its independent contractors as employees if it is able to prove, among other requirements (see Q 8676), that it had a reasonable basis for its classification of workers.

1. IRS Tax Topics No. 762.
2. Section 530 of the Revenue Act of 1978, P.L. 95-600 (as made permanent by the Tax Equity and Fiscal Responsibility Act of 1982 (TEFRA), P.L. 97-248.
3. See, for example, *303 West 42nd St. Enterprises, Inc. v. IRS*, 181 F.3d 272 (1999).
4. *Medical Emergency Care Associates v. Commissioner*, 120 TC 436 (2003).

The courts have found that the "reasonable basis" requirement is satisfied when the employer relies on one or more of the following:

(i) judicial precedent, published rulings or IRS letter rulings to the taxpayer (IRS rulings addressed to other taxpayers have been found insufficient);[1]

(ii) a past IRS audit of the employer where there was no assessment attributable to the treatment of individuals holding positions similarly situated to the individual at issue for employment tax purposes;

(iii) a longstanding recognized practice of a significant section of the industry in question;[2] or

(iv) as a catch-all, any other reasonable basis for not treating an individual as an employee.

The courts have found the reasonable basis requirement to be satisfied even in cases where the employer relied upon an IRS audit of one class of workers to justify independent contractor status for a second class. For example, the courts have allowed an employer to rely upon an audit of the classification of its landscaping staff in order to provide a reasonable basis for that same employer's treatment of its janitorial staff as independent contractors.[3] The relevant inquiry was into the relationship between the employer and the workers, in terms of control and supervision, rather than the actual type of work that was being performed.

An employer can also rely upon a "longstanding" custom used by a "significant section" of the industry to establish a reasonable basis for the workers' classification. The practice must be longstanding, and, under Section 530, an industry practice is longstanding if it has been in existence for at least 10 years (the statute does not *require* that the custom be in use for 10 years, but does preclude the courts from requiring a longer time period).[4]

A "significant section" of the industry means 25 percent of the industry, excluding the employer in question, though a lower percentage may apply if the facts and circumstances of the particular case show that such percentage is appropriate.[5] The taxpayer is not required to look to the practices in the industry on a nationwide basis. Instead, the courts have permitted taxpayers to look to the segment of the industry in which they practice, using factors such as the size of the employer and the geographic region in which it operates to determine the relevant comparison.[6]

Even if the employer has no precedential opinion, past IRS audit or industry custom to rely upon, it can still establish that it had a reasonable basis for classifying its workers as independent contractors if it can show that it had some *other* reasonable basis for the classification.[7] For example, employers who have relied upon professional advice (such as from an accountant

1. See *Darrell Harris, Inc. v. United States*, 770 F. Supp. 1492 (1991) (in which the taxpayer was not entitled to rely upon a letter ruling to satisfy the reasonable basis requirement because it was not issued directly to the taxpayer).
2. See *Nu-Look Design v. Commissioner*, 356 F.3d 290 (2004); *Greco v. United States*, 380 F. Supp. 2d 598 (2005).
3. *Lambert's Nursery and Landscaping, Inc. v. U.S.*, 894 F.2d 154 (1990).
4. Section 530(e)(2)(C)(i). See also, IRS Publication on the history of Section 530, available at: http://www.irs.gov/pub/irs-utl/irpac-br_530_relief_-_appendix_natrm_paper_09032009.pdf (last accessed June 4, 2017).
5. Section 530(e)(2)(C)(ii).
6. *General Inv. Corp. v. United States*, 823 F.2d 337 (1987); *J & J Cab Service, Inc. v. United States*, 75 AFTR 2d 618 (1995).
7. Rev. Proc. 85-18, 1985-13 IRB 27.

or attorney) in classifying workers as independent contractors may be able to use this advice as a reasonable basis for the classification.[1]

Some courts have also found that a reasonable basis for the classification existed when the common law factors (see Q 8669) weighed in favor of independent contractor classification.[2]

Planning Point: An IRS determination of a particular classification, made in response to a request made by a firm or worker on Form SS-8 (see Q 8675), would also constitute a reasonable basis for the classification under "(i)" above. A determination letter applies only to a worker (or a class of workers) requesting it, and the decision is binding on the IRS.

Note that in certain cases a formal determination will not be issued. Instead, an information letter may be issued. Although an information letter is advisory only and is not binding on the IRS, it may be used to assist the worker to fulfill his or her federal tax obligations.[3]

8678. Is a life insurance agent typically an employee or an independent contractor? How does this classification impact the agent's ability to deduct business expenses?

The amount of the deduction for a life insurance agent's expenses is directly related to the agent's status either as an independent contractor or an employee. Typically, whether an insurance agent is considered an independent contractor or an employee is determined on the basis of all the facts and circumstances involved. The IRS uses the same twenty factors discussed in Q 8669 in determining an individual's status as employee or self-employed person.[4]

Under the common law rules, most life insurance agents are self-employed individuals, and this is their status generally for tax purposes. Thus, in the usual case, a life insurance agent reports income as an independent contractor, using Schedule C of Form 1040 for business income and deductions. This means that he may deduct *most* of his business expenses directly from gross income.[5]

However, even a life insurance agent who is an *employee* under the common law rules may be permitted to deduct certain business expenses directly from gross income. This rule is limited to those expenses for which reimbursement has been included in the agent's gross income. Work expenses which are not fully reimbursed are generally deductible as miscellaneous itemized deductions; thus, they are permitted only to the extent that the aggregate exceeds 2 percent of adjusted gross income.[6]

The IRS has ruled that a full-time life insurance salesperson is not an "employee" for purposes of IRC Sections 62 and 67, even though he is treated as a "statutory employee" for Social Security tax purposes.[7]

1. *Smoky Mountain Secrets v. United States*, 910 F. Supp. 1316 (1995).
2. *In re Critical Care Support Services, Inc.*, 138 BR 378 (1992); *American Institute of Family Relations v. United States*, 79-1 USTC 9364 (1979).
3. General Instructions to IRS Form SS-8.
4. Rev. Rul. 87-41, 1987-1 CB 296.
5. IRC Sec. 62(a)(1).
6. IRC Secs. 62, 67.
7. Rev. Rul. 90-93, 1990-2 CB 33.

On the other hand, the IRS has found that a district manager of an insurance company was an employee of the company, and not an independent contractor.[1] The IRS found that regional and senior sales vice presidents of an insurance company (but who were not officers of the company) were independent contractors and not employees of the insurance company.[2]

The courts have also made decisions in various cases concerning an insurance agent's classification as an employee or independent contractor. As with other employment situations, where an employer has the right to control the manner and the means by which the agent performs services, an employer-employee relationship will generally be found.[3]

However, according to decisions from the Sixth and Eleventh Circuits, the fact that an insurance agent received certain employee benefits did not preclude his being considered an independent contractor, based on all the other facts and circumstances of the case. The Sixth Circuit rejected the IRS claim that a discharge provision in an agreement between agent and insurance company guaranteeing that the agent would not be fired for unsatisfactory performance unless he was first given notice that his work was unsatisfactory and his job in jeopardy, and was given the chance to bring his performance up to satisfactory levels, provided the company with the "right to control" the manner in which the agent performed his work. The court ruled that the provision simply reflected both the importance the company attached to sales productivity and its willingness to provide low -producing agents with a chance to bring productivity to acceptable levels before being terminated.[4]

Planning Point: Certain types of full-time insurance salesmen may qualify as "statutory employees" under IRC Section 3121(d)(3), rather than "common law employees," and, as such, may use Schedule C of Form 1040 to determine net profit or loss.[5] To qualify as a statutory employee under Section 3121(d)(3), the taxpayer must show: (1) that his entire or principal business activity was devoted to the solicitation of life insurance or annuity contracts; (2) that he did not have a substantial investment in the facilities used in connection with the performance of his services; and (3) that he is not a common law employee.[6]

8679. How are renewal commissions received by a life insurance agent taxed?

First year and renewal commissions are taxable to the agent as ordinary income. If the agent works on commission with a drawing account, the amount reported depends upon his contract with the insurance company. If the drawing account is a loan that must be repaid if he leaves, the agent reports only commissions actually received. If the drawing account is guaranteed compensation, he reports this compensation and any commissions received in excess of the amount that offsets his draw. This rule applies even if the agent uses the accrual method of accounting.[7]

1. TAM 9342001.
2. TAM 9736002.
3. See *Butts v. Commissioner*, TC Memo 1993-478; Let. Rul. 9306029.
4. *Butts v. Comm.*, above. See also *Ware v. United States*, 67 F.3d 574 (6th Cir. 1995).
5. Rev. Rul. 90-93, 1990-2 CB 33.
6. *In the Matter of Appeal of M and L Tofig*, No. 91R-0742-JV (California Board of Equalization 10/28/1993).
7. Rev. Rul. 75-541, 1975-2 CB 195; *Security Associates Agency Insurance Corp. v. Commissioner*, TC Memo 1987-317; *Dennis v. Commissioner*, TC Memo 1997-275.

Under certain circumstances an agent will not be required to recognize taxable income upon the sale of a life insurance policy. It has been held that an agent who is required to remit only "net premiums" (gross premium less the "basic commission" the company would allow him) to an insurance company, and who is under a contract with an insured to collect only an amount equal to the net premiums due, is not in constructive receipt of commissions usually earned on the sale of that policy. As a result, the agent is not taxed on the foregone commissions that would have been earned if a gross premium was collected.[1]

If the agent is not unconditionally obligated to repay advances, and any excess of advances over commissions earned would be recovered by the insurance company only by crediting earned commissions and renewals against such advances, amounts advanced to the agent are included in income in the year of receipt.[2] A life insurance agent's advance commissions received in previous years are taxable in the year the obligation to pay is discharged.[3]

With respect to commissions on credit life insurance, an accrual basis loan company which receives commissions on credit life insurance, but which may be required to refund a portion of the commission later if the loan is repaid and insurance coverage terminated before the end of the original term, includes the entire commission as income in the year the coverage was arranged. It may not spread the accrual over the term of the loan.[4]

When an agent purchases a policy for himself – on his own life or on the life of another – the agent must report the commissions as taxable income even though the commissions were never received. Such commissions are considered compensation and not a reduction in the cost of the policy.[5] This rule applies to brokers as well as to other life insurance salesmen. The agent or broker, or whatever title applies, is to receive or retain a percentage of the premiums on policies procured by him, called commissions, as compensation for his service to the company in obtaining the particular business for it. As such, the commissions were income within the meaning of IRC Section 61(a)(1).[6]

Similarly, if an agent sells a policy to a friend and waives his commissions, the agent must nevertheless report the commissions as taxable income.[7]

8680. How is the sale of a life insurance agent's renewal commissions taxed?

Generally, a bona fide, arm's length sale of a right to receive renewal commissions can successfully transfer the federal income tax liability on an insurance agent's renewal commissions to the purchaser. If an agent sells the right to renewal commissions, the agent must report the entire sale price as ordinary income in the year the sale is made.[8]

1. *Worden v. Commissioner*, 2 F.3d 359 (1993).
2. *George Blood Enterprises, Inc. v. Commissioner*, TC Memo 1976-102; Rev. Rul. 83-12, 1983-1 CB 99.
3. *Cox v. Commissioner*, TC Memo 1996-241.
4. Rev. Rul. 75-541, 1975-2 CB 195.
5. *Ostheimer v. United States*, 264 F.2d 789 (1959); Rev. Rul. 55-273, 1955-1 CB 221.
6. *Commissioner v. Minzer*, 279 F.2d 338 (1960); *Bailey v. Commissioner*, 41 TC 663 (1964).
7. *Mensik v. Commissioner*, 37 TC 703 (1962), *aff'd*, 328 F.2d 147 (7th Cir. 1964).
8. See *Cotlov v. Commissioner*, 228 F.2d 186; *Turner v. Commissioner*, 38 TC 304 (1962).

Renewals cannot be converted to capital gain by sale to a third party.[1] In addition, the Tax Court has held that amounts received by a district manager upon the termination of his agency contract are treated as ordinary income and not capital gain resulting from the sale of a capital asset, if the money received was compensation for the termination of the right to receive future income in the form of commissions.[2]

Apparently, the buyer must amortize his cost. In other words, the buyer can exclude from gross income in any year only that portion of the purchase price which the renewals received in that year bear to the total amount of anticipated renewals. The issue of whether the amount of deductible amortization is correctly determined requires consideration only of the contracts under which the buyer purchased the right to be general agent or purchased rights to renewal commissions.[3]

8681. Are there any circumstances where an insurance agent's commissions may be taxable to a company rather than to the agent?

Where an individual agent owns or controls a corporation which is related to the agent's insurance activities, questions may arise as to the proper allocation of income and deductions between the individual and his corporation.

Typically, income is taxed to the individual who earns it, and the income earner cannot avoid the result by assigning income or the right to receive it either before or after the income has been earned.[4]

In one situation, a life insurance agent assigned his commissions to his wholly owned pension consulting corporation, for which he worked as an employee. He did not (could not, under the insurer's rules) assign his agency contract. Since neither the corporation nor any of its other employees were authorized under the contract to submit applications, none of them had the right under the contract to earn commissions. All applications developed through the sales efforts of all employees were submitted through the agent and the insurance company paid the commissions under the assignment to the consulting firm. The IRS considered the arrangement an assignment of future income and ruled that the commissions were includable in the agent's gross income.

However, the agent was allowed to deduct (as a business expense) a part of the assigned commissions. Since the services of other employees of the corporation helped produce the commissions, part of the assigned commissions was treated as compensation to the corporation for its services and taxed to the corporation. The balance of the assigned commissions was treated as contributions to capital instead of income.[5]

The IRS distinguished this situation from one in which the corporation was held to have earned the income,[6] because there the agreements between the agent and insurance company were assigned to the corporation.

1. *Remington v. Commissioner*, 9 TC 99 (1947); *Davidson v. Commissioner*, 43 BTA 576 (1941).
2. *Clark v. Commissioner*, TC Memo 1994-278.
3. *Latendresse v. Commissioner*, 243 F.2d 577 (1957).
4. *Helvering v. Horst*, 311 U.S. 112 (1940).
5. Rev. Rul. 77-336, 1977-2 CB 202.
6. Rev. Rul. 54-34, 1954-1 CB 175.

In another case, a corporate life insurance agency tried to assign a contract to service a group medical insurance plan to its subsidiary, also an insurance agency. The parent corporation assigned the insurance commissions and service fees to the subsidiary, as well. However, the parent agency continued to perform all services to the group plan under the agreement, used its own office facilities and employees and paid all operating expenses. The subsidiary was unable to perform the agreement because of lack of staff, equipment and financing.

The Tax Court held that the parent earned the fees and commissions since it performed the services, and the subsidiary was unable to perform them. The parent agency argued that the assignment was of the agreement, as distinguished from the income. The argument failed because the parent was unable to submit proof. However, the court suggested that it would be hard to show an actual assignment of the agreement in view of the nature of the agreement, since it was one calling for performance of future services which the alleged assignee would be unable to perform.[1]

In *Davidson v. Commissioner*, the taxpayer was a successful salesman who specialized in estate planning sales. He formed a corporation to which he sold his insurance business, including all assets and good will, and provided in the instrument of transfer that all business done by him thereafter would be done for the benefit of the corporation. The taxpayer was to turn over to the corporation all of his first year commissions, keep his renewal commissions and be paid a salary as general manager of the corporation. The corporation carried on estate planning services acting through agents and employees other than the taxpayer, though the taxpayer worked jointly with some of these agents and personally received all commissions not retained by the other agents. The taxpayer endorsed over to the corporation commissions received by him pursuant to his agreement with the corporation, and did not include the commissions in his gross income, but did include them in the corporation's gross income in its return.[2]

Despite all these elaborate arrangements, the Tax Court held that all the commissions received by the taxpayer were taxable to him personally, not to the corporation. The court also rejected the taxpayer's argument that the commissions endorsed over to the corporation should be considered payments for services rendered by the corporation, and thus deductible as a business expense. The court held that the only amount deductible on such a basis would be an amount considered reasonable payment for such services had the taxpayer and the corporation bargained at arm's length.

In *American Savings Bank v. Comm.*, two individuals formed an insurance partnership authorized to solicit mortgage and credit life insurance in connection with loans made by banks in which they had interests. Insurance was sold on the bank premises primarily by officers of the banks who were individually licensed as insurance agents. By agreement between the partnership and the agents, commissions were divided 50-50 between the agents and the partnership. Later, the insurance business which, to that point, had been conducted as a partnership, was transferred to a corporation formed by the two partners. Commissions thenceforth were divided between

1. *Millette and Associates, Inc. v. Comm.*, TC Memo 1978-180.
2. 43 BTA 576 (1941).

the corporation and the agents just as had been done between the partnership and the agents. The issue in the case was whether the commissions received by the corporation were taxable to the corporation or to the two individuals.[1]

The court examined all surrounding facts and circumstances, and concluded that control over the company's earnings rested with the corporation. The court noted that nearly all commissions were generated by other agents of the company and the contracts authorizing sales of insurance were with the corporation rather than with the individuals. Therefore, the commissions were taxable to the corporation rather than to the two individuals.

In *Shaw v. Comm.*, the taxpayer owned and managed two corporations. He was also licensed as an insurance agent to sell credit life and health insurance to customers of his companies. Insurance was sold by employees to the corporations and applications were submitted in the taxpayer's name. Commissions on the insurance sold were paid to the taxpayer, who in turn endorsed the checks over to the corporations. In reaching its determination whether the commissions should be taxed to the taxpayer or to his corporations, the court first observed that the result would not be affected by the fact that, under state law, the corporations were prohibited from acting as insurance agents. Such a circumstance would not prevent the court from finding that the corporations should be taxed on the commissions if it determined that the corporations were actually in control of the insurance-selling enterprise. However, the court believed the facts of the case indicated that the taxpayer "was himself in the insurance business (admittedly to benefit his corporations) and used the corporations as his agents in the carrying out of the business of selling insurance." The court found, therefore, that the taxpayer, not his corporations, had earned the commission income and was liable for the taxes associated with it. However, the court recognized the fact that the corporations had performed services and expended funds in producing the insurance, and so allowed the taxpayer to deduct a large part of the commissions turned over to the corporations as a business expense.[2]

8682. Are partners and members of LLCs considered independent contractors or employees?

A general partner is treated as self-employed and income received from the partnership is, accordingly, treated as self-employment income.[3] Income received by a *limited* partner, on the other hand, is generally not treated as self-employment income *unless* that income represents a guaranteed payment to the limited partner within the meaning of IRC Section 707(c).[4] A payment will be considered "guaranteed" under Section 707(c) if it is made without regard to the income of the partnership.[5]

If an LLC is taxed as a partnership, its members are treated as partners for tax purposes (including determining whether their income represents self-employment income).[6]

1. 56 TC 828 (1971).
2. 59 TC 375 (1972).
3. See IRC Sec. 1402(a).
4. IRC Sec. 1402(a)(13).
5. IRC Sec. 707(c).
6. Let. Rul. 9432018.

Despite this, in the case of an LLC member, if a member who has contributed both services and capital to the organization receives a distribution, the distribution should represent self-employment income insofar as it relates to the *services* contributed by the member. The difficulty arises in determining whether a distribution relates to the services or a return of capital.

The Tax Court recently held that payments received by a taxpayer through his LLC were guaranteed payments, rather than partnership distributions, that gave rise to ordinary income tax liability because the payments were made without regard to the partnership's income and were made in exchange for the taxpayer's services, not as a return of partnership capital.

In this case, after the taxpayer's employer refused to treat him as an independent contractor, the taxpayer resigned and formed an LLC through which he could perform the same services as a subcontractor for his former employer. The taxpayer received all payments for these services through the conduit LLC, which was taxed as a partnership, and labeled them as partnership distributions—arguing that the payments were made in exchange for the use of capital.

The IRS disagreed with this characterization and instead reasoned that these payments represented guaranteed payments for services under IRC Section 707(c) and, therefore, generated ordinary income tax liability. The Tax Court agreed with the IRS, finding that the taxpayer here performed all services on behalf of the LLC, employed no employees and could not present any evidence that the payments, which were determined without regard to the partnership's income, were made in exchange for the use of partnership capital. As a result, the taxpayer was required to include the payments in calculating his ordinary income tax liability.[1]

While the IRS proposed regulations on the issue (see below), in 1997 Congress provided that the regulations would not be made final and the IRS has not proposed further regulations.[2] Because of this, it is uncertain whether a distribution to an LLC member will be subject to the self-employment tax (see Q 8670) in a situation where the distribution cannot be apportioned to show whether it relates to the member's services or capital contribution. Even in such a situation, the members of an LLC may still qualify as owner-employees for purposes of retirement plan qualification under the rules discussed in Q 8672.

Planning Point: Proposed Treasury Regulation Section 1.1402(a)-2 was originally issued by the IRS in 1997. However, because of controversy over the self-employment tax treatment of limited partners who are active in a partnership's business, Congress prohibited the IRS from making the regulations final before July 1, 1998, believing instead that Congress should formulate such rules. Since the expiration of the moratorium, neither Congress nor the IRS has acted to clarify the self-employment tax treatment of LLC members, leaving the proposed regulations as the only administrative guidance on the matter. Thus, while the proposed regulations are not precedential, they can be relied upon to avoid a penalty under IRC section 6406(f). There is also judicial precedent, in *Elkins*,[3] to reasonably conclude that the courts will sustain the position of a taxpayer who relies on proposed regulations.

1. *Seismic Support Services v. Comm.*, TC Memo 2014-78.
2. TRA 97, Sec. 935.
3. 81 TC 669 (1983).

PART VIII: BUSINESS EXPENSE DEDUCTIONS

8683. What is a business expense deduction?

A business expense deduction is a deduction allowed for ordinary and necessary expenses paid or incurred in connection with an individual's trade, business or profession.[1] The deduction allowed under IRC Section 62(a)(1) for expenses of a trade or business is the provision which technically allows for business income to be taxed on a net income basis, whether it be a corporate business or the business of individual taxpayers operating as sole proprietors or partners. In the case of a sole proprietorship or partnership, IRC Section 62(a)(1) operates to assure that all trade or business expenses, deductible as delineated under specific IRC Sections, are effectively allowed as above-the-line deductions, rather than itemized deductions. In the case of a sole proprietor, all but a few of these expenses are deducted in Schedule C of Form 1040.

For purposes of determining whether an expense may be deducted as a business expense, an expense is considered to be "ordinary" if it is one that is commonly incurred in the trade or occupation of the taxpayer. An expense is "necessary" if it is found to be appropriate or helpful to the taxpayer's business or occupation. Among the common expenses in this category are: employees' salaries; office rent; interest on business loans; the cost of supplies and utilities; traveling; entertainment; advertising; and automobile expenses.

Generally, business expenses of a self-employed individual (sole proprietor, independent contractor, or professional) may be deducted from gross income to arrive at adjusted gross income. The deductions are taken on Schedule C of Form 1040 in computing the net gain or loss from the taxpayer's business or profession.

The IRS has ruled that a full-time life insurance salesperson who is treated as a "statutory employee" for FICA purposes is *not* an "employee" for purposes of IRC Sections 62 and 67. Such individuals may thus treat unreimbursed business expenses as "above the line" deductions. This ruling was issued in part to clarify that taxpayers who are treated as "statutory employees" for FICA purposes (as are life insurance salespersons) are not necessarily treated as "employees" for other purposes.[2] The term "statutory employee" refers to certain individuals described in IRC Section 3121(d)(3)(B), who are subject to FICA withholding requirements (see Q 8668). The ruling's effect was essentially limited to those individuals.

See Q 8684 to Q 8699 for a detailed discussion of the various types of business expenses commonly deducted by taxpayers.

8684. Is a taxpayer entitled to deduct business travel expenses?

Generally, a taxpayer is entitled to deduct travel expenses when those expenses are incurred while the taxpayer is "away from home" for business reasons.[3] This is the case even though those

1. IRC Sec. 162(a).
2. Rev. Rul. 90-93, 1990-2 CB 33.
3. IRC Sec. 162(a)(2).

travel expenses would otherwise be personal expenses (such as food or lodging). There are three basic requirements that must be met before a taxpayer will be entitled to deduct business-related travel expenses:

(1) The expense must be a reasonable and necessary traveling expense;

(2) The expense must be incurred while "away from home;" and

(3) The expense must be incurred "in the pursuit of business."[1]

For an expense to be incurred in the pursuit of business, it must be directly connected to the trade or business of the taxpayer, and the expense must be necessary or appropriate to developing or pursuing the taxpayer's business or trade.[2]

Interpretation of the "away from home" requirement has been litigated extensively. Under the IRS interpretation, "away from home" for these purposes means that the taxpayer must be away from the taxpayer's principal place of business—not personal residence.[3] Several courts, however, have agreed with the contrasting opinion that the taxpayer's "home" is the taxpayer's residence.

Planning Point: If the taxpayer is engaged in business at two or more separate locations, the "tax home" for purposes of section 162(a)(2) is located at the principal place of business during the taxable year.[4]

See Q 8685 for a detailed discussion of the "away from home" requirement as it applies to taxpayers who travel frequently for business.

8685. When is a taxpayer considered to be "away from home" for purposes of deducting business travel expenses? What if the taxpayer is away for an extended period of time for business reasons?

As discussed in Q 8684, the IRS requires that a taxpayer be away from the company's principal place of business, rather than a residence, in order to deduct business travel expenses that would otherwise be personal in nature (such as food and lodging). The IRS has ruled that a taxpayer's tax "home"—meaning principal place of business—is not limited to a specific building or worksite, but instead encompasses the entire city or general area in which the business is located.[5]

In cases where a taxpayer is required to take extended business trips, determining the location of a taxpayer's primary place of business becomes difficult, though for most taxpayers, the determination is simple because many taxpayers maintain a residence in the general vicinity of their primary place of business. For taxpayers who are required to travel often for business, such extended business travel raises the question as to where that taxpayer's tax "home" is located.

1. *Comm. v. Flowers*, 326 U.S. 465 (1946); *Robertson v. Comm.*, 190 F.3d 392 (1999).
2. Rev. Rul. 54-147, 1954-1 CB 51.
3. See Rev. Rul. 75-432, 1975-2 CB 60.
4. *Markey v. Comm.*, 490 F.2d 1249 (6th Cir. 1974).
5. Rev. Rul. 56-49, 1956-1 CB 152.

Generally, in order for the taxpayer to deduct business-related travel expenses, the travel must be temporary in nature ("temporary" for these purposes has been statutorily interpreted to mean an employment period not exceeding one year[1]).

In other words, if a taxpayer is assigned to a new work location for an *indefinite* period of time, the taxpayer's principal place of business—and tax "home" for travel expense deduction purposes—is transferred to that new location.[2]

Often, the analysis of whether a taxpayer who travels for business has acquired a second "tax home" turns upon whether or not it would be reasonable to expect that taxpayer to relocate. For example, the Second Circuit has held that the real issue in a case where the taxpayer resided in Colorado, but had committed to a two year position in New York, was whether or not a reasonable person in her position would have relocated her residence to New York.[3]

Congress has clarified the issue so that Section 162 now specifically provides that a taxpayer will *not* be temporarily "away from home" for any period of employment that exceeds one year for tax years beginning after 1992.[4] If the taxpayer can show that the business travel was realistically expected to last for one year or less, and that travel in fact does last for one year or less, the travel will be considered temporary. On the other hand, if the travel is realistically expected to last for more than one year, or there is no realistic expectation that the travel will last for *less* than one year, the travel will be considered indefinite *regardless of whether it actually lasts for more than one year.*[5] A very narrow exception to this rule exists for federal employees who are travelling in connection with the investigation or prosecution of a federal crime.[6]

This statutory rule applies for taxpayers travelling for business reasons to a *single location* for more than one year. The distinction between indefinite and temporary business travel remains important in situations where the taxpayer's business travel may include *multiple* travel locations over a period that exceeds one year.

In *Wilson v. Commissioner*, for example, the taxpayer, who was from Idaho, was assigned by his employer to a series of temporary construction jobs in various locations in California over a period of time that exceeded one year. He claimed that, because each of these jobs was temporary, his principal place of business was in Idaho so that he should have been entitled to deduct his travel expenses while working in California. The Tax Court disagreed, finding that, while construction jobs are temporary by nature, all of the facts and circumstances had to be examined to determine whether the business travel was in fact indefinite. In this case, the overarching employment relationship was important and demonstrated an indefinite relationship so that the taxpayer could not reasonably argue that his travel could be segmented into individual construction jobs.[7]

1. Chief Counsel Memo 106447-98 (08-06-1998); Energy Policy Act of 1992 (1938), Pub. L. No. 102-486.
2. See *Peurifoy v. Comm.*, 358 U.S. 59 (1958).
3. *Six v. United States*, 450 F.2d 66 (1971).
4. IRC Sec. 162(a) (flush language).
5. *Rev. Rul. 93-86, 1993-2 CB 71.*
6. IRC Sec. 162(a) (flush language).
7. *Wilson v. Comm.*, TC Memo 2001-301.

8686. Can a taxpayer deduct business travel expenses if the taxpayer travels so frequently that the taxpayer has no "tax home" for determining whether the "away from home" requirement of Section 162 is met?

Yes. If a taxpayer travels constantly for business, it is possible that he or she may have no tax home for purposes of determining the deductibility of business travel expenses under Section 162.

For example, in *McNeill v. Commissioner*, the taxpayer was a truck driver who was travelling so frequently that the Tax Court found he had no principal place of business. Further, no significant expenses were incurred in connection with maintaining a principal residence, as he paid approximately $1,000 a year for a mobile home until he owned it in full and, for the tax years in question, the taxpayer only spent approximately twenty days per year in the mobile home. Though the taxpayer attempted to deduct all travel and meal expenses while he was "on the road," the Tax Court denied the deductions, finding that, in a case like this, the taxpayer was *never* "away from home" for tax purposes and, therefore, was not entitled to deduct any business travel expenses.[1]

Similarly, in *James v. United States*, the taxpayer was a traveling salesperson who spent so much time traveling that the Ninth Circuit found there were insufficient contacts with any location to determine a tax home. In this case, the court discussed whether a taxpayer was required to maintain a physical residence in order to *ever* be considered "away from home" for purposes of Section 162. Because the intent of Congress in allowing the deduction was to prevent the taxpayer from incurring duplicate (lodging) or higher (meal and lodging expenses tend to be higher in travel) expenses during business travel, the court found that the deduction should only apply in cases where the taxpayer has a "home" and must expend funds to maintain this home. Further, if a taxpayer has no permanent home, and must therefore obtain food and shelter in public restaurants and hotels whether or not the taxpayer is traveling, there is no justification for allowing the deduction for business travel expenses.[2]

Therefore, in rare cases, it is possible that the taxpayer will never be allowed to deduct business travel expenses whether or not they are incurred in the pursuit of a trade or business, because the taxpayer will never actually be "away from home." In other words, if a taxpayer is constantly on the move due to his work, he is never "away" from home.[3]

8687. Are business-related travel expenses deductible if a taxpayer resides in a location that is far from the taxpayer's principal place of business?

A taxpayer is entitled to deduct business travel expenses, but is not entitled to deduct the costs incurred in *commuting* between the taxpayer's principal residence and place of business.[4]

When a taxpayer chooses to reside in a location that is far from the taxpayer's principal place of business, the issue is not whether the taxpayer is "away from home" when travelling

1. TC Memo 2003-65.
2. *James v. United States*, 308 F.2d 204 (1962).
3. *Deamer v. Comm.*, 752 F.2d 337, 338 (8th Circuit 1985), affg, TC Memo 1984-63.
4. See, for example, *United States v. Tauferner*, 407 F.2d 243 (1969); *Sanders v. Comm.*, 439 F.2d 296 (1971).

between a residence and place of business, but whether or not the travel expenses are sufficiently connected to a trade or business as to be deductible under Section 162.

For example, the Tax Court has denied the taxpayer's travel expense deductions in a situation where the taxpayer maintained a residence in Tennessee with the taxpayer's family. The taxpayer was unable to find employment in Tennessee and accepted employment in North Carolina. The family continued to reside in Tennessee and the taxpayer incurred duplicate living expenses as a result, which he attempted to deduct as business travel expenses. The Tax Court denied the deductions, finding that the taxpayer's choice in maintaining his personal residence far from his principal place of business was not a business expense that was reasonable and necessarily connected to his business. Rather, these duplicate living expenses were the result of the taxpayer's personal choice to maintain a residence in Tennessee.[1]

Similarly, a postal employee who lived and worked in New York, but was promoted to a position (national president of the post office) that required him to spend approximately 300 hours per year in Washington, D.C., was unable to deduct his travel expenses between New York and Washington D.C. The taxpayer's wife continued to live in their New York residence and the taxpayer stayed in hotels and took his meals there while in Washington D.C. Even though the position required that the taxpayer spend significant time in Washington D.C., it did not require that he continue to maintain a residence in New York. Because of this, the expenses that he incurred while residing in Washington D.C. were found to be personal living expenses, rather than business travel expenses.[2]

8688. Is a taxpayer entitled to a deduction for travel expenses when the taxpayer has multiple places of business?

If a taxpayer regularly conducts business in more than one location, a determination must be made as to which location is the "principal" place of business. This determination must be made by examining all the facts and circumstances of the particular case, but the IRS has identified the following factors as important:

(1) The total time spent at each of the business locations;

(2) The degree of business activities conducted at each location; and

(3) Whether the financial return in each location is significant or insignificant.[3]

Though all three factors are important, the IRS generally considers the amount of time spent at each location to be the most important factor.[4]

For example, the Tax Court has held that a taxpayer who maintained a business in New York and another in Massachusetts was entitled to deduct expenses while travelling in

1. *Tucker v. Comm.*, 55 TC 783 (1971).
2. *McAvoy v. Comm.*, TC Memo 1965-289.
3. Rev. Rul. 54-147, 1954-1 CB 51.
4. See Rev. Rul. 63-82, 1963-1 CB 33; Rev. Rul. 61-67, 1961-1 CB 25.

New York because the taxpayer spent more of his time in Massachusetts.[1] In situations where the taxpayer's time is relatively evenly divided, all of the facts and circumstances will be analyzed to determine which place of business constitutes the taxpayer's "principal" place of business.[2]

Once the taxpayer's principal place of business is determined, the general rules applicable in determining whether travel expenses are deductible are applied. Thus, a taxpayer can deduct expenses for meals and lodging while conducting business in a secondary business location if an overnight trip is required. Transportation expenses can be deducted between the principal and secondary places of business even if an overnight stay is not required.[3] Expenses incurred while the taxpayer is in the vicinity of his principal place of business are not deductible.

8689. Can a taxpayer deduct travel expenses for a trip that has both business and personal elements?

The deduction for otherwise personal expenses incurred while a taxpayer is away from home for business purposes is only allowed to the extent that the travel is reasonable and necessary for a taxpayer's trade or business. However, because there have been many instances where a taxpayer attempts to deduct expenses for what essentially constitutes a personal vacation, the IRS has developed rules that govern a trip that combines both business and personal elements.

If the primary purpose behind a taxpayer's trip is personal, no travel expense deductions for expenses incurred in traveling to and from the destination will be permitted even if the taxpayer does, in fact, engage in some business activities during the course of the trip. However, if a trip has both business and personal elements, the taxpayer may deduct those expenses that are properly allocated to the business portion of the trip even if unable to deduct the expense of traveling to and from the destination because it is found that the trip was primarily undertaken for personal reasons.[4]

Whether a trip is primarily business-related or primarily personal is a question of fact. Though all facts and circumstances must be considered, the IRS has provided that an important factor is the amount of time spent on business compared to the amount of time spent on the taxpayer's personal activities.

Planning Point: If, for example, a taxpayer spends one week while at a destination on activities which are directly related to his trade or business and subsequently spends an additional five weeks for vacation or other personal activities, the trip will be considered primarily personal in nature in the absence of a clear showing to the contrary.[5]

Travel expenses for the taxpayer's spouse (or other family member) to accompany the taxpayer on a business-related trip are not deductible unless the taxpayer is able to show that

1. *Sherman v. Comm.*, 16 TC 332 (1951).
2. See, for example, *Bernard v. United States*, 87-1 USTC 1092 (1971).
3. Rev. Rul. 63-82, above.
4. Treas. Reg. §1.162-2(b)(1).
5. Treas. Reg. §1.162-2(b)(2).

there is a bona fide business purpose for the spouse or family member's presence. This is the case even if it is found that the taxpayer's trip is primarily business-related.[1]

Similar rules apply in the case of a taxpayer's travel expenses related to attendance at a convention—meaning that the expenses are not deductible if the reason for attending is not sufficiently related to the taxpayer's trade or business. However, the rules make clear that the fact that the taxpayer's attendance is voluntary will not impede the taxpayer's ability to deduct related travel expenses—even if the taxpayer actually uses vacation days in order to attend—so long as attendance at the convention is motivated by business reasons.[2]

8690. Do any special rules apply for a taxpayer who wishes to deduct business-related travel expenses for travel that takes place outside the United States?

Yes. IRC Section 274 applies to reduce the amount of otherwise allowable business travel deductions for taxpayers travelling for business outside of the United States unless one of the following are true:

(1) the trip has a duration of one week or less, or

(2) less than 25 percent of the trip is spent pursuing personal, nonbusiness activities.[3]

"One week" for this purpose means seven consecutive days, *not* including the day that travel begins but including the day that the taxpayer travels home.[4]

Unless the taxpayer establishes a more clear method of allocation that satisfies the IRS, whether or not the taxpayer spends less than 25 percent of the trip on personal activities must be determined on a per-day basis, meaning that each day will be considered a "business day" or a "nonbusiness day."[5]

"Transportation days," meaning days during which the taxpayer was engaged in travelling from the U.S. to a foreign destination in pursuit of business, are counted as business days unless the taxpayer does not take a reasonably direct route. If the taxpayer takes an indirect route for nonbusiness purposes, only the amount of time that would have been spent to travel by direct route using the same type of transportation will be considered business days.[6]

If the taxpayer is specifically required to be in the foreign location for a business purpose for the day in question (for example, to attend a business meeting), that day will be counted as a business day.[7] Further, if the taxpayer was primarily engaged in business activities during normal working hours, that day will be counted as a business day.[8] An intervening weekend

1. Treas. Reg. §1.162-2(c).
2. Treas. Reg. §1.162-2(d).
3. IRC Sec. 274(c).
4. Treas. Reg. §1.274-4(c).
5. Treas. Reg. §1.274-4(d)(2).
6. Treas. Reg. §1.274-4(d)(2)(i).
7. Treas. Reg. §1.274-4(d)(2)(ii).
8. Treas. Reg. §1.274-4(d)(2)(iii).

day or holiday can be counted as a business day even if no business was conducted on that day (see example 3, below).

Example 1: Mel leaves for a foreign business trip on Wednesday and returns the following Wednesday. She is considered to have been away from home for seven days. Because she has not been away from home for more than one week, the special rules applicable to foreign travel do not apply.

Example 2: Same facts as above, except Mel returns on the following Thursday. She is considered to have been away from home for eight days, so must allocate her travel expenses between business and personal expenses to determine the percent of time spent on personal activities. The day spent travelling on Wednesday will be counted as either a business or nonbusiness day in determining whether Mel meets the 25 percent test.

Example 3: Mel leaves for Paris on a Wednesday and returns the following Sunday. Mel attends business meetings on Thursday and Friday, and the following Monday through Friday, when her business concludes. The first weekend will be counted as business days even if no business is conducted because they are "intervening"—her business had not yet concluded at the beginning of the weekend. Her second Saturday in Paris will be counted as a personal day because her business had concluded the day before.

If Section 274 applies, the taxpayer's travel expense deduction will be disallowed to the extent of nonbusiness travel. The taxpayer will be required to multiply the total amount of travel expenses by a fraction, the numerator of which is the number of nonbusiness days occurring during the trip, and the denominator of which is the total number of days (business and nonbusiness) spent on the trip.[1]

Taxpayers who have no substantial control over arranging the business trip, such as in a case where the employer arranges a trip for an employee, may allocate all expenses of the trip to business travel (control over only the timing of the trip is not considered substantial control). Likewise, anyone traveling on an employer's behalf under a reimbursement or other expense allowance arrangement is considered not to have substantial control over arranging the trip provided the individual is neither a managing executive of the employer with authority to decide on the trip's business necessity, nor related to the employer within the meaning of IRC Section 267(b) (i.e., family members, an individual and his or her more-than-50 percent owned corporation, two corporate controlled-group members).[2]

8691. Can a taxpayer deduct business-related transportation expenses incurred when the taxpayer is not travelling away from home on business?

A taxpayer who is not considered to be "away from home" for purposes of deducting business-related travel expenses (see Q 8684 to Q 8690) may still be entitled to claim a deduction for business-related transportation expenses. A taxpayer is generally *not* entitled to deduct the cost of commuting from the taxpayer's residence to the taxpayer's primary place of business. However, business-related transportation costs other than commuting costs may be deducted as business expenses. Examples of such expenses include the following:

(1) Travelling from one business place to another business place within the general area that is considered a taxpayer's "tax home" (see Q 8685 and Q 8686);

(2) Visiting clients and customers;

1. Treas. Reg. §1.274-4(f)(1).
2. Treas. Reg. §1.274-4(f)(5)(i).

(3) Travelling to a business meeting outside of the taxpayer's principal place of business;

(4) Travel from the taxpayer's residence to a *temporary* workplace if the taxpayer has one or more *regular* workplaces. A work location is considered temporary if it is realistically expected to last (and does last) for one year or less, unless the circumstances indicate otherwise.[1]

If a taxpayer's residence is also the taxpayer's principal place of business, that taxpayer may deduct the costs of commuting between the residence and another place of business, whether or not that second place of business is considered "regular" or "temporary."[2]

Example: Brent is a representative for a cheese manufacturing company and works out of his home. He has no permanent office, but regularly must drive to visit clients who have questions about his company's cheese products. Brent may deduct the cost of driving between his home and client sites, even though these visits occur on a regular basis. If Brent were required to travel outside of his regular area of business on an overnight trip, those costs would be deductible as travel expenses, *not* transportation expenses. Because Brent travels by car, he can either deduct the actual costs of his car *or* the standard mileage rate for the year (54 cents per mile in 2016 and 53.5 cents per mile in 2017).[3]

As stated above, expenses incurred for commuting from the taxpayer's residence to place of business are generally nondeductible. This is the case even though the taxpayer works during the commute—for example, by taking work-related calls or discussing business while carpooling with a business associate.

8692. When is a taxpayer entitled to deduct moving expenses?

If certain conditions are met, a taxpayer may deduct reasonable moving expenses incurred in connection with beginning work at a new principal place of business, whether as an employee or self-employed person.[4] The following general requirements apply:

(1) The taxpayer must have incurred moving expenses;

(2) Those moving expenses must be related to the taxpayer's start of work at a new principal place of work;

(3) The taxpayer's new principal place of work must be at least fifty miles further from his principal residence than his former principal place of work *or*, if the taxpayer had no former principal place of work, at least fifty miles from his former residence;[5] and

(4) The taxpayer must work in the general location of the new principal place of work for a specified period. Specifically, this means that the taxpayer is either:

a. a full-time employee in the general location of the new principal place of work for at least thirty-nine weeks during the twelve-month period following his or her arrival *or*,

1. See IRS Publication 463, available at http://www.irs.gov/publications/p463/ch04.html (last accessed June 1, 2015).
2. IRS Pub. 463.
3. 2015-137 (Dec. 17, 2015), IR-2016-169 (December 13, 2016).
4. IRC Sec. 217(a).
5. IRC Sec. 217(c)(1).

b. in the twenty-four-month period following arrival, a full-time employee or self-employed individual (on a full-time basis) in the general location of the new principal place of work during at least seventy-eight weeks (thirty-nine weeks must be in the first twelve-month period). See Q 8668 and Q 8669 for a discussion of when a taxpayer is considered to be self-employed.[1]

For moving expenses that meet the requirements above to be "qualified," and thus deductible, they must relate to the expenses described below (the distinction also becomes important for determining whether the employee must include the costs of any employer-reimbursement in gross income, see Q 8693). "Qualified moving expenses" are:

(1) the costs incurred to move the taxpayer's household items from the first location to the second location; and

(2) the travel expenses (excluding meals, but including lodging) incurred by the taxpayer in travelling from the first location to the second location.[2]

The expenses described in (1), above, may include costs such as those related to packing, disconnecting and connecting utilities, and in-transit storage and insurance if incurred in the 30 day period after moving the goods from the taxpayer's former residence. The IRS specifically excludes costs such as losses sustained upon ending membership in clubs, wasted tuition fees, costs incurred in buying property or losses sustained upon selling property because of the move.[3]

Travel expenses described in (2), above, must be reasonable based on the facts and circumstances of the particular situation. Though the route travelled must usually be the shortest and most direct route, the taxpayer does not lose the deduction if the taxpayer incurs expenses that increase the cost of the move and are personal in nature. Instead, the deduction is reduced by the additional costs incurred for personal reasons.[4] The deduction is further reduced by any expenses deemed to be lavish or extravagant under the circumstances.

Example: Jeff is moving from Michigan to California for business reasons. He intends to drive but, rather than directly making the trip, he decides to stop and visit friends in St. Louis and Las Vegas along the way. Jeff is entitled to deduct the cost of moving from Michigan to California, minus any additional costs he incurs while visiting friends in other cities for personal reasons.

Planning Point: Travel expenses from the former to the new residence are deductible for one trip only. The trip must be made by the taxpayer and members of the taxpayer's household. It is not necessary, however, that the taxpayer and all household members travel together or at the same time.[5] The cost of traveling from a former home to a new one should be by the shortest, most direct route available using conventional transportation.[6]

1. IRC Sec. 217(c)(2).
2. IRC Sec. 217(b)(1).
3. Treas. Reg. §1.217-2(b)(3).
4. Treas. Reg. §1.217-2(b)(2).
5. Treas. Reg. §1.217-2(b)(4).
6. IRS Pub 521, Moving Expenses (2016).

A taxpayer is also entitled to deduct the moving expenses of other members of his household, provided that the household member's principal place of residence was both at the first location and at the second location.[1]

Generally, moving expenses are treated as "above the line" deductions; thus, if allowable, such expenses are deductible directly from gross income.[2]

8693. Can an employer deduct moving expenses for which it reimburses its employees? Are reimbursed moving expenses included in the taxpayer-employee's gross income?

Generally, if an employer reimburses an employee for business-related moving expenses (see Q 8692), that employer is entitled to deduct the reimbursed amount as an ordinary and necessary business expense under IRC Section 162.

If a taxpayer is reimbursed by the employer for non-qualified moving expenses (see Q 8692), the taxpayer must include those reimbursed amounts in gross income as compensation for services rendered.[3] A taxpayer is not required, however, to include amounts reimbursed for "qualified moving expenses" in gross income (see Q 8692). These qualified moving expenses are instead treated as a fringe benefit that is specifically excluded from an employee's income.[4]

In order for a moving expense reimbursement to be excludable from the employee's gross income, the reimbursement must be related to an expense that would be deductible by the employee (if the employee had paid it directly, see Q 8692) under IRC Section 217. If the employee actually did deduct the expense in a prior year, reimbursement for the expense is not excludable under Section 132.[5]

8694. Is a taxpayer entitled to claim a deduction for business-related education expenses?

An employee is generally entitled to deduct education-related expenses that meet the following requirements:

(1) The expense must relate to education that is designed to maintain or improve skills used by the taxpayer in his or her trade or business; or

(2) The education must be specifically required by the employer, or under applicable law or regulations, in order for the taxpayer to retain an established employment relationship, status or compensation level.[6]

1. IRC Sec. 217(b)(2). See also, *Shah v. United States*, 450 F. Supp. 1136 (1978).
2. IRC Sec. 62(a)(15).
3. IRC Sec. 82.
4. IRC Sec. 132(a)(6).
5. IRC Sec. 132(g).
6. Treas. Reg. §1.162-5(a).

Despite this, there are circumstances under which a taxpayer's educational expense deduction will not be permitted even if the qualifications described in (1) and (2) above are satisfied. Educational expenses will be considered personal, nondeductible expenses if:

(1) The expense is incurred in obtaining the minimum educational requirements for qualification in the taxpayer's business (for example, obtaining a law degree) though, once the employee has met the minimum educational standards upon entering his trade or business, he will be treated as continuing to meet those standards even if they are eventually changed;

Example: New Jersey requires all secondary school teachers to have a bachelor's degree that includes 30 credit hours of professional education courses. In New Jersey, if a school can certify that a qualified secondary school teacher with the requisite degree cannot be found, that school is permitted to hire a secondary school teacher who has completed at least 90 semester hours of college-level work, though such an individual is required to complete his or her degree within 3 years of hire to retain the position.

Annelise begins teaching in New Jersey with a bachelor's degree and thirty credit hours in professional education. Two years later, New Jersey adds the requirement that a secondary school teacher must complete a fifth year of education within ten years of beginning his or her employment to maintain certification. Annelise completes her fifth year of education three years later and obtains the required certificate. The fifth year of education is not part of the minimum educational requirements for secondary school teachers, so Annelise is entitled to deduct her expenses in obtaining the certificate.

Example: Same facts as above, except Annelise is hired during a period where there is a shortage of teachers and she has not yet completed her bachelor's degree. She completes her bachelor's degree within her first two years of employment. The expenses are not deductible, because a bachelor's degree is one of the minimum qualification requirements for secondary school teachers in New Jersey.[1]

(2) The expense is incurred in obtaining education that will qualify the taxpayer for entering a new trade or business. A "change of duties" does not constitute a new trade or business if the new duties involve the same general type of work involved in the taxpayer's present employment. For this purpose, all teaching and related duties are considered to involve the same general type of work.[2]

Example: Annelise is an elementary school teacher and, during the course of her employment, takes the classes necessary to qualify as a secondary school teacher. The educational expenses are deductible because they do not qualify Annelise for entering a new trade or business. Her husband, Kevin, is self-employed as an accountant and taking law school courses in the evenings. Kevin's education expenses are nondeductible, because they qualify him for entering a new trade or business.

8695. What special rules apply when a taxpayer deducts business-related entertainment expenses and meals?

Special restrictions apply when a taxpayer deducts business meal and entertainment expenses. A taxpayer is generally entitled to deduct the cost of a business meal if (a) the meal is not lavish or extravagant and (b) the taxpayer (or employee of the taxpayer) is present at the meal.[3]

1. Treas. Reg. §1.162-5(b)(2)(iii), Ex. 1.
2. Treas. Reg. §1.162-5(b)(3)(i).
3. IRC Sec. 274(k).

Entertainment expenses are typically only deductible if the taxpayer establishes that the activity is directly related to or associated with the taxpayer's trade or business.[1]

Generally, the deduction for the ordinary and necessary cost of business meals (i.e., those expenses which are not lavish and extravagant), are reduced by half, so that only 50 percent of allowable costs are deductible.[2] For certain taxpayers who are employed in the transportation industry, and are frequently required to have meals away from home (such as flight crews, interstate truck drivers, etc.), 80 percent of the cost of business meals is deductible for tax years beginning after 2007.[3]

In order to deduct the cost of business-related meals, taxpayers must also establish that the meal was either "directly related" or "associated with" the taxpayer's business (i.e., the taxpayer must show that the expense was incurred directly before, during, or after a bona fide business discussion) in order to deduct the cost.[4]

The deduction for business entertainment expenses is also generally limited to 50 percent of otherwise allowable costs.[5]

If the amount of the allowable deduction is reduced because the expense is found to be lavish or extravagant, the 50 percent limitation is applied *after* the cost has been reduced by the portion that is deemed to be unacceptable.[6]

If an employee is fully reimbursed for the expense of business meals and entertainment, such expenses are fully deductible by the employer, although the 50 percent limitation will apply to the employer's deduction.[7] However, if the expenses are not reimbursed, the employee is subject to the 50 percent limitation described above. Furthermore, the unreimbursed expenses that are deductible after that limitation are then subject to the 2 percent floor on miscellaneous itemized deductions.[8]

8696. When is a business-related entertainment or meal expense "ordinary and necessary" so that it may be deducted?

Whether a business-related entertainment or meal expense is ordinary and necessary is generally a question of fact. The courts have recognized that the taxpayer is entitled to exercise a certain degree of discretion in determining whether an expense is ordinary and necessary in the taxpayer's particular business.[9]

1. IRC Sec. 274(a).
2. IRC Sec. 274(n).
3. IRC Sec. 274(n)(3).
4. IRC Sec. 274(a)(1)(A).
5. IRC Sec. 274(n).
6. H.R. Rep. No. 841, 99th Cong., 2d Session at II-25 (1986).
7. IRC Sec. 274(n)(2)(A).
8. IRC Secs. 274(n)(1), 67(b).
9. *Cravens v. Comm.*, 272 F.2d 895 (1959).

Expenditures are generally found to be sufficiently necessary if, based on all the facts and circumstances, they are "appropriate and helpful" to the taxpayer's business.[1] Expenditures are generally found to be sufficiently ordinary if they are made for "sound and normal" business expenses of a nature and amount determined by general commercial standards.[2]

The Tax Court has allowed a deduction for entertainment expenses incurred by a bank that paid for private dinner parties at a country club (hosted by the bank's officers) for its significant customers ("key people" from among the bank's top five hundred clients and prospective clients in the upper echelon of the financial community).[3] The court noted that, in this case, there was evidence that these customers were not being reached by more direct methods, so it was not unreasonable for the bank to resort to private entertainment in order to entice their business.

On the other hand, when a public defender who supervised several attorneys attempted to deduct the cost of taking those attorneys to lunches at the public defender's country club, the Tax Court denied the deduction on the grounds that such expenses were not ordinary and necessary for a taxpayer who is engaged in the business of being a public defender. This was the case even though the court recognized that the lunches tended to boost morale and encourage efficient work. Also important was the Tax Court's recognition that these expenses might have been found to be ordinary and necessary were they incurred by a partner operating in a private law firm.[4]

8697. What limitations apply to prevent a taxpayer from deducting lavish or extravagant business-related entertainment expenses?

The prohibition on the deductibility of lavish or extravagant business-related expenses is tied to the notion that the expense must be reasonable in order to be deducted—a determination that is made based on the facts and circumstances of each individual case. Based on this premise, the courts have allowed taxpayers to deduct expenses that might be considered unreasonable in other contexts.

For example, the Tax Court has upheld a taxpayer's deduction for expenses incurred in using a chauffeured Cadillac to provide local transportation for securities analysts and investment advisors in New York.[5]

Conversely, the Tax Court has disallowed deductions for lease payments made on a Rolls Royce by a plastic surgeon. The court's opinion reflects the importance of whether the expense is reasonable, rather than the level of extravagance displayed. In this case, the taxpayer-surgeon claimed that the Rolls Royce was used in advertising and promoting the quality of his services, and that he only used the car for business travel between the hospital and medical

1. *First National Bank v. United States*, 276 F. Supp. 905 (1967).
2. *Byers v. Comm.*, 199 F.2d 273 (1952).
3. See *First National Bank*, above.
4. *Wells v. Comm.*, TC Memo 1977-419.
5. See *Denison v. Comm.*, TC Memo 1977-430.

conventions. The Tax Court rejected the petitioner's argument that the Rolls Royce would attract customers, finding that it had no reasonable relationship to his skill and performance as a plastic surgeon and that there was no evidence that any patients were attracted based on the leasing of the car.[1]

8698. What substantiation requirements apply when a taxpayer deducts business-related entertainment and meal expenses?

In order for a taxpayer to deduct business-related entertainment and meal expenses, the taxpayer must maintain records adequate to provide the following information:

(1) The amount of each separate entertainment (or meal) expense;

(2) The time and date upon which the expense was incurred;

(3) The name, address and/or location where the expense was incurred (if the location information does not make the type of entertainment apparent, the taxpayer must indicate whether it was a dinner, theater, sporting event, etc.);

(4) The business reason for the entertainment or the business benefit expected to be derived from the event, and (except in the case of business meals furnished on employer premises), the nature of any business discussion or activity;[2]

(5) A description of the business relationship between the taxpayer and the parties who were entertained (name, title or other description sufficient to establish the business relationship).[3]

The taxpayer's records must contain all of the above information or the deduction may be disallowed.[4] However, if the taxpayer entertains a large group of individuals, the taxpayer is not required to provide a name, title and description for each individual—a general description, such as "directors of Company X," will suffice if the group is homogeneous enough so that such a description will provide adequate identification. If, however, the taxpayer entertains a group that is so diverse that such a label will not identify the business relationship at issue, the IRS will require a listing on an individual basis.[5]

If a taxpayer holds season tickets for purposes of business entertaining, the event represented by each individual ticket must be treated as a separate entertainment event. For example, a taxpayer who holds season tickets for Boston Red Sox home baseball games must keep records providing the above information as it applies to each individual game.[6]

1. *Connelly v. Comm.*, TC Memo 1994-436.
2. IRC Sec. 274(e).
3. Treas. Reg. §1.274-5T(b)(3).
4. See, for example, *Newman v. Comm.*, TC Memo 1982-61 (deduction disallowed for insufficient substantiation because taxpayer failed to include location and business purpose information).
5. Rev. Proc. 63-4, 1963-1 CB 474.
6. Rev. Proc. 63-4, above, Q&A 17.

8699. When is a taxpayer entitled to deduct expenses incurred in maintaining a home office?

A taxpayer is only entitled to deduct expenses for a home office if the taxpayer is able to meet the restrictive requirements imposed by the IRC and the courts with regard to this business deduction. A deduction for use of a part of the taxpayer's residence as an office will not be allowed unless a portion of the dwelling is used exclusively and on a regular basis as (a) the principal place of business for any trade or business of the taxpayer; or (b) the place of business used by the taxpayer for meeting patients, clients or customers in the normal course of the taxpayer's business.[1] If the taxpayer uses a separate structure as a home office, the use requirements are less restrictive and the use must only be "in connection with" the taxpayer's trade or business.[2] A home office will qualify as a taxpayer's principal place of business if both of the following are true:

(1) The taxpayer uses the home office exclusively and regularly for administrative or management activities of the trade or business; and

(2) The taxpayer has no other fixed location for conducting substantial administrative or management activities of the trade or business.[3]

That a taxpayer chooses to have a third party perform administrative or management activities (such as billing) for the taxpayer will not, in itself, cause a disallowance of the deduction.

Example: Josh is an electrician who is self-employed. Most of his time is spent on-site with customers examining and repairing their electrical systems, but he maintains a small office in his home that is used exclusively and regularly for activities such as ordering supplies, calling his customers and keeping his books. Josh writes up estimates and records of work completed on-site at his customers' premises. He has engaged a local bookkeeping service for billing his customers, but he does not conduct any other substantial administrative or management activities outside of his home office. His home office will qualify for a home office deduction.

Planning Point: If the taxpayer is an employee and uses part of the taxpayer's home for business, the taxpayer must be able to show that, in addition to the requirements discussed above (1) the use is for the convenience of the employer and (2) no part of the home is rented to the employer and used to perform services as an employee for that employer.[4]

If the home office is merely appropriate and helpful, the deduction for home office expenses will be disallowed.[5]

For tax years beginning on or after January 1, 2013, the IRS has authorized an optional safe harbor method for calculating the amount of a taxpayer's home office deduction. The taxpayer calculates the home office deduction by multiplying the square footage of the home used for business purposes by a prescribed rate of $5.00. Under this safe harbor, the maximum allowable

1. IRC Sec. 280A(c)(1).
2. IRC Sec. 280A(c)(1)(C).
3. IRS Publication 587, Business Use of Your Home (2016).
4. IRS Pub. 587.
5. IRS Pub. 587, above.

portion of a home that may be used for qualified business purposes is 300 square feet, which results in a maximum allowable home office deduction of $1,500.[1]

8700. How does an employer's reimbursement or failure to reimburse an employee's expenses impact a taxpayer's business expense deductions?

The tax treatment of an employee's business expenses depends on whether the employee is reimbursed for them by the employer. The IRC provides that expenses paid or incurred by the taxpayer, in connection with the performance of services as an employee, under a reimbursement or other expense allowance arrangement with the employer are deductible in full from gross income, to arrive at adjusted gross income, so long as the expenses otherwise qualify as business expense deductions.[2] Generally, this deduction will be available only to the extent that the reimbursement is includable in the employee's gross income.[3]

Employers are generally required to report certain employee reimbursements for business expenses on Form W-2. The reporting requirements apply to the following groups:

(1) employers who do not require substantiation (or whose employees fail to substantiate expenses);

(2) employers who advance amounts for expenses and do not require the return of (or do not receive) unused amounts; and

(3) employers who reimburse a per diem or other fixed amount that exceeds government specified rates.

The rules, thus, generally apply only to reimbursements for unsubstantiated expenses and unreturned excess amounts.[4]

It is not uncommon for an employee to incur expenses in connection with work that are not reimbursed by the employer. Examples include an employee's use of his own automobile or subscriptions to work-related professional journals. In general, the same business expenses that are deductible by a self-employed person are deductible if incurred by an employee, but in the case of an employee, the deduction is allowable only as an itemized deduction. As such, it is treated as a so-called "miscellaneous itemized deduction."[5]

Miscellaneous itemized deductions are allowed only to the extent that the aggregate of such deductions exceeds 2 percent of the taxpayer's adjusted gross income.[6]

An employee cannot choose to forego reimbursement for a business expense for which his employer would pay and claim a deduction. "[A] business expense deduction is not allowable to an employee to the extent that the employee is entitled to reimbursement from the employer for an expenditure related to his status as an employee."[7]

1. Rev. Proc. 2013-13, 2013-6 IRB 478.
2. IRC Sec. 62(a)(2).
3. IRC Sec. 62(c), Treas. Reg. §§1.162-17(b)(2), 1.162-17(c).
4. Treas. Reg. §1.62-2.
5. Treas. Reg. §1.67-1T(a)(1)(i).
6. IRC Sec. 67.
7. *Lucas v. Comm.*, 79 TC 1 (1982).

PART IX: BAD DEBT AND WORTHLESS SECURITIES

8701. When can a taxpayer deduct losses sustained as a result of a bad debt? What is the difference between a business bad debt and a nonbusiness bad debt?

A bad debt is a specific obligation which can be deemed with reasonable certainty to have become totally or partially worthless. If this is the case, the creditor-taxpayer may be entitled to a deduction corresponding to the amount of the worthless debt.[1]

There are two kinds of bad debt deductions: (1) business bad debts and (2) nonbusiness bad debts. A business bad debt, as the name suggests, is a debt that is incurred in the conduct of the taxpayer's trade or business. A nonbusiness bad debt is defined, by exclusion, in IRC Section 166(d)(2) as a bad debt *other than* a debt (a) created in the conduct of the taxpayer's business[2] or (b) the loss from the worthlessness of which was incurred in the conduct of the taxpayer's trade or business.[3] The second exclusionary rule allows a taxpayer who was not the original creditor to claim a worthless debt that he acquired in the conduct of his business.

The classification as either a business or nonbusiness bad debt is important because only a business bad debt can be treated as a deduction from ordinary income, while nonbusiness bad debts receive a capital loss treatment.[4] Further, a taxpayer can claim a deduction for wholly or partially worthless business bad debts, while nonbusiness bad debts must be completely worthless for the deduction to be allowed (see Q 8704).[5]

Whether a debt is incurred in relation to a taxpayer's trade or business, so as to be classified as a business bad debt, is a question of fact.[6] In making the determination, it is important to note that a taxpayer is not restricted to one type of business and that there is no requirement that the loss be incurred in conducting the business in which the taxpayer spends the majority of taxpayer's time.[7]

A deduction for a loss sustained as the result of a bad debt will only be permitted in cases where both a valid debt and a true debtor-creditor relationship exist (see Q 8702). Whether a valid debt or a true debtor-creditor relationship exists is also a question of fact.[8]

A bad debt deduction will not be allowed in a situation where the debt is secured by collateral and the creditor has foreclosed on the collateral due to nonpayment.[9]

1. Treas. Reg. §1.166-1.
2. IRC Sec. 166(d)(2)(A); Treas. Reg. §1.166-5(b)(1).
3. IRC Sec. 166(d)(2)(B); Treas. Reg. §1.166-5(b)(2).
4. IRC Sec. 166(a) and (d).
5. IRC Sec. 166(d)(1).
6. *Commissioner v Smith*, 203 F.2d 310 (1953); *Nicholson v Commissioner*, 218 F.2d 240 (1954).
7. *Gliptis v United States*, 120 F. Supp. 3 (1954).
8. *Leuthold v. Commissioner*, 54 TCM 1308 (1987); *Lane v. United States*, 83-2 USTC 9524 (1983).
9. *Rose v Commissioner*, TC Memo 1987-19.

Bad debts of corporations, except for S corporations, are always classified as business bad debts.[1] An S corporation is required to separately state its nonbusiness bad debt, which is taxed under the rules applicable to short-term capital losses (see Q 8595).[2]

A discharge of one's obligation as a guarantor is considered a nonbusiness bad debt. The loss sustained by a guarantor unable to recover from the debtor is by its very nature a loss from a bad debt to which the guarantor becomes subrogated upon discharging his liability as guarantor.[3]

If the debt fails to qualify as a business bad debt, it can, in many cases, be treated as a nonbusiness bad debt.[4] If the *taxpayer fails to establish that a debt qualifies as a business bad debt under IRC Section* 166, he must be satisfied with treatment as a nonbusiness bad debt under that same section and may not look to IRC Section 165 (see Q 8706) for an alternative means of treating loss on the debt as an ordinary loss deduction.[5]

8702. When is a taxpayer entitled to claim a bad debt deduction?

A taxpayer may claim a bad debt deduction (whether it is a business bad debt or a nonbusiness bad debt, see Q 8701) for debt owed when the debt is a bona fide debt that has become worthless.[6]

A "bona fide debt" is one that arises from a debtor-creditor relationship involving a valid and enforceable agreement to pay a specific sum of money.[7] An agreement is considered to be a valid and enforceable agreement if it includes an unconditional promise by a debtor to pay the creditor.[8]

A taxpayer's voluntary undertaking to pay another debtor's obligations does not give rise to a valid and enforceable agreement for this purpose. Despite this, if the taxpayer volunteers to pay another person's obligation for a business purpose, and that debt subsequently becomes worthless, the taxpayer may be entitled to deduct the amount of the loss as a business expense under IRC Section 162.[9]

A bad debt can arise under a contractual agreement to pay a specific sum of money[10] or under an obligation created by law.[11] The requirements for determining whether a bad debt exists must be strictly met in order for the taxpayer to be entitled to claim the deduction.[12]

1. IRS Publication 535.
2. See Rev. Rul. 93-36, 1993-1 CB 187; Treas. Reg. §301.7701-2.
3. *Putnam v Commissioner*, 352 U.S. 82 (1956).
4. See *Krasnow v United States*, 508 F. Supp. 1099 (1981).
5. *Alsobrook v. United States*, 431 F. Supp. 1122 (E.D. Ark.), aff'd 566 F. 2d 628 (6th Circuit 1977).
6. *Anderson v. Commissioner*, 5 TC 482 (1945), aff'd, 156 F.2d 591 (1946).
7. Treas. Reg. §1.166-1(c). See, also, *Kavanaugh v. United States*, 575 F. Supp. 41 (1983); *Hynard v. IRS*, 233 F. Supp.2d 502 (2002); *Schneider v. Commissioner*, 42 TCM 1449 (1981); *Edgar v. Commissioner*, 39 TCM 816 (1979); *Fryer v. Commissioner*, 33 TCM 403 (1974); *Holman v. Commissioner*, 32 TCM 1323 (1973).
8. *Wortham Mach. v. United States*, 521 F.2d 160 (1975).
9. *Lutz v. Commissioner*, 282 F.2d 614 (1960).
10. *Community Research and Dev. Corp. v. Commissioner*, TC Memo 1979-264.
11. See Rev. Rul. 72-505, 1972-2 CB 102, Rev. Rul. 69-458 1969-2 CB 33.
12. *Robinson-Davis Lumber Co. v Crooks*, 50 F.2d 638 (1931).

Since it must be determined with reasonable certainty that the bad debt has become worthless, a bad debt deduction is typically not permitted if the creditor voluntarily forgives the debt.

A legal action is not required to establish that a debt is worthless or unrecoverable. Where the surrounding circumstances indicate that a debt is worthless and uncollectible and that legal action would in all probability not result in payment, a showing of these facts and circumstances will be sufficient evidence of the worthlessness of the debt.[1]

In determining whether a debt is worthless in whole or in part the IRS will consider all pertinent evidence, including the value of the collateral, if any, securing the debt and the financial condition of the debtor.[2]

A taxpayer must make a reasonable inquiry, however, to ascertain whether the debt can be collected before claiming the bad debt deduction.[3]

Planning Point: The parameters of what constitutes a "reasonable inquiry" into the collectability of a debt have certainly changed since the1938 court decision establishing that a "reasonable inference from information thus obtainable" satisfies the requirement. In today's digital age, apparently no less than a comprehensive credit check of the debtor and an assessment of economic conditions affecting the debtor's industry would likely suffice.

A bad debt deduction is claimed for the tax year in which the taxpayer determines that the debt is worthless, not in the year that the debt actually became worthless.[4] For example, if a debtor stopped making payments in 2017, but it was not until 2018 that the creditor-taxpayer determined that there was no reasonable chance that the debt would be paid, the bad debt deduction is properly claimed in 2018. A debtor's declaration of bankruptcy is generally treated as an indication that the debt has become at least partially worthless if the debt is unsecured and not a preferred debt.[5]

If a taxpayer finds that a debt is worthless, but later discovers that he may be able to recover all or a portion of the debt, the bad debt deduction is not invalidated.[6] Despite this, if a taxpayer has claimed a bad debt deduction, and subsequently finds that some amounts of the debt can be collected, the taxpayer is required to report any amounts collected on the debt as income.[7]

IRC Section 166(b) provides that the allowable deduction cannot exceed the creditor's basis in the debt as provided under Treasury Regulation Section 1.1011-1 (which outlines the rules for determining adjusted basis for purposes of calculating gain or loss). Though a taxpayer's basis in a debt may be equal to the face value of the debt, this is not always the case.

1. Treas. Reg. §1.166-2(b).
2. Treas. Reg. §1.166-2(a).
3. See *Freeman-Dent-Sullivan Co. v United States*, 21 F. Supp. 972 (1938).
4. See *Courier Journal Job Printing Co. v Glenn*, 37 F. Supp. 55 (1941).
5. Treas. Reg. §1.166-2(c).
6. See *Hamlen v Welch*, 116 F.2d 413 (1940).
7. Treas. Reg. §1.166-1(f).

The regulations identify certain situations where the deduction will not equal the face value of the debt (for instance, the deduction for worthless receivables is based on the price paid by the purchaser of the receivables and not on their face value).[1]

8703. What accounting methods are available for a taxpayer to use in accounting for bad debts?

The Tax Reform Act of 1986 repealed the reserve method of accounting for most taxpayers.[2] As a result, all taxpayers, except for certain financial institutions, must use the specific charge-off method in accounting for bad debts. Financial institutions may still be permitted to use the reserve method in accounting for bad debts.

Under the specific charge-off method, the taxpayer deducts amounts that were charged off on its books during the tax year in question. To "charge-off" an item, a taxpayer can use any method that shows the intent to remove the debt as an asset.[3] The taxpayer must be the creditor both at the time that the worthlessness was determined *and* at the time the debt was charged-off[4] (to allow otherwise would permit the taxpayer to claim a deduction for a loss that he did not own).

A debt that is "significantly modified" is deemed charged off.[5] A *modification* means any alteration of the legal rights or obligations of a lender or borrower, whether the alteration is evidenced by an express agreement (oral or written), conduct of the parties, or otherwise. A modification includes any total or partial deletion from, or addition to, such rights or obligations, but excludes an alteration that occurs by operation of the terms of a debt instrument (i.e., the annual resetting of an interest rate). As a general rule, a modification is a significant modification only if, based on all facts and circumstances, the legal rights or obligations that are altered and the degree to which they are altered are economically significant.[6] Treasury Regulation Section 1.1001-3(e)-(f) provides rules for determining when specific modifications are significant.[7]

The taxpayer must file a statement of facts substantiating the deduction along with the tax return containing the claim for the bad debt deduction.[8]

Financial institutions are also entitled to use the reserve method to account for losses resulting from bad debts. Instead of deducting specific bad debts from gross income, a financial institution can choose to deduct a reasonable amount as a reserve for bad debts. An account must be maintained for the bad debt reserves.[9] The reasonableness of the amount claimed is a question of fact. Factors that are often considered in making the reasonableness determination

1. Treas. Reg. §1.166- 1(d)(2)(i)(b).
2. P.L. 99-514, §805(a).
3. *Rubinkam v Commissioner*, 118 F.2d 148 (1941).
4. *Wachovia Bank & Trust Co. v United States*, 288 F.2d 750 (1961).
5. Treas. Reg. §§1.166- 3(3) and 1.1001-3 (definition of significantly modified debt).
6. Treas. Reg. 1.1001-3(e)(1).
7. Treas. Reg. §1.1001-3(c).
8. Treas. Reg. §1.166- 1(b).
9. Treas. Reg. §1.166- 4.

include the type of business involved and the amount of the bad debt.[1] What is reasonable in one business can vary from that which is reasonable for another business or in a different geographical area.

In using the reserve method, the taxpayer must file a statement of facts in support of the claim for the bad debt deduction. The statement must contain the following information:

(1) the amount of charge sales or other business transactions for the year and the percentage of the reserve from these sales;

(2) the total amount of the business' notes and accounts receivable at both the beginning and at the end of the tax year;

(3) the amount of debts that has become wholly or partially worthless and the amounts charged against the reserve account; and

(4) how the additional amount to the reserve account was determined.[2]

Special rules apply to certain banks claiming bad debt deductions.[3]

If a claim for a bad debt deduction is disallowed during one tax year, but subsequently the debt actually does become worthless, the taxpayer has seven years to file a claim for refund for the year that the debt actually became worthless.[4] This extension applies both to losses claimed under the specific charge-off method and under the reserve method[5]. This extended period does *not* apply to partially worthless debt (see Q 8704).[6]

8704. Is a bad debt deduction permitted when a debt is only partially worthless?

Certain taxpayers are entitled to claim a deduction for business bad debts that become only partially worthless during the tax year.[7] The allowable deduction cannot exceed the amount of the debt charged-off (see Q 8703) during the tax year.[8] The taxpayer must be able to clearly show the portion of the debt that has become partially worthless and must also show that the entire debt did not become worthless during the taxable year.

Despite this, a taxpayer is not *required* to charge-off and deduct partially worthless debts each year. Taxpayers are permitted to delay the bad debt deduction until the year in which the debt has become completely worthless.

Planning Point: Though a taxpayer is not required to claim a bad debt deduction in years when the debt is only partially worthless, the taxpayer is not permitted to claim the deduction for tax years beginning after the year in which the debt becomes *completely* worthless.[9]

1. Treas. Reg. §1.166- 4(b).
2. Treas. Reg. §1.166- 4(c).
3. Treas. Reg. §1.166- 4(d), See Treas. Reg. §§1.585-1 through 1.585-3.
4. IRC Sec. 6511(d)(1).
5. *Smith Elec. Co. v. United States*, 461 F.2d 790 (1972).
6. Treas. Reg. §301.6511(d)-1(c).
7. IRC Sec. 166(a)(2), Treas. Reg. §1.166-3.
8. Treas. Reg. §1.166-3(a)(2)(iii).
9. See IRS Publication 535.

If a taxpayer chooses to claim the deduction for partial worthlessness, the taxpayer's deduction in the year in which the debt becomes completely worthless is limited to the remaining basis in the debt.[1]

Not all taxpayers can claim a bad debt deduction if the debt is only partially worthless. IRC Section 166(d)(1) prohibits taxpayers "other than a corporation" from claiming a deduction for partially worthless *nonbusiness* debts.

If a debtor and a creditor reach a compromise agreement pursuant to which the creditor agrees to accept a lesser amount than what is owed, it is arguable that a partially worthless debt would result. However, the IRS has consistently refused to grant a deduction for partially worthless debts resulting from compromise agreements and the courts have agreed with this position.[2]

8705. Is a bad debt deduction permitted when a loan made between related parties becomes worthless?

A bad debt deduction may still be allowed in situations where the bad debt results from a loan made between related parties. The analysis of whether a worthless loan made between related parties gives rise to an allowable bad debt deduction is not the same as the analysis undertaken under IRC Section 267, however, which disallows certain losses on sales between related parties.[3]

Intrafamily transactions are subject to rigid scrutiny, and transfers between two spouses are presumed to be gifts. However, this presumption may be rebutted by an affirmative showing that there existed at the time of the transaction a real expectation of repayment and intent to enforce the collection of the indebtedness.[4]

The relevant inquiry in the bad debt context is whether the transaction was a valid loan or was instead a gift made between related parties. In making the determination, the courts examine all of the relevant facts and circumstances of the specific case.[5]

In connection with this facts and circumstances inquiry, it is important that both parties must intend and agree to treat the transaction as a loan, rather than as a disguised gift. Proper documentation of the transaction, while not strictly required, is helpful in proving the parties' intentions.[6] Regardless of whether the loan would have been extended had the parties not been related, the deduction should be sustained if, at the time the loan is made, there is a true intention amongst the parties that the debt will eventually be repaid.[7] See also Treasury Regulation Section 1.262-1(c)(4), which cites the IRC Section 166 bad debt deduction as one deduction that may be allowable despite the personal nature of the transaction.

1. IRC Sec. 166(b) and Treas. Reg. §1.166-3(a)(2)(iii), (b).
2. *Raffold Process Corp. v. Comm.*, 153 F.2d 168 (1946); *Bingham v. Comm.*, 105 F.2d 971 (1939); *Haskel v. Comm.*, TC Memo 1980-243. See *D'Alonzo v. Comm.*, 10 TCM 817 (1951); *Bohn v. Comm.*, 43 BTA 953 (1941).
3. See IRC Sec. 267 (disallowing certain losses on property sales and exchanges between related parties).
4. *Van Anda Est. v. Comm.* (1949), aff'd per curiam, 192 F. 2d 391(2nd Circuit 1951).
5. *Van Anda Est. v. Comm.*, 12 TC 1158, Id., *Mercil v. Comm.*, 24 TC 1150 (1955).
6. *Caligiuri v. Comm.*, 549 F.2d 1155 (8th Cir. 1977), aff'g TC Memo 1975-319. See also *Mellen v. Comm.*, TC Memo 1968-94, and *Cole v. Comm.*, TC Memo 1954-224.
7. *Oatman v. Comm.*, TC Memo 1982-684.

Planning Point: In the context of related-party transactions, it is important to note that the worthless debt will likely be classified as a nonbusiness debt. Completely worthless nonbusiness bad debts can only be claimed as short-term capital losses (see Q 8595).[1]

8706. When is a deduction permitted if a taxpayer owns securities that become worthless?

While IRC Section 166 does not apply to worthless securities,[2] IRC Section 165 allows a deduction for losses incurred based on ownership of securities that have become completely worthless during the year. The term "security" for purposes of IRC Section 165 includes shares of stock, stock rights or evidence of indebtedness issued by a corporation or a government.[3] The worthlessness of the security is a question of fact[4] and the loss will be disallowed unless the taxpayer is able to furnish proof of the original cost of the security.[5]

There are no fixed rules that apply when determining whether a security is completely worthless. The taxpayer is required to make a reasonable inquiry, and what is reasonable here is based on the inquiry that a reasonable person would make in order to determine the worthlessness of the securities.[6] Worthlessness must be determined objectively.[7]

The securities do not have to be sold to establish worthlessness,[8] but it is insufficient to show that the securities would have no value if sold.[9] Diminution in value is also not enough to establish worthlessness.[10]

Worthless securities also include securities that the taxpayer abandons after March 12, 2008. To abandon a security, all rights in the security must be permanently surrendered and relinquished and no consideration received in exchange for the security. All the facts and circumstances determine whether the transaction is properly characterized as an abandonment or other type of transaction, such as an actual sale or exchange, contribution to capital, dividend, or gift.[11]

The worthlessness of securities is generally established by a showing that an identifiable event (or series of events)[12] occurred, and that it is reasonably certain the event (or events) rendered the securities completely worthless. An identifiable event has been judicially defined as "… an incident or occurrence that points to or indicates a loss-an evidence of a loss. The evidence, though, may vary according to circumstances and conditions."[13] The Board of Tax Appeals also defined identifiable events as "… such events as would clearly evidence to the person of average

1. See Form 8949, Sales and Other Dispositions of Capital Assets; see also IRS Publication 550.
2. IRC Secs. 166(e), 165(g)(2)(C); Treas. Reg. §1.166-1(g).
3. IRC Sec. 165(g)(2); Treas. Reg. §1.165-5(a).
4. *Coyle v. Comm.*, 142 F.2d 580 (1944); *Superior Coal Co. v. Comm.*, 145 F.2d 597 (1944).
5. *Jankowsky v. Comm.*, 56 F.2d 1006 (1932).
6. *Green v. Comm.*, 133 F.2d 76 (1943).
7. *Beaudry v. Comm.*, 150 F.2d 20 (1945).
8. *De Loss v. Comm.*, 28 F.2d 803 (1928); *Peyser v. United States*, 58 F.Supp. 331 (1944); *Moyer v. Comm.*, 35 BTA 1155 (1937).
9. *Bullard v. United States*, 146 F.2d 386 (1944).
10. *Wyoming Inv. Co. v. Comm.*, 70 F.2d 191 (1934).
11. IRS Pub. 550, Investment Income and Expense (20162016).
12. *Rosing v. Corwin*, 88 F.2d 415 (1937).
13. *Industrial Rayon Corporation v. Comm.*, 94 F.2d 383 (1938).

intelligence, under the circumstances, that no probability of realization of anything of value from this investment, by sale, liquidation, or otherwise, thereafter existed."[1] The identifiable event may be an actual cancellation of the debt or it may be an event the applicable entity is required, solely for purposes of reporting to the IRS, to treat as a cancellation of debt.[2]

8707. Is a loss sustained as a result of worthless securities treated as an ordinary loss or a capital loss?

Generally, securities are classified as capital assets and any loss resulting from their disposal will receive a capital loss treatment.[3] As a capital loss, the loss is considered to have occurred on the last day of the taxable year, which may allow the conversion of a loss that otherwise would have been treated as short-term loss into long-term loss (see Q 8572 and Q 8696 for a discussion of capital loss treatment and the holding period requirement).[4]

Despite this, IRC Section 165(g)(3) allows domestic corporate taxpayers to treat losses sustained on worthless securities as ordinary losses if an affiliated corporation issued the securities. An "affiliated corporation" is one that meets the following ownership test:

(1) the corporate taxpayer owns at least 80 percent of the voting stock and value of the corporation;[5] and

(2) more than 90 percent of the affiliated corporation's aggregate gross receipts for all taxable years has been derived from sources other than royalties, rents, dividends, interest, annuities, and gains from sales or exchanges of stock and securities.

If the taxpayer is a bank which directly owns at least 80 percent of the stock of another bank, the stock will not be treated as a capital asset. Hence, any loss incurred on disposition of these stocks will be treated as ordinary loss.[6]

See Q 8708 for the special treatment of losses sustained upon the sale of certain small business stock.

8708. What special rules apply to the deductibility of losses incurred on small business stock?

Generally, shareholders will realize either a capital gain or loss upon the sale or disposition of stock (see Q 8707). However, the taxpayer treats the loss as an ordinary loss if it results from the disposition of certain small business stock under IRC Section 1244.[7] The loss could either arise from the sale of the small business stock, or from a determination that the stock is worthless. This ordinary loss treatment is applicable for both common and preferred stock.

1. *John H. Watson, Jr.*, 38 BTA 1026 (1938).
2. IRS Pub. 4681, Canceled Debts, Foreclosures, Repossessions, and Abandonments (20162016).
3. IRC Sec. 165(g).
4. Treas. Reg. §1.165-5(c).
5. IRC Sec. 1504(a)(2).
6. See IRC Secs. 165(m)(1) and 582(b).
7. Treas. Reg. §1.1244(a)-1.

Even though an individual may be entitled to ordinary loss treatment upon the sale of Section 1244 stock, the section does not apply to gains. Therefore, if a taxpayer realizes *gain* on the sale of Section 1244 stock, the gain is treated as a capital gain.

In a taxable year, the maximum amount of ordinary loss that can be claimed by a taxpayer under these provisions is $50,000 (or $100,000 for a married couple filing a joint tax return).[1] Any excess is treated as capital loss (see Q 8580 for a detailed explanation of the treatment of capital losses).

Stock in a domestic corporation is considered Section 1244 stock if the following requirements are met:[2]

(1) at the time the stock is issued, the corporation was a small business corporation (defined below);

(2) the stock was issued by the corporation in exchange for money or other property (excluding other stock and securities); and

(3) the corporation, during its five most recent tax years ending before the date the loss was sustained, derived more than 50 percent of its aggregate gross receipts from sources other than royalties, rents, dividends, interest, annuities, and sales or exchanges of stock or securities.[3]

A corporation qualifies as a small business corporation if the amount received by the corporation for stock does not exceed $1 million.[4]

Ordinary loss treatment is permissible if (1) the taxpayer was the shareholder to whom the stock of the small business corporation was issued and (2) the taxpayers are individual taxpayers who are partners in a partnership at the time the partnership acquired stocks in a small business corporation.[5]

Corporations (including S Corporations), trusts, and estates are not entitled to ordinary loss treatment under Section 1244 regardless of how the stock was acquired.[6] Individual taxpayers, other than the original holders of the stock, are also not entitled to ordinary loss treatment under Section 1244.[7] Stock is considered to have been issued once it has been fully paid for by the shareholder whether or not a certificate is prepared and delivered to the stockholder.[8]

Small business corporations should maintain adequate records to support any shareholder claims for ordinary loss treatment. The records should be sufficient to show:[9]

1. IRC Secs. 1244(b), 6013.
2. IRC Sec. 1244(c)(1); Treas. Reg. §1.1244(c)-1.
3. See *Snedeker v. Comm.*, TC Memo 1983-675.
4. IRC Sec. 1244(c)(3); Treas. Reg. §1.1244(c)-2.
5. Treas. Reg. §1.1244(a)-1(b).
6. See *Rath v. Comm.*, 101 TC 196 (1993).
7. *Rath v. Comm.*, above.
8. *Oppenheim v. Comm.*, TC Memo 1973-12; *Wesley H. Morgan*, 46 TC 878 (1966).
9. Treas. Reg. §1.1244(e)-1(a)(2).

(1) the persons to whom stock was issued, the date of issuance to these persons, and a description of the amount and type of consideration received from each;

(2) If the consideration received is property, the basis in the hands of the shareholder and the fair market value of the property when received by the corporation;

(3) The amount of money and the basis in the hands of the corporation of other property received for its stock, as a contribution to capital, and as paid-in surplus;

(4) Financial statements of the corporation, such as its income tax returns, that identify the source of the gross receipts of the corporation for the period consisting of the five most recent taxable years of the corporation, or, if the corporation has not been in existence for five taxable years, for the period of the corporation's existence; and

(5) Information relating to any tax-free stock dividend made with respect to Section 1244 stock and any reorganization in which stock is transferred by the corporation in exchange for Section 1244 stock.

In addition, a person who owns Section 1244 stock in a corporation must maintain records sufficient to distinguish such stock from any other stock he or she may own in the corporation.[1]

1. Treas. Reg. §1244(e)-1(b).

PART X: BUSINESS LIFE INSURANCE

8709. What is business life insurance?

As the name suggests, business life insurance is life insurance that is owned by a business, regardless of whether the business is organized as a sole proprietorship, partnership, or corporation. The insurance can serve a number of different purposes.

For example, business life insurance is often used to insure the life of a key employee, in order to mitigate the negative impact that the employee's death would have on the business. Business life insurance is also commonly used in the context of a buy-sell agreement, where the business is obligated to purchase the ownership interest of an owner who dies. The insurance also could be used to fund a non-qualified retirement package for a single employee or a number of employees.

8710. What is the income tax treatment to the insured of the premiums paid on business life insurance?

If the life insurance policy at issue is purchased for the benefit of the business and the insured has no ownership interest in the policy, the premiums generally are not taxable to the insured. Thus, premiums paid on key person life insurance, where an employer is both owner and beneficiary of the policy, are not taxable to the insured employee.[1]

If life insurance premiums are paid by an employer on a policy insuring the life of an employee and the proceeds are payable to the employee's beneficiary, some taxable income to the employee generally results.

8711. What rules govern the deductibility of payment of the premiums on business life insurance?

Life insurance premiums generally are not deductible if the premium payer has any interest in the policy or proceeds.

Under IRC Section 264(a)(1), no deduction is allowed for premiums paid on any life insurance policy, or endowment or annuity contract, if the taxpayer is directly or indirectly a beneficiary under the policy or contract. Where Section 264(a)(1) applies, the premiums are not deductible even though they otherwise would be deductible as ordinary and necessary business expenses.[2]

The rule under Section 264(a)(1) is an all or nothing rule, meaning that the entire premium will be nondeductible even though a premium payer has a right to receive only a portion of the proceeds. The deduction cannot be divided, and will either be allowed or disallowed in its entirety.[3] The rule under Section 264(a)(1) applies regardless of the form of insurance, so it makes no difference whether premiums are paid on term, ordinary life, or endowment policies.

1. *Casale v. Comm.*, 247 F.2d 440 (2d Cir. 1957); *Lacey v. Comm.*, 41 TC 329 (1963), *acq.* 1964-2 CB 6; Rev. Rul. 59-184, 1959-1 CB 65.
2. Treas. Reg. §1.264-1(a).
3. Rev. Rul. 66-203, 1966-2 CB 104.

Section 264(a)(1) clearly prohibits the deduction for premiums paid where a taxpayer is the premium payer and is also designated as the policy beneficiary. For example, premiums paid on key person insurance, where an employer normally is both owner (and premium payer) and beneficiary of a policy, are nondeductible under IRC Section 264(a)(1).

The deduction is also denied under Section 264(a)(1) where a premium payer is only indirectly a beneficiary under a policy. Thus, the deduction will be denied where a taxpayer, even though not a named beneficiary, has some beneficial interest in a policy, such as the right to change the beneficiary, to make loans, to surrender the policy for cash, or to draw against proceeds held in trust for the insured's spouse.[1]

An employer is permitted to deduct premiums paid on insurance covering the life of an employee if the employer is not directly or indirectly a beneficiary under the policy and the premiums represent additional reasonable compensation for services rendered by the employee. Thus, if an employer has no ownership rights or beneficial interest in a policy and proceeds are payable to an employee's estate or personal beneficiary, the employer may ordinarily deduct the premiums as additional compensation paid to the employee.[2] The deduction will not be denied merely because an employer may derive some indirect benefit, such as from the increased efficiency of the employee.[3]

8712. Can a corporation deduct the premiums it pays on a life insurance policy insuring the life of an employee or stockholder?

Based on the IRC Section 264(a)(1) prohibition, a corporation is not permitted to deduct the premiums it pays on a policy insuring the lives of its employee or stockholder if it either is directly or indirectly a beneficiary under the policy. The deduction is denied even if the corporation has only a partial beneficial interest in a policy.[4]

A corporation cannot deduct premiums it pays on key person insurance or on a policy insuring the life of a stockholder purchased to fund the corporation's redemption of the insured's stock. Normally, in these instances, the corporation is both owner and beneficiary of a policy, so a deduction is not allowed by reason of IRC Section 264(a)(1). If the policy proceeds are to be used to pay for stock that is to be surrendered to the corporation, that corporation cannot deduct the premiums even though it may have no right to the cash value of a policy and no right to name or change the beneficiary. In this case, the deduction is not allowed because the premium payments are treated as capital expenditures, rather than ordinary and necessary business expenses, because they are payments for the acquisition of a corporate asset: treasury stock.[5]

---

1. Rev. Rul. 70-148, 1970-1 CB 60; Rev. Rul. 66-203, supra.
2. IRC Sec. 162(a); Treas. Reg. §1.162-7.
3. Treas. Reg. §1.264-1(b).
4. *National Indus. Investors, Inc. v. Comm.*, TC Memo 1996-151.
5. Rev. Rul. 70-117, 1970-1 CB 30; Rev. Rul. 74-503, 1974-2 CB 117.

Conversely, if a corporation purchases life insurance for an employee and the corporation has no ownership rights or beneficial interest in the policy, premiums are ordinarily deductible as additional compensation for the employee's services.[1]

To be deductible, however, the premium payments must represent *reasonable* compensation.[2] The question of whether compensation is reasonable often arises in the case of a stockholder-employee of a closely-held corporation. If the total amount paid to and on behalf of a stockholder-employee is found to represent an unreasonable return for services, the IRS may treat the premium payments as a distribution of profits or dividends rather than as compensation. This also may be the result where the corporation has kept insufficient records so that there is no evidence, such as board of directors' minutes, to show that premium payments were intended as compensation.[3]

If the surrounding circumstances are sufficient to show that the premiums were not paid as compensation, the deduction will be disallowed. In *Atlas Heating & Ventilating Co. v. Comm.*,[4] for example, evidence showed that premiums actually were paid to fund a stock purchase agreement between individual stockholders. Consequently, the premiums were not compensation, but dividends. The policies were owned by the stockholder-employees and proceeds were payable to their personal beneficiaries. The insured individuals had agreed that, on each of their deaths, an amount of stock equal to the proceeds received by the deceased insured's beneficiaries would be turned in to the corporation and then distributed pro rata to the surviving stockholders.

For a discussion of the treatment of premiums paid by an S corporation on behalf of its shareholders or employees, see Q 8717.

8713. When a corporation owns a life insurance policy insuring the life of a key employee, are the premiums paid by the corporation taxable to the key employee?

No.[5] In *Casale v. Comm.*, the insured was president of the corporation and owned 98 percent of its stock. The corporation was both owner and beneficiary of a retirement income contract on the insured's life, which the corporation had purchased to hedge its obligation to the insured under a deferred compensation agreement. The Tax Court required the insured to include premiums paid by the corporation in his income. The Second Circuit reversed the Tax Court opinion, however, on the grounds that the corporation's separate entity could not be ignored and that the insured had received no current economic benefit that would constitute taxable income.

However, see *Goldsmith v. U.S.*, where the taxpayer, an independent contractor, was required to include the death and disability insurance features of a deferred compensation agreement in

1. IRC Sec. 162(a).
2. Treas. Reg. §1.162-7.
3. *Boecking v. Comm.*, TC Memo 1993-497; *Est. of Worster v. Comm.*, TC Memo 1984-123; *Champion Trophy Mfg. Corp. v. Comm.*, TC Memo 1972-250.
4. 18 BTA 389 (1929).
5. *Casale v. Comm.*, 247 F.2d 440 (2d Cir. 1957); Rev. Rul. 59-184, 1959-1 CB 65.

his income based on the court's finding that (a) those features conferred a current economic benefit on the taxpayer and (b) the current economic benefit of the insurance components were capable of valuation.[1]

The IRS, however, has agreed to follow the Second Circuit's decision as precedent in dealing with similar cases.[2]

8714. Are premiums paid by a corporation on life insurance to fund a stock redemption agreement taxable to an insured stockholder?

No. Even if the stockholder has the right to designate the policy beneficiary, the premiums are not income to the stockholder, provided that the beneficiary's right to receive the proceeds is conditioned on the transfer of stock to the corporation.[3]

Similarly, premiums are not taxable income to an insured stockholder when a trustee is named beneficiary, provided that the trustee is obligated to use the proceeds to purchase the insured's stock for transfer to the corporation.[4]

8715. Are life insurance premiums paid by an employer taxable income to an insured employee if the proceeds are payable to the employee's estate or personal beneficiary and the policy is owned by the employee?

Yes.[5] However, if dividends are applied to reduce current premiums, only the net premium must be included in the employee's taxable income.[6]

The premium payments are generally treated as additional compensation paid to the employee and are, therefore, deductible by the employer. However, if the employer is a closely-held corporation and the employee a stockholder, the IRS may challenge the arrangement on the grounds that the premiums are disguised dividends taxable to the insured, but not deductible by the corporation (see Q 8711).

Even where an insured employee and owner of the corporation was not the owner of the policy, but the employee's child or spouse was owner and beneficiary, payment of premiums on the policy was found to confer an economic benefit to the employee and, as such, was includable in the employee's gross income.[7]

Where a stockholder-employee argued that premiums paid by the corporation on the employee's personal insurance were merely loans, the premiums were treated as taxable dividends. This will be the result unless the employee can produce evidence to show that the employee intended to reimburse the corporation for the premium payments.[8]

1. 41 AFTR 2d 978 (Ct. Cl. 1978).
2. Rev. Rul. 59-184, supra. See also: *U.S. v. Leuschner*, 11 AFTR 2d 782 (S.D. Cal. 1962); *Lacey v. Comm.*, 41 TC 329 (1963), *acq.*, 1964-2 CB 6.
3. *Sanders v. Fox*, 253 F.2d 855 (10th Cir. 1958); *Prunier v. Comm.*, 248 F.2d 818 (1st Cir. 1957); Rev. Rul. 59-184, 1959-1 CB 65.
4. Rev. Rul. 70-117, 1970-1 CB 30.
5. Treas. Reg. §1.61-2(d)(2)(ii)(A); *Canaday v. Guitteau*, 86 F.2d 303 (6th Cir. 1936); *Yuengling v. Comm.*, 69 F.2d 971 (3rd Cir. 1934).
6. *Weeks v. Comm.*, 16 TC 248 (1951); *Sturgis v. Comm.*, TC Memo 1951, 10 TCM (CCH) 136.
7. *Brock v. Comm.*, TC Memo 1982-335; *Champion Trophy Mfg. Corp. v. Comm.*, TC Memo 1972-250; see IRC Sec. 301(c).
8. *Schwartz v. Comm.*, TC Memo 1963-340; *Jameson v. Comm.*, TC Memo 1942.

8716. Are life insurance premiums paid by an employer taxable income to an insured employee if the proceeds are payable to the employee's estate or personal beneficiary and the corporation owns the policy?

The tax results of an arrangement whereby an employer pays the premiums on a policy insuring the life of an employee are uncertain when the corporation owns the policy, unless the insured is a stockholder and the insurance is to be used to fund an agreement for the purchase of the insured's stock. The regulations provide: "Generally, life insurance premiums paid by an employer on the life of his employee where the proceeds of such insurance are payable to the beneficiary of such employee are part of the gross income of the employee."[1] This suggests that the entire premium is taxable to the employee.

However, the final regulations associated with the taxation of split dollar life insurance arrangements indicate that where (1) an employer pays all or any portion of the premiums on a life insurance contract insuring the employee and (2) the beneficiary of all or a portion of the death benefit is designated by the employee or is any person whom the employee would reasonably be expected to designate as the beneficiary, the employee must include the amount of the "economic benefit" associated with the life insurance coverage provided in the employee's income.[2] This economic benefit generally will be the cost of current life insurance provided to the employee as calculated using Table 2001 rates or using a carrier's alternative term rates.[3] The split dollar regulations are effective for split dollar arrangements entered into (or contracts that are materially modified) after September 17, 2003.[4]

8717. How are life insurance policy premiums paid by an S corporation to insure a shareholder or employee taxed?

An S corporation generally does not pay taxes at the entity level. Instead, items of income, deduction, loss, and credit are passed through to shareholders and taxes are calculated at the individual level. Payment of premiums by an S corporation should be characterized as a nondeductible expense, as deductible compensation, or as a nondeductible distribution of profits under the same general rules applicable to regular (C) corporations. However, the resulting tax treatment of the shareholders would differ in some instances.

If the premium payment is treated as a nondeductible expense, as it would be if a corporation were both owner and beneficiary of a key person policy, shareholders will be required to reduce the basis in their shares by their proportionate portion of the nondeductible expense.[5]

If particular premium payments are treated as employee compensation, such as in a case where an employee owns a policy or has a beneficial interest in it, the amount of compensation would be deductible in determining the S corporation's income or loss that is reported pro

1. Treas. Reg. §1.61-2(d)(2)(ii)(A).
2. Treas. Reg. §§1.61-22(b)(2)(ii); 1.61-22(d).
3. Treas. Reg. §1.61-22(d)(2)(i); Notice 2002-8, 2002-1 CB 398.
4. Treas. Reg. §1.61-22(j).
5. IRC Sec. 1367(a)(2)(D).

rata by each shareholder. The amount of compensation then must be included in income by the insured employee.[1]

When a premium payment is found to be a distribution with respect to stock to an individual shareholder, the tax treatment depends on whether the corporation has accumulated earnings and profits. If a corporation has no accumulated earnings and profits, the payment is treated first as a return of investment and then as capital gain. If a corporation has accumulated earnings and profits, part of the distribution might be treated as a dividend.[2] For example, an S corporation may have accumulated earnings and profits from years when it was a C corporation or as the result of a corporate acquisition.

The IRS has provided guidance on the effects of premiums paid by an S corporation on an employer-owned life insurance (EOLI) contract (see Q 8723) and the benefits received by reason of death of the insured on its accumulated adjustments account (AAA) under IRC Section 1368. The IRS ruled that premiums paid by an S corporation on an EOLI contract when the S corporation is directly or indirectly a beneficiary do not reduce the S corporation's AAA. Further, it ruled that benefits received by reason of the death of the insured from an EOLI contract that meets an exception under IRC Section 101(j)(2) do not increase the S corporation's AAA.[3]

8718. Are life insurance policy premiums deductible if paid by a partnership or an individual partner on the life of a copartner?

No. This is true regardless of who is named as policy beneficiary. Premiums paid for any life insurance, or endowment or annuity contract, are not deductible if a taxpayer is directly or indirectly a beneficiary under the policy or contract.[4] The premium paying partner will derive a benefit from the policy even if the insurance is purchased as a key person policy or to finance the purchase of an insured's partnership interest.[5]

The general rules governing the deductibility of life insurance premiums (see Q 8711) apply in the case of insurance purchased by a partnership on the life of an employee who is not a partner.

8719. Are life insurance premiums paid by a partner for insurance on the partner's own life deductible by the partner if the proceeds are payable to a partnership or to a copartner?

No, because of the general rule that premiums paid on any life insurance policy, or endowment or annuity contract, are not deductible if a taxpayer is directly or indirectly a beneficiary under the policy or contract.[6] When a policy is purchased as key person insurance or to finance the purchase of an insured's partnership interest, the insured's estate and, therefore, the insured, will benefit from the policy.

1. IRC Secs. 1363, 1366.
2. IRC Sec. 1368.
3. Rev. Rul. 2008-42, 2008-30 IRB 175.
4. IRC Sec. 264(a)(1).
5. Treas. Reg. §1.264-1.
6. IRC Sec. 264(a)(1).

Even if a partner takes out insurance on the partner's own life and irrevocably designates a copartner as beneficiary to induce the copartner to leave the copartner's investment in the firm, the insured partner is *indirectly* a beneficiary under the policy, and so the premiums cannot be deducted.[1]

8720. Can a sole proprietor deduct life insurance premiums paid for insurance on the sole proprietor's own life?

No. This is true regardless of who is beneficiary under the policy. In the case of a sole proprietorship, premium payments are treated as nondeductible personal expenses because a sole proprietor and the business are considered one and the same for tax purposes.[2]

The general rules governing the deductibility of life insurance premiums (see Q 8711) apply in the case of insurance purchased by a sole proprietor on the life of an employee.

8721. Can an employee of a sole proprietor deduct life insurance premiums the sole proprietor pays to insure the life of the sole proprietor?

No. The premiums are nondeductible because they either are personal expenses or expenses allocable to tax-exempt income (the death proceeds).[3]

8722. Are death proceeds of business life insurance exempt from income tax? Could receipt of tax-exempt income from insurance proceeds reduce an otherwise tax-deductible capital loss?

The general rules applicable to life insurance contracts also apply in the case of business life insurance. As such, the entire lump sum payable at an insured's death is exempt from regularly calculated income tax regardless of whether the beneficiary is an individual, a corporation, a partnership, a trust, or the insured's estate.[4]

See Q 8723 for rules pertaining to employer-owned life insurance contracts issued after August 17, 2006.

A portion of the death proceeds may be taxable if the proceeds are paid out under a life income or other installment option. In this case, the amount payable at death may be prorated and recovered from the payments in equal tax-free amounts over the payment period, but the interest earned on the proceeds over the distribution period is taxable.

Proceeds received by a partnership or by an S corporation retain their tax-exempt character when passed on to individual partners or shareholders. Proceeds received tax-free by a regular (C) corporation are, when paid out, usually taxable to the recipients as compensation or dividends.

Despite the general rule, there are some circumstances where death proceeds paid out in a lump sum are not wholly tax-exempt. For example, the IRC expressly provides that proceeds

1. Treas. Reg. §1.264-1.
2. IRC Sec. 262(a); Treas. Reg. §1.262-1(b)(1).
3. IRC Secs. 262(a), 265(a)(1); see *Whitaker v. Comm.*, 34 TC 106 (1960).
4. IRC Sec. 101(a); Treas. Reg. §1.101-1(a).

are taxable, under some circumstances, where a policy has previously been sold or otherwise transferred for a valuable consideration (see Q 8724 to Q 8727).

Under Section 101(a), in the case of proceeds payable under qualified pension or profit sharing plans, only the amount in excess of the cash surrender value is tax-exempt. The same rule applies to proceeds received under a tax sheltered annuity and proceeds received under individual retirement endowment contracts.

In some cases, the exemption may not be available because proceeds are not considered to be received as life insurance proceeds. These include proceeds that are taxable as dividends or compensation, proceeds that are taxable because of lack of insurable interest, proceeds taxable as a return of embezzled funds, and proceeds of creditor insurance.

Where liquidation of a business after a partner's death resulted in a loss, but life insurance on that partner had been purchased by the other partner for the purpose of protecting his capital investment in the business, the court ruled that because the loss was compensated for by insurance, it was not deductible. IRC Section 165(a) provides that "[t]here shall be allowed as a deduction any loss sustained during the taxable year *and not compensated for by insurance or otherwise*" (emphasis added).[1]

8723. For employer-owned life insurance contracts issued after August 17, 2006, are there any special requirements that must be met in order for the proceeds to be exempt from income tax?

An employer-owned life insurance contract is defined as a life insurance contract owned by a person or entity engaged in a trade or business under which that person or entity, or certain related persons, is a beneficiary under the contract, if the contract covers the life of an insured who is an employee when the contract is issued.[2] For life insurance contracts entered into after August 17, 2006, certain requirements must be met for death proceeds of an employer-owned life insurance contract to be received income-tax free.

First, before an employer-owned life insurance contract is issued, the employer must meet the following notice and consent requirements:

(1) The employer must notify the insured employee in writing that the employer intends to insure the employee's life;

(2) The employer must provide notice of the maximum face amount the employee's life could be insured for at the time the contract is issued;

(3) The employer must state that the policy owner will be the beneficiary of the death proceeds of the policy; and

(4) The insured also must give written consent to be the insured under the contract and consent to coverage continuing after the insured terminates employment.[3]

1. *Johnson v. Comm.*, 66 TC 897 (1976), *aff'd*, 78-1 USTC ¶9367 (4th Cir. 1978).
2. IRC Sec. 101(j)(3)(A).
3. IRC Sec. 101(j)(4).

Another set of requirements relates to an insured's status with an employer. The insured must have been (i) an employee at any time during the twelve month period before his or her death, or (ii) a director or highly compensated employee at the time the contract was issued. A "highly compensated employee" is one who is classified as highly compensated under the qualified plan rules of IRC Section 414(q) (except for the election regarding the top paid group), or under rules regarding self-insured medical expense reimbursement plans of IRC Section 105(h), except that the highest paid 35 percent instead of 25 percent will be considered highly compensated.[1]

In the alternative, death proceeds of employer-owned life insurance will not be included in an employer's income, assuming the notice and consent requirements are met, if the proceeds are paid to any of the following:

(1) A member of an insured's family, defined as a sibling, spouse, ancestor, or lineal descendent;

(2) Any individual who is the designated beneficiary of the insured under the contract (other than the policy owner);

(3) A trust that benefits a member of the family or designated beneficiary; or

(4) The estate of the insured.

Additionally, the proceeds will not be included in an employer's income if death proceeds are used to purchase an equity interest from a family member, beneficiary, trust, or estate.[2] The Pension Protection Act of 2006 ("PPA 2006") also imposes new reporting requirements on all employers owning one or more employer-owned life insurance contracts. Final reporting regulations were issued in November 2008.[3]

Further, the IRS released Notice 2009-48, which provides guidance on certain issues that may arise when dealing with employer-owned life insurance contracts with respect to IRC Section 101(j)'s notice and consent requirements and IRC Section 6039I's information reporting requirements. The guidance, which is presented in a question-and-answer format, is effective June 15, 2009, but the IRS has announced that it will not challenge a taxpayer who made a good faith effort to comply with IRC Section 101(j) based on a reasonable "interpretation of the provision before that date."

Reporting Requirements

All employers who own one or more life insurance contracts on the life of any employee that are considered employer-owned contracts under IRC 101(j) must file with the IRS an informational return, which includes the following information:

(1) The number of employees of the "applicable policy holder" (e.g. the employer) at the end of the year;

1. IRC Sec. 101(j)(2)(A).
2. IRC Sec. 101(j)(2)(B).
3. IRC Sec. 6039I; Treas. Reg. §1.6093I-1.

(2) The number of employees insured by employer-owned contracts at the end of the year;

(3) The total amount of insurance in force at the end of the year under such contracts,

(4) The name, address, and taxpayer ID number for the applicable policyholder and the type of business in which the policyholder is engaged; and

(5) That the applicable policyholder has a valid consent for each insured employee (or, if all such consents are not obtained, the number of insured employees for whom such consent was not obtained).[1]

These reporting requirements became effective for tax years ending after November 6, 2008. To comply with the reporting requirements, the applicable policyholder must provide the requested information by attaching Form 8925 to the policyholder's income tax return by the due date of that return.[2]

8724. When will the sale of a life insurance policy cause the loss of the income tax exemption for death proceeds? What is the transfer for value rule?

Under IRC Section 101(a)(2), if a life insurance policy or any interest in a policy is transferred for a valuable consideration, the death proceeds generally will be exempt only to the extent of the consideration paid by the transferee and net premiums, if any, paid by the transferee after the transfer. Any interest paid or accrued by the transferee on indebtedness with respect to the policy is added to the exempt amount if the interest is not deductible under IRC Section 264(a)(4).[3] This provision regarding interest paid or accrued applies to contracts issued after June 8, 1997. Further, for purposes of this provision, any material increase in a death benefit or other material change in a contract shall be treated as a new contract with certain limited exceptions.[4]

After subtracting the permissible exclusions outlined above, the balance of the death proceeds is taxable as ordinary income. This is known as the "transfer for value rule." If a sale or other transfer for value comes within any of the following exceptions to the transfer for value rule, the exemption is available despite the sale or other transfer for value:

(1) The sale or other transfer for value is to the insured individual;[5]

(2) The sale or other transfer for value is to a partner of the insured, to a partnership in which the insured is a partner, or to a corporation in which the insured is an

1. IRC Sec. 6093I; Treas. Reg. §1.6093I-1.
2. Treas. Reg. §1.6093I-1.
3. IRC Sec. 101(a)(2).
4. TRA '97, Sec. 1084(d).
5. IRC Sec. 101(a)(2)(B).

officer or shareholder.[1] Members of a limited liability company ("LLC") taxed as a partnership are considered to be partners for this purpose;[2] or

(3) If the basis for determining gain or loss in the hands of the transferee is determined in whole or in part by reference to the basis of the transferor. This occurs, for example, where a policy is transferred from one corporation to another in a tax–free reorganization, where a policy is transferred between spouses, or where a policy is acquired in part by gift.[3]

See Q 8725 for a more thorough discussion of when a life insurance policy is considered to have been transferred for value. See Q 8726 for a more thorough discussion of the exceptions to the transfer for value rule.

8725. When is a life insurance policy transferred for value?

A "transfer for value" occurs upon any transfer for a valuable consideration of a right to receive all or part of the proceeds of a life insurance policy. As such, the transfer for value rule extends far beyond straightforward sales of policies. The naming of a beneficiary in exchange for any kind of valuable consideration would constitute a transfer for value of an interest in the policy. Even the creation by a separate contract of a right to receive all or part of the proceeds would constitute a transfer for value.[4]

On the other hand, a transfer for value does not occur upon a mere pledging or assignment of a policy as collateral security.[5]

A corporation's transfer of a policy to a stockholder as a distribution in liquidation is a transfer for value.[6] A transfer for value can occur even though the policy transferred has no cash surrender value.[7] Even if there is no actual purchase price that is paid for the policy or interest in the policy, a transfer will be considered a transfer for value, provided the transferor receives some other valuable consideration.[8]

In one case, two policies were purchased on the life of an officer-stockholder, one by the insured and the other by the corporation. Subsequently, the insured entered into an agreement with two employees for the purchase of his stock at his death. The policies were transferred to a trustee for use in partially financing the agreement and the employees took over the payment of premiums. Upon the insured's death, the proceeds were applied to the purchase of his stock. The court held that the employees were transferees for value even though they had paid no purchase price for the policies. Their agreement to make premium payments and to purchase the stock constituted a valuable consideration. As a result, the employees were taxed on the

1. IRC Sec. 101(a)(2)(B).
2. Let. Rul. 9625013.
3. IRC Sec. 101(a)(2)(A); Rev. Rul. 69-187, 1969-1 CB 45; Let. Rul. 8951056.
4. Treas. Reg. §1.101-1(b)(4).
5. Treas. Reg. §1.101-1(b)(4).
6. *Lambeth v. Comm.*, 38 BTA 351 (1938).
7. *James F. Waters, Inc. v. Comm.*, 160 F.2d 596 (9th Cir. 1947).
8. *Monroe v. Patterson*, 8 AFTR 2d 5142 (N.D. Ala. 1961).

difference between the premiums they had paid and the proceeds applied toward their purchase of the insured's stock.[1]

A transfer for value occurred where two shareholders assigned to each other existing policies that had no cash values on their own lives to fund a cross-purchase agreement.[2]

Similarly, where a partnership named two partners as cross-beneficiaries on policies owned by the partnership, a transfer for value was found.[3] In that case, however, an exception to the transfer for value rule was present (i.e. the partnership exception) to exclude insurance proceeds from gross income.

On the other hand, if a transferor receives no valuable consideration whatsoever, there is no transfer for value.[4]

Because a transfer of a policy subject to a nonrecourse loan discharges the transferor of his or her obligation under the loan, the transferor is treated as receiving an amount equal to the discharged obligation.[5] Thus, there may be a transfer for value when a life insurance contract that is subject to a policy loan is transferred. Nonetheless, where the value of a policy exceeded the outstanding loan, a transfer was ruled in part a gift and within one of the exceptions to the transfer for value rule because the basis of the policy in the hands of the transferee was, in part, determined by reference to the basis of the policy in the hands of the transferor.[6]

The IRS has ruled that the gratuitous transfer of a policy subject to a nonrecourse loan was partially a gift and partially a sale. Because the transferor's basis was greater than the amount of the loan, the basis of the policy in the hands of the transferee was the basis in the hands of the transferor at the time of transfer. As a result, the transfer fell within the same exception to the transfer for value rule.[7]

The transfer of a policy to a grantor trust treated as owned by the transferor was not a transfer for value where the insured individuals, terms, conditions, benefits, and beneficial interests other than naming the trustee as beneficiary and nominal owner did not change.[8]

The transfer of a life insurance policy from one grantor trust to another grantor trust, where both trusts were treated as owned by the same taxpayer, will not be treated as a transfer for value.[9]

The replacement of a jointly owned policy with two separately owned policies is also not a transfer for value.[10]

1. *Monroe v. Patterson*, supra.
2. Let. Rul. 7734048.
3. Let. Rul. 9012063.
4. *Haverty Realty & Investment Co. v. Comm.*, 3 TC 161 (1944).
5. Treas. Reg. §1.1001-2(a).
6. Rev. Rul. 69-187, 1969-1 CB 45.
7. Let. Rul. 8951056. But see Let. Rul. 8628007.
8. Let. Rul. 9041052.
9. Rev. Rul. 2007-13, 2007-11 IRB 684.
10. Let. Rul. 9852041.

8726. What are the exceptions to the transfer for value rule that will permit a policy to be sold or otherwise transferred for value without the loss of the income tax exemption for death proceeds?

Several exceptions exist to allow proceeds of a life insurance contract to maintain their tax-exempt status even if there has been a transfer for value. If a sale or other transfer for value comes within any of the following exceptions to the transfer for value rule, the exemption from gross income is available despite the sale or other transfer for value:

(1) The sale or other transfer for value is to the insured individual;[1]

(2) The sale or other transfer for value is to a partner of the insured, to a partnership in which the insured is a partner, or to a corporation in which the insured is an officer or shareholder.[2] Members of a limited liability company ("LLC") taxed as a partnership are considered to be partners for this purpose;[3] or

(3) If the basis for determining gain or loss in the hands of the transferee is determined in whole or in part by reference to the basis of the transferor. This occurs, for example, where a policy is transferred from one corporation to another in a tax–free reorganization, where a policy is transferred between spouses, or where a policy is acquired in part by gift.[4]

For example, if a corporation purchases a policy insuring a key person and later sells it to the insured, the proceeds will be received wholly tax-exempt by the beneficiary despite the sale to the insured.[5]

Moreover, a transfer to a trust that is treated as owned wholly or in part by the insured comes within the exception as a transfer to the insured to the extent the insured is treated as owner.[6] An individual is treated as owner of a trust where the individual retains control over property the individual has transferred to the trust so that the income on that property is taxable to the individual under IRC Sections 671-679.

Where a policy is transferred more than once but the last transfer, or the last transfer for value, is to the insured, a partner of the insured, to a partnership in which the insured is a partner, or to a corporation in which the insured is a shareholder or officer, the proceeds will be wholly tax-exempt regardless of any previous sale or other transfer for value.[7] If the insured transfers the policy for a valuable consideration, and the transfer does not come within any of the exceptions to the transfer for value rule, the proceeds again will lose their tax-exempt status.

1. IRC Sec. 101(a)(2)(B).
2. IRC Sec. 101(a)(2)(B).
3. Let. Rul. 9625013.
4. IRC Secs. 101(a)(2)(A), 1041; Rev. Rul. 69-187, 1969-1 CB 45; Let. Rul. 8951056.
5. See Let. Rul. 8906034.
6. Rev. Rul. 2007-13; *Swanson v. Comm.*, 75-2 USTC ¶9528 (8th Cir. 1975).
7. Treas. Reg. §1.101-1(b)(3)(ii).

Example: X Corporation purchases an insurance policy for a single premium of $500 with a face amount of $1,000 upon the life of A, one of its employees, naming the X Corporation as beneficiary. The X Corporation transfers the policy to the Y Corporation in a tax-free reorganization (the policy having a basis for determining gain or loss in the hands of the Y Corporation determined by reference to its basis in the hands of the X Corporation). The Y Corporation later transfers the policy to the Z Corporation for $600. The Z Corporation receives the proceeds of $1,000 upon the death of A. The amount which the Z Corporation can exclude from its gross income is limited to $600 plus any premiums paid by the Z Corporation subsequent to the transfer of the policy to it.

If Z Corporation, however, before A's death, transfers the policy to the N Corporation, in which A is a shareholder, the N Corporation would receive the $1,000 proceeds upon A's death free from income taxes.[1]

8727. If an employer (or the employer's qualified plan) sells or distributes a policy that insures an employee's life to the insured's spouse or other family member, will the transfer cause the loss of the income tax exemption for death proceeds?

Yes, generally, unless the transferee is a partner of the insured. The exceptions to the transfer for value rule will not exempt this type of transaction from the general rule. Therefore, if a sale is involved, the death proceeds will be taxable to the extent that they exceed the consideration paid by the purchaser plus net premiums, if any, paid after the sale. Any interest paid or accrued by the transferee on policy indebtedness may be added to the exempt amount under certain circumstances.

Even if a spouse or family member pays nothing for a policy, a transfer may be considered a transfer for value based on the idea that the employee's past or promised future services constituted a valuable consideration for the transfer. The proceeds then probably would be taxable to the extent that they exceed the value of the contract at the time of transfer plus any subsequent premium payments and certain policy indebtedness.

The transfer for value rule would not cause taxation of the proceeds of a policy that is (i) transferred to an insured, followed by a gift from the insured to the insured's spouse or family member, or (ii) a sale to the insured's spouse after July 18, 1984.[2] A federal appeals court refused to treat a direct transfer by an employer to the wife of an insured employee for a consideration as two transfers merged into one: a transfer to the insured employee and then a gift from him to his wife.[3]

8728. What is a Section 79 plan?

IRC Section 79 allows an employer to provide up to $50,000 of tax-free group-term life insurance coverage to each of its employees.[4] More specifically, the employee may exclude the value of the group-term life insurance that does not exceed the sum of (a) $50,000 and (b) any amount paid by the employee toward the purchase of the insurance.[5]

1. Treas. Reg. §1.101-1(b)(5), Examples (3) and (5).
2. IRC Sec. 1041.
3. *Est. of Rath v. U.S.*, 79-2 USTC ¶9654 (6th Cir. 1979).
4. IRC Sec. 79(a)(1).
5. IRC Sec. 79(a).

Group-term life insurance that is excludable under Section 79 can also be offered through a cafeteria plan (see Q 8825).[1]

See Q 8729 for a discussion of how it is determined whether the value of the insurance exceeds the $50,000 limit and Q 8730 for a discussion of situations in which the $50,000 limit may not apply. See Q 8731 for the nondiscrimination requirements applicable to Section 79 plans.

8729. How is it determined whether the cost of group-term life insurance provided under a Section 79 plan exceeds the $50,000 excludable limit?

The cost of up to $50,000 of group-term life insurance coverage generally is tax-exempt under IRC Section 79 (see Q 8728). The cost of coverage in excess of $50,000 is taxable to the employee in most situations (see Q 8730 for a discussion of the exceptions).

In calculating the cost of coverage, an employee who has more than one employer must combine all group-term coverage and is entitled to exclude only $50,000 of the combined coverage. If an employee contributes toward the cost of the insurance, all of the employee's contribution for coverage will be subtracted from the amount that would otherwise be taxable.[2] The employee cannot carry over any unused portion of his or her contributions from year to year.

The taxable cost of coverage in excess of $50,000 must be calculated on a monthly basis. The steps are as follows:

(1) Determine the total amount of group-term life insurance coverage for the employee in each calendar month of the employee's taxable year, and if a change occurs during any month, take the average at the beginning and end of the month;

(2) Subtract $50,000 from each month's coverage;

(3) Apply the appropriate rate from the applicable tables of monthly premium rates (reproduced below) to the balance, if any, for each month;

(4) Subtract total employee contributions for the year, if any, from the sum of the monthly costs.[3]

The cost is determined on the basis of the life insurance protection provided to an employee during the employee's tax year, without regard to when the premiums are paid by an employer. The rates in the table provided immediately below should be used to compute the cost of excess group-term life insurance coverage.[4]

1. Prop. Treas. Reg. §1.125-1(k).
2. IRC Sec. 79.
3. Treas. Reg. §1.79-3.
4. Treas. Reg. §1.79-3(d)(2).

*Uniform Premiums for $1,000 of Group-Term Life Insurance Protection**
Rates Applicable to Cost of Group-Term Life Insurance Provided
After June 30, 1999

5-Year Age Bracket	Cost per $1,000 of Protection for One-Month Period
Under 25	$0.05
25 to 29	.06
30 to 34	.08
35 to 39	.09
40 to 44	.10
45 to 49	.15
50 to 54	.23
55 to 59	.43
60 to 64	.66
65 to 69	1.27
70 and above	2.06

*In using the above table, the age of the employee is the employee's attained age on the last day of the employee's taxable year.

8730. Are there any exceptions to the general rule that an employee may only exclude the first $50,000 of group-term life insurance provided under a Section 79 plan?

Yes. There are certain exceptions to the $50,000 ceiling on tax-exempt coverage. The cost of group-term life insurance, even for amounts over $50,000, is tax-exempt in the following situations:

(1) The insurance is provided to a former employee who:

(a) has terminated his or her employment as an employee with the employer and has become permanently disabled,

(b) has terminated his or her employment on or before January 1, 1984, and was covered by the plan or by a predecessor plan when he or she retired if the plan was in existence on January 1, 1984, or the plan is a comparable successor to such a plan, or

(c) has terminated employment as an employee after January 1, 1984, having attained age fifty-five on or before January 1, 1984, and having been employed by the employer at any time during 1983 if the plan was in existence on January 1, 1984, or the plan is a comparable successor to such a plan, *unless* the individual retired under the plan after 1986 and the plan is discriminatory after that date, not taking into account insurance provided to employees who retired before January 1, 1987;

(2) If a charitable organization is designated as policy beneficiary, where this designation may be made with respect to all or any portion of the proceeds, but no charitable contributions deduction is allowable for such a designation; or

(3) If an employer is beneficiary (directly or indirectly), unless the employer is required to pay proceeds over to an employee's estate or beneficiary.[1]

Any contribution toward group-term life insurance, but not toward permanent benefits, made by an employee during a taxable year generally reduces, dollar for dollar, the amount that otherwise would be included in the employee's gross income for term insurance. This reduction is not permitted, however, if the employee makes a prepayment for coverage after retirement or for payments allocable to insurance where the cost is not taxed because of one of the exceptions outlined above.[2]

The exemption of the cost of up to $50,000 of group-term life is not available with respect to group-term insurance purchased under a qualified employees' trust or annuity plan. The provisions of IRC Section 72(m)(3) and Treasury Regulation Section 1.72-16 apply to the cost of the protection purchased under qualified plans and no part of the cost is excludable from an employee's gross income.[3]

Premiums for supplemental insurance in excess of $50,000 provided by an employer under a group-term insurance plan are not taxable to an insured employee when paid by a family member to whom the employee has assigned the insurance.[4] If the cost of the coverage in excess of $50,000 is shared by an employer and assignee, the employer's portion of the cost is includable in the insured employee's gross income.[5]

8731. Do any nondiscrimination requirements apply to Section 79 plans?

Yes. If a Section 79 plan covers any key employees and the plan discriminates in favor of them either as to eligibility to participate or with respect to the kind or amount of benefits, the key employees may not exclude the cost of the first $50,000 of coverage (see Q 8728). If a plan is found to be discriminatory, the key employee must include the higher of the actual cost for such insurance or the cost as specified in the uniform premium Table I (see Q 8729). Employees who are not key employees may exclude the cost of $50,000 of coverage even if a plan is discriminatory.[6]

1. IRC Sec. 79(b); Treas. Reg. §1.79-2; TRA '84 Sec. 223(d), as amended by TRA '86, Sec. 1827(b)(1); Temp. Treas. Reg. §1.79-4T, A-1. See also Let. Rul. 9149010.
2. Treas. Reg. §§1.79-2(a)(2), 1.79-3(g)(2).
3. IRC Sec. 79(b)(3); Treas. Reg. §1.79-2(d).
4. Rev. Rul. 71-587, 1971-2 CB 89.
5. Rev. Rul. 73-174, 1973-1 CB 43.
6. IRC Sec. 79(d).

A plan is considered discriminatory in favor of key employees with respect to eligibility to participate *unless*:

(1) it benefits at least 70 percent of all employees;

(2) at least 85 percent of participants are not key employees;

(3) the plan benefits a class of employees found by the IRS not to be discriminatory; or

(4) if the plan is part of a cafeteria plan, the requirements for cafeteria plans are met (see Q 8825).[1]

Individuals who do not need to be counted for the purposes of determining whether a plan is discriminatory include:

(1) employees with fewer than three years of service;

(2) part-time and seasonal employees;

(3) employees excluded from a plan who are covered by a collective bargaining agreement if group-term life insurance was the subject of good faith bargaining, and

(4) certain nonresident aliens.[2]

Benefits are discriminatory unless all benefits that are made available to key employee participants are available to all other participants.[3] Benefits are not discriminatory if the plan provides a fixed amount of insurance that is the same for all covered employees or merely because the amount of insurance bears a uniform relationship to the total compensation of employees, or to their basic or regular rate of compensation.[4] In other circumstances, the determination of whether a plan is nondiscriminatory will be based on all the facts and circumstances.[5]

For purposes of determining whether an employer's group-term insurance plan is discriminatory, all policies providing group-term life insurance to a key employee or key employees carried directly or indirectly by an employer will be treated as a single plan. An employer may treat two or more policies that do not provide group-term life insurance to a common key employee as a single plan.[6] See Q 8732 for a discussion of who are considered key employees for purposes of these nondiscrimination rules.

1. IRC Sec. 79(d)(3)(A).
2. IRC Sec. 79(d)(3)(B).
3. IRC Sec. 79(d)(4).
4. IRC Sec. 79(d)(5); Treas. Reg. §1.79-4T, A-9.
5. Treas. Reg. §1.79-4T, A-9.
6. Treas. Reg. §1.79-4T, A-5.

Exemption for Church Plans

The nondiscrimination requirements discussed above do not apply to church plans for church employees. A church plan generally is one established by a church or convention or association of churches that is tax-exempt under IRC Section 501(c)(3). A church employee includes a minister, or an employee of an organization that is tax-exempt under IRC Section 501(c)(3), but does not include an employee of an educational organization above the secondary level, other than a school for religious training, or an employee of certain hospitals or medical research organizations.[1]

8732. Who are considered key employees for purposes of the nondiscrimination requirements that apply to Section 79 plans?

For purposes of the nondiscrimination requirements that apply to IRC Section 79 plans (see Q 8731), a key employee is an employee who, at any time during the employer's tax year was:

(1) an officer of an employer having annual compensation greater than $175,000 in 2018. No more than the greater of (a) three individuals or (b) 10 percent of employees need to be treated as officers, but in any event no more than fifty individuals may be considered officers;

(2) a more-than-5 percent owner of an employer; or

(3) a more-than-1 percent owner, determined without considering those employees who are not counted in testing for discriminatory eligibility, having an annual compensation from an employer of more than $150,000.[2]

A key employee also is any former employee who was a key employee when he or she retired or separated from service.[3]

For purposes of determining corporate ownership, the attribution rules of IRC Section 318 apply. Rules similar to the attribution rules apply to determine non-corporate ownership. In calculating attribution from a corporation, a 5 percent ownership test will apply rather than a 50 percent test.

In determining the percentages of ownership, only the particular employer is considered; other members of a controlled group of corporations or businesses under common control and other members of an affiliated service group are not aggregated. They are aggregated for purposes of determining the employee's compensation and in testing for discrimination.[4]

1. IRC Sec. 79(d)(7).
2. IRC Secs. 79(d)(6), 416(i).
3. IRC Sec. 79(d)(6).
4. IRC Sec. 414(t); see also Temp. Treas. Reg. §1.79-4T, A-5.

PART XI: EMPLOYER-SPONSORED ACCIDENT & HEALTH INSURANCE BENEFITS

8733. May an employer deduct as a business expense the cost of premiums paid for group accident and health insurance for employees?

An employer generally can treat accident and health insurance as a business expense, and can therefore deduct the cost of premiums paid for employees' coverage under a group health plan. This includes premiums for medical expense insurance, dismemberment and sight loss coverage for the employee, the employee's spouse and dependents, disability income for the employee, and accidental death coverage.

The employer is entitled to deduct these premiums if coverage is provided under a group policy, but is not permitted to reimburse employees for the cost of premiums for individual insurance purchased through the health insurance marketplace. The deduction will be disallowed if benefits are payable to the employer—the deduction for health insurance is allowable only if benefits are payable to employees or their beneficiaries.[1] However, if the employer's spouse is a bona fide employee and the employer is covered as a family member based on the spouse-employee's coverage, the premium is deductible.[2]

A corporation can deduct premiums it pays on group hospitalization coverage for commission salespersons, regardless of whether they are technically treated as employees or independent contractors.[3] The premiums paid, however, must qualify as additional reasonable compensation to the insured employees.[4]

A different rule applies for certain accrual basis employers that provide medical benefits to employees directly instead of through insurance or an intermediary fund. In this case, the employer may not deduct amounts estimated to be necessary to pay for medical care provided in the year, but for which no claims have been filed with the employer by the end of the year, if filing a claim is necessary to establish the employer's liability for payment.[5]

8734. What credit is available for small employers who contribute to employee health insurance costs?

Eligible small employers may take advantage of a tax credit for employee health insurance expenses for taxable years beginning after December 31, 2009, provided the employer offers health insurance to its employees and makes a non-elective contribution on behalf of each employee who participates in the plan.[6]

---

1. Treas. Reg. §1.162-10(a); Rev. Rul. 58-90, 1958-1 CB 88; Rev. Rul. 56-632, 1956-2 CB 101.
2. Rev. Rul. 71-588, 1971-2 CB 91; TAM 9409006.
3. Rev. Rul. 56-400, 1956-2 CB 116.
4. *Ernest Holdeman & Collet, Inc. v. Comm.*, TC Memo 1960-10. See Rev. Rul. 58-90, supra.
5. *U.S. v. General Dynamics Corp.*, 481 U.S. 239 (1987).
6. IRC Sec. 45R, as added by PPACA 2010.

An eligible small employer is defined as an employer that has no more than twenty-five full time employees, the average annual wages of whom do not exceed $53,400 (as adjusted for inflation in 2018; in 2017, the amount was $52,400, in 2016 the amount was $51,800; in 2015 the amount was $51,600; in 2014 the amount was $50,800, in 2010 to 2013 the amount was $50,000).[1]

In order to qualify, the employer must have a contribution arrangement for each employee who enrolls in the health plan offered by the employer through an exchange that requires that the employer make a non-elective contribution in an amount equal to a uniform percentage, not less than 50 percent, of the premium cost.[2]

Subject to phase-out[3] based on the number of employees and average wages, the amount of the credit is equal to 50 percent, and 35 percent in the case of tax-exempt organizations, of the lesser of:

(1) the aggregate amount of non-elective contributions made by the employer on behalf of its employees for health insurance premiums for health plans offered by the employer to employees through an exchange; or

(2) the aggregate amount of non-elective contributions the employer would have made if each employee had been enrolled in a health plan that had a premium equal to the average premium for the small group market in the ratings area.[4]

For years 2010 through 2013, the following modifications apply in determining the amount of the credit:

(1) The credit percentage is reduced to 35 percent (25 percent in the case of tax-exempt entities).[5]

(2) The amount under (1) is determined by reference to non-elective contributions for premiums paid for health insurance, and there is no exchange requirement.[6]

(3) The amount under (2) is determined by the average premium for the state small group market.[7]

The credit also is allowed against the alternative minimum tax.[8]

Planning Point: Proposed regulations explain how to calculate employer tax credits after 2013.[9] The regulations propose that the maximum credit for taxable years after 2014 (available for only two years) increase to 50 percent (35 percent for tax-exempt organizations), with some

1. IRC Sec. 45R(d), as added by PPACA 2010; IRC Sec. 45R(d)(3)(B), as amended by Section 10105(e)(1) of PPACA 2010.
2. IRC Sec. 45R(d)(4), as added by PPACA 2010.
3. IRC Sec. 45R(c), as added by PPACA 2010.
4. IRC Sec. 45R(b), as added by PPACA 2010.
5. IRC Sec. 45R(g)(2)(A), as added by PPACA 2010.
6. IRC Secs. 45R(g)(2)(B), 45R(g)(3), as added by PPACA 2010.
7. IRC Sec. 45R(g)(2)(C), as added by PPACA 2010.
8. IRC Sec. 38(c)(4)(B), as amended by PPACA 2010. The IRS has issued guidance; see Notice 2010-44, 2010-22 IRB 717; Notice 2010-82, 2010-51 IRB 1.
9. 2013 IRB LEXIS, 2013-38 IRB 211 (modifying Notice 2010-44, 2010-22 IRB 717; Notice 2010-82, 2010-51 IRB 1).

adjustments. There is a proposed phase out for small employers with more than ten employees or whose average annual wages exceed $25,000 (adjusted for inflation). In addition, the proposed regulations clarify that employer contributions to an HRA, FSA, or HSA are not considered premium payments[1] (See Q 8771.)

8735. Is the value of employer-provided coverage under accident or health insurance taxable income to an employee?

Generally, no. This includes medical expense and dismemberment and sight loss coverage for the employee, the employee's spouse and dependents, and coverage providing for disability income for the employee. Unlike the exclusion for group-term life insurance, there is no specific limit on the amount of employer-provided accident or health coverage that may be excluded from an employee's gross income. Further, coverage is tax-exempt to an employee when it is provided under a group insurance policy.[2] Similarly, the employee is not taxed on the value of critical illness coverage.

Accidental death coverage apparently also is excludable from an employee's gross income under IRC Section 106(a).[3]

The IRS has ruled privately that the value of consumer medical cards purchased by a partnership for its employees was excludable from the employees' income under IRC Section 106(a).[4]

Where an employer applies salary reduction amounts to the payment of health insurance premiums for employees, the salary reduction amounts are excludable from gross income under IRC Section 106.[5]

On the other hand, an employee must include in income payments received from an employer that *may* be used to pay the accident and health insurance premiums if those amounts are not *required* to be used for that purpose.[6] Employers are generally no longer permitted to reimburse employees for the cost of premiums for individual insurance policies purchased by the employee without incurring a penalty. Beginning in 2017, certain small employers may use a qualified small employer health reimbursement arrangement (QSEHRA) to reimburse employees for the cost of health coverage without incurring a penalty (see Q 8755).

Where a taxpayer's contribution to a fund providing retiree health benefits is deducted from the taxpayer's after-tax salary, it is considered an employee contribution and is includable in the taxpayer's income under IRC Section 61. In contrast, where an employer increases or grosses up a taxpayer's salary and then deducts the fund contribution from the taxpayer's after-tax salary, the contribution is considered to be an employer contribution that is excludable from the gross income of the taxpayer under IRC Section 106.[7]

1. Prop. Treas. Reg. §1.45R-3.
2. IRC Sec. 106(a). See also Treas. Reg. §1.106-1; Rev. Rul. 58-90, 1958-1 CB 88; Rev. Rul. 56-632, 1956-1 CB 101.
3. See Treas. Reg. §1.106-1; Treas. Reg. §1.79-1(f)(3); Let. Ruls. 8801015, 8922048.
4. Let. Rul. 9814023.
5. Rev. Rul. 2002-03, 2002-1 CB 316.
6. Rev. Rul. 75-241, 975-1 CB 316, Let. Rul. 9022060. See also Let. Rul. 9104050.
7. Let. Rul. 9625012.

The IRS has ruled privately that a return of a premium rider on a health insurance policy was a benefit in addition to accident and health benefits, so that the premium paid by the employer had to be included in the employee's taxable income.[1]

For purposes of determining the tax treatment of employer-provided accident and health insurance, full time life insurance salespersons are treated as employees if they are employees for Social Security purposes.[2] Coverage for other commission salespersons is taxable income to the salespersons, unless an employer-employee relationship exists.[3]

Discrimination generally does not affect exclusion of the value of coverage. Even if a self-insured medical expense reimbursement plan discriminates in favor of highly compensated employees, the value of coverage is not taxable; only reimbursements are affected.

For a discussion of the considerations applicable to S corporations, see Q 8882 to Q 8891.

8736. Is the value of employer-provided coverage under accident or health insurance taxable income to an employee if the employee has a choice as to whether to receive coverage or a higher salary?

Outside of the context of cafeteria plans, if an employer offers an employee a choice between a lower salary and employer-paid health insurance or a higher salary and no health insurance, the employee must include the full amount of the higher salary in income regardless of the employee's choice. If the employee selects the health insurance option, the IRS will deem the employee to have received the higher salary and, in turn, paid a portion of the salary equal to the health insurance premium to the insurance company.[4]

However, a federal district court faced with a similar fact situation ruled that for employees who accept employer-paid health insurance coverage, the difference between the higher salary and the lower one is not subject to FICA and FUTA taxes or to income tax withholding.[5]

8737. Is the value of employer-provided coverage under accident or health insurance taxable income to an employee when the coverage is provided for the employee's spouse, children or dependents?

Employer-provided accident and health coverage for an employee and the employee's spouse and dependents, both before and after retirement, and for the employee's surviving spouse and dependents after the employee's death, does not have to be included in gross income by the active or retired employee or, after the employee's death, by the employee's survivors.[6]

In 2010, the Affordable Care Act ("ACA"), expanded the exclusion from gross income for amounts expended on medical care to include employer-provided health coverage for any adult child of the taxpayer if the adult child has not attained the age of twenty-seven as of the end of

1. Let. Rul. 8804010.
2. IRC Sec. 7701(a)(20).
3. Rev. Rul. 56-400, 1956-2 CB 116; see also IRC Sec. 3508.
4. Let. Rul. 9406002. See also Let. Rul. 9513027.
5. *Express Oil Change, Inc. v. U.S.*, 25 F. Supp. 2d 1313 (N.D. Ala. 1996), *aff'd*, 162 F.3d 1290 (11th Cir. 1998).
6. Rev. Rul. 82-196, 1982-2 CB 53; GCM 38917 (11-17-82).

the taxable year. The IRS has released guidance indicating that the exclusion applies regardless of whether the adult child is eligible to be claimed as a dependent for tax purposes.[1]

8738. When will amounts received by an employee under employer-provided accident and health insurance be taxable income to the employee?

Amounts received by an employee under employer-provided accident or health insurance, group or individual, that reimburse the employee for hospital, surgical, and other medical expenses incurred for care of the employee or spouse and dependents are generally tax-exempt without limit.

Despite this, if the employee deducted the expense in a prior year and is later reimbursed, the reimbursement must be included in gross income. Moreover, if reimbursements exceed actual expenses, the excess must be included in gross income to the extent that it is attributable to employer contributions.[2]

Where an employer reimburses employees for salary reduction contributions applied to the payment of health insurance premiums, these amounts are not excludable under IRC Section 105(b) because there are no employee-paid premiums to reimburse.[3] Employers should note that, under the ACA, the employer may be liable for penalties if it chooses to reimburse employees for the cost of individual health insurance premiums. However, beginning in 2017, certain small employers may use a qualified small employer health reimbursement arrangement (QSEHRA) to reimburse employees for the cost of health coverage without incurring a penalty (see Q 8755).

Similarly, where an employer applies salary reduction contributions to the payment of health insurance premiums and then pays the amount of the salary reduction to employees regardless of whether the employee incurs expenses for medical care, these so-called "advance" reimbursements or loans are not excludable from gross income under IRC Section 105(b) and are subject to FICA and FUTA taxes.[4]

Critical Illness Benefits

If the value of an employer-provided critical illness insurance policy was not includable in the employee's gross income, amounts later received by the employee under the policy are includable in that employee's gross income. The exclusion from gross income under IRC Section 105(b) applies only to amounts paid specifically to reimburse medical care expenses. Because critical illness insurance policies pay a benefit irrespective of whether medical expenses are incurred, these amounts are not excludable under IRC Section 105(b).[5]

1. IRC Sec. 105(b), as amended by the Patient Protection and Affordable Care Act of 2010 and the Health Care and Education Reconciliation Act of 2010. Notice 2010-38, 2010-20 IRB 682.
2. IRC Sec. 105(b); Treas. Reg. §1.105-2; Rev. Rul. 69-154, 1969-1 CB 46.
3. Rev. Rul. 2002-3, 2002-1 CB 316.
4. Rev. Rul. 2002-80, 2002-2 CB 925.
5. See Treas. Reg. §§1.105-2, 1.213-1(e).

Wage Continuation and Disability Income

Sick pay, wage continuation payments, and disability income payments, both preretirement and postretirement, generally are fully includable in gross income and taxable to an employee.[1]

Sight Loss and Dismemberment

An employee is only entitled to exclude payments not related to absence from work for the permanent loss, or loss of use, of a member or function of the body, or permanent disfigurement of the employee or spouse or a dependent, if the amounts paid are computed with reference to the nature of the injury.[2]

An employee was entitled to exclude a lump-sum payment for incurable cancer under a group life-and-disability policy based upon this provision.[3]

However, if the benefits are determined based upon length of service rather than type and severity of injury, the exemption will not apply.[4] Similarly, if the benefits are determined as a percentage of the disabled employee's salary, rather than by the nature of the employee's injury, they are not excludable from income.[5] An employee who has permanently lost a bodily member or function, but who continues to work and draw a salary, cannot exclude a portion of that salary as payment for loss of the member or function if that portion was not computed with reference to the loss.[6]

8739. Are benefits paid under an employer-sponsored plan by reason of the employee's death received tax-free?

Accidental death benefits under an employer's plan are received income tax-free by an employee's beneficiary under IRC Section 101(a) as life insurance proceeds payable by reason of the insured's death.[7] Death benefits payable under life insurance contracts issued after December 31, 1984, are excludable if the contract meets the statutory definition of a life insurance contract in IRC Section 7702. See Q 8709 to Q 8731 for a detailed discussion of the tax treatment of life insurance death proceeds.

Survivors' Benefits

Benefits paid to a surviving spouse and dependents under an employer accident and health plan that provided coverage for an employee and the employee's spouse and dependents both before and after retirement, and to the employee's surviving spouse and dependents after the employee's death, are excludable to the extent that they would be if paid to the employee.[8]

1. See Let. Ruls. 9103043, 9036049.
2. IRC Sec. 105(c).
3. Rev. Rul. 63-181, 1963-2 CB 74.
4. *Beisler v. Comm.*, 814 F.2d 1304 (9th Cir. 1987); *West v. Comm.*, TC Memo 1992-617. See also *Rosen v. U.S.*, 829 F.2d 506 (4th Cir. 1987).
5. *Colton v. Comm.*, TC Memo 1995-275; *Webster v. Comm.*, 870 F. Supp. 202, 94-2 USTC ¶50,586 (M.D. Tenn. 1994).
6. *Laverty v. Comm.*, 61 TC 160 (1973) *aff'd*, 523 F.2d 479, 75-2 USTC ¶9712 (9th Cir. 1975).
7. Treas. Reg. §1.101-1(a).
8. Rev. Rul. 82-196, 1982-2 CB 53; GCM 38917 (11-17-82).

8740. Are benefits provided under an employer's noninsured accident and health plan excludable from an employee's income?

Although there is no particular legal form of plan required, uninsured benefits must be received under some sort of accident and health plan established by the employer for its employees in order to be tax-exempt on the same basis as insured plans.[1] An Ohio federal District Court described the "plan" requirement as follows: "there is no legal magic to a form; the essence of the arrangement must determine its legal character."[2]

A formal contract of insurance is not required if it is clear that, for an adequate consideration, the company has agreed and has become liable to pay and has paid sickness benefits based upon a reasonable plan of protection established for the benefit of its employees. For example, a provision for disability pay in an employment contract has been held to satisfy the condition.[3]

For tax purposes, it is not necessary for the plan to be in writing or even that an employee's rights to benefits under the plan be enforceable. For example, a plan has been found based on an employer's custom or policy of continuing wages during disability, which was generally known to employees.[4]

If an employee's rights are not enforceable, the employee must have been covered by a plan or a program, policy, or custom having the effect of a plan when the employee became sick or injured, and notice or knowledge of the plan must have been readily available to the employee.[5] Further, for a plan to exist an employer must commit to certain rules and regulations governing payment and these rules must be made known to employees as a definite policy before accident or sickness arises. *Ad hoc* payments that are made at the complete discretion of an employer do not qualify as a plan.[6]

The plan must be for employees. A plan may cover one or more employees and there may be different plans for different employees or classes of employees.[7] A plan that is found to cover individuals in a capacity other than their employee status, even though they are employees, is not a plan for employees. For purposes of determining the excludability of employer-provided accident and health benefits, self-employed individuals and certain shareholders owning more than 2 percent of the stock of an S corporation are not treated as employees.[8]

Further, uninsured medical expense reimbursement plans for employees must meet nondiscrimination requirements for medical expense reimbursements to be tax-free to highly compensated employees. See Q 8741 for a discussion of the nondiscrimination requirements applicable to employer-provided health insurance plans.

---

1. IRC Sec. 105(e).
2. *Epmeier v. U.S.*, 199 F.2d 508, 511 (7th Cir. 1959).
3. *Andress v. U.S.*, 198 F. Supp. 371 (N.D. Ohio 1961).
4. *Niekamp v. U.S.*, 240 F. Supp. 195 (E.D. Mo. 1965); *Pickle v. Comm.*, TC Memo 1971-304.
5. Treas. Reg. §1.105-5(a).
6. *Est. of Kaufman*, 35 TC 663 (1961), *aff'd*, 300 F.2d 128 (6th Cir. 1962); *Lang v. Comm.*, 41 TC 352 (1963); *Levine v. Comm.*, 50 TC 422 (1968); *Est. of Chism v. Comm.*, TC Memo 1962-6, *aff'd*, 322 F.2d 956 (9th Cir. 1963); *Burr v. Comm.*, TC Memo 1966-112; *Frazier v. Comm.*, TC Memo 1994-358; *Harris v. U.S.*, 77-1 USTC ¶9414 (E.D. Va. 1977).
7. Treas. Reg. §1.105-5(a); *Andress*, 198 F. Supp. 371 (1961).
8. IRC Sec. 105(g); Treas. Reg. §1.105-5(b).

8741. What nondiscrimination requirements apply to employer-provided health insurance plans?

Under current law, employer-provided health insurance plans are subject to nondiscrimination rules concerning discrimination based on health status under HIPAA '96. Though the HIPAA rules generally apply to both insured and uninsured plans, a plan that provides health benefits through an accident or health insurance policy need not meet the nondiscrimination requirements of IRC Section 105(h), which applies to amounts paid to highly compensated employees for coverage under *self-insured plans*, for covered employees to enjoy the tax benefits described in Q 8744.

For plan years beginning on or after September 23, 2010, which was six months after the date of enactment of the Affordable Care Act (ACA), insured plans that are not grandfathered were expected to become subject to the same nondiscrimination requirements as self-insured plans. On December 22, 2010, however, the IRS announced in Notice 2011-1 that compliance with nondiscrimination rules for health insurance plans will be delayed until regulations or other administrative guidance has been issued.[1] The IRS indicated that the guidance will not apply until plan years beginning a specified period after guidance is issued.

Affordable Care Act Rules

The ACA requires that a group health plan that is not a self-insured plan satisfy the requirements of IRC Section 105(h)(2). More specifically, the ACA provides that rules similar to the rules in IRC Section 105(h)(3) (nondiscriminatory eligibility classifications), Section 105(h)(4) (nondiscriminatory benefits), and Section 105(h)(8) (certain controlled groups) apply to insured plans. The term "highly compensated individual" has the meaning given that term by IRC Section 105(h)(5).[2] A detailed discussion of the applicable definition of highly compensated individual under Section 105 is provided in Q 8745.

A plan that reimburses employees for premiums paid under an insured plan does not have to satisfy nondiscrimination requirements.

8742. What is a self-insured health plan?

A self-insured plan is one in which reimbursement of medical expenses is not provided under a policy of accident and health insurance.[3] According to regulations, a plan underwritten by a cost-plus policy or a policy that, in effect, merely provides administrative or bookkeeping services is considered self-insured.[4]

An accident or health insurance policy may be an individual or a group policy issued by a licensed insurance company, or an arrangement in the nature of a prepaid health care plan regulated under federal or state law including an HMO. A plan will be found to be self-insured unless the policy involves shifting of risk to an unrelated third party.

1. 2011-1 CB 259.
2. Sec. 2716 of the Public Health Service Act, as added by Section 1001(5) of PPACA 2010, as amended by Section 10101(d) of PPACA 2010.
3. See IRC Sec. 105(h)(6).
4. Treas. Reg. §1.105-11(b).

A plan is not considered self-insured merely because prior claims experience is one factor in determining the premium.[1] Further, a policy of a captive insurance company is not considered self-insurance if, for the plan year, premiums paid to a captive insurer by unrelated companies are equal to at least one-half of the total premiums received and the policy is similar to those sold to unrelated companies.[2]

Withholding

An employer does not have to withhold income tax on an amount paid for any medical care reimbursement made to or for the benefit of an employee under a self-insured medical reimbursement plan within the meaning of IRC Section 105(h)(6).[3]

8743. Are reimbursements attributable to employee contributions to a self-insured health plan taxable to the employee?

Generally, reimbursements attributable to employee contributions are received tax-free. However, an employee must include any reimbursed amount to the extent that the employee has taken a deduction for the expense.

Amounts attributable to employer contributions are determined based on the ratio that employer contributions bear to total contributions for the calendar years immediately preceding the year of receipt (up to three years may be taken into account). If the plan has been in effect for less than a year, then the determination may be based upon the portion of the year, or such determination may be made periodically (such as monthly or quarterly) and used throughout the succeeding period.[4]

For example, if an employee leaves employment on April 15, 2018, and 2018 is the first year the plan was in effect, the determination may be based upon the contributions of the employer and the employees during the period beginning with January 1 and ending with April 15, or during the month of March, or during the quarter consisting of January, February, and March.

8744. What nondiscrimination requirements apply to self-insured health plans?

The nondiscrimination requirements set forth in IRC Section 105(h) apply to self-insured health benefits, although the IRS announced in Notice 2011-1 on December 22, 2010, that compliance with nondiscrimination rules for other health insurance plans will be delayed until regulations or other administrative guidance has been issued. The IRS indicated that the guidance will not apply until plan years beginning in a specified period after guidance is issued.

Benefits received pursuant to a self-insured plan are generally excludable from an employee's gross income. Despite this, if a self-insured medical expense reimbursement plan or the self-insured part of a partly-insured medical expense reimbursement plan discriminates in favor of

1. See, for example, Let. Rul. 8235047.
2. Treas. Reg. §1.105-11(b).
3. IRC Sec. 3401(a)(20).
4. Treas. Reg. §1.105-11(i).

highly compensated individuals, certain amounts paid to the highly compensated individuals will be taxable to those highly compensated individuals.

A medical expense reimbursement plan cannot be implemented retroactively because, if this were permitted, the nondiscrimination requirements of IRC Section 105 would be ineffective.[1]

A self-insured plan may not discriminate in favor of highly compensated individuals either with respect to eligibility to participate or benefits.

Eligibility

A plan discriminates as to eligibility to participate unless the plan benefits:

(1) 70 percent or more of all employees, or 80 percent or more of all the employees who are eligible to benefit under the plan if 70 percent or more of all employees are eligible to benefit under the plan; or

(2) employees who qualify under a classification set up by the employer and found by the IRS not to be discriminatory in favor of highly compensated individuals.[2]

For purposes of these eligibility requirements, an employer is not required to consider those employees who:

(1) have not completed three years of service at the beginning of the plan year; however, years of service during which an individual was ineligible under (2), (3), (4), or (5) below must be counted for this purpose;

(2) have not attained age twenty-five at the beginning of the plan year;

(3) are part-time or seasonal employees;

(4) are covered by a collective bargaining agreement if health benefits were the subject of good faith bargaining; or

(5) are nonresident aliens with no U.S.-source earned income.[3]

Part-time and Seasonal Workers

Part-time employees include those employees who are customarily employed for fewer than thirty-five hours per week. Seasonal employees are those who are customarily employed for fewer than nine months per year. In determining whether an employee is part-time or seasonal, the IRS will consider whether similarly situated employees of the employer (or employees in the same industry or location as the employer) are employed for substantially more hours or months, as applicable. A safe harbor rule provides that employees customarily employed for

1. *Wollenburg v. U.S.*, 75 F. Supp. 2d 1032, 1035 n.2 (D. Neb. 1999) (noting that "an employer can choose to benefit or hurt certain employees with much greater precision, with the benefit of hindsight."); *American Family Mut. Ins. Co. v. U.S.*, 815 F. Supp. 1206 (W.D. Wisc. 1992). See also Rev. Rul. 2002-58, 2002-38 IRB 541.
2. IRC Sec. 105(h)(3)(A).
3. IRC Sec. 105(h)(3)(B).

fewer than twenty-five hours per week or seven months per year may automatically be considered part-time or seasonal.[1]

Benefits

A plan discriminates as to benefits unless all benefits provided for participants who are highly compensated individuals are provided for all other participants.[2] If some participants become eligible for benefits immediately and others only after a waiting period, benefits are not considered to be available to all participants.[3] Benefits available to dependents of highly compensated employees must be equally available to dependents of all other participating employees. The test is applied to benefits subject to reimbursement, rather than to actual benefit payments or claims.

Any maximum limit on the amount of reimbursement must be uniform for all participants and for all dependents, regardless of years of service or age. Further, if the type or amount of benefits subject to reimbursement is offered in proportion to compensation and highly compensated employees are covered by the plan, the plan will be found to discriminate with regard to benefits.

A plan will not be considered discriminatory in operation merely because highly compensated participants use a broad range of plan benefits to a greater extent than other participants.[4]

The nondiscrimination rules are not violated merely because benefits under the plan are offset by benefits paid under a self-insured or insured plan of the employer, of another employer, or by benefits paid under Medicare or other federal or state law. A self-insured plan may take into account benefits provided under another plan only to the extent that the benefit is the same under both plans.[5] Benefits provided to a retired employee who was highly compensated must be the same as benefits provided to all other retired participants.

For purposes of applying the nondiscrimination rules, all employees of a controlled group of corporations, or employers under common control, and of members of an affiliated service group are treated as employed by a single employer.[6]

Highly Compensated Individual

An employee is a highly compensated individual if the employee falls into any one of the following three classifications:

(1) The employee is one of the five highest paid officers.

(2) The employee is a shareholder who owns, either actually or constructively through application of the attribution rules, more than 10 percent in value of the employer's stock.

1. Treas. Reg. §1.105-11(c).
2. IRC Sec. 105(h)(4).
3. Let. Ruls. 8411050, 8336065.
4. Treas. Reg. §1.105-11(c)(3).
5. Treas. Reg. §1.105-11(c)(1).
6. IRC Sec. 105(h).

(3) The employee is among the highest paid 25 percent, rounded to the nearest higher whole number, of all employees other than excludable employees who are not participants and not including retired participants.[1] Fiscal year plans may determine compensation on the basis of the calendar year ending in the plan year.

A participant's status as officer or stockholder with respect to a particular benefit is determined at the time when the benefit is provided.[2] See Q 8745 for a discussion of the tax consequences to a self-insured plan that is found to be discriminatory under these rules.

8745. What are the tax consequences for amounts paid by an employer to highly compensated employees under a discriminatory self-insured medical expense reimbursement plan?

If a self-insured medical reimbursement plan is found to be discriminatory in favor of highly compensated employees, those highly compensated employees may be taxed on reimbursed amounts provided under the plan. The taxable amount of payments is the "excess reimbursement."[3] The two situations discussed below will produce an excess reimbursement.

The first situation occurs when a benefit is available to a highly compensated individual but not to all other participants, or if the benefit otherwise discriminates in favor of highly compensated individuals. In this case, the total amount reimbursed under the plan to the employee with respect to that benefit is an excess reimbursement.

The second situation occurs when a plan discriminates as to participation, even though all benefits are available to all other participants and are not otherwise discriminatory. If this is the case, the excess reimbursement is determined by multiplying the total amount reimbursed to the highly compensated individual for the plan year by a fraction. The numerator of this fraction is the total amount reimbursed to all participants who are highly compensated individuals under the plan for the plan year and the denominator is the total amount reimbursed to all employees under the plan for such plan year. In determining the fraction, any reimbursement attributable to a benefit not available to all other participants is not taken into account.[4]

Multiple plans may be designated as a single plan for purposes of satisfying nondiscrimination requirements. If an employee elects to participate in an optional HMO offered by the plan, that employee is considered benefited by the plan only if the employer's contributions with respect to the employee are at least equal to what would have been made to the self-insured plan and the HMO is designated, with the self-insured plan, as a single plan.

Unless a plan provides otherwise, reimbursements will be attributed to the plan year in which payment is made. Accordingly, they will be subject to tax in an individual's tax year in which a plan year ends.

1. IRC Sec. 105(h)(5).
2. Treas. Reg. §1.105-11(d).
3. IRC Sec. 105(h)(1).
4. IRC Sec. 105(h)(7).

Amounts reimbursed for medical diagnostic procedures for employees, but not dependents, performed at a facility that provides only medical services are not considered a part of a plan and do not come within these rules requiring nondiscriminatory treatment.[1]

8746. Are premiums paid by a taxpayer for personal health insurance deductible?

A taxpayer may deduct premiums paid for medical care insurance (including hospital, surgical, and medical expense reimbursement coverage) as a medical expense to the extent that, when added to all other unreimbursed medical expenses, the total exceeds 10 percent of a taxpayer's adjusted gross income (7.5 percent for tax years beginning before 2013). The threshold is also 10 percent for alternative minimum tax purposes.

The Affordable Care Act increased the threshold to 10 percent of a taxpayer's adjusted gross income for taxpayers who are under the age of sixty-five effective in tax years beginning January 1, 2013. For taxpayers over the age of sixty-five, the threshold for deductibility remained at the 7.5 percent level from years 2013 to 2016.

A taxpayer must itemize his or her deductions in order to take a deduction for medical care premiums or any other medical expenses.[2] The reduction of itemized deductions for certain high-income individuals is not applicable to medical expenses deductible under IRC Section 213.[3]

The only premiums deductible as a medical expense are for medical care insurance. Premiums for non-medical benefits, such as disability income, accidental death and dismemberment, and waiver of premium under a life insurance policy, are not deductible.

The definition of "medical care" generally includes amounts paid for any qualified long-term care insurance contract or for qualified long-term care services and, thus, these expenses may be deducted, subject to certain limitations.[4]

Mandatory contributions to a state disability benefits fund are not deductible under the provisions applicable to medical expense deductions, but are deductible as taxes.[5] Employee contributions to an alternative employer plan providing disability benefits required by state law are nondeductible personal expenses.[6]

If a policy provides both medical and non-medical benefits, a deduction will be allowed for the medical portion of the premium only if the medical charge is reasonable in relation to the total premium. In order to take advantage of this bifurcated approach, the medical portion must be stated separately in either the policy or in a statement furnished by the insurance company.[7]

Similarly, where a premium provides for medical care for individuals other than the taxpayer, spouse and dependents (such as with automobile insurance), a deduction will not be

1. Treas. Reg. §1.105-11(g).
2. IRC Sec. 213(a).
3. IRC Sec. 68(c).
4. IRC Sec. 213(d)(1).
5. *McGowan v. Comm.*, 67 TC 599 (1976); *Trujillo v. Comm.*, 68 TC 670 (1977).
6. Rev. Rul. 81-192, 1981-2 CB 50 (citing N.Y. law); Rev. Rul. 81-193, 1981-2 CB 52 (citing N.J. law); Rev. Rul. 81-194, 1981-2 CB 54 (citing Cal. law).
7. IRC Sec. 213(d)(6).

allowed unless the policy separately states the portion that is applicable to the taxpayer, spouse and dependents.[1]

If a policy provides only indemnity for hospital and surgical expenses, premiums qualify as medical care premiums even though the benefits are stated amounts that will be paid without regard to the actual amount of expense incurred by the taxpayer.[2] Premiums paid for a hospital insurance policy that provides a specific payment for each week the insured is hospitalized, not to exceed a specified number of weeks, regardless of whether the insured receives other payments for reimbursement, do not qualify as medical care premiums and are not deductible.[3]

Because the benefit under a critical illness insurance policy is payable regardless of any actual medical expenses incurred or reimbursement received, the premiums paid for this type of policy would appear not to be deductible.[4]

A deduction also will be denied for employees' contributions to a plan that provides that employees absent from work because of sickness are to be paid a percentage of wages earned on that day by co-employees.[5]

A taxpayer may deduct premiums paid for a policy that reimburses the taxpayer for the cost of prescription drugs as medical care insurance premiums.[6]

Medicare premiums, paid by persons age sixty-five or older, under the supplementary medical insurance or prescription drug programs are deductible as medical care insurance premiums. However, the taxes paid by employees and self-employed individuals for basic hospital insurance under Medicare are not deductible.[7]

If a taxpayer prepays premiums before the taxpayer is sixty-five for insurance that will cover medical care for the taxpayer, spouse, and dependents *after* the taxpayer is sixty-five, these premiums are deductible when paid provided they are payable on a level-premium basis for ten years or more or until age sixty-five, but in no case for fewer than five years.[8]

Payments made to an institution for the provision of lifetime care are deductible under IRC Section 213(a) in the year paid to the extent that the payments are properly allocable to medical care, even if the care is to be provided in the future or possibly not provided at all.[9] The IRS has stated that its rulings should not be interpreted or expanded to permit a current deduction of payments for future medical care (including medical insurance provided beyond the current tax year) in situations where future lifetime care is not of the type associated with the ruling at issue.

1. Rev. Rul. 73-483, 1973-2 CB 75.
2. Rev. Rul. 58-602, 1958-2 CB 109, modified by Rev. Rul. 68-212, 1968-1 CB 91.
3. Rev. Rul. 68-451, 1968-2 CB 111.
4. See Treas. Reg. §1.213-1(e)(4).
5. Rev. Rul. 73-347, 1973-2 CB 25.
6. Rev. Rul. 68-433, 1968-2 CB 104.
7. IRC Sec. 213(d)(1)(D); Rev. Rul. 66-216, 1966-2 CB 100.
8. IRC Sec. 213(d)(7).
9. Rev. Rul. 76-481, 1976-2 CB 82; Rev. Rul. 75-303, 1975-2 CB 87; Rev. Rul. 75-302, 1975-2 CB 86.

8747. Are benefits received under a personal health insurance policy taxable income?

No. All kinds of benefits from personal health insurance generally are entirely exempt from income tax. This exemption applies to disability income, dismemberment and sight loss benefits, critical illness benefits,[1] and hospital, surgical, and other medical expense reimbursement. The taxpayer is not limited as to the amount of benefits, including the amount of disability income that he or she can receive tax-free under personally paid health insurance or under an arrangement having the effect of accident or health insurance.[2] However, courts have held that the IRC Section 104(a)(3) exclusion will be denied where a taxpayer's claims for insurance benefits were not made in good faith and were not based on a true illness or injury.[3]

If a health insurance policy provides for accidental death benefits, the proceeds of these death benefits may be tax-exempt to the policy beneficiary as death proceeds of life insurance.[4] A taxpayer may exclude from gross income disability benefits received for loss of income or earning capacity under no fault insurance.[5] The exclusion also has been applied where the policies were provided to the insured taxpayer by a professional service corporation in which the insured was the sole stockholder.[6]

Health insurance benefits are also tax-exempt if received by a person who has an insurable interest in the individual insured by the policy, rather than by that individual himself.[7]

Medical expense reimbursement benefits will impact the amount that a taxpayer is allowed to deduct for medical expenses. Because only unreimbursed expenses are deductible, the total amount of medical expenses paid during a taxable year must be reduced by the total amount of reimbursements received in that taxable year.[8]

Similarly, if the taxpayer deducts medical expenses in the year they are paid and then receives reimbursement in a later year, the taxpayer (or the taxpayer's estate, where the deduction is taken on the decedent's final return but later reimbursed to the taxpayer's estate) must include the reimbursement, to the extent of the prior year's deduction, in gross income for the later year.[9]

Where the value of a decedent's right to reimbursement proceeds, which is income in respect of a decedent,[10] is included in the decedent's estate, an income tax deduction is available for the portion of estate tax attributable to such value.

Disability income is not treated as reimbursement for medical expenses and, therefore, does not offset such expenses.[11]

1. See, e.g., Let Rul. 200903001.
2. IRC Sec. 104(a)(3); Rev. Rul. 55-331, 1955-1 CB 271, *modified by* Rev. Rul. 68-212, 1968-1 CB 91; Rev. Rul. 70-394, 1970-2 CB 34.
3. *Dodge v. Comm.*, 981 F.2d 350 (8th Cir. 1992).
4. IRC Sec. 101(a); Treas. Reg. §1.101-1(a).
5. Rev. Rul. 73-155, 1973-1 CB 50.
6. Let. Rul. 7751104.
7. See IRC Sec. 104; *Castner Garage, Ltd. v. Comm.*, 43 BTA 1 (1940), *acq.* 1941-1 CB 11.
8. Rev. Rul. 56-18, 1956-1 CB 135.
9. Treas. Reg. §§1.104-1, 1.213-1(g); Rev. Rul. 78-292, 1978-2 CB 233.
10. See Rev. Rul. 78-292, above.
11. *Deming v. Comm.*, 9 TC 383 (1947), *acq.* 1948-1 CB 1.

Example: Ryan, whose adjusted gross income for 2017 was $25,000, paid $4,000 in medical expenses during that year. On his 2017 return, he deducted medical expenses totaling $1,500 [$4,000 - $2,500 (10 percent of his adjusted gross income)]. In 2018, Ryan receives the following benefits from his health insurance: disability income of $1,200 and reimbursement for 2017 doctor and hospital bills of $400. He must report $400 as taxable income on his 2018 return. Had Ryan received the reimbursement in 2017, his medical expense deduction for that year would have been limited to $1,100 (4,000 - $400 [reimbursement] - $2,500 [10 percent of adjusted gross income]). Otherwise, he would have received the entire amount of insurance benefits, including the medical expense reimbursement, tax-free.

8748. How are accident or health benefits taxed for stockholder-employees of a closely-held C corporation?

An employer's accident or health plan must be established for *employees* in order to provide tax-free coverage and benefits.[1] The same is true with respect to amounts received under a state's sickness and disability fund under IRC Section 105(e)(2).

If a plan covers only stockholder-employees, the IRS can challenge tax benefits claimed under the plan on the ground that the plan is not for employees. The challenge for the closely-held C corporation is in establishing that the stockholder-employees are covered as employees, rather than in their capacity as stockholders. If this cannot be established, then premiums or benefits are likely to be treated as dividends. The result is that the premiums will be nondeductible by the corporation and the premiums or benefits will be includable in the gross incomes of covered stockholder-employees.[2]

Courts have found, however, that the tax benefits of employer-provided health insurance are available in a plan that covers only stockholder-employees. This is the case only if the plan covers a class of employees that can be segregated rationally from other employees, if any non-stockholder employees exist, on a criterion other than their being stockholders.[3]

The *Bogene, Smith, Seidel*, and *Epstein* cases, which were decided in favor of the taxpayers, all involved plans that covered only active and compensated officers of the corporation who also were stockholders. In *Smith* and *Seidel*, the officer-shareholders also were the only employees, though in *Bogene* and *Epstein* the corporations also employed other employees who were not shareholders and who were not covered by the plans.

The plan in *American Foundry*, where the plan was found to not be a plan for employees, covered only two of five active officers of a family corporation.[4]

The plan in *Sturgill* covered four officer-stockholders of a family corporation. Two of the four were not active or compensated as officer-employees and the plan was held not to be one for employees.[5]

1. IRC Sec. 105(e).
2. *Larkin v. Comm.*, 48 TC 629 (1967), *aff'd* 394 F.2d 494 (1st Cir. 1968); *Levine v. Comm.*, 50 TC 422 (1968); *Smithback v. Comm.*, TC Memo 1969-136; *Est. of Leidy v. Comm.*, 77-1 USTC ¶9144 (4th Cir. 1977).
3. *Bogene, Inc. v. Comm.*, TC Memo 1968-147, *acq.* 1968 AOD LEXIS 272; *Smith v. Comm.*, TC Memo 1970-243, *acq.* 1970 AOD LEXIS 245; *Seidel v. Comm.*, TC Memo 1971-238, *acq.* 972 AOD LEXIS 15; *Epstein v. Comm.*, TC Memo 1972-53, *acq.* 1972 AOD LEXIS 124; *Oleander Co., Inc. v. United States*, 82-1 USTC ¶9395 (E.D.N.C. 1981); *Giberson v. Comm.*, TC Memo 1982-338; *Est. of Leidy*, above; *Wigutow v. Comm.*, TC Memo 1983-620.
4. *American Foundry v. Comm.*, 76-1 USTC ¶9401 (9th Cir. 1976), acq. 1974-2 CB 1.
5. *Charlie Sturgill Motor Co. v. Comm.*, TC Memo 1973-281, *acq.* 1974 AOD LEXIS 151.

The plan in *Leidy* covered only the president, who was the sole stockholder, and the vice president, who was no longer active in the company.

In *American Foundry* and in *Sturgill*, courts allowed the corporations to deduct reimbursement payments to the active officers as reasonable compensation, even though the payments were not excludable by shareholder-employees under IRC Section 105.

8749. How is health insurance coverage for partners and sole proprietors taxed?

Partners and sole proprietors are self-employed individuals, not employees, and the rules for personal health insurance, rather than employer-provided health insurance, usually apply. Partners and sole proprietors, are, therefore, entitled to deduct 100 percent of amounts paid during a taxable year for insurance that provides medical care for the individual, spouse, and dependents during the tax year.

The insurance can also cover a child who was under age twenty-seven at the end of the tax year, even if the child did not qualify as the taxpayer's dependent. A "child" for this purpose is defined to include a taxpayer's child, stepchild, adopted child, or foster child. A foster child is any child placed with the taxpayer by an authorized placement agency or by judgment, decree, or other order of any court of competent jurisdiction.

In additional, certain premiums paid for long-term care insurance are eligible for this deduction.[1]

A partner or sole proprietor is not entitled to this deduction for any calendar month in which the partner or proprietor is eligible to participate in any subsidized health plan maintained by any employer of the self-employed individual or spouse. This rule is applied separately to plans that include coverage for qualified long-term care services or are qualified long-term care insurance contracts, and plans that do not include that coverage and are not those kinds of contracts.[2]

The deduction is allowable in calculating adjusted gross income and is limited to the self-employed individual's earned income for the tax year that is derived from the trade or business with respect to which the plan providing medical care coverage is established. Earned income means, in general, net earnings from self-employment with respect to a trade or business in which the personal services of the taxpayer are a material income-producing factor.

Any amounts paid for this kind of insurance may *not* be taken into account in computing:

(1) the amount of a medical expense deduction under IRC Section 213; and

(2) net-earnings from self-employment for the purpose of determining the tax on self-employment income.[3]

Additional considerations may apply in the case of a partnership. If a partnership pays accident and health insurance premiums for services rendered by partners in their capacity as

1. IRC Secs. 162(l); 213(d)(1).
2. IRC Sec. 162(l).
3. IRC Sec. 162(l).

partners and without regard to partnership income, premium payments are considered to be "guaranteed payments" under IRC Section 707(c). As such, the premiums are deductible by the partnership under IRC Section 162, subject to IRC Section 263, and must be included in partners' income under IRC Section 61.

A partner is not entitled to exclude premium payments from income under IRC Section 106 but may deduct payments to the extent allowable under IRC Section 162(l), as discussed above.[1] For partners, a policy can be either in the name of the partnership or in the name of the partner. The partner can either self-pay the premiums, or the partnership can pay them and report the premium amounts on Schedule K-1 (Form 1065) as guaranteed payments to be included in the partner's gross income. However, if the policy is in the partner's name and the partner self- pays the premiums, the partnership must reimburse the partner and report the premium amounts on Schedule K-1 (Form 1065) as guaranteed payments to be included in the partner's gross income. Otherwise, the insurance plan will not be considered to be established under the business.

The IRS has found that the cost of consumer medical cards purchased for partners is not deductible by the partners under either IRC Section 162(l) or IRC Section 213. This conclusion was based on the rationale that consumer medical cards that provide discounts on certain medical services and items are not actually insurance products.[2]

The IRS has also concluded that payments from a self-funded medical reimbursement plan set up by a partnership, and made to partners and their dependents, are excludable from partners' income. Premiums paid by partners for coverage under a self-funded plan are deductible, subject to the limits of IRC Section 162(l).[3]

There is no limit on the amount of benefits a partner or sole proprietor can receive tax-free.[4]

The IRS has also found that coverage purchased by a sole proprietor or partnership for non-owner-employees, including an owner's spouse, generally are subject to the same rules that apply in any other employer-employee situation.[5]

The IRS has issued settlement guidelines addressing whether a self-employed individual ("employer-spouse") may hire his or her spouse as an employee ("employee-spouse") and provide family health benefits to the employee-spouse, who then elects family coverage including the employer-spouse. The IRS position is that if an employee-spouse is a bona fide employee, the employer-spouse may deduct the cost of the coverage and the value of the coverage also is excludable from the employee-spouse's gross income.

However, the IRS will closely examine the situation to determine whether an employee-spouse qualifies as a bona fide employee. Part-time employment does not negate employee

1. Rev. Rul. 91-26, 1991-1 CB 184.
2. Let. Rul. 9814023.
3. Let. Rul. 200007025.
4. Rev. Rul. 56-326, 1956-2 CB 100; Rev. Rul. 58-90, 1958-1 CB 88.
5. Rev. Rul. 71-588, 1971-2 CB 91; TAM 9409006.

status, but nominal or insignificant services that have no economic substance or independent significance will be challenged.[1]

8750. How is health insurance coverage taxed for S corporation shareholders?

A shareholder-employee who owns more than 2 percent of the outstanding stock or voting power of an S corporation (based on direct ownership as well as attributed ownership) will be treated as a partner, not an employee (see Q 8749 for the rules applicable to partners).[2] Therefore, accident and health insurance premium payments for more-than-2 percent shareholders paid in consideration for services rendered are treated as guaranteed payments made to partners. The result is that an S corporation can deduct premiums under IRC Section 162 and a shareholder-employee must include premium payments in income under IRC Section 61. The shareholder-employee cannot exclude them under IRC Section 106, but may deduct the cost of the premiums to the extent permitted by IRC Section 162(l), as discussed in Q 8749.[3]

With respect to coverage purchased by an S corporation for employees who do not own any stock and for shareholder-employees who own 2 percent or less of the outstanding stock or voting power, the same rules apply as in any other employer-employee situation.

8751. What is a health reimbursement arrangement (HRA) and how is it taxed?

The IRS defines an HRA as an arrangement that:

(1) is solely employer-funded and not paid for directly or indirectly by salary reduction contributions under a cafeteria plan; and

(2) reimburses employees for substantiated medical care expenses incurred by the employee and the employee's spouse and dependents, as defined in IRC Section 152, up to a maximum dollar amount per coverage period. See Q 8754 for a discussion of the impact of the ACA on HRAs.

A taxpayer is entitled to carry forward any unused amounts in the individual's account to increase the maximum reimbursement amount in subsequent coverage periods.[4] HRAs are not available for self-employed individuals.

Employer-provided coverage and medical care reimbursement amounts under an HRA are excludable from an employee's gross income under IRC Section 106 and IRC Section 105(b), assuming all requirements for HRAs are met.[5]

1. IRS Settlement Guidelines, 2001 TNT 222-25 (Nov. 16, 2001); see also *Poyda v. Comm.*, TC Summary Opinion 2001-91.
2. IRC Sec. 1372.
3. Rev. Rul. 91-26, 1991-1 CB 184.
4. Notice 2002-45, 2002-2 CB 93; Rev. Rul. 2002-41, 2002-2 CB 75. See also IRS Publication 969 (2015) "Health Savings Accounts and Other Tax-Favored Health Plans."
5. Notice 2002-45, 2002-2 CB 93; Rev. Rul. 2002-41, 2002-2 CB 75.

Reimbursements for medicine are limited to doctor-prescribed drugs and insulin for tax years beginning after December 31, 2010. Consequently, over-the counter medicines are no longer qualified expenses unless prescribed by a doctor after 2010.[1]

An HRA is not permitted to offer cash-outs at any time, even on an employee's termination of service or retirement. However, it may continue to reimburse former employees for medical care expenses after such events even if the employee does not elect COBRA continuation coverage.[2] An HRA is a group health plan and, thus, is subject to COBRA continuation coverage requirements.

HRAs once could, on a one-time basis per HRA, make a qualified HSA distribution. A qualified HSA distribution is a rollover made before January 1, 2012 to a health savings account (see Q 8756), of an amount not exceeding the balance in the HRA as it existed on September 21, 2006.[3]

HRAs may not be used to reimburse expenses that were either incurred before the HRA was in existence or that are deductible under IRC Section 213 for a prior taxable year. An unreimbursed claim incurred in one coverage period may be reimbursed in a later coverage period, so long as the individual was covered under the HRA when the claim was incurred.[4]

The IRS has approved the use of employer-issued debit and credit cards to pay for medical expenses as incurred provided that the employer requires subsequent substantiation of the expenses or has in place sufficient procedures to substantiate the payments at the time of purchase.[5]

8752. What ordering rules for reimbursement apply if a taxpayer maintains both an HRA and a health FSA?

An employee may not be reimbursed for the same medical care expense by both an HRA and an IRC Section 125 health FSA (see Q 8765). Technically, ordering rules from the IRS specify that the HRA benefits must be exhausted before FSA reimbursements may be made. Despite this, HRAs can be drafted to specify that coverage under the HRA is available only after expenses exceeding the dollar amount of an IRC Section 125 FSA have been paid. Thus, an employee could exhaust FSA coverage, because FSA funds may only be carried over if the FSA specifically permits a carry over (and even then only up to $500 per year can be carried forward), before tapping into HRA coverage, which can be carried over.[6]

8753. Can HRA contributions be made via salary reduction or through a cafeteria plan?

Employer contributions to an HRA may not be attributable in any way to salary reductions. Thus, an HRA may not be offered under a cafeteria plan, but may be offered in connection with

1. IRC Sec. 106(f), as added by PPACA 2010.
2. Notice 2002-45, above.
3. IRC Sec. 106(e).
4. Notice 2002-45, 2002-2 CB 93.
5. Notice 2006-69, 2006-31 IRB 107; Rev. Proc. 2003-43, 2003-21 IRB 935, supplemented by Rev. Proc. 2007-62; 2007-2 CB 786. See also Notice 2007-2, 2007-2 IRB 254.
6. Notice 2002-45, 2002-2 CB 93.

a cafeteria plan. Where an HRA is offered in connection with another accident or health plan funded by a salary reduction plan, a facts and circumstances test is used to determine if salary reductions are attributable to the HRA. If a salary reduction amount for a coverage period to fund a non-HRA accident or health plan exceeds the actual cost of the non-specified accident or health plan coverage, the salary reduction will be attributed to the HRA. An example of the application of this rule can be found in Revenue Ruling 2002-41.[1]

Because an HRA may not be paid for through salary reduction, the following restrictions on health FSAs are not applicable to HRAs:

(1) The ban against a benefit that defers compensation by permitting employees to carry over an unlimited amount of unused elective contributions or plan benefits from one plan year to another plan year.

(2) The requirement that the maximum amount of reimbursement must be available at all times during the coverage period.

(3) The mandatory twelve month period of coverage.

(4) The limitation that reimbursed medical expenses must be incurred during the period of coverage.[2]

8754. Under the ACA, can a health reimbursement arrangement (HRA) be integrated with health insurance coverage without violating the prohibition on plans that place annual dollar limits on available benefits?

The IRS has issued guidance providing that a health reimbursement arrangement (HRA) cannot be integrated with individual coverage (whether purchased in the individual insurance markets or an exchange) in order to comply with the ACA prohibition against annual dollar limits on benefits available under a plan, eliminating the possibility that employers could use HRAs to subsidize employees' purchase of health insurance. This is the case unless certain specific criteria are met (see below).

IRS guidance provides the circumstances under which an HRA will be considered integrated with a health plan so that it does not violate the annual dollar limit prohibition. An HRA may be considered integrated with another health plan (and, thus, not in violation of the prohibition against annual dollar limits) if it meets one of two tests.

First, an HRA can be integrated if (1) the employer offers a second group health plan that does not consist solely of certain excepted benefits, (2) the employee receiving the HRA is actually enrolled in that group health plan or a spouse's plan, (3) the HRA is only available to employees enrolled in the non-HRA group coverage, (4) the HRA is only permitted to reimburse one or more of: co-payments, co-insurance, deductibles, and premiums under the non-HRA coverage, or medical expenses for non-essential benefits and (5) the employee is permitted to opt-out of the HRA.

1. 2002-2 CB 75.
2. Notice 2002-45, 2002-2 CB 93.

Under the second method, if the HRA does not limit reimbursements as required under the first method, (1) the employer must offer a group health plan in addition to the HRA that provides certain minimum value under IRC Section 36B, (2) the employee must actually be enrolled in that plan or a spouse's plan, (3) the HRA must only be available to employees enrolled in a non-HRA plan and (4) the employee must be permitted to opt-out.

An exception to these rules applies for employer sponsored HRAs offered to one participant or solely to retirees. These HRAs may be offered on a stand-alone basis without its participant(s) being covered by the employer's major medical health plan.

8755. What is a qualified small employer health reimbursement arrangement (QSEHRA)? Can a QSEHRA be used by employers to reimburse employees for the cost of individual health insurance premiums?

The 21st Century Cures Act introduced a new health reimbursement arrangement (HRA) that allows small employers to continue to reimburse employees for the cost of individual health insurance premiums. Small business employers will be able to offer qualified small employer health reimbursement arrangements (QSEHRAs) beginning in 2017 without incurring ACA penalties. QSEHRAs allow a small employer who is not an applicable large employer under the ACA (i.e., one that has fewer than 50 full-time employees) to reimburse employees for the purchase of individual health insurance policies using an HRA if the small employer does not also offer its employees group health coverage. The employer can contribute a maximum of $4,950 in 2018 for employees who purchase individual coverage, and a maximum of $10,000 if the employee purchases family coverage (both contribution limits will be indexed for inflation after 2017 and pro-rated amounts are used for years in which only partial coverage is offered).

QSEHRAs must generally be offered on the same basis to all comparable employees, though the employer can exclude employees who have yet to work 90 days, employees who have not reached age 25, employees who are covered by a collective bargaining agreement and employees who are nonresident aliens and have no earned income from U.S. sources. Small business employers who choose to offer QSEHRAs must provide a written notice to employees 90 days before the beginning of the year (the IRS extended the notice deadline for 2017 QSEHRAs[1]) that specifies the amount of the benefit that will be provided by the QSEHRA and informs participating employees that they must inform the health insurance exchanges of the benefit provided by the QSEHRA if the employee intends to apply for premium assistance.

The notice must also clearly inform the employee that if he or she does not purchase health insurance, ACA penalties may apply and any reimbursements from the QSEHRA may be included in gross income. Small employers must report the QSEHRA coverage on Form W-2, Box 12 (for informational purposes). Further, the employer must provide participating employees with Form 1095-B, and send the same data to the IRS on Form 1094-B.[2]

1. Notice 2017-20.
2. 21st Century Cures Act, HR 34.

8756. What is a health savings account (HSA) and how is it taxed?

A health savings account (HSA) is a trust created exclusively for the purpose of paying the qualified medical expenses of an account beneficiary.[1]

An HSA must be created by a written governing instrument that states:

(1) except in the case of certain rollover contributions, no contribution will be accepted:

a. unless it is in cash; and

b. to the extent that the contribution, when added to previous contributions for the calendar year, exceeds the contribution limit for the calendar year;

(2) the trustee is a bank, an insurance company, or a person who satisfies IRS requirements for administering the trust;

(3) no part of trust assets will be invested in life insurance contracts;

(4) trust assets will not be commingled with other property, with certain limited exceptions; and

(5) the interest of an individual in the balance of his or her account is non-forfeitable.[2]

HSAs are available to any employer or individual for an account beneficiary who participates in a high deductible health insurance plan. An eligible individual or an employer may establish an HSA with a qualified HSA custodian or trustee without IRS permission or authorization. As mentioned above, any insurance company or bank can act as a trustee and, additionally, any person already approved by the IRS to act as an individual retirement arrangement ("IRA") trustee or custodian automatically is approved to act in the same capacity for HSAs.[3]

HSAs are similar to IRAs in some respects although a taxpayer cannot use an IRA as an HSA, nor can a taxpayer combine an IRA with an HSA.[4]

Contributions to an HSA generally may be made either by an individual, by an individual's employer, or by both. If contributions are made by an individual taxpayer, they are deductible from income.[5] Contributions made by an employer are excluded from the employee's income.[6] The HSA itself is also exempt from income tax as long as it remains an HSA.[7] HSA contributions may be made through a cafeteria plan under IRC Section 125 (see Q 8751).[8]

1. IRC Sec. 223(d)(1).
2. IRC Sec. 223(d)(1).
3. Notice 2004-50, 2004-2 CB 196, A-72; Notice 2004-2, 2004-1 CB 269, A-9, A-10.
4. See Notice 2004-2, above.
5. IRC Sec. 223(a).
6. See IRC Sec. 106(d)(1).
7. IRC Sec. 223(e)(1).
8. IRC Sec. 125(d)(2)(D).

HSA distributions used exclusively to pay qualified medical expenses are not includable in gross income. Distributions used for other purposes are includable in gross income and may be subject to a penalty, with some exceptions.[1]

An employer's contributions to an HSA are not treated as part of a group health plan subject to COBRA continuation coverage requirements.[2] Therefore, a plan is not required to make COBRA continuation coverage available with respect to an HSA.[3]

According to IRS guidance, a levy to satisfy a tax liability under IRC Section 6331 extends to a taxpayer's interest in an HSA. A taxpayer is liable for the additional 20 percent tax (10 percent prior to January 1, 2011, under PPACA 2010) on the amount of the levy unless the taxpayer has attained age sixty-five or is disabled at the time of the levy.[4]

8757. Who is an eligible individual for purposes of maintaining an HSA?

An "eligible individual" for purposes of maintaining an HSA is an individual who, for any month, is covered under a high deductible health plan (HDHP) as of the first day of that month and is not also covered under a non-high deductible health plan providing coverage for any benefit covered under the HDHP.[5]

Individuals who are enrolled in Medicare Part A or Part B are not eligible to contribute to an HSA.[6] Mere *eligibility* for Medicare does not preclude HSA contributions.[7]

If an individual has received medical benefits through the Department of Veterans Affairs within the previous three months, the individual may not contribute to an HSA for the current month. Mere eligibility for VA medical benefits will not disqualify an otherwise eligible individual from making HSA contributions.[8]

If an individual is covered by a separate prescription drug plan that provides any benefits before a required high deductible is satisfied, the individual normally does not qualify as an eligible individual.[9] Despite this general rule, the IRS has ruled that if an individual's separate prescription drug plan does not provide benefits until an HDHP's minimum annual deductible amount has been met, then the individual will be an eligible individual under Section 223(c)(1)(A). For calendar years 2004 and 2005 only, the IRS provided transition relief such that an individual would not fail to be an eligible individual solely by virtue of coverage by a separate prescription drug plan.[10]

1. IRC Sec. 223(f).
2. See IRC Secs. 106(b)(5), 106(d)(2).
3. See Treas. Reg. §54.4980B-2, A-1 regarding Archer MSAs.
4. CCA 200927019.
5. IRC Sec. 223(c)(1)(A).
6. IRC Sec. 223(b)(7).
7. Notice 2004-50, 2004-2 CB 196, A-3.
8. Notice 2004-50, 2004-2 CB 196, A-5.
9. Rev. Rul. 2004-38, 2004-1 CB 717, modified by Rev. Proc. 2004-22; 2004-1 CB 727.
10. Rev. Proc. 2004-22, 2004-1 CB 727.

If an individual is covered under an Employee Assistance Program, disease management program, or wellness program, that individual will not fail to be an eligible individual based solely on this coverage if the program does not provide significant benefits in the nature of medical care or treatment.[1]

Certain types of insurance are not considered in determining whether an individual is eligible for an HSA. Specifically, insurance for a specific disease or illness, hospitalization insurance paying a fixed daily amount, and insurance providing coverage that relates to certain liabilities are disregarded.[2]

In addition, coverage provided by insurance or otherwise for accidents, disability, dental care, vision care, or long-term care will not adversely impact HSA eligibility.[3]

If an employer contributes to an eligible employee's HSA, in order to receive an employer comparable contribution the employee must:

(1) establish the HSA on or before the last day in February of the year following the year for which the contribution is being made and;

(2) notify the appropriate contact person of the HSA account information on or before the last day in February of the year described in (1) above and specify and provide HSA account information (such as the account number, name and address of trustee or custodian, etc.) as well as the method by which the account information will be provided (whether in writing, by e-mail, on a certain form, etc.).[4]

An eligible employee that establishes an HSA and provides the information required as described in (1) and (2) above will receive an HSA contribution, plus reasonable interest, for the year for which contribution is being made by April 15 of the following year.[5]

8758. Can an individual participate in both an HSA and a health FSA?

The IRS has issued guidance providing that taxpayers who participate in health flexible spending accounts (FSAs) that reimburse all qualified medical expenses are ineligible to also contribute to health savings accounts (HSAs) because participation in the FSA constitutes "other coverage" prohibited by the rules applicable to HSAs. This is the case even if the individual only participates in the FSA during the tax year because of a permitted carryover from the prior tax year.

In order to be eligible to contribute to an HSA, a taxpayer must have a high deductible health plan (HDHP), and can also have certain other types of permitted insurance and coverage, as well

1. Notice 2004-50, 2004-2 CB 196, A-10.
2. IRC Sec. 223(c)(3).
3. IRC Sec. 223(c)(1)(B).
4. Treas. Reg. §54.4980G-4 A-14(c).
5. TD 9393, 2008-20 IRB.

as preventative care coverage, but not "other coverage." For these purposes, a taxpayer is not eligible to contribute to an HSA if he or she is covered under a health plan that is not an HDHP that provides coverage for any benefit covered under the HDHP. A health FSA that reimburses for all qualified medical expenses falls within this prohibition.

This is the result even if participation in the FSA for the year is only because of a permitted carryover of up to $500 from the preceding tax year. The ineligibility for HSA contributions continues throughout the entire tax year, even if the carried over amounts are exhausted early in the year.

However, a taxpayer can elect to have unused FSA funds carried over into an HSA-compatible FSA (which is either a limited purpose FSA, a post-deductible FSA or a combination of the two). In this case, a taxpayer will be eligible to contribute to an HSA for the year.[1]

8759. What is a high deductible health plan for purposes of an HSA?

The requirements for a high deductible health plan (HDHP) differ depending on whether individual or family coverage is provided. In this context, family coverage includes any coverage other than self-only coverage.[2]

For 2018, an HDHP is a plan with an annual deductible of not less than $1,350 for self-only coverage ($1,300 in 2015-2017). The family coverage deductible limit is $2,700 in 2018 ($2,600 in 2015–2017). Annual out-of-pocket expenses for an HDHP cannot exceed $6,650 ($6,550 in 2016 and 2017) for self-only coverage. For family coverage, the annual out-of-pocket expense limitation is increased to $13,300 in 2018 ($13,100 for 2016 and 2017).[3] These annual deductible amounts and out-of-pocket expense amounts are adjusted for cost of living. Increases are made in multiples of $50.[4]

Deductible limits for HDHPs are based on a twelve month period. If a plan deductible may be satisfied over a period longer than twelve months, the minimum annual deductible under IRC Section 223(c)(2)(A) must be increased on a pro-rata basis to take the longer period into account.[5]

An HDHP may impose a reasonable lifetime limit on benefits provided under the plan as long as the lifetime limit on benefits is not designed to circumvent the maximum annual out-of-pocket limitation.[6] A plan with no limitation on out-of-pocket expenses, either by design or by its express terms, does not qualify as a high deductible health plan.[7] Beginning in 2016, the CMS has provided guidance stating that the self-only limitation applies to each individual,

1. ILM 201413005.
2. IRC Sec. 223(c)(5).
3. Rev. Proc. 2015-30, Rev. Proc. 2016-28, Rev. Proc. 2017-37.
4. IRC Sec. 223(g).
5. Notice 2004-50, 2004-2 CB 196, A-24.
6. Notice 2004-50, 2004-2 CB 196, A-14.
7. Notice 2004-50, 2004-2 CB 196, A-17.

regardless of whether the individual is enrolled in self-only or family coverage. This is the case even if the limitation for self-only coverage is below the family deductible limit. Family coverage can continue to be offered as long as the self-only limitation is applied separately to each individual under the plan.[1]

An HDHP may provide preventive care coverage without application of the annual deductible.[2] The IRS has provided guidance and safe harbor guidelines on what constitutes preventive care. Pursuant to the IRS safe harbor, preventive care includes, but is not limited to, periodic check-ups, routine prenatal and well-child care, immunizations, tobacco cessation programs, obesity weight-loss programs, and various health screening services. Preventive care may include drugs or medications taken to prevent the occurrence or reoccurrence of a disease that is not currently present.[3]

Notice 2013-57 clarifies that a health plan will not fail to qualify as an HDHP merely because it provides preventative services under the ACA without requiring a deductible.[4]

For months before January 1, 2006, a health plan would not fail to qualify as an HDHP solely based upon its compliance with state health insurance laws that mandate coverage without regard to a deductible or before the high deductible is satisfied.[5] This transition relief only applied to disqualifying benefits mandated by state laws that were in effect on January 1, 2004. This relief extended to non-calendar year health plans with benefit periods of twelve months or less that began before January 1, 2006.[6]

Out-of-pocket expenses include deductibles, co-payments, and other amounts that a participant must pay for covered benefits. Premiums are not considered out-of-pocket expenses.[7]

8760. What are the contribution limits on an HSA?

An eligible individual may deduct the aggregate amount paid in cash into an HSA during the taxable year, up to $3,450 for 2018 ($3,400 for 2017), for self-only coverage and $6,900 for 2018 (up from $6,750 in 2016) for family coverage. The HSA contribution limits for the 2018 taxable year and the six previous years are provided in the table below.[8]

	2012	2013	2014	2015	2016	2017	2018
Individual HSA Limit	$3,100	$3,250	$3,300	$3,350	$3,350	$3,400	$3,450
Family HSA Limit	$6,250	$6,450	$6,550	$6,650	$6,750	$6,750	$6,900

1. See DOL FAQ, available at www.dol.gov/ebsa/faqs/faq-aca27.html.
2. IRC Sec. 223(c)(2)(C).
3. Notice 2004-50, 2004-2 CB 196, A-27; Notice 2004-23, 2004-1 CB 725.
4. 2013 IRB LEXIS 465.
5. Notice 2004-43, 2004-2 CB 10
6. Notice 2005-83, 2005-2 CB 1075.
7. Notice 2004-2, 2004-1 CB 269, A-3; Notice 96-53, 1996-2 CB 219, A-4.
8. IRC Secs. 223(a), 223(b)(2); Rev. Proc. 2010-22, 2010-1 CB 747; Rev. Proc. 2009-29, 2009-1 CB 1050, Rev. Proc. 2015-53, Rev. Proc. 2016-28, Rev. Proc. 2017-37.

For years prior to 2007, the allowable contribution and deduction were limited to the lesser of the deductible under the applicable HDHP or the indexed annual limits for self-only coverage or family coverage.[1]

The determination of whether a plan offers self-only or family coverage is made as of the first day of the month. The limit is calculated on a monthly basis and the allowable deduction for a taxable year cannot exceed the sum of the monthly limitations. See Q 8761 for a discussion of the individual requirements for HSA eligibility. An example illustrating calculation of the HSA contribution limit is provided below.

> *Example:* Lola has self-only coverage under an HDHP in 2018 and wishes to contribute to an HSA. She has been an eligible individual for all of 2018, so her monthly contribution for self-only coverage is calculated by dividing the 2018 annual limit ($3,450) by the twelve months in her eligibility period. Lola can contribute $287.50 per month in 2018. If Lola was only an eligible individual for the first eight months of 2018, she still must first calculate her monthly contribution based on a twelve-month year. However, her annual contribution limit is prorated to $2,300 (her monthly $287.50 limit multiplied by the eight months of eligibility). Although the annual contribution level is determined for each month, Lola is entitled to contribute her entire annual contribution amount in a single payment, if desired.[2] If Lola had been an eligible individual for the last month of 2018, she would have been treated as though she were an eligible individual for the entire year.

Individuals who attain age fifty-five before the close of a taxable year are eligible for an additional "catch-up" contribution amount over and above that calculated under IRC Section 223(b)(1) and IRC Section 223(b)(2). The additional contribution amount is $1,000 for 2009 and later years.[3] In 2018, this would allow individuals age fifty-five and older to contribute up to $4,450 and the total contribution for a family would be $7,900.

An individual who becomes an eligible individual after the beginning of a taxable year and who is an eligible individual for the last month of the taxable year is treated as being an eligible individual for the entire taxable year. For example, a calendar-year taxpayer with self-only coverage under an HDHP who became an eligible individual for December 2018 would be able to contribute the full $3,450 to an HSA in that taxable year. If a taxpayer fails at any time during the following taxable year to be an eligible individual, the taxpayer must include in his or her gross income the aggregate amount of all HSA contributions made by the taxpayer that could not have been made under the general rule. The amount includable in gross income also is subject to a 10 percent penalty tax.[4]

For married individuals, if either spouse has family coverage, then both spouses are treated as having family coverage and the deduction limit is divided equally between them, unless they agree on a different division. If both spouses have family coverage under different plans, both spouses are treated as having only the family coverage with the lowest deductible.[5]

1. IRC Sec. 223(b)(2), prior to amendment by TRHCA 2006.
2. IRC Sec. 223(b); Notice 2004-2, 2004-1 CB 269, A-12.
3. IRC Sec. 223(b)(3).
4. IRC Sec. 223(b)(8).
5. IRC Sec. 223(b)(5).

An HSA may be offered in conjunction with a cafeteria plan. Both a HDHP and an HSA are qualified benefits under a cafeteria plan.[1]

Employer contributions to an HSA are treated as employer-provided coverage for medical expenses to the extent that contributions do not exceed the applicable amount of allowable HSA contributions.[2] Further, an employee is not required to include any amount in income simply because the employee may choose between employer contributions to an HSA and employer contributions to another health plan.[3]

An individual may not deduct any amount paid into an HSA. Instead, that amount is excludable from gross income under IRC Section 106(d).[4]

No deduction is allowed for any amount contributed to an HSA with respect to any individual for whom another taxpayer may take a deduction under IRC Section 151 (on dependency exemptions) for the taxable year.[5] See Q 8761 to Q 8765 for the rules governing employer contributions to employee HSAs. See Q 8768 for a discussion of the treatment of HSA distributions.

8761. What rules govern employer contributions to employee HSAs? Must an employer who offers HSAs to its employees contribute the same amount for each employee?

An employer offering HSAs to its employees is required to make comparable contributions to the HSAs for all comparable participating employees for each coverage period during the calendar year.[6] IRC Section 4980G incorporates the comparability rules of IRC Section 4980E by reference.[7]

"Comparable contributions" for this purpose are contributions that either are the same amount or the same percentage of the annual deductible limit under a high deductible health plan (HDHP).[8] "Comparable participating employees" include all employees who are in the same category of employee and have the same category of coverage.

Category of employee refers to full-time employees, part-time employees, and former employees.[9] Category of coverage refers to self-only coverage and family-type coverage. Family coverage may be subcategorized as self plus one, self plus two, and self plus three or more. Subcategories of family coverage may be tested separately, but an employer may not contribute less to a category of family coverage with more covered persons than to another category with fewer covered persons.[10]

1. IRC Sec. 125(d)(2)(D).
2. IRC Sec. 106(d)(1).
3. IRC Secs. 106(b)(2), 106(d)(2).
4. See IRC Sec. 223(b)(4).
5. IRC Sec. 223(b)(6).
6. IRC Secs. 4980E, 4980G.
7. Treas. Reg. §54.4980G-1, A-1.
8. IRC Sec. 4980E(d)(2); Treas. Reg. §54.4980G-4, A-1.
9. Treas. Reg. §54.4980G-3, A-5.
10. IRC Sec. 4980E(d)(3); Treas. Reg. §§54.4980G-1, A-2, 54.4980G-4, A-1.

For years beginning in 2007 and thereafter, participating highly compensated employees may not be treated as comparable to non-highly compensated employees.[1]

Employer contributions made to HSAs through a cafeteria plan, including matching contributions, are not subject to the comparability rules, but are instead subject to IRC Section 125 nondiscrimination rules.[2]

An employer may make contributions to HSAs of all eligible employees either:

(1) at the beginning of a calendar year;

(2) monthly, on a pay-as-you-go basis; or

(3) at the end of a calendar year, taking into account each month that an employee was a comparable participating employee.

An employer must use the same contribution method for all comparable participating employees.[3]

If an employer does not prefund HSA contributions, regulations provide that it may accelerate all or part of its contributions for an entire year to HSAs of employees who incur, during the calendar year, qualified medical expenses exceeding the employer's cumulative HSA contributions to date. If an employer permits accelerated contributions, the accelerated contributions must be available on a uniform basis to all eligible employees under reasonable requirements.[4] See Q 8762 for a detailed discussion of the rules that apply when an employee does not participate in the employer's HSA for the entire year.

8762. What are the contribution rules for employers who establish HSAs for employees when an employee has not established an HSA at the time the employer makes contributions or is not eligible to participate for the entire year?

If there are employees who have not established an HSA at the time the employer makes contributions, the employer must provide each such eligible employee a written notice containing certain information no later than January 15. The notice must explain that if the employee, by the last day of February, (a) establishes an HSA and (b) notifies the employer that he or she has done so, the employee will receive a comparable contribution to that HSA for the prior calendar year. This notice may be delivered electronically.

The employer must then make comparable contributions by April 15, taking into account each month that the employee was a comparable participating employee, for each eligible

1. IRC Sec. 4980G(d), as added by TRHCA 2006.
2. Notice 2004-50, 2004-2 CB 196, A-47; IRC Sec. 125 (b), (c), and (g); Treas. Reg. §1.125-1, A-19.
3. IRC Sec. 4980E(d)(3); Treas. Reg. §54.4980G-4, A-4.
4. IRC Sec. 4980E(d)(3); Treas. Reg. §54.4980G-4, A-15.

employee that notifies an employer that he or she has established an HSA. These retroactive comparable contributions must also include reasonable interest.[1]

There is a maximum contribution permitted for all employees who are eligible individuals during the last month of the taxable year. An employer may contribute up to the maximum annual contribution amount for the calendar year based on the employees' HDHP coverage to HSAs of all employees who are eligible individuals on the first day of the last month of the employees' taxable year. This rule also applies to employees who worked for the employer for less than the entire calendar year and employees who became eligible individuals after January 1 of the calendar year. For example, contributions may be made on behalf of an eligible individual who is hired after January 1 or an employee who becomes an eligible individual after January 1.[2]

Employers are only required to provide a pro rata contribution based on the number of months that an individual was an eligible individual and employed by the employer during the year. If an employer contributes more than a pro rata amount for a calendar year to an HSA of any eligible individual who is hired after January 1 of the calendar year, or any employee who becomes an eligible individual any time after January 1 of the calendar year, the employer must contribute that same amount on an equal and uniform basis to HSAs of all comparable participating employees who are hired or become eligible individuals after January 1 of the calendar year.[3]

Similarly, if an employer contributes the maximum annual contribution amount for the calendar year to an HSA of any eligible individual who is hired after January 1 of the calendar year or any employee who becomes an eligible individual any time after January 1 of the calendar year, the employer also must contribute the maximum annual contribution amount on an equal and uniform basis to HSAs of all comparable participating employees who are hired or become eligible individuals after January 1 of the calendar year.[4]

An employer who makes the maximum calendar year contribution or more than a pro rata contribution to HSAs of employees who become eligible individuals after the first day of the calendar year or to eligible individuals who are hired after the first day of the calendar year does not fail to satisfy comparability merely because some employees will have received more contributions on a monthly basis than employees who worked the entire calendar year.[5]

8763. Are there any exceptions to the comparability rules that govern employer contributions to employee HSAs?

Yes, the IRC provides an exception to the comparability rules that allows, but that does not require, employers to make larger contributions to HSAs of non-highly compensated employees than to HSAs of highly compensated employees.[6]

1. IRC Sec. 4980E(d)(3); Treas. Reg. §54.4980G-4, A-14.
2. Treas. Reg. §54.4980G-4.
3. Treas. Reg. §54.4980G-4.
4. Treas. Reg. §54.4980G-4.
5. Treas. Reg. §54.4980G-4.
6. IRC Sec. 4980G(d); Preamble, TD 9457, 74 Fed. Reg. 45994, 45995 (9-8-2009); see Treas. Reg. §54.4980G-6.

Regulations provide that employers may make larger HSA contributions for non-highly compensated employees who are comparable participating employees than for highly compensated employees who are comparable participating employees.[1] However, the reverse does not apply: employer contributions to HSAs for highly compensated employees who are comparable participating employees may *not* be larger than employer HSA contributions for non-highly compensated employees who are comparable participating employees.[2]

Comparability rules continue to apply with respect to contributions to HSAs of all non-highly compensated employees and all highly compensated employees. Thus, employers must make comparable contributions for a calendar year to the HSA of each non-highly compensated comparable participating employee and each highly compensated comparable participating employee.[3]

8764. Is there a penalty if an employer fails to meet the HSA comparability requirements with respect to contributions to employee HSAs?

If an employer fails to meet comparability requirements (see Q 8761), a penalty tax is imposed, equal to 35 percent of the aggregate amount contributed by an employer to HSAs of employees for their taxable years ending with or within the calendar year.[4]

8765. Can employers allow employees to roll funds into their HSAs from HRAs or FSAs? What is a qualified HSA distribution?

Employers may offer a rollover, known as a qualified HSA distribution, from a health reimbursement arrangement (HRA) or a health flexible spending arrangement (FSA) for any employee. However, if the employer offers a rollover option to one employee, it must offer a rollover to any eligible individual covered under an HDHP of the employer. Otherwise, the comparability requirements of IRC Section 4980G do not apply to qualified HSA distributions.[5]

There are special comparability rules for qualified HSA distributions contributed to HSAs on or after December 20, 2006, and before January 1, 2012. Effective January 1, 2010, the comparability rules of IRC Section 4980G do not apply to amounts contributed to employee HSAs through qualified HSA distributions.

To satisfy comparability rules, if an employer offers qualified HSA distributions to any employee who is an eligible individual covered under any HDHP, the employer must offer qualified HSA distributions to all employees who are eligible individuals covered under any HDHP. If an employer offers qualified HSA distributions only to employees who are eligible individuals covered under an employer's HDHP, the employer is not required to offer qualified

1. Treas. Reg. §54.4980G-6, Q&A-1.
2. Treas. Reg. §54.4980G-6, Q&A-2.
3. Treas. Reg. §54.4980G-6, Q&A-1.
4. IRC Secs. 4980E(a), 4980E(b), 4980G(b). For filing requirements for excise tax returns, see Treas. Reg. §§54.6011-2 (general requirement of return), 54.6061-1 (signing of return), 54.6071-1(c) (time for filing return), 54.6091-1 (place for filing return), and 54.6151-1 (time and place for paying tax shown on return).
5. IRC Sec. 106(e)(5).

HSA distributions to employees who are eligible individuals but are not covered under the employer's HDHP.[1]

8766. What is the penalty for making excess contributions to an HSA? How does an excess contribution impact the taxation of distributions from the HSA?

If an HSA receives excess contributions for a taxable year, distributions from the HSA are not includable in income to the extent that the distributions do not exceed the aggregate excess contributions to all HSAs of an individual for a taxable year if the following are true:

(1) The distribution is received by the individual on or before the last day for filing the individual's income tax return for the year including extensions.

(2) The distribution is accompanied by the amount of net income attributable to the excess contribution. Any net income must be included in an individual's gross income for the taxable year in which it is received.[2]

Excess contributions to an HSA are subject to a 6 percent tax. However, the penalty tax may not exceed 6 percent of the value of the account, as determined at the close of the taxable year.[3]

Excess contributions are defined, for this purpose, as the sum of:

(1) the aggregate amount contributed for the taxable year to the accounts, excluding rollover contributions, which is neither excludable from gross income under IRC Section 106(b) nor allowable as a deduction under IRC Section 223; and

(2) the amount calculated in (1), above, for the preceding taxable year *reduced by* the sum of (x) the distributions from the accounts that were included in gross income under IRC Section 223(f)(2), and (y) the excess of the maximum amount allowable as a deduction under IRC Section 223(b)(1), for the taxable year, over the amount contributed for the taxable year.[4]

For these purposes, any excess contributions distributed from an HSA are treated as amounts not contributed.[5]

8767. How are funds accumulated in an HSA taxed prior to distribution?

Funds accumulated in an HSA are generally exempt from income tax unless the account ceases to be an HSA.[6]

1. Treas. Reg. §54.4980G-7, Q&A-1.
2. IRC Sec. 223(f)(3)(A).
3. IRC Sec. 4973(a).
4. IRC Sec. 4973(g).
5. IRC Sec. 4973(g).
6. IRC Sec. 223(e)(1).

In addition, rules similar to those applicable to individual retirement arrangements (IRAs) regarding the loss of the income tax exemption for an account where an employee engages in a prohibited transaction[1] and those regarding the effect of pledging an account as security[2] apply to HSAs. Any amounts treated as distributed under these rules will be treated as not used to pay qualified medical expenses.[3]

8768. How are amounts distributed from HSAs taxed?

If a distribution from an HSA is used exclusively to pay the qualified medical expenses of an account holder, the distributed amount is not includable in gross income.[4] In contrast, any distribution from an HSA that is not used exclusively to pay qualified medical expenses of an account holder must be included in the account holder's gross income.[5]

In addition, a penalty tax applies to any distribution that is includable in income because it was not used to pay qualified medical expenses.[6] The penalty tax is 20 percent of includable income for a distribution from an HSA.[7] For distributions made prior to January 1, 2011, the additional tax on nonqualified distributions from HSAs was 10 percent of includable income.[8]

The penalty tax does not apply to includable distributions received after an HSA holder becomes disabled within the meaning of IRC Section 72(m)(7), dies, or reaches the age of Medicare eligibility.[9]

"Qualified medical expenses" are amounts paid by the account holder for medical care[10] for the individual, his or her spouse, and any dependent to the extent that expenses are not compensated by insurance or otherwise.[11] For tax years beginning after December 31, 2010, medicines constituting qualified medical expenses are limited to doctor-prescribed drugs and insulin. As a result, over-the counter medicines are no longer qualified expenses unless prescribed by a doctor after 2010.[12]

With several exceptions, the payment of insurance premiums is not a qualified medical expense. The exceptions include any expense for coverage under a health plan during a period of COBRA continuation coverage, a qualified long-term care insurance contract[13] or a health plan paid for during a period in which the individual is receiving unemployment compensation.[14]

An account holder may pay qualified long-term care insurance premiums with distributions from an HSA even if contributions to the HSA were made by salary reduction through a cafeteria

1. See IRC Sec. 408(e)(2).
2. See IRC Sec. 408(e)(4).
3. IRC Sec. 223(e)(2).
4. IRC Sec. 223(f)(1).
5. IRC Sec. 223(f)(2).
6. IRC Sec. 223(f)(4)(A).
7. IRC Sec. 223(f)(4)(A).
8. IRC Sec. 223(f)(4)(A), as amended by PPACA 2010, as further amended by HCERA 2010.
9. IRC Secs. 223(f)(4)(B), 223(f)(4)(C).
10. As defined in IRC Section 213(d).
11. IRC Sec. 223(d)(2).
12. IRC Sec. 106(f), as added by PPACA 2010.
13. As defined under IRC Section 7702B(b).
14. IRC Sec. 223(d)(2).

plan. Amounts of qualified long-term care insurance premiums that constitute qualified medical expenses are limited to the following age-based limits in 2018, which are adjusted annually: [1]

(1) for persons age forty or less, the limit is $420,

(2) for ages forty-one through fifty, the limit is $780;

(3) for ages fifty-one through sixty, the limit is $1,560;

(4) for ages sixty-one through seventy, the limit is $4,160; and

(5) for those over age seventy, the limit is $5,200.[2]

The age is the individual's attained age before the close of the taxable year.

An HSA account holder may make tax-free distributions to reimburse qualified medical expenses from prior tax years as long as the expenses were incurred after the HSA was established. There is no time limit on when a distribution must occur.[3]

HSA trustees, custodians, and employers need not determine whether a distribution is used for qualified medical expenses. This responsibility falls on individual account holders.[4]

8769. What is the Affordable Care Act? When did its provisions become effective?

The Affordable Care Act is a comprehensive health care reform law that President Obama signed into law on March 23, 2010.[5] The Patient Protection and Affordable Care Act significantly amends the IRC, ERISA, and the Public Health Service Act. The new law, known as the PPACA, ACA, or Affordable Care Act, focuses on expanding health care coverage, controlling health care costs, and improving the health care delivery system. It attempts to accomplish these goals in a variety of ways, as described in Q 8770 to Q 8776.

In many ways, the ACA is only a broad outline of the reforms that have taken place, or will take place, over several years, and many of the details either have been, or will be, filled in by regulators. The Department of Labor, the Department of Treasury, the IRS, and the Department of Health & Human Services have all proposed regulations, or will propose regulations, that outline the more detailed requirements of the ACA.

The ACA goes into effect between 2010 and 2018. The bulk of the provisions are effective beginning in 2011 through 2014. One provision, the tax on so-called "Cadillac" health care plans, goes into effect in 2020 (delayed from 2018).

1. Notice 2004-50, 2004-2 CB 196, A-40.
2. Rev. Proc. 2017-58.
3. Notice 2004-50, 2004-2 CB 196, A-39.
4. Notice 2004-2, 2004-1 CB 269, A-29, A-30.
5. Patient Protection and Affordable Care Act (P.L. 111-148).

8770. What kinds of health plans are governed by the Affordable Care Act?

The ACA covers insured and self-funded comprehensive medical health plans. In effect, the ACA governs major medical insurance and self-insured major medical plans.

Certain excepted benefits, which include standalone vision, standalone dental, cancer, long-term care insurance, Medigap insūrance, certain flexible spending accounts ("FSAs"), and accident and disability insurance that make payments directly to individuals, are generally not regulated under the ACA.

Similarly, plans that only impact retirees ("retiree-only plans") are not impacted by the ACA. Although the ACA removed the exemption for retiree-only plans and excepted benefit plans from the PHS Act, it left those exemptions in the IRC and ERISA. The preamble and footnote 2 of interim final grandfathered plan regulations explain that the exemption for retiree-only plans and excepted benefit plans still applies for those plans subject to the IRC and ERISA.

Federal regulators have determined that, with respect to retiree-only and excepted benefit plans, even though those provisions were removed by the ACA, they will read the PHS Act as if an exemption for retiree-only and excepted benefit plans were still in effect. Federal regulators have encouraged state insurance regulators to do the same, although in any given state it is possible, although unlikely, that regulators will decide to enforce the ACA mandates on all fully insured plans.

8771. What tax credit is available for employers who purchase health insurance? When does the credit become available?

The health insurance tax credit applies to for-profit and non-profit employers meeting certain requirements (see Q 8772). From 2010 through 2013, the amount of the credit for for-profit employers was 35 percent (25 percent for non-profit employers) of qualifying health insurance costs. The credit is increased for any two consecutive years beginning in 2014 to 50 percent of a for-profit employer's qualifying expenses and 35 percent for non-profit employers.[1]

The new tax credit is effective for 2010 and thereafter. Beginning in 2014, it is only available for two consecutive years. Thus, the maximum number of years that an employer can take advantage of this tax credit is six, namely 2010 through 2013, plus any two consecutive years beginning in or after 2014.[2]

8772. What employers are eligible for the new tax credit for health insurance under the Affordable Care Act?

The new health insurance tax credit[3] is designed to help approximately four million small for-profit businesses and tax-exempt organizations that primarily employ low and moderate-income workers. The credit is available to employers that both:

(1) have twenty-four or fewer eligible full time equivalent (FTE) employees, and

1. http://www.ncsl.org/documents/health/SBtaxCredits.pdf (last accessed June 1111, 2017). See also 2013 IRB LEXIS, 2013-38 IRB 211 (modifyingIRS Notice 2010-44, 2010-22 IRB 717; IRS Notice 2010-82, 2010-51 IRB 1).
2. http://www.ncsl.org/documents/health/SBtaxCredits.pdf (last accessed June 1111, 2017).
3. IRC Sec. 45R.

(2) pay wages averaging under $50,000 (this amount is indexed for inflation) per employee per year.[1]

IRC Section 45R provides a tax credit beginning in 2010 for a business with twenty-five or fewer eligible FTEs. Eligible employees do not include seasonal workers who work for an employer 120 days a year or fewer, owners, and owners' family members, where average compensation for the eligible employees is less than $50,000 and where the business pays 50 percent or more of employee-only (single person) health insurance costs. As a result, the compensation of owners and family members is not counted in determining average compensation, and the health insurance cost for these people is not eligible for the health insurance tax credit.[2]

The credit is largest if there are ten or fewer employees and average wages do not exceed $25,000. The amount of the credit phases out for businesses with more than ten eligible employees or average compensation of more than $25,000 and under $50,000. The amount of an employer's premium payments that counts for purposes of the credit is capped by the average premium for the small group market in the employer's geographic location, as determined by the Department of Health and Human Services.[3]

> *Example*: In 2018, a qualified employer has nine FTEs (excluding owners, owners' family members, and seasonal employees) with average annual wages of $24,000 per FTE. The employer pays $75,000 in health care premiums for these employees, which does not exceed the average premium for the small group market in the employer's state, and otherwise meets the requirements for the credit. The credit for 2018 equals $37,500 (50 percent x $75,000).[4]

8773. How does the Affordable Care Act impact the use of health savings accounts (HSAs)?

The ACA amended IRC Section 223(d)(2)(A) with respect to health savings accounts (HSAs), which now provides that, for amounts paid after December 31, 2010, a distribution from an HSA for a medicine or drug is a tax-free qualified medical expense only if the medicine or drug:

(1) requires a prescription;

(2) is an over-the-counter medicine or drug and the individual obtains a prescription; or

(3) is insulin.

If amounts are distributed from an HSA for any medicine or drug that does not satisfy these requirements, the amounts are treated as though they were distributed to pay for nonqualified medical expenses. Nonqualified medical expenses are includable in gross income and generally are subject to a 20 percent additional tax. This change does not affect HSA distributions for medicines or drugs made before January 1, 2011, nor does it affect distributions made after December 31, 2010, for medicines or drugs purchased on or before that date.

1. http://www.irs.gov/Affordable-Care-Act/Employers/Understanding-the-Small-Business-Health-Care-Tax-Credit (last accessed June 1, 2017).
2. http://www.irs.gov/newsroom/article/0,,id=220839,00.html (last accessed June 1, 2017).
3. http://www.irs.gov/newsroom/article/0,,id=220839,00.html (last accessed June 1, 2017).
4. Additional examples can be found online at http://www.irs.gov/pub/irs-utl/small_business_health_care_tax_credit_scenarios.pdf.

The IRS has provided guidance which makes it clear that these rules do not apply to items that are not medicines or drugs, including equipment such as crutches, supplies such as bandages, and diagnostic devices such as blood sugar test kits. These items may qualify as medical care if they otherwise meet the definition of medical care in IRC Section 213(d)(1), which includes expenses for the diagnosis, cure, mitigation, treatment, or prevention of disease, or for the purpose of affecting any structure or function of the body.

Expenses for items that are merely beneficial to the general health of an individual, such as expenditures for a vacation, are not expenses for medical care.[1]

8774. What penalties are imposed by the Affordable Care Act for employers who violate the health insurance nondiscrimination rules?

The health insurance nondiscrimination rules (see Q 8741 to Q 8743), the effective date of which has been delayed until regulations have been released and a new effective date has been announced by the IRS, have different sanctions than those applicable to self-insured plans that fall under IRC Section 105(h).

For discriminatory self-insured plans, highly compensated employees have taxable income based on the benefits paid by their employer. By contrast, with respect to the new health insurance nondiscrimination requirements, the sanction under IRC Section 4980D is a $100 per day excise tax on affected employees.[2]

Although the IRS has not yet issued regulations on the penalty, its request for comments indicates that the term "affected employees" means those who are not highly compensated. Thus, if an employer has an insured health plan that is not grandfathered and that violates these new nondiscrimination rules for a plan year beginning on or after September 23, 2010, and if that employer has twenty non-highly compensated employees, the penalty will be $2,000 per day as a result of having a discriminatory non-grandfathered health insurance plan.

IRC Section 4980(D)(d)(1) contains an exception to the excise tax for small employers, but the language is somewhat ambiguous. It states, "In the case of a group health plan of a small employer which provides health insurance coverage solely through a contract with a health insurance issuer, no tax shall be imposed by this section on the employer on any failure (other than a failure attributable to section 9811) which is solely because of the health insurance coverage offered by such issuer." It is not clear whether this exception applies to the new nondiscrimination rules or simply to a health insurance policy that does not meet federal requirements. For the purpose of this exception, a small employer is defined as two to fifty employees.[3]

There also is a 10 percent cap on the excise tax, that is, 10 percent of aggregate premiums paid by an employer, for inadvertent violations of the nondiscrimination rules.[4]

1. Treas. Reg. §1.213-1(e)(1)(ii).
2. IRC Sec. 4980D.
3. IRC Sec. 4980D(d)(1).
4. IRC Sec. 4980D(c)(3).

8775. What is the penalty if an employer fails to provide the required health insurance under the Affordable Care Act?

The shared responsibility penalty provisions became effective January 1, 2015, after a delay of one year. This delay was a result of the corresponding delay in the information reporting requirements applicable to certain employers, because that information was to be used to calculate the amount of an employer's shared responsibility payment.[1]

Beginning in 2015, employers with at least fifty full-time equivalent employees (FTEs) must offer health insurance coverage meeting specified requirements or pay a $2,000 per full-time worker penalty (after its first thirty employees) if any of its FTEs receive a federal premium subsidy through a state health insurance exchange (which would occur because the employee was not being offered sufficient coverage through the employer and, instead, purchased individual coverage through the exchanges). This penalty is adjusted annually for inflation ($2,080 per employee for 2015, $2,160 for 2016, $2,260 for 2017, and $3,480 for 2018).

A different penalty applies for employers of at least fifty FTEs that offer some type insurance coverage that is not sufficient to meet federal requirements. In this case, the penalty is $3,000 ($3,390 in 2017) per full-time employee who gets government assistance and buys coverage through an exchange, subject to a maximum penalty of $2,000 times the number of full-time employees in excess of the first thirty. Proposed regulations provide that an employer with a non-calendar year plan in existence on December 27, 2012 that offers employees affordable coverage, which satisfies the minimum value requirement by the first day of the plan year starting in 2014, will not be assessed a shared responsibility penalty for any period in 2014 prior to the beginning of the next plan year.[2]

The shared responsibility penalty that is imposed on employers for failing to provide minimum essential health insurance excludes excepted benefits under Public Health Service Act 2971(c). Excepted benefits include long-term care as well as standalone vision and standalone dental plans.

On June 28, 2012, the Supreme Court, in *National Federation of Independent Business v. Sebelius*,[3] upheld the constitutionality of the Affordable Care Act, with only minor changes to certain Medicaid provisions.

8776. What is the penalty if an individual fails to obtain the required health insurance under the Affordable Care Act?

Health care reform requires that most Americans have health insurance beginning in 2014, or a monetary penalty is imposed.

Unless exempt, individuals must have major medical health coverage provided by their employer or that they purchase themselves, or they must pay a fine that is the greater of a flat amount, or a percentage of income (above the tax filing threshold). The amounts are as follows:

(1) $95 or 1 percent of income in 2014;

1. Notice 2013-45, 2013 IRB Lexis 372.
2. 78 Fed. Reg. 218 (2013).
3. 132 S. Ct. 2566 (2012).

(2) $325 or 2 percent of income in 2015; and

(3) $695 or 2.5 percent of income in 2016-2018.[1]

Families will pay half the penalty amount for children under eighteen, up to a cap of $2,085 per family. After 2016, penalties are indexed to the Consumer Price Index.

Exemptions from the individual penalty will be granted for financial hardship, religious objections, American Indians, those without coverage for fewer than three months, undocumented immigrants, incarcerated individuals, those for whom the lowest cost plan option exceeds 8 percent of an individual's income, and those with incomes below the tax filing threshold.[2] See Q 8777 for a detailed discussion of these exemptions.

8777. When may a taxpayer be exempt from the rule that every taxpayer must obtain a certain level of health coverage or pay a penalty?

Beginning in 2014, taxpayers must obtain a certain minimum level of health coverage or pay a penalty (known as the shared responsibility provision) for failure to obtain minimum essential coverage unless the individual is statutorily exempted from this requirement. In general, the following exemptions may be applicable:

1. *Religious Exemption*. A taxpayer will be exempt from the shared responsibility provision if taxpayer (a) is a member of a recognized religious sect, the teachings of which render the taxpayer conscientiously opposed to accepting benefits provided by any public or private insurance provider that makes payments toward the expenses of obtaining medical care and (b) adheres to the established tenets or teaching of that sect.[3] The religious sect must have been in existence on December 31, 1950 and must be recognized by the Social Security Administration as one that is conscientiously opposed to accepting insurance benefits, including Medicare and Social Security.

2. *Foreign Persons Exemption*. A taxpayer will be exempt from the shared responsibility provision if not a citizen or national of the United States or an alien lawfully present in the United States.[4]

3. *Exemption for Incarcerated Individuals*. A taxpayer will be exempt from the shared responsibility provision during any month incarcerated, other than incarceration while awaiting the disposition of the charges that are pending against the taxpayer.[5]

4. *Affordability Exemption*. If an individual's required contribution for health coverage for the month exceeds 8 percent of the taxpayer's household income for the year (see Q 8780), the taxpayer will not be subject to the shared responsibility provision.[6]

1. IRC Sec. 5000A(c), Rev. Proc. 2016-55; Rev. Proc. 2017-58.
2. IRC Sec. 5000A(d), (e).
3. IRC Secs. 5000A(d)(2), 1402(g)(1).
4. IRC Sec. 5000A(d)(3).
5. IRC Sec. 5000A(d)(4).
6. IRC Sec. 5000A(e)(1).

5. *Exemption for Individuals not Required to File a Tax Return*. Individuals who are not required to file a federal tax return for the year because their income does not exceed the applicable filing thresholds (see Q 8501) are not subject to the shared responsibility provision.[1]

6. *Membership in an Indian Tribe*. Members of recognized Indian tribes are not subject to the shared responsibility provision.[2]

7. *Exemption for Short Coverage Gaps*. An individual will not be subject to the shared responsibility provision if there is a gap in health coverage for a period that is less than three months. However, if there is more than one such gap in coverage during the tax year, the exemption applies only to the first coverage gap.[3]

8. *Hardship Exemption*. The Secretary of Health and Human Services may allow exemptions from the shared responsibility provision on a case-by-case basis if it is determined that an individual has suffered a hardship and is thereby unable to obtain the required coverage.[4]

Both children and senior citizens are subject to the shared responsibility provision. If a child who can be claimed as a dependent does not qualify for an exemption, the taxpayer who can claim that child as a dependent is required to make the shared responsibility payment with respect to the child's failure to obtain the requisite coverage.[5] See Q 8778 for information on how to claim an applicable exemption.

8778. How does a taxpayer who may be exempt from the Affordable Care Act requirements obtain the exemption?

An individual who may be exempt from the ACA individual penalty provisions can often obtain a certificate of exemption from the health insurance exchanges. With respect to the religious and hardship exemptions, this is the only method of claiming the exemption. Individuals claiming the exemption based upon membership in an Indian tribe or incarceration may either obtain a certificate of exemption from the exchanges or claim the exemption on the federal tax return when the return is filed in the subsequent tax year. Exemptions for lack of affordable coverage, a short coverage gap, and certain hardships must be claimed on the taxpayer's federal income tax return.

Individuals who are exempt from the shared responsibility provision because their income for the year falls below the filing threshold, so that they are not required to file a federal tax return for the year, do not need to take any action in order to obtain the exemption.[6]

1. IRC Sec. 5000A(e)(2).
2. IRC Sec. 5000A(e)(3).
3. IRC Sec. 5000A(e)(4).
4. IRC Sec. 5000A(e)(5).
5. IRS Q&A on the Individual Shared Responsibility Provision, available at: http://www.irs.gov/uac/Questions-and-Answers-on-the-Individual-Shared-Responsibility-Provision (last accessed June 11, 2017).
6. See IRS Q&A on the Individual Shared Responsibility Provision, available at: http://www.irs.gov/uac/Questions-and-Answers-on-the-Individual-Shared-Responsibility-Provision (last accessed June 1111, 2017).

The IRS has also provided a list of the hardship exemptions that a taxpayer is entitled to claim without first obtaining a hardship exemption certification from the health insurance exchanges.[1] The hardship exemptions outlined in this notice are available if two or more members of a family have a combined cost of employer-provided health coverage that is deemed unaffordable, a taxpayer's gross income is below the applicable threshold for filing a tax return, or a taxpayer applied for minimum essential health coverage during the periods described in the notice, or applied for coverage and could not complete the process.

Further, the taxpayer is not required to obtain prior certification if (1) the taxpayer applied for coverage under the Children's Health Insurance Program and was found eligible, but had a gap in coverage before the program's effective date, (2) the taxpayer is eligible for services through an Indian healthcare provider or (3) the taxpayer resided in a state that did not expand Medicaid coverage and that taxpayer's household income is below 138 percent of the applicable poverty line. Taxpayers seeking to claim a hardship exemption that was not outlined by the IRS in Notice 2014-76 are still permitted to apply for an exemption through the health insurance marketplace.

8779. What are the requirements to claim the premium assistance tax credit under the Affordable Care Act?

The premium assistance tax credit is a subsidy that can be claimed by certain low-to-moderate income taxpayers in order to offset the cost of health insurance coverage. In order to be eligible to claim the premium assistance tax credit, a taxpayer must meet all of the following requirements:[2]

1. The taxpayer must purchase health insurance through the health insurance marketplace (also known as the health insurance exchanges).
2. The taxpayer must have income that falls within certain ranges (see Q 8780).
3. The taxpayer must not be able to obtain affordable coverage through an employer-provided health plan that provides minimum value (see Q 8812 for a discussion of what constitutes "affordable coverage" and Q 8814 for a discussion of plans that provide "minimum value").
4. The taxpayer must be ineligible for government-sponsored health care programs, such as Medicaid and Medicare.
5. Generally, a taxpayer who is married must file a joint return (though exceptions exist for certain victims of domestic violence).[3]
6. No other person may claim a dependency exemption with respect to the taxpayer for the tax year.

1. Notice 2014-76, 2014-50 IRB 946.
2. IRC Sec. 36B.
3. Notice 2014-23, 2014-16 IRB 942.

Individuals with household income (see Q 8780) that falls between 100 and 400 percent of the poverty line (as adjusted based on family size) may be eligible for the premium tax credit. The federal poverty guidelines that exist as of the first day of the annual open enrollment period are used to determine whether an individual is eligible for the credit, so that the 2017 guidelines are used to determine a taxpayer's credit for 2018.[1]

In 2017, the federal poverty guidelines for the forty-eight contiguous states (including Washington, D.C.) that determine eligibility in 2018 are:

- $12,060 (100 percent) to $48,240 (400 percent) for an individual;
- $16,240 (100 percent) to $64,960 (400 percent) for a family of two;
- $20,420 (100 percent) to $81,680 (400 percent) for a family of three; and
- $24,600 (100 percent) to $98,400 (400 percent) for a family of four.[2]

In 2016, the federal poverty guidelines for the forty-eight contiguous states (including Washington, D.C.) that determined eligibility in 2017 were:

- $11,770 (100 percent) to $47,080 (400 percent) for an individual;
- $15,930 (100 percent) to $63,720 (400 percent) for a family of two;
- $20,090 (100 percent) to $80,360 (400 percent) for a family of three; and
- $24,250 (100 percent) to $97,000 (400 percent) for a family of four.[3]

In 2015, the federal poverty guidelines for the forty-eight contiguous states (including Washington, D.C.) were:

- $11,770 (100 percent) to $47,080 (400 percent) for an individual;
- $15,930 (100 percent) to $63,720 (400 percent) for a family of two;
- $20,090 (100 percent) to $80,360 (400 percent) for a family of three; and
- $24,250 (100 percent) to $97,000 (400 percent) for a family of four.[4]

The federal poverty line is modified for taxpayers living in Alaska and Hawaii. If a taxpayer's primary residence during the tax year changes to a state with a different federal poverty line, or if married taxpayers reside in states with different federal poverty lines, the poverty line that applies

---

1. IRC Sec. 36B(d)(5).
2. See the Department of Health & Human Services website for the federal poverty guidelines that apply for families larger than four and the figures for Alaska and Hawaii, available at: http://aspe.hhs.gov/poverty-guidelines (last accessed June 11, 2017).
3. See the Department of Health & Human Services website for the federal poverty guidelines that apply for families larger than four and the figures for Alaska and Hawaii, available at: http://aspe.hhs.gov/poverty/14poverty.cfm (last accessed June 7, 2016).
4. See the Department of Health & Human Services website for the federal poverty guidelines that apply for families larger than four and the figures for Alaska and Hawaii, available at: http://aspe.hhs.gov/poverty/15poverty.cfm (last accessed June 7, 2016).

is the higher of the two guidelines.[1] Proposed regulations provide that if a taxpayer's household income is below 100 percent of the federal poverty line, so that he or she would generally be eligible to claim the premium tax credit, eligibility will be lost if the taxpayer intentionally or recklessly disregards the facts and provides incorrect information regarding household income to the exchanges.[2]

If a retired individual is offered health coverage, he or she may decline the offer of coverage and remain eligible for premium tax credit assistance if he or she is otherwise eligible based on household income. As discussed above, an active employee does not qualify for premium tax credit assistance if he or she is offered employer-sponsored health coverage that is affordable and provides minimum value, even if the employee declines the offer of coverage. A retiree is not considered to be eligible for employer-sponsored coverage unless he or she actually enrolls in the health plan. Further, family members of the retiree who are eligible to enroll in the health plan are not considered eligible for coverage unless they actually enroll in the plan.[3]

The U.S. Supreme Court, in *King v. Burwell*, held that the premium tax credits are available to all individuals who purchase insurance through an exchange, even if the individual purchased insurance through an exchange established by the federal government.[4]

8780. What is "household income" and how does it determine whether an individual is eligible for a premium assistance tax credit?

Household income is a taxpayer's modified adjusted gross income (MAGI, see below) plus the aggregate modified adjusted gross income of any other individual who was both (1) taken into account in determining the taxpayer's family size for purposes of determining qualification for the credit and (2) required to file a federal tax return for the tax year in question.[5] Because the taxpayer's family size is determined by counting any individual whom the taxpayer was entitled to claim as a dependent for the tax year,[6] it is essentially the case that any income of the taxpayer's dependents who are required to file a return for the year is included in calculating the taxpayer's MAGI.

A taxpayer's MAGI is the adjusted gross income shown on the taxpayer's federal income tax return for the year plus any excluded foreign income, nontaxable Social Security benefits and tax-exempt interest accrued or received during the tax year.[7] Supplemental Social Security income is not included in a taxpayer's MAGI.[8]

1. Treas. Reg. §1.36B-1(h).
2. Prop. Treas. Reg. §1.36B-2(b)(6)(ii).
3. TD 9745.
4. 135 S. Ct. 2480 (2015).
5. IRC Sec. 36B(d)(2).
6. IRC Sec. 36B(d)(1).
7. IRC Sec. 36B(d)(2)(B).
8. See IRS Questions and Answers on the Premium Tax Credit, available at: http://www.irs.gov/uac/Newsroom/Questions-and-Answers-on-the-Premium-Tax-Credit (last accessed June 11201711, 2017).

8781. If a taxpayer is eligible for the premium assistance tax credit, what happens if the household income level or family size changes during the tax year?

The amount of the allowable premium assistance tax credit varies based upon a taxpayer's annual household income and family size. If either the household income level or family size change throughout the tax year, the taxpayer's allowable credit will increase or decrease accordingly. This becomes important when a taxpayer has chosen to take the premium tax credit in advance (where the credit is paid directly to the insurance company to reduce premiums), rather than retroactively (where the credit is claimed on the taxpayer's federal income tax return for the year).[1]

If the actual allowable credit is less than the advance credit claimed, the difference will be deducted from the taxpayer's overpayment (tax refund) or added to the amount that the taxpayer owes to the IRS if no tax refund is forthcoming. If the actual allowable credit is more than the advance credit claimed, the reverse is true, so that the difference will be added to the taxpayer's refund or subtracted from the balance due to the IRS.[2]

The IRS has released guidance that advises taxpayers to notify the health insurance exchanges if any changes in circumstances have occurred that will alter the amount of the allowable credit in order to reduce the significance of the difference between the advance credit and actual allowable credit.[3] Changes in circumstances that can give rise to such a difference include the following:

1. Increases or decreases in household income
2. Marriage
3. Divorce
4. Birth or adoption of a child
5. Gaining or losing eligibility for government or employer-sponsored health insurance[4]

See Q 8780 for a discussion of how household income is calculated for purposes of the premium assistance tax credit.

8782. Can a taxpayer still qualify for a premium assistance tax credit if exempt from the shared responsibility penalty under the Affordable Care Act?

Yes, in some instances. Whether a taxpayer who is otherwise exempt from the shared responsibility penalty remains eligible to claim the premium assistance tax credit depends upon the type of exemption that applies. According to IRS guidance, taxpayers who are exempt

1. See IRS Pub. 5121 (rev. 1/2016).
2. Treas. Reg. §1.36B-4(a)
3. IRS Pub. 5120 (rev. 1/2016).
4. See IRS Questions and Answers on the Premium Tax Credit, available at: http://www.irs.gov/uac/Newsroom/Questions-and-Answers-on-the-Premium-Tax-Credit (last accessed June 11, 2017).

because they are incarcerated or not lawfully present in the U.S. are not eligible to claim the premium tax credit. This is the case, however, because these exempt individuals are not permitted to enroll in a health plan through the health insurance exchanges. Individuals who are exempt for other reasons, such as because a religious exemption or affordability exemption applies, will still be eligible to claim the premium tax credit if they otherwise meet the requirements for eligibility.[1]

See Q 8777 for a detailed discussion of the various exemptions that may apply. See Q 8779 for a discussion of the qualification requirements that apply in determining whether a taxpayer is generally eligible to claim the premium tax credit.

8783. Is a taxpayer eligible for a premium assistance tax credit if he or she is eligible for, or enrolled in, an insurance plan offered through an employer?

Generally, no. According to IRS guidance, a taxpayer is not eligible to receive a premium assistance tax credit even if enrolled in an employer-sponsored plan that is unaffordable or fails to provide minimum value.[2]

However, proposed regulations provide that if an individual declines to enroll in employer-sponsored coverage for the year, and does not have an opportunity to enroll in that coverage for one or more succeeding plan years, the individual is treated as ineligible for coverage in the years for which there is no enrollment opportunity (so that he or she will be eligible to claim the premium tax credit). Further, enrollment in an employer-sponsored plan that provides only excepted benefits will not disqualify an individual from receiving the premium tax credit because the individual must also be eligible for minimum essential health coverage (a plan providing only excepted benefits does not qualify as minimum essential coverage).[3]

Note that if an individual is receiving advance payment of the premium tax credit, he or she will be responsible for notifying the exchange if and when the individual becomes eligible to receive coverage from another source (such as an employer, or through a government sponsored program). Circumstances may exist where the individual notifies the exchange after the time that the exchange can discontinue the advance credit payment for the next month. In this case, the individual will be treated as eligible for the alternative coverage no earlier than the first day of the second month beginning after the month that the individual may enroll in the alternative coverage.[4]

8784. How does an eligible taxpayer obtain the premium assistance tax credit?

When a taxpayer applies for health coverage through an exchange, the exchange itself estimates the amount of credit that the taxpayer may be eligible to claim. The taxpayer then

1. See IRS Questions and Answers on the Individual Shared Responsibility Provision, available at: http://www.irs.gov/uac/Questions-and-Answers-on-the-Individual-Shared-Responsibility-Provision (last accessed June 11, 2017).
2. See IRS Questions and Answers on the Premium Tax Credit, available at: http://www.irs.gov/uac/Newsroom/Questions-and-Answers-on-the-Premium-Tax-Credit (last accessed June 11, 2017).
3. Prop. Treas. Reg. §1.36B-2(c)(3)(iii)(A).
4. Preamble to Proposed Regulations, REG-109086-15.

determines whether to apply the credit in advance (meaning that it is sent directly to the insurance company in order to offset premium payments) or retroactively (meaning that the taxpayer claims the premium credit on the federal tax return for the year).[1]

A taxpayer who receives a premium tax credit is required to file a federal tax return for the year in order to claim the credit. This is true even if the taxpayer would not otherwise be required to file a return because income does not exceed the applicable filing threshold (see Q 8501) for the tax year.[2]

On this return, the taxpayer must report the amount of premiums paid and any advance premium tax credit payments that have been forwarded to the insurance company on the taxpayer's behalf. If the taxpayer enrolls in a health insurance plan through the exchanges, the exchange will send the taxpayer a document that shows the amount of the taxpayer's annual premiums and any advance credit payments by January 31 of the year following the year of coverage.[3]

8785. How does an employer sponsored opt out arrangement impact a taxpayer's eligibility for the premium assistance tax credit?

Generally, the regulations provide that when determining whether employer-sponsored health coverage is affordable to an employee (so as to determine premium tax credit eligibility), the employee's required contribution to coverage is considered, and includes the amount by which the employee's salary would be reduced to enroll in the coverage.[4]

The IRS has recently released proposed regulations that address the effect of an offer of additional compensation in lieu of health coverage under a group health plan (known as "opt out" payments) on premium tax credit eligibility. The proposed regulations provide that if the opt out arrangement is unconditional, the amount made available pursuant to the arrangement increases the employee's required contribution for premium tax credit eligibility purposes.[5] This rule recognizes that the promise of additional compensation in exchange for foregoing health coverage is analogous to a salary reduction made in order to obtain coverage.

However, the regulations provide that amounts made available under a conditional opt out arrangement that is an "eligible opt out arrangement" are disregarded. An eligible opt out arrangement is one under which the employee's right to payment is conditioned on (1) the employee declining to enroll in employer-sponsored coverage, and (2) the employee providing reasonable evidence that he or she, and any dependents, will have coverage other than coverage obtained in the individual market (for example, a spouse's employer-sponsored coverage) for the year in question.

An employee's attestation that he or she has alternative coverage is considered reasonable evidence. An eligible opt out arrangement fails to be eligible, however, if the employer knows,

1. See IRS Questions and Answers on the Premium Tax Credit, available at: http://www.irs.gov/uac/Newsroom/Questions-and-Answers-on-the-Premium-Tax-Credit (last accessed June 11711, 2017).
2. IRS Pub. 5120 (rev. 1/2016).
3. See IRS Questions and Answers on the Premium Tax Credit, available at: http://www.irs.gov/uac/Newsroom/Questions-and-Answers-on-the-Premium-Tax-Credit (last accessed June 11711, 2017).
4. Treas. Reg. §§1.36B-2(c)(3)(v), 1.5000A-3(e)(3)(ii)(A).
5. See Notice 2015-87, 2015-52 IRB 889, Prop. Treas. Reg. §1.36B-2.

or has reason to know, that the employee does not have the alternative coverage. The employer must obtain this reasonable evidence no less often than each year to which the eligible opt out arrangement applies (i.e., as part of the annual open enrollment process).[1]

8786. If a taxpayer changes health coverage during a year and has a gap in coverage will the taxpayer be subject to the shared responsibility penalty?

A taxpayer is treated as having minimum essential health coverage for the month if covered for at least one day during that month. Therefore, if the coverage gap is less than one month, the taxpayer will not be treated as having a gap in coverage and will not be subject to the shared responsibility penalty.[2]

Further, an individual will not be subject to the shared responsibility penalty if the gap in coverage lasts for less than three months (see Q 8777). However, this exemption applies only to the first three-month gap in the tax year. If the taxpayer has more than one three-month coverage gap in the same tax year, he or she will be subject to the shared responsibility penalty with respect to the second coverage gap.[3]

8787. Are U.S. citizens who are not U.S. residents subject to the shared responsibility penalty?

In general, yes. However, a taxpayer may be exempt if he or she qualifies for the foreign earned income exclusion under IRC Section 911. Therefore, if a U.S. citizen who is living abroad has not been physically present in the U.S. for at least 330 full days within a twelve month period, the individual will be treated as having obtained minimum essential coverage for that twelve month period. Further, U.S. citizens who are bona fide residents of foreign countries for an entire tax year will be treated as having obtained minimum essential coverage for the year.[4]

U.S. citizens who do not meet the tests outlined above are required to maintain minimum essential health coverage (which can include group health coverage provided by a foreign employer), qualify for an otherwise applicable exemption (see Q 8777) or make the shared responsibility payment.

Employer Mandate

8788. How does an employer determine whether it is an applicable large employer and subject to the ACA employer shared responsibility provision?

Only employers who are "applicable large employers" are subject to the ACA employer shared responsibility provisions. An applicable large employer is one with at least fifty full-time equivalent employees (FTEs). These employers must offer health insurance coverage meeting

1. 81 FR 44561.
2. See IRS Questions and Answers on the Individual Shared Responsibility Provision, available at: http://www.irs.gov/uac/Questions-and-Answers-on-the-Individual-Shared-Responsibility-Provision (last accessed June 11, 2017).
3. IRC Sec. 5000A(e)(4).
4. IRC Sec. 911(d), TD 9632.

specified requirements or pay a $2,000 per full-time worker penalty (after its first thirty employees) if any of its FTEs receive a federal premium subsidy through a state health insurance exchange (which would occur because the employee was not being offered sufficient coverage through the employer) (see Q 8775).

Whether or not the employer is an applicable large employer that is subject to the shared responsibility provisions is based upon the number of FTEs employed by the employer in the preceding tax year (so that the employer's status as a large employer for 2018 is based on its FTEs during 2017).[1]

FTEs are determined based on each employee's hours of service. An employee is a full-time employee if he or she averages at least thirty hours of work per week.[2] However, an employee who averages 130 hours of work per month is treated as an employee who works at least thirty hours per week and, as such, is a full-time employee.[3]

An employer must also count as FTEs certain employees who do not work an average of thirty hours per week. This number is determined by dividing the total number of hours of service worked by employees who are *not* full-time employees in any month by 120. The resulting number must be added to the number of full-time employees as determined in the preceding paragraph.[4]

Seasonal employees are taken into consideration, but if any employer exceeds fifty FTEs for 120 days or fewer during the year and the employees in excess of fifty employed during the 120-day period are seasonal workers, the employer will not be treated as an applicable large employer.[5] The preamble to the regulations and IRS Q&A addressing the issue define "seasonal worker" as one who performs services on a seasonal basis as defined by the Secretary of Labor, and retail workers employed exclusively during holiday seasons, but also note that the employer is entitled to apply a reasonable, good faith interpretation of the term seasonal worker.

Employers should note that an optional "look-back" measurement period is available, but only for purposes of calculating the employer mandate penalty assessments. The look-back measurement cannot be used for purposes of determining whether the employer is an applicable large employer that is subject to the shared responsibility provisions.[6]

8789. How does an employer that has been in existence for less than one year determine whether it is subject to the ACA shared responsibility provisions?

In general, an employer's status as an applicable large employer is determined based on the number of full-time equivalent employees it employs in the previous year (see Q 8788). For an employer that was not in existence during the previous year, determination of whether

1. IRC Sec. 4980H(c).
2. IRC Sec. 4980H(c)(4).
3. Treas. Reg. §54.4980H-1(a)(21)(ii).
4. IRC Sec. 4980H(c)(2)(E).
5. IRC Sec. 4980H(c)(2)(B).
6. See IRS Q&A on the Employer Shared Responsibility Provisions Under the Affordable Care Act, available at: http://www.irs.gov/Affordable-Care-Act/Employers/Questions-and-Answers-on-Employer-Shared-Responsibility-Provisions-Under-the-Affordable-Care-Act)

it is an applicable large employer and thus subject to the ACA shared responsibility provisions is based upon the number of employees that it reasonably expects that it will employ during the current year. The penalty provisions will apply only if the employer *actually does* employ an average of fifty or more full-time employees (and equivalents) during its first year of existence.[1] An employer was not in existence during the previous calendar year only if it was not in existence on any business day during that year.[2]

An employer who was not in existence for the previous year is also entitled to exclude seasonal workers (see Q 8788) from its calculation if it reasonable expects to employ workers meeting the definition of seasonal worker during its first year of existence.[3]

8790. How does an employer that has a common owner with another employer determine whether it is subject to the ACA shared responsibility provisions?

Two or more employers who are controlled by the same owner or are otherwise related are considered to be a single employer if those employers are treated as a single employer under IRC Section 414.[4] IRC Section 414 treats two or more employers as one if they are: (1) part of a controlled group of corporations, (2) trades or businesses that are under common control, (3) affiliated service groups or (4) related through other arrangements generally having the same effect as in groups (1)-(3).[5]

These employers are combined in determining whether they collectively employ fifty or more full-time employees for purposes of applicable large employer status. If the combined total number of full-time employees exceeds fifty full-time employees (including equivalents), each employer is subject to the shared responsibility provisions even if no single employer crosses the threshold.

8791. Will an employer be subject to the ACA shared responsibility provisions if it offers employees and their dependents coverage that is both affordable and provides minimum value, but some of its employees, their spouses and/or dependents obtain coverage through the health insurance marketplace, Medicaid or Medicare?

No. If an applicable large employer offers coverage that is affordable and provides minimum value, the employer will not be subject to the shared responsibility provisions if some of its employees, or their spouses or dependents, obtain coverage from another source, such as through the insurance marketplace or through Medicare or Medicaid.

The employer will not be subject to the shared responsibility payment unless one of its employees receives a premium tax credit.[6] If the employer offers coverage that is both affordable

1. IRC Sec. 4980H(c)(2)(C)(ii).
2. Treas. Reg. §54.4980H-2(b)(3).
3. Treas. Reg. §54.4980H-2(b)(2).
4. IRC Sec. 4980H(c)(2)(C)(i).
5. IRC Secs. 414(b), (c), (m), (o).
6. IRC Sec. 4980H(a).

and provides minimum value to employees and their dependents, neither the employees nor their dependents will be eligible for the premium tax credit if they elect to purchase insurance through the exchanges. Employees (or dependents) who are eligible for Medicare or Medicaid are not eligible for a premium tax credit.[1]

8792. If an employer offers health coverage to fewer than 95 percent of its full-time employees, how is the employer shared responsibility payment amount calculated?

If the employer offers health coverage to fewer than 95 percent of its full-time employees, it may be subject to the shared responsibility provisions and owe a payment if any full-time employee purchased insurance through the exchanges and received a premium tax credit.[2]

To calculate this payment, the employer multiplies the number of full-time employees it employed for the year (minus up to thirty, and the number of full-time employees who were offered coverage) by $2,000.[3] For purposes of this calculation, a full-time employee does *not* include a full-time equivalent employee.

If the employer offers coverage for some months, but not for others, it must calculate its shared responsibility payment separately for the months in which coverage was not offered. The payment is equal to the number of full-time employees employed for the month (minus up to thirty, and the number of full-time employees who were offered coverage) multiplied by 1/12 of $2,000. If the employer does not offer coverage to a full-time employee on any day of a calendar month, that employee is treated as not having been offered coverage for the entire month.[4]

8793. If an employer offers health coverage to 95 percent or more of its full-time employees, but owes a shared responsibility penalty regardless, how is the amount of the payment owed calculated?

An employer who offers health coverage to at least 95 percent of its full-time employees, but owes a shared responsibility payment because one or more of its full-time employees received a premium tax credit, must calculate its liability separately for each month. This situation can arise, for example, if the employer offered coverage but that coverage was unaffordable or failed to provide minimum value for one or more full-time employees.

The payment amount is calculated by multiplying the number of full-time employees who receive a premium tax credit for the month by 1/12 of $3,000. There is, however, a payment cap equal the number of full-time employees for the month (minus up to thirty) multiplied by 1/12 or $2,000, which ensures that the penalty for employees that offer coverage never exceeds the penalty for employers who fail to offer coverage.[5]

1. See Preamble to the Final Regulations, TD 9655.
2. IRC Sec. 4980H(a).
3. Treas. Reg. §54.4980H-5(a).
4. Treas. Reg. §54.4980H-5(c).
5. IRC Sec. 4980H(b).

8794. When will employer-provided "wraparound" coverage constitute excepted benefits that are not subject to the ACA market reform provisions?

The departments of Treasury, Health and Human Services and Labor have released final rules that outline the requirements that certain limited health benefits, which are "wrapped around" employer-sponsored health coverage, must meet in order to qualify as excepted benefits that would not preclude the employee from claiming a premium tax credit.

The rules establish five requirements that employer-sponsored wraparound coverage offered in conjunction with an individually purchased health plan must satisfy in order to constitute an excepted benefit that would not jeopardize an employee's eligibility to claim a premium tax credit. The limited wraparound coverage must:

(1) Be specifically designed to supplement eligible individual health coverage by providing additional meaningful benefits;

(2) Be limited in amount. The final regulations set the limit as the greater of the maximum permitted annual salary reduction toward a health FSA or 15 percent of the cost of coverage under the primary plan;

(3) Satisfy certain nondiscrimination requirements by *not* (a) imposing preexisting condition exclusions, (b) discriminating based on any individual health factors or (c) being excludable from the employee's income under IRC Section 105;

(4) Provide that individuals who are eligible for the wraparound coverage cannot also be enrolled in excepted benefit coverage that is a health FSA, and meet certain standards with respect to eligibility designed prevent employers from failing to offer minimum essential health coverage to full-time employees as otherwise required by the ACA; and

(5) Satisfy certain reporting requirements by submitting certain information to the Office of Personnel Management that is sufficient to allow it to determine whether the coverage meets these requirements.

These rules apply as a pilot program with a sunset date, so that the wraparound coverage must be first offered no earlier than January 1, 2016 and no later than December 31, 2018, and end on the later of (1) the date that is three years after the date the wraparound coverage is first offered or (2) the date on which the last collective bargaining agreement relating to the plan terminates after the date the wraparound coverage is first offered.[1]

8795. How does an employer measure an employee's hours in determining whether that employee is a full-time employee for purposes of the ACA shared responsibility provisions?

The employer shared responsibility provisions imposed by the ACA only apply to employers with 50 or more full-time employees (or the equivalent of fifty or more full-time employees).

1. TD 9714.

Determining full-time status hinges on an employee's average hours of service (employees averaging at least thirty hours of service per week are considered full-time and regulations provide that 130 hours in a month is treated as the equivalent of thirty hours per week).[1]

An employer has the option of choosing one of two methods for measuring an employee's hours in order to determine full-time status. The first is a monthly measurement period under which the employer counts the employee's hours of service each month.[2] The second is called the "look-back" measurement period. The look-back measurement period, however, cannot be used to determine whether the employer is subject to the shared responsibility provisions in general (i.e, to determine whether the employer is an applicable large employer). The look-back measurement period is used instead (1) to determine whether an employer who is already offering health coverage has failed to satisfy the ACA standards so as to be liable for a penalty and (2) to calculate that penalty.[3]

The look-back measurement period allows an employer to determine the employee's status during a later period (the "stability period") based on the employee's hours of service during an earlier period (the "measurement period").[4] The measurement period must be a period of no more than twelve months and no less than three months, as determined by the employer. The employer can determine when the measurement period starts and ends, so long as that determination is made on a uniform and consistent basis for all employees in the same employment category (the regulations provide examples of permissible employment categories, including, among others, salaried and hourly employees, and collectively bargained and non-collectively bargained employees).[5]

If the employee is a full-time employee during the measurement period, he or she must be treated as a full-time employee during the stability period regardless of whether he or she would be a full-time employee based on hours of service during the stability period. The stability period must be at least six calendar months, but can in no event be shorter than the measurement period.[6] The final regulations note that an employer is entitled to treat additional employees as full-time employees even if their hours of service would not otherwise cause them to obtain full-time status under either of the measurement options.

8796. What constitutes an hour of service for purposes of determining whether an employee is a full-time employee in light of the ACA shared responsibility provisions?

An hour of service is generally each hour for which an employee is paid, or is entitled to receive payment, for the performance of services for the employer. An hour of service also includes any hours for which an employee is paid, or is entitled to receive payment, during a time period where no services are actually performed (for example, because the employee is entitled to paid vacation, paid sick leave, holiday pay, jury duty pay, etc.).[7]

1. IRC Sec. 4980H(c)(4).
2. Treas. Reg. §54.4980H-3(c).
3. See Preamble to the Final Regulations, TD 9655.
4. Treas. Reg. §54.4980H-3(d)(1)(i).
5. Treas. Reg. §54.4980H-3(d)(1)(i).
6. Treas. Reg. §54.4980H-3(d)(1)(iii).
7. Treas. Reg. §54.4980H-1(a)(24).

Hours of service do not include hours spent performing services for an employer as a volunteer or pursuant to a federal work-study program (or substantially similar program). To the extent payment for an employee's services comes from a non-U.S. source, the hours spent performing those services are also excluded.[1]

In some cases, an employee may be counted as a full-time employee for purposes of determining applicable large employer status even if that employee is not technically performing his or her job duties. If an employee is receiving short-term or long-term disability benefits, he or she may still be counted as a full-time employee if the employee retains his or her status as an employee *and* the disability benefits are paid for by the employer. Hours of service will result from employees receiving disability benefits under these circumstances even if the employee is not receiving his or her full compensation (for example, an employee receiving 80 percent of his or her compensation for forty hours per week will still be credited with forty hours of service per week, and will thus be a full-time employee). However, if the employee pays for the disability payment arrangement on an after-tax basis, no hours of service will result. Further, if the employee is not working, but is receiving workers compensation benefits, no hours of service will result.[2]

8797. How does a small employer who hires additional employees throughout the year determine whether it is subject to the ACA shared responsibility provisions if some of those employees are part-time employees?

An employer determines whether it employs fifty or more full-time employees (or full-time equivalents) during a year by calculating how many full-time employees it employed in the prior year. The employer first counts employees working at least thirty hours per week on a monthly basis as full-time employees. If the employer has part-time employees, it must also add full-time equivalent employees (which is determined by adding up the hours worked by all part-time employees and dividing by 120). The employer adds the totals for each month and divides by twelve to determine whether it employs fifty or more full-time employees for the year.[3]

Therefore, if an employer hires additional employees throughout the year, it may cause it to become subject to the ACA shared responsibility provisions in the following year if the additional employees' hours of service cause the employer to cross the fifty full-time employee threshold as calculated above.

8798. How does a small employer that purchases another business during the year determine whether it is subject to the ACA shared responsibility provisions if the new business is a separate business entity?

When one small employer purchases another business, even if the two businesses are separate legal entities, the employer must generally combine the number of full-time employees working for each business during the year in order to determine whether it is subject to the

1. Treas. Reg. §54.4980H-1(a)(24)(ii).
2. See Notice 2015-87.
3. See IRS Questions and Answers on the Employer Shared Responsibility Provisions, available at http://www.irs.gov/Affordable-Care-Act/Employers/Questions-and-Answers-on-Employer-Shared-Responsibility-Provisions-Under-the-Affordable-Care-Act.

shared responsibility provisions.[1] This is the case if the businesses are separate legal entities, but are controlled by the same business owner. The criteria for determining whether a group of businesses is a controlled group under IRC Section 1563 apply in determining whether two or more businesses must be aggregated for purposes of the shared responsibility provisions.

Therefore, a parent-subsidiary group must be aggregated if, within the group, stock representing 80 percent of the voting power of all stock in each corporation is owned by one or more of the other corporations in the group and the parent corporation owns at least 80 percent of voting power, or 80 percent of the total shares, of at least one other corporation in the group.

A "brother-sister" controlled group exists if five or fewer people who are individuals, estates or trusts own at least 50 percent of the combined voting power, or 50 percent or more of the stock value, of each corporation.[2] Similar ownership arrangements may also require aggregation in calculating whether the overall group employs fifty or more full-time employees and is thus subject to the shared responsibility provisions.

8799. If an employer with fewer than fifty full-time employees offers health coverage that is generally affordable and provides minimum value to employees, but for certain employees the coverage is not affordable and so those employees purchase health insurance through the market and receive premium tax credits, is that employer subject to the ACA shared responsibility provisions?

No. An employer with fewer than an average of fifty full-time employees on business days during the preceding calendar year is not subject to the shared responsibility provisions even if it offers health coverage that is not affordable to certain of its employees who, as a result, receive the premium tax credit.[3]

Further, for 2015, transition relief was available for employers with fewer than 100 full-time employees that offered coverage that was not affordable or did not provide minimum value. An employer was not subject to the shared responsibility provisions in 2015 (or, for non-calendar year plans, that portion of the plan year that fell within 2016) if the following conditions were satisfied:

1. The employer employed, on average, at least fifty full-time employees but fewer than one-hundred full-time employees in 2014.

2. The employer did not reduce its workforce or overall hours of employees' service between February 9, 2014 and December 31, 2014, unless such reduction was made for bona fide business purposes.

---

1. IRC 4980H(c)(2)(C).
2. IRC Secs. 4980H(c)(2)(C), 414(b), 1563.
3. IRC 4980H(b). See also IRS Questions and Answers on Employer Shared Responsibility Provisions Under the Affordable Care Act, available at: http://www.irs.gov/Affordable-Care-Act/Employers/Questions-and-Answers-on-Employer-Shared-Responsibility-Provisions-Under-the-Affordable-Care-Act.

3. The employer did not eliminate or materially reduce any health coverage that it offered as of February 9, 2014, before December 31, 2015.

4. The employer certified that it meets the eligibility requirements described above.[1]

8800. If an employer is subject to the shared responsibility provisions, but all of its employees obtain other health coverage, is that employer still required to offer health coverage?

Yes, an applicable large employer remains subject to the shared responsibility provisions even if all of its employees obtain coverage from other sources. However, the employer will only be required to pay the shared responsibility penalty if one or more of its employees receives a premium tax credit for purchasing individual health coverage. The shared responsibility penalty is calculated based on the number of full-time employees for the month in which an employee receives the premium tax credit.[2]

8801. If an employer offers health coverage to all full-time employees, but not to their dependents, is that employer subject to the ACA shared responsibility provisions?

Yes, if the employer is otherwise required to offer health coverage and fails to offer health coverage to the dependents of its employees, the employer will be subject to the shared responsibility penalty if one of those employees receives the premium tax credit for insurance purchased through the marketplace.

Planning Point: Note that IRS FAQ issued on the subject provides that an employer does not become liable for a shared responsibility penalty if only the *dependent* receives the premium tax credit.[3]

Despite this, the IRS provided transition relief for the 2014 and 2015 plan years for employers who offered coverage to employees but failed to offer dependent coverage so that the shared responsibility penalty was not assessed if the following were true:

1) The employer failed to offer dependent coverage.

2) The employer offered dependent coverage, but that coverage failed to constitute minimum essential coverage.

3) The employer offered dependent coverage to some, but not all, of its employees' dependents.

Further, the transition relief is only available to employers who did not offer dependent coverage in 2013 or 2014. The employer is required to take steps toward offering dependent coverage in 2014 or 2015 in order to take advantage of the transition relief.[4]

1. See Preamble to the Final Regulations, TD 9655, Section XV.D.6.
2. IRC 4980H(a)(2).
3. See IRS Questions and Answers on Employer Shared Responsibility Provisions Under the Affordable Care Act, available at: http://www.irs.gov/Affordable-Care-Act/Employers/Questions-and-Answers-on-Employer-Shared-Responsibility-Provisions-Under-the-Affordable-Care-Act.
4. Preamble to the final regulations, TD 9655.

8802. If a taxpayer owns a business and the only employees are that taxpayer and his or her spouse, is that taxpayer still eligible for the self-employment health insurance tax deduction with respect to health coverage purchased through the health insurance marketplace?

Yes, a self-employed owner of a small business is entitled to claim the self-employment health insurance tax deduction for health coverage purchased on the health insurance marketplace for the taxpayer and his or her family. This is the case if the taxpayer purchases the health insurance through the individual marketplace or through the small business (SHOP) marketplace. However, if the taxpayer claims the premium tax credit, the amount of the premium tax credit received cannot be deducted.[1]

8803. Does a retiree-only health reimbursement arrangement (HRA) provide minimum essential coverage under the ACA market reform provisions?

Yes. A retiree-only health reimbursement arrangement (HRA) is not subject to the annual dollar limit prohibitions because it is a plan with fewer than two current employees.[2] This is the case even if the retiree-only HRA is designed to reimburse the retiree for the cost of health coverage purchased through the individual health insurance exchanges.[3] Because a retiree-only HRA has fewer than two current employees, it provides minimum essential coverage for purposes of IRC Sections 5000A and 36B.

8804. Can an employer offer high-risk employees a choice between enrollment in a group health plan or cash without violating the Affordable Care Act market reform provisions?

No. The Department of Labor has released guidance providing that an employer who offers high-risk employees a choice between enrollment in a group health plan or cash violates the nondiscrimination requirements of the Affordable Care Act.[4] This is the case regardless of whether the cash payment is pre-tax or after-tax and regardless of whether the employee obtains individual health coverage from another source.[5]

8805. Will an employer receive a notification if it owes a shared responsibility penalty under the ACA?

Yes. According to IRS guidance, an employer will receive a notification if one or more of its employees has received the premium tax credit that can generate employer liability for a shared responsibility penalty. The IRS will then contact the employer with a determination of whether it owes a shared responsibility payment, giving the employer an opportunity to

1. See IRS Questions and Answers on Employer Shared Responsibility Provisions Under the Affordable Care Act, available at: http://www.irs.gov/Affordable-Care-Act/Employers/Questions-and-Answers-on-Employer-Shared-Responsibility-Provisions-Under-the-Affordable-Care-Act.
2. See DOL Technical Release No. 2013-03.
3. Preamble to the Interim Final Rules for Group Health Plans and Health Insurance Coverage Relating to Status as a Grandfathered Health Plan Under the Patient Protection and Affordable Care Act, 75 Fed. Reg. 34538, 34539.
4. IRC Sec. 9815.
5. See DOL FAQ About the Affordable Care Act Implementation (Part XXII), available at: http://www.dol.gov/ebsa/faqs/faq-aca22.html#footnote6

respond before a notice and demand for payment is made. Such contact will not be made, however, until after the due date for the individual employees' tax returns for the year, as this is how the individual employees will claim premium tax credits. The date of contact will also be delayed until after the filing deadline for the returns of applicable large employers that outline the number of full-time employees and any coverage offered.[1]

8806. How does an employer who owes a shared responsibility penalty make a payment?

IRS guidance indicates that an employer who owes a shared responsibility penalty will not be required to include payment when it files its tax return for the year. Instead, the IRS will send a notice and demand for payment that includes payment instructions for the employer to follow.[2]

8807. Are non-profit employers subject to the ACA shared responsibility provisions?

Yes. The shared responsibility provisions apply to all applicable large employers (those employers who employ an average of at least fifty full-time employees or full-time equivalents).[3] This includes both for-profit and non-profit entities.[4]

8808. How are employees who work for two separate employers that are under common control treated in determining whether an employer is subject to the ACA shared responsibility provisions?

The Affordable Care Act shared responsibility rules treat two or more employers that are under common control as a single employer for purposes of determining whether that employer is an applicable large employer so that the shared responsibility penalties may apply.[5] As a result, all of an employee's hours of service with each member of a group of employers that are under common control are added together in determining whether that employee is a full-time employee for purposes of applicable large employer status.

Conversely, if the employee works for two employers who are not under common control, the employee's hours of service with the first employer are not counted as hours of service with the second employer.[6]

1. See IRS Questions and Answers on Employer Shared Responsibility Provisions Under the Affordable Care Act, available at: http://www.irs.gov/Affordable-Care-Act/Employers/Questions-and-Answers-on-Employer-Shared-Responsibility-Provisions-Under-the-Affordable-Care-Act.
2. See IRS Questions and Answers on Employer Shared Responsibility Provisions Under the Affordable Care Act, available at: http://www.irs.gov/Affordable-Care-Act/Employers/Questions-and-Answers-on-Employer-Shared-Responsibility-Provisions-Under-the-Affordable-Care-Act.
3. IRC Sec. 4980H(c)(2)(A).
4. See IRS Questions & Answers on Employer Shared Responsibility Provisions Under the Affordable Care Act, available at: http://www.irs.gov/Affordable-Care-Act/Employers/Questions-and-Answers-on-Employer-Shared-Responsibility-Provisions-Under-the-Affordable-Care-Act.
5. IRC Sec. 4980(c)(2)(C)(i).
6. See IRS Questions & Answers on Employer Shared Responsibility Provisions Under the Affordable Care Act, available at: http://www.irs.gov/Affordable-Care-Act/Employers/Questions-and-Answers-on-Employer-Shared-Responsibility-Provisions-Under-the-Affordable-Care-Act.

8809. When is an employer considered to be part of a controlled group for purposes of the ACA shared responsibility provisions?

Companies that have a common owner will generally be combined for purposes of determining whether an employer is subject to the ACA shared responsibility provisions.[1] Whether or not a group of employers is treated as a single employer for ACA purposes is determined based upon the IRC Section 414 provisions that apply to aggregate certain employers for employment benefit purposes.

An employer is part of a controlled group if it is a parent-subsidiary controlled group of corporations and:

(1) stock possessing at least 80 percent of the voting power or value of all classes of stock in each of the corporations (except the parent) is owned by one or more of the other corporations, and

(2) the common parent corporation owns at least 80 percent of the total voting power or value of at least one of the other corporations.[2]

An employer is part of a brother-sister controlled group if five or fewer persons who are individuals, estates or trusts own stock possessing more than 50 percent of the combined voting power or value of all classes of stock of each corporation.[3]

Rules similar to the rules discussed above are applied in determining whether an employer that is not a corporation is treated as a member of a controlled group for purposes of the ACA shared responsibility provisions.[4] All employees of members of an affiliated service group are also treated as though employed by a single employer.[5]

8810. What types of employer-provided health coverage will be counted in determining whether the employer is liable for the Affordable Care Act Cadillac tax?

The IRS has issued preliminary guidance indicating that many types of employer-provided health benefits (in addition to traditional health insurance premiums) will be counted in determining whether the employer will be subject to the ACA "Cadillac tax" on high cost health coverage. An employer can become liable if it offers employer or salary reduction contributions to a health savings account (HSA) or health flexible spending account (FSA) that it administers.

Pre-tax contributions to HSAs are likely to be included in determining whether an employee's health coverage is subject to the Cadillac tax, but an employee's after-tax contributions are not included in the calculation. As a result, many employers will learn that the popular combination

1. IRC Sec. 4980H(c)(2)(C).
2. IRC Secs. 414(b), 1563(a)(1).
3. IRC Secs. 414(b), 1563(a)(2).
4. IRC Sec. 414(c).
5. IRC Sec. 414(m).

of high deductible health plans (HDHPs) and pre-tax HSA dollars may no longer be the most cost effective way to provide comprehensive coverage.

The cost of health FSAs, Archer MSAs, HRAs, retiree coverage and multi-employer plan coverage are also expected to be included when calculating whether the threshold that triggers the Cadillac tax has been crossed.[1]

8811. Can employment of summer interns cause an employer to become subject to the shared responsibility provisions?

Yes. However, in order to be counted as a full-time employee, an employee must be paid for his or her services—as a result, unpaid interns will *not* be counted as employees in determining whether an employer is subject to the shared responsibility provisions. An intern who is paid, however, will be counted in the same manner as any other employee.[2] Therefore, a paid intern who works an average of 30 hours per week must be offered health coverage within the period of time that it would be offered to any other full-time employee.

If the intern can legitimately be categorized as a seasonal employee (i.e, his or her duties are commonly only accomplished during a particular season), the employer may avoid offering health coverage to that intern. The employer can also avoid responsibility for offering health coverage to interns if the hours of those interns are capped at below 30 hours a week so that they are not treated as full-time employees under the ACA.

8812. What determines whether health coverage offered by an employer is "affordable" under the Affordable Care Act?

For purposes of the premium assistance tax credit (see Q 8779), employer-provided health coverage is deemed to be "affordable" if the taxpayer's required contribution toward the annual premium cost of self-only coverage does not exceed 9.5 percent (as indexed for inflation, 9.56 percent in 2018, down from 9.69 percent in 2017) of the taxpayer's household income (see Q 8780).[3] Any additional premium contributions that the taxpayer is required to make for family coverage are not included in determining whether the health coverage is affordable.

If an employer offers multiple health plan options, the affordability test applies to the lowest cost plan in which the taxpayer is eligible to participate.[4]

8813. Does an employer's contribution to a cafeteria plan or HRA impact whether health coverage is "affordable" under the Affordable Care Act?

The IRS has released final regulations that address the impact of employer contributions to cafeteria plans and health reimbursement arrangements (HRAs) upon the affordability of coverage and the employee's required contribution toward health coverage.

1. Notice 2015-16.
2. See Preamble to the Final Regulations, TD 9655.
3. IRC Sec. 36B(c)(2)(C)(i).
4. IRS Questions and Answers on the Premium Tax Credit, available at: http://www.irs.gov/uac/Newsroom/Questions-and-Answers-on-the-Premium-Tax-Credit (last June 11, 2017).

Pursuant to these regulations, an employee's required contribution toward health coverage is reduced by the amount of any employer contribution to an IRC Section 125 cafeteria plan that (1) may not be taken as a taxable benefit, (2) may be used to pay for minimum essential health coverage and (3) may only be used to pay for medical care.[1]

Employer contributions to an employee's HRA are used in determining the level of the employee's required contributions if the HRA is integrated with an employer-sponsored health plan and the employee is permitted to use the contributions to pay premiums. Further, the HRA amounts will count toward the employee's required contribution if the HRA would have been integrated with an employer-sponsored plan if the employee had enrolled in the primary health plan offered by that employer.[2]

The HRA funds are only taken into account in determining the employee's required contribution if both the HRA and the primary health plan are offered by the same employer.[3]

8814. When does employer-sponsored health coverage provide "minimum value" for purposes of the Affordable Care Act?

Employer-sponsored health coverage provides "minimum value," so that it also provides minimum essential coverage, if the plan covers at least 60 percent of the total allowed costs of benefits provided under the plan.[4] Beginning in 2014, an employer that offers health coverage to its employees is required to provide each employee with a Summary of Benefits and Coverage, which is a document that explains the benefits provided under the plan and must also include a statement as to whether the plan provides minimum value.

The Department of Health and Human Services and the IRS have provided guidance stating that a health plan that does not cover substantial hospital and physician services will not provide minimum value, and cannot satisfy an applicable large employer's obligation to provide health coverage to avoid the shared responsibility penalties.[5]

If an employee enrolls in a plan that does not provide minimum value, that employee is ineligible to claim the premium assistance tax credit even though the plan fails to provide the required coverage.

8815. Is there any transition relief for individuals with respect to the shared responsibility penalty provisions effective in 2014?

Yes. If an individual is eligible to enroll in an employer-sponsored health plan that has adopted a plan year that is not a calendar year, the individual is eligible for transition relief from the shared responsibility penalty if the plan year began in 2013 and ended in 2014. The transition relief began in January 2014 and continued through the month in which the plan

1. Treas. Reg. §1.5000A-3(e)(2)(E).
2. Treas. Reg. §1.5000A-3(e)(2)(D). See also Notice 2013-54, 2013-40 IRB 287.
3. Treas. Reg. §1.5000A-3(e)(2)(D).
4. IRC Sec. 36B(c)(2)(C)(ii).
5. Notice 2014-69, 2014-48 IRB 903.

year ended.[1] This rule was particularly important because many employer-sponsored health plans do not allow an employee to enroll in a plan after the beginning of the plan year. In the case of a 2013-2014 non-calendar year health plan, eligible employees would not be permitted to obtain the employer-sponsored coverage until after the start of 2014, when the shared responsibility penalty provision had already become effective. The transition relief prevented these taxpayers from becoming liable for the shared responsibility provision until the next plan year began in 2014.

The IRS also provided relief for taxpayers who are covered under certain limited-benefit government-sponsored health plans which may not provide minimum essential coverage (examples of this type of coverage include optional family planning coverage and pregnancy-related services that are offered through Medicaid). This transition relief applied to months in 2014 in which an individual was covered by one of the specifically enumerated plans that did not provide minimum essential coverage.[2]

1. Notice 2013-42, 2013-29 IRB 61.
2. Notice 2014-10, 2014-9 IRB 605.

PART XII: FRINGE BENEFITS

8816. How are funds provided to employees through an educational assistance program taxed?

An employee may generally exclude from income amounts received pursuant to an employer-sponsored Educational Assistance Program (EAP) that was established in order to fund employee education-related expenses, subject to the maximum limitation discussed below.[1] This exclusion was made permanent by EGTRRA 2001 following a number of extensions in preceding years. Amounts received under an EAP may be excluded whether or not the educational expenses are job related.[2] An employee cannot exclude from income more than $5,250 in educational assistance benefits in any calendar year.[3]

8817. What requirements must an education assistance program (EAP) meet in order to receive tax-preferred treatment?

The following requirements must be met by an employer-sponsored educational assistance program (EAP) to receive tax-preferred treatment:

1. *Written plan:* the program must be a separate written plan of the employer providing educational assistance for the exclusive benefit of the company's employees.[4] A sole proprietor may treat himself as employer and employee and a partnership will be treated as the employer of all self-employed partners.[5]

2. *Nondiscrimination*: the program must benefit employees who qualify under a classification set up by the employer that does not discriminate in favor of highly compensated employees, as defined in IRC Section 414(q). Generally, highly compensated employees are five percent owners or members of the top-paid group of employees. Employees covered by a collective bargaining agreement may be excluded if educational assistance benefits were the subject of good faith bargaining.[6]

3. *More than five percent owners*: the class of shareholders and their spouses and dependents, each of whom owns more than five percent of the employer's stock, cannot receive more than five percent of the educational benefit amounts.[7]

4. *Employee choice*: a program cannot offer employees a choice between educational assistance and other benefits that are includable in income.[8]

1. IRC Sec. 127(a)(1).
2. Treas. Reg. §1.127-2(c)(4).
3. IRC Sec. 127(a)(2).
4. IRC Sec. 127(b)(1).
5. IRC Sec. 127(c)(3).
6. IRC Sec. 127(b)(2).
7. IRC Sec. 127(b)(3).
8. IRC Sec. 127(b)(4).

5. *Funding*: an educational assistance program may be funded or unfunded.[1]

6. *Notification*: eligible employees must receive reasonable notification of the program's availability and benefits.[2]

A plan will still be considered in compliance with these requirements even though different types of educational assistance are used more than others or because successful completion of the course or obtaining a certain grade is required or considered in the process of obtaining reimbursement under the plan.[3]

Further, a plan will continue to meet the requirements of Section 127(b) even if it provides benefits to former employees. Included in the category of former employees are retirees, persons who were unable to work due to disability, persons whose positions were terminated due to a corporate downsizing, persons who left the employer voluntarily and employees who were involuntarily terminated from their positions.[4]

8818. What types of "educational assistance" may be provided on a tax-preferred basis through an employer-provided educational assistance program?

"Educational assistance," for purposes of an employer-sponsored educational assistance program (EAP), is generally defined in IRC Section 127 as an employer's payment of expenses incurred by an employee for education. Expenses such as tuition, fees, books, supplies, equipment and employer-provided courses of instruction including books, supplies and equipment are all included within this definition.[5]

Educational assistance does not include payments for tools or supplies that the employee may keep after finishing the course of instruction, as well as meals, lodging and transportation. Payment for any course or education involving sports, games or hobbies is not considered to be "educational assistance."[6]

The IRS, in interpreting the IRC definition, has defined a graduate level course as "... any course taken by an employee who has a bachelor's degree or is receiving credit toward a more advanced degree, if the particular course can be taken for credit by any individual in a program leading to a law, business, medical, or other advanced academic or professional degree."[7]

According to IRS guidance, a course will be considered to begin on the first regular day of class for the courses offered during that term. The date upon which a student registers for a course has no effect on the date the course is considered to have started for purposes of the Section 127 exclusion.

1. IRC Sec. 127(b)(5).
2. IRC Sec. 127(b)(6).
3. IRC Sec. 127(c)(5).
4. Treas. Reg. §1.127-2(h)(1); Rev. Rul. 96-41, 1996-2 CB 8.
5. IRC Sec. 127(c)(1).
6. IRC Sec. 127(c)(1).
7. Notice 96-68, 1996-2 CB 236.

8819. What reporting requirements apply to employers who provide assistance to employees through an educational assistance program?

Until 2002, an employer who maintains an Educational Assistance Program under IRC Section 127 was required to file an information return (Schedule F to the Form 5500) for each year that the program is in effect. The information return had to include the number of employees currently working, the number of employees eligible to participate in the plan, the number of employees actually participating, the total plan cost, and the number of highly compensated employees. In addition, the employer was required to identify itself and state the type of business in which it is engaged.[1]

Notice 2002-24, however, suspended these reporting requirements with respect to EAPs and certain other employee fringe benefits. Employers are relieved of the obligation to file under Section 6039D until the IRS provides further notice.[2]

Notice 2002-24 superseded Notice 90-24, which exempted plans under Section 127 from furnishing the additional information concerning highly compensated employees that was required by the TRA '86 amendments to Section 6039D.

This reporting relief applies to any plan year that begins prior to the issuance of further guidance on this subject by the IRS.[3]

8820. What is a dependent care assistance program?

A dependent care assistance program is a separate written plan of an employer for the exclusive benefit of providing employees with payment for or the provision of services that, if paid for by the employee, would be considered employment-related expenses under IRC Section 21(b)(2).[4]

"Employment-related expenses" are amounts incurred to permit the taxpayer to be gainfully employed while he or she has one or more dependents under age thirteen (for whom he or she is entitled to a personal exemption deduction under IRC Section 151(c)) or a dependent or spouse who cannot care for themselves. The expenses may be for household services or for the care of the dependents.[5]

The plan is not required to be funded.[6] A dependent care program may also be provided through a cafeteria plan.[7] See Q 8821 for a discussion of the tax treatment of employer contributions to a dependent care assistance program. See Q 8823 on the limitations to the amounts that an employee may exclude from income.

1. IRC Sec. 6039D.
2. 2002-16 IRB 785.
3. Notice 90-24, 1990-1 CB 355.
4. IRC Secs. 129(d)(1), 129(e)(1).
5. IRC Sec. 21(b)(2).
6. IRC Sec. 129(d)(5).
7. See Notice 2005-42, 2005-23 IRB 1204.

8821. Is dependent care assistance provided by an employer as a fringe benefit taxable income to the employee? Do any nondiscrimination requirements apply in order for these benefits to be received tax-free?

Non-highly compensated employees are permitted to exclude limited amounts (see Q 8823) received under an employer-sponsored dependent care assistance program for each tax year.[1] For highly compensated employees to enjoy the same income tax exclusion, the program must meet the following additional requirements:

(1) Plan contributions or benefits must not discriminate in favor of highly compensated employees as defined in IRC Section 414(q) or their dependents.

(2) The program must benefit employees in a classification that does not discriminate in favor of highly compensated employees or their dependents.

(3) No more than 25 percent of the amounts paid by the employer for dependent care assistance may be provided for the class of shareholders and owners, each of whom owns more than five percent of the stock or of the capital or profits interest in the employer (certain attribution rules under IRC Section 1563 apply).

(4) Reasonable notification of the availability and terms of the program must be provided to eligible employees.

(5) The plan must provide each employee, on or before January 31, with a written statement of the expenses or amounts paid by the employer in providing such employee with dependent care assistance during the previous calendar year.

(6) The average benefits provided to non-highly compensated employees under all plans of the employer must equal at least 55 percent of the average benefits provided to the highly compensated employees under all plans of the employer.[2]

The dependent care assistance plan may disregard any employee with compensation that is less than $25,000 annually for purposes of the 55 percent test if benefits are provided through a salary reduction agreement.[3] For this purpose, compensation is defined in IRC Section 414(q)(4), but regulations may permit an employer to elect to determine compensation on any other nondiscriminatory basis.[4]

For purposes of the eligibility and benefits requirements (described in items (2) and (6) above), the employer may exclude the following employees from consideration:

(1) Employees who have not attained age twenty-one and completed one year of service (provided all such employees are excluded).

(2) Employees covered by a collective bargaining agreement (provided there is evidence of good faith bargaining regarding dependent care assistance).[5]

1. IRC Sec. 129(d)(1).
2. IRC Sec. 129(d).
3. IRC Sec. 129(d)(8)(B).
4. IRC Sec. 129(d)(8)(B).
5. IRC Sec. 129(d)(9).

A program will not fail to meet the requirements above, other than the 25 percent test applicable to more than five percent shareholders, or the 55 percent test applicable to benefits, merely because of the utilization rates for different types of assistance available under the program. The 55 percent test may be applied on a separate line of business basis.[1]

8822. Is the employer entitled to a deduction for amounts paid to employees under a dependent care assistance program?

Yes. The employer's expenses incurred in providing benefits under a dependent care assistance program generally are deductible to the employer as ordinary and necessary business expenses under IRC Section 162.

8823. Is there a limit to the amount that an employee may exclude for payments paid by an employer under a dependent care assistance program?

An employee may exclude up to $5,000 paid by the employer for dependent care assistance provided during a tax year.[2] The excludable amount is reduced to $2,500 for a married individual filing separately. Additionally, the excludable amount cannot exceed the earned income of an unmarried employee or the lesser of the earned income of a married employee or the earned income of the employee's spouse.[3]

An employee cannot exclude from gross income any amount paid to an individual with respect to whom the employee or the employee's spouse is entitled to take a personal exemption deduction under IRC Section 151(c) or who is a child of the employee under nineteen years of age at the close of the taxable year, or the spouse.[4]

If the dependent care assistance is provided by way of on-site facilities (such as an on-site day care center), the amount of dependent care assistance excluded is based on a dependent's use of the facilities and the value of the services provided with respect to that dependent.[5]

The amount of employment-related expenses available in calculating the dependent care credit of IRC Section 21 is reduced by the amount excludable from gross income under IRC Section 129.[6]

8824. What reporting requirements apply in connection with amounts paid by an employer under a dependent care assistance program?

The employee must identify on the tax return all persons or organizations that provide care for the employee's dependent. This includes the name, address, and taxpayer identification number of the person (name and address in the case of a tax-exempt 501(c)(3) organization) providing the services. If the employee does not have the information, then the employee can use

1. See IRC Sec. 414(r).
2. IRC Sec. 129(a). See IRS Pub. 503.
3. IRC Sec. 129(b).
4. IRC Sec. 129(c).
5. IRC Sec. 129(e)(8).
6. IRC Sec. 21(c).

form W-10, Dependent Care Provider's Identification and Certification to request this information from the provider. The IRS may disallow a credit to an employee who fails to provide this information unless the taxpayer can show that he or she exercised due diligence in attempting to obtain the information. To show due diligence, the taxpayer should attach a statement explaining that the provider refused to complete the W-10.[1]

As is the case with employer-provided educational assistance programs, the IRS has suspended the reporting requirements that are otherwise applicable to dependent care programs until further notice.[2]

Prior to this suspension, IRC Section 6039D generally required an employer maintaining a dependent care assistance plan to file an information return with the IRS that provided:

(1) its number of employees;

(2) the number of employees eligible to participate in the plan;

(3) the number of employees participating in the plan;

(4) the number of highly compensated employees ("HCEs") of the employer;

(5) the number of HCEs eligible to participate in the plan;

(6) the number of HCEs actually participating in the plan;

(7) the cost of the plan;

(8) the identity of the employer; and

(9) the type of business in which it is engaged.

8825. What is a cafeteria plan? What information must an employer provide in order to establish a cafeteria plan for its employees?

A cafeteria plan (or "flexible benefit plan") is a written plan that gives employees the option of choosing between cash and "qualified benefits." With certain limited exceptions, a cafeteria plan cannot provide for deferred compensation, which generally means that the taxpayer-employee must use all benefits within the tax year.[3]

Some cafeteria plans provide for salary reduction contributions by the employee and others provide benefits in addition to salary. In either case, the employee-participants are given the opportunity to purchase certain benefits with pre-tax dollars.

1. IRC Sec. 129(e)(9).
2. Notice 2002-24, 2002-16 IRB 785; Notice 90-24, 1990-1 CB 335.
3. IRC Sec. 125(d).

A plan may provide for automatic enrollment whereby an employee's salary is reduced to pay for "qualified benefits" unless the employee affirmatively elects cash.[1]

Under the 2007 proposed regulations (effective for plan years beginning on or after January 1, 2009), the written plan document must contain:

(1) a specific description of the benefits, including periods of coverage;

(2) the rules regarding eligibility for participation;

(3) the procedures governing elections;

(4) the manner in which employer contributions are to be made, such as by salary reduction or non-elective employer contributions;

(5) the plan year;

(6) the maximum amount of employer contributions available to any employee stated as (a) a maximum dollar amount or maximum percentage of compensation or (b) the method for determining the maximum amount or percentage;

(7) a description of whether the plan offers paid time off, and the required ordering rules for use of non-elective and elective paid time off;

(8) the plan's provisions related to any flexible spending arrangements (FSA) included in the plan;

(9) the plan's provisions related to any grace period offered under the plan; and

(10) the rules governing distributions from a health FSA to employee health savings accounts (HSAs), if the plan permits such distributions (see Q 8765).[2]

The plan document need not be self-contained, but may incorporate by reference separate written plans.[3]

Participants should note that, under the Patient Protection and Affordable Care Act, for purchases made in 2011 and thereafter, the cost of an over-the-counter medicine or drug cannot be reimbursed from FSAs (Q 8830), HRAs (Q 8751) or HSAs (Q 8756) unless a prescription is obtained.[4] These new rules do not affect insulin, even if purchased without a prescription, or other health care expenses such as medical devices, eye glasses, contact lenses, co-pays and deductibles. FSA and HRA participants may continue using debit cards to buy prescribed over-the-counter medicines, if certain requirements are met (see Q 8751).[5] In addition, starting in 2013, there are new rules about the $2,500 limit (as indexed for inflation) on the amount that

1. Rev. Rul. 2002-27, 2002-1 CB 925.
2. Prop. Treas. Reg. §1.125-1(c), 72 F.R. 43938 (Aug. 6, 2007).
3. Prop. Treas. Reg. §1.125-1(c)(4).
4. P.L. 111-148.
5. IRS News Release IR-2010-128 (Dec. 23, 2010).

can be contributed to an FSA (see Q 8830) and, beginning in 2014, the new optional $500 carryover provision that can be incorporated into a health FSA.[1]

Former employees may participate in an employer's cafeteria plan (although the plan may not be established predominantly for their benefit), but self-employed individuals may not.[2] A full-time life insurance salesperson who is treated as an employee for Social Security purposes will also be considered an employee for cafeteria plan purposes (see Q 8678).[3]

See Q 8826 for an explanation of benefits that may be offered through cafeteria plans. See Q 8827 for a discussion of the nondiscrimination requirements that apply to cafeteria plans. See Q 8828 for a discussion of "simple" cafeteria plans.

8826. How can a cafeteria plan be used by employers to offer employee benefits?

An employer may offer employees who are participants in a cafeteria plan a choice among two or more benefits consisting of cash and qualified benefits.[4] A cash benefit is not strictly limited to cash, but includes a benefit that may be purchased with after-tax dollars or the value of which is generally treated as taxable compensation to the employee (provided the benefit does not constitute deferred compensation).[5]

A qualified benefit is a benefit that is not includable in the gross income of the employee because of an express statutory exclusion and because the benefit constitutes deferred compensation. Contributions to Archer Medical Savings Accounts, qualified scholarships, educational assistance programs, or excludable fringe benefits are not qualified benefits. Products that are advertised, marketed, or offered as long-term care insurance similarly do not qualify as qualified benefits.[6]

When insurance benefits, such as those provided under accident and health plans and group term life insurance plans, are provided through a cafeteria plan, the benefit is the coverage under the plan. Accident and health benefits are qualified benefits to the extent that coverage is excludable under IRC Section 106.[7] Accidental death coverage offered in a cafeteria plan under an individual accident insurance policy is excludable from the employee's income under IRC Section 106.[8]

Group term life insurance coverage on employee-participants can be offered through a cafeteria plan. Coverage may be offered through the plan even if it exceeds the $50,000 excludable limit under IRC Section 79.[9] The application of IRC Section 79 to group term life insurance and IRC Section 106 to accident or health benefits is explained in Q 8735 to Q 8738.

1. Notice 2012-40, 2012-26 IRB 1046.
2. Prop. Treas. Reg. §1.125-1(g)(2).
3. IRC Sec. 7701(a)(20); Prop. Treas. Reg. §1.125-1(g)(1)(iii).
4. IRC Sec. 125(d)(1)(B).
5. Prop. Treas. Reg. §1.125-1(a)(2).
6. IRC Sec. 125(f); Prop. Treas. Reg. §1.125-1(q).
7. Prop. Treas. Reg. §1.125-1(h)(2).
8. Let. Ruls. 8801015, 8922048.
9. Prop. Treas. Reg. §1.125-1(k).

Accident and health coverage, group term life insurance coverage, and benefits under a dependent care assistance program are still counted as "qualified" benefits even if they must be included in income because a nondiscrimination requirement has been violated.[1]

For tax years beginning after 2012, a health flexible spending arrangement (FSA) offered under a cafeteria plan is not a qualified benefit unless the plan limits employees to no more than $2,500 in salary reduction contributions for each tax year.[2] Beginning in 2014, up to $500 of the balance of a health FSA may be carried forward to the subsequent tax year if the FSA incorporates a provision that permits such a carryover.

A cafeteria plan generally cannot provide for deferred compensation, permit participants to carry over unused benefits or contributions from one plan year to another, or permit participants to purchase a benefit that will be provided in a subsequent plan year. A cafeteria plan, however, may permit a participant in a profit sharing, stock bonus, or rural cooperative plan that has a qualified cash or deferred arrangement to elect to have the employer contribute on the employee's behalf to the plan.[3] After-tax employee contributions to an IRC Section 401(m) qualified plan are permissible benefits under a cafeteria plan, even if the employer makes matching contributions.[4]

A cafeteria plan may permit a participant to elect to have the employer contribute to a health savings account (HSA) on the participant's behalf (see Q 8756 to Q 8768).[5] Unlike other benefits, HSA balances may be carried over from one year to another even if they are funded through a cafeteria plan.

Generally, life, health, disability, or long-term care insurance with an investment feature, such as whole life insurance, or an arrangement that reimburses premium payments for other accident or health coverage extending beyond the end of the plan year cannot be provided under a cafeteria plan.[6] Supplemental health insurance policies that provide coverage for cancer and other specific diseases are not treated as providing deferral of compensation and are properly considered accident and health benefits under IRC Section 106.[7]

Participants in a cafeteria plan maintained by an educational organization described in IRC Section 170(b)(1)(A)(ii) (i.e., one with a regular curriculum and an on-site faculty and student body) can be permitted to elect postretirement term life insurance coverage. The postretirement life insurance coverage must be fully paid up on retirement and must not have a cash surrender value at any time. Postretirement life insurance coverage meeting these conditions will be treated as group term life insurance under IRC Section 79 (see Q 8628 to Q 8631).[8]

1. IRC Sec. 129(d); Prop. Treas. Reg. §1.125-1(b)(2).
2. IRC Sec. 125(i).
3. IRC Sec. 125(d)(2).
4. Prop. Treas. Reg. §1.125-1(o)(3)(ii).
5. IRC Sec. 125(d)(2)(D).
6. Prop. Treas. Reg. §1.125-1(p)(1)(ii).
7. TAM 199936046.
8. IRC Sec. 125(d)(2)(C).

Under the Affordable Care Act, plans and issuers that offer dependent coverage must make this coverage available until a child reaches the age of twenty-six.[1] Even if a cafeteria plan has not yet been amended to provide coverage for children under age twenty-seven, the ACA allows employers with cafeteria plans to permit employees to immediately make pre-tax salary reduction contributions to provide coverage for these children in order to assist with implementation of the expanded coverage requirements.

Both married and unmarried children qualify for this coverage. This rule applies to all plans in the individual market and to new employer plans, as well as to existing employer plans unless the adult child has another offer of employer-based coverage. Beginning in 2014, children up to age twenty-six can stay on their parent's employer plan even if they have another offer of coverage through an employer.

Employees are eligible for the new tax benefit beginning March 30, 2010 and thereafter if the children are already covered under the employer's plan or are added to the employer's plan at any time. For this purpose, a child includes a son, daughter, stepchild, adopted child, or eligible foster child. This "up to age twenty-six" standard replaces the lower age limits that applied under prior tax law, as well as the requirement that a child generally qualify as a dependent for tax purposes.

8827. What nondiscrimination requirements apply to cafeteria plans that provide benefits to highly compensated or key employees?

If a cafeteria plan discriminates in favor of highly compensated individuals as to eligibility to participate or as to contributions or benefits, highly compensated participants will be considered in constructive receipt of the available cash benefit, which will prevent these employees from excluding the amounts from income.[2]

"Highly compensated" individuals are officers, shareholders owning more than five percent of the voting power or value of all classes of stock, those who are "highly compensated," and any of their spouses or dependents. For this purpose, "highly compensated" means (1) any individual or participant who, for the preceding plan year (or the current plan year in the case of the first year of employment), had compensation from the employer in excess of the compensation amount specified in IRC Section 414(q)(1)(B) ($120,000 for 2015-2018 and $115,000 for 2012-2014), and, (2) if elected by the employer, also was in the top-paid group of employees (determined by reference to Section 414(q)(3)) for such preceding plan year (or for the current plan year in the case of the first year of employment).[3]

Participation will be nondiscriminatory if the following requirements are satisfied:

(1) The plan benefits a classification of employees found by the Secretary of Treasury not to discriminate in favor of employees who are officers, shareholders, or highly compensated.

1. See IRC Sec. 105(b); Notice 2010-38, 2010-1 CB 682.
2. IRC Sec. 125(b)(1); Prop. Treas. Reg. §1.125-7(m)(2).
3. IRC Sec. 125(e); Prop. Treas. Reg. §1.125-7(a)(3); IRS News Release IR-2011-103 (Oct. 20, 2011), IR-2012-77 (Oct. 18, 2012); IR-2013-86 (Oct. 31, 2013), IR-2014-99 (Oct. 23, 2014); IR-2015-118 (Oct. 21, 2015), Rev. Proc. 2016-55, Rev. Proc. 2017-58.

(2) No more than three years of employment are required for participation and the employment requirement for each employee is the same.

(3) Eligible employees begin participation by the first day of the first plan year after the employment requirement is satisfied.[1]

Under the proposed regulations, a cafeteria plan does not discriminate in favor of highly compensated individuals if the plan benefits a group of employees who qualify under a reasonable classification established by the employer and the group of employees included in the classification satisfies the safe harbor percentage test or the unsafe harbor percentage test.[2]

If a cafeteria plan offers health benefits, the plan is not discriminatory as to contributions and benefits if:

(1) contributions for each participant include an amount that either:

(x) equals 100 percent of the cost of the health benefit coverage under the plan of the majority of the highly compensated participants who are similarly situated (e.g., same family size); or

(y) equals or exceeds 75 percent of the cost of the most expensive health benefit coverage elected by any similarly-situated participant; and

(2) contributions or benefits in excess of (1) above bear a uniform relationship to compensation.[3]

A plan is considered to satisfy all discrimination tests if it is maintained under a collective bargaining agreement between employee representatives and one or more employers.[4]

Further, a "key employee," as defined for purposes of the top-heavy rules, is treated as though he or she is in constructive receipt of the available cash benefit option in any plan year in which nontaxable benefits provided under the plan to key employees exceed 25 percent of the aggregate of such benefits provided to all employees under the plan. In making this calculation, excess group term life insurance coverage that is includable in income (see Q 8728 and Q 8729) is not considered a nontaxable benefit.[5]

Employees of a controlled group of corporations, employers under common control, or members of an "affiliated service group" are treated as employed by a single employer.[6]

Employer contributions include amounts that the employer contributes to a cafeteria plan pursuant to a salary reduction agreement to the extent that the agreement relates to compensation that has not been actually or constructively received by the employee as of the date of

1. IRC Sec. 125(g)(3); Prop. Treas. Reg. §1.125-7(b).
2. Prop. Treas. Reg. §1.125-7(b)(1).
3. IRC Sec. 125(g)(2); Prop. Treas. Reg. §1.125-7(e).
4. IRC Sec. 125(g)(1).
5. IRC Sec. 125(b)(2).
6. IRC Sec. 125(g)(4).

the agreement if such compensation does not subsequently become currently available to the employee.[1]

See Q 8828 for the application of the nondiscrimination requirements to simple cafeteria plans.

8828. What is a simple cafeteria plan for small businesses?

A "simple cafeteria plan" is a cafeteria plan that is established and maintained by an eligible employer and with respect to which contribution, eligibility, and participation requirements are met.[2]

For years beginning in 2011 and thereafter, the Patient Protection and Affordable Care Act (ACA) creates a safe harbor "simple cafeteria plan" under which an "eligible employer" (generally an employer with fewer than 100 employees) is treated as meeting any applicable nondiscrimination requirements (Q 8827) for the year.[3]

The employer is required to make contributions on behalf of each "qualified employee" in an amount equal:

(1) a uniform percentage (not less than two percent) of the employee's compensation; or

(2) an amount not less than the lesser of (x) six percent of the employee's compensation for the plan year, or (y) twice the amount of salary deduction contributions of each qualified employee.[4]

Contribution requirement option (2) is not met if the rate of contributions with respect to the salary contributions of any highly compensated or key employee at any rate of contribution is greater than that with respect to an employee who is not a highly compensated or key employee.[5]

All employees with at least 1,000 hours of service during the preceding plan year must be eligible to participate. Further, each employee who is eligible to participate must be able to select any benefit available under the plan.[6] An employee can be excluded if the employee:

(1) is under age twenty-one;

(2) has less than one year of service;

(3) is covered by a collective bargaining agreement and the benefits of the cafeteria plan were the subject of good faith bargaining; or

(4) the employee is a nonresident alien working outside of the United States.[7]

1. Prop. Treas. Reg. §1.125-1(r).
2. IRC Sec. 125(j)(2), as added by PPACA 2010; IRS Publication 15-B.
3. IRC Sec. 125(j)(1), as added by PPACA 2010.
4. IRC Sec. 125(j)(3)(A), as added by PPACA 2010.
5. IRC Sec. 125(j)(3)(B), as added by PPACA 2010.
6. IRC Sec. 125(j)(4)(A), as added by PPACA 2010.
7. IRC Sec. 125(j)(4)(B), as added by PPACA 2010.

To implement a simple cafeteria plan, an employer must be an "eligible employer," which is, with respect to any year, any employer that employed an average of 100 or fewer employees on business days during either of the two preceding years.[1] An employer that initially qualifies for a simple cafeteria plan ceases to qualify in the year after the number of employees reaches 200.[2]

A qualified employee is any employee who is eligible to participate in the cafeteria plan and who is not a highly compensated or key employee.[3]

8829. What are the tax benefits that can be realized by providing employee benefits through a cafeteria plan?

As a general rule, a participant in a cafeteria plan is not treated as being in constructive receipt of taxable income solely because he has the opportunity – before a cash benefit becomes available – to elect among cash and "qualified" benefits (generally, nontaxable benefits).[4]

A participant must elect the qualified benefits before the cash benefit becomes currently available in order to avoid taxation. That is, the election must be made before the specified period for which the benefit will be provided begins—generally, the plan year.[5]

A cafeteria plan may, but is not required to, provide default elections for one or more qualified benefits for new employees or for current employees who fail to timely elect between permitted taxable and qualified benefits.[6]

Benefits provided under a cafeteria plan through employer contributions to a health flexible spending arrangement (FSA) are not treated as qualified unless the plan provides that an employee may not elect to have salary reduction contributions in excess of $2,500 (this amount is indexed annually for inflation, see Q 8830) made to the FSA for any tax year.[7] Under IRS Notice 2012-40:

(1) the $2,500 limit does not apply for plan years that begin before 2013;

(2) the term "taxable year" in IRC Section 125(i) refers to the plan year of the cafeteria plan, as this is the period for which salary reduction elections are made;

(3) plans may adopt the required amendments to reflect the $2,500 limit at any time through the end of calendar year 2014;

(4) in the case of a plan providing a grace period (which may be up to two months and fifteen days), unused salary reduction contributions to the health FSA for plan years beginning in 2012 or later that are carried over into the grace period for that plan year will not count against the $2,500 limit for the subsequent plan year; and

1. IRC Sec. 125(j)(5)(A), as added by PPACA 2010.
2. IRC Sec. 125(j)(5)(C), as added by PPACA 2010.
3. IRC Sec. 125(j)(3)(D), as added by PPACA 2010.
4. IRC Sec. 125; Prop. Treas. Reg. §1.125-1.
5. Prop. Treas. Reg. §1.125-2.
6. Prop. Treas. Reg. §1.125-2(b).
7. IRC Sec. 125(i).

(5) unless a plan's benefits are under examination by the IRS, relief is provided for certain salary reduction contributions exceeding the $2,500 limit that are due to a reasonable mistake and not willful neglect, and that are corrected by the employer.

Under IRS Notice 2013-71, heath FSAs may now be amended so that $500 of unused amounts remaining at the end of the plan year may be carried forward to the next plan year. However, plans that incorporate the carry forward provision may not also offer the grace period that would otherwise allow FSA participants an additional period after the end of the plan year to exhaust account funds.[1]

8830. What is a health flexible spending arrangement (FSA)?

Editor's Note: The Affordable Care Act ("ACA") imposes an annual limitation on contributions to a health FSA. For taxable years beginning after 2012, FSA contributions will not be treated as a qualified benefit unless the cafeteria plan provides that an employee may not elect for any taxable year to have salary reduction contributions in excess of $2,500 made to the arrangement. The limit will be indexed for inflation ($2,650 in 2018).[2]

A health flexible spending arrangement (FSA) is a program that is established under IRC Section 125 to provide for the reimbursement of certain expenses that have already been incurred. This benefit may be provided as a stand-alone plan or as part of a traditional cafeteria plan.

Health coverage under an FSA is not required to be provided under commercial insurance plans, but the coverage that is provided must demonstrate the risk shifting and risk distribution characteristics of insurance. Reimbursements under a health FSA must be paid specifically to reimburse medical expenses that have been incurred previously.

A health FSA cannot provide coverage only for periods during which the participants expect to incur medical expenses if the period is shorter than a plan year. Further, the maximum reimbursement amount must be available at all times throughout the period of coverage (properly reduced for prior reimbursements for the same period of coverage).

This must be true without regard to the extent to which the participant has paid the required premiums for the coverage period, and without a premium payment schedule based on the rate or amount of covered claims incurred in the coverage period.[3] Though there was no statutory limit on contributions to a health FSA prior to 2013, most employers imposed a limit to protect themselves against large claims that had not yet been funded by salary reductions.

The period of coverage must be twelve months, or in the case of a short first plan year, the entire first year (or the short plan year where the plan year is changed). Elections to increase or decrease coverage may not be made during a coverage year, but prospective changes may be allowed consistent with certain changes in family status.

1. Notice 2013-71, 2013-47 IRB 532.
2. IRC Sec. 125(i), as added by PPACA 2010; Notice 2012-40, 2012-1 CB 1046; Rev. Proc. 2017-58.
3. Prop. Treas. Reg. §1.125-5(d).

The plan may permit the period of coverage to be terminated if the employee fails to pay premiums, provided that the terms of the plan prohibit the employee from making a new election during the remaining period of coverage. The plan may permit revocation of existing elections by an employee who terminated service.[1]

As is the case with a cafeteria plan, a health FSA may provide a grace period of no more than 2½ months following the end of the plan year for participants to incur and submit expenses for reimbursement. The grace period must apply to all participants in the plan. Plans may adopt a grace period for the current plan year by amending the plan document before the end of the current plan year.[2]

For tax years beginning in 2014 and beyond, a health FSA may be amended so that $500 of unused amounts remaining at the end of the plan year may be carried forward to the next plan year. However, plans that incorporate the carry forward provision may not also offer the grace period.[3]

The plan may not reimburse premiums paid for other health plan coverage, but it may reimburse medical expenses of the kind described under IRC Section 213(d).[4] Beginning in 2011, reimbursements for medicine are limited to doctor-prescribed drugs and insulin. Over-the-counter medicines are no longer qualified expenses unless the participant obtains a doctor's prescription.[5]

The reimbursed medical expenses must be expenses incurred to obtain medical care during the period of coverage. The employee must provide substantiation that the expense claimed has been incurred and is not reimbursable under other health coverage.[6] The IRS has approved the use of employer-issued debit and credit cards to pay for medical expenses as incurred, provided that the employer requires subsequent substantiation of the expenses or has in place sufficient procedures to substantiate the payments at the time of purchase.[7] On a one-time basis, a plan may allow a qualified HSA distribution (see Q 8765).

An employee must include the value of employer-provided coverage for qualified long-term care services provided through an FSA in gross income.[8]

8831. What is a dependent care flexible spending arrangement (FSA)?

A dependent care flexible spending arrangement (FSA) is a program that is established under IRC Section 125 to provide for the reimbursement of certain expenses related to dependent care that have already been incurred. This benefit may be provided as a stand-alone plan or as part of a traditional cafeteria plan.

1. Prop. Treas. Reg. §1.125-5(e).
2. Prop. Treas. Reg. §1.125-1(e); Notice 2005-42, 2005-1 CB 1204; Notice 2012-40, 2012-1 CB 1046.
3. Notice 2013-71, 2013-47 IRB 532.
4. Prop. Treas. Reg. §1.125-5(k).
5. IRC Sec. 106(f), as added by PPACA 2010.
6. Prop. Treas. Reg. §1.125-6(b); Rev. Proc. 2003-43, 2003-1 CB 935; superseded and modified by Notice 2013-30, 2013-21 IRB 1099. See *Grande v. Allison Engine Co.*, 2000 U.S Dist. LEXIS 12220 (S.D. Ind. 2000).
7. Notice 2006-69, 2006-2 CB 107. See also Notice 2007-2, 2007-1 CB 254.
8. IRC Sec. 106(c)(1).

Substantially the same rules apply to dependent care FSAs as health FSAs (see Q 8830), except that the maximum amount of reimbursement need not be available throughout the entire period of coverage. A plan may limit a participant's reimbursement to amounts that were actually contributed to the plan and that are still available in the participant's account.[1] Contributions to a dependent care FSA may not exceed $5,000 (or $2,500 for a married individual filing a separate return) during a taxable year.[2]

Like a health FSA, a dependent care FSA may permit a grace period of no more than 2½ months following the end of the plan year for participants to incur and submit expenses for reimbursement.[3] A dependent care FSA may not, however, permit the same $500 carryfoward option that is now permitted in the context of health FSAs.

The IRS has also approved the use of employer-issued debit and credit cards to reimburse for recurring dependent care expenses. Because expenses may not be reimbursed until the dependent care services are provided, reimbursements through debit cards must flow in arrears of expenses incurred.[4]

8832. Is a surviving spouse of an employee taxed on the value of death benefits paid under a plan of the employer?

A surviving spouse who receives death benefits payable under a contract, or pursuant to an established plan of the employer, must include such amounts in income.[5] However, if the employee death benefits are payable because of the death of certain terrorist attack victims or astronauts, they may be excluded from gross income.[6]

Frequently, death benefits are funded by insurance on the life of the employee, with the insurance owned by and payable to the employer. These death benefits do not become tax-exempt to the employee's surviving spouse simply because the proceeds of the insurance policy are received tax-free by the employer. While the employer receives the proceeds as life insurance proceeds, the surviving spouse receives them as compensation payments from the employer.[7] As a result, employee death benefits rarely qualify as life insurance benefits wholly excludable under IRC Section 101(a).[8] Death benefits payable to an employee's surviving spouse under a split-dollar arrangement, however, may be received free of income tax obligations.

Contractual death benefits are treated as "income in respect of a decedent."[9] As a result, where an estate tax has been paid, the recipient of the death payments is entitled to an income tax deduction for that portion of the estate tax attributable to the value of the payments.

1. Prop. Treas. Reg. §1.125-5.
2. IRC Sec. 129(a)(2)(A); Notice 2012-40, 2012-1 CB 1046.
3. Notice 2005-42, 2005-1 CB 1204; Notice 2012-40, 2012-1 CB 1046.
4. Notice 2006-69, 2006-2 CB 107.
5. *Simpson v. U.S.*, 261 F.2d 497 (7th Cir. 1958); *Robinson v. Comm.*, 42 TC 403 (1964).
6. IRC Sec. 101(i).
7. *Essenfeld v. Comm.*, 311 F.2d 208 (2d Cir. 1962).
8. See *Edgar v. Comm.*, TC Memo 1979-524.
9. *Est. of Wright v. Comm.*, 336 F.2d 121 (2d Cir. 1964).

8833. What types of benefits can an employer provide in the form of services that do not require an employee to include the value of the benefit in income?

Generally, fringe benefits not expressly excluded from income by the Code must be included in gross income for income tax purposes and in wages for purposes of FICA and FUTA.[1] IRC Section 132 provides that certain fringe benefits that are classified as "no-additional-cost-services" may be excluded from income.[2]

As the name suggests, a "no-additional-cost-service" is one offered by the employer at no substantial additional cost (including foregone revenue) to the employer for providing such service to the employee and such service is offered to customers in the ordinary course of the line of business of the employer in which the employee is working.

For example, the cost of a flight provided to an airline employee traveling on a space-available basis is an excess capacity service and is eligible for treatment as a no-additional-cost-service. In addition, the services of a flight attendant and the cost of in-flight meals given to the airline employee traveling on a space-available basis are merely incidental to the services being provided (i.e. the flight) and, thus, the employee does not have to include them in income.[3] Reciprocity is allowed between unrelated employers if certain conditions are met.[4]

The no-additional-cost services exclusion applies to services provided to retired and disabled employees, spouses and dependent children, as well as to current employees. Widowers and widows of employees who died while employed also qualify for the exclusion.[5] A partner who performs services for a partnership will be considered employed by the partnership.[6]

The no-additional-cost services exclusion is not available to highly compensated employees unless the service is provided on substantially the same terms to each member of a group of employees which is defined under a reasonable classification set up by the employer which does not discriminate in favor of highly compensated employees.[7] For this purpose, "highly compensated employee" has the same meaning as provided in Code Section 414(q) for qualified plans.[8] Generally, a highly compensated employee is any employee:

(1) who was a five percent owner at any time during the year or the preceding year; or

(2) for the preceding year had compensation in excess of $80,000 (as indexed, $120,000 in 2015-2018 and $115,000 in 2014) and was in the top-paid group of employees for the preceding year.

1. IRC Sec. 61(a)(1).
2. IRC Sec. 132.
3. Treas. Reg. §1.132-2(a)(5).
4. See Treas. Reg. §1.132-2(b).
5. IRC Sec. 132(h).
6. Treas. Reg. §1.132-1(b).
7. IRC Sec. 132(j)(1).
8. IRC Sec. 132(j)(6).

8834. What types of tax-preferred transportation-related fringe benefits can an employer provide to its employees?

Editor's Note: Congress recently placed mass transit benefits on par with employer-provided parking expenses, so that a taxpayer may exclude up to $250 a month in employer-provided transportation in a commuter vehicle or employer-provided transit passes. Congress retroactively extended this parity for the 2015 tax year. The Protecting Americans Against Tax Hikes Act of 2015 (PATH) made these provisions permanent.

A "qualified transportation fringe" is a benefit provided by an employer to employees, and includes:

(1) transportation in a commuter highway vehicle that is used in connection with travel between an employee's home and place of work;

(2) any transit pass; or

(3) qualified parking.[1]

A cash reimbursement from an employer to an employee for one of these items also falls within the qualified transportation fringe definition if the transit passes are not readily available in the employer's area.[2] A transit pass may still be readily available if the transportation provider only accepts a certain form of payment (i.e., the transportation provider only accepts cash or checks, and the employer has provided a debit card to pay for transit expenses). The IRS has indicated that payment restrictions, unless combined with other restrictions, are not sufficient to cause a transit pass to fail to be readily available.[3]

Self-employed individuals and owner-employees are not considered employees for purposes of qualified transportation fringes.[4]

Code Section 132 places a limit on the amount that may be excluded from income for a qualified transportation fringe. These limitation amounts are adjusted for inflation.[5]

An employee can exclude up to $250 per month in (combined) employer-provided transportation in a commuter vehicle or for transit passes. An employee may exclude $250 per month for qualified parking expenses.[6] The limits are indexed for inflation annually (the 2018 amount is $260).

For purposes of Section 132, a "commuter highway vehicle" is defined as any highway vehicle that seats at least six persons and which is used at least 80 percent of the time for transporting employees between their homes and places of work.[7]

1. IRC Sec. 132(f)(1).
2. IRC Sec. 132(f)(3).
3. IRS INFO 2016-0007.
4. IRC Sec. 132(f)(5)(E).
5. IRC Sec. 132(f)(6).
6. IRC Sec. 132(f)(2), IRS Publication 15-B.
7. IRC Sec. 132(f)(5)(B).

A "transit pass" is any pass, token, fare card, voucher or similar item which entitles an individual to transportation on mass transit facilities or in commuter highway vehicles.[1]

"Qualified parking" is defined as parking provided to an employee on or near the employer's business location or near a location from which an employee commutes to work by mass transit, commuter highway vehicle, or carpool. It does not include any parking near the employer's place of business that the employee uses for residential parking.[2]

The IRS has released a program manager technical assistance providing guidance for employers that choose to make cash reimbursements to employees to compensate them for retroactive increases in the amount of transit benefits that may be excluded from income under IRC Section 132(f). Many employers wished to reimburse employees to account for the increased permissible benefit level in past years. Typically, cash payments made by employers for transit benefits are only excludable from an employee's income if transit passes are not readily available in the employer's area. The IRS has indicated that cash amounts that exceed the monthly maximum limit (in any month) will be taxed as wages, even if those amounts are paid because of the retroactive increase in the monthly amount for past years.[3]

8835. Can an employee exclude from income the value of employee discounts offered by the employer?

The "qualified employee discount" exclusion applies to employee discounts provided by the employer on any property (other than real property or personal property of a kind held for investment) or services which are offered for sale to customers in the ordinary course of the line of business of the employer for which the employee works. For the benefit to be excludable from income, the discount may not exceed:

(1) the gross profit percentage of the price at which the property is being offered by the employer to customers in the case of property; or

(2) 20 percent of the price at which services are offered by the employer to customers, in the case of services.[4]

For purposes of this provision, an insurance policy or a commission or similar fee charged by a brokerage house or an underwriter on sales of securities is considered a service.[5] The qualified employee discount will generally be available for employees of leased sections of department stores.[6] The same nondiscrimination rules apply to qualified employee discounts as apply to no-additional-cost services (see Q 8833).[7]

1. IRC Sec. 132(f)(5)(A).
2. IRC Sec. 132(f)(5)(C).
3. PMTA 2016-001.
4. IRC Sec. 132(c).
5. Treas. Reg. §1.132-2(a)(2).
6. IRC Sec. 132(j)(2).
7. IRC Sec. 132(j)(1).

8836. What is a "working condition" fringe benefit?

A "working condition fringe" benefit is defined as property or services provided by the employer to the extent that, if the employee paid for such property or services, he or she would be able to deduct the expenses as a business expense.[1]

For example, qualified automobile demonstration is considered to be a working condition fringe benefit and is defined as the use of an auto by a full-time auto salesman in the area where the dealer's sales office is located provided that the auto is used to aid the salesman in his job and personal use is substantially restricted.[2]

This exclusion is generally available to any current employee, any partner who performs services for the partnership, any director of the employer, and any independent contractor who performs services for the employer.[3] There is no nondiscrimination requirement.

8837. What is a "de minimis" fringe benefit?

The "de minimis fringe" exception allows an employee to exclude from income any property or services provided by the employer, if the value of such property or services is so small as to make accounting for it unreasonable or administratively impractical.[4]

For example, an employer-operated eating facility is considered a de minimis fringe if it is located on or near the business premises and the revenue from the facility equals or exceeds its operating costs. These rules are applicable to highly-compensated employees only if access to the facility is available on substantially the same terms to each member of a group of employees which is defined under a reasonable classification set up by the employer which does not discriminate in favor of highly compensated employees (see Q 8833).[5]

The frequency with which the employer provides the benefit at issue must be taken into account in determining whether the value is de minimis. The benefits provided must be calculated on a per-employee basis. For example, if an employer provides one meal to only one employee on a daily basis, the value of the free daily meal would not be de minimis to that individual employee, even though the provision of one daily meal to one employee would be de minimis with respect to the employer's entire workforce.[6]

If, however, it would be administratively difficult to determine the frequency with which the employer provides the fringe benefit to an individual employee, the employer may measure frequency based on the frequency for the provision of the fringe benefit to all employees. The regulations use the example of an employer who uses reasonable means to restrict use of employer-provided copy machines to business-related use and is successful in ensuring that 85 percent of the copying is for business use. Any personal use of the copy machine by a particular

1. IRC Sec. 132(d).
2. IRC Sec. 132(j)(3).
3. Treas. Reg. §1.132-1(b)(2).
4. IRC Sec. 132(e)(1).
5. IRC Sec. 132(e)(2).
6. Treas. Reg. §1.132-6(b)(1).

employee will be considered a de minimis fringe because it would be administratively difficult for the employer to measure usage on a per-employee basis.[1]

An employer may provide meals, money for meals or local transportation fare as de minimis benefits if the following conditions are satisfied:

(1) The benefit is provided on an occasional basis, determined by examining the availability of the benefit and the regularity with which the benefit is provided to the employee. If an employer provides one of these benefits, or a combination of the three benefits, on a regular or routine basis, they are not provided on an occasional basis.

(2) The benefit is provided because of overtime work that requires an extension of the employee's work schedule, even if the conditions giving rise to the need for overtime are reasonably foreseeable.

(3) In the case of a meal or meal money, the benefit is provided to enable the employee to work overtime hours.

Meal money and local transportation fare will not qualify as de minimis benefits if the amounts provided are calculated based on the number of hours that the employee works.[2]

8838. How is the value of a fringe benefit that is not excludable under IRC Section 132 determined for purposes of determining the amount that must be included in the employee's income?

A fringe benefit not excludable under the rules discussed in Q 8833 to Q 8837 (no-additional-cost, transportation, employee discount and de minimis fringe benefits) is included in the gross income of the employee to the extent that the fair market value of the benefit exceeds the sum of (a) the amount, if any, paid by the employee for the benefit and (b) the amount, if any, specifically excluded by some other section of the IRC.[3]

Therefore, if the employee pays fair market value for the benefit, no amount must be included in gross income.[4]

The fair market value of a fringe benefit is determined on the basis of objective facts and circumstances. The amount that an individual would have to pay for the fringe benefit in an arm's length transaction is considered in determining the fair market value.[5] The regulations specifically provide that in calculating fair market value, any special relationship that exists between the employer and employee must be disregarded.[6]

1. Treas. Reg. §1.132-6(b)(2).
2. Treas. Reg. §1.132-6(d)(2).
3. Treas. Reg. §1.61-21(b)(1).
4. Treas. Reg. §1.61-21(b)(1).
5. Treas. Reg. §1.61-21(b)(2).
6. Treas. Reg. §1.61-21(b)(2).

Special optional rules are available for determining the fair market value of employer-provided automobiles. Specifically, the fair market value is based on the amount that the employee would be required to pay in order to lease the same or comparable vehicle, under comparable conditions (for example, taking use restrictions into consideration) in an arm's length transaction in the same geographic area.[1]

8839. Can an employer provide employee fringe benefits through a stock bonus plan?

Yes, an employer can provide employees with benefits through a stock bonus plan. Generally, a stock bonus plan is a profit sharing plan that holds employer securities and generally distributes those securities to participants when benefits are paid.[2]

Stock bonus plans can be funded through an employer's contribution of employer securities, cash, or both. Traditionally, the IRS has taken the position that the distribution must be in the form of employer stock (except for the value of a fractional share).[3] The Tax Court has agreed with the IRS position.[4] A stock bonus plan may provide for payment of benefits in cash if certain conditions are met (see Q 8840). For the purpose of allocating contributions and distributing benefits, the plan is subject to the same requirements as a profit sharing plan.

8840. What special requirements apply to a stock bonus plan offered by an employer?

In addition to meeting all of the requirements of IRC Section 401(a) and the requirements outlined below, employee stock bonus plans must meet certain distribution (Q 8841) and voting (Q 8842) requirements as to employer stock that is held by the plan.[5]

If the employer securities held within the plan are not readily traded on a public market, any transactions involving stock require an independent valuation of the stock for that transaction. A stock bonus plan generally is required to give participants the right to demand benefits in the form of employer securities. If employer securities are not readily tradable on an established market, the participant must be given the right to require the employer (not the plan) to repurchase employer securities under a fair valuation formula (a "put option").[6]

The requirement that participants have the right to demand benefits in the form of employer securities does not apply in situations where the charter or bylaws of the employer restrict the ownership of substantially all outstanding employer securities to employees, to a qualified plan trust, or to an S corporation.[7]

1. Treas. Reg. §1.61-21(b)(4).
2. Treas. Reg. §1.401-1(a)(2)(iii).
3. Rev. Rul. 71-256, 1971-1 CB 118.
4. *Miller v. Comm.*, 76 TC 433 (1981).
5. IRC Secs. 401(a)(23), 4975(e)(7).
6. IRC Sec. 409(h).
7. IRC Sec. 409(h)(2)(B).

The employer must make this put option available for at least sixty days following distribution of the stock and, if it is not exercised within that time, it must be made available for another sixty day period (at a minimum) in the following year.[1]

The plan may repurchase the stock instead of the employer, but the plan cannot be required to do so. Certain banks that are prohibited by law from redeeming or purchasing their own shares are not subject to the requirement that they give participants a put option.[2]

If, pursuant to a put option, an employer is required to repurchase securities distributed to an employee as part of a "total distribution," the amount paid for the securities must be paid in substantially equal periodic payments (at least annually), over a period beginning within thirty days after the exercise of the put option, and not exceeding five years. The employer must provide adequate security and reasonable interest must be paid on any unpaid amounts. A total distribution is a distribution to the recipient within one taxable year of the balance to the credit in his or her account.[3] If an employer is required to repurchase securities distributed to an employee as part of an "installment distribution," the amount paid for the securities must be paid within thirty days after the put option is exercised.[4]

8841. What rules govern distributions from an employer-sponsored stock bonus plan?

Distributions from a stock bonus plan are subject to mandatory 20 percent withholding, unless the employee elects a direct rollover.[5] The mandatory withholding requirement does not apply to any distribution that consists only of securities of the employer-corporation and cash of up to $200 that is received in lieu of stock. The maximum amount to be withheld under the mandatory withholding rules may not exceed the sum of the amount of money received and the fair market value of property other than securities of the employer corporation received in the distribution.[6]

The plan must provide that if a participant, with the consent of his or her spouse, so elects, the distribution of the account balance will begin within one year after the plan year:

(1) in which the participant separates from service by reason of attainment of the normal retirement age under the plan, disability, or death; or

(2) which is the fifth plan year following the plan year in which the participant otherwise separated from service.

Distribution under (2) will not be required if the participant is re-employed by the employer before distributions actually begin under (2).[7]

1. IRC Sec. 409(h)(4).
2. IRC Sec. 409(h)(3).
3. IRC Sec. 409(h)(5).
4. IRC Sec. 409(h)(6).
5. IRC Sec. 3405(c).
6. IRC Sec. 3405(e)(8).
7. IRC Sec. 409(o)(1)(A).

The plan also must provide that, unless the participant elects otherwise, distribution of the participant's account balance will be made in substantially equal periodic payments (at least annually) over a period not longer than the greater of (1) five years, or (2) in the case of a participant with an account balance in excess of $1,105,000 as indexed in 2018, five years plus one additional year (not to exceed five additional years) for each $220,000 in 2018, or fraction thereof, by which the employee's account balance exceeds $1,105,000.[1]

Planning Point: An employer whose stock is not publicly traded, and therefore is subject to the employer's potential obligation to repurchase its stock from terminating plan participants, should be concerned about the impact that obligation could have on its cash flow. The employer should consider writing its plan to take the maximum time allowed, generally five years, to begin the process of distributing stock from the plan and then repurchasing that stock from former employees. *Martin Silfen, J.D., Brown Brothers Harriman Trust Co., LLC.*

Notwithstanding these requirements, if the general rules for commencement of distributions from qualified plans require distributions to begin at an earlier date, those general rules control.[2]

8842. Does participation in an employer's stock bonus plan entitle the employee-participant to voting privileges?

A stock bonus plan is required to pass through certain voting rights to participants or beneficiaries. If an employer's securities are "registration-type," each participant or beneficiary generally must be entitled to direct the plan as to how securities allocated to him or her are to be voted.[3] "Registration-type" securities are securities that must be registered under Section 12 of the Securities and Exchange Act of 1934 or that would be required to be registered except for an exemption in that law.[4]

If securities are not "registration-type" and more than 10 percent of a plan's assets are invested in securities of the employer, each participant (or beneficiary) must be permitted to direct voting rights under securities allocated to his or her account with respect to approval of corporate mergers, consolidations, recapitalizations, reclassifications, liquidations, dissolutions, sales of substantially all of the business's assets, and similar transactions as provided in future regulations.[5]

If the plan contains non-registration-type securities, the plan satisfies this requirement if each participant is given one vote with respect to an issue and the trustee votes the shares held by the plan in a proportion that takes this vote into account.[6]

1. IRC Sec. 409(o)(1)(C); Notice 2017-64.
2. See General Explanation of TRA '86, p. 840.
3. IRC Secs. 401(a)(28), 4975(e)(7), 409(e)(2).
4. IRC Sec. 12(g)(2)(H).
5. IRC Sec. 409(e)(3).
6. IRC Secs. 401(a)(22), 409(e)(3), 409(e)(5).

PART XIII: CHOICE OF ENTITY AND THE SMALL BUSINESS

8843. What is a sole proprietorship and how is it formed?

A sole proprietorship is an unincorporated business entity that is owned by a single business owner. The primary distinguishing feature of the sole proprietorship is that only one person owns and manages the business. The business exists as an extension of the proprietor.[1]

Because of this, the structure of the sole proprietorship is simple and relatively easy to establish. The proprietor usually need only buy some stock-in-trade, possibly rent some business space, and open his door for business. In some states it will be necessary for the proprietor to file or record what is commonly called a "fictitious business name"; d/b/a or "doing business as"; or "assumed name" registration if the business owner intends to operate the business under a different name than the owner's name. The proprietor may also be required to obtain state and local licenses, if any are applicable to the business.

Planning Point: In some states, simply filing a fictitious business name does not provide any ownership interest in the name. Whether or not this filing confers any ownership interest must be determined under the laws of the applicable state where the business is located.

However, the owner largely avoids the complexity and expense involved in organizing a partnership (see Q 8845), limited liability company (see Q 8892), S corporation (see Q 8882) or C corporation (see Q 8868). A proprietor is not required to draft a partnership agreement, LLC operating agreement or articles of incorporation and bylaws. Therefore, the sole proprietor can avoid the cost of attorney's fees, filing, publication, and recording and annual administrative maintenance costs.

In some cases, however, these advantages are outweighed by the risk of increased liability, an important disadvantage to the proprietorship structure. Since the business is an extension of the proprietor and not a separate legal entity, the liabilities or losses of the business are the personal liabilities and losses of the proprietor. No legal distinction is made between a proprietor's personal liabilities and those created as a proprietor. Therefore, liability for these business obligations is unlimited and unshared. If business assets are insufficient to cover these business liabilities, creditors may reach the proprietor's personal assets to satisfy their claims. A sole proprietorship can also be more difficult to transfer in that the ownership of the enterprise cannot be divided into separate shares.

8844. How is a sole proprietorship taxed?

Legally, a sole proprietorship is not an entity separate from its owner (see Q 8843). As a result, for tax purposes, the proprietor and the enterprise are treated as one indivisible unit. The proprietorship, as such, is not a tax paying entity.

1. See *Williams v. McGowan*, 152 F.2d 570 (1945).

The proprietor reports income and expenses on an individual return (Form 1040). For this purpose, a separate Schedule C is filed, including total proprietorship receipts, inventory, costs, and deductions, to arrive at proprietorship net profit or loss. This net profit or loss from Schedule C is carried to Form 1040, and included in taxable income.[1]

In addition to the regular income tax applicable to the proprietorship net income, the Schedule C net income is also subjected to a separate self-employment tax (on Schedule SE), which is intended as a substitute for the Social Security taxes which would have been imposed if the income had been salary or wages paid by an employer (see Q 8552 and Q 8555). Since a sole proprietor is, in effect, both employer and employee, the self-employment tax encompasses both the employer and employee portions of the Social Security taxes on wages.

The estate of a sole proprietor is treated in the same manner as the estate of any other decedent. Unless specific assets pass by trust, contract or survivorship, they will be included within the proprietor's estate and potentially subject to estate taxation. Since the proprietor's business is not a separate entity, the business assets and liabilities also are subject to the estate administration process. This can be of a particular concern if the estate owns some assets which may be risky from a liability perspective.

A "qualified joint venture" that is carried out by two spouses may elect to treat their business as two sole proprietorships and not as a partnership for tax purposes. A qualified joint venture is any joint venture conducting a trade or business where the only owners are two spouses, both spouses materially participate in the business, and both spouses elect to opt out of the partnership taxation rules. Items of income, gain, loss, deduction, and credit must be divided between the spouses according to their respective interests in the business.[2] See Q 8848 to Q 8866 for a discussion of the tax treatment of partnerships.

8845. What is a partnership and how is it formed?

A partnership is an arrangement in which two or more parties join together, usually for some profit-motivated activity. Whereas a corporation is recognized as an independently functioning legal entity, separate and apart from its owners (stockholders), the status of a partnership falls somewhere in between that of a separate independent entity and a mere contractual association between participants. It is analogous to a sole proprietorship with multiple owners.

For tax purposes, however, the partnership is not treated as a separately taxable entity (even though it will still have to file a tax return). Instead, the income or loss realized by a partnership is passed through and taxed directly to the parties who are the partners of the partnership at their individual level.[3] This basic approach is the same as the tax treatment of S corporations (see Q 8883 and Q 8884). As is the case with S corporations, the pass-through approach eliminates the double-taxation effect of taxing the same income at the entity level and again when it

1. See IRS Guidance on Sole Proprietorships, available at http://www.irs.gov/Businesses/Small-Businesses-&-Self-Employed/Sole-Proprietorships (last accessed June 11, 2017).
2. IRC Sec. 761(f).
3. IRC Sec. 701.

is distributed to the owners of the entity. Many of the issues which arise in applying this pass-through approach are common to both S corporations and partnerships.

For tax purposes, the term "partnership" may include a general partnership, limited partnership, joint venture, limited liability company, or other unincorporated organization. Beginning in 1997, the IRS replaced the complicated set of rules that existed for use in for determining whether an association or entity was to be treated as a corporation or as a partnership for tax purposes with a single taxpayer election approach, known as a "check the box" approach. As a result, non-corporate organizations may file an election to be treated as a corporation or as a partnership for purposes of determining the tax rules to which they will be subject. This is done on IRS Form 8832.

A partnership is formed under an agreement known as the "partnership agreement." The partnership agreement is a written agreement between the partners, covering the organization, conduct, and termination of their common enterprise. This partnership agreement typically also governs the method that will be used for allocating partnership income, loss, deductions and credits among the individual partners. It may also include many provisions associated with a buy-sell agreement (see Q 8903).

8846. How does a partner acquire interests in a partnership? Is the allocation of income amongst partners impacted if a partner acquires a partnership interest by gift?

A person becomes a partner in a partnership through the ownership of a capital interest in a partnership in which capital is a material income-producing factor, whether the interest is acquired by purchase or gift.[1] Generally, such a person will be taxed on his or her share of partnership profits or losses. If capital is not an income-producing factor in the partnership, the transfer of a partnership interest to a family member may be disregarded as an ineffective assignment of income, rather than an assignment of property from which income is derived.

Generally, the partnership agreement will provide how income and losses will be allocated. However, where an interest is acquired by gift (an interest purchased by one family member from another is considered to have been acquired by gift), the allocation of income, as set forth in the partnership agreement, will not control to the extent that:

(1) it does not allow for a reasonable salary for services rendered to the partnership by the donor of the interest; or

(2) the income attributable to the capital share of the donee is proportionately greater than the income attributable to the donor's capital share.[2]

The transfer must be complete and the family member donee must have control over the partnership interest consistent with the status of partner. If the donee is not old enough to serve in the capacity of partner, the interest must be controlled by a fiduciary for his benefit.

1. IRC Sec. 704(e)(1).
2. IRC Sec. 704(e)(2).

8847. Is a partnership entitled to deduct its organizational expenses?

A partnership may deduct up to $5,000 of organizational expenses in the year the partnership begins business. The $5,000 amount is reduced (but not below zero) by the amount of organizational expenses that exceed $50,000. If any organizational expenses remain, they may be deducted over a 180-month period beginning with the month that the partnership begins business.[1]

Organizational expenses which may typically be deducted include legal fees for services incident to organization, fees for establishment of the partnership accounting system, and necessary filing fees.[2]

The determination of the date the partnership begins business is a question of fact, but ordinarily it begins when the partnership starts the business operations for which it was organized. For example, the acquisition of operating assets that are necessary to the type of business to be carried on by the partnership may constitute "beginning business." The mere signing of a partnership agreement, however, is not sufficient to show the beginning of business.[3]

8848. How is a partnership taxed?

With the exception of certain publicly traded partnerships, a partnership is not taxed at the entity level.[4] Despite this, the partnership must file an information return on Form 1065 that shows its taxable ordinary income or loss and capital gain or loss. Unlike in the case of a sole proprietorship (see Q 8843), the partnership is regarded as a separate entity for the purpose of computing taxable income, and business expenses of the partnership may be deducted.

In general, a partnership calculates taxable income in the same manner as individuals, except that the standard deduction, personal exemptions, and expenses of a purely personal nature are not allowed.[5] The partnership may also be entitled to a deduction for production activities. Each partner must report his share of partnership profits, whether distributed or not, on his individual return.

In general, after the partnership calculates its taxable income, items of income, gain, loss, deduction or credit are allocated among the partners pursuant to the partnership agreement's provisions, and the partners are taxed on those distributions individually.[6] These tax items are commonly allocated among the partners in direct proportion to their respective percentage ownership interests in the partnership (see Q 8849).

Planning Point: As part of the partnership's income tax return, the partnership is required to issue a Form K-1 to each of the partners. This Form advises each partner how income, loss and other "pass through" items should be reported on the partner's personal income tax return. Therefore, if an individual owns an interest in a partnership (or other "flow through entity," such as an S Corporation or LLC), the individual cannot file a personal income tax return until after the partnership (or entity level) return has been completed.

1. IRC Sec. 709(b).
2. Treas. Reg. §1.709-2(a).
3. Treas. Reg. §1.709-2(c).
4. IRC Sec. 701.
5. IRC Secs. 703(a), 63(c)(6)(D).
6. IRC Sec. 704(a).

The situation becomes more complicated, however, when the partnership provides for allocation of income and other cash distributions or losses in a manner which differs from the partners' relative percentage interests in capital. Limited partnerships have long been used as a vehicle for so-called tax-sheltered investments. These ventures are typically structured to produce losses and/or tax credits, through liberal use of deductions for depreciation, natural resources depletion or exploration, and other provisions. The partnership agreements spell out the method for allocation of these tax benefits among the various classes of partners.

Thus, depending upon the objectives of the various partners, the tax allocation provisions of the partnership agreement might be drafted in order to allocate tax losses and/or credits to a particular partner or class of partners. Typically, the general partner(s), who are the organizers and managers of a venture will be treated differently from the limited partners, who are the principal providers of capital to the project. Prior to extensive reforms enacted in 1986 (see Q 8634 and Q 8635), these types of tax shelter partnerships were widely promoted, with the partnerships' typically substantial tax losses being allocated primarily, if not exclusively, to the passive investors.

Under current law, the allocation specified under the agreement must have a "substantial economic effect." Essentially, this means that the IRS will scrutinize and revise the allocation of tax items among the partners to the extent necessary to be in accordance with each partner's true economic interest in the partnership.[1] See Q 8849 for a detailed discussion of the allocation of income and loss among partners.

Special allocation rules apply where the partner's interest changes during the year.[2]

A partnership which is traded on an established securities market, known as a publicly traded partnership, is taxed differently than a partnership in some instances (see Q 8863 and Q 8864).[3] See Q 8855 for special considerations that may apply in the context of a family partnership.

8849. How is partnership income and loss allocated among partners? What is the "substantial economic effect test"?

The partnership agreement often provides for the allocation of separately stated items of partnership income, gain, loss, deductions and credits among the partners (known as a partner's distributive share), and sometimes provides for an allocation system that is disproportionate to the capital contributions of the partners (a so-called "special allocation"). Despite this, if the method of allocation lacks "substantial economic effect" (or if no allocation is specified), the distributive shares will be determined in accordance with the partner's interest in the partnership, based on all the facts and circumstances.[4]

1. Treas. Reg. §1.704-1(b).
2. IRC Secs. 706(d), 704(b).
3. IRC Sec. 7704.
4. IRC Secs. 704(a), 704(b).

The substantial economic effect test exists in order to "prevent use of special allocations for tax avoidance purposes, while allowing their use for bona fide business purposes."[1] Under the regulations, generally, an allocation will not have economic effect unless the partners' capital accounts are maintained properly, liquidation proceeds are required to be distributed based on the partners' capital account balances and, following distribution of such proceeds, partners are required to restore any deficits in their capital accounts to the partnership. Further, the economic effect will generally not be considered substantial unless the allocation has a reasonable possibility of substantially impacting the dollar amounts received by partners, independent of tax consequences. Allocations are also insubstantial if they merely shift tax consequences within a partnership tax year or are likely to be offset by other allocations in subsequent tax years.[2]

If a partner contributes property to a partnership, allocations must generally be made to that partner to reflect any variation between the basis of the property to the partnership and its fair market value at the time of contribution.[3] When contributed property is distributed to a partner who did not contribute that property, the contributing partner must recognize gain or loss upon distributions occurring within seven years of the contribution.[4] A contributing partner, however, is treated as receiving property which the partner contributed (and no gain or loss will therefore be recognized on the distribution) if the property contributed is distributed to another partner and like-kind property is distributed to the contributing partner within the earlier of (1) 180 days after the distribution to the other partner, or (2) the partner's tax return due date (including extensions) for the year in which the distribution to the other partner occurs.[5]

For contributions of property made after October 22, 2004, if the property has a built-in loss, the loss is considered only in determining the items allocated to the contributing partner. Also, when determining items allocated to other partners, the basis of the property is its fair market value at the time it was contributed to the partnership.[6]

The IRS is entitled to reallocate income and deductions attributable to distributions of property from a partnership to an individual and the individual's controlled corporation to prevent distortions of income.[7] See Q 8850 for special rules that apply to allocations attributable to nonrecourse allocations.

8850. How are partnership losses and deductions attributable to nonrecourse obligations allocated among partners?

Special rules apply to the allocation of losses and deductions attributable to nonrecourse obligations after 1991. If, however, the partnership agreement has not been substantially modified after 1991, transitional rules may permit the use of the earlier regulations under certain circumstances.[8] See below for a discussion of the rules that applied prior to 1992.

1. Sen. Fin. Comm. Report No. 938, 94th Cong., 2d Sess. 100 (1976).
2. Treas. Reg. §1.704-1(b)(1)(i). See also Treas. Reg. §1.704-1(b)(2)(ii) and (iii).
3. IRC Sec. 704(c)(1)(A).
4. IRC Sec. 704(c)(1)(B).
5. IRC Sec. 704(c)(2).
6. IRC Sec. 704(c)(1)(C).
7. IRC Sec. 482; *Dolese v. Commissioner*, 811 F.2d 543, 87-1 USTC ¶9175 (10th Cir. 1987).
8. See Treas. Reg. §1.704-2(l).

For purposes of this discussion, the term "nonrecourse debt" refers to the traditional concept of nonrecourse—where a creditor's right to repayment is limited to one or more assets of the partnership. Nonrecourse liability means partnership liability with respect to which no partner bears the economic risk of loss. If a partner bears the economic risk of loss with respect to nonrecourse debt, deductions and losses allocable to such nonrecourse debt must be allocated to such partner.[1] In contrast, recourse debt refers to debt for which an individual partner is liable.

Special rules have been developed to govern the treatment of nonrecourse liabilities in the partnership context, because an allocation of a loss or deduction attributable to the nonrecourse liabilities of a partnership ("nonrecourse deductions") cannot have economic effect with respect to a partner. This is because it is the nonrecourse lender, rather than the partner, that bears the risk of economic loss with respect to the deductions.[2] The amount of nonrecourse deductions for a partnership year is equal to the excess, if any, of the net increase in "partnership minimum gain" for the year over the amount of any distributions of proceeds of nonrecourse liabilities allocable to an increase in "partnership minimum gain."[3]

"Partnership minimum gain" is the amount of gain which would be realized in the aggregate if the partnership were to sell each property that is subject to a nonrecourse liability for an amount equal to the nonrecourse liability.[4]

Generally, nonrecourse deductions will be considered to have been allocated in accordance with the partners' interests in the partnership (and the allocation will therefore be honored), if the following requirements are met:

(1) Nonrecourse deductions are allocated in a manner that is consistent with allocations that have substantial economic effect of some other significant partnership item attributable to the property securing the nonrecourse financing.

(2) All other material allocations and basis adjustments either have economic effect or are allocated in accordance with the partners' interests in the partnership.

(3) The partners' capital accounts are maintained properly.

(4) Liquidation proceeds are required to be distributed based upon the partners' capital account balances.

(5) Following distribution of liquidation proceeds, partners are required to either (a) restore any deficits in their capital accounts to the partnership or (b) allocate income or gain sufficient to eliminate any deficit.

(6) If there is a net decrease in partnership minimum gain during a year, each partner must be allocated items of partnership income and gain ("minimum gain chargeback")

1. Treas. Reg. §1.704-2(i).
2. Treas. Reg. §1.704-2(b)(1).
3. Treas. Reg. §1.704-2(c).
4. Treas. Reg. §1.704-2(d).

for that year equal to that partner's share of the net decrease in partnership minimum gain. (This requirement does not apply to the extent that a partner's share of the net decrease in minimum gain is caused by a guarantee, refinancing, or other change in the debt instrument causing it to become partially or wholly recourse debt or partner nonrecourse debt, and the partner bears the risk of economic loss for the liability. Further, it does not apply to the extent that a partner contributes capital to the partnership to repay the nonrecourse liability and the partner's share of net decrease in minimum gain results from the repayment).[1]

Years Beginning After December 29, 1988 and Before December 28, 1991

For those partnerships which qualified under the 1989-1991 rules and which choose to remain grandfathered under such rules, nonrecourse debt is treated under the rules described above.[2] Nonrecourse deductions will be deemed to be allocated in accordance with the partners' interests in the partnership if the requirements (1)-(4) and part (a) of the fifth of the requirements, described above, are met, and if the partnership agreement contains a clause complying with the minimum gain chargeback requirements contained in former Temporary Treasury Regulation Section 1.704-1T(b)(4)(iv). Those requirements provide that if there is a net decrease in partnership minimum gain during a year, each partner must be allocated a minimum gain chargeback equal to the greater of (1) the partner's share of the net decrease in minimum gain attributable to a disposition of property securing nonrecourse liabilities, or (2) the partner's deficit capital account.[3]

Years Beginning Before December 30, 1988

For partnerships which qualified under the rules that applied before December 30, 1988, and choose to remain grandfathered under such rules, nonrecourse debt is treated under the rules described in former Temporary Treasury Regulation Section 1.704-1T(b)(4)(iv),[4] except that:

(1) the amount of nonrecourse deductions for a partnership year is equal to the net increase in partnership minimum gain for the year. There is no reduction for certain distributions as there was under the former temporary regulations; and

(2) nonrecourse deductions need not be allocated in accordance with the partners' interests in the partnership if current requirements (1) through (4) are met and either: (1) following distribution of liquidation proceeds, partners are required to restore any deficits in their capital accounts to the partnership; or (2) if there is a net decrease in partnership minimum gain during a year, each partner must be allocated items of partnership income and gain for that year equal to that partner's share of the net decrease in partnership minimum gain.

1. Treas. Reg. §§1.704-2(b)(1); 1.704-2(e); 1.704-2(f).
2. Former Treas. Reg. §1.704-1T(b)(4)(iv).
3. Former Treas. Reg. §1.704-1T(b)(4)(iv).
4. Former Treas. Reg. §1.704-1(b)(4)(iv).

8851. How is the tax treatment of a partner's distributive share determined? When does a partner report income and loss?

The character of any item of income, gain, loss, deduction, or credit in the hands of a partner is determined as if such item were realized directly from the source from which it was realized by the partnership, or incurred in the same manner as incurred by the partnership. For example, a partner's distributive share of gain that stems from the sale of depreciable property used in the trade or business of the partnership is treated as though it was gain from the sale of the depreciable property in the hands of the partner. Similarly, a partner's distributive share of partnership "hobby losses"[1] or his distributive share of the partnership's charitable contributions retains such character in the hands of the partner.[2]

Where it is necessary to determine the amount or character of a partner's gross income, the partner's gross income includes the partner's distributive share of the gross income of the partnership. This means the amount of partnership gross income from which the partner's distributive share of partnership taxable income or loss was derived (including the various items listed above). For example, a partner is required to include his distributive share of partnership gross income in measuring his gross income for purposes of determining whether a partner is required to file a return.[3]

A partner's distributive share of partnership loss (including capital loss) is deductible only to the extent of the adjusted basis of such partner's interest in the partnership (see Q 8852). Any excess of such loss over such basis may be deducted only if and when the excess is actually repaid to the partnership.[4]

The partner must include the distributive share of partnership items of income, gain, loss, deductions, and credits on his return for the partnership year that ends in or at the same time as the partner's own individual tax year. Since most individuals report on a calendar year basis, an individual partner generally includes partnership income for the same calendar year as a partnership that reports on the calendar year basis. If the partnership uses a non-calendar fiscal year, the calendar year partner includes partnership income, gains, losses, deductions, and credits for the partnership year that *ends* in the partner's calendar year.[5]

8852. How is a partner's basis in the partnership calculated?

A partner's "basis" in the partnership interest is the partner's interest in the partnership for tax purposes. It is used to determine the tax imposed upon cash distributions, gain or loss on sale, and the limit on loss deduction (see Q 8851).

Initially, the partner's basis is the amount of money plus the adjusted basis of any property the partner has contributed to the partnership, though it is subject to various adjustments

1. IRC Sec. 702.
2. Treas. Reg. §1.702-1(b).
3. IRC Sec. 6012(a).
4. IRC Sec. 704(d).
5. IRC Sec. 706(a); Treas. Reg. §1.706-1(a).

thereafter.[1] The basis is increased by any further contributions and by the partner's distributive share of taxable income, tax-exempt income, and the excess of the deductions for depletion over the basis of the property subject to depletion.[2] The basis is decreased (but not below zero) by current distributions from the partnership, by the partner's distributive share of losses and nondeductible expenditures not properly chargeable to capital and by the amount of the partner's deduction for depletion with respect to oil and gas wells.[3]

A partner's basis also includes his or her share of partnership liabilities (see Q 8853). Basis is increased by any increase in the share of partnership liabilities, as though the partner had made an additional cash contribution.[4] A partner is deemed to receive a cash distribution to the extent that the partner's share of partnership liabilities decreases. As a result, basis decreases if the share of partnership liabilities decreases.[5]

If a limited partner contributes a personal note to the partnership, the basis in the partnership interest is not increased, however, because it is treated as a contribution of property in which the partner has no basis.[6] When the note is paid, the amount becomes an additional contribution that is added to basis.

Planning Point: A partner's basis is very much of a "moving target" and must be reexamined every time the owner wants to engage in tax planning.

8853. What liabilities are included in determining a partner's adjusted basis in a partnership interest?

A partner's basis includes the partner's share of partnership liabilities.[7] An economic risk of loss analysis is used to determine which liabilities are included in a partner's adjusted basis.

A partnership liability is treated as a recourse liability to the extent that any partner bears the economic risk of loss for that liability.[8] A partner bears the economic risk of loss for a partnership liability to the extent that the partner (or certain related parties) would be obligated to make a payment to any person or make a contribution to the partnership with respect to a partnership liability (and would not be entitled to reimbursement by another partner, certain parties related to another partner, or the partnership) if the partnership were to undergo a "constructive liquidation."

A "constructive liquidation" would treat:

(1) all of the partnership's liabilities as due and payable in full;

(2) all of the partnership assets (including money), except those contributed to secure a partnership liability, as worthless;

1. IRC Secs. 722, 705.
2. IRC Sec. 705(a)(1), Treas. Reg. §1.705-1(a)(2).
3. IRC Secs. 705(a)(2), 705(a)(3).
4. IRC Secs. 752(a), 705(a).
5. IRC Secs. 752(b), 705(a)(2).
6. *Oden v. Comm.*, TC Memo 1981-184; Rev. Rul. 80-235, 1980-2 CB 229.
7. IRC Secs. 752, 705(a).
8. Treas. Reg. §1.752-1(a)(1).

(3) all of the partnership assets as disposed of in a fully taxable transaction for no consideration (other than relief from certain liabilities);

(4) all items of partnership income, gain, loss, and deduction for the year as allocated among the partners; and

(5) the partner's interests in the enterprise as liquidated.[1]

If one or more partners (or related persons) guarantee the payment of more than 25 percent of the interest that will accrue on a partnership nonrecourse liability over its remaining term, the loan will be deemed to be recourse with respect to the guarantor to the extent of the present value of the future interest payments if it is reasonable to expect that the guarantor will be required to pay substantially all of the guaranteed interest if the partnership fails to do so.[2]

An obligation will be considered recourse with respect to a partner to the extent of the value of any property that the partner (or related party in the case of a direct pledge) directly or indirectly pledges as security for the partnership liability.[3] Further, if a partner (or related party) makes a nonrecourse loan, or obtains an interest in such a loan to the partnership and the economic risk of loss is not borne by another partner, the obligation will be considered recourse as to that partner.[4]

A recourse liability allocated to a partner under these rules is included in the partner's basis.

However, a limited partner generally does not bear the economic risk of loss for any partnership recourse liability because limited partners are not typically obligated to make additional contributions and do not typically guarantee interest, pledge property, or make loans to the partnership. Otherwise, a limited partner can include a share of a partnership liability in his basis only if it is nonrecourse liability (see below).

A partnership liability is treated as a *nonrecourse* liability if no partner bears the economic risk of loss (see above) for that liability. Generally, partners share nonrecourse liability in the same proportion as they share profits. However, nonrecourse liabilities are first allocated among partners to reflect each partner's share of (1) any partnership minimum gain or (2) IRC Section 704(c) minimum gain.

Partnership minimum gain is the amount of gain that would be realized if the partnership were to sell all of its property that is subject to nonrecourse liabilities in full satisfaction of such liabilities and for no other consideration. IRC Section 704(c) minimum gain is the amount of gain that would be allocated under IRC Section 704(c) to a partner who contributed property to the partnership if the partnership were to sell all of its property that is subject to nonrecourse liabilities in full satisfaction of such liabilities and for no other consideration.[5]

1. Treas. Reg. §1.752-2(b)(1).
2. Treas. Reg. §1.752-2(e).
3. Treas. Reg. §1.752-2(h).
4. Treas. Reg. §1.752-2(c).
5. Treas. Reg. §§1.752-3(a), 1.704-2(d).

These rules apply to any liability incurred on or after December 28, 1991, except for those incurred or assumed pursuant to a written binding contract that was effective before that date and at all times thereafter. A partnership may elect to apply the provisions of the regulations to liabilities incurred or assumed prior to December 28, 1991, as of the beginning of the first taxable year ending on or after that date.[1]

Similar rules apply to liabilities incurred or assumed by a partnership after January 29, 1989, and before December 28, 1991, unless the liability was incurred or assumed pursuant to a written binding contract that was effective prior to December 29, 1988 and at all times thereafter.[2] They also apply to partner loans and to guarantees of partnership liabilities that were incurred or assumed by a partnership after February 29, 1984, and before December 28, 1991, beginning on the later of March 1, 1984, or the first date on which the partner bore the economic risk of loss with respect to a liability because of his status as a creditor or guarantor of such liability.[3] A partnership could elect to extend application of the temporary regulations to all of its liabilities as of the beginning of its first taxable year ending after December 29, 1988, and before December 28, 1991, subject to certain consistency rules.[4]

8854. How is a sale of partnership interests taxed?

As a practical matter, limited partnership interests are often not freely transferable because there is a lack of a market for the interests. However, in the event that an interest is sold, gain recognized by a limited partner on the sale of an interest is taxed as a long-term capital gain (see Q 8567). Any portion of that gain that is attributable to a limited partner's share of the partnership's IRC Section 751 "unrealized receivables" and "substantially appreciated inventory" items is subject to treatment as ordinary income.

In addition to any requirements in the partnership agreement that must be met upon the transfer of an interest, the IRC requires the transferor-partner to promptly notify the partnership of a transfer of a unit that occurs at a time when the partnership holds unrealized receivables or inventory items that have substantially appreciated in value. A penalty is imposed for a failure to make this notification, unless the failure is due to reasonable cause and not to willful neglect. Once the partnership has been notified, it is required to inform the buyer, the seller and the IRS of the names, addresses and taxpayer identification numbers of the parties to the transfer.

Upon the sale or exchange of, or certain distributions with respect to a partnership unit, the partnership will be treated as owning its proportionate share of the property owned by any other partnership in which it is a partner. Therefore, if gain is realized upon the sale or exchange of, or certain distributions with respect to, a unit, a portion of the gain may be treated as ordinary income rather than capital gain to the extent it is attributable to unrealized receivables and substantially appreciated inventory held, not only by the partnership, but also by any partnership in which the partnership holds an interest.

1. Treas. Reg. §1.752-5.
2. Temp. Treas. Reg. §1.752-4T(a), prior to removal by TD 8380.
3. Temp. Treas. Reg. §1.752-4T(b), prior to removal by TD 8380.
4. Temp. Treas. Reg. §1.752-4T(c), prior to removal by TD 8380.

If it is found that a limited partner holds an interest primarily for sale to customers in the ordinary course of business, rather than for investment purposes, all gain recognized by that partner upon sale is taxable as ordinary income under the theory that the units are actually inventory held for sale in the ordinary course of business.

The amount of gain recognized by a limited partner on the sale of partnership units is equal to the excess of: (a) the amount realized on the sale of a unit, over (b) the adjusted tax basis of the interest. The amount realized includes cash, the fair market value of other property received on the sale and the partners' share of any qualifying nonrecourse liability of the partnership. Because nonrecourse liabilities must generally be taken into account, it is possible for a partner to be subject to a tax liability that exceeds the actual proceeds received upon the sale of a partnership interest. This is frequently referred to as "phantom income."

The partnership agreement may permit the general partner to make a special election under IRC Section 754 to adjust the basis of partnership property when there is a transfer of a unit or a distribution of partnership assets that takes into account the basis in the partnership unit. If the value of the partnership property has increased, this election would result in the transferee partner having an increased basis in the allocable share of partnership assets and, therefore, the partner would receive more favorable tax treatment (greater cost recovery) if the partnership filed the Section 754 election. A general partner may choose *not* to make this election, however, because of the complexities and added expenses of the tax accounting required. In some cases, this may adversely affect the marketability of partnership interests and the price that a prospective purchaser would be willing to pay for a partnership unit. However, when a partner dies, a Section 754 election allows for a step up in basis for the partner's interest in the partnership's assets. This can be a valuable tax benefit for estates which own interests in partnerships.

Planning Point: In the event a partner in a partnership were to die, the partnership agreement should be examined to determine if a Section 754 election is authorized or required. Next, the general partner should be contacted to determine if an election is already in effect. Once an election is in effect under Section 754, it remains in effect for future years and can only be revoked with the consent of the IRS.[1]

8855. What is a family partnership? What special considerations apply in the context of a family partnership?

In the income tax context, a business owner may wish to reduce tax liability by allocating a portion of the business income to minor children, essentially engaging in "income shifting." To this effect, the owner may form a family partnership between the parent and the children in which the children own an interest in the partnership that entitles them to specified portions of the partnership's income.

In theory, if this income was taxable to the children separately, it would be taxed at a lower rate bracket. Today, however, this tax reduction technique has very limited applicability because of the so-called "kiddie tax" (see Q 8562). The kiddie tax requires that "unearned" income of a child under age eighteen, or twenty-four for certain students, be taxed at the parent's tax rate.

1. Treas. Reg. §1.754-1(c).

"Unearned income" is essentially any income other than that received for personal services rendered by the child.

Generally, family partnerships will be recognized for tax purposes only if the following special requirements are met:

(1) A family member, in general, will be deemed to be a partner only if the family member owns a capital interest in partnership property (such as machinery and equipment, real property or inventory) where the business of the partnership is such that capital is a material income-producing factor, whether or not such interest was derived by purchase or gift.[1] If the partnership business is such that personal services are a material income-producing factor, a family member who regularly renders valuable personal service to the business will generally be eligible for partner status for tax purposes.[2]

(2) Where the partner receives the partnership interest as a gift, and capital is a material income-producing factor, the donee's distributable partnership share will be included in taxable income except to the extent of:

a. the donor's reasonable compensation for services rendered to the partnership; and

b. a proportionately greater distributive share attributable to donated capital compared to the donor's capital.[3] Thus, although a proportionate share of income attributable to a gifted capital interest may be shifted to a family member, compensation for personal services may not be shifted in such a manner, nor may distributive shares based on capital interests be arbitrarily realigned without proportional reference to the underlying capital interest. This means that where the donor-partner performed all or nearly all of the personal services rendered in connection with partnership activities, income allocated to the donee would be reduced (and taxed to the partner who performed the services) by the reasonable value of the services.

(3) Where an interest in a family partnership is acquired by purchase from another family member, the interest is treated as if it was acquired by gift from the seller unless it can be shown that the sale was a bona fide arm's-length transaction.[4] If the transfer is a gift, the purchaser's (donee's) basis in the interest is limited to the fair market value of the interest and not the purchase price.

For purposes of applying these rules to "family" partnerships, IRC Section 704(e)(3) defines the "family" as including only a spouse, ancestors (including an individual's parents and

1. IRC Sec. 704(e)(1).
2. Treas. Reg. §1.704-1(e)(1)(ii).
3. IRC Sec. 704(e)(2); Treas. Reg. §1.704-1(e)(3).
4. IRC Sec. 704(e)(3), Treas. Reg. §1.704-1(e)(4).

grandparents), lineal descendants (including children and grandchildren); and trusts, if the primary beneficiaries are any of the above.

As a general rule, a family partnership may consist of two or more of the following: spouses, children, grandchildren, grandparents, or a trust for the benefit of any of those individuals. A partnership formed only by siblings, in-laws, or uncles and aunts is subject only to the rules applicable to partnerships in general, and are not limited by the more restrictive rules imposed on family partnerships.

Although as a general rule, minor children will not be afforded treatment as partners for purposes of Section 704(e), two narrow and limited exceptions do exist for children age 18 and older:

(1) If the minor child can be shown to be competent to manage and own property and to participate in the partnership activities in a manner consistent with the management of such property interests, partnership status may be afforded with the result that the child's distributive share of partnership income will be taxed to the child rather than, for example, to a parent-partner.[1]

(2) Where the exception above cannot be shown to exist, a minor child may still qualify as a partner to the extent partnership income is "earned income."

8856. What is a family limited partnership?

A family limited partnership (FLP) is a partnership consisting of family members that, when properly formed and maintained, can be used to achieve both the lifetime and estate planning goals of an individual seeking to transfer wealth. When contemplating transferring wealth, a person's lifetime goals often include retaining control of assets before death and protecting assets from creditors, while estate planning goals are often centered upon minimizing taxes and providing financial security to future generations.

The structure of a FLP provides an opportunity to accomplish both categories of goals and is identical to other limited partnerships in that it must consist of at least one general and one or more limited partners. The general partner in a FLP manages the partnership and makes all business decisions, thus retaining control of the assets, but is exposed to unlimited personal liability for the debts of the FLP. Conversely, the limited partner is afforded limited liability but cannot participate in management of the partnership.

The general partner is usually the asset owner who wishes to transfer his/her assets to future generations in a tax-advantaged manner. Conceptually, transferring assets using a FLP involves two steps: (1) the general partner contributes assets to a newly formed FLP in exchange for a fractional general partnership interest (usually 1-2 percent) and a substantial limited partnership interest (usually 98-99 percent) and (2) gifting the limited partnership interest(s) to the desired family members.

1. Treas. Reg. §1.704-1(e)(2)(viii).

The gifting of limited *partnership interests* (as opposed to *interest in an asset*) is the foundation for potentially realizing tax savings because limited partners' interests can be subject to certain discounts for transfer tax purposes. Special valuation rules relating to transfers of a partnership interest between family members will generally not apply if the general partner and limited partner interests are properly structured in partnership agreement and the agreement is followed by the partners.[1]

Planning Point: As recent cases have shown, the FLP must serve a "legitimate non-tax purpose"[2] and be property maintained for the entity to be respected for tax purposes. Legitimate non-tax purposes and partnership formalities are discussed in further detail in Q 8859. *Tim G. Skinner, JD, CPA.*

8857. How can a taxpayer establish a family limited partnership (FLP)?

The creation of a partnership involves several steps that should be followed in order to ensure that the partnership is properly formed and that the entity structure is respected. A FLP is a product of state law. Therefore, the laws of the state in which the entity is formed will govern the creation of the entity.

As long as the entity is formed for a legitimate business purpose, properly formed, and properly maintained under applicable state law, the entity should be respected for tax purposes. Although the exact steps for creating a partnership vary from state to state, the general steps required to form a partnership, or a limited liability company that elects partnership taxation, are as follows:

1. ***Create a name for the partnership.*** The partnership name should be approved by the office of the Secretary of State in the state in which the partnership is being formed. Any partnership filings will not be accepted if the partnership name is found to be impermissibly similar to another name already on file.

2. ***Draft a Limited Partnership Agreement.*** The importance of the provisions in this agreement cannot be overstated and are discussed in further detail in Q 8858.

3. ***Designate a registered agent.*** The registered agent must be authorized to conduct business in the state where the entity is formed. The agent must have a physical street address in the state.

4. ***File a Certificate of Limited Partnership with the Secretary of State.*** The Certificate will request the name and addresses of the partners, as well as the agent's name and address.

5. ***Pay required fees.*** A filing fee must generally be paid to the Secretary of State in the state where the entity is formed.

1. IRC Sec. 2701; Let. Rul. 9415007 (providing that retained interests by the transferor will generally not apply where the only difference between the GP and LP interest is management and liability).
2. *Estate of Purdue v. Comm.*, 145 TC Memo 249, 19 (2015).

6. ***Register for an Employer Identification Number ("EIN")***. The EIN number is assigned to the partnership by the IRS and is needed conduct business transactions. IRS Form SS-4 can be used to apply for an EIN, or individuals may choose to complete an online application.[1]

7. ***Register for a State ID Number***. A State ID number is similar to the federal EIN number for business classification purposes.

8858. Why is it important that the requirements for properly forming and maintaining a family limited partnership (FLP) are followed?

Establishing a legitimate non-tax motive for forming a FLP and respecting the partnership structure once the entity is established are critical to ensuring that the partnership structure will be respected. If the partnership is disregarded by the IRS for gift tax purposes due to illegitimate use or improper maintenance, the gift that is transferred will be classified as an interest in the *assets* of the entity instead of an interest in the *partnership*.[2] As a result, gifts of assets are valued at fair market value and not subject to discounts,[3] so that the strategy will fail to achieve estate planning goals of preferential tax treatment.

Recent case law has highlighted the importance of establishing a non-tax motive for forming a FLP to ensure that the assets in the FLP escape inclusion in the taxpayer's estate under IRC Section 2036.[4] For example, in *Purdue v. Commissioner*,[5] the court found that "consolidating investments into a family asset managed by a single advisor" established one of several legitimate non-tax motives for transferring property to the FLP.[6] The court relied on centralized asset management from prior cases to support the taxpayer's position that the FLP served a legitimate non-tax purpose.[7] The court also noted the change in asset management after the FLP was formed, specifically that the assets became part of an "overall, well-coordinated professional investment strategy."[8] Prior to formation of the FLP, Mr. Purdue had handled all financial decisions, but the children jointly made investment decisions after the entity was formed.[9] The change in asset management pre-FLP and post-FLP was a significant point of focus for the court and bolstered the Purdue's claim that the FLP served a legitimate business purpose.[10]

On the other hand, in *Holiday v. Commissioner* the court did not find for the taxpayer where a FLP was formed for (1) protection from litigator's claims (where the taxpayer had never been sued), (2) protection against undue influence of caregivers (the taxpayer's sons were her caregivers), and (3) preservation of assets for the decedent's heirs (the taxpayer was not involved in

1. The online application is available at https://sa.www4.irs.gov/modiein/individual/index.jsp.
2. David T. Lewis & Andrew C. Chomakos, The Family Limited Partnership Deskbook, 127 (2nd ed. 2007).
3. IRC Sec. 2512(a) ("The value at the date of the gift shall be considered the amount of the gift").
4. See IRC Sec. 2036(a) ("The gross estate includes the value of all property ... except in case of a bona fide sale for an adequate and full consideration").
5. *Estate of Purdue v. Comm.*, 145 TC Memo 249 (2015).
6. *Id.* at 19.
7. *Id.* at 18-19. (*See e.g., Estate of Schutt v. Comm.*, TC Memo 2005-126; *Estate of Bongard v. Comm.*, 124 TC; *Estate of Stone v. Comm.*, TC Memo 2012-48, slip op. at 18; *Estate of Mirowski v. Comm.*, TC Memo 2008-74).
8. *Estate of Purdue v. Comm.*, TC Memo 2015-249.
9. *Id.* at 18.
10. *Id.* at 19 (See e.g., *Estate of Hurford v. Comm.*, TC Memo 2008-278).

selecting the structure used to preserve the assets). The taxpayer's stated purposes for forming the FLP were unsupported by his circumstances and management of his assets in the FLP was nearly identical to the management of the assets before the partnership was established—nothing changed. As a result, the court agreed with the IRS and found that the FLP was not to be respected, so that all transfers occurring under the FLP structure should be treated as asset transfers valued without discounts.[1]

8859. What are the requirements for properly forming and maintaining a family limited partnership (FLP)?

While the IRS does not provide a list of what constitutes proper maintenance of a partnership, case law has developed certain requirements that should be followed. These requirements generally fall into one of two categories—administrative requirements and filing requirements.

Administratively, the newly formed entity must establish and respect its valid business purpose (as discussed in Q 8858 and which should be clearly stated in the partnership agreement). In finding for the taxpayer that the FLP had been properly maintained and respected in *Purdue v. Commissioner*, the court noted that the taxpayer kept personal and FLP funds separate, kept adequate records with respect to the entity, established all financial accounts in the name of the entity, conducted meetings at least annually to discuss the partnership's business and kept written minutes of those meetings, and maintained separate books and records for the entity. Importantly, in *Purdue* the business was managed as a legitimate business: the children heard presentations from the investment manager, approved annual cash distributions and generally operated the business according to the operating agreement. Further, the family was not financially dependent upon the business –the decedent had sufficient funds outside of the structure for her living expenses at her death.[2]

Conversely, in *Holiday v. Commissioner*, the court emphasized that the necessary formalities of the partnership were not followed. Specifically, books and records for the partnership were not kept, required distributions per the partnership agreement were not followed, and meetings along with meeting minutes were not kept. Unsurprisingly, the court held that it was apparent that the FLP was formed for the sole purpose of achieving a valuation discount.[3]

There are also federal and state filing requirements for partnerships that must be strictly followed. Each partnership is required to file an annual information tax return,[4] Form 1065, by the 15th day of the third month (March 15) following the close of the partnership's tax year.[5] As part of this filing, each member or partner of the entity should be furnished with a Form K-1 that provides information regarding the distributive share of partnership income or loss for each member or partner.[6]

1. *Estate of Holiday v. Comm.*, TC Memo 2016-51.
2. *Estate of Purdue v. Comm.*, TC Memo 2015-249.
3. *Estate of Holiday v. Comm.*, TC Memo 2016-51.
4. IRC Sec. 6031(a).
5. IRS Publication 4163.
6. IRC Sec. 6031(b).

Planning Point: Depending on the state in which the partnership is formed, additional state tax returns may be required. *Tim G. Skinner, JD, CPA.*

8860. What estate and gift tax planning opportunities are available through use of the family limited partnership structure?

In order to appreciate the tax planning opportunities afforded by using a family limited partnership (FLP), the estate tax and the current limitations on transferring wealth in a tax-advantaged manner warrant a brief overview. In *Holiday v. Commissioner*,[1] the tax court succinctly described the relevant estate tax code provisions when examining transfers:

> Estate tax is imposed on the transfer of a decedent's taxable estate.[2] The taxable estate consists of the value of the gross estate after applicable deductions.[3] Except to the extent provided in sections 2033 through 2046, the gross estate includes "all property, real or personal, tangible or intangible, wherever situated."[4] The value of the gross estate includes the value of such property, to the extent of the decedent's interest in it, at the time of death.[5]
>
> Section 2036 is intended to include in a decedent's gross estate inter vivos transfers that were testamentary in nature. Accordingly, a decedent's gross estate includes the value of all property that the decedent transferred but retained the possession or enjoyment of, or the right to the income from, for the decedent's life.[6] This rule, however, does not apply in cases where the transfer was a bona fide sale for adequate and full consideration.[7]

The core concept in estate planning is simple: estate is taxed is levied upon asset transfers at death. Therefore, to reduce the tax burden on one's estate, a taxpayer often seeks to transfer value outside of his estate prior to death. Gifting property eliminates future growth of the estate and any income produced from gifted property is not included in the donor's estate.

However, individuals seeking to transfer wealth face a common problem—the amount he or she is able to transfer that is exempt from gift tax is limited by the annual gift tax exclusion and gift tax credit. The annual gift tax exclusion for 2018 is $15,000, which allows an individual to give away up $15,000 per year ($30,000 for a married couple that elects split gift treatment) per donee without triggering the gift tax.[8] The lifetime transfer tax exemption for 2018 is $5.6 million, which means that the first $5.6 million of a decedent's estate is exempt from transfer taxes.[9]

1. *Estate of Holiday v. Comm.*, TC Memo 2016-51.
2. IRC Sec. 2001(a).
3. IRC Sec. 2051.
4. IRC Sec. 2031(a).
5. IRC Sec. 2033.
6. IRC Sec. 2036(a).
7. *Estate of Holiday v. Comm.*, TC Memo 2016-51.
8. Rev. Proc. 2017-58.
9. Rev. Proc. 2016-55.

Because the value of the decedent's gross estate includes the value of property at the time of death,[1] estate and gift tax planning strategies aim to accomplish two goals: reduce the gross estate through transferring assets prior to death and minimize transfer taxation. For high net worth individuals, the annual gift tax exclusion and lifetime transfer tax exemption may be insufficient for accomplishing these goals.

Accordingly, FLPs have developed to provide taxpayers a new avenue to transfer wealth and minimize transfer taxes while also accomplishing non-tax goals. The tax advantages of a FLP are best illustrated with a simple example involving A and his two children, B and C. A contributes real estate valued at $10,000,000 to a newly formed partnership. In exchange for his contribution of assets, A receives a 1 percent general partner interest and a 99 percent limited partner interest in the partnership. A then transfers a 49.5 percent limited partner interest to both B and C. Assume that the discount for lack of control is 10 percent and the discount for lack of marketability is 15 percent. This transfer would be valued for estate and gift taxes purposes at $7,500,000, ($10M - ($10M x 25%)). The value of the underlying real estate is still worth $10,000,000, but the value for transfer tax purposes has been reduced by the combined 25 percent discount. Further, A still has control over the management of and cash flow of the property as the general partner. Assuming A is successful in substantiating his 25 percent discount, he as removed $2,500,000 from his taxable estate with no diminishing value to the asset transferred to his children. Further discussion regarding the available discounts to FLP interests are discussed in Q 8861.

8861. What valuation discounts may be available to family limited partnership interests and how are the discounts applied?

Transfers of property are generally valued at the fair market value of the asset being transferred. The term fair market value has been defined in the regulations as "the price at which the property would change hands between a willing buyer and a willing seller, neither being under any compulsion to buy or sell and both having reasonable knowledge of the facts."[2] However, the interests of a properly structured FLP can be subject to discounts relative to fair market value. The two most common discounts available to FLP interests are the discount for minority interests and the discount for lack of marketability.

The discount for minority interests reflects the notion that the owner of such an interest lacks the ability to exert complete control over the asset. For example, minority owners lack control over management of the asset, disposition or liquidation, and distributions. Valuing an interest is a fact-specific question that turns on an assessment of the particular asset being valued and, therefore, there is not a fixed minority discount amount that can be anticipated (and, in fact, minority discounts are not guaranteed if the courts find they are not warranted based on the particular facts and circumstances of the case). Although minority discounts are not uniformly applied, case law has shown that the typical minority interest discount ranges from 10 percent

1. IRC Sec. 2031(a).
2. See Treas. Reg. §§1.2031-(1)(b) and 25.2512-1.

to 30 percent.[1] For example, a 10 percent minority interest in a business worth $1,000,000 might be valued at less than $100,000 (*i.e.*, less than the minority interest owner's pro-rata share of the asset).

Planning Point: The transfer tax value is based on the fair market value taking into account discounts, which allows a grantor to gift assets while paying tax on a value that is less than the underlying value of the asset. *Tim G. Skinner, JD, CPA.*

In the example above, if the appropriate discount for the minority interest is 20 percent, the donee receives an asset worth $100,000, but the value transferred for estate tax purpose is $80,000 (($100,000 – ($100,000 × 20%)). The $20,000 is not included in the estate tax base and therefore escapes taxation, yet the underlying value of the asset in the hands of the transferee is unchanged.

The second discount potentially available to FLPs is the discount for lack of marketability, which reflects the idea that a ready market does not exist for the interest being valued. In terms of the fair value definition discussed above, a "willing buyer" will take into account the cost and effort involved in eventually converting his minority interest to cash. In other words, the degree to which an ownership interest can be converted to cash is diminished and the illiquidity associated with the interest warrants a discount. Similar to the minority interest discount, the discount for lack of marketability requires an assessment of the facts and circumstances and, therefore, a fixed lack of marketability discount does not apply. However, case law has shown that the typical minority interest discount ranges from 15 percent to 40 percent.

For example, in *Estate of Barudin v. Commissioner*, the court allowed a 26 percent marketability discount in the decedent's minority interest in a general partnership owning real estate. Further, in *Estate of Lauder v. Commissioner*, the decedent received a 40 percent discount in his minority interest in a corporation. The courts have also allowed the lack of marketability discount where the decedent owned a controlling interest and all of the interests in an asset or business. In *Estate of Luton v. Commissioner*,[2] the decedent's 78 percent interest in an unincorporated ranch received a 20 percent marketability discount. Notably, the court also allowed a 25 percent discount to the decedent's 100 percent ownership of the stock of a holding company.[3] Given the prevalence of closely held businesses in the context of FLPs, the court in *Mandelbaum v. Commissioner*[4] discussed a list of factors to assess when valuing a closely held business that should prove useful to a taxpayer trying to establish the appropriate marketability discount for a closely held business. The case law that has developed around the lack of marketability discount emphasizes that when an interest holder cannot readily liquidate his investment, a discount is appropriate.

1. *Wheeler v. U.S.*, 77 AFTR 2d 96-1405 (10 percent discount); *Estate of Berg v. Comm.*, 61 TCM (CCH) 2949 (1991) (20 percent discount); *Estate of Newhouse v. Comm.*, 94 TC No. 14 (1990) (35 percent discount).
2. *Estate of Luton v. Comm.*, 72 TC Memo 1994-539.
3. *Estate of Dougherty v. Comm.*, TC Memo 1990-274.
4. *Mandelbaum v. Comm.*, TC Memo 1995-255.

8862. Are there any disadvantages to using the family limited partnership (FLP) structure?

As discussed in Q 8858, properly forming and maintaining a FLP as a genuine business entity is critical to ensuring that the benefits of the structure can be realized. One of the primary disadvantages of the FLP structure is that these formation and maintenance requirements can be complicated, and a family seeking to form a FLP will have to engage a team of advisors to provide expert advice (attorneys, CPAs, investment advisors and appraisers should all be consulted, both at the time of formation and throughout the life of the FLP). Because of this, FLPs are often very expensive to establish and maintain.

These costs can escalate during the life of the FLP. Whenever assets are transferred to the FLP, they should be appraised by a professional—generating additional expenses as more and more of the parent generation's assets are transferred into the FLP.

Another disadvantage to the FLP structure is potential liability for the general partners. Because the general partners will remain liable for any liabilities of the partnership (i.e., a lawsuit brought against the FLP), only certain assets should be held by the FLP. Therefore, if the family wishes to transfer assets that could potentially generate liability for the general partners to the FLP, it is advisable that the actual FLP general partner be an LLC that is owned by the parent generation. If the FLP wishes to conduct active business that could result in liability, that business should be conducted through a corporation or LLC that the family partnership owns. Establishing these multiple tiers will generate additional costs and complexity.

Importantly, the presence of a FLP tends to attract the attention of the IRS, meaning that an estate tax return that includes a transfer of FLP interests may generate additional scrutiny. On a gift tax return, the taxpayer must specify whether the reported gifts were subject to a valuation discount (one of the primary advantages of the FLP, see Q 8861, making it easier for the IRS to identify the transfer as one deserving extra scrutiny.

8863. What is a publicly traded partnership?

A publicly traded partnership is a partnership that is either (1) traded on an established securities market, or (2) is readily tradable on a secondary market or the substantial equivalent thereof (discussed below).[1]

Generally, a partnership that is not traded on an established securities market will be treated as readily tradable on a secondary market or the substantial equivalent thereof if, taking into account all of the facts and circumstances, the partners are readily able to buy, sell, or exchange their partnership interests in a manner that is comparable, economically, to trading on an established securities market. This occurs if any of the following are true:

(1) Partnership interests are regularly quoted by any person making a market in the interests.

1. IRC Sec. 7704(b).

(2) Any person regularly makes bids or offers quotes pertaining to the interests available to the public and stands ready to effect buy or sell transactions regarding same for itself or on behalf of others.

(3) A partnership interest holder has a readily available, regular, and ongoing opportunity to sell or exchange the interest through a public means of obtaining or providing information of offers to buy, sell, or exchange interests in the partnership.

(4) Prospective buyers and sellers have the opportunity to buy, sell, or exchange partnership interests in a time frame and with the regularity and continuity that is comparable to that described in (1)-(3) above.[1]

Despite this, interests in a partnership are not readily tradable on a secondary market or the substantial equivalent thereof unless (1) the partnership participates in the establishment of the market or the inclusion of its interests thereon, or (2) the partnership recognizes transfers made on that market.[2]

Generally, both general and limited partnership interests are included in calculations of percentage of partnership interests. However, if at any time during the taxable year, the general partner (and certain related persons under IRC Section 267(b) or IRC Section 707(b)(1)) own more than 10 percent of the outstanding interests in partnership capital and profit, the calculations are made without regard to interests owned by the general partner and the related persons.[3]

The percentage of partnership interests that are traded in a tax year is equal to the sum of the monthly percentages. The percentage of partnership interests traded during a month is determined by reference to partnership interests outstanding during the month. Any monthly convention may be used (e.g., first of month, 15th of month, end of month), so long as it is reasonable and used consistently.

In the case of "block transfers," the determination of percentage of partnership interests traded during a thirty day period is made with reference to partnership interests outstanding immediately prior to the block transfer.[4] A block transfer occurs when a partner transfers interests exceeding 2 percent of total interests in partnership capital and profit during a thirty day period.

These rules apply to the taxable years of a partnership beginning after December 31, 1995, unless the partnership was actively engaged in an activity before December 4, 1995. In that case, these rules apply to taxable years beginning after December 31, 2005, unless the partnership added a substantial new line of business[5] after December 4, 1995, in which case these rules

1. Treas. Reg. §1.7704-1(c).
2. Treas. Reg. §1.7704-1(d).
3. Treas. Reg. §1.7704-1(k)(1).
4. Treas. Reg. §§1.7704-1(k)(2) to 1.7704-1(k)(4).
5. Treas. Reg. §1.7704-2.

apply to taxable years beginning on or after the addition of the new line of business.[1] Different transitional rules applied to certain pre-1996 partnerships.[2]

8864. What special rules apply in the tax treatment of a publicly traded partnership?

A publicly traded partnership will be taxed as a corporation unless 90 percent of the partnership's income is passive-type income and has been passive-type income for all taxable years beginning after 1987 during which the partnership (or any predecessor) was in existence. For this purpose, a partnership (or a predecessor) is not treated as being "in existence" until the taxable year in which it is first publicly traded (see Q 8855).[3]

On the first day that a publicly traded partnership is treated as a corporation under these rules, the partnership is treated as though it transferred all assets (subject to its liabilities) to a new corporation in exchange for stock in the corporation, followed by a distribution of the stock to its partners in liquidation of their partnership interests.[4]

In general, "passive-type income" includes interest, dividends, real property rents, gain from the sale of real property, income and gain from certain mineral or natural resource activities, and gain from sale of a capital or IRC Section 1231 asset.[5] ("Passive-type income" for these purposes is different from income derived from a passive activity under the passive activity loss rules, see Q 8644.)

The passive-type income exception is not available if the partnership would be treated as a regulated investment company[6] if the partnership were a domestic corporation. The IRS has the authority to provide otherwise if the principal activity of the partnership involves certain commodity transactions.[7]

A partnership that fails to meet the passive-type income requirement may be treated as continuing to meet the requirement if the following are true:

(1) The IRS finds that the failure was inadvertent.

(2) Steps are taken so that the partnership once more meets the passive-type income requirement within a reasonable time after the discovery of the failure.

(3) The partnership and each individual holder agree to make whatever adjustments or pay whatever amounts that the IRS may require with respect to the period in which the partnership inadvertently failed to meet the requirement.[8]

1. Treas. Reg. §1.7704-1(l). Notice 88-75, 1988-2 CB 386, (see below) generally applies to partnerships exempted from the rules in this section.
2. See Notice 88-75, 1988-2 CB 386.
3. IRC Sec. 7704(c)(1); Notice 98-3, 1998-1 CB 333.
4. IRC Sec. 7704(f).
5. IRC Sec. 7704(d)(1).
6. See IRC Sec. 851(a).
7. IRC Sec. 7704(c)(3).
8. IRC Sec. 7704(e).

A grandfather rule provided that partnerships that were publicly traded, or for which registrations were filed with certain regulatory agencies, on December 17, 1987 ("existing partnerships"), were exempt from treatment as a corporation until tax years beginning after 1997. Adding a substantial line of business to an existing partnership after December 17, 1987 would terminate the exemption. For purposes of the 90 percent passive-type income requirement above, an existing partnership is not treated as being in existence before the earlier of (1) the first taxable year beginning after 1997 or (2) such a termination of exemption due to the addition of a substantial new line of business. This means that an existing partnership was not required to meet the 90 percent requirement while it was exempt under the transitional rules in order to meet the 90 percent requirement when its exemption expired.[1]

A publicly traded partnership taxed as a corporation under the above rules is treated, in general, as a taxable entity and tax benefits are taken at the entity level. Individual investors, therefore, are unable to realize certain tax benefits, such as depreciation deductions and tax credits, on their individual tax returns.

A publicly traded partnership that is taxed as a corporation should not be subject to the "at risk" rules (see Q 8704) or the "passive loss" rules (see Q 8642). Also, a publicly traded partnership would not qualify to make an election to be treated as an S corporation (see Q 8882).

See Q 8865 for safe harbor rules that can allow a partnership to avoid taxation as a publicly traded partnership. See Q 8871 for the tax rules that apply to corporations.

8865. Are there any safe harbor provisions that allow a partnership to avoid taxation as a publicly traded partnership based on a finding that its shares are traded on a secondary market (or the equivalent thereof)?

Several safe harbors exist that allow a partnership to avoid taxation as a publicly traded partnership. Under the "*Private Transfers Safe Harbor,*" certain transfers not involving trading (private transfers) are disregarded in determining whether interests in a partnership are readily tradable on a secondary market or the substantial equivalent thereof.[2] These transfers include:

(1) transfers in which the basis of the partnership interest in the hands of the transferee is determined by reference to the transferor's basis or is determined under IRC Section 732;

(2) transfers at death, including transfers from an estate or testamentary trust;

(3) transfers between family members, as defined in IRC Section 267(c)(4);

(4) the issuance of partnership interests for cash, property, or services;

(5) distributions from a qualified retirement plan or individual retirement account;

1. TRA '87, Sec. 10211(c), as amended by TAMRA '88, Sec. 2004(f)(2).
2. Treas. Reg. §1.7704-1(e).

(6) a partner's transfer of interests exceeding 2 percent of total interests in partnership capital and profit during a thirty day period ("block transfers");

(7) transfers under redemption or repurchase agreements that can only be exercised upon:

(a) death, disability, or mental incompetence of the partner, or

(b) the retirement or termination of service of a person actively involved in managing the partnership or in providing full time services to the partnership;

(8) transfers of an interest in a closed end partnership pursuant to a redemption agreement if the partnership does not issue any interest after the initial offering (and substantially identical investments are not available through the general partner or certain related parties under IRC Section 267(b) and IRC Section 707(b)(1));

(9) transfers of at least 50 percent of the total interests in partnership capital and profits in one transaction or a series of related transactions; and

(10) transfers not recognized by the partnership.

The "*Redemption and Repurchase Agreements Safe Harbor*" allows transfers involving redemption and repurchase agreements (other than those described in (7) and (8) of "Private Transfers Safe Harbor," above) to be disregarded in determining whether interests in the partnership are readily tradable on a secondary market or the substantial equivalent thereof if the following requirements are met:

(1) The agreement provides that the partner must give written notice to the partnership at least sixty days prior to the redemption or repurchase date.

(2) Either (a) the agreement provides that the redemption or repurchase price cannot be established until at least sixty days after such notification, or (b) the redemption or repurchase price is not established more than four times during the partnership's taxable year.

(3) No more than 10 percent of partnership interests are traded during a taxable year (disregarding only private transfers, see above).[1]

The "*Private Placement Safe Harbor*" provides that interests in a partnership will not be treated as publicly traded if: (1) all interests in such partnership were issued in transactions that were not required to be registered under the Securities Act of 1933, and (2) the partnership has one-hundred partners or fewer at all times during the taxable year. Each person indirectly owning an interest in the partnership through a partnership, S corporation, or grantor trust is treated as a partner if (1) substantially all of the value of the owner's interest in the entity is attributable to

1. Treas. Reg. §1.7704-1(f).

its interest in the partnership, and (2) a principal purpose of the tiered arrangement is to satisfy the 100 partner limitation.[1]

A "*Two Percent Safe Harbor*" provides that interests are not tradable on a secondary market or the substantial equivalent thereof if less than 2 percent of the percentage interests in partnership capital or profits are transferred during the taxable year (disregarding certain transfers involving private transfers, those involving qualified matching services, and certain redemption and repurchase agreements).[2]

8866. What is an LLP? How is an LLP taxed?

Many state laws now provide for so-called limited liability partnerships (LLP), a form of partnership which is particularly well-suited for professional partnerships (such as partnerships of attorneys or doctors). To organize as an LLP, the partnership must file a statement of qualification with the relevant state agency.[3]

The LLP form is particularly useful to professional partners because, as the name suggests, it limits the liability of the partners. Traditional partnerships involve unlimited liability of all general partners personally for the obligations and liabilities of the partnership. In a professional partnership of attorneys, for example, this would potentially subject partner A to personal liability for malpractice even though the malpractice is committed by partner B. It is important to understand that while this structure does provide some protection, it does not provide protection from a partner's own malpractice.

If the state in which the partnership operates has an LLP statute, the partnership may choose to register as a LLP in order to eliminate the liability of the general partners for acts or omissions of the other partners, though the general partners will remain liable for their own wrongful acts.[4]

LLPs are taxed in the same manner as a traditional partnership, in that the partners are taxed at the individual level, rather than at the entity level.

Another variation of the LLP is the limited liability limited partnership (LLLP), which provides the typical limited liability to the limited partners, but also limits the liability of the general partners in the same manner (meaning that the assets of those partners are not reachable by creditors of the partnership). However, only certain states authorize creation of the LLLP.[5]

8867. What is a C corporation?

A corporation is a business entity that is treated as an artificial "person" created under state law and granted the right to engage in business by a charter issued by the state.

1. Treas. Reg. §1.7704-1(h).
2. Treas. Reg. §1.7704-1(j).
3. Revised Uniform Partnership Act ("RUPA"), Secs.101(5), 1001.
4. RUPA, Sec. 306(c).
5. See, for example, Del. Code Ann., Title 6, §17-1105.

Planning Point: The corporation will have a "corporate designator" in its name so that people who do business with the entity will know it is a corporation. Some corporate designators include: incorporated, corporation, company, limited, or an abbreviation thereof. These designators must appear at the end of the corporate name. The idea is to let people who are doing business with an entity know the form of entity with which they are dealing. These designators should also be on the stationary and business cards of the corporation.

As a person, the corporation may sue and be sued, it may buy, sell, and own property in its corporate name, and it may carry on any activities appropriate to the conduct of its business. Thus, property of the corporation along with its debts and liabilities are those of the corporation—not those of the stockholders who own it. As a result, the corporation is also taxed as a separate entity—its tax liabilities are separate and distinct from its stockholder-owners.[1]

The corporation's existence is separate from the individuals who own and manage it. It has only the powers expressly or impliedly conferred upon it by the state. A corporation is considered to be a "C" corporation if it is an entity that is incorporated under the laws of one or more states *unless* it has filed an election to be treated as an "S" corporation (see Q 8882). In general, this discussion will refer to C corporations as "corporations" and S corporations as "S corporations." Whether a corporation is a C corporation or an S corporation depends upon a tax election. The non-tax characteristics of these two types of corporations are the same.

Both publicly traded and closely held corporations may be organized as C corporations. A closely held corporation (also referred to as a "close" or "closed" corporation) is one that is owned by one individual or a small number of individuals. The stock of a closely held corporation has a very limited market and will not ordinarily change hands except at the death or retirement of a stockholder or in the case of some other major realignment within the company.

The opposite of the closely held corporation is the "publicly held corporation." A publicly held corporation is owned by a substantial number of shareholders, most of whom take no part in the active management of the corporation. Typically, a publicly held corporation is a large corporation whose stock is traded on a stock exchange or on the over-the-counter market.

See Q 8868 for a discussion of the formation of a corporation. Q 8871 discusses the tax treatment of a corporation. See Q 8882 to Q 8891 for a discussion of issues specifically applicable to S corporations.

8868. How is a C corporation formed?

The requirements that apply in forming a corporation vary from state to state. Several states have adopted the Model Business Corporation Act, which can serve to illustrate the basic provisions generally found in individual state statutes.

While a partnership is governed by its partnership agreement, a corporation is governed by its certificate of incorporation (also known as its charter) and bylaws. In the past, for the protection of investors and the general public, business conducted by the corporation was limited strictly to those types of transactions specifically authorized by the corporate charter. Today, most

1. See IRC Sec. 11.

states only require that the purpose of the business, as stated in the charter, be to engage in any lawful business activity. Subject to state law and the terms of the charter, most basic corporate activities are governed by an official set of bylaws.

Planning Point: The bylaws set forth the mechanics as to how the corporation is to function. For example, the bylaws will specify how directors are elected; how meetings are called and whether business can be conducted without the formality of a meeting. The bylaws can set forth the specific authority of the directors and the officers. Typically, the statutes for the state where the corporation is formed will fill in any gaps which the bylaws may not address.

To obtain the authority to conduct business as a corporation, the person organizing the corporation must file certain information with the state of incorporation. Generally, filing requirements include articles of incorporation, a filing fee and written appointment of a statutory agent (for service of process) within the state of incorporation. Most states will provide copies of the relevant forms on a governmental website. Delaware, which is an extremely common state for corporate formations partially because of its well-developed case law and streamlined formation process, provides links to PDF documents that must be filed based on the type of corporation that will be formed (e.g., stock corporations, public benefit corporations, close corporations, non-profit corporations).[1]

8869. What provisions must generally be included in a C corporation's articles of incorporation?

The following elements typically must be included in the articles of incorporation, however, each state may vary this information to some extent:

(1) Name of corporation. The selected corporate name must not be in present use within the state, and must be one which connotes a corporate status (e.g., ABC Company, Inc.; XYZ Corporation). Many states provide a separate process by which a corporation may reserve a corporate name.

(2) Place of business. The complete address of the principal place of business and, often, the address of a registered agent (i.e. the person designated to receive official communications with the corporation) within the state of formation, must be included.

(3) Purpose of business. The essential purpose of the business can be briefly stated (with reliance upon broadly-written state statutes, which generally grant broad operating authority), or a lengthy description of numerous operations may be included. Generally, it seems advisable to add to the present business purpose those closely related operations that might reasonably be entered into at some future date. As a result, should the corporation later broaden its activities, such operations will not constitute *ultra vires* acts of the corporation, nor serve as a basis for dissenting minority stockholder suits. The Delaware forms pre-fill this information with "any lawful act or activity for which corporations may be organized." Other states permit similar approaches.

1. Delaware filing forms may be accessed at http://corp.delaware.gov/corpformscorp09.shtml (last accessed June 12, 2016).

(4) Number of authorized shares. This means the number of shares that the corporation is permitted to authorize. This does not mean "issued" shares or sold shares, but rather the total number of shares that can be issued at a later date. Often times, the documentation may authorize 1,000 shares and have 100 shares being issued at the inception of the corporation. The 100 issued shares allow the ownership to be held in percentage increments, and there are still 900 shares which can be issued at a later date if necessary. This clause should further state whether the authorized shares carry a par or non-par value.

(5) Minimum stated capital. Some state statutes prescribe a minimum stated capital for the business, usually $500, before the corporation can commence business. Operating before this stated capital is deposited exposes incorporators to personal liability.

Optional Provisions

In addition to the essential information that must be included in a filing, in some states, the additional information may be optional, and is most commonly provided in the corporation's bylaws:

(1) Express terms of shares. Where all of the authorized shares are common stock, it is unnecessary to define their terms. However, if there is more than one class of stock, it is important that the following terms be defined (often in the corporation's bylaws): rights to dividends; voting rights; preference on liquidation; preemptive rights to purchase additional stock.

(2) Self-dealing of stockholders. In a closely held business, it is not unusual for stockholders or directors to sell property to or purchase property from the corporation. To preclude dissenting minority stockholder suits, specific authority for such acts should be included in the Articles.

(3) Corporate authority to purchase its own shares. Though many state statues permit the corporation to purchase its own shares, by director action, these permitted purchases are rather narrowly defined. To add flexibility for the stockholders, specific language can be added providing broad authority for such purchases.

8870. Is a corporation entitled to a deduction for the expenses it incurs in organizing as a corporation?

A corporation's expenses of organization (such as filing fees and attorney costs) are not deductible when incurred. However, the corporation may treat these as deferred expenses and deduct them ratably over the 180 month period beginning when the corporation starts business.[1]

1. IRC Sec. 248; Treas. Reg. §1.248-1.

8871. How is a C corporation taxed?

Unlike in the partnership context, a corporation is required to file a tax return and pay taxes at the entity level. The owners of the corporation (its shareholders) also pay taxes at the individual level based on any distributions received as dividend income based on stock ownership.

A corporation pays tax according to a graduated rate schedule, which can result in a lower tax rate for corporations with relatively modest earnings. The corporate tax rates range from 15 percent to 35 percent. The first $50,000 of a corporation's earnings is taxed at the 15 percent rate, but the next $25,000 of earnings is taxed at 25 percent. Earnings above $75,000, but below $10,000,000, are subject to a 34 percent rate. A 35 percent rate applies to corporate earnings above the $10,000,000 level. [1]

Taxable income is computed for a corporation in much the same way as for an individual. Generally, a corporation may take the same deductions as an individual, except those of a personal nature (such as deductions for medical expenses and the personal exemptions). A corporation also does not receive a standard deduction.

Some deductions are allowed specifically for corporations, however, including a deduction equal to 70 percent of dividends received from other domestic corporations, 80 percent of dividends received from a 20 percent owned company, and 100 percent for dividends received from affiliated corporations (see Q 8872 for a detailed discussion of the deductions available with respect to dividends).[2] A corporation may deduct contributions to charitable organizations to the extent of 10 percent of taxable income (with certain adjustments).[3] Generally, charitable contributions in excess of the 10 percent limit may be carried over for five years.[4]

A corporation is also allowed a deduction for production activities. This deduction is equal to nine percent of a taxpayer's qualified production activities income (or, if less, the taxpayer's taxable income). The deduction is limited to 50 percent of the W-2 wages paid by the taxpayer for the year. The definition of "production activities" is broad and includes construction activities, energy production, and the creation of computer software.[5]

Capital gains and losses are netted for a corporation in the same manner as for an individual (see Q 8578) and net short-term capital gain, to the extent it exceeds net long-term capital loss, if any, is taxed at the corporation's regular tax rates.

A corporation reporting a net capital gain (where net long-term capital gain exceeds net short-term capital loss) is taxed under one of the two following methods, depending on which produces the lower tax:

1. *Regular method.* Net capital gain is included in gross income and taxed at the corporation's regular tax rates.

---

1. IRC Sec. 11(b).
2. IRC Sec. 243.
3. IRC Sec. 170(b)(2).
4. IRC Sec. 170(d)(2).
5. IRC Sec. 199.

2. *Alternative method*. First, a tax on the corporation's taxable income, exclusive of net capital gain, is calculated at the corporation's regular tax rates. Then a second tax on the net capital gain (or, if less, taxable income) for the year is calculated at the rate of 35 percent. The tax on income exclusive of net capital gain and the tax on net capital gain are added to arrive at the corporation's total tax. For certain gains from timber, the maximum rate is 23.8 percent (15 percent before 2016).[1]

8872. What is the corporate dividend exclusion?

A corporation, as a legal entity, may own shares in other corporations in the same manner as individuals, and is entitled to receive any dividends on such shares.

However, in computing its taxable income, a corporation, unlike an individual, may deduct 80 percent of dividends received from domestic corporations if it owns at least 20 percent but less than 80 percent of the stock.[2] For corporations that own less than 20 percent of the distributing corporation the deduction is limited to 70 percent of the dividends received.[3] Dividends received are 100 percent deductible if the recipient is a small business investment company operating under the Small Business Investment Act, or, subject to certain conditions, if the recipient is a member of the same affiliated group of corporations as the issuer of the dividends (generally meaning 80 percent or more common ownership).[4]

In order to prevent abuse of the dividends-received deduction through extremely short-term investments designed only to capture imminent dividends on a tax-free basis, the deduction is available only if the stock is held for a minimum period, depending on the type of stock involved.

Debt-Financed Portfolio Stock

The dividends-received deduction is further limited with respect to dividends received from debt-financed portfolio stock. In general, the otherwise allowable deduction (after applying the other limitations) must be reduced by a percentage equal to the percentage of the cost of the dividend-yielding stock which was debt-financed.[5]

8873. How are dividends from a foreign corporation taxed when they are received by a domestic corporation?

Dividends received by a domestic corporation which owns at least 10 percent of a foreign corporation are subject to a domestic corporation deduction only to the extent that the dividends are deemed attributable to U.S. source income of the foreign corporation. This is computed by applying to the dividends received a ratio equal to the ratio of U.S. source income to total income of the foreign corporation. Once the U.S.-source portion is determined, the deduction is then limited, depending on the percentage ownership of the foreign corporation.

1. IRC Secs. 1201, 1222.
2. IRC Sec. 243(c).
3. IRC Sec. 243(a)(1).
4. IRC Sec. 243(a)(3).
5. IRC Sec. 246(a).

If the domestic corporation owns at least 10 percent, but less than 20 percent, the deduction is 70 percent of the U.S.-source portion of the dividends received. If the percentage ownership is at least 20 percent, the portion deductible increases to 80 percent of the U.S.-source dividends received.

A 100 percent deduction is allowed for dividends received from a foreign wholly-owned subsidiary of a domestic corporation, provided that all of the subsidiary's income is effectively connected with a U.S. trade or business. Special rules apply in the case of dividends received from certain foreign sales corporations (FSCs).[1]

8874. How is a C corporation shareholder taxed upon the sale of the shareholder's stock in the corporation?

Generally, a shareholder who sells or exchanges stock for other property realizes a capital gain or loss.[2] Whether such gain or loss is short-term or long-term usually depends on how long the shareholder held the stock before selling (or exchanging) the stock.[3] For an explanation of how the holding period is calculated, see Q 8573; for the treatment of capital gains and losses, including the current tax rates applicable for capital gains, see Q 8566 to Q 8581.

When shares of stock are sold, the amount of gain (or loss) is the difference between the selling price and the shareholder's tax basis in the shares at the time of sale. If the shares are exchanged for property, or for property and cash, the amount of gain (or loss) is the difference between the fair market value of the property plus the cash received in the exchange and the shareholder's tax basis.[4]

Despite this, if common stock in a corporation is exchanged for common stock in the same corporation, or if preferred stock is exchanged for preferred stock in the same corporation, gain or loss is generally not recognized unless cash or other property is also received. In this case, the exchange is taxed in substantially the same manner as a "like-kind" exchange.

The exchange of shares of different corporations and exchanges of common for preferred do *not* qualify for the general "like-kind" exchange rules, even if the shares are similar in all respects.[5] The nonrecognition rules of IRC Section 1036 apply to exchanges of common stock for common stock in the same corporation, even though the shares are of a different class and have different voting, preemptive, or dividend rights.[6]

For an explanation of "like-kind" exchanges, see Q 8612. See Q 8875 for considerations that apply in determining a stockholder's basis in corporate stock.

1. IRC Sec. 245.
2. See IRC Secs. 1221, 1222.
3. See IRC Secs. 1222, 1223.
4. See IRC Sec. 1001.
5. IRC Sec. 1036; Treas. Reg. §1.1036-1. See IRC Sec. 1031(a).
6. Rev. Rul. 72-199, 1972-1 CB 228. See Treas. Reg. §1.1036-1.

8875. What special considerations apply in determining a stockholder's basis in securities, such as corporate stock?

If an individual's holdings in a particular security were all acquired on the same day and at the same price, there is little difficulty in establishing the tax basis and holding period of the securities subject to the sale or exchange. When an individual sells or otherwise transfers securities from holdings that were purchased or acquired on different dates or at different prices (or at different tax bases), the process becomes more difficult. See Q 8570 for a discussion of the general rules applicable in determining a taxpayer's basis in an asset.

In the context of corporate securities, the individual must generally be able to identify the lot from which the transferred security originated in order to determine tax basis and holding period. Unless the individual can "adequately identify" the lot from which the securities being sold originated, the securities sold will be deemed to have come from the earliest of such lots purchased or acquired, by a "first-in, first-out" (FIFO) method.[1] However, in cases involving mutual fund shares, the selling shareholder may be permitted to use an "average basis" method to determine tax basis and holding period in the securities transferred.

Generally, identification is determined by the certificate delivered to the buyer or other transferee. The security represented by the certificate is deemed to be the security sold or transferred. This is true even if the taxpayer intended to sell securities from another lot or instructed a broker to sell securities from another lot.[2]

The following are exceptions to the general rule of adequate identification:

(1) The securities are left in the custody of a broker or other agent. If the seller specifies to the broker which securities to sell or transfer, and if the broker or agent sends a written confirmation of the specified securities within a reasonable time, then the specified securities are the securities sold or transferred, even though different certificates are delivered to the buyer or other transferee.[3]

(2) The taxpayer holds a single certificate representing securities from different lots. If the taxpayer sells part of the securities represented by the certificate through a broker, adequate identification is made if the taxpayer specifies to the broker which securities to sell, and if the broker sends a written confirmation of the specified securities within a reasonable time. If the taxpayer sells the securities, then there is adequate identification if there is a written record identifying the particular securities intended for sale.[4]

(3) The securities are held by a trustee, or by an executor or administrator of an estate. An adequate identification is made if the trustee, executor, or administrator specifies in writing in the books or records of the trust or estate the securities to be sold,

1. Treas. Reg. §1.1012-1(c)(1).
2. Treas. Reg. §1.1012-1(c)(2).
3. Treas. Reg. §1.1012-1(c)(3)(i).
4. Treas. Reg. §1.1012-1(c)(3)(ii).

transferred, or distributed. In the case of a distribution, the trustee, executor, or administrator must give the distributee a written document specifying the particular securities distributed. Here, the specified securities are the securities sold, transferred, or distributed, even if certificates from a different lot were delivered to the purchaser, transferee, or distributee.[1]

In the case of stock which is inherited, the basis is equal to the value of the stock on the date of the decedent's death (and subject to certain exceptions, including the election to apply the alternate valuation date).[2] Since the new basis is generally equal to the date of death value of the stock, this adjustment can result in either a step up or a step down in basis. Therefore, unrealized gains and losses disappear at the time of death.

Planning Point: If the taxpayer has unrealized gains and is not expect to live long; it is better to get the step up in basis under IRC Section 1014. Conversely, if there are unrealized losses, which would be lost at death, consideration should be given to determine if the unrealized losses can be used during lifetime.

8876. What is the accumulated earnings tax that a C corporation may be subject to? When does the tax apply?

In addition to the graduated tax rate schedule outlined in Q 8871, a corporation will be subject to a penalty tax if, for the purpose of preventing the imposition of income tax upon its shareholders, it accumulates earnings instead of distributing them as dividends.[3] The tax is 20 percent of the corporation's *accumulated taxable income* (15 percent for tax years beginning prior to 2013).[4]

"Accumulated taxable income" is taxable income for the year (after certain adjustments) minus the federal income tax, dividends paid to stockholders (during the taxable year or within 2½ months after the close of the taxable year), and the "accumulated earnings credit."[5]

A corporation is permitted to retain amounts required to meet the reasonable needs of the business—the tax will only be imposed upon amounts in excess of these amounts. To facilitate this permitted retention, an accumulated earnings credit is allowed. A corporation must demonstrate a specific, definite and feasible plan for the use of the accumulated funds in order to avoid the tax.[6]

The use of accumulated funds for the personal use of a shareholder and family is evidence that the accumulation was to prevent the imposition of income tax upon its shareholders.[7] In deciding whether a family owned bank was subject to the accumulated earnings tax, the IRS took into account the regulatory scheme the bank was operating under to determine its reasonable needs.[8]

1. Treas. Reg. §1.1012-1(c)(4).
2. IRC Secs. 1014, 2032.
3. IRC Secs. 531-537; *GPD, Inc. v. Comm.*, 75-1 USTC ¶9142 (6th Cir. 1974).
4. IRC Sec. 531, as amended by ATRA.
5. IRC Sec. 535.
6. *Eyefull Inc. v. Comm.*, TC Memo 1996-238.
7. *Northwestern Ind. Tel. Co. v. Comm.*, 127 F. 3d 643, 97-2 USTC ¶50,859 (7th Cir. 1997).
8. TAM 9822009.

Most corporations are allowed a minimum accumulated earnings credit equal to the amount by which $250,000 ($150,000 in the case of service corporations in health, law, engineering, architecture, accounting, actuarial science, performing arts or consulting) exceeds the accumulated earnings and profits of the corporation at the close of the previous taxable year.[1] Consequently, an aggregate of $250,000 (or $150,000) may be accumulated for any purpose without danger of incurring the penalty tax.

Tax-exempt income is not included in the accumulated taxable income of the corporation, but will be included in earnings and profits in determining whether there has been an accumulation beyond the reasonable needs of the business.[2] However, a distribution in redemption of stock to pay death taxes which is treated as a dividend does not qualify for the "dividends paid" deduction (Q 8872) in computing accumulated taxable income.[3]

The accumulated earnings tax applies to all C corporations, without regard to the number of shareholders in taxable years beginning after July 18, 1984.[4]

8877. What is the personal holding company tax that a C corporation may be subject to? When does the tax apply?

In addition to the typical corporate tax rates (Q 8871) and accumulated earnings penalty tax (Q 8876), a second penalty tax, called the personal holding company (PHC) tax, may be imposed to prevent shareholders from avoiding personal income taxes on securities and other income-producing property placed in a corporation to avoid higher personal income tax rates. The PHC tax is 20 percent (15 percent for tax years beginning prior to 2013) of the corporation's undistributed PHC income (taxable income adjusted to reflect its net economic income for the year, minus dividends distributed to shareholders), if the corporation meets both the "stock ownership" and "PHC income" tests.[5]

A corporation meets the "stock ownership" test if more than 50 percent of the value of its stock is owned, directly or indirectly, by or for not more than five shareholders.[6] Certain stock owned by families, trusts, estates, partners, partnerships, and corporations may be attributed to individuals for purposes of this rule.[7]

A corporation meets the "PHC income" requirement if 60 percent or more of its adjusted ordinary gross income is PHC income, generally defined to include the following: (1) dividends, interest, royalties, and annuities; (2) rents; (3) mineral, oil, and gas royalties; (4) copyright royalties; (5) produced film rents (amounts derived from film properties acquired before substantial completion of the production); (6) compensation from use of corporate property by shareholders; (7) personal service contracts; and (8) income from estates and trusts.[8]

1. IRC Sec. 535(c)(2).
2. Rev. Rul. 70-497, 1970-2 CB 128.
3. Rev. Rul. 70-642, 1970-2 CB 131.
4. IRC Sec. 532(c).
5. IRC Secs. 541, as amended by ATRA, 542, 545.
6. IRC Sec. 542(a)(2).
7. IRC Sec. 544.
8. IRC Secs. 542(a)(1), 543(a).

8878. Are C corporations subject to the alternative minimum tax? How is the corporate alternative minimum tax calculated?

A corporate taxpayer must calculate its liability under the regular tax and a tentative minimum tax, and then add to its regular tax the amount of tentative minimum tax as exceeds the regular tax. The amount added is the corporate alternative minimum tax (AMT).[1]

To calculate its AMT, a corporation first calculates its "alternative minimum taxable income" (AMTI), as explained below.[2] The corporation must then calculate its "adjusted current earnings" (ACE), also explained below. The corporation increases its AMTI by 75 percent of the amount by which ACE exceeds AMTI (or reduces its AMTI by 75 percent of the amount by which AMTI exceeds ACE).[3] The tax itself is a flat 20 percent rate, applied to the corporation's AMTI after it is adjusted based on ACE.[4]

Each corporation receives a $40,000 exemption, similarly to the AMT exemption applicable to individuals (see Q 8560). The corporate exemption amount, however, is reduced by 25 percent of the amount by which AMTI exceeds $150,000 (phasing out completely at $310,000).[5]

AMTI is regular taxable income determined with certain adjustments and increased by tax preferences.[6] "Tax preferences" for corporations are the same as for other taxpayers. Adjustments to income include:

(1) property is generally depreciated under a less accelerated or a straight line method over a longer period, except that a longer period is not required for property placed in service after 1998;

(2) mining exploration and development costs are amortized over ten years;

(3) a percentage of completion method is required for long-term contracts;

(4) net operating loss deductions are generally limited to 90 percent of AMTI (although some relief was available in 2001 and 2002);

(5) certified pollution control facilities are depreciated under the alternative depreciation system except those that are placed in service after 1998, which will use the straight line method; and

(6) the adjustment based on the corporation's ACE.[7]

1. IRC Secs. 55-59.
2. IRC Sec. 55(b)(2).
3. IRC Sec. 56(g).
4. IRC Sec. 55(b)(1)(B).
5. IRC Secs. 55(d)(2), 55(d)(3).
6. IRC Sec. 55(b)(2).
7. IRC Secs. 56(a), 56(c), 56(d).

To calculate ACE, a corporation begins with AMTI (determined without regard to ACE or the AMT net operating loss) and makes additional adjustments. These adjustments include adding certain amounts of income that are includable in earnings and profits but not in AMTI (including income on life insurance policies and receipt of key person insurance death proceeds). The amount of any such income added to AMTI is reduced by any deductions that would have been allowed in calculating AMTI had the item been included in gross income. The corporation is generally not allowed a deduction for ACE purposes if that deduction would not have been allowed for earnings and profits purposes, though a deduction is allowed for certain dividends received by a corporation. Generally, for property placed into service after 1989 but before 1994, the corporation must recalculate depreciation according to specified methods for ACE purposes. For ACE purposes, earnings and profits are adjusted further for certain purposes such as the treatment of intangible drilling costs, amortization of certain expenses, installment sales, and depletion.[1]

A corporation subject to the AMT in one year may be allowed a minimum tax credit against regular tax liability in subsequent years. The credit is equal to the excess of the adjusted net minimum taxes imposed in prior years over the amount of minimum tax credits allowable in prior years.[2] However, the amount of the credit cannot be greater than the excess of the corporation's regular tax liability (reduced by certain credits such as certain business related credits and certain investment credits) over its tentative minimum tax.[3]

8879. Are there any exceptions to the rule that corporations may be subject to the alternative minimum tax? Can small corporations be exempt from AMT requirements?

Certain small corporations are deemed to have a tentative minimum tax of zero and are, therefore, exempt from the AMT.[4] To qualify, the corporation must meet a $5 million gross receipts test for its first taxable year beginning after 1996, under which average annual gross receipts for the previous three years must not exceed $5 million. If the corporation has not existed for three full years, the years the corporation was in existence are substituted for the three years (with annualization of any short taxable year). The corporation must continue to meet this test in each subsequent tax year to remain exempt, but with $7.5 million substituted for $5 million.[5]

Gross receipts means those receipts properly recognized under the taxpayer's method of accounting for federal income tax purposes. Gross receipts include total sales (net of returns and allowances) and all amounts received for services. It also includes all investment income such as interest, dividends, rents and royalties. Gross receipts are generally reduced by the adjusted basis of capital assets or property sold in a trade or business.[6]

1. IRC. Sec. 56(g); the tax is reported on Form 4626.
2. IRC Sec. 53(b).
3. IRC Sec. 53(c).
4. IRC Sec. 55(e).
5. IRC Secs. 55(e)(1), 448(c).
6. Treas. Reg. §1.448-1T(f)(2)(iv).

If a corporation loses its AMT exemption, certain adjustments used to determine the corporation's AMTI will be applied for only those transactions entered into or property placed in service in tax years beginning with the tax year in which the corporation ceases to be a small corporation and tax years thereafter.[1]

A corporation exempt from the AMT because of the small corporation provision may be limited in the amount of credit it may take for AMT paid in previous years. In computing the AMT credit, the corporation's regular tax liability (reduced by applicable credits) used to calculate the credit is reduced by 25 percent of the amount that such liability exceeds $25,000.[2]

8880. What is a controlled group of corporations?

The controlled group rules aggregate several entities (this rule applies to corporations, but also to proprietorships and partnerships) into a single employer for meeting various qualification requirements of the IRC. In general, the determination of whether a group is a controlled group of corporations or under common control considers stock ownership by value or voting power. All employees of a group of employers that are members of a controlled group of corporations or, in the case of partnerships and proprietorships, are under common control will be treated as employed by a single employer.[3]

A controlled group may be a parent-subsidiary controlled group, a brother-sister controlled group, or a combined group, as follows:[4]

(1) A parent-subsidiary controlled group is composed of one or more chains of subsidiary corporations connected through stock ownership with a common parent corporation. A parent-subsidiary group exists if at least 80 percent of the stock of each subsidiary corporation is owned by one or more of the other corporations in the group and the parent corporation owns at least 80 percent of the stock of at least one of the subsidiary corporations. When determining whether a parent owns 80 percent of the stock of a subsidiary corporation, all stock of that corporation owned directly by other subsidiaries is disregarded.

(2) A brother-sister controlled group is two or more corporations in which five or fewer individuals, estates, or trusts own stock consisting of 80 percent or more of each corporation, and more than 50 percent of each corporation when taking into account each stockholder's interest only to the extent each stockholder has identical interests in each corporation. For purposes of the 80 percent test, a stockholder's interest is considered only if the stockholder owns some interest in each corporation of the group.[5]

1. IRC Sec. 55(e)(2).
2. IRC Sec. 55(e)(5).
3. IRC Secs. 414(b), 414(c).
4. Treas. Reg. §1.414(b)-1.
5. *U.S. v. Vogel Fertilizer Co.*, 455 U.S. 16 (1982); Treas. Reg. §1.1563-1(a)(3).

(3) A combined group is three or more corporations, each of which is a member of a parent-subsidiary group or a brother-sister group (above) and one of which is both a parent of a parent-subsidiary group and a member of a brother-sister group.[1]

Special rules apply for determining stock ownership, including special constructive ownership rules, when determining the existence of a controlled group.[2] Community property rules, where present, also apply.[3]

For purposes of qualification, the test for a controlled group is strictly mechanical. Once the existence of a group is established, aggregation of employees is required and will not be negated by showing that the controlled group and plans were not created or were manipulated for the purpose of avoiding the qualification requirements.[4]

8881. How is the treatment of transactions between corporations impacted by membership in a controlled group? How are corporate members of a controlled group taxed?

IRC Section 482 allows the IRS to distribute, apportion or allocate income, deductions, credits or allowances among a controlled group of corporations (see Q 8880) in order to prevent tax evasion or to more accurately reflect the actual income of the entity. While the provision applies to all entities, it is especially relevant in the context of a corporation that may engage in transactions with other corporations in the controlled group that are not considered to be arm's length. In such a situation, special rules may govern transactions that take place between members of the controlled group.

To reflect the fact that such a sale or exchange between members of a controlled group may not have resulted from arm's length negotiations, loss on a sale or exchange (other than of inventory) between two corporations that are members of the same controlled group (using a 50 percent test instead of 80 percent, see Q 8880), though generally not denied, is deferred until the property is transferred outside the controlled group.[5]

Further, the controlled group rules prevent a single business owner from taking advantage of the graduated rate schedule that applies to corporations through use of multiple corporations that would spread taxable income among corporations in order to cause all income to become subject to the low 15 percent corporate tax rate.[6] Similarly, a controlled group of corporations is entitled to only one accumulated earnings tax credit (Q 8876) and only one $40,000 AMT exemption (Q 8878).[7]

1. IRC Secs. 414(b), 1563; Treas. Reg. §1.414(b)-1.
2. IRC Sec. 1563(d); Treas. Reg. §1.414(b)-1.
3. *Aero Indus. Co., Inc. v. Comm.*, TC Memo 1980-116.
4. *Fujinon Optical, Inc. v. Comm.*, 76 TC 499 (1981).
5. IRC Sec. 267(f).
6. IRC Sec. 1561(a)(1).
7. IRC Sec. 1561(a)(2), (3).

8882. What is an S corporation and how is it formed?

An S corporation is a corporation that files an election to be treated as an S corporation, which, generally, means that it will be treated as a pass-through entity that is taxed similarly to a partnership, thus avoiding most tax at the corporate level.[1] To be eligible to make the election, a corporation must meet certain requirements as to the kind and number of shareholders (Q 8887), classes of stock (Q 8890), and sources of income. However, the decision to be an S corporation is a tax election. Therefore, an S corporation will be treated the same as any other corporation for purposes of the applicable state corporation law as well as the liability protection associated with the corporate form.

An S corporation must be a domestic corporation with only a single class of stock and may have up to 100 shareholders (none of whom are nonresident aliens) who are individuals, estates, and certain trusts. An S corporation may not be an ineligible corporation.

An ineligible corporation is one of the following: (1) a financial institution that uses the reserve method of accounting for bad debts; (2) an insurance company; (3) a corporation electing (under IRC Section 936) credits for certain tax attributable to income from Puerto Rico and other U.S. possessions; or (4) a current or former domestic international sales corporation (DISC). Qualified plans and certain charitable organizations may be S corporation shareholders.[2]

While an S corporation can only have one class of stock, it is permitted to have a second class of stock if the only difference is the ability to vote.[3]

Planning Point: In order to qualify as an S corporation, an election must be filed in order to be treated as such. These elections are made on IRS Form 2553, and must be made within two months and fifteen days after the effective date of the election. The IRS has recently issued Revenue Procedure 2013-30, which will extend this time period for up to three years for certain situations.

8883. How is an S corporation taxed? When may S corporation income be taxed at the corporate level?

An S corporation is generally not subject to tax at the corporate level.[4] However, a tax is imposed at the corporate level under certain circumstances. When an S corporation disposes of property within five years after the S election was made, gain attributable to pre-election appreciation of the property (built in gain) is taxed at the corporate level to the extent such gain does not exceed the amount of taxable income imposed on the corporation if it were not an S corporation.[5]

1. See IRC Secs. 1361, 1362, 1363.
2. IRC Sec. 1361.
3. IRC Sec. 1361(c)(4).
4. IRC Sec. 1363(a).
5. IRC Sec. 1374. The PATH Act permanently reduced the holding period requirement to five years.

For S elections made after December 17, 1987, a corporation switching from C corporation status to S corporation status may also be required to recapture certain amounts at the corporate level in connection with goods previously inventoried under a LIFO method.[1]

In addition, a tax is imposed at the corporate level on *excess* "net passive income" of an S corporation (passive investment income reduced by certain expenses connected with the production of such income) but only if the following are true:

(1) The corporation, at the end of the tax year, has accumulated earnings and profits (either carried over from a year in which it was a nonelecting corporation or due to an acquisition of a C corporation).

(2) Passive investment income exceeds 25 percent of gross receipts.

The highest corporate tax rate (currently 35 percent) applies.[2] "Passive investment income" means rents, royalties, dividends, interest, and annuities.[3] The following items are excluded from the definition of passive investment income for this purpose:

(1) Rents for the use of corporate property if the corporation also provides substantial services or incurs substantial cost in the rental business;[4]

(2) Interest on obligations acquired from the sale of a capital asset or the performance of services in the ordinary course of a trade or business of selling the property or performing the services;

(3) Gross receipts derived in the ordinary course of a trade or business of lending or financing; dealing in property; purchasing or discounting accounts receivable, notes, or installment obligations; or servicing mortgages;[5]

(4) If an S corporation owns 80 percent or more of a C corporation, dividends from the C corporation to the extent the dividends are attributable to the earnings and profits of the C corporation derived from the active conduct of a trade or business.[6]

If amounts are subject to tax both as built-in gain and as excess net passive income, an adjustment will be made in the amount taxed as passive income.[7]

Also, tax is imposed at the corporate level if investment credit attributable to years for which the corporation was not an S corporation is required to be recaptured.[8]

1. IRC Sec. 1363(d).
2. IRC Sec. 1375(a).
3. IRC Secs. 1362(d)(3), 1375(b)(3).
4. See Let. Ruls. 9837003, 9611009, 9610016, 9548012, 9534024, 9514005.
5. Treas. Reg. §1.1362-2(c)(5).
6. Treas. Reg. §1.1362-8(a).
7. IRC Sec. 1375(b)(4).
8. IRC Sec. 1371(d).

Furthermore, an S corporation may be required to make an accelerated tax payment on behalf of its shareholders if the S corporation elects not to use a required taxable year.[1] The corporation is also subject to estimated tax requirements with respect to the tax on built-in gain, the tax on excess net passive income and any tax attributable to recapture of investment credit.[2]

8884. How is the shareholder of an S corporation taxed?

Like a partnership, an S corporation computes its taxable income and allocates it to an individual, with the exception that certain personal and other deductions are allowed to the S corporation shareholder, but not to the S corporation itself. Further, the S corporation may elect to amortize organizational expenses (see Q 8870).[3]

Each shareholder then reports on his individual return the shareholder's proportionate share of the corporation's items of income, loss, deductions and credits. These items retain their character when they are passed through from the S corporation to the shareholder.[4]

Planning Point: The shareholder receives a Form K-1 from the S corporation every year which states the shareholder's proportionate share of such items. The individual shareholder cannot complete their personal income tax return until they receive the Form K-1 from the corporation.

Certain items of income, loss, deduction or credit must be passed through as separate items because they may have an effect on each individual shareholder's tax liability. For example, net capital gains and losses pass through as such to be included with the shareholder's own net capital gain or loss. Any gains and losses on certain property used in a trade or business are passed through separately to be aggregated with the shareholder's other IRC Section 1231 gains and losses. (Gains passed through are reduced by any tax at the corporate level on gains, see Q 8883).

Miscellaneous itemized deductions pass through to be combined with the individual's miscellaneous deductions for purposes of the 2 percent floor on such deductions. Charitable contributions pass through to shareholders separately subject to the individual shareholder's percentage limitations on deductibility.

Tax-exempt income passes through as such. Items involving determination of credits pass through separately.[5] Before pass-through, each item of passive investment income is reduced by its proportionate share of the tax at the corporate level on excess net passive investment income (see Q 8883).[6]

Items that do not need to be passed through separately are aggregated on the corporation's tax return and each shareholder reports his share of such nonseparately computed net income or

1. IRC Sec. 7519.
2. IRC Sec. 6655(g)(4).
3. IRC Sec. 1363(b).
4. IRC Secs. 1366(a), 1366(b).
5. IRC Sec. 1366(a)(1).
6. IRC Sec. 1366(f)(3).

loss on the shareholder's individual return.[1] Items of income, deductions, and credits (whether or not separately stated) that flow through to the shareholder are subject to the "passive loss" rule (see Q 8642 to Q 8651) if the activity is passive with respect to the shareholder. Items taxed at the corporate level are not subject to the passive loss rule unless the corporation is either closely held or a personal service corporation.

Thus, whether amounts are distributed to them or not, shareholders are taxed on the corporation's taxable income. Shareholders take into account their shares of income, loss, deduction and credit on a per-share, per-day basis.[2] The S corporation income must also be included on a current basis by shareholders for purposes of the estimated tax provisions.[3]

The Tax Court determined that when an S corporation shareholder files for bankruptcy, all the gains and losses for that year flowed through to the bankruptcy estate. The gains and losses should not be divided based on the time before the bankruptcy was filed.[4]

8885. What special considerations apply in determining a shareholder's basis in S corporation stock?

The basis of each shareholder's stock is *increased* by his share of items of separately stated income (including tax-exempt income), any nonseparately computed income, and by any excess of deductions for depletion over basis in property subject to depletion.[5]

An S corporation shareholder may *not* increase tax basis due to excluded discharge of indebtedness income.[6] The basis of each shareholder's stock is *decreased* (not below zero) by:

(1) items of distributions from the corporation that are not includable in the income of the shareholder;

(2) separately stated loss and deductions and nonseparately computed loss;

(3) any expense of the corporation not deductible in computing taxable income and not properly chargeable to the capital account; and

(4) any depletion deduction with respect to oil and gas property to the extent that the deduction does not exceed the shareholder's proportionate share of the property's adjusted basis.

For tax years beginning after 2005, if an S corporation makes a charitable contribution of property, each shareholder's basis was reduced by the pro rata share of basis in the property.[7] If the aggregate of these amounts exceeds the basis in his stock, the excess reduced the shareholder's

1. IRC Sec. 1366(a).
2. IRC Sec. 1377(a).
3. Let. Rul. 8542034.
4. *Williams v. Comm.*, 123 TC 144 (2004).
5. IRC Sec. 1367(a)(1).
6. IRC Sec. 108(d)(7)(A).
7. IRC Sec. 1367(a)(2), as amended by TEAMTRA 2008, ATRA and PATH.

basis in any indebtedness of the corporation to the shareholder.[1] A shareholder may not take deductions and losses of the S corporation that, when aggregated, exceed the basis in S corporation stock plus his basis in any indebtedness of the corporation to the shareholder.[2] Such disallowed deductions and losses may be carried over.[3] In other words, the shareholder may not deduct in any tax year more than the shareholder has "at risk" in the corporation.

8886. How are S corporation distributions taxed?

Generally, earnings of an S corporation are not treated as earnings and profits. However, an S corporation may have accumulated earnings and profits for any year in which a valid election was not in effect or as the result of a corporate acquisition in which there is a carryover of earnings and profits under IRC Section 381.[4] Corporations that were S corporations before 1983 but were not S corporations in the first tax year after 1996 are able to eliminate earnings and profits that were accumulated before 1983 in their first tax year beginning after May 25, 2007.[5]

A distribution from an S corporation that does not have accumulated earnings and profits lowers the shareholder's basis in the corporation's stock.[6] Any excess distribution is generally treated as gain.[7]

If the S corporation does have earnings and profits, distributions are treated as distributions by a corporation without earnings and profits, to the extent of the shareholder's share of an accumulated adjustment account (i.e., post-1982 gross receipts less deductible expenses, which have not been distributed).

Any excess distribution is treated under the usual corporate rules. That is, the distribution is treated as a dividend up to the amount of the accumulated earnings and profits. Any excess is applied to reduce the shareholder's basis. Finally, any remainder is treated as a gain.[8] However, in any tax year, shareholders receiving the distribution may, if all agree, elect to have all distributions in the year treated first as dividends to the extent of earnings and profits and then as return of investment to the extent of adjusted basis and any excess as capital gain.[9] If the IRC Section 1368(e)(3) election is made, it will apply to all distributions made in the tax year.[10]

Certain distributions from an S corporation in redemption of stock are treated as a sale or exchange. Generally, only gain or loss, if any, is recognized in a sale. In general, redemptions that qualify for "exchange" treatment include redemptions that are not essentially equivalent to a dividend, substantially disproportionate redemptions of stock, complete redemptions of stock, certain partial liquidations, and redemptions of stock to pay estate taxes.[11]

1. IRC. Sec. 1367(b)(2)(A).
2. IRC Sec. 1366(d)(1).
3. IRC Sec. 1366(d)(2).
4. IRC Sec. 1371(c).
5. SBWOTA 2007 Sec. 8235.
6. IRC Sec. 1367(a)(2)(A).
7. IRC Sec. 1368(b).
8. IRC Sec. 1368(c).
9. IRC Sec. 1368(e)(3).
10. Let. Rul. 8935013.
11. See IRC Secs. 302, 303.

If the S corporation distributes appreciated property to a shareholder, gain will be recognized by the corporation as if the property had been sold at fair market value, and the gain will pass through to shareholders like any other gain.[1]

8887. Who can be a shareholder in an S corporation? What restrictions apply to 2 percent shareholders in an S corporation?

An S corporation may have up to 100 shareholders (none of whom are nonresident aliens) who are individuals, estates, and certain trusts.

Members of a family are treated as one shareholder. "Members of a family," for this purpose, means "the common ancestor, lineal descendants of the common ancestor, and the spouses (or former spouses) of such lineal descendants or common ancestor." Generally, the common ancestor may not be more than six generations removed from the youngest generation of shareholders who would be considered members of the family.[2]

Only certain trusts can qualify as S corporation shareholders. These trusts include: (1) a trust all of which is treated as owned by an individual who is a citizen or resident of the United States under the grantor trust rules; (2) a trust that was described in (1) above immediately prior to the deemed owner's death that continues in existence after such death may continue to be an S corporation shareholder for up to two years after the owner's death; (3) a trust to which stock is transferred pursuant to a will may be an S corporation shareholder for up to two years after the date of the stock transfer; (4) a trust created primarily to exercise the voting power of stock transferred to it; (5) a qualified subchapter S trust (QSST), see Q 8888; (6) an electing small business trust (ESBT), see Q 8889; and (7) in the case of an S corporation that is a bank, an IRA or Roth IRA.[3] An estate can continue to be an eligible shareholder during the reasonable period of administration. This can continue for the duration of payments being made under IRC Section 6166 (relating to the deferral of the estate tax for certain estates containing closely held business interests).[4]

8888. What is a qualified subchapter S trust (QSST)?

A QSST is a trust that has only one current income beneficiary (who must be a citizen or resident of the U.S.), all income must be distributed currently, and the trust corpus may not be distributed to anyone else during the life of such beneficiary. The income interest must terminate upon the earlier of the beneficiary's death or termination of the trust. If the trust terminates during the lifetime of the income beneficiary, all trust assets must be distributed to that beneficiary. The beneficiary must make an election for the trust to be treated as a QSST.[5]

Planning Point: When the stock is initially transferred to the trust, the taxpayer must file a separate S corporation election. For both the QSST and the electing small business trust (ESBT, see Q8879), the election must be filed "within the sixteen day and two month period beginning on the day that the stock is transferred to the trust.[6]

1. IRC Secs. 1371(a), 311(b).
2. IRC Sec. 1361(c)(1).
3. IRC Secs. 1361(c)(2), 1361(d).
4. IRC Sec. 1361(b)(1)(B); Rev. Rul. 76-23; Let. Rul. 200226031.
5. IRC Sec. 1361(d).
6. Treas. Reg. §§1.1361-1(j)(6)(iii); 1.1361-1 (m)(2)(iii).

8889. What is an electing small business trust (ESBT)?

An ESBT is a trust in which all of the beneficiaries are individuals, estates, or charitable organizations.[1] Each potential current beneficiary of an ESBT is treated as a shareholder for purposes of the 100 shareholder limitation.[2] A potential current beneficiary is generally, with respect to any period, someone who is entitled to, or in the discretion of any person may receive, a distribution of principal or interest of the trust. In addition, a person treated as an owner of a trust under the grantor trust rules is a potential current beneficiary.[3] If there is no potential current beneficiary of an ESBT during any period, the ESBT itself is treated as the S corporation shareholder.[4] Trusts exempt from income tax, QSSTs (Q 8888), charitable remainder annuity trusts (CRATs), and charitable remainder unitrusts (CRUTs) may not be ESBTs. An interest in an ESBT may not be obtained by purchase.[5] If any portion of the basis in the beneficiary's interest is determined under the cost basis rules, the interest is treated as though it was acquired by purchase.[6] An ESBT is taxed at the highest individual income tax rate (39.6 percent in 2013 and beyond).[7]

Planning Point: When the stock is initially transferred to the trust, the taxpayer must file a separate S corporation election. For both the QSST and the ESBT, the election must be filed "within the sixteen day and two month period beginning on the day that the stock is transferred to the trust.[8]

8890. What restrictions apply to an S corporation's ability to issue stock?

An S corporation must be a domestic corporation with only a single class of stock.

A corporation will be treated as having one class of stock if all of its outstanding shares confer identical rights to distribution and liquidation proceeds.[9] Also, it is permissible to have two classes of stock if the only difference between the two classes is the ability to vote.[10] "Bona fide agreements to redeem or purchase stock at the time of death, disability or termination of employment" will be disregarded for purposes of the one-class rule unless a principal purpose of the arrangement is to circumvent the one-class rule and they establish a purchase price that is not substantially above or below the fair market value of the stock.

Agreements that provide for a purchase price or redemption of stock at book value or a price between book value and fair market value will not be considered to establish a price that is substantially above or below fair market value.[11] Agreements triggered by divorce and forfeiture provisions that cause a share of stock to be substantially nonvested are disregarded

1. IRC Sec. 1361(e).
2. IRC Sec. 1361(c)(2)(B)(v).
3. Treas. Reg. §1.1361-1(m)(4).
4. Treas. Reg. §1.1361-1(h)(3)(i)(F).
5. IRC Sec. 1361(e).
6. Treas. Reg. §1.1361-1(m)(1)(iii).
7. IRC Secs. 641(c), 1(e).
8. Treas. Reg. §§1.1361-1(j)(6)(iii); 1361-1 (m)(2)(iii).
9. Treas. Reg. §1.1361-1(l)(1).
10. IRC Sec. 1361(c)(4).
11. Treas. Reg. §1.1361-1(l)(2)(iii). See IRC Secs. 1361, 1362.

in determining whether a corporation's shares confer identical rights to distribution and liquidation proceeds.[1]

Planning Point: The application of the second class of stock rules can sometimes arise in unexpected situations. For example, employment agreements or buy sell agreements may contain provisions which establish a different purchase/sale price for different shareholders or situations. These contractual rights could potentially be construed to violate the prohibition against having a second class of stock. Therefore, care must be given to the consequences which one agreement may have upon another.

8891. What is a qualified subchapter S subsidiary (QSSS)?

An S corporation may own a qualified subchapter S subsidiary (QSSS). A QSSS is a domestic corporation that is not an ineligible corporation (see Q 8882), if 100 percent of its stock is owned by the parent S corporation and the parent S corporation elects to treat it as a QSSS.

A QSSS is generally not treated as a separate corporation and its assets, liabilities, and items of income, deduction, and credit are treated as those of the parent S corporation.[2] If the S corporation or its QSSS is a bank, special rules provide for the recognition of a QSSS as a separate entity for tax purposes.[3] A QSSS will also be treated as a separate corporation for purposes of employment taxes and certain excise taxes.[4] For tax years beginning after 2014, a QSSS will be treated as a separate corporation for purposes of the shared responsibility provisions of the Affordable Care Act.[5]

If a QSSS ceases to meet the above requirements, it will be treated as a new corporation acquiring all assets and liabilities from the parent S corporation in exchange for its stock. If the corporation's status as a QSSS terminates, the corporation is generally prohibited from being a QSSS or an S corporation for five years.[6] In certain cases following a termination of a corporation's QSSS election, the corporation may be allowed to elect QSSS or S corporation status without waiting five years if, immediately following the termination, the corporation is otherwise eligible to make an S corporation election or QSSS election, and the election is effective immediately following the termination of the QSSS election. For example, this rule may apply when an S corporation sells all of its QSSS stock to another S corporation, or an S corporation distributes all of its QSSS stock to its shareholders, and the former QSSS makes an S election.[7]

8892. What is an LLC and how is an LLC formed?

A limited liability company (LLC) is a noncorporate business entity. There are no provisions that provide for LLCs in the IRC, as there are with respect to partnerships and corporations.

1. Treas. Reg. §1.1361-1(l)(2)(iii)(B).
2. IRC Sec. 1361(b)(3).
3. Treas. Reg. §1.1361-4(a)(3).
4. Treas. Reg. §§1.1361-4(a)(7); 1.1361-4(a)(8).
5. Treas. Reg. §1.1361-4(a)(8)(E).
6. IRC Sec. 1361(b)(3).
7. Treas. Reg. §1.1361-5(c).

An LLC is created strictly at the state level with the enactment by the state legislature of an LLC Act or Code.

An LLC, by its nature, provides limited liability for its members, absent personal guarantees. Generally, all members may participate in the management of an LLC. Most state statutes provide that an LLC must have at least two members, although a few states allow one-member LLCs. An LLC is formed by drafting a document called the articles of organization and filing it with the appropriate state agency. This initiating document is similar in scope to a C corporation's articles of incorporation (see Q 8868).

The LLC will also create an operating agreement that generally dictates how the organization will be operated and sets out the rules that govern interaction between its members. The contents of both documents set out the framework for the LLC. The way these documents are drafted becomes especially critical in states that have flexible LLC statutes, since the wording of these documents may determine whether the entity will be classified as a partnership or a corporation for federal tax purposes.

The operating agreement, unlike the articles of organization with respect to a corporation, generally is not filed with a state agency. The operating agreement is similar in scope to corporate by-laws, a partnership agreement or limited partnership agreement in that it sets out the rights, duties and responsibilities of the members. It provides the guidelines by which the LLC will operate on a day to day basis.

The contents of the operating agreement have proven crucial in determining whether an LLC lacks a preponderance of corporate characteristics and may be afforded partnership tax treatment. Revenue Procedure 95-10[1] provides valuable guidance in drafting an operating agreement so as to avoid a preponderance of the corporate characteristics. In states with flexible LLC statutes, the IRS will look to the particular LLC's operating agreement in order to determine the existence or nonexistence of the corporate characteristics.

The operating agreement will typically contain provisions relating to:

- name, purpose and term of the LLC;
- names and addresses of the members;
- rights, powers and duties of the members and their scope of authority;
- scope of authority of the managers and how the managers are to be chosen;
- capital contributions of members;
- approval of transactions;
- allocation of income, profits, losses, expenses, equity and distributions;

1. 1995-3 IRB 20.

- compensation of members and/or managers;
- provisions for holding meetings, voting and other formalities;
- how fiscal matters such as books, records, accounting methods, etc., will be handled;
- how interests in the LLC may or may not be transferred;
- limitation of liability and indemnification; and
- any other provisions applicable to the operation of the organization.

One of the unique characteristics of an LLC is that it is a business entity that may provide for management by all of its members. Unlike an S corporation, an LLC has no restrictions on the number or types of owners and multiple classes of ownership are generally permitted. Management status may be determined by the particular state's LLC act, but most likely will be determined by the LLC's operating agreement.

Planning Point: It is also possible to structure the entity to be "manager managed." Under this approach, certain individuals are designated to manage the entity. This is analogous to having voting and non-voting stock in the corporate context or with a limited partnership (which is managed solely by its general partner).

If the LLC is treated as a partnership, it combines the liability shield of a corporation with the tax advantages of a partnership (see Q 8848).

8893. How is an LLC taxed? How is it determined whether an LLC is taxed as a partnership or corporation?

An LLC may be treated as either a corporation (see Q 8871), partnership (see Q 8848), or sole proprietorship (see Q 8844) for tax purposes. An *eligible entity* (a business entity not subject to automatic classification as a corporation, see below) may elect corporate taxation by filing an entity classification form, otherwise it will be taxed as either a partnership or sole proprietorship depending upon how many owners are involved. Eligible entities can elect how they would like to be classified for tax purposes on IRS Form 8832.

Certain entities, such as corporations organized under a federal or state statute, insurance companies, joint stock companies, and organizations engaged in banking activities, are automatically classified as corporations. An LLC with only one owner will be considered a corporation or a sole proprietorship. In order to be classified as a partnership, the entity must have at least two owners.[1]

If a newly-formed domestic eligible entity with more than one owner does not elect to be taxed as a corporation, it will be classified as a partnership. Likewise, if a newly-formed single-member eligible entity does not elect to be taxed as a corporation, it will be taxed as a sole proprietorship with its profit and loss being reported on Schedule C of the owner's personal

1. Treas. Reg. §301.7701-2.
2. See instructions for form SS-4.

income tax return. Therefore, no separate federal return is required. But even though there is no federal return, some states may still require a separate tax return. Also, under most circumstances, a corporation in existence on January 1, 1997 does not need to file an election in order to retain its corporate status.[1]

If a business entity elects to change its classification, rules are provided for how the change is treated for tax purposes.[2]

Revenue Ruling 95-37[3] provides that a partnership converting to a domestic LLC will be treated as a partnership-to-partnership conversion (and therefore be "tax-free") provided that the LLC is classified as a partnership for federal tax purposes. The partnership will not be considered terminated under IRC Section 708(b) upon its conversion to an LLC so long as the business of the partnership is continued after the conversion. Further, there will be no gain or loss recognized on the transfer of assets and liabilities so long as each partner's percentage of profits, losses and capital remains the same after the conversion. The same is true for a limited partnership converting to an LLC.[4]

An LLC formed by two S corporations was classified as a partnership for federal tax purposes.[5] An S corporation may merge into an LLC without adverse tax consequences provided the LLC would not be treated as an investment company under IRC Section 351 and the S corporation would not realize a net decrease in liabilities exceeding its basis in the transferred assets pursuant to Treasury Regulation Section 1.752-1(f). Neither the S corporation nor the LLC would incur gain or loss upon the contribution of assets by the S corporation to the LLC in exchange for interests therein pursuant to IRC Section 721.[6] A corporation will retain its S election when it transfers all assets to an LLC, which is classified as a corporation for federal tax purposes due to a preponderance of corporate characteristics (see below), provided the transfer qualifies as a reorganization under IRC Section 368(a)(1)(F) and the LLC meets the requirements of an S corporation under IRC Section 1361.[7]

An LLC that was in existence prior to January 1, 1997, may continue under its previous claimed classification if it meets the following requirements: (1) it had a reasonable basis for the classification; (2) the entity and its members recognized the consequences of any change in classification within the sixty months prior to January 1, 1997; and (3) neither the entity nor its members had been notified that the classification was under examination by the IRS.[8]

Prior to January 1, 1997, whether an LLC was treated as a corporation or partnership for federal income tax purposes depended on the existence or nonexistence of a preponderance of six corporate characteristics: (1) associates; (2) an objective to carry on a business and divide

1. Treas. Reg. §301.7701-3.
2. Treas. Reg. §301.7701-3(g).
3. 1995-1 CB 130.
4. Let. Rul. 9607006.
5. Let. Rul. 9529015.
6. Let. Rul. 9543017.
7. Let. Rul. 9636007.
8. Treas. Reg. §301.7701-3(h)(2).

the gains from it; (3) limited liability; (4) free transferability of interests; (5) continuity of life; and (6) centralized management.[1]

Characteristics (1) and (2) above are common to both corporations and partnerships and were generally discounted when determining whether an organization was treated as a corporation or partnership.[2] These former regulations provided an example of a business entity that possessed the characteristics of numbers (1), (2), (4) and (6) above, noting that since numbers (1) and (2) were common to both corporations and partnerships, these did not receive any significant consideration. The business entity did not possess characteristics (3) and (5) above and, accordingly, was labeled a partnership.[3]

8894. What is a professional corporation (PC)? Is there any difference between the tax treatment of C corporations and PCs?

Organizations of physicians, lawyers, and other professional people organized under state professional corporation or association acts are generally treated as corporations for tax purposes.[4] A key distinguishing fact of the PC is that the entity is taxed at a flat rate of 35 percent (rather than a graduated rate schedule that otherwise applies to corporations) if it is characterized as a personal service corporation by the IRS (as most are). However, to be treated as a corporation, a professional organization must be both organized and *operated* as a corporation.[5] Although professional corporations are generally treated as corporations for tax purposes, they are not generally taxed in the same manner as regular C corporations (Q 8871). Note that if a professional corporation has elected S corporation status, the shareholders will be treated as S corporation shareholders (see Q 8882).

Although a professional corporation is recognized as a taxable entity separate and apart from the professional individual or individuals who form it, the IRS may under some circumstances reallocate income, deductions, credits, exclusions, or other allowances between the corporation and its owners in order to prevent evasion or avoidance of tax or to properly reflect the income of the parties.

Under IRC Section 482, such reallocation may be made only where the individual owner operates a second business distinct from the business of the professional corporation. Reallocation may not be made where the individual works exclusively for the professional corporation.[6]

8895. What are the requirements for establishing a professional corporation (PC)?

Professional corporations are governed by state law, so the requirements will vary from state to state. In many states, each member of the PC must be licensed in the same profession

1. Treas. Reg. §301.7701-2(a)(1), as in effect prior to January 1, 1997.
2. Treas. Reg. §301.7701-2(a)(2), as in effect prior to January 1, 1997.
3. Treas. Reg. §301.7701-2(a)(3), as in effect prior to January 1, 1997.
4. Rev. Rul. 77-31, 1977-1 CB 409.
5. *Roubik v. Comm.*, 53 TC 365 (1969).
6. *Foglesong v. Comm.*, 82-2 USTC ¶9650 (7th Cir. 1982).

(i.e., law or medicine) and many states require the PC to submit proof of licensing and obtain state approval upon formation. Some states also require that the PC obtain approval from their state licensing body at the time of formation.

The letters "PC" must generally follow the name of the professional corporation. Depending upon the state and the industry, requirements may also apply to the actual name of the PC (for example, while a group of lawyers will often be required to use some form of "professional corporation" after the corporate name, a group of doctors may be required to use "medical corporation").

Unlike traditional corporations, some (or all) of the officers and directors of a professional corporation often must be licensed to perform the activity that the PC is engaged in. States may specify the number of directors that must be on the PC's board (for example, in California, three directors are required unless the PC has fewer than three shareholders).

To form the PC, articles of incorporation must generally be filed in the same manner as required of a traditional corporation. In fact, most states require that a professional corporation take the same formation steps as a traditional corporation. In Delaware, for example, the PC is required to select an official address and registered agent for the PC, choose a board of directors and officers, file a certificate of incorporation with the state, obtain a federal employer identification number and issue stock certificates to initial shareholders. The board of directors must meet to adopt official bylaws, and shareholder and director meetings must be held annually. For more information on the formation requirements that apply to C corporations, see Q 8868.

8896. What are some of the advantages and disadvantages of the professional corporation (PC) structure?

In certain states, groups of professionals performing services in specified fields (such as medicine, accounting and law) are not permitted to establish a traditional corporation that would eliminate the personal liability of the individual professionals entirely. These groups may wish to form a professional corporation in order to obtain some of the benefits of a corporation, such as personal protection against corporate debts, although each individual can still be held liable for his or her own malpractice. While the PC structure does not allow the individual to escape liability for his or her own professional malpractice, it does protect each individual from liability incurred by other members of the group.

Further, the PC structure allows the group to obtain the benefit of perpetual corporate existence, so that the business will continue if one or more members leaves the PC (in the partnership context, there is always the possibility that the partnership may need to be dissolved if one or more partners leaves or dies).

Like any other corporation, double taxation is a primary disadvantage of the PC structure. The PC itself is subject to tax, and the individual owners are subject to tax when the PC profits are distributed.

8897. What is a B corporation?

A B corporation is a relatively new type of corporation that has gained popularity in recent years. A "B" corporation, also known as a "benefit corporation," is a corporation that is formed with the express purpose of fulfilling some type of socially responsible mission that is intended to create a general public benefit. Not all states have passed legislation that makes the benefit corporation a separate legal entity that taxpayers can consider in their choice of entity analysis. Maryland, California, Hawaii, New Jersey, New York, Vermont and Virginia are among those that have passed legislation.[1]

A B corporation is not a unique type of entity—rather; it is a corporation where the charter provides that it will be operated as a benefit corporation. The charter will typically provide the specific socially responsible purpose that the B corporation exists to fulfill. Essentially, the B corporation's officers and directors will be liable not only for operating the corporation in order to achieve a profit, but also to fulfill the specified social purpose.

Although not required at formation, since a B corporation is essentially formed as a C corporation, several nonprofit groups exist to provide certification, as well as guidance and assistance in determining the public benefit structure of a B corporation. One of these, a nonprofit group called "B Labs" provides an assessment test that the corporation takes in order to determine its social and environmental impact and goals.[2] Once the corporation "passes" this test, as long as it meets all of the legal requirements applicable to validly formed corporations (Q 8868) and signs a declaration that it will operate as a B corporation, it becomes certified.

Some state statutes provide for a cause of action by the B corporation, directly or through its shareholders, against a B corporation's officers and directors for failure to pursue the public benefit purpose that is specified in its charter.[3] Further, state statutes require the B corporation to describe its activities relating to the specified public benefit in its annual report to shareholders. As such, a B corporation is essentially a type of C corporation that is subject to certain additional requirements, which vary by state, related to the performance of some public good.

8898. How is a B corporation taxed?

The IRS has yet to provide guidance as to the tax treatment of B corporations. As such, a B corporation is subject to the same tax rules that govern C corporations (see Q 8867 to Q 8881), until the IRS releases guidance to the contrary.

8899. How might the losses incurred during operation of a business impact choice of entity decisions?

For many business owners, the opportunity to limit personal liability may be the most attractive feature of the corporate form. This can be an advantage and even a necessity for a business

1. A B corporation group provides a state-by-state analysis of the legislative status of B corporations at www.benefitcorp.net/state-by-state-legislative-status. Delaware passed its legislation pertaining to B corporations as recently as July 17, 2013, so the rules pertaining to B corporations are still in the very early developmental phases.
2. See "Performance Requirements," available at http://www.bcorporation.net/become-a-b-corp/how-to-become-a-b-corp/performance-requirements (last accessed June 22, 2017).
3. See, for example, Article 1 of New Jersey legislation authorizing B corporations, available at http://www.njleg.state.nj.us/2010/Bills/A4000/3595_I1.PDF (last accessed June 22, 2017).

that faces substantial liability for the actions of its agents, the hazardous nature of its business, or the liability exposure of its products. Also, any venture has an inherent risk of loss, especially in the early years. Shareholders in a corporation (as well as members of a limited liability company and limited partners in a limited partnership) are not liable for the corporation's actions beyond the amount of their capital contribution to the corporation. However, there are still important considerations that must be noted, because limited liability is not absolute.

First, the corporation and its shareholders must follow strict state law requirements relating to shareholder meetings, election of a board of directors, directors' meetings, and other matters of internal governance required by the corporation's articles of incorporation and the state of incorporation's laws. These are not mere formalities—a corporation which fails to follow these rules may lose its status as a corporation and limited liability in a process known as "piercing the corporate veil." However, many states have close corporation statutes relaxing these rules and giving shareholders in a closely held corporation greater freedom to determine their own internal governance.

Second, a shareholder's limited liability may be illusory for bank financing, because most lending institutions demand that stockholders personally guarantee close corporation indebtedness.

Finally, potential incorporators who wish to do business under an umbrella of limited liability can find other ways to do so without incorporating. One way to do so may be to set up a limited partnership with an existing corporation, S corporation or LLC as the general partner.

8900. What considerations regarding transferability of interests in an entity should be taken into account when choosing the business entity form?

Free transferability of interests is a factor that must be considered when a business owner is determining which business entity structure to choose. Shares in a corporation may be simpler to transfer than an interest in a partnership or a proprietorship. This can be attractive if, for example, an older shareholder wishes to dispose of his interest to finance his retirement, but younger members want to keep operating the business (see Q 8903 to Q 8934, which address issues in business succession planning). A corporation can also be recapitalized to freeze the value of an estate and pass a family business to a younger generation. As is the case with limited liability, free transferability of interests, particularly in a closely held corporation, is not absolute.

Planning Point: Note that with an LLC, you can have free transferability of interests and still be treated as a partnership. The LLC interests can also be documented through share certificates, as with a corporation.

First, there may be a limited market for minority interests in a closely-held or family business, even one that is organized as a corporation. Prospective investors may simply refuse to risk being frozen out of management decisions and profits, and may be reluctant to upset the balance of personalities and interests already existing in any company. Second, it may be extremely difficult to value the shares in the business. Third, a sale to an inappropriate shareholder may jeopardize a business' status as an S corporation. The solution to many of these problems is to restrict transferability of shares to those within a family, those approved by all other shareholders, or those who would not jeopardize the business' S corporation election. These restrictions, of course, destroy the same free transferability of interests that some incorporators may find attractive.

Finally, increased prestige and image may be a factor to consider. A new corporation may find it easier to attract bank financing and venture capital than a partnership or proprietorship, even if the shareholders must personally guarantee the debt. This advantage comes, however, at the higher price of establishing a corporation than for a partnership or proprietorship. State filing fees and attorney and accountant's fees all add to the cost of starting the venture. However, a corporation may amortize its organizational expenses over 60 months from the month in which the corporation begins business.[1]

8901. Can the treatment of employment benefits in an entity structure impact choice of entity?

Yes. While S corporations and partnerships are able to offer many of the same employment type benefits, such as qualified pension and profit-sharing plans and accident and health insurance, the tax treatment differs in some cases. Many of the IRC provisions that create tax preferences for employment benefits do so only for plans that provide benefits for *employees*. Partners in a partnership are generally subject to different rules. Rather than being treated as employees, 2 percent shareholders in an S corporation are treated as partners for certain employment benefit purposes.[2]

For example, premiums paid for accident and health insurance paid on behalf of 2 percent shareholders and partners are deductible by the entity, but are includable in the recipient's gross income.[3] This is because in order for premiums paid by the employer on behalf of the recipient to be excludable from that recipient's income, he or she must be considered an employee. For purposes of determining the excludability of employer-provided accident and health benefits, self-employed individuals and certain shareholders owning more than 2 percent of the stock of an S corporation are not treated as employees.[4]

Despite this, sole proprietors, partners, and 2 percent shareholder-employees of an S corporation may generally deduct up to 100 percent of their health insurance premiums on their individual returns.[5]

See Q 8733 to Q 8815 for a discussion of the treatment of various health-related benefits provided in an employment context. Q 8816 to Q 8842 discusses the treatment of various employment "fringe" benefits.

1. IRC Sec. 248.
2. IRC Sec. 1372.
3. Rev. Rul. 91-26, 1991-1 CB 184.
4. IRC Sec. 105(g); Treas. Reg. §1.105-5(b).
5. IRC Sec. 162(l).

8902. When can estate planning considerations impact a choice of entity decision?

Both C corporations and S corporations may take advantage of opportunities to provide liquidity and reduce estate taxes at a shareholder's death. These techniques include:

Section 303 stock redemptions. IRC Section 303, designed to provide liquidity and prevent the forced sale of businesses to pay income and estate taxes, provides that income from certain partial redemptions of stock to pay death taxes will be treated as a sale of stock rather than a dividend. Where stock included in the adjusted gross estate of a shareholder (without regard to family attribution-of-ownership rules) equals a certain percentage of the gross estate, the corporation can redeem from the estate a quantity of stock equal in value to the total of the deceased's federal estate tax, state death taxes, and funeral and administrative taxes.

Gifts of stock. Because corporate ownership is easily divisible, shareholders can give close corporation stock to family members, charities, etc. These gifts can shift income to lower-bracket family members, remove future appreciation from the shareholder's future estate, and even provide an income tax deduction in the case of charitable gifts. S corporation shareholders must take care to insure that such gifts do not jeopardize S corporation eligibility. Unlike an S corporation, there are no restrictions on the ability of a trust to own interests in an LLC.

Planning Point: When making gifts of stock, it is important to review any shareholders agreements which may exist in order to make sure the stock is transferable in the desired manner. It may be necessary to obtain certain consents from the corporation or other shareholders in order to complete the transfer.

Planning Point: Since, however, it is permissible for an S corporation to issue non-voting stock, estate planning opportunities exist whereby the non-voting stock can be transferred without relinquishing control. Also, since the transferred stock in this context is non-voting, it is entitled to an adjustment to reflect the lower value associated with this type of stock.

Estate freeze techniques. Some shareholders in closely-held corporations may reduce their eventual taxable estate by recapitalizing the corporation to "freeze" the value of stock included in their estates and pass future appreciation on to family members. Interests transferred in this fashion will be treated as gifts and valued according to special valuation rules (see Q 8946).

See Q 8903 to Q 8934 for a discussion of business succession techniques, including buy-sell agreements and redemptions that may be useful in the small business context.

Planning Point: If, however, an S corporation is going to pass through an estate, consideration should be given as to whether the stock is going to pass into a trust. If so, the trust must qualify as either a QSST or ESBT.

PART XIV: BUSINESS SUCCESSION PLANNING

8903. What is a buy-sell agreement?

Buy-sell agreements are often used in business succession planning where the business is owned by a relatively small group of owners who would otherwise have a limited market in which to sell their business interests (most commonly represented by their stock in the enterprise). A buy-sell agreement can provide the remaining shareholders or co-owners with the option of purchasing the business interests of a deceased or withdrawing co-owner before the business interest is sold to a third party. Business entities such as closely held corporations (Q 8867), LLCs (Q 8892), and partnerships (Q 8845) frequently rely upon buy-sell agreements when creating future business succession plans. A buy-sell agreement is essentially a contract to buy and sell a departing business owner's interests in a business at some point in the future, usually upon the occurrence of one or more specified events. The most common of the events that can trigger the repurchase are the stockholder's death or, if also an employee, retirement or the voluntary or involuntary termination of employment.[1]

A buy-sell agreement is typically structured as either a cross-purchase agreement or a redemption agreement. A cross-purchase agreement is an agreement among co-owners to purchase each other's business interests upon the death, or other withdrawal from the business, of one or more owners. These agreements typically specify a predetermined purchase price and, in some cases, are funded by life insurance purchased to insure the lives of the various business owners.

The typical buy-sell agreement also specifies the method to be used to determine the repurchase price of the shares, selecting from such options as an agreed price with periodic revisions, a formula price based on book value or capitalization of earnings, or third party appraisal or arbitration.

A redemption agreement allows the business entity to purchase the interest of a deceased or withdrawing business owner upon the occurrence of previously agreed upon "triggering events." See Q 8910 for a discussion of the different considerations that apply depending upon whether the agreement is structured as a cross-purchase or redemption agreement.

It is also possible to structure a buy-sell agreement so that it combines features of the cross-purchase agreement and redemption agreement.[2] In addition, the buy-sell agreement can involve a contract to sell to a third party or another entity.

See Q 8904 for a discussion of the importance of buy-sell agreements in business succession planning. Q 8905 outlines the primary methods for funding a buy-sell agreement and Q 8906 outlines the use of life insurance in funding the agreement. Q 8910 to Q 8912 provide an in-depth analysis of the differences between the redemption and the cross-purchase forms of agreements.

---

1. *Stephenson v. Drever*, 16 Cal. 4th 1167 (1997).
2. See *Jacobs v. Comm.*, TC Memo 1981-81, Rev. Rul. 69-608, 1969-2 CB 42.

8904. Why are buy-sell agreements often used in business succession planning?

Use of a buy-sell agreement in the business succession planning context can mean the difference between the orderly withdrawal of a partner, whether by death or otherwise, and possible loss of control over a business by the remaining co-owners.[1] In general, business succession planning is intended to ensure that the following goals are met:

(1) Preserving a deceased co-owner's wealth and providing liquidity for the estate.

(2) Providing the remaining owners with the security of knowing they will maintain control of the business without unwanted third-party intervention.

(3) Ensuring business continuity, if so desired by the remaining business owners.

(4) Fixing the value[2] of the business interest for estate tax purposes to avoid potential IRS intervention.

The courts have consistently considered the foregoing goals bona fide business reasons for entering into buy-sell agreements, as have the goals of maintaining exclusive family control over a business, assuring continuity of company management policies, and retaining key employees. However, the courts have also noted that "legitimate business purposes" are often 'inextricably mixed' with testamentary objectives where the parties to a restrictive stock agreement are all members of the same immediate families, and, as a result, have required taxpayers to satisfy both business purpose and nontestamentary disposition tests for purposes of valuing closely held stock for estate tax purposes.[3]

Interests in closely held corporations, LLCs, partnerships and sole proprietorships can have very limited markets for sale. This is particularly problematic when a deceased co-owner either has no heirs to inherit the deceased owner's interest or has heirs who are poorly equipped or unwilling to take over the business. If the deceased business owner passes the interests to children who are not interested in continuing the business, they may be forced to sell their inherited interests at a discounted price to a third party. Executing a buy-sell agreement ensures that the business owner controls the disposition of business interests by allowing that owner to choose the buyer in advance. This type of succession planning also protects the value of the business as a whole and ensures that this value will pass to the owner's estate without the need for protracted post-death negotiation.

Use of a buy-sell agreement can also ensure that the remaining business owners can continue the business without interference from a deceased owner's heirs or the need for a third party investor following that owner's death or early withdrawal from the business. The existence of the agreement will prevent a small business owner from selling the owner's interests to outside investors who may not share the business vision of the remaining co-owners.

1. See Treas. Reg. §20.2031-2(h); *True v. Comm.*, TC Memo 2001-167.
2. See IRC Sec. 2031 and Treas. Reg. §20.2031-2(h).
3. *Lauder II*, TC Memo 1992-736, *True v. Comm.*, TC Memo 2001-67.

Another individual may hold an option or contract to buy securities owned by a decedent at the time of death. The effect, if any, that is given to the option or contract price in determining the value of the securities for estate tax purposes depends upon the circumstances of the particular case, with little weight being accorded to a price contained in an option or contract under which the decedent is free to dispose of the underlying securities at any price during the decedent's lifetime. For example, this is the effect of a shareholder's agreement to buy whatever shares of stock the decedent may own at the time of death.[1]

8905. How is a buy-sell agreement funded?

A buy-sell agreement can be funded through the use of the prospective buyer's own funds, accumulated earnings, debt instruments or insurance (either life or disability).

While self-funding on the part of the buyer is possible, many selling business owners may prefer the certainty that is provided through other funding methods. Self-funding presents the possibility that the buyer may be unable to obtain the funds upon the selling owner's death or withdrawal.

As a result, many buy-sell agreements are funded with insurance. The type of insurance that is required will depend upon the triggering events specified in the buy-sell agreement itself (see Q 8909). If a right to purchase under the agreement is triggered by the seller's death, the buyer or business may fund the agreement by purchasing life insurance that insures the life of the selling business owner (see Q 8906). Death, however, is not the only type of event that may trigger a buy-sell agreement. If the triggering event is the selling owner's disability or retirement from the business, funding may be provided more effectively through a disability insurance policy or a permanent life insurance policy that provides the potential for tax-free loans during the life of the insured. It is also common to treat an "involuntary transfer" as a triggering event. Essentially, this will become applicable if a creditor of an owner attempts to seize an interest in the business in pursuit of the collection of a debt. This can occur if an actual debt is owed to a third party or if one of the owners is party to a divorce (or other) proceeding and the interest in the business is being transferred to a spouse who is not an owner. In the event that an involuntary transfer is a triggering event, insurance will not likely be available to fund the purchase.

If the parties have entered into a cross-purchase agreement, insurance funding is accomplished by the business owners purchasing insurance on the lives of each participating co-owner.

The entity itself may also set aside accumulated earnings to fund a buy-sell agreement. In a closely held corporation, however, it might be difficult to set aside adequate funds when the operation of the business could benefit from the use of these funds. Further, in case of a C corporation, accumulated earnings above $250,000 can be subject to the accumulated earnings 15 percent penalty tax (see Q 8876).[2] (The limit is $150,000 in the case of a business whose principal function is performing services in the fields of accounting, actuarial science, architecture, consulting, engineering, health, law, and the performing arts.)[3] While accumulation of

1. Treas. Reg. §20.2031-2(h).
2. IRC Sec. 535(c)(1, *United States v. Donruss Co.*, 393 U.S. 297 (1969).
3. IRC Sec. 535(c)(2).

earnings and profits to meet the reasonable needs of the corporation is permissible, the parties must carefully evaluate the strategy to avoid the penalty tax, which may prove time consuming.[1]

If insurance funding or accumulation of earnings has not been accomplished in advance, and the buying owners have insufficient cash on hand to fund the buy-sell agreement upon occurrence of a triggering event, a debt instrument can be used. The buying owners may be able to negotiate a series of payments to the selling owner or the estate. In choosing this option, the owners must consider whether the sale will be taxed under the installment sale rules[2] and the possible taxation (or deductibility) of the interest payments (see Q 8918 for a discussion of the installment sale rules).[3]

Planning Point: It is also important to consider the terms of the promissory notes. Examples include how long the term will extend, if there will be security for the note (i.e. a pledge of the stock being purchased) and if the note is due upon the sale of the business by the remaining owners. It is often good practice to attach a sample of a proposed note to be used for the payout.

8906. What types of insurance can be used to fund a buy-sell agreement?

Many business owners who structure a buy-sell agreement prefer to use insurance to fund the agreement. The insurance provides certainty that the purchase price will be funded, as it can be structured to pay out upon the occurrence of the triggering event(s), usually the death, retirement or permanent disability of the seller. A buy-sell agreement funded through insurance can raise several tax and nontax issues, however.

Various types of insurance can be used to fund a buy-sell agreement, including the following:

(1) *Term life insurance*. Term life insurance, which provides life insurance coverage for a set amount of time, is a possible funding mechanism, but because the insured may outlive the pre-set term of the policy, it may not present the best option for younger business owners. If the insured outlives the term, the policy may expire and the investment may be lost.

(2) *Cash value life insurance*. Various types of permanent life insurance that allow for a build-up of cash value within the policy may be used to fund a buy-sell agreement, and may be especially useful where the triggering event is *not* the departing business owner's death. This type of insurance provides for a build-up of cash value over time and permits the policy owner to withdraw a portion of the cash value tax-free. As a result, if the buy-sell agreement is triggered by an event such as the departing owner's retirement or disagreement over S corporation dividend distributions, for example, the remaining owners can still access the cash value to fund the purchase.

(3) *Disability insurance*. Disability insurance can be used to fund a buy-sell agreement where the triggering event is the disability of the departing business owner and, as

1. IRC Sec. 537(a)(2).
2. See IRC Sec. 453, *American Taxpayer Relief Act of 2012*, Pub. L. No. 112-240 (which increased the maximum tax rate for long-term capital gains from 15 to 20 percent).
3. IRC Sec. 163(a).

provided in most disability policies, the owner becomes totally disabled while he is engaged in active full-time work and his ownership interest is purchased pursuant to the agreement.[1]

Q 8709 through Q 8731 provide an in-depth discussion of the tax treatment of the use of life insurance in a business context. Q 8713 discusses the tax treatment of the policy from the standpoint of the insured-employee, and Q 8711 and Q 8712 outline the deductibility of premiums paid by the employer-business entity.

See Q 8909 for a discussion of some of the various triggers that may be used in the context of a buy-sell agreement.

8907. Can the use of life insurance to fund a cross-purchase buy-sell agreement cause the premiums to be treated as constructive dividends to shareholders in a closely-held C corporation? How can this result be avoided?

Unless the transaction is properly structured, funding a cross-purchase agreement with life insurance can result in adverse tax consequences if the corporation pays the policy premiums. In the case of a cross-purchase buy-sell agreement between individual shareholders, a shareholder will often purchase life insurance on the lives of the other shareholders in order to fund the agreement (see Q 8906). In many cases, however, the premiums are paid out of corporate resources.

In the C corporation context, these premium payments may be treated as distributions with respect to stock in the corporation for tax purposes. As a result, the shareholders will be taxed on the premiums paid as though the premiums were dividends that were constructively received by those shareholders.[2]

To avoid this result, as long as the corporation itself has no ownership rights or beneficial interest in the policy, it is possible that the corporation could instead pay the policy premium to the policy owner in the form of a bonus. In this case, the shareholders can avoid the constructive dividend tax issue and the corporation will be able to deduct the cost of the premiums paid so long as the payments can be characterized as "reasonable compensation."[3] Reasonable compensation is "such amount as would ordinarily be paid for like services by like enterprises under like circumstances. The circumstances to be taken into consideration are those existing at the date when the contract for services was made, rather than those existing at the date when the contract is questioned"[4] A salary that exceeds what is customarily paid for such services is considered unreasonable or excessive.

If the total amount paid to and on behalf of a stockholder-employee is an unreasonable return for his or her services, the IRS may treat the premium payments as a distribution of

1. See *Oak Rd. Family Dentistry, P.C. v. Provident Life & Accident Ins. Co.*, 370 F. Supp. 2d 1317(2005).
2. See, for example, *Johnson v. Comm.*, 74 TC 1316 (1980).
3. IRC Sec. 162(a), Treas. Reg. §1.162-7.
4. Treas. Reg. §1.162-7(b)(3).

profits or dividends rather than as compensation. This also may be the result where there is no evidence, such as board of directors' meeting minutes, to show that premium payments were intended as compensation.[1]

The deduction will be disallowed where surrounding circumstances affirmatively show that premiums were not paid as compensation. In *Atlas Heating &Ventilating Co. v. Comm.*,[2] for example, evidence showed that premiums actually were paid to fund a stock purchase agreement between individual stockholders. Consequently, they were not compensation, but dividends. The policies were owned by the stockholder-employees and proceeds were payable to their personal beneficiaries. The insured individuals had agreed that, on each of their deaths, an amount of stock equal to the proceeds received by the deceased insured's beneficiaries would be turned in to the corporation and then distributed pro rata to the surviving stockholders.

See Q 8903 to Q 8910 for a discussion of buy-sell agreements in the context of C corporations generally.

8908. What potential tax consequences arise if the corporation owns the life insurance policy on a majority shareholder's life used to fund a buy-sell agreement, but the named beneficiary is a party other than the corporation?

Potential adverse estate tax consequences may result if a life insurance policy used to fund a buy-sell agreement is actually owned by the corporation itself, but the policy beneficiary is someone other than the corporation. If, at the time of death, the insured owns more than 50 percent of the corporation's voting stock, the entire value of the death benefit paid out under the policy may be included in the insured's estate.[3] This is because, as a majority shareholder in the corporation that owns the actual policy, the insured will be deemed to have retained incidents of ownership in the policy that are sufficient to warrant inclusion of the death benefit in his or her estate.

These adverse tax consequences only exist if three circumstances are present: (1) the corporation is the named owner of the policy, (2) the insured owns more than a 50 percent interest at death and (3) the policy beneficiary is *not* the corporation.

Any proceeds payable to a third party for a valid business purpose (for example, satisfaction of the corporation's business debt), so that the corporation's net worth is increased by the amount of the proceeds, will be deemed to be payable to the corporation and so will not be attributed to the decedent.

In order to avoid the inclusion of the death benefit in the insured's estate, the corporation could name itself as policy beneficiary or could take steps to ensure that the insured owns less than 50 percent of the corporation's voting stock upon his or her death.

1. See, for example, *Boecking v. Comm.*, TC Memo 1993-497; *Est. of Worster v. Comm.*, TC Memo 1984-123; *Champion Trophy Mfg. Corp. v. Comm.*, TC Memo 1972-250.
2. 18 BTA 389 (1929).
3. Treas. Reg. §20.2042-1(c)(6).

8909. When is a buy-sell agreement triggered? What are the differences between mandatory and optional buyout triggers?

A buy-sell agreement is triggered upon the occurrence of certain specified "triggering events." The parties to the agreement may build one or more triggering events into their particular buy-sell agreement, depending upon the anticipated succession issues.[1] Typical triggering events include the death, loss of required professional license, retirement or disability of an owner or shareholder, or an involuntary transfer.

If the buy-sell agreement is triggered by an owner's disability, the owners should include a definition of "disability" in the agreement to minimize disagreement between the buying and selling owners. Further, if using disability insurance to fund the agreement, the policy itself should contain a corresponding definition of disability that all parties understand.

Planning Point: This can also be done by reference. For example, the agreement could provide that the definition of disability will be as set forth within certain specified disability insurance policies.

This minimizes the risk that the buy-sell agreement will be triggered in the minds of the parties, but the insurance will not cover the disability that has actually occurred. Both the Uniform Probate Code and the Social Security Administration provide definitions of "disability" that may provide useful information to small business owners negotiating contract provisions.[2]

Planning Point: While it may seem convenient to incorporate the definition of "disability" in a buy-sell agreement by reference to a frequently referred to government description, this approach is not always wise. For example, Section 223(d) of the Social Security Act defines disability as "inability to engage in any substantial gainful activity by reason of any medically determinable physical or mental impairment which has lasted or can be expected to last for a continuous period of not less than twelve months." [3] While this definition may seem unequivocal, it has been the subject of litigation in a number of cases. In one case, the Plaintiff unsuccessfully argued that the position of the word "which" in the definition supported his claim that only the impairment is required to extend over the one-year period, and that this requirement does not apply to the term, "inability to engage in any substantial gainful activity."[4] Incorporation by reference is no substitute for precise draftmanship.

Buy-sell agreements are perhaps most frequently triggered by the death or retirement of a business owner in the small business context (see Q 8904 for a discussion of the motivations behind using a buy-sell agreement to plan for these triggering events).

A triggering event can be either mandatory or optional. After the triggering events have been determined, the parties must determine whether they wish to provide that occurrence of the event makes purchase mandatory, or merely creates a right or an option to purchase under the buy-sell agreement. Like any other contract, the parties have freedom to negotiate the

1. E.g., *Maxx Private Invs., LLC v. Drew/Core Dev., LLC*, 24 Mass. L. Rep. 456, 2008 Mass. Super. LEXIS 298 (2008).
2. See Uniform Probate Code §5-103(f), Social Security Law 42 USCA §416(i)(1).
3. 42 U.S.C. Section 423(d).
4. *Alexander v. Richardson*, 451 F. 2d 1185 (10th Circuit 1971).

contract terms in a buy-sell agreement in order to reflect the specific needs of the business. There are three common rights that are negotiated in the context of buy-sell agreements, including (1) mandatory purchase requirements, (2) "call"-type options and (3) "put"-type options.

As the name suggests, if the parties provide for a mandatory purchase, all parties to the agreement will be obligated to complete the sale once the triggering event has occurred.[1]

The agreement can also provide for a call-type option, under which the buyer is given the *option* to purchase upon the occurrence of the triggering event. In this case, if the buyer exercises the option, the selling owner is required to sell the interests.

Conversely, the agreement can provide for a "put" type option, under which the *seller* is given the option to sell upon the occurrence of a triggering event, and the buyer will then be required to purchase the interests.

In any of these three situations, the triggering event will be crucial to determining whether the provisions of the buy-sell agreement are activated.[2] The parties must consider the fact that, as in any other option contract, if the rights are structured similarly to put or call options, the party giving the option will be free to exercise the option or *not to* exercise the option upon occurrence of the triggering event. On the other hand, the party who gave the option is *bound* to perform once the option is exercised within the terms of the agreement.[3]

8910. What is the "redemption" type buy-sell agreement? How is this different from a cross-purchase buy-sell agreement?

A "redemption" type agreement is structured so that it is the business entity (usually a corporation), rather than the individual owners, that agrees to purchase the business interests of an owner under a buy-sell agreement.[4] A cross-purchase agreement is an agreement among owners to purchase the business interests of another co-owner.[5]

In many respects, structuring a redemption-style buy-sell agreement may be much simpler because there is only one buyer, the corporation or business entity. Conversely, in a cross-purchase agreement, multiple buyers may be involved, depending on the number of co-owners involved in the business. Funding a cross-purchase agreement can also prove more complicated than in a redemption context, especially if the agreement is funded by insurance policies owned by multiple shareholders, rather than the entity itself.

Choosing between a redemption or cross-purchase style agreement may trigger many non-tax issues. For example, state laws may restrict a corporation's redemption of its own stock[6] in cases where the redemption can risk the corporation's insolvency or impair its capital.[7]

1. *True v. Comm.*, TC Memo 2001-167, 2001 TCM LEXIS 199 (2001).
2. E.g., *Thomas by & Through Schmidt v. Thomas*, 532 N.W.2d 676(1995).
3. *Fries v. Fries*, 470 N.W.2d 232 (1991), *Wessels v. Whetstone*, 338 N.W.2d 830 (1983).
4. E.g., *Glacier State Electric Supply Co. v. Comm.*, 80 TC 1047 (1983), IRC Sec. 302.
5. E.g., *Rodeo Family Enters., LLC v Matte*, 2011 N.Y. Misc. LEXIS 2004 (2011).
6. See Revised Model Business Corp. Act. §6.40 (1984); Del. Code Ann. tit. 8, §160 (1974).
7. See, e.g., Fla. Stat. Ch. 607.06401, N.C. Gen. Stat. §55-6-40, 11 Vt. Stat. Ann. 11A, §6.40.

Conversely, there are no similar restrictions upon the sale of one stockholder's shares to another stockholder under a cross-purchase agreement.

Sale of stock between the shareholders of a corporation under a cross-purchase agreement creates the same tax consequences as would the sale of the securities in any other context (see Q 8874 and Q 8736).

However, if the corporation participates in the purchase, as it does in a redemption agreement, the purchase may be treated as a dividend distribution.[1] See Q 8911 for a discussion of IRC Section 302 redemptions and Q 8912 for a discussion of IRC Section 303 redemptions.

As a general rule, any payment by a corporation other than an S corporation to a shareholder will be treated as a dividend rather than a capital transaction even if the payment is made to redeem stock.[2]

In any case where an amount received in redemption of stock is treated as a dividend distribution, the basis of the remaining stock is adjusted with respect to the stock redeemed. For example, A, an individual, buys all of the stock of Corporation X for $100,000. Thereafter, the corporation redeems half of the stock for $150,000, and it is determined that this amount constitutes a dividend. The remaining stock of Corporation X held by A has a basis of $100,000.[3]

In the context of closely held corporations, characterization as a stock redemption is important for at least two additional reasons. First, if a redemption is treated as a sale or exchange, the basis of the shares retained by the seller, if any, is unaffected by the transaction. If redemption is treated as a dividend, the basis of the shares redeemed is added to the basis of the shares retained.[4]

Second, if redemption is treated as a sale or exchange, the part of the distribution properly chargeable to earnings and profits is an amount not in excess of the ratable share of earnings and profits of the corporation attributable to the redeemed stock.[5] If a redemption is treated as a dividend, earnings and profits of the corporation are reduced by the amount of money or other property distributed by the corporation.[6]

8911. What is an IRC Section 302 stock redemption?

One of the exceptions to dividend treatment (discussed in Q 8910) is contained in IRC Section 302(b)(3). IRC Section 302(b)(3) provides that if a corporation redeems all of a shareholder's remaining shares so that a shareholder's interest in the corporation is terminated, the amount paid by the corporation will be treated as a payment in exchange for the stock, not as

1. See IRC Sec. 304(a)(1).
2. IRC Sec. 301(a), Rev. Rul. 55-515, 1955-2 CB 222.
3. Treas Reg. §1.302-2(c) Example 1.
4. Treas. Reg. §1.302-2(c).
5. IRC Sec. 312(n)(7).
6. IRC Secs. 312(a), 316(a).

a dividend. In other words, the redemption will be treated as a capital transaction (see Q 8565 to Q 8581).[1]

There will be no taxable dividend, then, if a corporation redeems all of its stock owned by an estate. In determining what stock is owned by an estate, the constructive ownership or attribution-of-ownership rules contained in IRC Section 318 must be applied.

Consequently, to achieve non-dividend treatment under IRC Section 302(b)(3), a corporation must redeem not only all of its shares actually owned by an estate, but also all of its shares constructively owned by the estate.

One of these constructive ownership rules provides that shares owned by a beneficiary of an estate are considered owned by the estate. For example, assume that a decedent owned 250 shares of Corporation X's stock, so that the decedent's estate now actually owns 250 shares. Assume further that a beneficiary of the decedent's estate owns fifty shares. Because the estate constructively owns the beneficiary's fifty shares, the estate is deemed to own a total of 300 shares. Redemption of the 250 shares actually owned, therefore, will not affect a redemption of all the stock owned by the estate.

Further, stock owned by a close family member of a beneficiary of an estate may be attributed to an estate beneficiary, because of the family constructive ownership rules, and through the estate beneficiary to the estate. An estate beneficiary would be considered to own, by way of family attribution rules, shares owned by the decedent's spouse, children, grandchildren, and parents.[2] There are two ways in which the family attribution rules can be addressed.

First, the First Circuit has held that where, because of hostility among family members, a redeeming shareholder is prevented from exercising control over stock that the individual would be deemed to own constructively under attribution rules, the attribution rules will not be applied to the individual.[3]

On the other hand, the IRS has indicated it will not follow this decision and has ruled that the existence of family hostility will not affect its application of attribution rules.

If certain conditions are met, however, the IRS will not apply the ruling to taxpayers who have acted in reliance on the IRS' previously announced position on this issue.[4] The Fifth Circuit also has taken the position that the existence of family hostility does not prevent application of attribution rules, thus creating disagreement between the two circuit courts that have ruled on the question.[5] The Tax Court consistently has held that hostility within a family does not affect application of attribution rules.[6]

1. Rev. Rul. 77-455, 1977-2 CB 93.
2. IRC Sec. 318(a).
3. *Robin Haft Trust v. Comm.*, 75-1 USTC ¶9209 (1st Cir. 1975).
4. Rev. Rul. 80-26, 1980-1 CB 66; IRC Sec. 7805(b).
5. *David Metzger Trust v. Comm.*, 82-2 USTC ¶9718 (5th Cir. 1982), *cert. den.*, 463 U.S. 1207 (1983).
6. See *Cerone v. Comm.*, 87 TC 1 (1986).

The second way in which the family attribution rules can be addressed is if the sale of the departing owner's interest qualifies as a complete termination of the shareholder's interest.[1] A family member, as well as entities such as estates and trusts, can accomplish a complete termination by waiving the family attribution rules if (1) the departing owner has no interest in the corporation immediately after the sale, (2) the owner does not acquire any such interest within 10 years from the date of the sale (other than stock acquired by gift or inheritance), and (3) the owner agrees in writing to notify the IRS of any acquisition described in (2).[2]

Constructive ownership rules are complicated and their application requires expert legal advice. It generally may be said that a danger of dividend tax treatment exists in every case involving a family-owned corporation engaging in a stock redemption. There are, however, means available in some cases to avoid the harsh operation of the rule. A partial redemption may be able to escape dividend tax treatment even in a family-owned corporation.

8912. What is an IRC Section 303 stock redemption? How is a Section 303 redemption useful in the context of a closely-held corporation?

IRC Section 303 was enacted expressly to help solve the liquidity problems frequently faced by estates that are comprised largely of stock in a closely-held corporation, and to protect small businesses from forced liquidations or mergers due to the impact of estate taxes. Within the limits of IRC Section 303, surplus can be withdrawn from the corporation income tax-free.

In certain instances, stock of a public corporation also may be redeemed under IRC Section 303.

Any payments by a corporation to a shareholder generally are treated as dividends (see Q 8910). Despite this, under certain circumstances IRC Section 303 allows a corporation to redeem part of a deceased stockholder's shares without the redemption being treated as a dividend. Instead, the redemption price will be treated as payment in exchange for the stock in a capital transaction.

An IRC Section 303 redemption can safely be used in connection with the stock of a family-owned corporation because the constructive ownership rules (see Q 8911) are not applied in an IRC Section 303 redemption.[3]

The following conditions must be met if a stock redemption is to qualify under IRC Section 303 for non-dividend treatment:

(1) The stock that is to be redeemed must be includable in the decedent's gross estate for federal estate tax purposes.

(2) The value for federal estate tax purposes of all stock of a redeeming corporation that is includable in a decedent's gross estate must comprise more than 35 percent

1. IRC Sec. 302(b)(3); see IRC Sec. 302(c)(2) for situations in which constructive ownership rules of IRC Sec. 318(a)(1) will not apply.
2. IRC Section 302(c)(2).
3. IRC Secs. 318(a)-(b).

of the value of the decedent's adjusted gross estate.[1] The "adjusted gross estate" for this purpose is the gross estate less deductions for estate expenses, indebtedness and taxes[2] and for unreimbursed casualty and theft losses.[3] The total value of all classes of stock includable in a gross estate is taken into account to determine whether this 35 percent test is met, regardless of which class of stock is to be redeemed.[4]

IRC Section 303(b) provides that a corporate distribution in redemption of stock will qualify as an IRC Section 303 redemption if all the stock of the corporation that is included in determining the value of a gross estate exceeds 35 percent of the adjusted gross estate. Although most gifts made by a donor within three years of death are not brought back into the donor's gross estate under IRC Section 2035, certain kinds of gifts are brought back. These are the "first kind of exception" gifts. Gifts of corporate stock that fall within this classification are part of a gross estate for purposes of computing the 35 percent requirement (or the 20 percent requirement discussed below) and a corporation's redemption of this stock will qualify as a sale or exchange if all other requirements of IRC Section 303 are satisfied. IRC Section 2035(c)(1)(A) states generally that the three year rule will apply for the purposes of IRC Section 303(b). This is generally interpreted as follows: If a decedent makes a gift of any kind of property within three years of his or her death, the value of the property given will be included in the decedent's gross estate for purposes of determining whether the value of the corporate stock in question exceeds 35 percent of the value of the gross estate, but a distribution in redemption of that stock will not qualify as an IRC Section 303 redemption unless the stock redeemed actually is a part of the decedent's gross estate.[5]

The stock of two or more corporations will be treated as that of a single corporation, provided that 20 percent or more of the value of all of the outstanding stock of each corporation is includable in a decedent's gross estate.[6] Only stock directly owned is taken into account in determining whether the 20 percent test has been met; constructive ownership rules do not apply even when they would benefit a taxpayer.[7] Stock that, at a decedent's death, represents the surviving spouse's interest in property held by the decedent and the surviving spouse as community property or as joint tenants, tenants by the entirety, or tenants in common is considered to be includable in a decedent's gross estate for the purpose of meeting the 20 percent requirement.[8] The 20 percent test is not an elective provision, meaning that if a distribution in redemption of stock qualifies under IRC Section 303 only by reason of the application of the 20 percent test and also qualifies for sale treatment under

1. IRC Sec. 303(b)(2)(A).
2. IRC Sec. 2053.
3. IRC Sec. 2054.
4. Treas. Reg. §1.303-2(c)(1).
5. Rev. Rul. 84-76, 1984-1 CB 91.
6. IRC Sec. 303(b)(2)(B).
7. *Est. of Byrd v. Comm.*, 21 AFTR 2d 313 (5th Cir. 1967).
8. IRC Sec. 303(b)(2)(B).

another section of the IRC, the executor may not elect to have only the latter section of the IRC apply and thus retain the undiminished IRC Section 303 limits for later use. All distributions that qualify under IRC Section 303 are treated as IRC Section 303 redemptions in the order they are made.[1]

(3) The dollar amount that can be paid out by a corporation under protection of IRC Section 303 is limited to an amount equal to the sum of (x) all estate taxes, including the generation-skipping transfer tax imposed by reason of the decedent's death, and federal and state inheritance taxes attributable to a decedent's death, plus interest, if any, collected on these taxes, and (y) funeral and administration expenses allowable as estate deductions under IRC Section 2053.[2]

(4) The stock must be redeemed not later than (x) three years and ninety days after the estate tax return is filed (the return must be filed within nine months after a decedent's death), (y) sixty days after a Tax Court decision on an estate tax deficiency becomes final, or (z) if an extension of time for payment of tax is elected under IRC Section 6166, the time determined under the applicable section for payment of the installments. For any redemption made more than four years after a decedent's death, however, capital gains treatment is available only for a distribution in an amount that is the lesser of the amount of the qualifying death taxes and funeral and administration expenses that are unpaid immediately before the distribution, or the aggregate of these amounts that are paid within one year after the distribution.[3]

(5) The shareholder from whom stock is redeemed must be one whose interest is reduced directly, or through a binding obligation to contribute, by payment of qualifying death taxes and funeral and administration expenses, and the redemption will qualify for capital gains treatment only to the extent of that reduction.[4] That is, "the party whose shares are redeemed [must actually have] a liability for estate taxes, state death taxes, or funeral and administration expenses in an amount at least equal to the amount of the redemption."[5]

The stock of any corporation, including an S corporation, may qualify for IRC Section 303 redemption. Moreover, any class of stock may be redeemed under IRC Section 303. Thus, a nonvoting stock, common or preferred, issued as a stock dividend or issued in a lifetime or post-death recapitalization can qualify for the redemption.[6]

8913. How are interests subject to a buy-sell agreement valued?

One of the most difficult areas in negotiating a buy-sell agreement is determining the purchase price for the interests that are the subject of the agreement. Advance agreement upon

1. Treas. Reg. §1.303-2(g); Rev. Rul. 79-401, 1979-2 CB 128.
2. IRC Secs. 303(a), 303(d).
3. IRC Secs. 303(b)(1), 303(b)(4).
4. IRC Sec. 303(b)(3).
5. H.R. Rep. No. 94-1380 at 35 (Estate and Gift Tax Reform Act of 1976), *reprinted in* 1976-3 CB (Vol. 3) 735 at 769.
6. Treas. Reg. §1.303-2(d).

the purchase price, or the method for determining the purchase price, is important, because failure to include pricing terms may make enforcement of the agreement problematic. There are three common methods used in determining the purchase price. The parties may either (1) set a fixed price; (2) use a formula to determine price; or (3) obtain an independent appraisal.

The valuation provided under the buy-sell agreement is not always determinative of the parties' final tax liabilities, however, especially in the case of a closely-held company where the IRS could argue that the interests were undervalued and attempt to impose penalties under Section 6662.[1] Use of an independent appraiser can help to alleviate this concern for some companies.

However, if the valuation in the buy-sell agreement complies with the "price term control test," the purchase price in the buy-sell agreement will generally control the value of the asset for *estate* tax purposes.[2] For the terms of the buy-sell agreement to control for estate tax purposes, therefore, it is important that the agreement prohibit the decedent from transferring shares outside of the buy-sell agreement for any other price than that which is specified in the agreement. Further, the parties must be able to demonstrate that, based on the specific circumstances of the case, the buy-sell agreement represents a legitimate business arrangement, rather than a disguised scheme to pass the shares at an artificially low value to the deceased owner's children or other natural beneficiaries. If, however, the parties fail to show that the buy-sell agreement represents such a legitimate arrangement, the price of the underlying securities may be disregarded in arriving at the value of the stock[3]

It is also necessary to address the requirements of IRC Section 2703. Under Section 2703, the IRS will disregard the price established in the buy-sell agreement for establishing the fair market value of the interest being sold unless certain requirements are met. Specifically, (i) the agreement must be a bona fide business arrangement, (ii) the agreement must not be a device to transfer property to members of the decedent's family for less than full and adequate consideration, and (iii) the terms must be comparable to similar arrangements entered into by persons in an arms' length transaction.[4]

Planning Point: While using a fixed price may be the simplest method for the parties, it is important that the agreement is reviewed at regular intervals to ensure that the price still accurately reflects the value of the business to avoid IRS intervention. On a practical level, clients frequently fail to update these stipulated values.

If the parties develop a formula to determine the pricing under a buy-sell agreement[5] it is important that they clearly define all terms necessary to determine the price under that formula. Further, they should be aware that the courts may set aside the formula in certain cases, including cases where the formula was not determined in an arm's length negotiation or is found to be against public policy.[6]

1. See also *True v. Comm.*, 2001 TCM LEXIS 199 (2001) for an illustration of understatement penalties that may apply.
2. See Treas. Reg. §20.2031-2(h); *True v. Comm.*, above.
3. Treas. Reg. §20.2031-2(h).
4. IRC Sec. 2703(b).
5. See e.g., *Anderson v. Comm.*, 1970 TCM LEXIS 10 (1970).
6. See e.g., *Hendrix v. Comm.*, TC Memo 2011-133 (in this case the pricing was upheld, but the court discussed the circumstances that might cause it to be set aside).

Planning Point: Some agreements provide for a stipulated value. However, if the stipulated value is not updated with a specified period of time (i.e., 2 years), then a formula is used to determine the value.

See Q 8914 for a discussion of the use of so-called "showdown clauses" in pricing under a buy-sell agreement.

8914. What is a "showdown clause" in the context of a buy-sell agreement? When should one be used?

A showdown clause, also known as "shoot out," "slice-of-the-pie," "Russian roulette" or "Chinese wall" clauses, essentially allows one party to name a price upon the occurrence of a triggering event under a buy-sell agreement. Upon occurrence of the triggering event, one party specifies a price at which the party would buy (or sell) the business interests at issue, and the others decide whether to buy the interests (or sell their interests) to the naming party.

When a business owner invokes a showdown clause, this is essentially expressing a decision to exit the business. This provision works best if both sides are in an equal financial position because, if the parties are on unequal footing, the clause may provide a route for one owner to unjustifiably "chase out" a co-owner from the business. A showdown clause is frequently invoked in a situation where a deadlock in management or another similar issue exists among the various business owners that cannot be resolved through other methods.[1]

In *Wilcox v. Styles*,[2] a showdown clause was enforced by the courts, leading to an eventual dissolution of the business due to a deadlock over management issues that occurred between the two business owners of a closely-held corporation. The court upheld both the agreement containing the showdown clause and the pricing specified under the agreement, which was supported in part by an independent expert appraisal. The court in this case emphasized the importance of the written agreement—a mere oral agreement would be insufficient.[3]

Generally, offers made pursuant to a showdown clause cannot be used to establish the value of the business interest for estate tax purposes. By their nature, showdown clauses involve voluntary lifetime transfers of property, and do not prevent the interests from being sold at a higher price than that specified in the buy-sell agreement (see Q 8913).

8915. How can the fact that a business owner holds a minority or majority interest in an entity impact the use of a buy-sell agreement?

Control premiums and minority discounts are especially important in the small business context where the business is owned by a small group of individuals who may also be significantly involved in the day-to-day operations of the business. Control and minority issues may be important in establishing the value of business interests that are subject to a buy-sell agreement.

Normally, an interest in a business is valued in proportion to the entire value of the business. However, application of a premium that reflects one owner's (or a group of owners') ability to

1. *RS & P/WC Fields Ltd. Partnership v. BOSP Invs.*, 829 F. Supp. 928 (1993).
2. 127 Or. App. 671 (1994).
3. *Bruce v. Cole*, 854 So. 2d 47 (2003).

control business affairs, including the ability to withdraw business assets, has been recognized in many cases.[1] In other cases, premium pricing has been found appropriate in a context where one owner functions as the "swing vote" within the business, in recognition of the substantial influence that the owner has over the business' affairs.[2]

A premium is not always available, however in the swing vote context, as it involves a fact-intensive analysis. For example, the Ninth Circuit did not allow a premium for swing vote status in the case of *Simplot v. Commissioner*, reversing the Tax Court's determination of value that was based largely on scenarios constructed by the court to prove the value of the particular owner's influence and control. The Ninth Circuit found that it was an error for the Tax Court to base value on fictional potential purchasers, rather than concrete facts.[3]

A valuation discount has often been applied in the context of minority ownership interests in order to reflect the *lack* of control that these owners may influence over business affairs.[4] In certain cases, a minority discount is combined with a discount for lack of marketability that is generally found in the small business context.[5] (It should be noted that the discount for lack of marketability is often available even for majority interests in a closely-held business.)[6]

Minority discounts will generally be disallowed, however, in the context of larger companies, where securities are marketable and there are multiple business owners.[7]

Planning Point: It becomes a client decision as to whether or not the valuation approach should account for any premiums or discounts associated with a minority or controlling interest in the business. For example, the agreement can be drafted to determine a value for the overall business, with this value to be multiplied by the percentage interest in the business being sold. This approach does not reflect any premium or discount. In the alternative, the valuation can be calculated to reflect the value of a specific percentage interest of the business (i.e. the fair market value of a 30 percent interest in the business). This approach will take into account discounts or premiums.

8916. What is a right of first refusal? What is the difference between a right of first refusal and a buy-sell agreement?

A right of first refusal requires that a selling business owner give his or her co-owners or the business entity itself the opportunity to purchase certain business interests at the same price that

1. On control premiums generally, see *Estate of Bright v. United States*, 658 F.2d 999 (1981); *Estate of Desmond v. Comm.*, TC Memo 1999-76 (majority stock interest in an S corporation was subject to a control premium); *Rakow v Comm.*, TC Memo 1999-177 (controlling interest in corporation was subject to a control premium).
2. *Estate of Winkler v. Comm.*, TC Memo 1989-231 and Let. Rul. 9436005.
3. *Estate of Simplot v. Comm.*, 249 F.3d 1191 (2001), rev'g 112 TC 130 (1999).
4. See, e.g., *Knott v. Comm.*, TC Memo 1987-597; *Estate of Berg v. Comm.*, TC Memo 1991-279; *Moore v. Comm.*, TC Memo 1991-546 (minority interest in a general partnership). But see also *Ahmanson Found. v. United States*, 674 F.2d 761 (1981); *Estate of Curry v. United States*, 706 F.2d 1424 (1983); *Citizens Bank & Trust Co. v. Comm.*, 839 F.2d 1249 (1988) (no discount for nonvoting interest if the same decedent held majority of voting interest).
5. *Estate of Hecksher v. Comm.*, 63 TC 485 (1975); *Estate of Titus* v. *Comm.*, TC Memo 1989-466; *Moore v. Comm.*, TC Memo 1991-546 (minority discount); *Mandelbaum v. Comm.*, TC Memo 1995-255 (lack of marketability discount) and *McCormick Estate v. Comm.*, TC Memo 1995-371 (minority discount and lack of marketability discount); *Gross v. Comm.*, TC Memo 1999-254 (minority interest in S corporation was given a combined minority and lack of marketability discount).
6. *Estate of Bennett v. Comm.*, TC Memo 1993-34; *Estate of Andrews v. Comm.*, 79 TC 938 (1982).
7. *Snyder v. Comm.*, 93 TC 529 (1989); *Estate of Dougherty v. Comm.*, TC Memo 1990-274; *Citizens Bank & Trust Co. v. Comm.*, 839 F.2d 1249 (1988).

he or she is able to obtain from a third party investor.[1] The co-owners will be given the option of matching the terms of the competing offer before the selling owner is able to sell his or her interests to a third party. Though the agreed upon price may not fix the value of the interest for estate and gift tax purposes,[2] it can be considered as one of the factors that could determine its value. Likewise, the depressive effect of a restrictive agreement such as a right of first refusal is one of the factors that should be considered in valuing a gift of stock.[3]

While a right of first refusal may provide comfort to all business owners in that they know they will have a right to purchase a departing business owner's shares before third parties are given the right, business owners must remember that in the context of a closely-held business, there is often a very limited market for the shares. Even if a business owner is able to find a third party buyer, the remaining business owners will then be forced to come up with a matching purchase offer, which may prove difficult in the small business context when funds are more limited.

Further, a right of first refusal often gives a departing business owner the power to find a willing buyer that the remaining business owners may be forced to accept in the event that they are unable to match the purchase price. As the departing business owner will no longer be involved in the business' operations, he or she may not be the person best suited to choose a replacement owner.

In the context of a buy-sell agreement, if the triggering event is the withdrawal of one business owner, only the remaining owners or entity itself have the right to purchase the departing owner's interests. The price or method for determining the price will be fixed by the agreement, and the agreement has often been pre-funded with insurance or accumulated earnings in order to ensure that the remaining owners are able to make the purchase. Therefore, the buy-sell agreement is often the more advantageous method for planning a departing business owner's transition.

8917. What special considerations apply when an S corporation uses a buy-sell agreement?

Owners of S corporations, like C corporations, can execute buy-sell agreements to provide for the transition of a business owner's interests based upon one or more triggering events. The S corporation also may choose to structure the agreement as either a cross-purchase or redemption agreement. In addition to the factors that are important to any business, S corporations must consider the following factors: (1) preservation of the S corporation status; (2) requiring distributions to ensure shareholders have adequate funds to pay for the S corporation's income taxes at the shareholder level; and (3) protecting its fiscal year.

When an S corporation[4] fails to qualify as an S corporation, it automatically becomes a C corporation.[5] Because S corporation qualification is tied to the number and types of

1. See *True v. Comm.*, 390 F.3d 1210 (2004); *Oldcastle Materials, Inc. v. Rohlin*, 343 F. Supp. 2d 762 (2004).
2. *Fry Est. v. Comm.*, 9 TC 503 (1947).
3. *James v. United States*, 148 F.2d 236 (1945).
4. IRC Sec. 1361(b).
5. IRC Sec. 1362(d).

shareholders, the use of a properly structured buy-sell agreement may be critical to protecting the business' qualification as an S corporation.[1] Provisions prohibiting certain transfers and acts should be included in the buy-sell agreement, including:[2]

(1) prohibitions on the transfer of stock to a prohibited S corporation shareholder, such as a corporation, foreign individual or ineligible trust; and

(2) prohibitions on the transfer of stock to an additional new shareholder if the transfer would bring the total number of shareholders above the permitted number (currently 100).

Further, an S corporation buy-sell agreement may contain different triggering events than those commonly used for a C corporation or partnership. An S corporation must make a variety of elections that can impact all of its shareholders. The fact that an S corporation is limited to issuing one class of stock (see Q 8890) often means that rights to liquidation proceeds and distribution requirements must be uniform for all shareholders so that variances are not found to create a second class of stock and disqualify the S corporation. A corporation is treated as having only one class of stock if all of the corporation's outstanding shares confer identical rights to distribution and liquidation proceeds [3] A buy-sell agreement could be structured so that remaining business owners have the right to purchase the interests of a shareholder who disagrees with the rights created with respect to the S corporation's single class of stock.

Because S corporations are taxed at the individual shareholder level, rather than at the entity level, regardless of whether the S corporation actually distributes dividends, a buy-sell agreement can be used to ensure the shareholders' ability to pay their income tax liabilities.[4] A provision that triggers a buyout upon failure of the S corporation to meet its dividend obligations could be used to protect the interests of less wealthy shareholders.

Buy-sell agreements may also be useful in protecting the fiscal year of the S corporation. Generally, an S corporation is required to observe a calendar year as its tax year unless it can establish a valid reason for adopting a fiscal year.[5] If more than 50 percent of the S corporation's shares are transferred, it must change to a calendar year or reestablish its entitlement to a fiscal year.[6] To prevent this occurrence, an S corporation's buy-sell agreement should contain provisions that would prevent shareholders from transferring enough shares to disqualify the S corporation from its current use of a fiscal year, if desired.

8918. How can an installment sale be used to "fund" a buy-sell agreement?

Any disposition of property where at least one payment will be received after the close of the tax year of disposition may be treated as an installment sale.[7] Generally, however, the installment

1. *Hunt v. Data Mgmt. Resources, Inc.*, 985 P.2d 730 (1999).
2. See *Minton v. Comm.*, TC Memo 2007-372 (example of binding shareholder agreement).
3. Treas. Reg. §1.1361-1(l)(2)(iv), (Ex. 6).
4. IRC Secs. 7519, 444.
5. IRC Sec. 1378. See also Rev. Proc. 87-57, 1987-2 CB 687, Rev. Proc. 87-32, 1987-2 CB 396, regarding what constitutes a sufficient business purpose for adopting a fiscal year that does not end on December 31.
6. Tax Reform Act of 1986, Pub. L. No. 99-514, Sec. 806(e).
7. IRC Sec. 453(b)(1).

method of taxation (see below) is not available for sales between certain related parties unless they can clearly establish that the transaction was not intended to avoid tax.[1]

Gain on an installment sale is required to be reported under the installment method unless the taxpayer "elects out" of using the method by the due date for filing a return (including extensions) for the year of the sale. Taxpayers may elect out by reporting all the gain as income in the year of the sale on Form 4797 (*Sales of Business Property*), or on Form 1040, Schedule D (*Capital Gains and Losses*), and Form 8949 (*Sales and Other Dispositions of Capital Assets*).[2]

Installment sales are often used in the context of a buy-sell agreement where the business owners have not planned in advance to fund the purchase through the use of insurance or otherwise (see Q 8905 and Q 8906). Though installment sales may be used to purchase the interests of a departing business owner, they do not provide the immediate liquidity to the retiring owner or deceased owner's estate that can be realized through a life insurance strategy or by using accumulated earnings to purchase the interest outright.

Planning Point: Practically, an installment sale may be the only means of purchasing a departing business owner's interests if the buy-sell agreement was not funded in another manner.

Essentially, an installment sale requires the corporation (or shareholders if the buy-sell agreement is structured as a cross-purchase agreement, see Q 8910) to purchase the interests of the departing business owner using a note, under which it will pay for the interests over time. The departing business owner (or that owner's estate) reports gain on the sale using the "installment method," which means that the gain for any given year equals the part of the gain that is actually received (or considered to have been received) during that tax year. The departing business owner must also report as income the amount of the payments received in the year that are deemed to represent interest income. The portion that is deemed to be a return of the owner's adjusted basis in the interests is excluded as in any other sale.[3] See Q 8570, Q 8852 and Q 8875 for a discussion of determining basis in various contexts.

The departing owner can elect out of the installment sale method and report the entire amount of gain in the year of sale, even though he or she has not yet received all of the proceeds.

The installment method cannot be used if the business interests at issue are securities that are publicly traded on an established market.[4]

8919. What are the tax consequences of using an asset sale to liquidate a C corporation, rather than transitioning the business through some other form of succession planning?

Liquidation is the winding down of a corporation's affairs until it is completely divested of all assets. A status of liquidation exists when the corporation ceases to be a going concern and its

1. IRC Sec. 453(g)(2). If the buyer disposes of the asset within 2 years of the purchase, there are additional restrictions in IRC Sec. 453(e), also called the anti-Rushing Rule, see *Rushing v Comm.*, 441 F.2d 593 (1971).
2. IRS Tax Topics 705 (May 28, 2015).
3. See IRS Publication 537.
4. IRS Pub. 537, above.

activities are merely for the purpose of winding up its affairs, paying its debts, and distributing any remaining balance to shareholders.[1]

If a corporation decides that the best option is to liquidate, rather than transition ownership of the company through another form of succession planning, there are a variety of methods that can be used in such liquidation.

Similarly to the corporation's taxation while operating as an active business, the liquidated company is generally subject to double taxation because both the corporation and shareholders will be liable for taxes on the sale proceeds. In an asset sale, the corporation sells all of its assets to a buyer, recognizing gain on the transaction as the difference between its basis in the assets and the amount realized.[2] After taxes and expenses, the corporation distributes any excess to its shareholders, who are then subject to tax at the individual level.[3]

The asset sale can also be structured as an installment asset sale, which allows the buyer to purchase the company over a period of time using a note or other debt obligation (see Q 8918 for a discussion of the installment method of taxation).[4] Despite this, if the entire business is sold through an installment sale, a special rule applies that requires the business to allocate the selling price and payments between three classes of assets: (1) assets sold at a loss, (2) real and personal property eligible for the installment method of taxation, and (3) property that is ineligible to be sold in an installment sale, such as publicly traded securities and inventory. Gain on the sale of property that is ineligible for the installment method of taxation must be reported in the year of sale, rather than over the time period in which the installment payments are made.[5]

8920. What tax considerations make the liquidation of an S corporation different than the liquidation of a C corporation?

IRC Section 1371 provides that an S corporation is subject to the same rules that apply in the context of a C corporation unless there is a specific rule that has been developed for S corporations. Despite this, one of the primary differences between an S corporation and a C corporation is their basic tax treatment, which has an important impact upon the issues that the entity will face during liquidation. Because S corporations are taxed at a single level, taxation of a sale or other liquidation of the business will usually occur only at the individual level, unlike in the context of the C corporation, where the corporation itself will be required to pay taxes on any gain before passing the profits through to shareholders, who will also be taxed on the amounts they receive.

Many S corporation shareholders will have a higher stock basis than that of a C corporation shareholder. This is because the basis of an S corporation shareholder's stock is increased by any

1. Treas. Reg. §1.332-2(c).
2. IRC Sec. 336(a).
3. IRC Sec. 331(a).
4. IRC Sec. 453B(a).
5. See IRS Pub. 537.

earnings of the S corporation that are passed through for tax purposes.[1] Depending upon how long the corporation had existed as an S corporation, and the level of earnings that were passed through to shareholders, S corporation shareholders may have substantially higher tax bases upon sale. Because tax basis decreases the amount of gain that the shareholders are required to recognize upon sale, the S corporation shareholder's total tax liability will often be lower than the C corporation shareholder's upon liquidation of the company.

If the S corporation was ever a C corporation, however, the S corporation will be required to account for any built-in gains, which are taxed at the highest rate applicable to C corporations (see Q 8871).[2] The tax on built-in gains is designed to preserve a part of the double tax structure for certain S corporations that were formerly C corporations. The built-in gains tax applies if the S corporation sells an asset within a five year period (formerly ten years) following its S corporation election.[3] The tax on built-in gains is imposed at the S corporation level, in addition to any taxes that are paid by the S corporation's shareholders. This tax will only apply in situations where the S corporation was formerly a C corporation and liquidates within ten years of making its S election.

8921. What gift tax concerns apply in the family business context when planning for business succession?

In many cases, the retiring business owner in a family owned small business will want to transition the business to the owner's children using a gifting strategy, rather than a traditional sale. Because the American Taxpayer Relief Act increased the top estate and gift tax rate to 40 percent for tax years beginning after 2012, avoiding this tax will often be a top priority for small business owners.[4]

Each taxpayer is allowed to exclude $5.6 million (in 2018, as indexed for inflation) from transfer taxation during the taxpayer's lifetime (gifts made during life and post-mortem are aggregated for purposes of determining the exempted amount).[5]

Further, a $15,000 (in 2018, up from $14,000 in 2013-2017, and $13,000 for 2011 and 2012) annual exclusion is available for present interest gifts on a per donor/donee basis.

Establishing value for purposes of the exemption and exclusion amounts will be a primary concern for many exiting business owners because, in the small business context, there is often no established market value for the interests being transferred. In the context of the family owned business, the transfer of business interests from one generation to the next is often not accomplished as a result of arm's length negotiations that result in a purchase price that reflects any actual market value of the company.

1. IRC Secs. 1367(a), 1366(a)(1)(A).
2. IRC Sec. 1374(b)(1).
3. IRC Sec. 1374(d)(7), as amended by PATH.
4. American Taxpayer Relief Act of 2012, Pub. Law No. 112-240, Sec. 101, IR 2015-118 (Oct. 21, 2015), Rev. Proc. 2017-58.
5. Rev. Proc. 2017-58.

Thus, when a business owner transfers his ownership interests, a valuation will be required to determine the worth of company shares and the applicable amount of taxes upon the transfer of those shares. Often, however, the lack of established market makes it difficult to accurately determine the value of the transferred interests, opening the business owner to an IRS challenge and potential future gift tax liability for undervalued shares.

Wandry vs. Commissioner was a case where taxpayers were able to establish the value of business interests that were transferred to their children by creating a transaction that capped the annual gift at the annual exclusion amount, rather than specifying a percentage or number of interests subject to transfer. Because the value of the business had not yet been ascertained, the taxpayers specified that the gifts were not to exceed the annual exclusion amount in the documents governing the transfers of the business interests. The taxpayers used their existing gift tax exemption in making the gifts. In *Wandry*, the court approved a formula gift clause that viewed the gift as being of a fixed dollar amount with this fixed dollar amount being expressed as a percentage of the business value. To the extent that the valuation was not correct, the gifted interests were reallocated among the owners of the business. Part of the significance of the case is the court's finding that, with respect to the reallocation of the partnership interests, it did not matter if some of the reallocated interests reverted to the grantor.

Outright gifts are not the only type of transaction that can give rise to gift tax concerns in the family business context, however. Shareholders of nonparticipating preferred stock in profitable family held corporations have been held to have made gifts to the common stockholders (typically descendants of the preferred shareholder) by waiving payment of dividends or simply by failing to exercise conversion rights or other options available to a preferred stockholder to preserve his position.[1] The Tax Court has held that the failure to convert noncumulative preferred stock to cumulative preferred stock did not give rise to a gift, but that thereafter a gift was made each time a dividend would have accumulated. However, the failure to exercise a put option at par plus accumulated dividends plus interest was not treated as a gift of foregone interest.[2]

A transaction involving the nonexercise of an option by a son under a cross-purchase buy-sell agreement followed by the sale of the same stock by the father to a third party when the fair market value of the stock was substantially higher than the option price was treated as a gift from the son to the father.[3] Also, a father indirectly made a gift to his son to the extent that the fair market value of stock exceeded its redemption price when the father failed to exercise his right under a buy-sell agreement to have a corporation redeem all of the available shares held by his brother-in-law's estate and the stock passed to the son.[4]

8922. How can a grantor retained annuity trust be used in family business succession planning?

Trust entities can be useful in business succession planning, whether the trusts are revocable or irrevocable. The two forms of trust are not mutually exclusive, and in many

1. TAMs 8723007, 8726005.
2. *Snyder v. Comm.*, 93 TC 529 (1989).
3. Let. Rul. 9117035.
4. TAM 9315005.

instances, a succession plan may contain more than one trust entity. The decision to have one or both depends on the business owner's goals, how much control the senior generation wants, when the assets will be transferred to the heirs and other restraints that are imposed.

A grantor retained annuity trust (GRAT) is an irrevocable trust to which the business owner transfers shares in his business while retaining the right to a fixed annual annuity payout for a stated term of years.

Planning Point: In response to a comment on the IRS's proposed GRAT regulations, the final regulations include and use interchangeably both the term "GRAT" (which does not appear in the statutes or the regulations) and its Treasury Regulation citation, §25.2702-3(b).[1]

At the end of the term, the property remaining in the GRAT (the appreciation and income in excess of the annuity amount that is to be paid to the business owner) will pass to the trust beneficiaries (often the owner's children or grandchildren). Only the value of the remainder interest is subject to gift tax.

The amount of the taxable gift to the beneficiaries can be reduced by structuring the trust with a larger annuity payout or a longer stated term. Further, the value is dependent on the IRS Section 7520 interest rate in effect at the time the trust is established—a lower interest rate can also reduce the value of the taxable gift.

A GRAT may be structured so that there is little or no gift tax payable on the value of the remainder interest that passes to the trust beneficiaries. For gift tax purposes, this is known as a "zeroed-out" GRAT. If the zeroed-out GRAT produces a return in excess of the annuity amount payable to the business owner, the GRAT will succeed in passing on the reminder interest (the trust's excess income and appreciation) to the trust beneficiaries at little or no gift tax cost to the business owner. If the zeroed-out GRAT fails to produce a return in excess of the annuity amount and the remainder beneficiaries receive nothing, there is minimal downside risk since there was little or no gift tax cost to the business owner upon establishing the zeroed-out GRAT. The primary risk of using a GRAT (especially a short term GRAT) to transfer business interests is that if the business owner fails to survive the stated term, the GRAT may be included in his estate and subject to estate taxes.

See Q 8923 for a discussion of the use of intentionally defective grantor trusts in family business succession planning.

8923. How can an intentionally defective grantor trust be used in family business succession planning?

A trust structure called an intentionally defective grantor trust (IDGT) is another trust structure that can be used by a small business owner to transfer business interests to the next generation. In using this strategy, the business owner actually sells all interests in the business to the IDGT, naming the children or other heirs as beneficiaries of the trust.

1. TD 9414, 2008-35 IRB.

An IDGT is an irrevocable trust that is valid for estate tax purposes, but "defective" for income tax purposes. This means the business owner (as the grantor of the IDGT) is the owner of the IDGT for income-tax purposes, but is not treated as the owner of the IDGT for estate tax purposes. Since the business interests are sold to the IDGT, there are no gift taxes.

Further, there are no capital gains taxes to the business owner because sales between a grantor and an IDGT are disregarded for income tax purposes. Typically, the business owner will structure the sale so that there is no down payment by the IDGT, annual interest payments are at the lowest rate permitted by the IRS, and a balloon principal payment is due in nine or more years. This technique is similar to a GRAT, but without the mortality risk. The value of the business is taken outside of the business owner's estate for estate tax purposes, because future appreciation and interest are sheltered within the IDGT. The business owner's estate is also reduced by the income and capital gains taxes to be paid on the IDGT's income. In other words, the business owner is not taxed separately on the interest payments but instead is taxed on all of the capital gains and income realized by the IDGT. The taxes paid by the business owner on the IDGT's income and capital gains are effectively tax-free gifts to the beneficiaries of the IDGT.

The viability of IDGTs as wealth transfer vehicles is supported by the IRS in Revenue Ruling 2008-22,[1] although in a somewhat different context. In the ruling, a grantor of an inter vivos trust retained the power, exercisable in a non-fiduciary capacity, to acquire property held in the trust by substituting other property of equivalent value. The ruling provides that, for estate tax purposes, the substitution power will not, by itself, cause the value of the trust corpus to be includible in the grantor's gross estate, provided the trustee has a fiduciary obligation (under the local law) to ensure the grantor's compliance with the terms of this power by satisfying itself that the properties acquired and substituted by the grantor are in fact of equivalent value, and further provided that the substitution power cannot be exercised in a manner that can shift benefits among the trust beneficiaries.

8924. What are self-cancelling installment notes (SCINs)? How can SCINs be used in family business succession planning?

Under a self-cancelling installment note (SCIN), the selling business owner agrees to sell property to a buyer (often, the owner's children or other beneficiaries) in exchange for an installment note that expires either when the seller receives the maximum price for the property or upon the occurrence of a cancellation event, such as the seller's death. This is a form of installment sale transaction (see Q 8918). It allows the seller to secure the purchase for the business interest, while still retaining the ability to defer part of the gain.[2] In turn, the buyer can claim an interest deduction with respect to the payments made.[3]

Under a SCIN, if the cancelling event is the selling business owner's death, all remaining payments under the note are canceled upon the seller's death, similar to a private annuity.

1. 2008-16 IRB (April 21, 2008).
2. IRC Sec. 453(f)(3).
3. IRC Sec. 163(d)(5); Treas. Reg. §1.163-8T(b)(3) (investment expenditure).

Typically, the purchaser pays a premium for this cancellation feature in the form of either a higher interest rate or a larger purchase price. Gain under a SCIN is recognized by the selling business owner as payments are received. However, when the seller dies, any unrecognized (i.e., cancelled) gain at the seller's death under the SCIN is reportable either on the seller's final IRS Form 1040 or on the seller's estate's IRS Form 1041.

In order for the IRS to recognize the SCIN, the term of the note must be shorter than the seller's life expectancy at the time of the sale, based on IRS mortality tables.[1] The advantage of using a SCIN, as opposed to other installment sale methods or an intentionally defective grantor trust (see Q 8923), is that the unpaid balance is not included in the seller's estate.[2]

However, if no payments are made under the SCIN before the death of the seller, the IRS may argue that the value of the SCIN is zero and should only reduce the value of the note.[3] A SCIN signed by a family member is presumed to be a gift rather than a bona fide transaction.[4]

SCINs are particularly useful if the seller has a relatively short remaining life expectancy because if the selling owner outlives the term of the note, the estate tax benefit will have been lost and the owner may actually have incurred additional expenses in the form of higher income taxes or gift tax liability.

8925. Are there any special provisions available to allow the estate of a small business owner to defer payment of estate taxes?

Section 6166 was added to the Internal Revenue Code to allow estates to pay estate taxes attributable to substantial closely-held business interests in installments. Prior to that time, the IRS had discretion to permit installment payments, but such discretion was rarely exercised. Consequently, Congress acted to provide certain estates with the right to defer estate tax payments if the requirements of Section 6166 were met.

In general, IRC Section 6166 provides for an elective five-year deferral, ten-year installment payment method of liquidating the estate tax liability. An estate is eligible for the Section 6166 election if the value of a closely-held business that is includible in the gross estate exceeds 35 percent of the adjusted gross estate.[5]

If the Section 6166 election is made, no payments of the tax are required for an initial five-year period, though interest payments must be made.[6] The estate tax liability itself may then be paid in ten equal annual installments in years six through fifteen, with interest continuing to run on the unpaid balance. Interest on the deferred amount is 2 percent (subject to a limitation discussed below).

1. GCM 39503.
2. See *Frane vs. Comm.*, 998 F.2d 567 (1993); *Moss v. Comm.*, 74 TC 1239 (1980).
3. See *Estate of Costanza v. Comm.*, 320 F.3d 595 (2003); *Robert Dallas*, TC Memo 2006-212.
4. *Estate of Costanza v. Comm.*, 320 F.3d 595 (2003); *Estate of Labombarde v. Comm.*, 58 TC 745 (1972).
5. IRC Sec. 6166(a)(1).
6. IRC Sec. 6166(a)(3), (f)(1).

This deferral treatment is allowed only for estates comprised of "interests in a closely-held business." Whether or not the business interests contained in an estate meet this standard is determined by the "business interest test," which is satisfied as follows:

(1) If the decedent was a sole proprietor the business interest test is satisfied.

(2) If the business was a partnership, the business interest test is satisfied only if:

(i) there were no more than forty-five partners in the partnership, or

(ii) the decedent's interest in partnership capital was at least 20 percent.

(3) If the business was a corporation, the business interest test is satisfied only if:

(i) there were no more than forty-five shareholders, or

(ii) the decedent's ownership of voting stock was at least 20 percent.

Interests or shares owned by the decedent's spouse, siblings, ancestors, and descendants are treated as owned by the decedent for purposes of applying the forty-five partner or shareholder test. Interests owned jointly by two spouses are counted as one partner or shareholder.

In applying the 20 percent interest test, the estate may elect to have interests owned by the decedent's spouse, siblings, ancestors, and descendants counted as part of the decedent's interest. However, if this is the method through which decedent's interest qualifies for the deferral, then

(1) the five-year deferral period is lost (i.e., the ten-year payment period starts immediately), and

(2) the favorable 2 percent interest rate is not available on deferred amounts.

The value of the business interest must be more than 35 percent of the "adjusted gross estate." The adjusted gross estate is the gross estate minus deductions for expenses, debts, taxes, and losses.

8926. What issues arise when a family partnership is considering its small business succession strategy?

The preferred solution to the problem of transferring family partnership interests at death depends upon the particular type of family partnership and the circumstances surrounding it. A family partnership may be between two spouses, a parent and his or her adult child or children, the entire family, or the parent and a trustee or trustees, the latter acting for minor children. In some instances, disposition of the partnership interests by will may be a satisfactory solution. In most instances, a buy-sell agreement will be the preferred solution. Except in the case of two spouses, the income tax savings that result from the family partnership, by reason of spreading the business income, will more than pay the premiums on the life insurance used to finance the agreement.

When a family partnership has been formed by two spouses, it is sometimes assumed that there is no need for a buy-sell agreement to take effect at death. The spouse-partners may take the position that a buy-sell agreement is unnecessary because the survivor (assuming there are no children or other heirs) will take the interest in the business from the first-to-die under the intestacy laws of the state in the absence of a will. Moreover, in most states, each has a statutory right to one-third of the property owned at death by the other, and this right cannot be eliminated even by a will to the contrary.

Notwithstanding the circumstances that exist so far as inheritance is concerned between the spouses, a buy-sell agreement is practical and in some instances may be necessary in order to avoid serious problems upon the death of the first-to-die. See Q 8927 for a detailed discussion of the use of buy-sell agreements in the context of a family partnership.

Where two spouses are partners in a partnership business, they may execute wills leaving their interests in the business to each other. This procedure will sometimes eliminate any liquidation problems at death because the surviving spouse will own the entire business by virtue of the duly executed will, and it eliminates any doubts or problems so far as the surviving spouse's rights are concerned.

There are several major problems, however, that require serious consideration, even though the spouses have executed wills leaving their business interests to each other. The decedent may have personal creditors pressing claims against the estate. Such claims must be satisfied before the surviving spouse can take over the decedent's business interest.

Aside from personal creditors of the decedent, the business itself may be faced with substantial liabilities. Any such claims, if pressed for settlement, will need to be satisfied by the surviving spouse.

There is always the chance that the decedent's will may be contested by other potential heirs, and if set aside will leave the surviving spouse in the same position as if no will had ever been executed. Consequently, if the will is set aside for one reason or another, the surviving spouse will then take under the intestacy laws of the particular state involved, which may give a large portion of the decedent's business interest to heirs other than the surviving spouse. And if any of these heirs are minors, liquidation of the business could become necessary.[1]

8927. How can a buy-sell agreement be useful in transitioning a family partnership?

If a family partnership is formed between two spouses, in order to eliminate the possible problems and uncertainties that may arise, a buy-sell agreement should be formed between the partners. Moreover, each spouse should be assured there will be ample capital in order to purchase the decedent's business interest. This may become necessary through failure of the decedent's will (see Q 8926), if no will had been executed, through a change in a previously executed will, or because of creditors' claims.

1. *Spivak v. Bronstein*, 79 A. 2d 205 (1951).

Family members (or any other person) will be recognized as partners only if one of the following requirements is satisfied: (1) if capital is a material income-producing factor, they acquired their capital interest in a bona fide transaction (even if by gift or purchase from another family member), actually own the partnership interest, and actually control the interest; (2) if capital is not a material income-producing factor, they joined together in good faith to conduct a business. They agreed that contributions of each entitle them to a share in the profits, and some capital or service has been (or is) provided by each partner.[1]

One of the advantages of the buy-sell agreement is that the value of the business may be established through a valuation formula contained in the agreement (the valuation of shares is a frequent subject of litigation, with the IRS often taking the position that the estate has undervalued the reported value). If properly established, the stated value should be accepted for federal estate tax purposes. A recommended method in the case of a family partnership is to have an independent certified public accountant establish and certify the true value, and to attach this certificate to the buy-sell agreement. See Q 8937 for a detailed discussion of valuation issues that arise in the context of a buy-sell agreement.

Adequate life insurance is as essential in financing the buy-sell agreement, as would be the case were the parties unrelated. Since the spouses are partners in the business, each should carry life insurance upon the life of the other.

If the surviving spouse is to carry on the business after the death of the first-to-die as legatee, rather than as purchaser under a buy-sell agreement, insurance on his or her life payable to the surviving spouse for business purposes is advisable, if not essential. Without a special fund available to satisfy partnership creditors and to hire the assistance necessary to do some of the work previously performed by the first-to-die, the surviving spouse may find it difficult to continue the business. With adequate life insurance proceeds at his or her disposal, and with adequate experience in the business gained as an active partner, the surviving spouse is given an opportunity to continue the business successfully.

8928. What special considerations arise when developing a business succession plan for a family partnership that is formed between a parent and adult children?

In this type of partnership, disposition of partnership interests by will on the death of a partner is seldom a satisfactory solution. In the case of a married child, a bequest of his or her partnership interest often would be made to a surviving spouse, and in many instances might lead to the liquidation of the business as being preferable to taking the surviving spouse into the firm. The same result could follow should the parent bequeath his or her partnership interest to the surviving spouse. On the other hand, if the parent bequeaths his or her interest to the children and such interest comprises the major part of the estate, the surviving spouse may be able to elect to take against the will and thereby upset the bequest of the partnership interest.

1. IRS Publication 541 (Rev. January 2016).

A specially designed buy-sell agreement usually will be a desirable solution. Under such an agreement the children will agree to purchase their parent's partnership interest upon death and to maintain insurance on the parent's life with which to finance the purchase. The insurance proceeds will be collected by the children, or by a trustee acting for them, and paid over to the executor of the parent's estate to meet the cash needs of estate administration and to fulfill bequests to the surviving spouse of the balance of the funds.

Thus, the surviving spouse will be assured adequate income and will not be able to upset the plan, even though there is little other estate property. Where division of the estate is not a problem and the parent wishes to leave something to the children, the plan may be modified by giving the children a bargain price in the agreement, or by having them purchase a portion of the parent's interest while he or she bequeaths the remaining portion to them.

In the case of a partnership between a parent and his married child, in most instances there should be a traditional cross-purchase agreement (see Q 8903 to Q 8910). Where there are at least two children as partners with their parent, the parent may not desire to increase his or her interest in the firm if a child dies first. In this case, the agreement should provide for a cross-purchase between the children in the event of the death of one of them.

8929. How can the existence of preferred stock complicate business succession planning in the context of a family-owned business?

In the context of a family-owned business, many business owners may consider creating a class of preferred stock to help provide for a smooth transition of business ownership to the next generation of family members. This can actually create problems that can complicate the transition process.

First, small business owners must be advised that the creation of a second class of stock can cause a currently existing S corporation to lose its S corporation status, because S corporations are only permitted to issue a single class of stock.[1] Second, if a currently existing corporation wishes to convert to S corporation status in the future, the existence of the class of preferred stock will make the conversion impossible unless all existing preferred shareholders agree to exchange those shares for a single class of stock that is generally available to all shareholders.

Further, the rules contained in IRC Section 2701 can thwart a business owner's plans to transfer interests gift tax-free to family members by setting the value of any retained preferred business interest (known as an "applicable retained interest," see below) that does not contain a right to receive a "qualified payment" at zero if there is a transfer of a common equity interest in the business to a family member.[2]

Essentially, these rules require that the transferring family member treat the retained preferred stock interests as a taxable gift to the family member to whom the common stock interests are

1. IRC Sec. 1361(b)(1)(D).
2. IRC Sec. 2701(a)(3).

sold. The rules imposed under IRC Section 2701 are designed to prevent a scenario where the older generation creates a class of preferred shares (which is retained) in order to avoid paying gift taxes on common shares (which he or she transfers to the younger generation).

For example, before the enactment of Section 2701, a business owner may have created a class of preferred shares with a value that was equal to the current value of the business, retaining these preferred shares. The business owner could then transfer a class of common shares to the child that had no current value, and thus generated no gift tax liability. By fixing the value of an applicable retained interest at zero (in the absence of a qualified payment right), Section 2701 seeks to prevent this result. Essentially, the rules provide that the taxable gift can only be avoided if the parent who retains the preferred stock receives a qualified dividend payment (which will establish the value of the preferred stock) on a fixed basis (either as a set amount or specified percentage of the stock value) going forward, and that such dividends are actually paid. This can create additional tax liability for the parent and also reduce the operating capital of the company itself.

Where an applicable retained interest includes a distribution right which consists of the right to receive a qualified payment and there are one or more liquidation, put, call, or conversion rights with respect to such interest, the value of all such rights is to be determined by assuming that each such liquidation, put, call, or conversion right is exercised in a manner which results in the lowest value.[1] IRC Section 2701 does not apply to distribution rights with respect to qualified payments where there is no liquidation, put, call, or conversion right with respect to the distribution right.[2]

The rules imposed under IRC Section 2701 also do not apply if, for either the transferred interest or the applicable retained interest, market quotations are readily available (as of the date of transfer) on an established securities market. Further, the rules do not apply if the applicable retained interest is of the same class as the transferred interest, or if the applicable retained interest is proportionally the same as the transferred interest (disregarding nonlapsing differences with respect to voting in the case of a corporation, or with respect to management and limitations on liability in the case of a partnership).[3] An exception from the rules is also provided for a transfer of a vertical slice of interests in an entity (defined as a proportionate reduction of each class of equity interest held by the transferor and "applicable family members" (defined below) in the aggregate). For example, Section 2701 does not apply if John owns 50 percent of each class of equity interest in a corporation and transfers a portion of each class to his child in a way that reduces each of John's interests, as well as the aggregate interests held by any applicable family members, by 10 percent. This is so even if the transfer does not proportionately reduce John's interest in each class.[4]

Definitions

An "applicable retained interest" is any interest in an entity with respect to which there is (1) a distribution right and the transferor and family members control the entity immediately

1. IRC Sec. 2701(a)(3)(B).
2. IRC Sec. 2701(a)(3)(C).
3. IRC Sec. 2701(a)(2).
4. Treas. Reg. §25.2701-1(c)(4).

before the transfer, or (2) a liquidation, put, call, or conversion right (i.e, rights commonly granted to holders of preferred stock).[1]

A "qualified payment" means any dividend payable on a periodic basis at a fixed rate (including rates tied to specific market rates) on any cumulative preferred stock (or comparable payment with respect to a partnership). With respect to the transferor, an otherwise qualified payment is to be treated as such unless the transferor elects otherwise. With respect to applicable family members, an otherwise qualified payment is not to be treated as such unless the family member so elects. A transferor or a family member can make an irrevocable election to treat any distribution right (which is otherwise not a qualified payment) as a qualified payment, payable at such times and in such amounts as provided in the election (such times and amounts not to be inconsistent with any underlying legal instruments creating such rights).[2] The value assigned to a right for which an election is made cannot exceed fair market value (determined without regard to IRC Section 2701).[3]

A "member of the transferor's family" includes the transferor's spouse, lineal descendants of the transferor or transferor's spouse, and the spouse of any such descendant.[4] An "applicable family member" with respect to a transferor includes the transferor's spouse, an ancestor of the transferor or transferor's spouse, and the spouse of any such ancestor.[5] An individual is treated as holding interests held indirectly through a corporation, partnership, trust, or other entity.[6] In the case of a corporation, "control" means 50 percent ownership (by vote or value) of the stock. In the case of a partnership, "control" means 50 percent ownership of the capital or profits interests, or in the case of a limited partnership, the ownership of any interest as a general partner.[7] When determining control, an individual is treated as holding any interest held by an applicable family member (see above), including (for this purpose) any lineal descendant of any parent of the transferor or the transferor's spouse.[8]

8930. How can the existence of voting stock create adverse estate tax consequences in the context of a transfer of stock in a controlled corporation?

When a taxpayer transfers property in which certain rights are retained, the value of that property will be included in the estate for estate tax purposes.[9] IRC Section 2036 specifically provides that retaining the right to vote shares in certain corporations constitutes a right that will generate estate tax inclusion even if the shares themselves are actually transferred. This is the case whether the right to vote is retained directly or indirectly (such as through the use of a trust entity or informal agreement).[10]

1. IRC Sec. 2701(b).
2. IRC Sec. 2701(c)(3).
3. Treas. Reg. §25.2701-2(c)(2).
4. IRC Sec. 2701(e)(1).
5. IRC Sec. 2701(e)(2).
6. IRC Sec. 2701(e)(3).
7. IRC Sec. 2701(b)(2).
8. IRC Sec. 2701(b)(2)(C).
9. IRC Sec. 2036(a).
10. IRC Sec. 2036(b).

In order for the value of transferred voting stock to be included in the original shareholder's estate, the corporation must be considered a "controlled corporation." A corporation is a controlled corporation if, at any time after the transfer and during the three-year period ending on the date of the decedent's death, the decedent-transferor owned at least 20 percent of the combined voting power of all classes of the corporation's stock. In determining the 20 percent ownership test, the family attribution rules of IRC Section 318 apply.[1]

As a result, the transferring owner will be treated as though he or she owns (1) any stock owned (either directly or indirectly) by the spouse, children, grandchildren or parents, (2) a proportionate share of any stock owned by a partnership or estate in which the transferor is either a partner or beneficiary, (3) a proportionate share of any stock owned by a trust of which he or she is a beneficiary or grantor and (4) stock owned by a corporation if the transferring owner owns 50 percent or more of the value of that corporation. These broad attribution rules expand the reach of IRC Section 2036, making the transfer of nonvoting stock the most effective way to avoid the risk that the value of the shares will eventually be included in the transferor's estate.

8931. Can a qualified terminable interest property (QTIP) trust be useful in reducing the estate tax burden in a family business' succession plan?

Yes. In the context of a family-owned business owned by one spouse, a qualified terminable interest property trust is a tool that may be used in reducing the estate tax burden upon the death of the first-to-die spouse if the business interests would otherwise be included in the taxable estate. Essentially, this strategy is used to remove a portion of the first-to-die spouse's interests from his or her estate so that the value of that estate is reduced to below the applicable estate tax exemption amount ($5.6 million in 2018).

A qualified terminable interest property trust is a trust containing "qualified terminable interest property" (QTIP), which is property (1) which passes from the decedent, (2) in which the surviving spouse has a "qualifying income interest for life," and (3) as to which the executor makes an irrevocable election on the federal estate tax return to have the marital deduction apply.

The surviving spouse has a "qualifying income interest for life" if (1) the surviving spouse is entitled to all the income from the property, payable annually or at more frequent intervals, and (2) no person has a power to appoint any part of the property to any person other than the surviving spouse unless the power is exercisable only at or after the death of the surviving spouse.[2] Apparently, the last requirement is violated even if it is the surviving spouse who is given the lifetime power to appoint to someone other than the surviving spouse.[3]

An executor can elect under Code Section 2056(b)(7) to treat an individual retirement account and a trust as QTIP if the trustee is the named beneficiary of decedent's IRA and the

1. IRC Sec. 2036(b)(2).
2. IRC Sec. 2056(b)(7).
3. TAM 200234017.

surviving spouse can compel the trustee to withdraw from the IRA an amount equal to all the income earned on the IRA assets at least annually and to distribute that amount to the spouse. No person can have a power to appoint any part of the trust property to any person other than the spouse.[1]

Importantly, this strategy allows the spouse who actually controlled the business to direct how the *principal* (the actual business shares) will be disposed of after the death of the surviving spouse. However, if the QTIP trust is funded with a minority interest in the business, and the estate contains a controlling interest, it is possible that a control premium and minority discount (see Q 8945) may impact the valuation of the shares for estate tax purposes. In this case, the shares that form the controlling interest may be given a higher value than anticipated (and the shares included in the QTIP trust may be given a *lower* value than anticipated), thus increasing the estate value while correspondingly decreasing the value of the martial deduction that will result from the use of the QTIP strategy.

As a result, the business owner should consider the impact of the control premium and minority discount valuation issues, and either (1) transfer additional assets from the estate to the QTIP trust in order to reduce the value of the estate to below the exemption level or (2) ensure that sufficient shares are transferred into the QTIP trust so that the estate will not be deemed to hold a controlling interest in the business.

See Q 8932 for a discussion of the implications of using a QTIP trust to transfer small business interests in the context of a buy-sell agreement.

8932. Can a qualified terminable interest property (QTIP) trust be used in a family business succession plan if the business interests at issue are subject to a buy-sell agreement?

Using a qualified terminable interest property (QTIP) trust where the business interests at issue are subject to a buy-sell agreement can create estate tax problems if the stock value set by the buy-sell agreement does not meet the requirements of IRC Section 2703 (see Q 8937). Generally, if the requirements of Section 2703 are satisfied, the price specified under the buy-sell agreement will control for estate tax purposes.[2]

If the requirements are not satisfied, however, the price may be adjusted so that it reflects the true fair market value of the stock. As a result, if the value is adjusted upward, the shareholders who are subject to the buy-sell agreement may be deemed to have received an economic benefit from the surviving spouse's QTIP because those shareholders were granted the right to purchase the shares at a lower price.

To qualify as QTIP property, no person may be given a power to appoint any part of the property to any person other than the surviving spouse unless the power is exercisable only at or after the death of the surviving spouse (see Q 8931).[3] If a third party is given the power to

1. Rev. Rul. 2000-2, 2000-1 CB 305.
2. See, for example, *Slocum v. U.S.*, 256 F. Supp. 753 (S.D.N.Y. 1966).
3. IRC Sec. 2056(b)(5).

purchase shares that would otherwise be QTIP at a price that is eventually found to be lower than fair market value, the QTIP trust may be ineligible for QTIP treatment because, effectively, the difference between the lower price specified in the buy-sell agreement and the higher true fair market value is treated as income that is derived from the shares and granted to a party other than the surviving spouse.[1]

Similarly, if the buy-sell agreement prohibits the QTIP trust from selling the stock without the consent of a third party, the shares will likely fail to qualify as QTIP. One of the essential requirements of a QTIP trust is that it must entitle the surviving spouse to receive all of the income derived from the trust principal. In order to give effect to this requirement, the regulations provide that the surviving spouse must be given the power to require that the trustee convert any unproductive property into income-producing property. Such a power will not disqualify the property as QTIP so long as applicable trust administration rules require the trustee to use the judgment and care in the exercise of the power that a prudent man would use if he were owner of the property. What's more, a power to retain a residence or other property for the spouse's personal use will not disqualify the interest passing in trust, [2] If stock contained in a QTIP trust cannot be sold without the permission of a third party, the surviving spouse's income rights are not absolute and the property may fail to qualify for the marital deduction.[3]

8933. Should the transfer of stock to a successor generation pursuant to a family business succession plan be structured as gifts or compensation?

While each small business is different, many family-owned businesses prefer to structure the transfer of stock to the next generation as compensation, rather than making the transfer by gifts.

The compensation structure, while generating taxable income for the successor generation, offers a tax deduction to the company that will often offset any income tax liability that is created.[4] While the income tax liability may be deferred under IRC Section 83 if the transferred stock is subject to a substantial risk of forfeiture, in the family business context, the income tax liability incurred by the successor-employee can often be eliminated through a bonus or other additional compensation.

The compensation structure may be preferable to transferring stock to the successor generation via gifts because the successor-employee will receive a basis in the stock that is equal to its fair market value on the date of transfer.[5] Conversely, if the transaction is structured as a gift, the successor-employee will receive a basis in the stock that is equal to its basis in the hands of the transferor (a carryover basis).[6] For stock that has appreciated with time, this can

1. See TAM 9147065, where it was found that the first-to-die spouse granted an option for his sons to grant themselves the excess of the fair market value of the shares over the option price, thus defeating the property's QTIP status.
2. Treas. Reg. §20.2056(b)-5(f)(4).
3. TAM 9147065.
4. IRC Secs. 83(a), 83(h), 162(a).
5. IRC Sec. 1012; Treas. Reg. §1.83-4(b).
6. IRC Sec. 1015(a).

reduce any gains that the successor would be required to recognize should the stock eventually be transferred again in the future.

Further, the compensation structure eliminates any gift tax liability that would be incurred if the transfer were made through gifts. By structuring the transfer of company stock as compensation, the parent generation is not required to use up any of its gift tax annual exclusion or lifetime exemption amount by making the transfer—leaving it free to reduce its taxable estate further by making other gifts of property to the successor generation.

However, as a practical matter, the higher estate and gift tax exemptions are reducing the number of individuals who will have difficulties in transferring their business free of estate and gift tax. Also, with respect to the compensation approach to transferring the business, the taxpayer is essentially trading the estate tax for the income tax. Since the estate tax rate is currently 40 percent and the income tax rates are less, this approach can be viable to the extent the federal estate tax is applicable.

8934. How can a three-year grantor retained income trust (GRIT) be used in family business succession planning?

A grantor retained income trust (GRIT) is an irrevocable trust created by the grantor allowing the grantor to retain an income interest for a term of years. At the end of the term, the property held in trust is distributed to, or remains in trust for, the named beneficiaries. If the grantor survives beyond the retained income term, then the property transferred in trust—the remainder interest in the trust property—is not included in the grantor's estate. Although the transfer of a remainder interest is a taxable gift—a gift tax is due when the transfer is made—a GRIT can reduce a grantor's overall transfer tax liability because the gift tax is based on the value of the remainder when transferred. Thus, any appreciation in the remainder property (from the date of the gift to the date of the grantor's death) is effectively transferred estate tax-free. However, if the grantor dies before the retained income period expires, the trust property is included in the grantor's estate and will be subject to estate tax.

A three-year GRIT is simply a GRIT whose specified term is three years—a time period that stems from the general rule that gifts that are made within three years of a donor's death will be brought back into the donor's estate.[1] In this context, a gift of stock is transferred to a GRIT that provides that all income from the trust will be paid to the parent generation for a period of three years. Because this income right is not a fixed amount or fixed percentage of the fair market value of the stock transferred, it is not a "qualified interest,"[2] so that the value of the income interest—or the "retained interest"—will be zero.[3] This means that, for gift tax purposes, the value of the interest that remains at the end of the term will be the entire value of the stock transferred.[4] Effectively, this strategy is most valuable when the parent generation

1. IRC Sec. 2035.
2. Treas. Reg. §25.2702-3(b).
3. Treas. Reg. §25.2702-1.
4. IRC Sec. 2702; Treas. Reg. §25.2702-1(b).

has determined that it is willing to pay the gift taxes on the stock transfer currently in order to avoid the inclusion of the appreciated stock in their estate.

At the end of the three-year period, the stock will pass to the next generation. The risk of this strategy is that, if the parent generation dies within the three-year period, the value of the stock (including any appreciation that occurs within the three-year period) and all gift taxes paid will be included in the parent's estate (although the estate will receive a credit for the gift taxes already paid). If the parent outlives the three-year period, this risk is eliminated and any appreciation in the stock is transferred estate tax-free.

The ability to use this technique has been limited with the advent of IRC Section 2702. This section provides that the retained interest is valued at zero, unless the retained interest is a "qualified retained interest." The rules of Section 2702 apply with respect to transfers to family members.[1] Therefore, the ability to implement a GRIT is limited to those parties that are not family members within the statutory definition. This technique may have applicability to same sex couples who do not get married and other unrelated parties within the definition.

1. Treas. Reg. §25.2702-2(a)(1) for definition of "member of the family." This regulation defines member of the family as the individual's spouse, any ancestor or lineal descendant of the individual or the individual's spouse, any brother or sister of the individual, and any spouse of the foregoing. However, there are a few exceptions which will permit these transfers with retained interests among family members. These are GRATs and GRUTs, personal residence trusts and the qualified personal residence trusts.

PART XV: SMALL BUSINESS VALUATION

8935. How is the value of a small business determined? Why is valuing a small business different from valuation in other business contexts?

Small business value, as in other valuation contexts, is usually defined in terms of "market value" or "fair market value," which means the amount a willing buyer would pay a willing seller for property (the individual business interests) or a business enterprise, assuming that each party to the transaction has reasonable knowledge of all material facts and that neither is under a compulsion to buy or sell. In the small business context, valuation is often problematic because, typically, there is no established secondary market in which the business interests are bought and sold, whereas a larger entity may be traded on an established market so that its fair market value is easily established by current trading prices.

Further, the business owners are typically very involved in the day-to-day operations and management of a small business—meaning that the current owners' exit from the business can dramatically impact the business' future operations and, thus, its current value.

Often, valuation issues in the small business context become important when the owner-managers seek to transfer their interests in the business to related parties—typically children or grandchildren. Even if these business succession plans are structured as bona fide sales, rather than outright gifts, the IRS is more likely to closely scrutinize the transaction in order to ensure that the interests were valued based on their market value, however limited, to avoid transitioning the business using artificially low values in order to disguise a gift transaction.

Similarly, estate tax valuation is often important in the small business context because of the lack of an established market to provide an objective valuation benchmark for determining the value that must be included in a deceased owner's taxable estate.

Because of these factors, the IRS has recognized that there is no one exact formula that can be used in valuing a small business, and that the valuation process, by its nature, requires a fact intensive inquiry over which even independent expert appraisers might disagree.[1] Despite this, a series of general principles governing valuation of small business interests has emerged to provide guidance to the small business owner. At a high level, three methods of business valuation exist: asset valuation, income valuation and market valuation. The asset valuation approach (an asset sale) is often the default if no action is taken by the business owner and/or if the business owner dies while in business. Although the details can get complicated as it applies to specific fact situations, this method simply involves taking the sum of the assets and subtracting the liabilities to find the value of the business. This method is not appropriate for certain types of businesses. In the case of professional service organizations comprised of professionals such as attorneys, doctors, accountants and financial planners, the business' tangible assets can be of negligible value, which could cause a vast undervaluation of the business.

Income valuation and market valuation are discussed at Q 8939 and Q 8940.

1. Rev. Rul. 59-60, 1959-1 CB 237.

General valuation principles are discussed in Q 8936, while Q 8937 outlines the potential impact of a buy-sell agreement upon valuation. Q 8938 addresses some of the more specific issues that arise when the business interests are composed of corporate stock.

Special estate tax valuation rules are discussed in Q 8946. See Q 8903 to Q 8934 for a discussion of business succession planning in general.

8936. What general principles govern small business valuation for estate and gift tax purposes?

The fair market value of any interest in an "unmarketable business," whether it is structured as a partnership, corporation, limited liability company, or a proprietorship, is the amount that a willing buyer, whether an individual or a corporation, would pay for the interest to a willing seller, neither being under any compulsion to buy or to sell and both having reasonable knowledge of the relevant facts. The net value is determined on the basis of all relevant factors, including the following:

(1) The value of all the assets of the business, tangible and intangible, including goodwill (see Q 8941 and Q 8942);

(2) The demonstrated earning capacity of the business; and

(3) The other factors set forth in the regulations[1] relating to valuation of corporate stock, to the extent applicable.

Adequately determining the value of a small business' "goodwill" requires special attention, as it is an especially fact intensive determination. Complete financial and other data upon which the valuation is based should be submitted with the relevant tax return, including copies of reports of examinations of the business made by accountants, engineers, or any technical experts as close to the applicable valuation date as possible.[2]

Professional appraisers, courts and the IRS generally follow the principles laid out in Revenue Ruling 59-60 when valuing the stock of a closely-held corporation or the stock of corporations where market quotations are not readily available. The factors outlined in Revenue Ruling 59-60 also apply in valuing interests of other business entities, such as closely-held partnerships or LLCs, for gift tax or estate tax purposes.

In the case of small business stock, where actual sale prices and bona fide bid and asked prices of the security of a closely held or other corporation are unavailable, fair market value (fmv) of the security is determined by taking into consideration the soundness of the security, the interest yield, the date of maturity and other relevant factors. In the case of shares of stock, fmv is determined by taking the company's net worth, prospective earning power and dividend-paying capacity, and other relevant factors into consideration. In each case, "other relevant factors" include, but are not limited to: the goodwill of the business; the economic outlook of the

1. See Treas. Reg. §§20.2031-2(f), 20.2031-2(h), 25.2512-2(f).
2. Treas. Reg. §§20.2031-3, 25.2512-3.

particular industry; the company's position in the industry and its management; the degree of control of the business represented by the block of stock to be valued; and the values of securities of corporations engaged in the same or similar lines of business which are listed on a stock exchange.[1]

Typically, in a valuation challenge today, the courts will adopt a "winner take all" approach, rather than seeking a compromise position between the two parties' competing valuation proposals. This is because the Tax Court has found that the "compromise the difference" approach that was historically used by the courts merely encouraged the parties to assert extreme values, forcing the courts to determine a reasonable middle ground between those two extreme positions.

The Tax Court adopted its "winner take all" approach in a 1980 valuation decision, *Buffalo Tool & Die Manufacturing Company, Inc. v. Commissioner*,[2] finding that the parties were fully capable of reaching an agreement themselves in order to avoid the judicial process (and the related expenses) altogether. Therefore, the court reasoned that the threat that the other party's valuation approach would be adopted in its entirety would motivate more careful analysis by the parties before resulting to judicial intervention. This is the approach that the majority of courts now take with respect to valuation decisions.[3]

8937. How does the existence of a buy-sell agreement impact small business valuation?

As discussed in Q 8903 to Q 8918, a buy-sell agreement can function as an important business succession planning tool, as it allows the business owners to plan for the orderly withdrawal of one or more business owners and will specify a predetermined method for determining the price of the business interests. Despite this, IRC Section 2703 provides that the value of any interest must be determined without regard to any option, agreement, or other right to acquire or use the property at a price less than the fair market value of the property (without regard to the option, agreement, or other restrictions) or any restriction on the right to sell or use the property (i.e., buy-sell agreement), unless the agreement meets the following requirements:

(1) It is a bona fide business arrangement;

(2) It is not a device to transfer the property to members of the decedent's family for less than full or adequate consideration; and

(3) It has terms comparable to those entered into by persons in an arm's length transaction.[4]

Assuming these requirements are met, it is possible that the *estate tax* value of a business interest (including closely-held stock) may be controlled by the price or formula contained in a buy-sell agreement.

1. Treas. Reg. §25.2512-2(f).
2. 74 TC 441.
3. *Est. of McGill v. Comm.*, TC Memo 1984-292 (voting trust certificates); *Est. of Gallo v. Comm.*, TC Memo 1985-363 (closely held stock); *Est. of Gillet v. Comm.*, TC Memo 1985-394 (closely held stock); *Est. of Rubish v. Comm.*, TC memo 1985-406 (ranch); *Est. of Watts v. Comm.*, TC Memo 1985-595 (partnership interest).
4. IRC Sec. 2703.

Though the facts of each case must be examined to determine whether the agreement price will be accepted for estate tax purposes,[1] case law has established that if the following conditions are met, the agreement price will hold, even though the fair market value of the business interest may be substantially more at the valuation date than the agreement price:

(1) The estate must be obligated to sell at death (under either a mandatory purchase agreement or an option held by the designated purchaser, see Q 8909);

(2) The agreement must prohibit the owner from disposing of his interest during his lifetime at a price higher than the contract or option price;

(3) The price must be fixed by the terms of the agreement or the agreement must contain a formula or method for determining the price; and

(4) The agreement must be an arm's length business transaction and not a gift. Thus, the purchase price must be fair and adequate at the time the agreement is made, particularly if the parties are closely related.[2]

Therefore, the price set in a buy-sell agreement was found to control valuation issues in a number of cases involving estate tax valuation where these requirements were satisfied.[3] For gift tax purposes, however, an agreement restricting lifetime sale will be considered with all other pertinent factors, and may tend to lower the value of the business interest.[4]

If a business purchase agreement calls for shares to be purchased from an estate with installment purchase notes bearing a rate of interest lower than the market rate at the date of death, an executor may be allowed to discount the value of the shares by the difference between the interest rate called for in the buy-sell agreement and the prevailing rate at the date of death. The IRS has ruled privately that it was relevant that (1) the purchaser was to buy the stock by means of installment payments plus interest over a thirty-year period, and (2) the market rate of interest increased substantially from the time of the buy-sell agreement to the time of the decedent's death. The estate had no right to the payment of interest or principal on the promissory note until each installment came due.[5]

A first-offer agreement, under which survivors have no enforceable right to purchase the business interest and can purchase the interest only if the executor wishes to sell, does not fix the value of the interest for estate tax purposes.[6]

1. Treas. Reg. §§20.2031-2(h), 20.2031-3; Rev. Rul. 59-60, 1959-1 CB 237.
2. *Slocum v. U.S.*, 256 F. Supp. 753 (S.D.N.Y. 1966).
3. *Brodrick v. Gore*, 224 F.2d 892 (10th Cir. 1955); *May v. McGowan*, 194 F.2d 396 (2nd Cir. 1952); *Comm. v. Child's Estate*, 147 F.2d 368 (2nd Cir. 1952); *Comm. v. Bensel*, 100 F.2d 639 (3rd Cir. 1939); *Lomb v. Sugden*, 82 F.2d 166 (2nd Cir. 1936); *Wilson v. Bowers*, 57 F.2d 682 (2nd Cir. 1932); *Mandel v. Sturr*, 266 F.2d 321 (2nd Cir. 1959); *Fiorito v. Comm.*, 33 TC 440, acq. 1960-1 CB 4; *Est. of Littick*, 31 TC 181, acq. in result, 1984-2 CB 1; *Est. of Weil*, 22 TC 1267, acq. 1955-2 CB 10; *Est. of Salt*, 17 TC 92, acq. 1952-1 CB 4; *Est. of Maddock*, 16 TC 324, acq. 1951-2 CB 3. See also Treas. Reg. §§20.2031-2(h), 20.2031-3.
4. *Est. of James v. Comm.*, 148 F.2d 236 (2nd Cir. 1945); *Kline v. Comm.*, 130 F.2d 742 (3rd Cir. 1942); *Krauss v. U.S.*, 140 F.2d 510 (5th Cir. 1944); *Comm. v. McCann*, 146 F.2d 385 (2nd Cir. 1944); *Spitzer v. Comm.*, 153 F.2d 967 (8th Cir. 1946).
5. Let. Rul. 8245007.
6. *Worcester County Trust Co. v. Comm.*, 134 F.2d 578 (1st Cir. 1943); *City Bank Farmers Trust Co. v. Comm.*, 23 BTA 663 (1931), acq. 1932-1 CB 2; *Michigan Trust Co. v. Comm.*, 27 BTA 556 (1933).

If an agreement is between closely related persons and is found to be merely a scheme for avoiding estate taxes, the price set in the agreement will not control.[1] A buy-sell agreement is not binding unless it represents a bona fide business agreement and is not testamentary in nature.[2] An agreement may be found to be a scheme for avoiding estate taxes, however, even if it also serves a bona-fide business purpose.[3]

No effect will be given to an option or contract under which a decedent is free to dispose of the interest or shares at any price he or she chooses during life.[4]

On the other hand, an agreement that restricts sale during life, but not at death, also will fail to fix the estate tax value.[5]

8938. How are shares of stock valued in a closely-held corporation?

IRC Section 2031(b) governs valuation, for estate tax purposes, of unlisted stocks and securities. Essentially, this provision provides that the value of securities of corporations involved in the same or similar business may be considered in cases where the small business at issue has no readily available market price because its interests are neither listed on a public exchange nor frequently traded.

Revenue Ruling 59-60 contains a broad discussion of factors that the IRS believes should be considered in valuing shares of stock in closely-held corporations or in corporations where market quotations are either lacking or too scarce to be recognized.[6] The IRS has found that in these cases, all available financial data, as well as all relevant factors affecting the fair market value, should be considered. The following nonexhaustive list of factors are important in this analysis:

(1) The nature of the business and the history of the enterprise from its inception;

(2) The economic outlook in general and the condition and outlook of the specific industry in particular (see Q 8943);

(3) The book value of the stock and the financial condition of the business;

(4) The business' earning capacity;

(5) The business' dividend-paying capacity;

(6) Any goodwill or other intangible value that can be attributed to the business (see Q 8941 and Q 8942);

(7) Sales of the stock and the size of the block of stock to be valued (see Q 8945); and

1. *Slocum v. U.S.*, 256 F. Supp. 753 (S.D.N.Y. 1966).
2. *Est. of True v. Comm.*, 2004-2 USTC ¶60,495 (10th Cir. 2004).
3. *St. Louis County Bank v. U.S.*, 49 AFTR 2d ¶1509 (8th Cir. 1982).
4. *Est. of Caplan v. Comm.*, TC Memo 1974-39; *Est. of Gannon v. Comm.*, 21 TC 1073 (1954); *Est. of Trammell v. Comm.*, 18 TC 662 (1952), acq. 1953-1 CB 6; *Est. of Matthews v. Comm.*, 3 TC 525 (1944); *Hoffman v. Comm.*, 2 TC 1160 (1943); *Est. of Tompkins v. Comm.*, 13 TC 1054 (1949); Rev. Rul. 59-60, 1959-1 CB 237.
5. *Land v. U.S.*, 303 F.2d 170 (5th Cir. 1962).
6. 1959-1 CB 237.

(8) The market price of stock of corporations engaged in the same or a similar line of business having their stock actively traded in a free and open market, either on an exchange or over-the-counter (see Q 8939).[1]

In general, when valuing an operating company that sells goods and services, primary consideration is given to earnings, and when valuing a company that merely holds investments, primary consideration is given to asset values. However, if a company is not easily characterized as one or the other, both earnings and assets must be considered.[2] For a discussion of the impact of a buy-sell agreement on valuation, see Q 8550.

8939. What is the market valuation approach used in valuing closely-held business interests?

The market valuation approach to valuing closely-held business interests attempts to determine the value of stock in a closely-held corporation by comparing it to the price of publicly traded shares in a comparable business. Revenue Ruling 59-60 guidelines (discussed in Q 8938) suggest that comparable business entities in the same or similar line of business must be identified as a starting point in this analysis. Once one or more comparable entities are located, their price/earnings (P/E) ratio must be determined. The P/E ratio is the price per share divided by the earnings of the applicable stock over the most recent 12 month period. This ratio illustrates the investor interest in the stock based on its current selling price on a recognized exchange or on the over-the-counter market.

When evaluating stock of a comparable publicly traded company, it should be remembered that only a small portion of the capital stock issued and outstanding is traded daily. As a result, such trades represent only minority-interest trading. Nevertheless, the P/E ratio of stock in a comparable publicly traded company is relevant because unlike closely-held shares, publicly traded stock has daily marketability through the exchanges, so price is always a known factor.

P/E ratios may fluctuate due to special situations—extraordinary losses or gains may occur in one year or the sale of a subsidiary may cause fluctuations. Moderate P/E fluctuations should be disregarded. However, if a company exhibits wide variations due to extraordinary losses or gains, it may be too volatile to be used as a meaningful basis for comparison.

Marketability Discount

The discussion concerning market valuation assumes that what is being sold or purchased is some type of minority share value with daily marketability. However, there is rarely a ready market for shares in a closely-held company. In addition, most closely-held companies do not provide financial data to the public and may not even provide it to minority shareholders. Finally, closely-held companies frequently place restrictions on stock.

All these "unknowns" work to limit the marketability of closely-held stock and introduce a marketability discount. Such discounts may range anywhere from 10 percent to 50 percent

1. Rev. Rul. 59-60, Sec. 4.01.
2. *Martin v. Comm.*, TC Memo 1985-424.

or more. (The larger discounts usually apply to minority blocks as opposed to controlling interests.) Marketability discounts must be determined on a case by case basis. Ultimately, the exact amount of the discount may not be known until the seller and buyer agree on a price per share. Nonetheless, it should be remembered that closely-held stock will almost always be valued at a lower rate than comparable publicly traded stock because of the marketability discount associated with closely-held companies (see Q 8935). See Q 8945 for a detailed discussion of the application of control premiums and minority discounts in small business valuation.

8940. What is the income valuation approach that is used in valuing closely-held business interests?

The income approach to valuing closely-held business interests is primarily based on an estimation of future earnings capacity. The first step in the process of calculating future earnings is to obtain any financial plans prepared by the company. The next step is to project the company's cash flow for a minimum of five years. These projections should be based on information about the recent past, including the company's profit-and-loss statements. Company sales and income are also frequently used to predict future cash flow.

In cases where the company has an erratic history of sales and earnings, the process may become more complex. In these situations, the reason behind the irregular financial past must be determined. An important element in this analysis involves determining whether the company is operating in a cyclical industry prone to yearly swings in sales and income. If so, other industry firms can be expected to show similar cyclical behavior. Recognizing an industry cycle should provide clues to future financial performance.

If the industry is non-cyclical, firm records must be reviewed to determine the specific reasons or events that caused the erratic history. Questions to ask include:

(1) Does the company face heavy debt and/or potentially substantial litigation costs?

(2) Is management lacking in experience or depth?

(3) Have products not been brought to market in a timely manner?

(4) Has growth been too rapid?

(5) Was expansion poorly planned?

A problem in any of these areas may signal problems in the future as well.

When predicting cash flow, the standard practice is to forecast five years into the future and discount each year's cash flow back to present value, by using a market-indicated rate of return. Risks faced generally by the industry in which the company operates should also be factored into this equation. The fifth year value of the company must be estimated by capitalizing the fifth-year cash flow, using an appropriate rate of return that considers both company and industry risk. The fifth year value is translated into present value by using a discount rate derived from the market rate.

The sum of the discounted cash flows for five years and the present value of the capitalized fifth year results in the fair market value of the company under this valuation approach.

8941. How is "goodwill" important in valuing small business interests?

Goodwill is an intangible business asset that includes attributes such as the business' reputation, client and supplier relationships and potential for repeat business. In the closely-held business context, IRS Revenue Ruling 59-60 specifically identifies goodwill as a factor that must be valued in order to determine the company's overall fair market value.

An important consideration in determining the presence of goodwill, and whether this goodwill is transferable, involves whether the general performance of the business depends upon a certain individual or a group of individuals. If this is the case, this goodwill may be lost if the business is sold without the continued participation of these individuals. Reduction in the value of goodwill can be exacerbated if those individuals not only leave the business, but also begin to compete against it. In the case of *Norwalk v. Commissioner*, a Tax Court case involving the liquidation of an accounting practice, the Court said that "[i]t is well-established ...that the transfer of the 'goodwill' of a professional practice generally requires an enforceable covenant not to compete in order to be fully effective"[1]

Though the IRS has recognized that the personal skill of one owner or a group of owners often cannot (or will not) be sold along with the business,[2] it has recognized that such skill can add substantially to the value of the business by enhancing the reputation of that business.[3] However, in order for the value of the business to be increased by the goodwill established by departing business owners, the IRS requires that those departing owners relinquish all rights to that goodwill. Therefore, for example, if a business owner or group of owners sell their business without allowing the purchasers to use their existing business name, no goodwill has been transferred that would increase the value of the business.[4]

8942. What factors are used in determining the intangible value of a small business?

As is typical in small business valuation, the IRS has indicated that the extent to which a business' value is attributable to intangible value in the form of goodwill must be determined on a case by case basis.[5] At its most basic level, the value that exceeds the value of the business' tangible assets is attributed to its goodwill. Goodwill is determined by deciding how much a purchaser would pay for this excess value, which is the product of intangibles such as reputation and market position (see Q 8941).

Because of the fact-intensive nature of the inquiry, there are no specific factors that must be considered in determining the goodwill of a small business. Often, the value of goodwill will depend upon the business' earning capacity and projected future earning capacity, but it can also

1. See *Zorniger v. Comm.*, 62 TC 435 (1974); *Akers v. Comm.*, 6 TC 693 (1946); *Norwalk v. Comm.*, TC Memo 1998-279.
2. See *Providence Mill Supply Co. v. Comm.*, 2 BTA 791 (1925).
3. Rev. Rul. 64-235, 19641964-2 CB 18.
4. Rev. Rul. 57-480, 1957-2 CB 47.
5. Rev. Rul. 64-235, above.

include value attributable to the business' prestige, whether it owns a trademark or brand name and its record of successful operation over a prolonged period of time.[1]

A business that derives much of its success from the services provided by its owners, such as a group of doctors or accountants, will often assign significant value to the goodwill generated by the reputations of these professionals. Conversely, if the business is primarily asset-driven, where the physical equipment or structures producing a product may be more important than the personal services of a business owner, goodwill may be assigned a lesser value. However, even in a product-driven business, if the reputation of concrete products produced by the business provides motivation for repeat business, the business' goodwill should be assigned a higher value.

The courts have held that the value of personal relationships established by a shareholder-employee or other business owner are generally not corporate assets, and therefore may not be considered in determining the value of goodwill, unless the individual has committed to continuing services to the business, whether contractually or otherwise. In this context, non-compete agreements and traditional employment agreements may be useful in establishing such a commitment[2] (see Q 8941).

Because the standards for valuing goodwill are so amorphous, the IRS has proposed a formula that may be used to value goodwill in the event that the parties are unable to assign value based upon past earnings performance and perceived reputational value. Under this formulaic approach, the owners must first determine the return on the average annual value of the business' tangible assets over a period of time (the IRS recommends five years). The percentage of returns that are based on tangible assets is subtracted from the total average earnings of the business over the same period of time. The remaining value is considered to represent earnings from the business' intangible assets, including goodwill. This value is then capitalized (at a suggested rate of 15 to 20 percent, depending upon the individual level of business risk) to allocate a value to those intangible assets.[3]

Any abnormal years should be excluded from the period used for averaging under this formula. In determining the rate of capitalization that is most appropriate, the IRS has indicated that the owners must consider factors such as (1) the nature of the business, (2) the risks involved in the business and (3) the stability or irregularity of earnings.

It is important to note that the IRS only recommends use of this formula if the parties are unable to otherwise realistically assign value to a business' goodwill through another reasonable approach that is based on factors more specific to the particular business. The IRS advises that the formula approach should not be used if there is better evidence available from which the value of intangibles can be determined. If the assets of a going business are sold upon the basis of a rate of capitalization that can be substantiated as being realistic, though it is not within the range of figures indicated here as the ones ordinarily to be adopted, the same rate of capitalization should be used in determining the value of intangibles.[4]

1. Rev. Rul. 59-60, 1959-1 CB 237.
2. *Martin Ice Cream Co. v. Comm.*, 110 TC 189 (1998).
3. Rev. Rul. 68-609, 1968-2 CB 327.
4. Rev. Rul. 68-609, 1968-2 CB 327. Prepared pursuant to Rev. Proc. 67-6, 1967-1 CB 576.

8943. What types of external risks are important in determining the value of a small business?

As in any other business context, the value of a small business may be substantially impacted by external pressures and risk factors. As such, the IRS recognizes that the general economic outlook and industry-specific risk factors must be considered in determining the overall value of the business.[1]

In this analysis, it is important to identify industry trends that have emerged, and whether the business' management is aware of these trends and planning to take advantage of them in their future business plans. While general economic outlook is an important consideration in assigning value to a business, the parties must also consider whether the small business in question tends to prosper in proportion to general economic conditions, or whether its performance is counter-cyclical. If the business' performance is counter-cyclical, valuation must account for the fact that a general market downturn could represent a period of growth within the industry that the business operates.

Investor perceptions toward the industry in which the business operates can also serve as a predictor of current and future business value. To this end, examination of comparable businesses that are traded more regularly can aid in determining the potential for increased value in the small business based on industry performance. The IRS, therefore, recognizes that the market prices of stock in corporations engaged in the same or similar lines of business with actively traded stock, either on an exchange or over-the-counter, can be important in determining investor perceptions that can influence future value.[2]

Further, it is important to identify the business' position in the industry with respect to its competitors. In this analysis, whether the individual business is more or less successful than competitors is important, but it is also important to determine whether the industry in which that business operates is competitive with respect to other industries. It must also be determined whether a company that is more successful than its competitors is poised to continue this success. For example, if a company's success is based largely upon the fact that it has developed a product that is new to the market, whether it can maintain this advantage is critical to anticipating future success.[3]

The courts have also made clear that, in any analysis that determines value partially based upon other business' performance, the comparable businesses that are selected must be appropriately comparable to the small business valuation at issue. For example, the performance of the securities of a holding company, where the primary issue is asset performance, are not appropriately comparable to the potential performance of an operating company, where the primary concern is earnings capacity, and thus should not be used to determine value.[4] According to the Tax Court, "[i]n general, the appraiser will accord primary consideration

1. Rev. Rul. 59-60.
2. See also the IRS' Business Valuation Guidelines IRM 4.48.4.2.3 (July 1, 2006).
3. Rev. Rul. 59-60.
4. *Estate of Ford v. Comm.*, TC Memo 1993-580.

to earnings when valuing stocks of companies which sell products or services to the public. Conversely, in the investment or holding type of company, the appraiser may accord the greatest weight to the assets underlying the security to be valued."[1]

While there is no formula for determining the impact of various external factors upon the value of a particular small business, the fact-intensive inquiry generally includes an evaluation of the following nonexhaustive list of issues:

(1) Status of the local labor market;

(2) The company's reliance on other entities for goods or services;

(3) The risk or anticipation of merger or acquisition;

(4) The existence of pending or potential litigation,

(5) The local, regional and national economies and forecasts; and

(6) The nature and extent of competition within the company's field.[2]

Both the relevance and the weight accorded to any one of these factors will depend upon the nature of the business and the industry and geographic location in which it operates.

8944. How does the current management structure of a small business impact valuation?

Generally, when the future prospects of a small business are completely dependent on the current management team, the business is at a much greater risk and, as a result, less valuable than a company with good management backup and a well-organized system of delegation. The organizational structure of the small business and the degree of control that the business owners exercise over the actual operations are important in determining the impact that the current management structure will have on the value of the business.

As discussed in Q 8941 and Q 8942, in a business where emphasis is placed on the performance of services by specified individuals, rather than the supply of goods through use of tangible assets owned by the business, the presence or absence of these individuals has a much more substantial impact on the business' value.[3] Similarly, where, as is common with many small businesses, operations are directed entirely by a small group, retention of these individuals can be key to maintaining the value of the business. The loss of individuals who have been key to a business' success can reduce the value that should be assigned to that business, especially if there is no succession plan in place.[4]

The IRS has recognized, however, that such losses can be offset, such as through the use of insurance funding, as in a buy-sell agreement where the company has purchased insurance

1. *Estate of Newhouse* v. *Comm.*, 94 TC 193 (1990).
2. Klaris, "*Valuing the Family Business,*" 129 Tr. & Est. 18 (Feb. 1990).
3. See *Providence Mill Supply Co. v. Comm.*, 2 BTA 791 (1925); Rev. Rul. 64-235, above.
4. Rev. Rul. 59-60.

to help sustain operations if a key owner dies or otherwise withdraws from the business (see Q 8906).[1] Such an offset must, therefore, be taken into account when assigning weight to the valuation impact of the current management structure, whether through the retention or loss of certain individuals' services.

8945. How can a majority or minority interest impact the value of a small business interest?

If a block of stock represents a controlling interest in a corporation, a "control premium" may add to the value of the stock. If, however, the shares constitute a minority ownership interest, a "minority discount" is often applied to the value. For example, in *Martin v. Commissioner*,[2] discounts were applied to shares of stock representing a minority interest in a holding company that, in turn, held minority interests in seven operating companies. In this case, lack of control over both the holding and operating companies, combined with a lack of marketability (see Q 8939), led the court to allow a combined 70 percent discount in valuing the interests.

A premium may also attach for swing vote attributes where one block of stock may exercise control by joining with another block of stock.[3] The IRS has valued stock included in the gross estate at a premium as a controlling interest, while applying a minority discount to the marital deduction portion which passed to the surviving spouse.[4]

However, the fact that an interest being valued is a minority interest does not always mean that a minority discount is available. Courts have held that, even though the interests at issue are minority interests, a minority discount is not appropriate if there is nothing lost through the minority ownership position. For example, in a case where the decedent owned minority interests in five partnerships, no discount was available because the partnership agreement required the partnerships to distribute cash flow annually based on a predetermined formula. Therefore, the majority partners would not be able to prevent or alter the partnership distributions and there was no risk that the minority owner would not receive an annual payout.[5]

If a donor transfers shares in a corporation to each of the donor's children, the IRS will no longer consider family control when valuing the gift under IRC Section 2512. Thus, a minority discount will not be disallowed solely because a transferred interest would be part of a controlling interest if such interest were aggregated with interests held by the person to whom the interest was transferred who was already a controlling shareholder.[6]

The Tax Court has determined that an estate would not be allowed a minority discount where the decedent transferred a small amount of stock immediately prior to death for the sole purpose of reducing her interest from a controlling interest to a minority interest for valuation purposes.[7] Also, a partnership or LLC may be included in the gross estate under IRC Section 2036

1. Rev. Rul. 59-60, above.
2. TC Memo 1985-424.
3. TAM 9436005.
4. TAM 9403005.
5. *Godley v. Comm.*, 2002-1 USTC ¶60,436 (2002) (partnerships held housing projects subject to long-term government contracts).
6. TAM 9432001.
7. *Est. of Murphy v. Comm.*, TC Memo 1990-472.

without the benefit of discounts if a decedent transfers all of his or her assets to the partnership or LLC and retains complete control over the income of the partnership or LLC.[1]

8946. What special estate tax valuation issues must be considered in the small business context?

In recognition of the limited marketability of closely-held family businesses, and in an effort to encourage the continued operation of these businesses after the death of the business owner, Congress enacted IRC Section 2032A to potentially ease the estate tax liability of successors to family businesses. If the family business includes ownership of real estate used in the business, the estate may be able to take advantage of this special use valuation provision in valuing the real property for inclusion in the gross estate.

Generally, real property is valued based upon its "highest and best use," which typically leads to a valuation that reflects the upper limit of the property's potential value. However, a "current use" approach is available for qualified real property used for farming purposes or in certain trades or businesses. "Qualified real property" used in a closely-held business may also qualify for special use valuation.[2] An estate's executor can elect to value qualified real property used in a closely-held business on the basis of its *actual* use in the business, rather than its highest and best use, if the requirements of IRC Section 2032A, discussed below, are satisfied.

Planning Point: As it applies to real property, farmers and ranchers often feel asset rich and cash poor. The estate tax issues they face are significant and not easily solved. One option to consider are "land grant" non-profit organizations that preserve the ranching/farming heritage and avoid liquidation due to taxes.

The aggregate decrease in the business value permitted through special use valuation under Section 2032A is $1,140,000 for decedents dying in 2018, as indexed annually for inflation.[3]

Section 2032A valuation may be elected if: (1) the qualified property is owned by a U.S. citizen or resident and (2) the executor makes the election under Section 2032A(d)(2).[4] Qualified real property is real property located in the United States where the following additional conditions are satisfied:

(1) *Substantial and historical usage.* The IRC Section 2032A election is only available to estates in which a farming or other closely held business comprises a substantial part of the estate. The following requirements apply:

 (a) (i) 25 percent or more of the adjusted value of the decedent's gross estate must consist of the adjusted value of real property used in the business, and (ii) 50 percent or more of the adjusted value of the gross estate must consist of the adjusted value of real or personal property used in the business;[5] and

1. *Est. of Strangi v. Comm.*, TC Memo 2003-145; *Kimbell v. U.S.*, 2003-1 USTC ¶60,455 (2003).
2. IRC Sec. 2032A(a)(1).
3. Rev. Proc. 2017-58.
4. IRC Sec. 2032A(b).
5. IRC Sec. 2032A(b)(1)(A) and (B).

(b) During the eight years immediately preceding the decedent's death, the decedent, or a member of his family, must have (i) owned and used the property[1] and (ii) materially participated in the business.[2]

(2) *Future usage to prevent recapture*. Because IRC Section 2032A is intended to encourage continued future use of the property, each person with an interest in the property must sign a written consent to a special recapture tax set forth in IRC Section 2032A(c).[3] This requirement is imposed in furtherance of the goal of encouraging the decedent's heirs to continue the business rather than being forced to sell in order to meet tax liabilities.[4]

The recapture tax is imposed if the heir (1) disposes of any interest in the qualified small business property to a non-family member or (2) ceases to use the property for a qualified use (meaning use within the closely-held business) within ten years of the death of the decedent and before the death of the qualified heir.[5] Essentially, a "qualified heir" is an heir who is either (1) a surviving spouse; (2) an heir who has not yet reached the age of twenty-one; (3) a disabled individual; or (4) a student.[6]

The numerous requirements imposed under IRC Section 2032A, along with its limited applicability in the estate tax context, naturally mean that the valuation approach will only be useful in limited circumstances.

1. IRC Sec. 2032A(b)(1)(C) and (A)(i); Treas. Reg. §20.2032A-3(c)(1) and (d).
2. IRC Sec. 2032A(e)(6) provides that material participation will be determined as under IRC Sec. 1402(a)(1).
3. IRC Sec. 2032A(d)(2).
4. See *Stovall v. Commissioner*, 101 TC 140 (1993).
5. IRC Sec. 2032A(c).
6. IRC Sec. 2032A(c)(7)(C).

PART XVI: ACCOUNTING

8947. What is an accounting period?

An accounting period is the taxable period that is used to determine a taxpayer's income tax liability.[1] An accounting period can be measured as either a calendar year[2] or a fiscal year.[3] In either case, the taxable year cannot exceed a period of twelve months.[4] Despite this, it is not sufficient for a taxpayer who is a business owner to merely begin an accounting period on the date the business began and end it twelve months later. This is because the accounting period does not end on the last day of December to qualify as a calendar year, does not end on the last day of the month to qualify as a fiscal year, and does not satisfy the fifty-two to fifty-three week requirements.[5]

Certain taxpayers are not permitted to choose their accounting period. The regulations require that most entities adopt a specific required tax year in order to prevent the manipulation of the tax year in order to artificially defer a taxpayer's tax liabilities.[6]

A calendar year accounting period is a period of twelve months that starts on January 1st and ends on December 31st. Any taxpayer can adopt the calendar year accounting period, though certain taxpayers are required to adopt a calendar year accounting period if any of the following are true:

(1) the taxpayer keeps no books;

(2) the taxpayer does not have an annual accounting period; or

(3) the taxpayer has an annual accounting period, but such period does not qualify as a fiscal year.[7]

If the taxpayer maintains records that are sufficient to adequately reflect the taxpayer's income on the basis of an annual accounting period, the taxpayer is considered to have "kept books."[8]

A fiscal year is any twelve month period that ends on the last day of any month other than December. The taxpayer must keep accounts and report income and expenses using the same period that corresponds to the chosen fiscal year.[9]

A taxpayer may also elect, as a variation of the fiscal year period, a tax year consisting of fifty-two to fifty-three weeks, where the annual accounting period varies between fifty-two and fifty-three weeks, but always ends on the same day of the week and, additionally, always ends on:

(1) Whatever date this same day of the week last occurs in a calendar month; or

---

1. IRC Sec. 441(c), 7701(a)(23), IRS Pub. 538.
2. IRC Sec. 441(d).
3. IRC Secs. 441(e), 7701(a)(24).
4. Treas. Reg. §1.441-1(a)(2).
5. IRC Sec. 441, Rev. Rul. 85-22, (1985)-1 CB 154.
6. Treas. Reg. §1.441-1(b)(2).
7. IRC Sec. 441 (g), IRS Pub. 538.
8. Treas. Reg. §1.441-1(b)(7).
9. IRC Secs. 441(e), 706(b). See also IRS Pub. 538.

(2) Whatever date this same day of the week falls that is nearest to the last day of the calendar month.[1]

Planning Point: Cyclical businesses, like retail stores, may have several months (holiday season) with large sales but many months where expenses exceed sales. Quarterly tax payments still must be made off the entire year's estimated revenues and not increased (for example, in the holiday season) and decreased as sales decrease. Moving the accounting period forward to the end of January (or later) enables retail stores to recognize the sales, less the returned items, and more accurately prepare for the upcoming year's tax obligations.

8948. How is a partnership's accounting period determined?

A partnership is one of the entities that is generally required to adopt a particular accounting period as specified under the regulations.[2] A partnership's accounting period is determined by reference to the partner's required accounting period(s).[3] The partnership's "required taxable year" can either be:

(1) The tax year of the majority partnership interest;

(2) The tax year of all the principal partners; or

(3) If it cannot be established based on the majority partnership interest or principal partners, a calendar year.[4]

For these purposes, when a partnership's accounting period is determined by reference to the majority interest, it means that it is determined based on the tax year of a partner or group of partners having an aggregate interest in partnership profits or capital of more than 50 percent.[5]

A "principal partner" is a partner who has an interest of five percent or more in partnership profits or capital.[6] Once it is established that a partner is a principal partner, that principal partner is required to maintain the same calendar year established by the partnership unless that principal partner is able to demonstrate a valid business purpose for the deviation.

See Q 8951 for a discussion of the business purpose test that must be satisfied to allow a principal partner to adopt an alternate accounting period. This business purpose test must also be satisfied in order for the partnership to adopt an accounting period that deviates from the requirements set forth in (1)-(3), above.

8949. How is an S corporation's accounting period determined?

An S corporation is generally required to adopt a calendar year accounting period (meaning that its tax year ends on December 31, see Q 8947) unless it can establish a valid business purpose for adopting an alternate accounting period.[7]

1. IRC Sec. 441(f).
2. Treas. Reg. §1.1441-4(b)(2)(i)(G), IRC Sec. 706.
3. IRC Secs. 444, 706.
4. IRC Sec. 706(b). See also Treas. Reg. §1.706-1(b)(2).
5. IRC Sec. 706(b)(4).
6. IRC Sec. 706(b)(3).
7. IRC Sec. 1378(b).

The business purpose test, applicable in the context of both partnerships and S corporations, is discussed in Q 8951.

8950. When can a partnership or S corporation elect an otherwise impermissible accounting period?

Partnerships and S corporations are entities that are generally required to adopt a taxable year in accordance with certain specified requirements, as set forth in the Internal Revenue Code and Treasury Regulations.[1] See Q 8948 (partnerships) and Q 8949 (S corporations) for the general rules applicable in establishing the accounting periods for these entities.

A partnership or S corporation is entitled to adopt an accounting period that varies from the otherwise specified requirements in the following cases:

(1) The entity establishes a valid business purpose for adopting a different accounting period (see Q 8951);[2]

(2) The entity elects a fifty-two to fifty-three week taxable year[3] (see Q 8947);

(3) The entity is entitled to use a grandfathered accounting period.

A grandfathered accounting period is an accounting period that either the partnership or S corporation has received permission to use on or before July 1, 1974 in an IRS letter ruling.[4]

The IRS will consider all of the facts and circumstances when determining whether to permit the adoption of an alternate tax year, including the tax consequences that would result from such a change.

In addition, a partnership or S corporation can elect to adopt a tax year other than its required year under Section 444 as long as the required accounting period is deferred for no more than three months.[5] An entity that makes this election is required to make certain payments under Section 7519 that are based on a formula derived from the entity's income for the year and the highest tax rate currently applicable under IRC Section 1 (39.6 percent for 2013 and beyond).[6]

8951. How does a partnership or S corporation establish that it has a valid business purpose for adopting an accounting period that deviates from its required accounting period?

A valid business purpose will generally be found to exist if the requested tax year coincides with the entity's ownership tax year (in the case of an S corporation) or natural business year.[7]

1. IRC Sec. 444(e).
2. IRC Secs. 706(b)(1)(C), 1378(b), Treas. Reg. §1.706-1(b)(2)(ii), (7).
3. Treas. Reg. §1.441-1(b)(2)(ii)(A).
4. Treas. Reg. §1.441-1(b)(6).
5. IRC Sec. 444(b).
6. IRC Sec. 7519(b).
7. Treas. Reg. §1.442-1(b)(2).

An S corporation can establish an ownership tax year as the tax year that constitutes the tax year of an S corporation shareholder holding more than 50 percent of the corporation's issued and outstanding stock, disregarding certain shareholders who are tax-exempt under IRC Section 501.[1] A partnership or S corporation can establish the term of its natural business year by satisfying one of the tests discussed below.

In general, the IRS has developed three tests that are used in determining whether a valid business purpose has been established:

(1) 25 percent gross receipts test;[2]

(2) Annual business cycle test; and[3]

(3) Seasonal business test.[4]

If the entity is able to establish that its requested accounting period corresponds to a natural business year that is supported by the 25 percent gross receipts test, the IRS will automatically approve the requested accounting period under Revenue Procedure 2006-46. The annual business cycle test and seasonal business test are subject to discretionary approval.

To satisfy the 25 percent gross receipts test, a taxpayer[5] must establish that it has earned at least 25 percent of its gross receipts from sales and services during the last two months of the requested accounting period, using its gross receipts for the preceding three years. The taxpayer must demonstrate that this 25 percent or more threshold is met by calculating the timing of its earnings as though the requested accounting period had been in effect for three years.[6] However, even if the taxpayer's requested accounting period satisfies this 25 percent gross receipts test, the taxpayer must determine whether another accounting period would also satisfy the 25 percent gross receipts test. If any accounting period *other than* the requested accounting period would produce the aggregation of a higher percentage of the entity's earnings in the final two months of the period, then the requested accounting period cannot automatically qualify as the taxpayer's natural business year. [7]

The taxpayer must use the same *method* as is used in filing that taxpayer's current tax return in calculating its gross receipts for purposes of the 25 percent gross receipts test. If an entity does not have at least a forty-seven month period of gross receipts, then it is not entitled to establish its natural business year under the gross receipts test. [8]

Under the annual business cycle test, a taxpayer must demonstrate that its business operates cyclically, in that it is subject to peak and non-peak periods. The taxpayer's natural business year

1. Rev. Proc. 2006-46, 2006-45 IRB 859.
2. Rev. Proc. 2006-46.
3. Rev. Proc. 2002-39, 2002-22 IRB 1046.
4. Rev. Proc. 2002-39.
5. Partnerships, S corporations or personal service corporations.
6. Rev. Proc. 2006-46, Rev. Proc. 2002-39.
7. Rev. Proc. 2006-46, Rev. Proc. 2002-39.
8. Rev. Proc. 2006-46, Rev. Proc. 2002-39.

may be found to end at the conclusion of its highest peak period of business, or soon thereafter.[1] Revenue Procedure 2002-39 provides a safe harbor rule that treats one month after the end of a business' peak season as "soon after" the close of the peak season. A business that has steady income throughout the year will not be able to satisfy this test.

The seasonal business test applies to entities that operate only during part of the year for one reason or another (for example, because of weather conditions) so that the entity's gross receipts for periods outside of its operational season are found to be insignificant. Under the seasonal business test, the entity's natural business year is deemed to end at the end of, or soon after, its seasonal operation.[2] If the entity earns 10 percent or less of its income outside of its operational season, such amounts are automatically deemed to be insignificant for purposes of this rule. One month after the end of the entity's operational season is deemed to be "soon after" the end of its season.

If a taxpayer is unable to satisfy any of the three tests described above, he or she may attempt to demonstrate a valid business purpose based on individual facts and circumstances by showing that there are compelling tax or non-tax reasons for adopting an alternative accounting period.[3] However, it is insufficient that the non-tax reasons asserted merely create a tax year that is more convenient for the taxpayer. As such, reasons that are considered insufficient include:

(1) The hiring patterns of the business;

(2) Use of a particular year for administrative purposes, such as the admission or retirement of partners or shareholders; or

(3) The fact that the business uses price lists or model years that change on an annual basis.

Further, if the tax consequences of the alternate period result in deferral or distortion, the requested change will often be denied unless the taxpayer is able to demonstrate compelling non-tax reasons for the change. The IRS has found that compelling non-tax reasons for an alternate accounting period exist in situations where the entity closed down operations for ten years for reasons beyond its control or when the entity's business was impacted by a strike, for example.[4]

Planning Point: Before changing accounting periods, a business owner should find out what the norm is for the business owner's industry. Changing accounting periods can also have unintended consequences. For example, accounting period changes can affect the calculations that go into the valuation of a business if the owner later chooses to sell it. Changing periods can also cause non-revenue generating paperwork for the acquirer which could affect negotiations.

1. Rev. Proc. 2002-39.
2. Rev. Proc. 2002-39.
3. Rev. Proc. 2002-39. See also Rev. Rul. 87-57, 1987-2 CB 117, illustrating the application of this test.
4. Rev. Rul. 87-57.

8952. When is it permissible for a taxpayer to adopt an accounting period that is less than twelve months?

A taxpayer may adopt an accounting period that is less than a full twelve month period, known as a short period, in certain limited circumstances.[1] A taxpayer may adopt a short period if:

(1) The taxpayer's short period has been specifically approved by the IRS;[2] or

(2) The taxpayer was only in existence during part of what would otherwise constitute the applicable accounting period.[3]

If a taxpayer obtains approval to adopt a short period under (1), above, the taxpayer must annualize taxable income by determining annual income and dividing that amount by the number of months in the short period.[4] Further, if the taxpayer is an individual, the amount of the taxpayer's personal exemption must be reduced so that it bears the same ratio to the full exemption as the number of months in the short period bears to twelve.[5]

Option (2), above, generally occurs in situations where a business entity only operated for a portion of the otherwise required tax year. For example, a business that liquidates before the close of its tax year is entitled to use the period of its existence during that accounting period as its short accounting period.[6]

8953. Can an accounting period be changed once chosen?

Yes. A taxpayer can change its accounting period if it has obtained the approval of the IRS unless the taxpayer is authorized under the Internal Revenue Code or the regulations to change the accounting period without prior approval.[7] (See Q 8954.)

Individual taxpayers are entitled to change accounting periods (e.g., from a calendar year to a fiscal year) by filing Form 1128 with the IRS.[8] Pass-through entities, such as partnerships and S corporations, are not entitled to change accounting periods using this form.

Partnerships and S corporations can obtain automatic approval to change to an alternate accounting period if the requirements set forth in Revenue Procedure 2006-46 are satisfied, meaning that the entity:[9]

(1) Is changing to a required taxable year (Q 8948 and Q 8949) or to a 52-53 week accounting period ending in reference to its required taxable year (Q 8947);

1. IRC Sec. 443(a).
2. IRC Sec. 443(a)(1).
3. IRC Sec. 443(a)(2).
4. IRC Sec. 443(b)(1).
5. IRC Sec. 443(c).
6. See IRC Secs 708 (termination of partnerships) and 1362 (termination of S corporation status).
7. IRC Sec. 442, Treas. Reg. §1.442-1(a).
8. Rev. Proc. 2002-39, Rev. Proc. 2003-62.
9. Rev. Proc. 2006-46.

(2) Satisfies the 25 percent gross receipts test (Q 8951);[1]

(3) Is an S corporation (or is planning to make an S election) changing to its ownership tax year (Q 8951);

(4) Wishes to change from a fifty-two to fifty-three-week taxable year to a non-fifty-two to fifty-three-week taxable year that ends on the last day of the same calendar month that is an otherwise permitted taxable year, and vice versa.[2]

Typically, the IRS will establish conditions that the taxpayer must satisfy in order to change its accounting period when it consents to the change.[3] In addition to any terms established by the IRS, the taxpayer will be required to maintain its records and compute its income based on the requested accounting period.

Generally the taxpayer must use Form 1128, "Application to Adopt, Change or Retain a Tax Year" to file for a change of accounting period. The taxpayer may not request to retroactively change an accounting period even to change to a required accounting period for a prior tax year.[4]

8954. Are there any circumstances that allow a small business taxpayer to change its accounting method without IRS approval?

Yes. The IRS has released guidance providing that small business taxpayers (see below) may make certain tangible property changes in methods of accounting in order to take into account only amounts paid or incurred, and dispositions made, in tax years beginning on or after January 1, 2014. For the tax year beginning on or after January 1, 2014, small business taxpayers are permitted to make such changes without filing Form 3115.[5]

For purposes of this exception, a "small business taxpayer" is a taxpayer with one or more distinct trades or businesses that has:

(1) Total assets of less than $10 million as of the first day of the tax year for which a change in accounting method under the final tangible property regulations and related guidance is effective; or

(2) Average annual gross receipts of $10 million or less for the prior three tax years.

This exception applies only to small business taxpayers electing to make changes in accounting methods in order to prospectively apply the final tangible property regulations. While these taxpayers are still permitted to file the Form 3115 in order to make this change, the IRS guidance allows small business taxpayers to simply make the change on a federal income tax return. This guidance is meant to ease the burden of changing accounting methods for small business taxpayers by effectively allowing them to make the change on a cut-off basis.

1. Rev. Proc. 2006-46.
2. Rev. Proc. 2006-46.
3. Rev. Proc. 2002-39.
4. Rev. Proc. 2006-45, 2006-45 IRB 851.
5. Rev. Proc. 2015-20, modifying Rev. Proc. 2015-14.

If a small business taxpayer has already filed a Form 3115 with respect to accounting changes applying the tangible property regulations, the taxpayer may withdraw the form by filing an amended return on or before the due date of the original tax return (including extensions).[1]

8955. What is the cash basis method of accounting?

The cash basis method of accounting is the most widely used accounting method for individual taxpayers, and is often used by many business entities, as well.[2] Cash basis taxpayers recognize all gross income, whether in the form of cash, property or services, in the year that the income is actually or constructively received.[3]

"Constructive receipt" is considered to have occurred when income is made available to a taxpayer without restrictions.[4] For example, a cash basis taxpayer cannot avoid reporting income simply because he refused to deposit a check. Conversely, if a taxpayer's employer provides the taxpayer with a stock bonus, but conditions are imposed so that the bonus is not available to the taxpayer until a future date, the corporation's reporting such bonus on its books does not constitute constructive receipt on the part of the taxpayer-employee.

Similarly, a taxpayer is entitled to claim any deductions for the year in which the expenses that gave rise to the deduction were actually paid.[5] There is no "constructive payment" type doctrine that corresponds to the constructive receipt doctrine discussed above, however.[6]

Though a cash basis taxpayer's receipt of income in the form of cash is simple to recognize, complications may arise when the income is received in the form of non-cash property or a right to receive income based on future services. As such, the IRS has developed the doctrines of "cash equivalence" and "economic benefit" to address the receipt of property and services. When income is received in the form of property, the cash basis taxpayer must include the fair market value of such property in income if rights to the income are (1) freely transferable, (2) readily marketable and (3) immediately convertible into cash.[7]

On the other hand, if a taxpayer contracts to perform services for a specified amount of income that will be received in installments over the period of service, the taxpayer does not report the value of the installment payments in the year the contract is entered. This is because the taxpayer does not receive a cash equivalent at the time of contracting, but rather obtains only the right to receive such cash payments in the future dependent on performance of the required services.[8]

Under the economic benefit theory, a taxpayer is required to recognize income if an economic benefit has been conferred upon the taxpayer, even if the taxpayer has no ability to currently access

1. Rev. Proc. 2015-20.
2. IRC Sec. 446(c)(1).
3. Treas. Reg. §1.446-1(c)(1)(i).
4. Treas. Reg. §1.451-2(a).
5. Treas. Reg. §1.461-1(a)(1).
6. See *Massachusetts Mutual Life Insurance Co. v. U.S.*, 288 U.S. 269 (1933).
7. See Rev. Rul. 73-173, 1973-1 CB 40.
8. Rev. Rul. 73-173; *Shuster v. Helvering*, 121 F.2d 643 (1941).

the cash or non-cash property providing such benefit.[1] For the cash basis taxpayer to recognize income under the economic benefit theory, the property must be transferred for the benefit of the taxpayer[2] and confer vested, nonforfeitable rights[3] to the taxpayer. For example, a taxpayer was required to recognize income when his employer transferred certain amounts into a trust for his future benefit where the employer's payment was irrevocable, even though the taxpayer was not currently able to access the funds in the trust.[4] Therefore, unlike the cash equivalence theory, the property that is irrevocably transferred and held for the taxpayer's benefit does not have to be transferrable by the taxpayer.[5] The taxpayer is required to include the fair market value of non-cash property, or present value of any cash, that is transferred in income for the year such property or cash is transferred.[6]

Planning Point: Generally speaking, the cash basis method of accounting works best for organizations that prefer simplicity over predictability. Cash basis is like balancing a checkbook; if the money is there, then the money affects the tax obligations. Large and unanticipated increases in revenues can lead to large tax obligations—and potentially large cash outflows—that small business owners may not be prepared for. Quarterly estimated tax payments may be more difficult to predict in a cash basis business with large, infrequent sales.

8956. What is the accrual method of accounting?

Taxpayers who use the accrual method of accounting generally report income in the year that it is earned, rather than in the year it is received.[7] Under this method, income is recognized in the year when (1) all events have occurred to fix the taxpayer's right to receive the income and (2) the amount of income that the taxpayer will be entitled to receive can be determined with reasonable accuracy. Because the relevant inquiry is when the income is *earned*, rather than when the income is *received*, compensation agreed upon with respect to the performance of future services is not recognized until those services have actually been performed (at the time the taxpayer has earned the compensation).[8]

Pursuant to the "all events test,"[9] income is recognized when all of the events that are required for the taxpayer's right to the income to be vested have occurred so that the amount of the taxpayer's entitlement can be determined with reasonable certainty.[10] It is possible for a taxpayer to report income although no payment has yet been received.[11]

Similarly, an accrual basis taxpayer's expenses are deductible for the taxable year in which the liability for payment becomes definite and the amounts payable become ascertainable with

1. See *Spoul v. Comm.*, 16 TC 244 (1951). See also *Thomas v. U.S.*, 45 F. Supp.2d 618 (1999).
2. Compare *Sproull*, and *Jacuzzi v. Comm.*, 61 TC 262 (1973) (economic benefit upon transfer to trust), with *Casale v. Comm.*, 247 F.2d 440, 445 (2d Cir. 1957) (no economic benefit); *Centre v. Comm.*, 55 TC 16 (1970); Rev. Rul. 72-25, 1972-1 CB 127 (no economic benefit).
3. See *e.g., Robertson vs. Comm.*, 6 TC 1060 (1946), *acq.* 1946-2 CB 4.
4. *Jacuzzi v. Comm.*, 61 TC 262 (1973).
5. *Hackett v. Comm.*, 159 F.2d 121 (1st Cir. 1946); *Brodie v. Comm.*, 1 TC 275 (1942).
6. *212 Corp. v. Comm.*, 70 TC 788 (1978); *Bell Est. v. Comm.*, 60 TC 469 (1973).
7. IRC Sec. 446(c)(2).
8. Treas. Reg. §1.451-1(a).
9. IRC Sec. 448(h)(4).
10. Treas. Reg. §1.446-1(c)(1)(ii).
11. *Comm. v Hansen*, 360 U.S. 446 (1959).

reasonable certainty, but only to the extent that economic performance with respect to the item has occurred.[1]

In general, an accrual basis taxpayer will include amounts in income upon the earliest of the following events: (1) payment is actually received, (2) the income amount becomes due to the taxpayer, (3) the taxpayer earns the income, or (4) title to property has passed to the taxpayer.[2]

An accrual basis taxpayer who enters into an agreement to provide future services may postpone reporting advance payments under the agreement if the services relate to property the taxpayer owns, leases, builds or installs, but only if the agreement relates to servicing property the taxpayer ordinarily owns, leases, builds or installs in the ordinary course of business *without* such a service agreement. Recognition of advance payments is not permitted when (1) the taxpayer will perform any part of the service after the end of the tax year immediately following the year of payment or (2) the service will be performed at an unspecified future date that *might* be after the end of the tax year immediately following the year of payment.[3]

> *Example 1:* Scott owns a computer sales business. In 2017, he receives payment for a one-year service contract on a computer that he sold. If Scott normally sells computers without the service contract, he can postpone until 2018 recognition of any income he did not earn in 2017 because, by the terms of the agreement, the services will be performed within one year.

> *Example 2:* Lauren owns a dance studio and, on October 1, 2017, receives payment for a one year contract for forty-eight dance lessons. The one-year period begins on October 1. Lauren gives eight dance lessons in 2017. She is required to recognize one-sixth (8/48) of the advance payment in 2017, because she has earned that portion. Further, she is required to recognize the remainder of the income in 2018, even if she does not give all of the lessons in 2018.

The IRS has released guidance that provides a safe harbor for accrual basis taxpayers to treat economic performance as occurring ratably over the life of contracts that provide for services to be provided over time. Under this safe harbor, taxpayers who enter into ratable service contracts are now permitted to expense the cost of regularly provided services as those services are provided over the life of the contract. One example provided in the guidance makes clear that, in the case of ratable service contracts, a payment made in December 2017 for services to be performed in January 2018 can be expensed in 2017, when payment is made. A contract qualifies for treatment as a ratable service contract if (1) it provides for the provision of services on a regular basis (weekly, monthly, etc.), (2) each occurrence of services provides independent value and (3) the contract term is for twelve months or less (excluding extensions).[4]

If the accrual basis taxpayer must give up certain rights in order to receive the agreed upon amounts, accrual of that income will be prevented. For example, the courts have held that, in the case of an insurance claim resulting from property damage where the insured held two different insurance policies, a clause in policy A that prevented the payout unless the taxpayer agreed

1. IRC Sec. 461(h).
2. IRS Publication 538.
3. IRS Pub. 538.
4. Rev. Proc. 2015-39, 2015-22 IRB 195.

to forego his right to the proceeds of policy B prevented accrual. Even though all events that would give rise to the taxpayer's rights to the amounts receivable under policy A had occurred and the amount could be determined, attachment of the condition prevented accrual of the amounts involved.[1] The right to receive an amount must be enforceable by the recipient with no strings attached.

Planning Point: Generally speaking, the accrual method of accounting normalizes, or smooths out, the revenues and expenses of a business, making it easier to do year over year comparisons and forecasts. A company that wins a large deal may get paid an up-front cash amount for products that are delivered for years to come. Accrual tax accounting allows the tax obligations to be paid over longer periods of time, giving the business owner more choice and control over how, and when, taxes are paid.

8957. Are any taxpayers required to use the accrual method of accounting, rather than the cash basis method?

Yes with some exceptions. Generally, C corporations, partnerships in which a C corporation is a partner and tax shelter arrangements (see Q 8634) are required to use the accrual basis method of accounting.[2]

However, several exceptions exist to permit certain C corporations and partnerships with C corporation shareholders to use the cash basis method. Farming businesses[3] that are organized as C corporations are permitted to use the cash basis method of accounting. Similarly, small businesses organized as C corporations are permitted to use the cash basis method if the corporation (or partnership with C corporation shareholder) has annual gross receipts that do not exceed $5,000,000.[4]

Certain personal service corporations are also permitted to use the cash basis method of accounting. Further, the IRS has specifically determined that the prohibition on C corporations using the cash basis accounting method does not apply to limited liability companies.[5]

Generally, taxpayers that maintain inventory are required to use the accrual basis method with respect to purchases and sales of that inventory unless the taxpayer obtains the IRS' consent to use the cash basis method. Typically, the IRS will consent to such a change if the cash basis method clearly reflects the taxpayer's income.[6] See Q 8967 for a more specific discussion of the methods that may be used to account for inventory.

The cash basis method may also be used by most other taxpayers whose average annual gross receipts do not exceed $1 million[7] and may be used by select taxpayers whose average annual gross receipts do not exceed $10 million.[8]

1. *Maryland Ship- building & Drydock Co. v. U.S.*, 409 F.2d 1363 (Ct. Cl. 1969).
2. IRC Sec. 448(a).
3. IRC Sec. 263A.
4. IRC Sec. 448(b).
5. Let. Ruls. 9328005, 9321007.
6. Treas. Reg. §1.446-1(c)(2)(i).
7. Rev Proc. 2001-10, 2001-2 IRB 272.
8. Rev. Proc. 2002-28, 2002-18, IRB 815.

8958. Can a taxpayer choose to use both the cash basis and accrual methods of accounting?

Under IRC Section 446(c), a taxpayer may use any combination of the permissible accounting methods to compute taxable income if the combination clearly reflects the taxpayer's income and is consistently used. For example, a taxpayer is permitted to use the cash basis method to account for income and expenses, but the accrual method to account for purchases and sales. Despite this, a taxpayer is *not* permitted to use one method to account for income and a different method to account for expenses.[1]

Though the regulations require that a taxpayer use the accrual method to account for purchases and sales if inventories are maintained, that taxpayer may wish to use the cash basis method for income and expenses because the required calculation may be simpler.[2]

A taxpayer is also permitted to use one accounting method to determine tax liability for income arising from a trade or business and another method to account for income that is not related to a trade or business.[3] Taxpayers engaged in different trades or businesses can also use a different method of accounting for each trade or business in which the taxpayer participates.[4]

8959. Can a taxpayer change an accounting method once it has been chosen?

Though a taxpayer does not need IRS consent to choose its initial accounting period, generally, the taxpayer must seek the consent of the IRS to change its accounting method. This is the case even if the taxpayer's current accounting method is an impermissible one (for example, if a partnership with C corporation shareholders has chosen the cash basis method, see Q 8957).[5] The IRS can also require the taxpayer to change its accounting method[6] if it is determined that the chosen accounting method does not clearly and accurately reflect the taxpayer's income.[7]

Certain specific accounting changes do not require IRS consent. Revenue Procedure 2011-14 provides a list of circumstances in which automatic approval for changes in accounting methods will be granted. For example, a taxpayer who is improperly using the reserve method of accounting to account for bad debts may automatically switch to the specific charge-off method (see Q 8703).[8]

In order to obtain IRS approval to change a taxpayer's current accounting method, the taxpayer must file Form 3115, "Application for a Change in Accounting Method" with the IRS. The instructions to Form 3115 provide a brief description of the situations in which a taxpayer may obtain automatic IRS approval for a change in accounting method.[9]

1. Treas. Reg. §1.446-1(c)(1)(iv); *Grider v Comm.*, TC Memo 1999-417.
2. Treas. Reg. §§1.446-1(a)(4)(i), 1.446-1(c)(2)(i). See also *Gustafson v Comm.*, TC Memo 1988-82.
3. Treas. Reg. §1.446-1(c)(1)(iv)(b).
4. Treas. Reg. §1.446-1(d).
5. Treas. Reg. §1.446-1(e)(2)(i).
6. IRC Sec. 446(e), Treas. Reg. §1.446-1(e)(2)(i).
7. IRC Sec. 446(b).
8. Rev. Proc. 2011-14, 2011-1 CB 330, as modified by Rev. Proc. 2015-14 and Rev Proc. 2015-20.
9. Instructions to Form 3115, available at http://www.irs.gov/pub/irs-pdf/i3115.pdf (last accessed June 26, 2017).

Once the taxpayer either determines that automatic change is available or obtains IRS consent to change from one method of accounting to another, the taxpayer is required to make any adjustments to items of income or expense that are necessary to prevent duplication or omission of amounts based on the change.[1]

Taxpayers may also wish to change the accounting for one or more material items of income or deduction, rather than the overall method of accounting.[2] A "material item" is defined in the regulations as any item that involves the proper time for the inclusion of the item in income or the taking of a deduction.[3] Changing the accounting method for a material item, rather than the overall method of accounting, also requires that the taxpayer obtain consent if the change is not subject to automatic approval. For example, a taxpayer must obtain consent in order to change the method of depreciation or amortization of items, except for certain changes to the straight-line method depreciation that are subject to automatic approval under Revenue Procedure 2011-14.[4]

8960. What is the installment method of accounting and when is it used?

In cases where a taxpayer does not receive payment immediately after a sale, the taxpayer may be able to recognize the income from those sales over a period of time, rather than when the sale is made. The installment method may be used to account for gains (but not losses) if the taxpayer has sold property and will receive at least one payment with respect to that sale after the close of the tax year in which the sale occurs.[5] Under the installment method, for each year in which payments are due, the taxpayer will recognize a proportionate amount of the payments as they are actually received over the payment term.[6]

Despite this, a taxpayer is not entitled to use the installment method of accounting if the transaction is a dealer disposition or involves the sale of property that is held as inventory in the ordinary course of the taxpayer's trade or business (see Q 8967 for a discussion of inventory accounting).[7] A dealer disposition is a sale of personal property by a person who regularly sells or otherwise disposes of property using an installment plan or a disposition of real property that is held by the taxpayer for sale to customers in the ordinary course of a trade or business.[8] Certain farm property and the sale of timeshares and residential lots are excluded from the definition of dealer disposition.[9]

Section 453 only affects the timing of income recognition and does not impact the characterization of the income (for example, as a capital gain or ordinary income).[10]

1. IRC Sec. 481(a).
2. Treas. Reg. §1.446-1(a)(1).
3. Treas. Reg. §1.446-1(e)(2)(ii).
4. See IRS Pub. 538.
5. IRC Sec. 453(b)(1).
6. IRC Sec. 453(c).
7. IRC Sec. 453(b)(2).
8. IRC Sec. 453(l).
9. IRC Sec. 453(l)(2).
10. *Murray v. United States*, 192 Ct Cl 63 (1970).

See Q 8918 for more information on using the installment method of accounting in the context of small business dispositions. Q 8962 discusses the special rules that apply in the context of related party sales under the installment method.

8961. What interest requirements apply when a taxpayer uses the installment method of accounting?

Generally, when a taxpayer uses the installment method of accounting (see Q 8960), if the sale price is over $3,000 and any payment is deferred for more than one year, interest must be charged on payments due more than six months after the sale. Interest must be charged at a rate that is at least 100 percent of the "applicable federal rate," (AFR) compounded semiannually, or interest will be imputed at that rate.[1] However, the following exceptions to this general rule apply:

(1) If less than 100 percent of the AFR, a rate of no greater than 9 percent, compounded semiannually, will be imputed in the case of sales of property (other than new IRC Section 38 property) if the stated principal amount of the debt instrument does not exceed $5,717,471 in 2017 (as indexed annually for inflation);[2]

(2) If less than 100 percent of the AFR, a rate of no greater than 6 percent, compounded semiannually, is imputed on aggregate sales of land during a calendar year between an individual and a member of the individual's family (i.e., brothers, sisters, spouses, ancestors, and lineal descendants) to the extent the aggregate sales do not exceed $500,000 (the general rule of 100 percent of the AFR, compounded semiannually, applies to the excess);[3] and

(3) A rate of 110 percent of the AFR, compounded semiannually, applies to sales or exchanges of property if, pursuant to a plan, the transferor or any related person leases a portion of the property after the sale or exchange ("sale-leaseback" transactions).[4]

The applicable federal rate applied will be the lowest of the AFRs in effect for any month in the 3-month period ending with the first calendar month in which there is a binding contract in writing.[5]

All interest received by the taxpayer is taxed as ordinary income.[6] In some cases, depending on the property and amount involved, the interest (or imputed interest) to be paid over the period of the loan must be reported as "original issue discount" that accrues in daily portions; in other cases the interest is allocated among the payments and that much of each payment is treated as interest includable and deductible according to the accounting method of the buyer and seller.

1. IRC Sec. 483.
2. IRC Sec. 1274A; Rev. Rul. 2016522016-52.
3. IRC Sec. 483(e)(3).
4. IRC Sec. 1274(e).
5. IRC Sec. 1274(d)(2)(B).
6. Treas. Reg. §1.483-1.

8962. What special accounting rules apply in the installment sale context if the sale involves related parties?

Under IRC Section 453(e)(1), if a taxpayer ("first seller") disposes of property to a related person in an installment sale ("first sale"), and the related party in turn sells the property in a second sale before the first seller receives all payments under the first sale, the amount realized in the second sale will be treated as received by the first seller. This is the case even though the first seller has actually not received all payments due with respect to the first sale.[1]

Essentially, the payments received from the second sale are treated as though they were used to pay off the first sale even if, in reality, the second seller has made no payments. The purpose of this treatment is to prevent a taxpayer from improperly deferring gain on the sale of property by using the installment method of accounting.

In order for the related party rules to apply, the second sale must occur within two years of the first sale unless the property at issue consists of marketable securities.[2]

For purposes of the installment sale rules, "related party" includes the seller's siblings, ancestors, lineal descendants, certain controlled corporations (see Q 8880) and estates, trusts and partnerships in which the seller has an interest.[3]

If the second sale occurs as a result of an involuntary conversion under IRC Section 1033 (see Q 8617), the second sale will not be treated as a "second sale" under these rules if the first sale was made before the threat of the involuntary conversion arose.[4] Further, a second sale will not be deemed to have occurred for purposes of these rules if the sale occurs after the death of either the first seller or the related party who acquires the property in the first sale.[5] If the parties are able to prove that the sales were not motivated by tax avoidance, the related party rules will not apply.[6]

8963. Is a taxpayer required to use the installment method to account for an installment sale?

In situations where the installment method applies, the taxpayer is required to use the installment method unless an election is made to opt out of this treatment. If the taxpayer does not affirmatively elect out, the installment method is the default method of accounting for transactions covered by the installment sale rules (see Q 8960 and Q 8962). The opt-out election must be made on or before the due date for filing the taxpayer's return for the year. Once the election is made, the taxpayer may only revoke the election with the IRS' consent.[7]

1. IRC Sec. 453(e).
2. IRC Sec. 453(e)(2).
3. IRC Secs. 453(f), 318(a), 267(b).
4. IRC Sec. 453(e)(6).
5. IRC Sec. 453(e)(6)(C).
6. IRC Sec. 453(e)(7).
7. IRC Sec. 453(d).

8964. What types of contracts are considered "long-term contracts" for purposes of determining the proper method of accounting?

A long-term contract is any contract that provides for the manufacture, building, installation, or construction of property that will not be completed within the taxable year that the contract was executed.[1]

Despite this general definition, a manufacturing contract is only treated as a long-term contract if it provides for the manufacture of:[2]

(1) Unique items which are not normally carried as finished goods inventory; or

(2) Items which would normally require more than a twelve month production period to complete (regardless of the duration of the actual contract).[3]

An item is considered "unique" if it was designed to meet the needs of a specific customer and is generally not suitable for the use of other customers without significant modification.[4] A taxpayer can use the IRS' safe harbor to show that a product is not unique in the following circumstances:

(1) *Short production period*. If an item could normally be manufactured within ninety days or less, then it is not considered to be a unique item. If multiple orders are involved, this test is satisfied if each unit can be manufactured within ninety days;[5]

(2) *Customized item*. An item is not considered unique if 10 percent or less of the total contract cost is attributed to the cost of customizing the item;[6]

(3) *Inventoried item*. An item that might otherwise be considered unique ceases to be unique when the taxpayer begins to normally include similar items in its finished goods inventory.[7]

The item's production period begins when the taxpayer has incurred at least 5 percent of the total contract cost and ends when the item is ready for sale and all reasonably expected production activities have been completed.[8]

Construction contracts, for this purpose, include the improvement or building of real property, reconstruction or rehabilitation of real property, contracts for the installation of an integral component to real property, and contracts for the improvement of real property.[9]

See Q 8965 for the rules governing accounting for long-term contracts.

1. IRC Sec. 460(f)(1); Treas. Reg. §1.460-1(b)(1).
2. IRC Sec. 460(f)(2); Treas. Reg. §1.460-2(a).
3. IRC Sec. 460(f)(2)(B); Treas. Reg. §1.460-2(a)(2).
4. Treas. Reg. §1.460-2(b)(1); *Sierracin Corp. v. Comm.*, 90 TC 341 (1988).
5. Treas. Reg. §1.460-2(b)(2)(i).
6. Treas. Reg. §1.460-2(b)(2)(ii).
7. Treas. Reg. §1.460-2(b)(2)(iii).
8. Treas. Reg. §1.460-2(c)(1).
9. Treas. Reg. §1.460-3(a).

8965. How does a taxpayer account for revenue and costs under a long-term contract?

If the contract is found to be a long-term contract (see Q 8964), the taxpayer will be required to use the percentage of completion method to account for revenue under that contract, unless an exception applies to allow use of the completed contract method. Generally, the completed contract method may only be used for certain home construction and other real estate construction contracts (see Q 8966), so the exception is very limited.[1]

The percentage of completion method requires the taxpayer to include the portion of the total contract price that corresponds to the percentage of the entire contract that has been completed during that tax year.[2] The aim of this method is to include a portion of income during each year as the work under the contract progresses.

To determine the income that must be recognized under a long-term contract, a taxpayer uses the following steps:[3]

(1) The completion factor for the contract, which is the ratio of the cumulative allocable contract costs that the taxpayer has incurred through the end of the taxable year to the estimated total allocable contract costs that the taxpayer reasonably expects to incur under the contract, is computed;

(2) The amount of cumulative gross receipts from the contract is computed by multiplying the completion factor by the total contract price;

(3) The amount of current-year gross receipts is computed, which is the difference between the amount of cumulative gross receipts for the current taxable year and the amount of cumulative gross receipts for the immediately preceding taxable year (whether positive or negative); and

(4) Both the current-year gross receipts and the allocable contract costs incurred during the current year are taken into account in computing taxable income.

If this method does not result in the taxpayer including the total contract price in income by the time the contract is completed, the taxpayer must include any remaining amounts in income for the tax year following the year of completion.[4]

A de minimis rule allows a taxpayer to defer recognition of income under a long-term contract for any year in which less than 10 percent of the estimated contract costs have been incurred by the end of the year. This income and related costs must then be recognized in a later year in which at least 10 percent of the contract has been completed.[5]

1. IRC Sec. 460(a); Treas. Reg. §1.451-3(b).
2. IRC Sec. 460(b)(1); Treas. Reg. §1.460-4(b)(1).
3. Treas. Reg. §1.460-4(b)(2).
4. Treas. Reg. §1.460-4(b)(3).
5. IRC Sec. 460(b)(5).

8966. Are there any exceptions to the rule that a taxpayer must use the percentage of completion method in accounting for long-term contracts?

Yes. The percentage of completion method (Q 8965) is not required to be used in the case of (1) construction contracts entered into by small contractors and (2) home construction contracts.[1]

The exemption for small contractors will apply if the following criteria are met:[2]

(1) The long-term contract must be a construction contract;[3]

(2) At the time the contract was entered into, it is estimated that the contract will be completed within two years. However, if the contract takes longer than two years to complete due to factors beyond the taxpayer's control, the small contractor's exception may still be used;[4] and

(3) The contractor or its predecessor's average annual gross receipts for the three years preceding the year in which the construction contract was entered into is $10 million or less.[5]

The home construction contract exemption applies to any construction contract under which at least 80 percent of the estimated total contract costs are reasonably attributed to the building construction, reconstruction or rehabilitation of: (1) dwelling units[6] in a building containing four or fewer dwelling units or (2) improvements to real property directly related to such dwelling units and located on the site of such dwelling units.[7] If the construction involves both dwelling units and commercial units, costs must be reasonably allocated to determine the contract costs attributable to the dwelling units in order to determine whether the contract will qualify for the exemption.

8967. What is inventory accounting? What methods are generally used by taxpayers to account for inventory?

Inventory accounting is generally required in any case where the IRS feels it is necessary in order to accurately reflect a taxpayer's income. Inventory accounting usually becomes important in cases where the taxpayer's business involves the production and sale of goods or the purchase and resale of goods.

As a general principle, IRC Section 471 requires that a taxpayer's inventory accounting method must: (1) conform as closely as reasonably possible to the best accounting practice used in the taxpayer's business[8] and (2) clearly reflect the taxpayer's income.[9] Under the regulations,

1. IRC Sec. 460(e).
2. IRC Sec. 460(e)(1)(B); Treas. Reg. §1.460-3(b)(1).
3. IRC Sec. 460(e)(4); Treas. Reg. §1.460-3(a).
4. Treas. Reg. §§1.460-3(b)(1)(ii), 1.460-1(f)(4).
5. IRC Sec. 460(e)(1)(B)(ii); Treas. Reg. §1.460-3(b)(3).
6. Dwelling unit is defined in IRC Sec. 168(e)(2)(A)(ii)(I).
7. IRC Sec. 460(e)(6)(A); Treas. Reg. §1.460-3(b)(2)(i).
8. See *Geometric Stamping Co. v. Comm.*, 26 TC 301 (1956), acq., 1958-1 CB 4 (re: importance of consistency).
9. Treas. Reg. §1.471-2(c). See also *Walmart v. Comm.*, TC Memo 1997-1 (8th Cir. 1998) (upholding the estimate for inventory shrinkage).

therefore, there is no one particular accounting method that must be used in all circumstances to account for inventory. Instead, the method chosen must reflect the realities of the taxpayer's business. As such, greater weight is given to consistency than to the actual valuation method chosen.[1]

There are various methods of inventory accounting, including first-in, first-out (FIFO), last-in, first-out (LIFO) and specific identification methods.

The FIFO method of accounting assumes that the first items of inventory purchased by the taxpayer are the first items that are sold. As such, the inventory that remains at the end of the taxpayer's accounting period is valued based on the most recent purchase price.[2]

Conversely, under the LIFO method, the most recent items of inventory that are purchased are considered to be the first items sold. Under the LIFO method, inventory is valued based on its cost, rather than its market value.[3]

Rather than focusing on the flow of inventory, the specific identification method requires that the taxpayer keep records so that it may assign a specific cost to each item of inventory.[4]

Certain taxpayers are either prohibited or are given the option to not use the inventory method of accounting. They include:

(1) Real estate dealers – A taxpayer that is in the business of selling real properties is not permitted to use the inventory method;[5]

(2) Farmers – A taxpayer engaged in a farming business may use either the inventory or the cash method in reporting income;[6]

(3) Real estate investment mortgage units are exclusively governed by Sections 860A through 860G.[7] These entities are not permitted to use the inventory methods under Section 471.

Though greater weight is given to consistency than to the method of inventory accounting chosen, certain inventory accounting methods are specifically prohibited under Treasury Regulation Section 1.471-2(f), including the following:

(1) Deducting a reserve for price changes or an estimated depreciation in the value of inventory;

(2) Carrying inventory at a nominal price or at less than its proper value;

1. Treas. Reg. §1.471-2(b).
2. See Treas. Reg. §1.471-2(d); ARB No. 43, Chapter 4, Statement 4 (AICPA, 1953) (FASB Accounting Standards Codification 330-10-30).
3. IRC Sec. 472(b)(2).
4. Treas. Reg. §1.471-2(d).
5. Rev. Rul. 69-536, 1969-2 CB 109, amplified in Rev. Rul. 86-149, 1986-2 CB 67; *Atlantic Coast Realty Co. v. Comm.*, 11 BTA 416 (1928); *Miller Development Co. v. Comm.*, 81 TC 619 (1983).
6. Treas. Reg. §1.471-6(a).
7. Rev. Rul. 95-81.

(3) Omitting portions of the inventory;

(4) Using a base-stock method based on a normal quantity and constant price;

(5) Including in-transit goods in inventory where title to such goods is not yet vested in the taxpayer;

(6) Using a direct cost method by a manufacturer, under which only direct production costs and variable overhead costs are allocated to inventory; and

(7) Using a prime cost method by manufacturer, under which only direct production costs are allocated to inventory.

If a taxpayer has used a prohibited inventory method, IRS consent is still required to change the method unless automatic approval is available under Revenue Procedure 2011-14 (see Q 8953).[1]

Planning Point: FIFO or LIFO? Choosing LIFO is enticing in a capital-heavy business when the costs of the goods sold are increasing. This will reduce the current tax burden. However, LIFO often increases administrative time and paperwork. LIFO can affect valuation in the sale of a business as it postpones the inevitable until the sale of the business. Technology businesses often exist in a deflationary world, where the costs of their inventory decrease as computing power (and other technologies) increase year over year. FIFO is also accepted by the International Financial Reporting Standards Board (IFRS), and LIFO is not.

1. See Treas. Reg. §1.446-1(e)(2)(i).

PART XVII: CHARITABLE GIVING

8968. What deduction is an individual allowed to take with respect to gifts made to charitable organizations?

An individual may deduct certain amounts for charitable contributions.[1] The allowable deduction for a contribution of property other than money is generally equal to the fair market value of the property.[2] However, under certain circumstances, the deduction for a gift of property must be reduced (see Q 8980). See Q 8970 for a discussion of the fair market value determination.

The amount that may be deducted in any one year is subject to certain income percentage limits that depend on the type of property, the type of charitable organization to which the gift is made, and whether the contribution is made directly "to" the charity or "for the use of" the charity (see Q 8973). Taxpayers are required to itemize deductions in order to take a charitable deduction.

Generally, a gift of less than an individual's entire interest in property is not deductible, though certain exceptions to this rule exist (see Q 8979 and Q 8980).

For a charitable contribution to be deductible, the charity must receive some benefit from the donated property.[3] In addition, the donor cannot expect to receive an economic benefit (aside from the tax deduction) from the charity in return for the donation.[4] For instance, if a taxpayer contributes substantially appreciated property, and later reacquires it from the charity under a prearranged transaction, or if the charity sells the appreciated property and uses the proceeds to purchase other property from the taxpayer under a similar arrangement, the taxpayer is required to recognize gain on the contribution.[5] However, where there is no arrangement and no duty on the part of the charity to return the property to the donor, the taxpayer is entitled to the deduction. In addition, if the charity does return the property, the taxpayer receives a new basis in the property (i.e., the price he paid to reacquire it).[6]

In determining whether a payment that is partly in consideration for goods or services (i.e., a quid pro quo contribution) qualifies as a charitable deduction, the IRS has adopted the 2-part test set forth in *United States v. American Bar Endowment*.[7] Under these circumstances, for a charitable contribution to be deductible, a taxpayer must:

(1) Intend to make a payment in excess of the fair market value of the goods or services received; and

(2) Actually make a payment in an amount that exceeds the fair market value of the goods or services.[8]

---

1. IRC Sec. 170(a).
2. Treas. Reg. §1.170A-1(c)(1).
3. See *Winthrop v. Meisels*, 180 F.Supp. 29 (DC NY 1959), aff'd 281 F.2d 694 (2d Cir. 1960).
4. *Stubbs v. U.S.*, 70-2 USTC ¶9468 (9th Cir.), cert. den. 400 U.S. 1009 (1971).
5. *Blake v. Comm.*, 83-1 USTC ¶9121 (2nd Cir. 1982).
6. *Sheppard v. U.S.*, 361 F.2d 972 (Ct. Cl. 1966).
7. 477 U.S. 105 (1986).
8. Treas. Reg. §1.170A-1(h)(1).

The deduction amount may not exceed the excess of (1) the amount of any cash paid and the fair market value of the goods or services over (2) the fair market value of the goods or services provided in return.[1]

The Tax Court has held that tuition payments paid by taxpayers to religious day schools for the secular and religious education of their children were not deductible as a charitable contribution, including amounts paid to one of the schools for after-school religious education classes.[2]

Certain goods or services received in return for a charitable contribution may be disregarded for purposes of determining whether a taxpayer has made a charitable contribution, the amount of any charitable contribution, and whether any goods or services have been provided that must be substantiated or disclosed.[3] These items include goods or services that have an insubstantial value under IRS guidelines, certain annual membership benefits received for a payment of $10.90 or less (in 2018, as indexed annually for inflation) and certain admissions to events.[4]

If a taxpayer makes an otherwise deductible charitable contribution to a university (or other institution of higher learning) that directly or indirectly entitles the donor to purchase tickets for athletic events in the institution's stadium, the contribution is only 80 percent deductible and to the extent that the contribution is not found to be a payment for the tickets themselves.[5] The IRS has determined that the portion of the payment made to a state university's foundation was deductible under IRC Section 170(l) even though the donor (an S corporation) received the right to purchase tickets for seating in a skybox at events in an athletic stadium of the university. The IRS reasoned that the portion of the payment to the foundation for the right to buy the tickets for seating was considered as being paid for the benefit of the university and, as such, 80 percent of such portion was deductible. The IRS found that the remainder of the payment (consisting of the ticket purchase, the right to use the skybox, the passes to visit the skybox, and the parking privileges) was not deductible.[6]

The IRS has found that contributions made to a university for the purpose of constructing a building providing meeting space for campus organizations qualified for a charitable deduction under IRC Section 170. With the exception of the meeting rooms leased to individual sororities, the facilities in the building would be open to all students. Because the facts indicated that the contributions were indeed gifts to the college, and not gifts to the sororities using the college as a conduit, the IRS determined that the requirements of Revenue Ruling 60-367,[7] which discussed the circumstances under which donations that benefitted a college fraternity would be considered a gift to an educational institution, had been satisfied.[8]

1. Treas. Reg. §1.170A-1(h)(2).
2. See *Sklar v. Comm.*, 125 TC 281 (2005); see also *Sklar v. Comm.*, 282 F.3d 610 (9th Cir. 2002), aff'g TC Memo 2000-118.
3. Treas. Reg. §§1.170A-1(h), 1.170A-13(f)(8).
4. Treas. Reg. §1.170A-13(f)(8). See also Rev Proc. 2017-58.
5. IRC Sec. 170(l).
6. See TAM 200004001.
7. 1960-2 CB 73.
8. Let. Rul. 9829053. See also Let. Ruls. 200003013, 199929050.

8969. How is the value of property donated to charity determined?

Where property other than money is donated to charity, it is necessary to calculate the property's fair market value in order to determine the amount of the allowable charitable deduction.

As in other circumstances, fair market value for this purpose is "the price at which the property would change hands between a willing buyer and a willing seller, neither being under any compulsion to buy or sell and both having reasonable knowledge of relevant facts."[1] The willing buyer has often been viewed as a retail consumer, not a middleman.[2] However, there are certain circumstances where the retail consumer is not the proper benchmark. For example, in the case of unset gemstones, the ultimate consumer is generally a jeweler engaged in incorporating the gems into jewelry. Therefore, the fair market value is based on the price that a jeweler would pay a wholesaler to acquire such stones.[3]

Often, taxpayers rely on expert appraisals in determining the fair market value of property.[4] For some gifts to charity, an appraisal is required (see Q 8970). However, the value assigned by an appraiser is not always controlling and the IRS or the Tax Court may consider factors in addition to those considered by the taxpayer's appraiser(s) which may reduce the value of the gift and, thus, the charitable deduction.[5] The IRS has warned taxpayers that some promoters are likely to inflate the value of a charitable deduction for gemstones and lithographs, thus subjecting the taxpayer to higher taxes and possible penalties.[6] Earlier case law has indicated that an auction price may be helpful in determining the value of art.[7]

The taxpayer claiming the charitable deduction has the burden of proof in establishing the fair market value of the property donated.[8]

Evidence of what an organization is willing to pay for copies of a manuscript may be used by the taxpayer as evidence of the value of the original manuscript, but it is not conclusive.[9] Similarly, the price paid by a bankruptcy trustee may provide evidence of the fair market value, but in at least one case, the courts have found that the substantially higher value established by an appraiser was determinative of the property's value.[10]

For property that is transferred to a charity and subject to an option to repurchase, fair market value under IRC Section 170 is the value of the property upon the expiration of the option.[11]

1. Treas. Reg. §1.170A-1(c); Rev. Rul. 68-69, 1968-1 CB 80.
2. See *Goldman v. Comm.*, 388 F.2d 476 (6th Cir. 1967).
3. *Anselmo v. Comm.*, 80 TC 872 (1983), aff'd 757 F.2d 1208 (11th Cir. 1985).
4. See *Tripp v. Comm.*, 337 F.2d 432 (7th Cir. 1964); *Est. of DeBie v. Comm.*, 56 TC 876 (1971), acq. 1972-2 CB 1 and 1972-2 CB 2.
5. See *Williford v. Comm.*, TC Memo 1992-450 (involving oversized artwork); *Doherty v. Comm.*, TC Memo 1992-98 (involving artwork of questionable quality and authenticity); *Arbini v. Comm.*, TC Memo 2001-141 (involving newspapers and holding that the appropriate market for purposes of determining the fair market value of the newspapers is the wholesale market).
6. IR 83-89.
7. *Mathias v. Comm.*, 50 TC 994 (1968), acq. 1969-2 CB xxiv. But see *McGuire v. Comm.*, 44 TC 801 (1965), acq. in result 1966-2 CB 6.
8. See *Weil v. Comm.*, TC Memo 1967-78; *Schapiro v. Comm.*, TC Memo 1968-44.
9. *Barringer v. Comm.*, TC Memo 1972-234. See also *Kerner v. Comm.*, TC Memo 1976-12.
10. *Herman v. U.S.* and *Brown v. U.S.* (consolidated actions), 99-2 USTC ¶50,889 (E.D. Tenn. 1999).
11. TAM 9828001.

Guidelines for valuing property generally can be found in Revenue Procedure 66-49,[1] and Announcement 2001-22.[2] See also *Crocker v. Comm.*[3] (describing the three methods of determining fair market value of commercial real estate: (1) the replacement method, (2) the comparable sales method, and (3) the income capitalization method).

Planning Point: The fair market value of publicly traded securities is equal to the average value of the high and low stock values on the date of delivery of the stock multiplied by the number of shares given to charity. The date of delivery depends on how the stock was delivered: hand delivered, mailed or electronically transferred.

A taxpayer is not entitled to a charitable deduction for a contribution of clothing or a household item unless the property is in good used condition or better. A deduction for a contribution of clothing or a household item may be denied in circumstances where the donated item has minimal monetary value. These rules do not apply to a contribution of a single item if a deduction of more than $500 is claimed and a qualified appraisal is included with the return. Household items include furniture, furnishings, electronics, linens, appliances, and similar items; but not food, art, jewelry, and collections.[4]

Planning Point: It is a good idea to take photographs of household items prior to donation to document that they are in good used condition or better.

Intellectual property. The American Jobs Creation Act of 2004 (AJCA 2004) provides strict rules for charitable donations of patents and intellectual property.[5] For the temporary regulations providing guidance for the filing of information returns by donees relating to qualified intellectual property contributions, see Temporary Treasury Regulation Section 1.6050L-2T; TD 9206;[6] and Announcement 2005-49.[7]

8970. What verification is required to substantiate a deduction for a charitable donation?

A charitable contribution is allowable as a deduction only if verified as required under regulations.[8] The required substantiation varies based upon the type and value of the contribution.

A charitable deduction is not allowed for any contribution of a check, cash, or other monetary gift unless the donor retains a bank record or a written communication from the charity showing the name of the charity and the date and the amount of the contribution.[9]

A taxpayer who donates cash or property to charity that has a value of $250 or more must obtain substantiation in the form of a contemporaneous written acknowledgment of the

1. 1966-2 CB 1257, as modified by Rev. Proc. 96-15, 1996-2 CB 627.
2. 2001-11 IRB 895.
3. TC Memo 1998-204.
4. IRC Sec. 170(f)(16), as added by PPA 2006.
5. See IRC Secs. 170(e)(1)(B), 6050L; IRC Sec. 170(m). See also Rev. Rul. 2003-28, 2003-11 IRB 594; Notice 2005-41, 2005-23 IRB 1203; Notice 2004-7, 2004-3 IRB 310; and IRS News Release IR-2003-141 (12-22-2003).
6. 70 Fed. Reg. 29450 (5-23-2005).
7. 2005-29 IRB 119. See also Notice 2005-41, 2005-23 IRB 1203.
8. IRC Sec. 170(a)(1).
9. IRC Sec. 170(f)(17), as added by PPA 2006.

contribution that is supplied by the charitable organization.[1] This acknowledgment must include the following information: (1) the amount of cash contributed and a description (excluding value) of any property contributed, (2) a statement of whether the charitable organization provided any goods or services in consideration for the contribution, and (3) a description and good faith estimate of the value of any such goods or services, or (4) a statement to the effect that the goods or services provided consisted solely of intangible religious benefits.[2] The acknowledgment will be considered "contemporaneous" if it is obtained by the taxpayer on or before the earlier of (1) the date the taxpayer files his return for the year, or (2) the due date (including extensions) for filing the return.[3] Substantiation is not required if the information is reported on a return filed by the charitable organization.[4] An organization can provide the acknowledgement electronically, such as via an e-mail addressed to the donor.[5]

For contributions of property other than money, the taxpayer is generally required to maintain a receipt from the donee organization showing the name of the donee, the date and location of the contribution, and a description of the property. The value does not have to be stated on the receipt.[6]

If a taxpayer donates property with a value that exceeds $500, the taxpayer must satisfy certain appraisal requirements in addition to the property description requirements outlined below.[7] The appraisal requirements that generally apply to property valued at more than $5,000 and at more than $500,000 do not apply to readily valued property, such as cash, publicly traded securities and certain qualified vehicles for which an acknowledgement is provided. Further, the general appraisal requirement does not apply if the taxpayer can show that the failure was due to reasonable cause and not willful neglect.[8] For purposes of the valuation thresholds, property (and all similar items of property) donated to one charity will be treated as one property.[9]

If the claimed value of the donated property exceeds $500, the taxpayer must include with the tax return a *description of the property*.[10] Specifically, the taxpayer must attach a completed Form 8283 to the relevant tax return (Noncash Charitable Contributions), which includes a property description and an acknowledgment by the organization of the amount and value of the gift. (The property description requirement does not apply to a C corporation that is not a personal service corporation or a closely-held C corporation.) In addition, a *qualified appraisal* must be obtained when the claimed value of the property exceeds $5,000 or $500,000.[11] See Q 8971 for a detailed discussion of the appraisal requirements that must be satisfied for certain charitable donations.

1. IRC Sec. 170(f)(8)(A).
2. IRC Sec. 170(f)(8)(B); Treas. Reg. §1.170A-13(f)(2).
3. IRC Sec. 170(f)(8)(C); Treas. Reg. §1.170A-13(f)(3).
4. IRC Sec. 170(f)(8)(D).
5. Publication 1771.
6. Treas. Reg. §1.170A-13(b)(1).
7. IRC Sec. 170(f)(11)(A)(i).
8. IRC Sec. 170(f)(11)(A)(ii).
9. IRC Sec. 170(f)(11)(F).
10. IRC Sec. 170(f)(11)(B).
11. IRC Secs. 170(f)(11)(C), 170(f)(11)(D).

Under the special rule for pass-through entities (partnerships or S corporations), the above requirements will be applied at the entity level; however, the deduction will be denied at the partner or shareholder level.[1]

8971. What appraisal requirements may be required in connection with substantiating a charitable deduction that exceeds certain valuation thresholds?

In addition to satisfying the requirements described in Q 8970, a qualified appraisal is required in connection with the charitable donation of certain highly valued property. The *qualified appraisal* requirement for contributions of property for which a deduction of more than $5,000 is claimed is met if the individual, partnership, or corporation:

(1) Obtains a qualified appraisal of the property; and

(2) Attaches to the tax return information regarding the property and the appraisal (as the Secretary may require).[2]

Donors who claim a deduction for a charitable gift of property (except publicly traded securities) valued in excess of $5,000 ($10,000 for nonpublicly traded stock) are required to obtain a qualified appraisal report, attach an appraisal summary (containing the information specified in regulations) to their return for the year in which the deduction is claimed, and maintain records of certain information related to the contribution.[3]

If a taxpayer fails to obtain the required appraisal for a gift of nonpublicly traded stock, the IRS may deny the deduction even if it does not dispute the value of the gift.[4] The Tax Court distinguished its holding in *Hewitt* from a 1993 decision in which it had permitted a deduction to a taxpayer who substantially, though not fully, complied with the appraisal requirement. In the earlier ruling, the taxpayer had obtained an appraisal from a qualified appraiser, completed and attached Form 8283, but had failed to include all the information required of an appraisal summary.[5] The Fourth Circuit agreed with the Tax Court's analysis, stating that "*Bond* does not suggest that a taxpayer who completely fails to observe the appraisal regulations has substantially complied with them." The Fourth Circuit further found that a deduction may still be permitted in situations where the taxpayers make a good faith effort to comply with the appraisal requirements, but that the deduction will be denied for taxpayers who ignore the requirement entirely. (For more information about the appraisal and summary requirements, see the instructions for Schedule A, Form 1040, and IRS Publication 526, Charitable Contributions.)

A qualified appraiser must not be the taxpayer, a party to the transaction in which the taxpayer acquired the property, the donee, an employee of any of the above, any other person who might appear not to be totally independent, or one who is regularly used by the taxpayer, a party to the transaction or the charity, and does not perform a majority of appraisals for

1. IRC Sec. 170(f)(11)(G).
2. IRC Secs. 170(f)(11)(C), 170(f)(11)(E).
3. Treas. Reg. §1.170A-13(c)(2).
4. *Hewitt v. Comm.*, 109 TC 258 (1997), *aff'd*, 166 F.3d 332 (4th Cir. 1998).
5. See *Bond v. Comm.*, 100 TC 32 (1993).

other persons.[1] See, for example, *Davis v. Commissioner*,[2] where appraisals were upheld where the appraiser was determined to be financially independent of the donor, and no conspiracy or collusive relationship was established.

In *Wortmann v. Commissioner*,[3] the Tax Court substantially reduced the taxpayers' charitable deduction (from $475,000 to $76,200) after it concluded that the property appraisal was dubious and not well supported by valuation methodology.

An appraisal will not be upheld if the appraiser bases his fee on a percentage of the appraisal value, unless the fee is based on a sliding scale that is paid to a generally recognized association regulating appraisers.[4]

If the donor gives similar items of property (such as books, stamps, paintings, etc.) to the same donee during the taxable year, only one appraisal and summary is required. If similar items of property are given during the same taxable year to several donees, and the aggregate value of the donations exceeds $5,000, a separate appraisal and summary must be made for each donation.[5] The appraisal summary must be signed and dated by the donee as an acknowledgement of the donation.[6]

Taxpayers making contributions of art appraised at $50,000 or more may wish to request a "Statement of Value" from the IRS (which is the equivalent of a letter ruling as to the value of a particular transfer that is made at death, by inter vivos gift, or as a charitable contribution).[7] The request must include specified information, including a description of the artwork, the cost, manner and date of acquisition, and a copy of an appraisal (which meets requirements set forth in Section 8 of the revenue procedure). The IRS charges a fee of $2,500 for obtaining a Statement of Value that can cover up to three items of art.[8]

The regulations state that taxpayers are not required to obtain a qualified appraisal of securities whose claimed value exceeds $5,000 if the donated property meets the definition of "publicly traded securities." Publicly traded securities are (1) listed on a stock exchange in which quotations are published on a daily basis or (2) regularly traded in a national or regional over-the-counter market for which published quotations are available.[9]

Securities that do not meet the above requirements may still be considered publicly traded securities if they meet the following five requirements:

(1) The issue is regularly traded during the computational period in a market that is reflected by the existence of an interdealer quotation system for the issue;

1. Treas. Reg. §1.170A-13(c)(5)(iv).
2. TC Memo 1999-250.
3. TC Memo 2005-227.
4. Treas. Reg. §1.170A-13(c)(6).
5. Treas. Reg. §1.170A-13(c)(4)(iv)(B).
6. Treas. Reg. §1.170A-13(c)(4)(iii).
7. See Rev. Proc. 96-15, 1996-1 CB 627, as modified by Ann. 2001-22, 2001-11 IRB 895.
8. Rev. Proc. 96-15, above, Sec. 7.01(2).
9. Treas. Reg. §1.170A-13(c)(7)(ix)(A).

(2) The issuer or its agent computes the issue's average trading price for the computational period;

(3) The average price and total volume of the issue during the computational period are published in a newspaper of general circulation throughout the U.S. not later than the last day of the month following the end of the calendar quarter in which the computational period ends;

(4) The issuer or its agent keeps books and records that list for each transaction during the computational period involving each issue covered by this procedure the date of the settlement of the transaction, the name and address of the broker or dealer making the market in which the transaction occurred, and the trading price and volume; and

(5) The issuer or agent permits the IRS to review the books and records.[1]

The "computational period" is weekly during October through December and monthly during January through September. Taxpayers who are exempted from obtaining a qualified appraisal because the securities meet these five requirements must attach a partially completed appraisal summary (section B of Form 8283) to the appropriate returns. The summary must contain the information required by parts I and II of the Form.[2]

For property contributions for which a deduction of more than $500,000 is claimed, the individual, partnership, or corporation must attach the qualified appraisal of the property to the tax return for the taxable year.[3]

8972. Are the substantiation requirements impacted if the charity disposes of the donated property after the taxpayer has already claimed a charitable deduction?

If the charitable donee disposes of "charitable deduction property" that is subject to the rules set forth in Q 8971 within three years after its receipt, the donee must provide an information return to the IRS.

Charitable deduction property includes any property (other than publicly traded securities) for which a charitable deduction was taken under IRC Section 170 where the claimed value of the property (plus the claimed value of all similar items of property donated by the donor to one or more donees) exceeded $5,000.[4] The return must show the name, address, and taxpayer identification number of the donor, a description of the property, the date of the contribution, the date of disposition, and the amount received on disposition. A copy of the return must be provided to the donor.

1. Treas. Reg. §1.170A-13(c)(7)(ix)(B).
2. Ann. 86-4, 1986-4 IRB 51.
3. IRC Secs. 170(f)(11)(D), 170(f)(11)(E).
4. IRC Sec. 6050L.

Example: If a charity accepts ownership of real estate worth $300,000 in 2017 from a donor as a charitable gift and later sells the real estate to another party in 2019, the charity will need to provide IRS Form 8282 to the IRS and the donor with the required information.

Failure to file the return may subject the donee to a penalty.[1] However, donee reporting is not required upon disposition of donated property within three years of receipt if the value of the property (as stated in the donor's appraisal summary) was not more than $5,000 at the time the donee signed the summary. In addition, no reporting will be required if the donee consumes or distributes property without receiving anything in exchange and the consumption or distribution is in furtherance of the donee's charitable purpose (such as the distribution of medical supplies by a tax-exempt relief agency).[2]

8973. What are the penalties if a taxpayer overvalues property donated to charity?

If a taxpayer underpays his tax because of a substantial valuation misstatement of property donated to charity, the taxpayer may be subject to a penalty of 20 percent of the underpayment attributable to the misstatement.[3] However, this penalty applies only if the underpayment attributable to the misstatement exceeds $5,000 ($10,000 for a corporation other than an S corporation or a personal holding company).[4] A "substantial valuation misstatement" exists if the value claimed is 150 percent or more of the amount determined to be correct.[5] If the value claimed is 200 percent or more of the amount determined to be correct, there is a "gross valuation misstatement," which is subject to a 40 percent underpayment penalty.[6]

8974. What are the income percentage limits for deductions of a charitable contribution?

The amount of a taxpayer's allowable deduction for charitable contributions will depend upon the taxpayer's adjusted gross income (AGI), the type of asset donated, as well as the type of organization to which the donation is made. Further, the IRC distinguishes between gifts "to" a charitable organization and gifts "for the use of" a charitable organization (see below).

50 percent limit. Generally, an individual is allowed a charitable deduction of up to 50 percent of AGI for cash and certain other contributions (other than certain property, see Q 8977) *to:* churches, schools, hospitals or medical research organizations, groups that normally receive a substantial part of their support from federal, state, or local governments or from the general public and that aid any of the above organizations as well as federal, state, and local governments. Also included in this list is a limited category of private foundations (i.e., private operating foundations and conduit foundations)[7] that generally direct their support to public charities. The above organizations are often referred to as "50 percent -type organizations."[8]

1. IRC Sec. 6721; Treas. Reg. §1.6050L-1. See SCA 200101031.
2. Instructions for IRS Form 8282.
3. IRC Secs. 6662(a), 6662(b)(3).
4. See IRC Sec. 6662(d).
5. IRC Sec. 6662(e)(1)(A), as amended by PPA 2006.
6. IRC Sec. 6662(h)(2)(A)(i), as amended by PPA 2006.
7. See IRC Sec. 170(b)(1)(E).
8. IRC Sec. 170(b)(1)(A).

30 percent limit. The deduction for contributions of most long-term capital gain property to the above "50 percent-type organizations," contributions *for the use of* any of the above organizations, as well as contributions (other than long-term capital gain property) *to* or *for the use of* any other types of charitable organizations (i.e., most private foundations) is limited to the lesser of (a) 30 percent of the taxpayer's AGI, or (b) 50 percent of AGI minus the amount of charitable contributions allowed for contributions to the 50 percent -type charities.[1]

20 percent limit. The deduction for contributions of long-term capital gain property to most private foundations is limited to the lesser of (a) 20 percent of the taxpayer's AGI, or (b) 30 percent of AGI minus the amount of charitable contributions allowed for contributions to the 30 percent -type charities.[2]

Deductions denied because of the 50 percent, 30 percent, or 20 percent limits may be carried over and deducted over the next five years, retaining their character as 50 percent, 30 percent, or 20 percent type deductions.[3]

Gifts are "to" a charitable organization if made directly to the organization. Even though the gift may be intended to be used by the charity, and the charity may use it, if it is given *directly* to the charity, it is a gift to the charity and not "for the use of" the charity, for purposes of the deduction limits. Unreimbursed out-of-pocket expenses incurred on behalf of an organization (e.g., unreimbursed travel expenses of volunteers) are deductible as contributions "to" the organization if they are directly related to performing services for the organization (and, in the case of travel expenses, there is no significant element of personal pleasure, recreation, or vacation in such travel).[4]

"For the use of" applies to indirect contributions to a charitable organization.[5] The term "for the use of" does not refer to a gift of the right to use property. Such a gift would generally be a nondeductible gift of less than the donor's entire interest. See Q 8981 for a discussion of the permissible deduction when a taxpayer donates only the right to use property, rather than an ownership interest in such property.

8975. When is the deduction for charitable donations taken?

Generally, the deduction for a contribution is taken in the year the gift is made.[6] However, if the contribution is a future interest in tangible personal property (such as stamps, artwork, etc.), the contribution is considered made (and the deduction allowable) only "when all intervening interests in, and rights to the actual possession or enjoyment of, the property have expired" or are held by parties unrelated to the donor.[7]

1. IRC Secs. 170(b)(1)(B), 170(b)(1)(C).
2. IRC Sec. 170(b)(1)(D).
3. IRC Secs. 170(d)(1), 170(b)(1)(D)(ii); Treas. Reg. §1.170A-10(b).
4. IRC Sec. 170(j); *Rockefeller v. Comm.*, 676 F.2d 35 (2nd Cir. 1982), aff'g 76 TC 178 (1981), acq. in part 1984-2 CB 2; Rev. Rul. 84-61, 1984-1 CB 39. See Rev. Rul. 58-279, 1958-1 CB 145.
5. See Treas. Reg. §1.170A-8(a)(2). See *Davis v. United States*, 495 U.S. 472 (1990).
6. IRC Sec. 170(a)(1).
7. IRC Sec. 170(a)(3). See also Treas. Reg. §1.170A-5.

Example: If a donor creates a charitable remainder trust and funds it with a piece of artwork, the donor may not take a charitable income tax deduction for the contribution to the charitable remainder trust until the year the trustee sells the artwork.

This rule does not apply to gifts of undivided present interests, or to gifts of future interests in real property or in intangible personal property.[1] A grant of stock options by a company to a charitable trust resulted in a deduction in the year in which the options were exercised.[2] Where real estate was transferred to a charity and subject to an option to repurchase, the IRS determined that fair market value under IRC Section 170 was equal to the value of the property *upon the expiration of the option*.[3] A fixture that is to be severed from real property is treated as tangible personal property.[4] The deduction for a charitable contribution made by an accrual basis (see Q 8956) S corporation is properly passed through to shareholders and taken in the year that the contribution is actually paid.[5]

See Q 8980 for an explanation of the treatment given to gifts of partial interests.

8976. Can an individual deduct the fair market value of appreciated real estate or intangible personal property such as stocks or bonds given to a charity?

If an individual makes a charitable contribution of real property or intangible personal property to a public charity, the sale of which would have resulted in long-term capital gain (see below), the taxpayer is generally entitled to deduct the full fair market value of the property. However, the deduction for the gift is limited to the lesser of 30 percent of adjusted gross income or the unused portion of the 50 percent limit (see Q 8974).[6]

A deduction denied because it exceeds 30 percent of the individual's adjusted gross income may be carried over and treated as a contribution of capital gain property in each of the next five years.[7]

Example: In 2017, Jaclyn had adjusted gross income of $600,000. She made a charitable contribution of long-term capital gain stock worth $200,000 to her church. Her deduction is limited to $180,000 (30 percent of $600,000). In 2018, Jaclyn's adjusted gross income is $700,000. She contributes $100,000 worth of long-term capital gain bonds to the church. She may deduct $120,000 in 2018 ($100,000 plus $20,000 carried forward from 2017), since the total does not exceed 30 percent of her adjusted gross income for 2018 ($210,000).

An individual may elect to take a gift of long-term capital gain property into account at its adjusted basis instead of its fair market value. If the taxpayer makes this election, the income percentage limit for the contribution is increased to 50 percent instead of 30 percent. However, such an election applies to all such contributions made during the taxable year.[8] The election is generally irrevocable.[9]

1. Treas. Reg. §§1.170A-5(a)(2), 1.170A-5(a)(3).
2. Let. Ruls. 200202034, 8849018.
3. TAM 9828001.
4. IRC Sec. 170(a)(3).
5. TAM 200004001. See also Rev. Rul. 2000-43, 2000-2 CB 333.
6. See IRC Sec. 170(b)(1)(C); Treas. Reg. §1.170A-8(d)(1).
7. IRC Secs. 170(b)(1)(C); Treas. Reg. §1.170A-10(c).
8. IRC Secs. 170(b)(1)(C)(iii), 170(e)(1).
9. *Woodbury v. Comm.*, 90-1 USTC ¶50,199 (10th Cir. 1990), aff'g TC Memo 1988-272.

If the charitable contribution consists of property that, if sold at the time of the contribution, would result in income that would not otherwise qualify for long-term capital gain treatment (such as short-term capital gain property), the deduction must be reduced by the amount of gain that would not be long-term capital gain.[1] If the entire gain would be income other than long-term capital gain, the allowable deduction would be limited to the taxpayer's adjusted basis in the contributed property.

Special rules apply to charitable contributions of S corporation stock in determining whether gain on the stock would have been long-term capital gain if the stock were sold by the taxpayer.[2]

Donors making charitable contributions of the long-term capital gain portion of futures contracts must mark the contracts to market as of the dates the contracts are transferred to the donee and recognize the accrued long-term capital gains as income.[3] The amount of taxable gain or deductible loss recognized by the transferor at the time of the charitable transfer equals the difference between the fair market value of the futures contract at the time of the transfer and the transferor's tax basis in the futures contract, as adjusted under IRC Section 1256(a)(2), to account for gains and losses already recognized in prior tax years under the mark to market rules.[4]

In one case, taxpayers who transferred appreciated stock to charitable organizations in the midst of an ongoing tender offer and merger were taxed on the gain on the stock under the "anticipatory assignment of income doctrine" where the charitable gifts occurred after the taxpayers' interests in a corporation had ripened into rights to receive cash.[5] But where taxpayers assigned warrants to four charities after receiving a letter announcing that all issued and outstanding stock of the company would be purchased, the Tax Court held that under Revenue Ruling 78-197[6] the IRS could treat the proceeds of the sales of the warrants by the charities as income to the donors *only if* at the time the assignments took place, the charitable donees were legally bound or could be compelled to sell the warrants.[7]

A taxpayer who donated stock to a supporting organization where the voting rights had been transferred for a business purpose to a third party many years ago was permitted to claim a charitable deduction.[8]

8977. Is a charitable deduction available for the donation of appreciated tangible personal property, such as art, stamps, coins and gems?

It depends upon whether the use of the gift is *related* to the exempt purpose of the charity to which the property is given. Generally, if the sale of appreciated tangible personal property

1. IRC Sec. 170(e)(1)(A); Treas. Reg. §1.170A-4(a).
2. IRC Sec. 170(e)(1).
3. *Greene v. U.S.*, 79 F.3d 1348 (2nd Cir. 1996).
4. *Greene v. U.S.*, 185 F.3d 67, 84 AFTR 2d 99-5415 (2nd Cir. 1999).
5. See *Ferguson v. Comm.*, 174 F.3d 997 (9th Cir. 1999).
6. 1978-1 CB 83.
7. *Rauenhorst v. Comm.*, 119 TC 157 (2002).
8. Let Rul. 200108012.

would result in long-term capital gain (see below), a taxpayer is entitled to deduct the property's full fair market value up to 30 percent of the individual's adjusted gross income, *if* the charity makes use of the property in a way that is related to its charitable purpose or function (i.e., it is a "related-use" gift).[1] The limit is generally 20 percent in the case of private foundations. However, if the use by the charity is unrelated to its charitable purpose or function, the amount of the charitable contribution taken into account is generally limited to the donor's adjusted basis in the donated property.[2]

The following example illustrates the meaning of "unrelated use": "[I]f a painting contributed to an educational institution is used by that organization for educational purposes by being placed in its library for display and study by art students, the use is not an unrelated use; but if the painting is sold and the proceeds used by the organization for educational purposes, the use of the property is an unrelated use." In addition, the regulations state that contributions of furnishings used by the charitable organization in its offices and buildings in the course of carrying out its functions will be considered a related use gift.[3]

Planning Point: The charitable organization will state on IRS Form 8283, Part IV (which the donor provides to the IRS as part of the donor's income tax return) whether it intends to use the item for an unrelated use.

The IRS has determined that a gift of seeds, plants, and greenhouses to an IRC Section 501(c)(3) school's plant science curriculum was a related use gift, and that a gift of a violin to a charitable organization whose exempt purpose included loaning instruments to music students was a related use gift.[4] The IRS has also found that contributions of art to a Jewish community center for use in the center's recreational, educational, and social activities were related use gifts.[5]

If the taxpayer contributes long-term capital gain "related use" property to public charities, the taxpayer may elect to value the gift at its adjusted basis instead of its fair market value. If this election is made, the 30 percent of adjusted gross income limit does not apply. Instead, the donor may deduct the amount of his adjusted basis in the gift, up to 50 percent of adjusted gross income. If the taxpayer makes the election, it applies to all gifts of long-term capital gain property during the year.[6] Such an election is generally irrevocable.[7]

The amount of the deduction for a contribution of tangible personal property must be reduced by the amount of gain that would *not* be long-term capital gain (gain on a capital asset held for more than one year, see Q 8572) if the contributed property had been sold at its fair market value at the time of the contribution. Thus, for example, if the entire gain would be ordinary income, the allowable deduction would be limited to the taxpayer's adjusted basis in

1. IRC Sec. 170(b)(1)(C); Treas. Reg. §1.170A-8(d)(1).
2. IRC Sec. 170(e)(1)(B).
3. Treas. Reg. §1.170A-4(b)(3)(i).
4. Let. Ruls. 9131052, 9147049.
5. Let. Rul. 9833011.
6. IRC Secs. 170(b)(1)(C)(iii), 170(e)(1).
7. *Woodbury v. Comm.*, 900 F.2d 1457, 90-1 USTC ¶50,199 (10th Cir. 1990), aff'g TC Memo 1988-272.

the contributed property. It makes no difference whether or not the property is put to a related use.[1] Ordinary income property includes a work of art created by the donor.[2]

Planning Point: If an artist makes a charitable gift of the artist's own artwork, the artist will only be able to deduct the costs of creating the art (e.g., paper, paint, etc.).

The charitable deduction is recaptured by the donor on certain dispositions by the charity of tangible personal property identified by the charity as related use property for which a deduction in excess of basis was allowed. Unless the charity makes the appropriate certification, recapture applies if the charity disposes of the property after the taxable year the property was contributed, but before the end of the three-year period starting on the date of contribution (see Q 8972). The certification must be in writing and signed under penalty of perjury by an officer of the charity. The written statement must (1) certify that the use of the property was related and describe the use of the property or (2) state the intended use at the time of contribution and certify that the intended use has become impossible or infeasible to implement. The amount recaptured (included in income) in the year of disposition is equal to the amount of the charitable deduction minus the donor's basis in the property at the time of contribution.[3]

Example. Amy contributes a painting to an art museum in December 2017. The museum intends to display the painting. Amy claims a charitable deduction for the painting's fair market value of $100,000 for 2017. Amy's basis in the painting was $40,000. In 2018 (within three years of the contribution), the museum sells the painting. Amy must include $60,000 ($100,000 charitable deduction - $40,000 basis) in income in 2018.

A charity is required to report any disposition of property (other than publicly traded securities) within three years after its receipt to the IRS, if the claimed value of the property (plus the claimed value of all similar items of property by the donor to one or more charities) exceeds $5,000. A copy of the related use certification (see above) must be included with this return.[4] Any person who identifies tangible personal property as related use property and knows that the property is not intended for such use is subject to a $10,000 penalty.[5]

8978. How is the charitable contribution deduction computed when property is sold to a charity at a reduced price (in a "bargain sale")?

If property is sold to a charity for less than its fair market value (a bargain sale), the individual must first determine whether a charitable deduction is allowable under the general rules governing charitable deductions (see Q 8968). The taxpayer must then determine the amounts of the allowable deduction and gain (if any) that will result from the transaction. The taxpayer first calculates the percentage of the property's fair market value that is being contributed and what percentage is being sold. (The fair market value of the contributed portion is the fair market value of the entire property less the amount realized on the sale.[6] The fair market value of the portion sold is the amount realized on the sale.)

1. See IRC Sec. 170(e)(1)(A); Treas. Reg. §1.170A-4(a).
2. Treas. Reg. §1.170A-4(b)(1).
3. IRC Sec. 170(e)(7), as added by PPA 2006.
4. IRC Sec. 6050L, as added by PPA 2006.
5. IRC Sec. 6720B, as added by PPA 2006.
6. Treas. Reg. §1.170A-4(c)(3).

To determine the permissibility and the amount of the deduction for the contributed portion, the value of the contributed portion must be reduced by any gain that would *not* have been realized as long-term capital gain had the contributed portion been sold, taking into account the basis allocated to it.[1] If the sale of the contributed portion by the donor would have resulted in long-term capital gain (see example 2, below), no reduction is required unless the gift is tangible personal property and the use of the gift will be unrelated to the function of the charity.[2]

After any such reduction required by IRC Section 170(e)(1) has been made, the remaining amount of the contribution is the allowable deduction.

The taxpayer's adjusted basis in the property is then allocated to each portion in these proportions.[3] It is allocated between the portions contributed and sold, based on their relative proportions of the property's fair market value.[4] Gain is recognized on the sale portion to the extent the amount realized exceeds the allocated basis. However, no loss is recognized if the sale amount is less than the allocated basis of the sold portion.[5] The amount of the deduction for the contributed portion is determined as if property having the allocated basis and allocated fair market value were given.

The end result of this analysis is that essentially two separate transactions take place: (1) a sale of property that may result in taxable income, and (2) a deductible contribution of property to the charity. In some cases, the application of these rules may result in a taxable gain in excess of the allowed deduction. If the property is subject to a liability, the amount of the liability is treated as an amount realized.[6]

Example 1. Dale sells ordinary income property to his church for $4,000, which is the amount of his adjusted basis. The property has a fair market value of $10,000. The contribution portion of the transaction has a value of $6,000 ($10,000 fair market value less $4,000 amount realized) that represents 60 percent of the value of the property. The amount realized represents 40 percent of the value of the property ($4,000/$10,000). The adjusted basis ($4,000) is therefore allocated as follows: 40 percent of it ($1,600) becomes Dale's basis in the "sold" portion and 60 percent of it ($2,400) becomes his basis in the "contributed" portion. The $6,000 "contribution portion" of the transaction has an allocated basis of $2,400. If it were sold, he would recognize $3,600 of ordinary income. The deduction for the $6,000 contribution is therefore reduced by $3,600. Dale has a charitable deduction of $2,400. Because Dale is receiving $4,000 for the "sold" portion and has an allocated basis in it of $1,600, he recognizes $2,400 of ordinary income with respect to the sale part of the transaction. The church's basis in the property received will be $6,400; this consists of the sum of the bargain sale price ($4,000) and the amount of Dale's basis ($2,400) in the gift portion.[7]

Example 2. The facts are the same as in Example 1, except that the property was long-term capital gain stock. Dale's allocations of basis are the same as above; therefore, he recognizes $2,400 on the sale portion of the transaction. However the contributed portion is not subject to a reduction; thus, he is permitted a deduction of $6,000. The church's basis in the stock will be $6,400, determined the same way as in Example 1.

1. IRC Sec. 170(e)(1)(A); Treas. Reg. §1.1011-2(a).
2. IRC Sec. 170(e)(1)(B).
3. IRC Sec. 1011(b); Treas. Reg. §§1.170A-4(c)(2)(i), 1.1011-2.
4. IRC Secs. 170(e)(2), 1011(b); Treas. Reg. §1.170A-4(c)(2).
5. Treas. Reg. §1.1001-1(e).
6. Treas. Reg. §1.1011-2(a)(3).
7. See Treas. Reg. §1.170A-4(d), Example 5.

A taxpayer who makes charitable contributions of long-term capital gain property may elect to apply the provisions of IRC Section 170(e)(1) to all such contributions, thus using adjusted basis instead of fair market value to determine the value of the gifts. This election permits the individual to take a higher proportion of income as charitable deductions than would otherwise be allowed (see Q 8974).

In the context of a bargain sale, the Tax Court has found that the charitable deduction was properly claimed in the year that the sale was completed, because sufficient benefits and burdens of ownership had passed to the charitable organization in that year.[1] Bargain sale treatment was denied to a taxpayer who inflated his valuation to a figure that would enable him to recover his original investment in his property (in the form of cash plus tax savings from the inflated tax deduction).[2]

8979. How is the amount of a charitable contribution determined when a taxpayer donates property subject to a mortgage or other debt?

When property subject to a liability, such as a mortgage or other debt, is contributed to a charity, the amount of the liability is treated as an amount realized, even if the charity does not assume or pay the debt.[3] The property is considered sold for the amount realized, and the contribution is subject to the bargain sale rules (see Q 8978).

If the charity assumes a liability or if property is donated that is subject to a liability, the amount of the charitable contribution may not include any interest paid (or to be paid) by the donor for any period after the contribution if the donor is allowed an interest deduction for the amount.[4] If the property is a bond, the contribution must be reduced by the amount of interest paid by the taxpayer on indebtedness incurred to purchase or carry the bond that is attributable to any period before the making of the contribution. However, the amount of such a reduction is limited to the interest or interest equivalent (e.g., bond discount) on the bond that is not includable in the donor's income.[5]

> *Example:* (a) On January 1, 2008, Jen, an individual using the cash receipts and disbursements method of accounting, purchased for $9,280 a 5½ percent, $10,000, 20-year Omega Corporation bond, the interest on which was payable semi-annually on June 30 and December 31. The Omega Corporation had issued the bond on January 1, 2008, at a discount of $720 from the principal amount. On December 1, 2018, Jen donated the bond to a charitable organization, and, in connection with the contribution, the charitable organization assumed an indebtedness of $7,000 that Jen had incurred to purchase and carry the bond.
>
> (b) During the 2018 calendar year, Jen paid accrued interest of $330 on the indebtedness for the period from January 1, 2018, to December 1, 2018, and an interest deduction of $330 is allowable for such amount. Of the bond discount of $36 a year ($720 divided by 20 years), $33 (11/12 of $36) is includable in Jen's income. Of the $550 of annual interest receivable on the bond, she will include in income only the June 30, 2018, payment of $275.
>
> (c) The market value of the Omega Corporation bond on December 1, 2018, was $9,902. This value includes $229 of interest receivable that had accrued from July 1 to December 1, 2018.

1. See *Musgrave v. Comm.*, TC Memo 2000-285.
2. *Styron v. Comm.*, TC Summ. Op. 2001-64.
3. Treas. Reg. §1.1001-2; Rev. Rul. 81-163, 1981-1 CB 433. See Let. Rul. 9329017; *Guest v. Comm.*, 77 TC 9 (1981), *acq.* 1982-2 CB 1; *Crane v. Comm.*, 331 U.S. 1 (1947).
4. IRC Sec. 170(f)(5); Treas. Reg. §1.170A-3(a).
5. IRC Sec. 170(f)(5)(B); Treas. Reg. §1.170A-3(c).

(d) The amount of the charitable contribution determined without regard to the reduction required by IRC Section 170(f)(5) is $2,902 ($9,902, the value of the property on the date of gift, less $7,000, the amount of the liability assumed by the charitable organization). In determining the amount of the allowable charitable deduction, the value of the gift ($2,902) must be reduced to eliminate from the deduction that portion for which Jen has been allowed an interest deduction. Although the amount of such interest deduction was $330, the reduction required by this section is limited to $229, since the reduction is not to exceed the amount of interest income on the bond that is not includable in Jen's income.[1]

8980. Can a deduction be taken for a charitable contribution of less than the donor's entire interest in property?

Usually not. Generally, a taxpayer may not deduct a charitable contribution that is less than the entire interest in property unless the contribution is made in trust. (A deduction of a partial interest will be allowed to the extent a deduction would be allowed if the interest had been transferred in trust.[2]) However, a taxpayer may deduct contributions of partial interests if they are made to each of several charities, with the result that the entire interest in the property has been given to charitable organizations. An individual may make a gift of a partial interest in property if that is the individual's entire interest, but not if partial interests were created to avoid the application of the rule prohibiting gifts of less than the individual's entire interest.[3]

Exceptions: A deduction *is* allowed for a contribution of less than the donor's entire interest in property in the following instances:

(1) The taxpayer donates an irrevocable remainder interest in a personal residence or farm;[4]

(2) The taxpayer makes a qualified conservation contribution;[5] or

(3) The taxpayer donates an undivided portion of his entire interest.[6] An undivided portion is a fraction or percentage of each and every substantial interest or right owned by the donor in property and the fraction or percentage extends over the entire term of the donor's interest in the property and in other property into which that property is converted.[7] The *right* to possession of an undivided portion of the taxpayer's entire interest has been held sufficient to constitute a charitable gift, even where the donee did not actually choose to take possession.[8] The possibility that a charity's undivided fractional interest may be divested upon the

1. See Treas. Reg. §1.170A-3(d) Example (2).
2. IRC Sec. 170(f)(3)(A); Treas. Reg. §1.170A-7(a).
3. Treas. Reg. §1.170A-7(a)(2)(i).
4. IRC Sec. 170(f)(3)(B)(i); Treas. Reg. §§1.170A-7(b)(3), 1.170A-7(b)(4).
5. IRC Sec. 170(f)(3)(B)(iii).
6. IRC Sec. 170(f)(3)(B)(ii).
7. Treas. Reg. §1.170A-7(b)(1). See Rev. Rul. 57-293, 1957-2 CB 153 (undivided ¼ ownership and ¼ possession of art object); Rev. Rul. 72-419, 1972-2 CB 104 (undivided 20 percent remainder interest which was the donor's only interest in the property). See also See Let. Ruls. 8145055, 8639019.
8. See *Winokur v. Comm.*, 90 TC 733 (1988), acq. 1989-1 CB 1. See also Let. Ruls. 200223013, 200223014 (the gift of a fractional interest in any work of the donors' collection accepted by the donee (subject to the gift and loan agreement) would qualify as a gift of an undivided portion of the donors' entire interest in the work, relying on *Winokur*, above; thus, the undivided fractional interest would be deductible).

occurrence or nonoccurrence of some event has been determined not to defeat an otherwise deductible contribution where the possibility is deemed so remote as to be negligible.[1]

The IRS has also found that a charitable gift of an "overriding royalty interest" or a "net profits interest" in an oil and gas lease did not constitute an undivided portion of the donor's entire interest in an oil and gas lease where the donor owned a working interest under the lease.[2]

The IRS has ruled privately that a donor's transfer of a life insurance policy to a charity, where the donor retained bare legal title, was not a retention of a substantial interest for purposes of the partial interest rule. Thus, the donor did not violate the partial interest rule, and was allowed to claim the charitable contribution deduction on the first day following the end of the 30-day cancellation period.[3]

In a case involving the contribution of a patent to a qualified charity, the IRS found that no deduction is allowed if: (1) the taxpayer retains any substantial right in the patent; or (2) the taxpayer's contribution of a patent is subject to a conditional reversion, unless the likelihood of the reversion is so remote as to be negligible. On the other hand, a contribution of a patent subject to a license or transfer restriction will be deductible, but the restriction *reduces* what would otherwise be the fair market value of the patent at the time of the contribution and, therefore, *reduces* the amount of the charitable contribution.[4]

A charitable deduction is not allowed for a contribution of an undivided portion of the donor's entire interest in tangible personal property unless, before the contribution, all interests in the property were held by the donor or the donor and the charity. In the case of any additional contribution of interests in the same property, the fair market value (FMV) of such contributions will be equal to the lesser of (1) the FMV at the time of the initial fractional contribution, or (2) the FMV at the time of the additional contribution.[5]

Example. Mark contributed 10 percent of a painting valued at $100,000 to an art museum in 2017 (a related use gift). The charitable deduction for the 10 percent interest was $10,000 in 2017. In 2018, Mark contributes another 10 percent interest in the painting to the art museum when the painting is valued at $110,000. However, for charitable deduction purposes, the fair market value of the painting cannot exceed the $100,000 value at the time of the initial contribution. Therefore, the charitable deduction is limited to $10,000 (10 percent of $100,000) in 2018.

The charitable deduction for a contribution of an undivided portion of the donor's entire interest in tangible personal property is recaptured (plus interest) if the donor does not contribute all of the remaining interests in the property to charity within ten years of the initial fractional contribution or before death, whichever is earlier. Recapture is also required if the charity did not have substantial physical possession or make related use of the property during that period. The income tax on the recaptured amount is increased by 10 percent of the amount recaptured.[6]

1. Let. Rul. 9303007.
2. See Rev. Rul. 88-37, 1988-1 CB 522.
3. Let. Rul. 200209020.
4. Rev. Rul. 2003-28, 2003-1 CB 594.
5. IRC Sec. 170(o), as added by PPA 2006.
6. IRC Sec. 170(o)(3)(B).

8981. What deduction is available when a taxpayer only grants the charity the right to use property, rather than donating an ownership interest in the property?

The right to use property is less than the entire interest in property owned by an individual and is subject to the rules governing a charitable contribution of less than the donor's entire interest (see Q 8980).[1] Therefore, generally no deduction will be allowed.

> *Example:* Stephen owns a beautiful vacation home on the beach. He typically rents it for $3,000 per week. He offers his favorite nonprofit the right to use his vacation homes for a week-long board retreat. Stephen is not, however, able to deduct $3,000 for the nonprofit's use of the vacation home for the week.

However, in some cases, a deduction has been allowed for the costs of repairing and maintaining property owned by the taxpayer but used by the charity. These deductions have been allowed as contributions "for the use of" the charity.[2] Despite this, the IRS has denied a deduction for maintenance and repair costs in other situations.[3] To be deductible, the costs must be unreimbursed expenses "directly attributable to the performance of ... volunteer services."[4]

A taxpayer was not permitted a deduction when he donated a week's use of his vacation home in connection with a charitable auction, the proceeds of which benefitted charitable organizations. The IRS also noted that the successful bidder would not be permitted a charitable deduction to the extent that valuable consideration is received in return (i.e., the bidder paid fair rental for a week's use of the home).[5]

Tenant-stockholders were allowed to exclude $500,000 of gain from the disposition of their shares of stock in a cooperative apartment which was coordinated with a donation of the same shares to a charitable organization.[6]

8982. What are the tax consequences of a charitable contribution of partnership interests?

A partnership interest is a capital asset that, if sold, would be given capital gain or loss treatment except to the extent of the partner's share of certain partnership property that, if sold by the partnership, would produce ordinary gain (i.e., the partner's share of "unrealized receivables" and "substantially appreciated inventory").[7] (See Q 8566 and Q 8567 regarding the treatment of capital gains and losses.) Thus, if a taxpayer makes a charitable contribution of a partnership interest, and if the taxpayer has held the interest for long enough to qualify for long-term capital gain treatment (i.e., more than one year, see Q 8572), a deduction is permitted in the amount of the full fair market value of the interest less the amount of ordinary gain, if any, that would have been realized by the partnership for the partnership's share of "unrealized

1. IRC Sec. 170(f)(3)(A).
2. See *Est. of Carroll v. Comm.*, 38 TC 868 (1962); Rev. Rul. 58-279, 1958-1 CB 145.
3. Rev. Rul. 58-279, above; Rev. Rul. 69-239, 1969-1 CB 198.
4. Rev. Rul. 58-279, above.
5. Rev. Rul. 89-51, 1989-1 CB 89.
6. See FSA 200149007.
7. IRC Sec. 741.

receivables" and "substantially appreciated inventory." (The deduction is subject to the otherwise applicable limits discussed in Q 8974.)

If the partnership interest includes a liability (mortgage, etc.), the amount of the liability is treated as an amount realized on the disposition of the partnership interest.[1] Thus, the contribution is subject to the bargain sale rules, and the transfer will be treated, in part at least, as a sale (see Q 8978).[2] (If the partner's share of the partnership liabilities exceeds the fair market value of his partnership interest, the partner may have taxable income, but no deduction under the bargain sale rules.) In *Goodman v. United States*,[3] the taxpayer contributed her partnership interest to charity, subject to her share of partnership debt. The district court held that the taxpayer recognized gain on the transfer that was equal to the excess of the amount realized over that portion of the adjusted basis of the partnership interest (at the time of the transfer) allocable to the sale under IRC Section 1011(b).[4]

The following steps must be taken to determine the taxpayer's taxable income and the amount of the charitable deduction under the bargain sale rules:

1. *Determine the taxable gain on the sale portion*. Under the bargain sale rules, part of the donor's basis is allocated to the portion sold. The basis allocated to the sold portion is the amount of basis that bears the same ratio to the entire basis as the amount realized bears to the market value of the property. Presumably, the sold portion includes the same proportionate part of the donor's share of unrealized receivables and substantially appreciated inventory as it does basis.

   Example: Adam owns a 10 percent interest in a partnership that he has held for three years. The fair market value of his interest is $100,000 and his adjusted basis is $50,000. His share of a mortgage on partnership property is $40,000, and his share of "unrealized receivables" (potential depreciation recapture on the mortgaged property) is $5,000 in which the partnership's basis is zero. He donates his entire interest to charity. He is deemed to have received $40,000, his share of partnership liabilities, on the transfer. In effect there are two transactions–a sale for $40,000 and a contribution of $60,000.

   Of Adam's $50,000 basis in his partnership interest, $20,000 is allocated to the sale portion: $40,000 (amount realized)/$100,000 (fair market value) × $50,000 (total adjusted basis). The fair market value of the sold portion is $40,000 (amount realized). Adam must recognize a gain of $20,000 ($40,000 realized less $20,000 adjusted basis allocated to the sold portion). Of that gain, $2,000 is allocable to unrealized receivables ($5,000 unrealized receivables × $40,000/$100,000). Because the partnership has no basis in the unrealized receivables, the entire $2,000 would be ordinary income. Adam must report a taxable long-term capital gain of $18,000 and a taxable ordinary gain of $2,000.

2. *Determine the charitable contribution deduction*. Generally, the fair market value of the portion given to charity is deductible except to the extent the property would have generated ordinary income if sold. Consequently, the allowable deduction for the

1. Treas. Reg. §1.1001-2. See *Crane v. Comm.*, 331 U.S. 1 (1947).
2. Rev. Rul. 75-194, 1975-1 CB 80.
3. 2000-1 USTC ¶50,162 (S.D. Fl. 1999).
4. Citing Rev. Rul. 75-194 and Treas. Reg. §1.1001-2.

gift portion must be reduced to the extent the portion of the partnership interest given to the charity would produce ordinary income if sold.

Example: The fair market value of Adam's gift to charity is $60,000. Because 60 percent of the partnership interest was given to the charity ($60,000/$100,000), 60 percent of Adam's share of partnership "unrealized receivables," or $3,000 ($5,000 × 60 percent = $3,000), is considered included in the gift. The balance of the gift would be long-term capital gain on sale. Because $3,000 would be ordinary income on a sale, Adam's contribution is reduced by $3,000, and his charitable contribution deduction is $57,000.

Other special rules may apply under certain circumstances, for example, if the partnership owns property subject to tax credit recapture, if it has made installment sales, or (as might occur in the case of an oil and gas partnership) if it is receiving income in the form of "production payments."

PART XVIII: ASSET PROTECTION TRUSTS

8983. What is a domestic asset protection trust? Why might an individual wish to establish an asset protection trust?

A domestic asset protection trust is an irrevocable trust that is established in a U.S. jurisdiction that is designed to protect the assets of the individual who creates the trust. These trusts are unique in that the individual who transfers assets to the trust (the trust settlor) is generally also a trust beneficiary, so that he or she retains the economic benefit of the assets that are transferred into the trust while simultaneously protecting those assets from the claims of creditors.

The underlying reasons for establishing a domestic asset protection trust can vary. Some high net worth individuals may wish to establish the trust in order to protect assets from the claims of traditional creditors, while others establish these trusts in order to protect assets from the threat of future liabilities stemming from litigation. For example, individuals with high-risk exposure levels, including doctors, lawyers and directors and officers of public companies, may wish to shield their assets from the threat of future lawsuits. Others may wish to protect the assets that will eventually be inherited by a "spendthrift" heir (see Q 8995 to Q 8997) or a disabled individual (see Q 8998 to Q 8999 for a discussion of qualified disability trusts). Asset protection trusts can also be used as a tool in marital planning, perhaps replacing a prenuptial agreement (Q 9001) by placing certain assets beyond the reach of a future spouse.

While asset protection is generally the primary motive in establishing these trusts, the irrevocable nature of the trust also means that the trust assets can be excluded from the settlor's estate.

Not every state has enacted a statute that authorizes domestic asset protection trusts. Some states do not allow establishment of these trusts because of the public policy concerns over allowing an individual to establish a trust in order to shield assets from the valid claims of creditors. However, many individuals will establish domestic asset protection trusts in states that do authorize these trusts, such as Delaware (Q 8986) or Alaska (Q 8987), regardless of whether the individual actually resides in that state.

See Q 8984 for a discussion of the necessary elements of an effectively designed asset protection trust and Q 8985 for some of the important issues that an individual should consider when determining whether to establish such a trust.

8984. What are the important elements of an effectively designed domestic asset protection trust?

First, a domestic asset protection trust must be irrevocable in order to effectively protect the assets of the trust creator (settlor) against the claims of future creditors. The trust settlor is named as a trust beneficiary (additional beneficiaries may also be named), resulting in what is known as a self-settled trust. Second, a trustee (whether an individual or a corporation) who is a resident of the state in which the trust is established must be appointed and given discretionary authority over trust administration and distributions.

Importantly, a domestic asset protection trust must contain a "spendthrift" clause in order to protect the trust settlor's assets against the claims of creditors. See Q 8996 for an in depth discussion of the types of language that can constitute a valid spendthrift clause.

Some of the important considerations that an individual must be aware of when determining whether a domestic asset protection strategy is appropriate are discussed in Q 8985.

8985. What issues should an individual consider when establishing a domestic asset protection trust?

It is important for an individual who is considering establishing a domestic asset protection trust to remember that the validity of the arrangement may be challenged in court regardless of whether he or she has established a trust that meets all of the requirements discussed in Q 8984. Since these trusts are relatively new, issues surrounding their validity have not been extensively litigated, so a variety of potential grounds for challenge still exist.

Because of the public policy concerns surrounding these trusts, and the fact that not every state authorizes their creation, a creditor may challenge the validity of a trust established in a state other than the settlor's state of residence by claiming that the laws of the settlor's state of residence should apply. The trust must clearly specify which state law will govern. Further, in order to minimize the potential success of such a claim, a trustee who is resident in the state where the trust was formed must be chosen—merely directing a nonresident trustee to apply the laws of the state could be insufficient. If possible, the assets should actually be transferred to the state in which the trust is formed (meaning that real estate located in another state may not be an ideal trust asset).

A valid and enforceable asset protection trust should avoid even the appearance that the assets were fraudulently transferred into the trust in order to evade the claims of a specific creditor. Often, preexisting creditors may reach the assets despite the presence of a valid trust (see Q 8989, Q 8992 and Q 8997 for a discussion of situations in which assets held in an asset protection trust may be reached). The issue may result in litigation even if the settlor could reasonably foresee that the claim or liability would arise in the future.

The settlor should also be aware that most state laws will not allow a domestic asset protection trust to shield assets from claims for child support.

8986. What is a Delaware dynasty trust?

A Delaware dynasty trust is essentially an irrevocable trust established under Delaware law in order to reduce or eliminate a taxpayer's estate, gift and generation skipping transfer (GST) tax liability. A dynasty trust gets its name because the trust is intended to benefit multiple generations of beneficiaries. However, some taxpayers may structure these trusts as asset protection trusts by naming themselves as beneficiaries in order to receive distributions at the trustee's discretion if the need arises.

Delaware trust law is favorable to trusts and is one of the few states allowing the creation of a trust that never expires, permitting the trust assets to pass from generation to generation without the imposition of transfer taxes. Many other states adopt the traditional rule against perpetuities, which provides that a trust can only last as long as the lifetimes of individuals who are currently living (or a specified term of years), plus twenty-one years.

Further, and importantly, Delaware provides protection against creditors for assets placed in a trust created under Delaware law, unless the transfer was made specifically to defraud a taxpayer's creditors.[1]

Planning Point: The Delaware statutory scheme provides protection from most creditors, but does allow the assets in a Delaware dynasty trust to be reached in order to satisfy alimony or child support obligations. A person who has suffered death, personal injury or property damage on or before the date the assets were transferred to trust may also be able to reach the trust assets if the trust creator is found liable for the damages caused.[2]

If a Delaware dynasty trust does not have any Delaware beneficiaries, no Delaware state income or capital gains taxes are imposed upon the trust accumulations and taxes are imposed only when distributions are made.

Planning Point: Individuals should be advised that though Delaware may exempt trust income from state tax, their own state of residence may impose income or capital gains taxes.

These trusts can be funded with cash, stock or other assets. Many wealthy taxpayers fund the trust with assets that equal the current transfer tax exemption amount ($5.6 million in 2018) in order to avoid transfer taxation. Both the amount that is initially contributed and any subsequent appreciation is removed from the taxpayer-settlor's estate.

See Q 8983 to Q 8985 for a discussion of domestic asset protection trusts generally. See Q 8987 to Q 8990 for a more detailed discussion of asset protection trusts established in Delaware. Alaska asset protection trust rules are discussed in Q 8991 to Q 8994.

8987. How can a Delaware dynasty trust be used in the context of business succession planning?

A Delaware dynasty trust can be used to transfer business interests from one generation to future generations while minimizing tax liability. Essentially, the trust is funded with the business interests. If the value of the business interests does not exceed the transfer tax exemption amount in the year of transfer ($5.6 million in 2018), the transferred interests will, theoretically, increase in value within the trust and the appreciation will also be transferred without transfer tax liability.

Delaware is one of the few states that allow a trust to continue indefinitely, so that the trust creator and business owner can ensure that the business interests will benefit the heirs into future generations. Further, because the trusts are irrevocable and are generally protected from a taxpayer's creditors, the business owner can ensure that his or her business is protected from the beneficiaries' creditors even after death.

---

1. 12 Del. C. § 3572(a).
2. 12 Del. C. § 3573.

Planning Point: Creating a Delaware dynasty trust is a complex undertaking and requires expert legal advice in order to ensure that the trust document clearly meets Delaware statutory requirements.

8988. What are the requirements under Delaware law for establishing a Delaware dynasty trust that limits the ability of creditors to reach the trust assets?

A Delaware dynasty trust can often be used as an asset protection trust in order to protect the trust assets from the creditors of the beneficiaries. Under Delaware law, the ability of creditors to reach trust assets is limited if a qualified disposition to a qualified trustee has been made.

A qualified disposition is a transfer of property to a qualified trustee of an irrevocable trust that expressly provides that Delaware law will govern. There may be multiple trustees, so long as one of the trustees is a qualified trustee.[1]

A qualified trustee is an individual, other than the transferor, who is a Delaware resident or a financial institution that is authorized to act as a trustee under Delaware law. A portion of the trust property must be maintained under Delaware law and the trustee must materially participate in the trust administration. The trust may also provide that a trust protector or trust advisor may be appointed, and the transferor may hold the trust advisor position so long as he or she does not have any additional authority over the trust.[2]

8989. If the Delaware law requirements limiting the ability of creditors to reach trust assets have been satisfied, can a creditor still bring a claim against those assets?

Yes, but if a qualified disposition has been made, a creditor whose claims existed at the time of the disposition must bring a claim within four years following the disposition or, if later, within one year following the date the creditor discovered the disposition or the date the creditor reasonably could have discovered the disposition.[3] For creditors whose claims arose after the qualified disposition, no claims may be brought unless the transfer was made with actual intent to defraud the creditor.[4]

If the transferor has made more than one qualified disposition to the trust, a subsequent disposition is disregarded in determining whether a creditor's claim with respect to a prior qualified disposition is time-barred. Further, any distributions to a beneficiary are considered as having been made from the latest qualified disposition.[5]

Certain claims are not subject to the time limitations discussed above. For example, claims for child support and alimony cannot be avoided. Further, claims by persons who suffered death,

1. Del. Code. Ann. Tit. 12, Sec. 3570(4).
2. Del. Code. Ann. Tit. 12, Sec. 3570(8).
3. Del. Code. Ann. Tit. 12, Sec. 3572(b).
4. Del. Code. Ann. Tit. 12, Sec. 3572(a).
5. Del. Code. Ann. Tit. 12, Sec. 3572(f).

physical injury or property damages on or before the date of the qualified disposition are not barred.[1]

8990. If the Delaware law requirements limiting the ability of creditors to reach trust assets have been satisfied and a creditor makes a claim against those assets, what are the results if the beneficiary has already received a trust distribution?

If a beneficiary of a Delaware trust has not acted in bad faith, the beneficiary may retain any distributions from the trust that are made before a creditor brings a claim against the trust assets.[2] Under Delaware law, it is presumed that the beneficiary (including a beneficiary who is also the transferor) did not act in bad faith, and the creditor has the burden of proving the existence of bad faith.[3]

8991. What is an Alaska Trust?

Like a Delaware trust (see Q 8986 to Q 8990), an Alaska trust is a form of domestic asset protection trust that is formed under the favorable trust laws developed by Alaska. If the assets are transferred to the trust pursuant to a written document that provides that the interests of the trust beneficiary in the trust assets cannot be voluntarily or involuntarily transferred before the interests are paid or delivered to the beneficiary, the assets will be protected from the beneficiary's creditors.

This means creditors that exist when the trust is created, or those who become creditors after the trust is created, are unable to satisfy their claims from the beneficiary's interest in the trust in most circumstances.[4]

This is the case even if the trust beneficiary is also the settlor of the trust.[5] The settlor can also permissibly serve as co-trustee or trust advisor, as long as the settlor does not have authority over discretionary trust distributions.[6] A non-settlor trust beneficiary may serve as sole trustee, co-trustee or advisor without jeopardizing the validity of the transfer restrictions.[7]

"Payment or delivery" of trust assets, for these purposes, does not include a beneficiary's use or occupancy of either real property or tangible personal property owned by the trust, so long as the use is in accordance with the trustee's discretionary authority as specified in the trust document.[8]

See Q 8992 for a discussion of situations where a creditor can reach assets held in an Alaska trust despite proper structuring of the trust. See Q 8983 to Q 8985 for a discussion of domestic asset protection trusts generally. The rules governing asset protection trusts established in Delaware are discussed in Q 8987 to Q 8990.

1. Del. Code. Ann. Tit. 12, Sec. 3573.
2. Del. Code. Ann. Tit. 12, Sec. 3574(b)(2).
3. Del. Code. Ann. Tit. 12, Sec. 3574(c).
4. Alaska Stat. 34.40.110(b).
5. Alaska Stat. 34.40.110(a).
6. Alaska Stat. 34.40.110(f).
7. Alaska Stat. 34.40.110(g).
8. Alaska Stat. 34.40.110(a).

8992. Are there any situations where a creditor can reach assets held for a beneficiary in an Alaska trust?

Yes. There are circumstances under which a creditor can reach the assets held in a valid Alaska trust when the creditor is a creditor of the settlor. First, a creditor of the settlor may reach Alaska trust assets if the creditor establishes that the transfer of property to the trust was made with the intent to defraud the creditor (a settlor's expressed intent to protect the assets from the beneficiary's potential future creditors does not show an intent to defraud).[1] A creditor may reach trust assets under this exception if the creditor was a creditor before the assets were transferred, and an action to prove intent to defraud is brought within either:

1. four years after the transfer was made, or
2. within one year after the transfer is (or reasonably could have been) discovered by the creditor *if* (a) the creditor can demonstrate that it brought a specific claim against the settlor before the transfer or (b) the creditor files another action (other than one asserting an intent to defraud) that is based on an act or omission of the settlor that occurred before the transfer, and an action asserting an intent to defraud is filed within four years of the transfer.[2]

A creditor who became a creditor subsequent to the asset transfer may only reach the assets if it brings an action claiming intent to defraud within four years of the transfer.[3]

A creditor who is a creditor of the settlor may also reach trust assets if the trust provides that the settlor may revoke or terminate all or part of the trust without the beneficiary's consent, and the trust interest would be adversely affected if the settlor exercised the power to revoke or terminate. A settlor is not considered to have retained these powers if he or she has the right to veto a trust distribution, or if he or she holds a non-general power of appointment. Retention of the rights to receive income in the circumstances discussed below also does not constitute a power to revoke or terminate trust interests.[4]

If the trust provides that all or a part of the trust income or principal must be distributed to the settlor, a creditor of the settlor may reach trust assets unless the distribution is one of the following types of distribution:

1. a distribution of income or principal from a charitable remainder annuity trust or charitable remainder unitrust;
2. a distribution of a percentage of the value of the trust each year as determined each year under the trust document;
3. actual or potential use of real property held under a qualified personal residence trust;
4. a distribution of income or principal from a grantor retained annuity trust or grantor retained unitrust.[5]

1. Alaska Stat. 34.40.110(b)(1).
2. Alaska Stat. 34.40.110(d).
3. Alaska Stat. 34.40.110(d)(2).
4. Alaska Stat. 34.40.110(b)(2).
5. Alaska Stat. 34.40.110(b)(3).

A creditor of the settlor may also reach trust assets if the settlor is, at the time of transfer, in default for thirty days or more in making child support payments that are due under a valid support judgment or order.[1]

8993. What special requirements apply to an Alaska trust where the settlor is also named as trust beneficiary?

The settlor of an Alaska trust who is also named trust beneficiary is required to sign a sworn affidavit before the assets are transferred to the trust. This affidavit must state that the settlor has full right, title and authority to transfer the assets to the trust, and that the transfer will not render the settlor insolvent. The settlor must also verify that he or she does not plan on filing for bankruptcy relief.

Further, the affidavit must state that the settlor does not intent to defraud any creditors through the transfer, and that no pending or threatened court actions exist (unless the actions are identified and attached to the affidavit). Similarly, the settlor must verify that he or she is not involved in any administrative proceedings unless they are identified and attached to the affidavit.

The settlor must also verify that the settlor is not in default on child support payments by more than thirty days, and that the assets being transferred were not obtained from unlawful activities.[2]

8994. How does a beneficiary's divorce impact interests in an Alaska trust?

Generally, the beneficiary's interest in an Alaska trust is not considered marital property that is subject to division. However, unless the parties otherwise agree in writing, this general rule does not apply if the settlor is the beneficiary and the assets were transferred to the trust (1) after the settlor-beneficiary's marriage or (2) within thirty days before the settlor-beneficiary's marriage, unless the settlor gives written notice of the transfer to the future spouse.[3]

8995. What is a spendthrift trust?

A spendthrift is an individual who is prone to using property in an excessive or frivolous manner. Thus, a spendthrift trust serves two important purposes: (1) it protects the beneficiary of the trust from himself or herself; and (2) it prevents the beneficiary's creditors from accessing the beneficiary's interest in the trust.

A spendthrift provision protects the beneficiary by preventing voluntary or involuntary alienation by the beneficiary.[4] The beneficiary cannot sell, give away, exchange, or otherwise transfer the beneficiary's interest. A settlor typically does this to protect the beneficiary from misfortune or incapacity.

In addition, the spendthrift provision also allows the settlor to carry out the intent of benefitting the beneficiary, rather than the beneficiary's creditors or assignees. A spendthrift trust

1. Alaska Stat. 34.40.110(b)(4).
2. Alaska Stat. 34.40.110(j).
3. Alaska Stat. 34.40.110(l).
4. Restatement (Third) of Trusts § 58 cmt. a (2003).

does not require that the beneficiary be a "spendthrift" or declared incompetent under the law.[1] It is enough that the settlor has a concern about the beneficiary's ability to manage their finances in a responsible manner.

Most states have now codified the law of spendthrift trusts. Some states make all trusts spendthrift trusts unless the settlor specifically provides otherwise. In addition, some states may restrain involuntary, but not voluntary, alienation for all trusts.[2]

See Q 8983 to Q 8985 for a discussion of domestic asset protection trusts generally.

8996. What provisions must a spendthrift trust contain to be enforceable?

A settlor must intend to create a spendthrift trust, and, as such, the trust must contain a spendthrift clause that restrains both voluntary and involuntary alienation.[3] A provision as simple as "This is a spendthrift trust" is generally enough to satisfy the courts. Other examples include:

> "To B for life. Her right to these payments is not to be transferable."
>
> "A beneficiary shall not have the right or power to anticipate, by assignment or otherwise, any income or principal given to the beneficiary by this Will or to sell, transfer, encumber or in otherwise charge his interest in income or principal in advance of actually receiving that income or principal. Neither the income nor the principal shall be subject to execution, garnishment, attachment, insolvency, bankruptcy or other legal proceeding of any character, or legal sequestration, levy or sale or at any time be applicable or subject to, voluntarily or involuntarily, the payment of a beneficiary's debts, including, without limitation, any claims for alimony or support."

A settlor's intent may also be implied. The Restatement 3rd of Trusts provides that language in a trust instrument that restrains only voluntary alienation is sufficient to create a spendthrift trust that also implicates involuntary alienation.[4]

8997. Are there any circumstances under which a beneficiary's interests in a spendthrift trust may be reached by creditors or other third parties?

Invalid Trust or Spendthrift Provision

The first and fairly obvious way a third party may reach a beneficiary's interest in a spendthrift trust is if the trust itself is invalid or the spendthrift provision is invalid. If a trust does not exist, then a spendthrift provision does not protect any of the beneficiary's interests. Furthermore, a spendthrift provision is invalid if it does not manifest the settlor's intent to create the spendthrift trust.

1. Restatement (Third) of Trusts § 58 cmt. a (2003).
2. Restatement (Third) of Trusts § 58 cmt. a (2003).
3. Restatement (Third) of Trusts § 58 cmt. a (2003) at cmt. b(3).
4. Restatement (Third) of Trusts § 58 (2003).

After a Distribution is made to Beneficiary

In addition, the interest is only protected while properly held in trust. Once the trustee makes a distribution to the beneficiary, creditors may reach the interest through the same procedures that apply generally to property of the beneficiary.

Supplies & Necessities for the Protection of Beneficiary's Interest in the Trust

A claim by someone who renders necessary services or gives necessary supplies to the beneficiary can also access the beneficiary's interest in a spendthrift trust.[1] To refuse recovery for providing necessities to the beneficiary would frustrate the settlor's purpose of protecting and providing for the beneficiary.[2]

In addition, a beneficiary may find it difficult to obtain services essential to protecting and enforcing his or her rights under the spendthrift trust if claimants who provided assistance had no means of recovering from the trust.[3] Thus, a claimant who has an enforceable unjust enrichment claim may reach a beneficiary's interest in a spendthrift trust.[4] This includes those who provide services or materials for preserving the beneficiary's interest in the trust, or for goods and services that increased the value of the beneficiary's interest.[5]

Example: S's will leaves his residuary estate to T upon a spendthrift trust for B for life, remainder to R or R's issue. Shortly before death, S amended the trust by a codicil by which C is added as a life beneficiary to share the benefits of the trust with B. B institutes an action to contest the codicil. C employs attorney A to represent him in the action, and the codicil is upheld. Although subject to a spendthrift restraint, C's interest in the trust can be reached by A in payment for her services in protecting that interest. It is within the discretion of the court to determine how much of each distribution A should receive as a matter of fairness both to her and to C.[6]

Public Policy

Occasionally, public policy calls for a spendthrift provision to be invalid. The following examples are not an exclusive list because courts continue to define what exactly violates public policy based on special circumstances and evolving policy. This section will explore common instances.

If the Settlor is Also the Beneficiary

A settlor of a spendthrift trust cannot also be the beneficiary of the trust.[7] The most common reason a settlor attempts this is to protect his personal estate from issues concerning a business. However, it is against public policy to allow a settlor to enjoy his own property but not be responsible for the liabilities and debts that he creates.

1. Restatement (Third) of Trusts § 59 cmt. c (2003).
2. Restatement (Third) of Trusts § 59 cmt. c (2003).
3. Restatement (Third) of Trusts § 59 cmt. c (2003) at (d).
4. Restatement (Third) of Trusts § 59 cmt. c (2003).
5. Restatement (Third) of Trusts § 59 cmt. c (2003).
6. *Id.*
7. Restatement (Third) of Trusts § 58 cmt. b (2003).

A small number of states have recognized a rare exception where a settlor may also be the beneficiary. If a settlor/beneficiary is a prisoner, a few states have recognized it does not violate public policy for such a person to tie up his property because he is not in a position to defraud creditors. Rather, a prisoner has an interest in protecting his estate from those who may try to take advantage of him because of his current incarceration.[1]

Spousal or Child Support

An enforceable claim by the beneficiary's spouse or children for support can invalidate a spendthrift provision.[2] On public policy grounds, typically a beneficiary cannot enjoy a favorable interest while neglecting to support his dependents.[3]

Alimony

In states that provide for spousal support, a spendthrift provision may be invalid to protect against an ex-spouse's enforceable claim for support.[4]

Federal Tax Obligations of the Beneficiary

A government claimant can reach a beneficiary's interest to the extent provided by federal law or an applicable state statute.[5] Bankruptcy, however, generally respects the spendthrift trust.[6]

Tort Claimants

In some jurisdictions, tort claimants have been able to access a beneficiary's interest within a spendthrift trust. When a tort claimant is an innocent party that has suffered harm, a court is not likely to protect a beneficiary's trust interest, especially when the beneficiary acted willfully or fraudulently.[7]

8998. What is a qualified disability trust?

A qualified disability trust is a non-grantor trust (meaning that a qualified disability trust generally cannot be a grantor trust) where all of the beneficiaries of the trust are disabled at some point during the year, as determined at the close of the tax year by the Commissioner of Social Security.[8] The trust must also qualify as one described in Section 1917 of the Social Security Act, meaning that it is a trust that was established solely for the benefit of an individual under sixty-five years of age who is disabled.[9]

As a rule, a qualified disability trust will be a discretionary trust, meaning that qualified disability trusts do not require distribution of all income each year.

1. See *Booth v. Chadwick*, 154 S.W.2d 268 (Tex. Civ. App.–Galveston 1941).
2. Restatement (Third) of Trusts § 58 cmt. b (2003).
3. Restatement (Third) of Trusts § 58 cmt. b (2003).
4. Restatement (Third) of Trusts § 59 cmt. b (2003).
5. *Id.* at a(1).
6. Restatement (Third) of Trusts § 58 comment a (2003).
7. Restatement (Third) of Trusts § 59 comment a(2) (2003).
8. IRC Sec. 642(b)(2)(C)(ii)(II).
9. 42 USCS 1396p(c)(2)(B)(iv).

A trust will not fail to qualify as a qualified disability trust merely because the trust assets will revert to an individual who is not disabled after the trust no longer has any beneficiaries who are disabled.[1]

See Q 8999 for a discussion of the tax treatment of qualified disability trusts. For a discussion of the ABLE account rules that allow taxpayers to create savings accounts for disabled individuals without jeopardizing qualification for Social Security and Medicaid benefits, see Q 393. See Q 8983 to Q 8985 for a discussion of domestic asset protection trusts generally.

8999. What special tax treatment applies to a trust if it qualifies as a qualified disability trust?

If a trust is a qualified disability trust, it is entitled to claim a personal exemption under IRC Section 151(d) (typically, trusts are not entitled to the personal exemption deduction because they are not individuals). In the case of a qualified disability trust, the trust is treated as an individual and IRC Section 67(e) is used to determine its adjusted gross income.[2]

Generally, this means that the trust's adjusted gross income is determined in the same manner as if it were an individual, except that deductions for costs and expenses in trust administration that would not have been incurred were the assets not held in trust are allowable.[3] Further, the deduction for trusts that distribute current income only[4] and the deduction for trusts that accumulate income or distribute trust principal[5] may be allowed, as relevant.

Because of these provisions, qualified disability trusts are typically much more favorable from a tax perspective than a standard irrevocable trust, which receives a much lower annual exemption than the personal exemption available to individuals. However, in some cases (often depending upon the taxpayer's income tax bracket and the needs of the beneficiary), it may be more advantageous to structure the trust as a grantor trust, where the tax liability "flows through" to the grantor of the trust.

For a discussion of the ABLE account rules that allow taxpayers to create savings accounts for disabled individuals without jeopardizing qualification for Social Security and Medicaid benefits, see Q 393.

9000. What filing requirements apply to qualified disability trusts?

A qualified disability trust will generally be responsible for filing a tax return in the same manner as any other trust. The filing is made on Form 1041, and must be made if any one of three circumstances applies: (1) the trust has taxable income for the year, (2) the trust had gross income of $600 or more for the year regardless of whether it had taxable income or (3) the trust has a beneficiary who is a non-resident alien. Form 1041 is due at the same time that personal income tax returns are due for the year (a five month extension may be available upon request).

1. IRC Sec. 642(b)(2)(C)(ii) (flush language).
2. IRC Sec. 642(b)(2)(C)(i).
3. IRC Sec. 67(e).
4. IRC Sec. 651.
5. IRC Sec. 661.

PART XIX: MARRIAGE AND DIVORCE

9001. What is a prenuptial agreement?

A prenuptial (or antenuptial) agreement is an agreement entered into before marriage by two individuals who plan to become spouses. These agreements are generally entered into in contemplation of the possibility of a future divorce, and most commonly provide the terms for disposition of property upon divorce.[1] A prenuptial agreement may provide for the disposition of property held as separate property by each spouse before the marriage, and often provides a description of the property that one or both spouses are entitled to receive in the event of a divorce.

In some cases, prenuptial agreements also govern one spouse's rights to property upon the death of the second spouse (for example, the agreement may bar the surviving spouse's right to elect against enforcement of the deceased spouse's will, which would generally allow the surviving spouse to receive property despite the terms of the decedent's will to the contrary).[2]

Prenuptial agreements also commonly provide that certain provisions of the agreement itself (or the entire agreement) will terminate after the spouses have been married for a certain number of years, or that the agreement will only be triggered if one spouse engages in certain specified behaviors that lead to a divorce (i.e., infidelity, substance abuse, financial irresponsibility).

For more information on the general requirements for establishing a valid prenuptial agreement, see Q 9002. For information on separation agreements and postnuptial agreements, see Q 9004 to Q 9006.

9002. What are the general requirements for establishing a valid prenuptial agreement?

While state law generally governs the formation and validity of prenuptial agreements, many states have adopted the Uniform Premarital Agreement Act (the Uniform Act) to govern enforcement issues relating to prenuptial agreements.[3] Like any other contract, a valid prenuptial agreement must, in most jurisdictions, be a written contract signed by both prospective spouses in order to be valid.[4]

While a typical contract would require "consideration" (i.e., something of value exchanged by the parties, whether tangible or intangible) in order to be valid, the Uniform Act provides that there is no consideration requirement with respect to prenuptial agreements. However, most states that do require consideration find that sufficient consideration exists if the parties to the contract actually do marry, or because the contract itself contains waivers of rights that constitute sufficient consideration.

1. See, for example, *Daugherty v. Daugherty*, 816 N.E.2d 1180 (2004); *Owen v. Owen*, 759 S.E.2d 468 (2014).
2. NY CLS Dom. Rel. 236B(3).
3. 9B ULA 372.
4. See, for example, Cal. Fam. Code 1611; Idaho Code Ann. 32-917.

Some states also require that the contract be executed a certain number of days before the marriage actually takes place. These statutes can vary—for example, Minnesota requires only that the contract be executed "prior to" the marriage.[1]

It is also common for state law to provide that the agreement must be entered into voluntarily, and that it will not be enforceable if it was unconscionable (i.e., unacceptably unfair) at the time it was entered into. This may be the case as, for example, in Delaware, because one party (1) was not provided fair and reasonable disclosure of the property or other financial obligations of the other party, (2) did not expressly waive his or her rights to this disclosure and (3) did not have, or reasonably could not have had, knowledge of the property or financial obligations at issue.[2] Disclosure of pertinent financial information is a requirement in most states, though the Uniform Act requires both (1) that the disclosures were not made and (2) that the terms of the agreement were unconscionable (some adopting states have modified the Uniform Act provision in order to mandate disclosure regardless of unconscionable contract terms).[3]

These types of statutory provisions generally reflect the concern that it would be against public policy to enforce a contract that was unconscionable at the time it was entered into. Some states specifically require that the parties to the contract obtain independent legal representation in order for certain provisions of a prenuptial agreement to be enforceable. California law provides that provisions regarding spousal support will not be enforceable if the party was not represented by independent counsel. Generally, this law permits a premarital waiver of spousal support upon divorce if the contracting parties knew the effect of such a provision at the time the contract was entered into, but would otherwise find the provision unconscionable and, thus, unenforceable.[4]

Certain states will not permit the parties to waive spousal support entirely in a prenuptial agreement, or will not permit such a waiver if the lack of spousal support would require the waiving spouse to receive public assistance. In these cases, the courts will generally be permitted to modify the support provisions of the agreement, rather than invalidating it entirely.[5] Provisions in a prenuptial agreement that provide for child support or custody that may not be in the best interests of the children may also be challenged on public policy grounds.

Prenuptial agreements have also been challenged on the public policy grounds that they were drafted in order to encourage divorce, though the viability of such a challenge would depend upon the specific state law and egregiousness of the contract terms. Many courts will reject these challenges in the absence of extreme circumstances and/or unconscionable contract terms.

9003. What are the requirements for drafting a valid separation agreement?

A separation agreement (sometimes referred to as a property settlement agreement) is an agreement between two married spouses who have decided to separate, and may be especially

1. Minn. Stat. Ann. 519.11.
2. See 13 Del. Code. Sec. 326
3. VA Code Ann. Sec. 20-151.
4. Cal. Fam. Code. Sec. 1612.
5. See, for example, Fla. Stat. § 61.14.

appropriate in cases where the spouses share custody of a child. Most state statutes require that a separation agreement be in writing,[1] although this requirement is not as strictly construed as in the case of prenuptial (Q 9001 to Q 9002) or postnuptial (Q 9004 to Q 9005) agreements (for example, some New York courts permit oral separation agreements to be made while the parties are in court).[2]

Planning Point: These rules vary based on state law, so the relevant state law should be carefully examined in determining whether an oral separation agreement will be enforceable.

Many of the same fairness issues that apply in determining the validity of a prenuptial agreement also apply in the case of separation agreements. Therefore, the separation agreement generally must be entered into voluntarily[3] (without the presence of fraud; general contract principles apply in determining whether duress or undue influence prevent a finding of voluntariness) and many states require that full financial disclosures be made between the parties.[4]

Some states require that the terms of the agreement be substantively "fair" in all cases,[5] while other states only impose such a substantive fairness requirement if the parties have not satisfied otherwise applicable financial disclosure requirements.[6]

A separation agreement that purports to waive child support obligations may be challenged on the grounds that it is against public policy and is thus unenforceable.[7]

9004. What is a postnuptial agreement?

Generally, a postnuptial agreement is an agreement entered into between two spouses who plan to continue their marriage—meaning that a postnuptial agreement is not the same as a separation agreement or a property settlement agreement. Postnuptial agreements are also referred to as reconciliation agreements, because they are commonly entered into after the spouses have experienced a period of marital discord that has alerted the parties to the possibility of future separation or divorce.

Like a prenuptial agreement, postnuptial agreements commonly deal with the financial consequences of a separation or divorce, or the death of one spouse. As a result, and because of the relationship between the parties, the rules governing prenuptial agreements (Q 9001 to Q 9002) will govern postnuptial agreement disputes in many states.

9005. What are the general requirements for drafting a valid postnuptial agreement?

As with prenuptial agreements (Q 9001 to Q 9002), a common challenge to a valid postnuptial agreement is that the agreement is unenforceable because it is against public policy, and

1. See, for example, Cal. Fam. Code Sec. 2550; Tex. Fam. Code Sec. 3.631(a).
2. *Sanders v. Copley*, 151 A.D.2d 350 (1989).
3. See *Hall v. Hall*, 171 So. 3d 817 (2015).
4. Cal. Fam. Code ß 1100(e); *In re Marriage of Brewer & Federici*, 93 Cal. App. 4th 1334 (2001).
5. *Sharp v. Sharp*, 877 P.2d 304 (Ariz. Ct. App. 1994).
6. *Casto v. Casto*, 508 So. 2d 330 (1987).
7. See, for example, *Rueckert v. Rueckert*, 499 N.W.2d 863 (1993).

whether the agreement will be enforced depends upon both the terms of the agreement and the applicable state law. For example, a spouse's agreement in a postnuptial agreement to never bring a lawsuit against her spouse for any reason whatsoever was deemed to be against public policy and, therefore, the provision was unenforceable.[1]

However, provisions providing for property division have generally been held enforceable absent unconscionable terms,[2] and provisions providing for forfeiture of equitable property division rights have been upheld if the waiving spouse engaged in certain specified behaviors (i.e., infidelity, substance abuse or financial irresponsibility).[3]

See Q 9003 for a discussion of separation agreements.

9006. What is a qualified domestic relations order (QDRO) and how can a QDRO impact an individual's retirement benefits?

A qualified domestic relations order ("QDRO") is a judgment, decree, or order (including an approval of a property settlement agreement) that awards all or a portion of a participant's benefits to an alternate payee and that meets all the requirements specified by the IRS for being qualified.

A plan may distribute, segregate, or otherwise recognize the attachment of any portion of a participant's benefits in favor of the participant's spouse, former spouse, or dependents without violating the restrictions on alienation of benefits (Q 3876) only if such action is mandated by a QDRO.[4] Only a spouse, former spouse, child, or other dependent of a participant may be classified as an alternate payee under a QDRO.

The following requirements must be met for a domestic relations order ("DRO") to be qualified:

(1) it must relate to the provision of child support, alimony, or property rights to a spouse, former spouse, child, or other dependent;

(2) it must be made under a state's community property or other domestic relations law;

(3) it must create, recognize, or assign to the spouse, former spouse, child, or other dependent of the participant the right to receive all or a portion of a participant's plan benefits;

(4) it must clearly specify the names and, unless the plan administrator has reason to know them, the addresses of the participant and each alternate payee, the amount or percentage of the participant's benefit to be paid to each alternate payee (or a method for determining the amount), the number of payments or the period to which the order applies, and each plan to which the order applies; and

1. *Towles v. Towles*, 256 S.C. 307 (1971).
2. See, for example, *Gilley v. Gilley*, 778 S.W.2d 862 (1989).
3. *Laudig v. Laudig*, 624 A.2d 651 (1993).
4. IRC Secs. 401(a)(13)(B), 414(p).

(5) it may not require the plan to provide any type or form of benefit or benefit option not otherwise provided under the plan, to pay increased benefits, or to provide increased benefits to an alternate payee that are required to be paid to another alternate payee under another previously ordered qualified DRO.[1]

9007. What is alimony?

A payment received by (or on behalf of) a recipient spouse pursuant to a divorce or separation instrument (see below) executed after 1984 is an alimony or separate maintenance payment if:

(1) The payment is made in cash to a (former) spouse recognized under applicable state law, including a same-sex spouse;[2]

(2) The divorce or separation instrument does not designate the payment as *not* includable or deductible as alimony;[3]

(3) There is no liability to make the payments after the death of the recipient,[4] (the Tax Court has held that "substitute" payments – i.e., post-death payments that would begin as a result of the death of the taxpayer's ex-spouse, and would substitute for a continuation of the payments that terminated on her death, and that otherwise qualified as alimony – were not deductible alimony payments);

(4) The individuals do not file a joint federal income tax return;

(5) If the individuals are legally separated under a decree of divorce or separate maintenance, the spouses are not members of the same household at the time the payment is made.[5]

A divorce or separation instrument includes any decree of divorce or separate maintenance or a written instrument incident to such, a written separation agreement, or other decree requiring spousal support or maintenance payments.[6] The failure of the divorce or separation instrument to provide for termination of payments at the death of the recipient will not disqualify payments from alimony treatment.[7] However, if both the divorce or separation instrument *and* state law fail to unambiguously provide for the termination of payments upon death, such payments may be disqualified from receiving alimony treatment.[8]

1. IRC Sec. 414(p)(1).
2. Rev. Rul. 58-66, 1958-1 CB 60; Rev. Rul. 2013-17, 2013-2 CB 201.
3. See *Richardson v. Comm.*, 125 F.3d 551 (7th Cir. 1997), *aff'g* T.C. Memo 1995-554; see also Let. Rul. 200141036.
4. See, e.g., *Okerson v. Comm.*, 123 TC 258 (2004).
5. IRC Sec. 71(b).
6. IRC Sec. 71(b)(2).
7. See IRC Sec. 71(b)(1)(D); TRA '86 Conf. Rept. at page 849.
8. *Hoover v. Comm.*, 102 F.3d 842, 97-1 USTC ¶50,111 (6th Cir. 1996); *Ribera v. Comm.*, TC Memo 1997-38. See *Mukherjee v. Comm.*, TC Memo 2004-98; *Lovejoy v. Comm.*, 293 F.3d 1208 (10th Cir. 2002); *Thomas D. Berry v. Comm.*, 36 Fed. Appx. 400, 2002 U.S. App. LEXIS 10785 (10th Cir. 2002). But see *Kean v. Comm.*, 407 F. 3d 186, 2005-1 USTC ¶50,397 (3rd Cir. 2005); *Michael K. Berry v. Comm.*, TC Memo 2005-91.

Payment of housing costs generally does not qualify as alimony to the extent of the payor's interest in the property (although payments do qualify as alimony to the extent of the payee's interest in the property).[1]

9008. How are alimony payments taxed?

Alimony and separate maintenance payments generally are taxable to the recipient and deductible from gross income by the payor (even if the payor does not itemize).[2] Alimony payments are deductible regardless of whether the payment is made from taxable income (i.e., the deduction is still allowed even if the payor used savings in order to make the payment).

The individuals may agree in the written divorce instrument or separation agreement that the alimony payments will be excludable by the recipient and nondeductible by the payor, and[3] a state court may also order this treatment.

Payments of arrearages from prior years are taxed to a cash basis taxpayer in the year of receipt.[4] Furthermore, the Tenth Circuit Court of Appeals has held that an alimony arrearage paid to the estate of a former spouse was taxable as income in respect of a decedent.[5]

9009. What is a common law marriage?

The rules governing common law marriage vary by state, and only a handful of states currently recognize common law marriage. However, common law marriage is recognized as marriage for federal tax purposes. Individuals in a common law marriage may be treated as being legally married for federal tax purposes if they live together in a state that recognizes common law marriage, or if they live in a state where the common law marriage began.

Currently, common law marriage is recognized only in Alabama, Colorado, the District of Columbia, Iowa, Kansas, Montana, New Hampshire (only for inheritance purposes), Oklahoma, Rhode Island, South Carolina, Texas and Utah. In certain other states, such as Pennsylvania, Georgia and Ohio, a common law marriage may be recognized if it was entered into before the date on which common law marriage was abolished by the state.

To enter into a common law marriage, a couple must hold themselves out to the public as being "married". Factors to be considered in making this determination include whether the couple uses the same last name, whether the community believes the couple are married and whether the couple files a joint tax return. One factor that a court may consider in determining whether a common law marriage is the length of time that a couple has lived together, holding themselves out as married. No specific length of time applies; the time period must only be "significant".

1. Temp. Treas. Reg. §1.71-1T(b); Let. Rul. 8710089.
2. IRC Secs. 71(a), 215(a).
3. Treas. Reg. §1.71-1T(b); *Tucker v. Comm.*, TC Summ. Op. 2013-94.
4. *Coleman v. Comm.*, TC Memo 1988-442.
5. *Kitch v. Comm.*, 103 F.3d 104, 97-1 USTC ¶50,124 (10th Cir. 1996).

9010. What are domestic partnerships?

A domestic partnership (also referred to as a civil union in some states) is an option for couples who wish to formalize their relationship, but do not wish to enter into a legal marriage (prior to the legalization of same-sex marriage in *Obergefell v. Hodges*, many same-sex couples opted for domestic partner status). In order to enter into a domestic partnership, two individuals must visit a courthouse or other government office (depending upon the state of residence), and generally must submit an application and pay a fee similar to the fee that is required when applying for a marriage license.

Individuals who are in registered domestic partnerships or civil unions are not treated as spouses for federal tax purposes, but are often entitled to some of the benefits afforded to legally married couples, including employment-related benefits (see Q 9012). Further, while domestic partners are not treated as married for federal purposes, they may be entitled to certain state benefits. For example, certain counties in California extend benefits that married spouses are entitled to receive to individuals in domestic partnerships, while in Delaware no specific state provision exists to extend such rights. States generally maintain a domestic partnership registry to keep track of couples who have entered into these arrangements.[1]

It has been noted, however, that the availability of domestic partner benefits may be curtailed after the holding in *Obergefell*, because now all couples have the right to be legally married and, theoretically, domestic partner status is no longer as necessary as it was prior to that ruling. Though the California state domestic partnership statute has not yet been changed, one requirement of the statute is that either (a) both persons must be members of the same sex or (b) one or both persons must qualify for Social Security old age benefits (meaning that one person in an opposite sex couple must be at least 62 years of age to qualify for domestic partnership status in California).[2] This indicates that the domestic partnership law of even one of the more liberal states in the country was intended to provide equal benefits to same-sex couples. Now that same-sex couples are entitled to equal benefits at the federal level, it is unclear whether this statute will be amended.

9011. What are domestic partner employment benefits and how are they taxed?

Domestic partner benefits are benefits that an employer voluntarily offers to an employee's unmarried partner. An employee's domestic partner may be of the same sex or the opposite sex. An employer determines the scope of its plan's definition of domestic partner.

Employers may offer a range of domestic partnership benefits, such as family, bereavement, sick leave, and relocation benefits. In general, most people mean employer-provided health insurance coverage when they speak of domestic partnership benefits.

An employee is taxed on the value of employer-provided health benefits for his or her domestic partner unless the domestic partner qualifies as the employee's dependent under IRC

1. See, for example, California's domestic partnership registry, available at http://www.sos.ca.gov/registries/domestic-partners-registry/.
2. Cal. Fam. Code Sec. 297(b)(4).

Section 151. The tax is determined by assessing the fair market value of the coverage provided to the domestic partner. This amount then is reported on the employee's W-2 form and is subjected to Social Security (FICA) and federal income tax withholding.

Any amount received by a domestic partner as payment or reimbursement of plan benefits will not be included in the income of the employee or the domestic partner to the extent that the coverage provided to the domestic partner was paid for by the employee's plan contributions or the fair market value of the coverage was included in the employee's income under IRC Section 104(a)(3).[1]

Coverage of domestic partners, whether or not they qualify as dependents, under an employer-provided health plan will not otherwise affect the ability of employees to exclude amounts paid, directly or indirectly, by a plan to reimburse employees for expenses incurred for medical care of the employees, their spouses, and dependents.

Same-sex couples who are legally married in any state are treated as spouses for all federal law purposes (including employment-related retirement benefits, see Q 9013), regardless of where they live.[2] As a result, many domestic partners have chosen to legally marry, and, therefore, some expect that fewer employers will offer domestic partner benefits in the future.

9012. How are employer-sponsored retirement benefits impacted when an employee is married?

Certain spousal survivor benefits (discussed below) apply in the case of retirement benefits that are provided to a married employee. Further, special attention must be paid to the beneficiary designations of certain plans, and it may be more difficult for a married plan participant to take out a plan loan without spousal consent.

Certain types of plans are required to provide automatic survivor benefits in the form of qualified joint and survivor annuities (QJSA) or qualified preretirement survivor annuities (QPSA) as the typical form of retirement benefit for married participants unless both the employee and the spouse consent to waive this requirement. The requirement that a plan provide the QJSA and QPSA forms of benefit generally applies to all defined benefit plans, to all defined contribution plans that are subject to minimum funding standards (e.g., target benefit and money purchase pensions), and to profit sharing plans that include annuity provisions as the normal form of benefit (see Q 3846, Q 3847).[3]

A QJSA is an annuity (1) for the life of the participant, with a survivor annuity for the life of his or her spouse that is not less than one-half (nor greater than 100 percent) of the amount of the annuity payable during the joint lives of the participant and his or her spouse, and (2) that is the actuarial equivalent of a single annuity for the life of the participant.[4] The QJSA must be at least as valuable as any other optional form of benefit payable under the plan at the same time (see Q 3848).

1. Let. Ruls. 200846001, 9850011, 9717018, 9603011. See also Let. Ruls. 9109060, 9034048. See also Field Service Advice 199911012.
2. *United States v. Windsor*, 133 S. Ct. 2675 (2013); *Obergefell v. Hodges*, 135 S.Ct. 2584 (2015); Notice 2014-19, 2014-17 IRB 979.
3. IRC Sec. 401(a)(11)(B).
4. IRC Sec. 417(b).

A QPSA is a survivor annuity for the life of the surviving spouse of the participant under which payments are to begin no later than the month in which the participant would have reached the earliest retirement age provided under the plan and that also meets the following requirements with respect to the amount of the annuity:

(1) In the case of a defined contribution plan, the survivor annuity is the actuarial equivalent of the participant's account and must not be less than one-half of the participant's vested account balance as of the date of his or her death unless waived by the participant and spouse.[1]

(2) In the case of all other plans, (x) if the participant died after the date the participant attained the earliest retirement age provided under the plan, the payments to the surviving spouse must not be less than the amounts that would have been payable under the survivor portion of a qualified joint and survivor annuity had the participant retired with an immediate qualified joint and survivor annuity on the day before he died, or (y) if the participant died on or before the date the participant would have reached the earliest retirement age, the payments to the surviving spouse must not be less than the amounts that would have been paid under the survivor portion of a QJSA had the participant separated from service on the earlier of the actual time of separation or death, survived to the earliest retirement age, retired with an immediate qualified joint and survivor annuity at the earliest retirement age, and died on the day after he or she reached the earliest retirement age.[2] In any case, payments to the surviving spouse must not violate the incidental benefit rule (Q 3795).[3]

If the retirement plan is covered by ERISA, the participant's spouse may automatically be the beneficiary, which means that if a spouse wishes for the benefits to be transferred to a non-spousal beneficiary (such as a child) upon his or her death, the beneficiary must now affirmatively make the election.

If a plan participant is married and wishes to take out a loan from a retirement plan, the participant's spouse must generally consent. Further, plans must comply with qualified domestic relations orders (QDROs, see Q 9006), which are often used to divide retirement plan assets in a divorce proceeding.

Same-sex spouses are now entitled to all of these rights under various retirement plans.

9013. What special rules apply with respect to IRA contributions between spouses who are legally married?

A married individual may make contributions to a traditional IRA for a non-working spouse if (1) the non-working spouse and working spouse file a joint return for the taxable year, and (2) the amount of compensation (if any) includable in the non-working spouse's gross income

1. Treas. Reg. §1.401(a)-20, A-20.
2. IRC Sec. 417(c); Treas. Reg. §1.401(a)-20, A-18.
3. Sen. Fin. Comm. Rep. to P.L. 98-397. See Rev. Rul. 85-15, 1985-1 CB 132.

for the taxable year is less than the compensation includable in the working spouse's gross income for the taxable year.[1] The deductibility of such contributions depends on whether the non-working spouse or working spouse is an "active participant" (see below) and on the married couple's adjusted gross income.[2] Community property laws are disregarded for purposes of this deduction.[3]

In the case of a defined benefit plan, an individual who is not excluded under the eligibility provisions of the plan for the plan year ending with or within the individual's taxable year is an active participant in the plan, regardless of whether such individual has elected to decline participation in the plan, has failed to make a mandatory contribution specified under the plan, or has failed to perform the minimum service required to accrue a benefit under the plan.[4] An individual in a plan under which accruals all have ceased is not an active participant. Where benefits may vary with future compensation, all accruals are not considered to have ceased.[5]

In the case of a profit sharing or stock bonus plan, an individual is an active participant if any employer contribution is deemed added or any forfeiture is allocated to the individual's account during the individual's taxable year.[6] A contribution is treated as made to an individual's account on the later of the date the contribution is made or allocated.[7]

A married individual may make contributions to a Roth IRA plan for a non-working spouse if (a) statements (1) and (2) above apply, and (b) the adjusted gross income of the married couple is less than the applicable limits discussed in Q 3638.[8] "Compensation" is generally earned compensation, such as wages or self-employment income, rather than interest income or Social Security benefits. The joint return rule implicitly requires that, except where one or both have died, the contributing individual and the contributing individual's spouse have identical taxable years.[9]

An eligible individual may make contributions to a spousal IRA even if the individual does not own or contribute to an IRA for himself or herself.

If the earner spouse dies during the taxable year, the non-working spouse may contribute to the spousal IRA if a joint return is filed for the year. No amount may be contributed to the IRA of a deceased spouse.[10]

The contributing individual must have been married to his or her spouse as of the last day of their tax year. An individual legally separated under a decree of divorce or separate maintenance is not married for these purposes.[11]

1. IRC Sec. 219(c)(2).
2. IRC Sec. 219(g).
3. IRC Sec. 219(f)(2).
4. Notice 87-16, 1987-1 CB 446, A-15; Treas. Reg. §1.219-2(b)(1); see *Nicolai v. Comm.*, TC Memo 1997-108.
5. Notice 87-16, 1987-1 CB 446, A-16; Treas. Reg. §1.219-2(b)(3); Let. Rul. 8948008
6. Treas. Reg. §1.219-2(d)(1); see *Tolley v. Comm.*, TC Memo 1997-244.
7. Treas. Reg. §1.219-2(d)(1).
8. IRC Secs. 219(c)(2), 408A(c)(3).
9. IRC Sec. 6013.
10. Let. Rul. 8527083.
11. IRC Sec. 6013(d)(2).

9014. What benefits apply to IRAs that are inherited by a surviving spouse?

A surviving spouse is entitled to roll over IRA funds that are inherited from a deceased spouse into his or her own account, delaying required minimum distributions (and the associated tax liability) until the surviving spouse reaches age 70 ½. A non-spousal beneficiary, on the other hand, is not entitled to delay distributions and must take distributions over his or her life expectancy (or a five-year period, whichever method is elected).

Any minimum distribution that was required to be made to the deceased owner, but had not been made before the owner's death, must be made to the surviving spouse in the year of death, but in all other respects, required distributions after the owner's death are determined as if the surviving spouse were the owner.[1]

9015. What are the income tax consequences that should be considered by a couple before they legally marry?

Married couples have the right to file both joint federal and state income tax returns, rather than two separate returns, for the current tax year, as well as for all other open years. In the case of same-sex couples who had filed separate federal returns for simplicity because they lived in a state that did not recognize same-sex marriage, amending a past year's return could lead to higher refunds in some cases.

In some cases, however, choosing to marry and file a joint return can actually increase tax liability. Unmarried couples generally have the opportunity to file two single (or two head-of-household) tax returns without worrying about the "marriage penalty" for filing separately that applies to a legally married couple.

As a result of the Supreme Court's ruling in *Obergefell v. Hodges*, same-sex couples now must make the same cost-benefit analysis that applies to opposite-sex couples in determining whether to file jointly. A single taxpayer crosses the earnings threshold into the 39.6 percent tax bracket when he or she earns more than $400,000 for the year (this amount is adjusted annually for inflation)—meaning that two single taxpayers could live together and earn approximately $800,000 before entering into the highest income tax bracket. Two married people, on the other hand, become subject to the 39.6 percent rate when they have combined earnings of only approximately $450,000 (as adjusted for inflation) for the year.

Similarly, if a couple is not married, they can earn $400,000 ($200,000 each) before their itemized deductions and personal exemptions become subject to the phaseout rules that gradually reduce their value. Once that same couple is married, however, the penalties apply once combined income between the spouses reaches $250,000.

The investment income tax will also apply to a married couple earning a combined $250,000 (while two unmarried taxpayers could earn $400,000 before crossing the threshold). See Q 8582 to Q 8603 for a discussion of the investment income tax.

1. Treas. Reg. §1.408-8, A-5(a).

9016. What are the estate tax implications when a couple legally marries?

Federal estate tax rules have evolved in recent years to make it easier for legally married couples to avoid transfer taxes when passing wealth from one spouse to another spouse after death. Both same-sex and opposite-sex couples are now able to take advantage of these special rules.

For example, the $5.6 (in 2018) exemption is portable between spouses if an election is made on a properly filed estate tax return, meaning that legally married couples can now rely on shielding a combined $11.2 million from estate taxes without having to engage in complex and expensive estate planning in order to determine which spouse should technically own marital assets.

Because same-sex married couples are now entitled to this federal tax treatment, these couples should be advised to review their estate planning documents to take into account the fact that these taxpayers are now entitled to both the portability election (see Q 17) and the marital deduction.

9017. What is portability?

Portability is essentially the right of a surviving spouse to use any of a deceased spouse's unused transfer tax exemption amount—thereby increasing his or her own estate and gift tax exemption amount in order to exclude more of his or her assets from transfer tax liability. The portability provision was made permanent by the American Taxpayer Reform Act of 2012.

Generally, a surviving spouse may apply the deceased spouse's unused estate tax exclusion amount to the surviving spouse's own transfers if portability is elected by filing a timely estate tax return (typically, within nine months of the date of death, with an automatic extension of six months). While an estate that does not exceed the estate tax exemption amount is not generally required to file an estate tax return, a return is required in order to elect portability.[1] If an estate tax return is not required because of the estate's value, the IRS has provided a simplified method for requesting an extension of time to elect portability. The extension is available if the decedent was survived by a spouse, died after 2010 and was a U.S. citizen. In order to obtain the extension, the executor must file a completed Form 706 (the estate tax return) on or before the later of January 2, 2018 or the second anniversary of the decedent's date of death. At the top of Form 706, the executor must state that the return is "Filed pursuant to Rev. Proc. 2017-34 to elect portability under § 2010(c)(5)(A)".[2]

9018. How can life insurance be used in estate planning for unmarried partners?

Prior to the legalization of same-sex marriage for all federal tax purposes, unmarried couples often used life insurance in order to provide income to the surviving partner upon the death of the first partner (because Social Security survivor benefits were unavailable, as were federally

1. Treas. Reg. §20.2010-2.
2. Rev. Proc. 2017-34.

mandated retirement account survivor benefits). This planning technique often produced favorable tax results, because proceeds of life insurance are generally received income tax-free,[1] and are also estate tax-free unless the insured retained incidents of ownership over the policy or the proceeds were paid to the insured's estate.[2]

Placing the life insurance policy in an irrevocable trust is one way that an insured can avoid retaining incidents of ownership in the policy (however, if the insured retains a right to the cash surrender value of the policy, he or she will have retained incidents of ownership that could cause estate tax consequences;[3] see Q 178 for a more detailed discussion of this potential result).

While life insurance can prove to be a valuable estate planning tool in some cases, if a same-sex couple purchased individual life insurance policies designed to provide a surviving partner with liquidity upon the death of a first-to-die partner in order to pay estate taxes, the couple may wish to revise this plan in light of the portability and unlimited marital deduction options available to married couples.

If the couple chooses to legally marry, a survivorship policy, which pays benefits upon the death of the second spouse and may be less expensive, may be more appropriate if the goal of the married couple is to provide benefits to children or other heirs upon the death of the second spouse. This is because portability now allows a married couple to shield a combined $10.9 million in assets from estate tax, so that most married couples will not be subject to estate tax liability upon the death of the first-to-die spouse.

9019. What are the gift tax implications when a couple legally marries?

Legally married couples are permitted to pool their $15,000 (in 2018) annual gift tax exclusion so that each couple is able to make annual tax-free gifts of up to $30,000 per donee.[4] If a gift is treated as a split gift for gift tax purposes, it will also be treated as a split gift for generation skipping transfer (GST) tax purposes.[5]

9020. What are the potential gift and estate tax consequences when unmarried partners own property jointly?

Two unmarried partners may own property jointly as a joint tenancy with a right of survivorship, meaning generally that each individual is a co-owner of the property and that upon the first partner's death, the survivor retains his or her right to the property.[6] While this can be a beneficial estate planning strategy for unmarried taxpayers, gift tax liability can arise when one party contributes more of the purchase price than the other. The amount of the taxable gift in such a situation generally equals the value of the gift that exceeds the contributing party's

1. IRC Sec. 101(a)(1).
2. IRC Sec. 2042.
3. *St. Louis Union Trust Co. v. U.S.*, 262 F. Supp. 27 (1966).
4. IRC Sec. 2513; Treas. Reg. §25.2513-1.
5. IRC Sec. 2652(a)(2).
6. IRC Sec. 2040.

unused gift tax annual exclusion amount ($15,000 in 2018).[1] This assumes that no legally binding obligation to support exists between the parties, as often exists in the case of a domestic partnership or civil union.

Further, the property may be included entirely in the deceased partner's estate upon his or her death unless the surviving partner is able to show that he or she contributed to the purchase price of the asset.[2] On the other hand, a legally married couple is able to take advantage of both the marital deduction and portability options when jointly owned property is involved.

9021. Does the marital status of two individuals who own property together impact the ability to deduct mortgage interest?

Generally, there is a limitation of $1,000,000 on the amount of aggregate debt that may be treated as "acquisition indebtedness," for purposes of deducting mortgage-related interest, but the amount of refinanced debt that may be treated as acquisition indebtedness is limited to the amount of debt being refinanced.[3] The deductibility of interest incurred on "home equity indebtedness" is limited to debt of $100,000, or the amount of equity (that is, the fair market value of the home less the acquisition indebtedness), whichever is less.[4] This essentially results in a maximum deduction for interest paid on up to $1.1 million of mortgages taken to build or buy houses (the first $1,000,000 of "acquisition indebtedness" + the first $100,000 of "home equity indebtedness").

However, unmarried taxpayers may be entitled to double this generally applicable $1.1 million limit. The Ninth Circuit recently reversed a Tax Court holding that two unmarried home co-owners could not each deduct interest on $1.1 million of personal residence indebtedness, because the debt limitations are residence-based, rather than taxpayer-based. The Tax Court found that the taxpayers could deduct only the interest incurred on a total of $1.1 million of debt ($1 million of acquisition indebtedness and $100,000 of home equity indebtedness), even if they owned two residences. The Ninth Circuit reversed this decision, holding that the debt limit applied on a per-taxpayer basis to unmarried co-owners of a qualified residence.[5] The IRS acquiesced in the Ninth Circuit's decision in 2016.[6]

1. IRC Sec. 2503; Treas Reg. §25.2511-1(h)(5).
2. See Treas. Reg. §20.2040-1(a)(2).
3. IRC Sec. 163(h)(3)(B); Notice 88-74, 1988-2 CB 385.
4. IRC Sec. 163(h)(3)(C).
5. *Sophy v. Comm.*, 138 TC 204 (2012); *Voss v. Comm.*, 796 F.3d 1051 (2015).
6. AOD 2016-02, 2016-31 IRB 193.

PART XX: BLENDED FAMILIES

9022. What is a blended family?

The term "blended family" can encompass any number of modern family structures. Most commonly, the term refers to individuals who have remarried after prior marriages have ended in divorce. These couples may have children from prior marriages, and may have children together, potentially resulting in a situation where individuals may wish to provide for children from both current and prior marriages, and also stepchildren. Each client may wish to ensure that his or her own children (rather than stepchildren) are provided for in the event that they are the first-to-die spouse, but may concurrently wish to provide for their surviving spouse even if their own children are the ultimate beneficiaries.

9023. What basic planning considerations must be accounted for in blended family situations?

When an individual enters into a second or subsequent marriage, it is entirely possible that he or she has entered into agreements with a prior spouse (whether in the form of prenuptial or postnuptial agreements, divorce or property settlement agreements, see Q 9001 to Q 9005 that must be taken into account when entering into estate planning strategies in contemplation of providing for a spouse from a subsequent marriage. These existing agreements could provide for continuing support obligations, required funding of life insurance policies for the benefit of a former spouse or previously agreed upon beneficiary designations on retirement accounts or other financial products.

Importantly, many individuals who enter into second or subsequent marriages already have children from a prior marriage, and may wish to ensure that those children are provided for before leaving any assets to stepchildren. Both accurate, updated beneficiary designations Q 9024 and trust arrangements (Q 9032 to Q 9033) can be useful in this context.

Other issues can arise when there is a disparity in wealth or age between the spouses. Disparities in wealth can require planning to fully use the federal estate tax exemption (i.e., either through trust arrangements or by taking advantage of portability (Q 9030 to Q 9031) of both the wealthier and less wealthy spouse. Disparities in age can lead to conflicts between adult children from prior marriages and stepparents that should be addressed in estate planning (i.e., via trust planning and open conversation) in order to ensure that a decedent's wishes are properly carried out.

9024. Why are beneficiary designations especially important in blended family scenarios?

When an individual remarries, it can become especially important to review his or her beneficiary designations to ensure they are current. Beneficiary designations in existing retirement plans, life insurance policies, annuities and other financial accounts must be carefully examined in order to determine who the individual intends to benefit, and whether any waivers will be required from a current or former spouse in order to make those intended designations effective.

Planning Point: Importantly, beneficiary designations will override any instructions that the individual provides in his or her will, so it is crucial that each relevant plan and policy be examined to ensure beneficiary designations are accurate.

While in some cases changes in beneficiary designation can be effected unilaterally, it is more complicated to change beneficiary designations in a qualified retirement plan that is subject to the automatic survivor benefit rules (i.e., ERISA plans, those which automatically provide benefits to a surviving spouse). These plans typically must provide that participants can only elect to waive the survivor benefits during a designated election period (see Q 3855).[1] This type of waiver must be in writing, must specify a new beneficiary (or provide that the plan participant is allowed to change or name the beneficiary without the spouse's consent), must acknowledge the effect of the waiver and must be witnessed or notarized.[2]

Planning Point: Clients should be advised to carefully follow the procedures set forth by the relevant retirement or pension plan in order to ensure that the intended beneficiary designations become effective, as recent court decisions have made clear that even substantial compliance is insufficient. This has been the case even where the intention to change beneficiaries was clear and where the intended new beneficiaries could be identified.[3]

If the plan is a nonqualified plan (such as an IRA or SEP IRA), the account owner is free to name whoever he or she wishes as beneficiary. However, if community property rules apply, the plan will be subject to the relevant community property rules, which could give each spouse a one-half interest in the account value (or any growth in the account that occurred during the marriage).

The account owner can designate multiple beneficiaries and provide that each will receive a share of his or her account value (it is generally advisable to specify percentages, rather than dollar amounts, that each beneficiary will receive to account for growth in value).

Further, existing agreements or orders (i.e., prenuptial agreements, postnuptial agreements, qualified domestic relations orders (QDROs), divorce settlements, etc.) can interfere with an individual's ability to unilaterally change the beneficiary designation on his or her accounts.

9025. What is the impact of divorce and remarriage on Social Security planning?

Typically, a surviving spouse may be entitled to receive Social Security survivor benefits based upon the earnings record of the deceased spouse. In the case of divorce, however, if one spouse remarries before age sixty, he or she may no longer be entitled to claim survivor benefits based on the prior marriage unless the subsequent marriage ends. This is the case unless the prior marriage lasted for at least ten years.[4]

1. IRC Sec. 417(a)(1)(a).
2. IRC Sec. 417(a)(2); Treas. Reg. §1.401(a)-20.
3. *See*, for example, *Kennedy v. DuPont Savings and Investment Plan*, 55 U.S. 285 (2009), in which the Supreme Court held that a waiver of beneficiary rights contained in a divorce decree did not override the actual beneficiary designation contained in the plan.
4. 20 CFR 404.331(a)(2).

Social Security survivor benefits are not impacted if the surviving spouse remarried after he or she reached age sixty.[1] In certain cases where the surviving spouse remarries after age fifty, but before age sixty, that spouse may remain entitled to a prior spouse's Social Security benefits if he or she was disabled at the time of the remarriage.[2]

Planning Point: Practically, the Social Security rules provide that a divorced surviving spouse will not be entitled to receive Social Security survivor benefits based on a prior spouse's earnings record unless he or she is unmarried or has remarried after reaching age sixty (unless the disability exception applies).

9026. What gift and estate tax issues typically arise in the case of couples who have divorced and remarried?

It is common for couples who have been divorced and remarried to have children from prior marriages, complicating the transfer of wealth both during life and upon death. In some cases, an individual may have some idea of the specific assets he or she wishes to transfer to a particular child, or may wish to provide more generous gifts to heirs who are less able to provide for themselves. In other cases, the goal of the individual is to create some level of equality in each heir's inheritance and minimize conflict in general. In any event, federal transfer taxes (estate, gift and generation skipping transfer taxes) must be taken into account in order to minimize tax liability.

If the individual plans to begin making gifts during life (perhaps in order to minimize the necessity for complicated estate planning or to ensure that specific tangible assets pass to a certain beneficiary), he or she should attempt to take advantage of the $15,000 (in 2018) per donor/donee annual gift tax exclusion amount (if the spouse consents, up to $30,000 per donee can be sheltered each year).[3] The exclusion amount applies only to present interest gifts (i.e., it does not apply to gifts where the donee only has the right to enjoy the property in the future (see Q 872). Generally, if the gifts exceed the annual exclusion amount, the donor is responsible for paying gift tax on the fair market value of the property transferred and must file a gift tax return (Form 709) by April 15 in the year following the year in which the gift is made.[4]

Individuals who choose not to transfer wealth gradually during life should plan for the estate tax and the generation skipping transfer tax (GSTT; applicable if the individual wishes to "skip" a generation in making his or her bequests).

With respect to the estate tax, individuals should note that most transfers between spouses fall within the unlimited marital deduction, so will not be subject to estate tax.[5] Transfers to certain types of trusts (QTIP trusts, see Q 9032 and Q 9033) also qualify for the marital deduction.[6] Estates that are valued at below the transfer tax exemption amount ($5.6 million in 2018) are also exempt from the estate tax. In the blended family context (where age and wealth disparity

1. 20 CFR 404.335(e)(1).
2. 20 CFR 404.335(e)(2).
3. Rev. Proc. 2017-58; IRC Sec. 2513; Treas. Reg. §25.2513-2.
4. IRC Sec. 6019.
5. IRC Sec. 2056.
6. See IRC Sec. 2056(b)(7).

are often factors), it can be important to plan to make use of both spouses' exemption amounts (either through portability or trust planning (see Q 9029 to Q 9031).

If an individual wishes to transfer wealth to a "skip" generation (i.e., his or her grandchildren or great-grandchildren), GSTT planning becomes important. The transfer tax exemption amount discussed above also applies to the GSTT. In many cases, the individual may wish to transfer assets into a trust, allocating a portion of his or her GSTT exemption to the transfer. In this case, the assets in the trust can be allowed to grow sheltered from any GSTT and provide for grandchildren and great-grandchildren in the future while using up only a minimal amount of the transferor's GSTT exemption. Of course, for direct transfers to skip generations made during life, the $15,000 per donor/donee gift tax annual exclusion amount is available. See Q 841 to Q 858 for an in-depth discussion of the GSTT.

9027. What considerations should be accounted for in choosing a trustee when a blended family is involved?

Many individuals who are engaged in estate planning for a blended family choose to establish trusts to ensure that their wishes in providing for various heirs are carried out. In these cases, it is important to carefully consider who will serve as trustee in carrying out those wishes.

Many remarried individuals may be tempted to appoint their surviving spouse as trustee, but the relationship between the surviving spouse and any children from prior marriages should be considered before making this choice. Animosity between these parties can make trust administration difficult, and can lead to dissatisfaction among the children that the deceased spouse intended to benefit. The same issues can arise if another family member is named as trustee. These issues are magnified if the trust provides for discretionary distributions, as many trusts do. For this reason, a corporate or institutional trustee may provide the best option in order to minimize conflict in blended family situations in that an impartial third-party will be making decisions regarding trust distributions and general administration.

9028. What is a spouse's elective share? How can a spouse's election impact estate planning in a blended family?

Pursuant to state law, a surviving spouse is entitled to claim a portion of his or her deceased spouse's estate in lieu of the inheritance that the decedent chose to leave for the survivor (whether via will, trust or otherwise). In the traditional family context, this is often not an issue because the first-to-die spouse simply leaves his or her entire estate to the survivor with the understanding that the surviving spouse has sufficient incentive to provide for the couple's mutual children or other heirs.

In the blended family context, a deceased spouse may choose to leave certain of the assets to children from a prior marriage, with only a specified portion of the estate passing to the surviving spouse. This can create a problem when such a scenario intersects with state elective share rules, which may provide that the surviving spouse is entitled to a greater portion of the estate than the decedent directed. As a result, the elective share rules must be considered when engaging in estate planning for a blended family.

In many cases, blended families will use a qualified terminable interest property (QTIP) trust (see Q 9032 to Q 9033) to ensure that the surviving spouse is satisfied with his or her inheritance while still providing for children from a prior marriage.

9029. What issues involving the use of spouses' estate tax exemption amounts can arise in a blended family? What is portability?

Although the issue of wealth disparity can present an issue in any marital context, more extreme differences in both age and wealth tend to become important in the blended family context (where individuals may be entering a second or third marriage, potentially later in life). In these cases, estate planning must take into account the potential use of a less wealthy spouse's estate tax exemption, especially if the couple intends to keep their assets relatively separate.

For some couples, portability makes it easier to make full use of both spouses' estate tax exemptions even in the face of wealth disparity. Portability, which is the right of a surviving spouse to use any of a deceased spouse's unused transfer tax exemption amount, allows the surviving spouse to increase his or her own estate and gift tax exemption amount in order to exclude more of his or her assets from transfer tax liability (essentially excluding $11.2 million from estate tax liability per couple in 2018).[1]

In a first marriage, portability can be useful because the assets of the first-to-die spouse will typically pass directly to the surviving spouse (sheltered by the marital deduction), so that the first-to-die spouse will use none of his or her exemption. Portability ensures that the surviving spouse (whose eventual estate may be larger because he or she has inherited the assets of the first-to-die spouse) can make use of both spouses' exemption amounts.

In the case of a subsequent marriage/blended family scenario, however, using portability may not be ideal because the spouses may wish to leave more property to children from previous marriages rather than leaving all assets to the surviving spouse. As a result, trust options may provide a more attractive strategy to allow spouses in a blended family to make full use of both spouses' estate tax exemption amounts. See Q 9030 to Q 9032 for a discussion of some of the trust options that can be used by spouses in a blended family.

Planning Point: Clients should be aware that only the estate tax exemption of the most recent spouse can be used via portability.[2] Therefore, if a client's spouse predeceases him or her and the client chooses to remarry, the exemption amount of the first spouse will be lost if the subsequent spouse dies before the client. However, the client can continue to use his or her first spouse's exemption for lifetime gifts made before the death of the subsequent spouse.

Portability is also discussed in Q 9017.

1. Rev. Proc. 2017-58. Portability was introduced in the Tax Relief, Unemployment Reauthorization and Job Creation Act of 2010, and was made permanent by the American Taxpayer Relief Act of 2012.
2. Treas. Reg. §§20.2010-3(a), 20.2010-1(d)(5).

9030. What issues need to be weighed when a blended family is choosing whether to rely upon portability or trust options to ensure that both spouses' estate tax exemptions are fully used?

As discussed in Q 9029, portability can allow a surviving spouse to take advantage of both his or her federal estate tax exemption and the exemption of the first-to-die spouse (the generation skipping transfer tax exemption is not portable). For some couples, portability is appealing because of its simplicity—the executor of the estate is only required to file an estate tax return and elect portability.[1] Using portability to take advantage of both spouses' estate tax exemptions also avoids the necessity of forming a trust, which can be expensive to establish.

However, if an individual does not wish to leave the bulk of his or her assets to the surviving spouse, a trust option can prove more effective for carrying out the individual's wishes. Using trusts to provide for various family members' inheritances can also help prevent family conflict after the first-to-die spouse's death, as all heirs (including the surviving spouse, adult children and grandchildren) can be informed ahead of time to avoid unpleasant surprises that can lead to disagreement and even lawsuits.

Using a trust instead of portability can also create adverse tax consequences, however. As a general rule, the basis of property that has been acquired from a decedent is the fair market value of the property at the date of the decedent's death (i.e., the basis is "stepped up" or "stepped down," as the case may be, to the fair market value for estate tax valuation purposes). When portability is elected, the assets in the estate receive two basis adjustments—one after the death of the first-to-die spouse and one after the death of the surviving spouse, assuming the assets remain in the surviving spouse's estate. When the same assets are held in a trust, the assets do not receive a step-up in basis at the death of the surviving spouse (assuming they are excluded from the surviving spouse's estate, which is the goal of many trust options in blended family situations). If the assets appreciate substantially in value between the deaths of the two spouses, receiving a second step-up in basis can result in tax savings.[2]

Further, if the family resides in a state that imposes its own estate or inheritance tax, federal portability rules will not apply to those state-level taxes. The rates, exemption levels and how these taxes are imposed can vary significantly from state to state (i.e., the rate can vary based upon who inherits the property).

9031. How can members of a blended family use trusts in estate planning to fully use the exemption of both spouses when relying on portability is undesirable?

As discussed in Q 9029, many individuals in a second or subsequent marriage may not wish to rely on portability in order to make use of both spouses' federal estate tax exemption amounts. If the first-to-die spouse were to leave all assets outright to the surviving spouse (in order to take advantage of portability), that surviving spouse would have total control over those assets,

1. IRC Sec. 2010(c)(5); Treas. Reg. §20.2010-2.
2. IRC Sec. 1014(a).

including the ability to disinherit children from a prior marriage or even leave the first-to-die spouse's assets to a new spouse.

In this case, an *inter vivos* trust may be desirable, as it can allow the first-to-die spouse to control the ultimate disposition of his or her assets, and can also provide the spouse with income during life.

One example of such a trust provides the less wealthy spouse with a testamentary general power of appointment over the trust assets in the amount necessary to use that spouse's estate tax exemption if he or she is the first-to-die spouse. This type of trust can also continue to provide the grantor of the trust (the wealthier spouse) with income rights during life. These trusts can be revocable, so as to provide protection in the event of a divorce.[1] One downside to these types of trusts is that the power of appointment allows the poorer spouse to provide an inheritance to whomever he or she chooses (this feature avoids gift tax issues that would otherwise arise to make the trust structure undesirable).

Planning Point: Because these types of trusts are not specifically approved by IRS regulation, competent professional advice must be sought out in order to weigh the potential risks and benefits of the many available types of trust structures.

A joint revocable trust is another type of revocable trust that can be used to ensure both spouses' exemptions are used, but this type of trust requires both spouses to contribute the assets (in the case of wealth disparity, this would mean that the wealthy spouse makes gifts to the poorer spouse to fund the trust).

With both of these types of trust, a risk also exists that the IRS will determine that one spouse actually made the gift after his or her spouse's death, causing potential problems in claiming the marital deduction. While a lifetime power of appointment may avoid this problem, it causes another in that the poorer spouse then has the lifetime power to appoint to whomever he or she chooses, unless the spouses agree that the spouse either exercise the power immediately in writing (with testamentary effect, becoming effective on the wealthier spouse's death) or release the power. Because of these complications, many individuals prefer to use the qualified terminable interest property (QTIP) trust structure, which is governed by specific IRS regulations, discussed in Q 9032 and Q 9033.

See Q 9034 for a discussion of "A-B trusts". Q 9035 discusses some of the potential uses of an irrevocable life insurance trust (ILIT).

9032. What is a qualified terminable interest property (QTIP) trust and how can QTIP trusts be useful in planning for the blended family?

In many cases, an individual may wish to provide security for a surviving spouse during that spouse's lifetime, but simultaneously wish to ensure that his or her children are the ultimate trust beneficiaries. In a blended family, this issue becomes even more pronounced because a surviving spouse may have his or her own children from a prior marriage, or may remarry and

1. For examples of these types of trusts, see Let. Ruls. 200403094 and 200604028.

have additional children after a prior spouse has died. Unlike trusts that grant the poorer spouse a power of appointment over trust assets, a qualified terminable interest property (QTIP) trust provides the surviving spouse with only a lifetime interest in trust assets, helping to ensure that the first-to-die spouse's wishes are carried out. Unlike the trusts discussed in Q 9033, however, a QTIP trust is irrevocable

Planning Point: If a substantial age disparity exists between the spouses, a QTIP trust may not be an attractive option, as it requires that the decedent's children and other heirs wait until the death of a much younger spouse before receiving property that may form the bulk of their inheritance.

A QTIP trust is a trust that contains qualified terminable interest property. "Qualified terminable interest property" means property (1) which passes from the decedent, (2) in which the surviving spouse has a "qualifying income interest for life," and (3) as to which the executor makes an irrevocable election on the federal estate tax return to have the marital deduction apply.

The surviving spouse has a "qualifying income interest for life" if (1) the surviving spouse is entitled to all the income from the property, payable annually or at more frequent intervals, and (2) no person has a power to appoint any part of the property to any person other than the surviving spouse unless the power is exercisable only at or after the death of the surviving spouse.[1] The last requirement may be violated even if it is the surviving spouse who is given the lifetime power to appoint to someone other than the surviving spouse.[2] A QTIP allows a decedent to provide for a surviving spouse, receive the marital deduction, and pass the remainder to beneficiaries the decedent selects in his or her will.

Planning Point: A QTIP election is irrevocable, so that the property transferred to the QTIP trust will be included in the surviving spouse's gross estate.

An executor can elect under IRC Section 2056(b)(7) to treat an individual retirement account and a trust as QTIP if the trustee is the named beneficiary of decedent's IRA and the surviving spouse can compel the trustee to withdraw from the IRA an amount equal to all the income earned on the IRA assets at least annually and to distribute that amount to the spouse. No person can have a power to appoint any part of the trust property to any person other than the spouse.[3]

Certain "terminable interests" in property do not qualify for the marital deduction. The purpose of this rule is to ensure inclusion in the surviving spouse's estate of any property remaining in the estate at his or her death which escaped the initial tax in the predeceased spouse's estate.

A "terminable interest" in property is an interest which will terminate or fail on the lapse of time or on the occurrence or the failure to occur of some contingency. Life estates, terms for

1. IRC Sec. 2056(b)(7).
2. TAM 200234017.
3. Rev. Rul. 2000-2, 2000-1 CB 305.

years, annuities, patents, and copyrights are therefore terminable interests.[1] Some terminable interests are deductible and some are nondeductible under the marital deduction law. In general, a "terminable interest" is nondeductible if (1) another interest in the same property passes (for less than an adequate consideration) from the decedent to someone other than his or her spouse (or that spouse's estate), and (2) the other person may possess or enjoy any part of the property after the spouse's interest ends.

See Q 9033 for a discussion of some of the considerations that should be taken into account in deciding whether to create an *inter vivos* or testamentary QTIP trust.

9033. What are some of the considerations that should be taken into account when deciding whether to use an inter vivos or a testamentary QTIP trust?

The difference between an *inter vivos* and testamentary qualified terminable interest property (QTIP) trust is that the *inter vivos* trust is created and funded during the grantor's life, while the testamentary trust only becomes effective at the grantor's death (i.e., his or her will provides for creation of the trust).

Planning Point: Note that with an *inter vivos* QTIP trust, the trust documents can provide that the funding spouse will actually become the trust beneficiary if the less wealthy spouse is the first-to-die spouse. This option, however, still requires that the grantor not be given the right to amend, alter, revoke or terminate the trust.[2] This strategy also carries the risk that the trust could be treated as a self-settled trust reachable by the grantor's creditors.

An *inter vivos* trust can also provide asset protection to the couple while both spouses are still living. Further, an *inter vivos* QTIP trust is "defective" for income tax purposes for the lives of both spouses—this eliminates the need to file separate income tax returns for the trust.

Property held in the *inter vivos* trust is valued separately from property held individually by the surviving spouse for his or her benefit. This generally means that if, for example, a portion of a piece of property is held in the QTIP trust and a portion remains outside of the trust, each portion of the property could potentially be eligible for any applicable valuation discounts that may be available.[3]

One primary disadvantage to the *inter vivos* QTIP trust is that it is not revocable upon divorce. Therefore, once created, the divorced spouse remains entitled to the benefit of the QTIP trust assets if he or she survives the trust creator. Despite this, the trust document can limit the trustee's power to invade the trust principal by providing that such a discretionary right is available only if the beneficiary was married to the trust creator at his or her death. After divorce, income from the trust is includable only in the income of the beneficiary spouse.[4] Because the testamentary QTIP trust only becomes effective at death, the grantor is able to modify his or her will following a divorce so that a prior spouse does not receive the benefit of the QTIP trust.

1. IRC Sec. 2056(b); Treas. Reg. §20.2056(b)-1(b).
2. Treas. Reg. §25.2523(f)-1(d).
3. See, for example, *Estate of Mellinger v. Comm.*, 112 TC 26 (1999).
4. IRC Sec. 682(a).

9034. How can an A-B trust be used by individuals in a blended family to plan for inheritances by children from prior marriages?

Planning for wealth transfer in a blended family can become complicated because, without proper planning, a surviving spouse could inherit all of a first-to-die spouse's assets and gain complete control over how those assets will be distributed upon his or her death. If the first-to-die spouse has children from a first marriage, he or she may prefer that the assets benefit those children, rather than any children (or future children) of the surviving spouse. In the end, many individuals will wish to provide for a surviving spouse during life, but ultimately want to control the distribution of their assets upon the death of that surviving spouse.

In order to accomplish this, many individuals use trusts in order to ensure that a surviving spouse has sufficient income for life, but that the first-to-die spouse's assets ultimately pass to his or her biological children (rather than to any stepchildren or future spouses of the surviving spouse). Creating what is known as an "A-B trust" (also known as a bypass trust, which were typically created to avoid estate taxes prior to the increase of the federal estate tax exemption and introduction of portability, see Q 9031) can ensure that both the spouse and decedent's children benefit from a decedent's estate according to his or her wishes.

The A-B trust can really take many forms, depending upon the parties' wishes. For example, the decedent can leave a portion of his or her estate in the "A trust", typically a revocable grantor trust that gives the surviving spouse use of the trust income for life, but often leaves the remainder (trust principal) to the decedent's children. The "B trust" is an irrevocable trust that would contain a portion of the decedent's estate to either immediately benefit his or her own children, or to provide income to the surviving spouse with the trust principal preserved for the children (depending upon the wishes of the decedent).

While the surviving spouse may have the ability to modify the beneficiaries of the A trust and retain some control over the principal of that trust (depending upon trust terms), the B trust is irrevocable. In this manner, both the surviving spouse and decedent's children are protected. Further, the client has ensured that at least a portion of his or her assets will ultimately pass to his or her own children, rather than to stepchildren or as the surviving spouse directs.

This type of trust structure also helps very wealthy families minimize estate taxes. The portion of the trust that does not pass unfettered to the surviving spouse is funded with an amount equal to the federal exemption amount to shield those assets from estate taxes, while the "marital" portion of the trust can be funded with whatever amount of assets the first-to-die spouse wishes (and will be sheltered from estate tax by the marital deduction).

In these scenarios, the A trust is typically established as a grantor trust, which is taxed to the individual grantor. The B trust is irrevocable, so is taxed according to general trust rules and must file a Form 1041. Because the B trust is irrevocable, it could also potentially be used to protect the assets of the first-to-die spouse from a financially irresponsible surviving spouse (i.e., from the surviving spouse's creditors, see Q 8983 to Q 8997 for a discussion of asset protection trusts).

See Q 9032 to Q 9033 for a discussion of qualified terminable interest property (QTIP) trusts, which are another option that can be useful in the blended family context.

9035. What is an irrevocable life insurance trust (ILIT) and how can an ILIT be useful in a blended family's estate plan?

An irrevocable life insurance trust (ILIT) is a trust funded by life insurance that cannot be modified, amended or revoked without the permission of the beneficiary. It is mechanism used in estate planning in which a grantor effectively removes all of his or her rights of ownership to the assets that have been transferred to the trust. The primary purpose of an ILIT is to reduce a decedent's estate tax liability (while simultaneously providing for heirs) by removing a life insurance policy from the decedent's gross estate.

An ILIT can be a valuable tool both for providing for children from a first marriage or a surviving spouse, and for reducing a decedent's taxable estate. Prenuptial agreements (Q 9001 to Q 9002) can be helpful in providing that a surviving spouse's inheritance will be limited to proceeds from the life insurance policy held by the ILIT. A prenuptial agreement can also provide that if the couple divorces, the beneficiary-spouse must forfeit all rights to the trust assets (which would presumably then pass to the insured's children or other heirs).

An ILIT allows a decedent to control who receives the proceeds of the life insurance policy because the proceeds are actually paid to the trust, and the governing trust documents then provide specific details as to who should receive the proceeds and under what circumstances. This strategy can also allow a decedent to protect an inheritance from the beneficiary's creditors.

For individuals who wish to benefit a generation of beneficiaries that is more than one removed (so that the generation skipping transfer (GST) tax would apply), a portion of the GST exemption amount ($5.6 million in 2018)[1] can be applied to the transfers to the trust (thereby sheltering the entire amount of the proceeds from the GST tax). It should be noted that this can provide a valuable strategy for wealthy individuals who anticipate transferring wealth in excess of the exemption amount, as only the cash actually transferred to the trust to fund the life insurance policy premiums must be exempted. By allocating the GST tax exemption to those cash transfers, the larger value of the life insurance proceeds can be paid out entirely GST tax-free, while leaving a greater proportion of the exemption for allocation to other assets.

9036. In the blended family context, what issues should be considered in planning for who will be responsible for payment of any transfer tax liability?

In the blended family context, an individual is likely to spend more time in his or her estate planning because of the inherent complications that can arise in these scenarios. Despite this, many may forget that any estate tax liability can reduce the carefully planned out inheritances that the decedent's heirs will actually receive—generating potential conflict despite the most careful trust and gifting strategies.

In most cases, the decedent can specify in his or her will how estate taxes should be apportioned among the beneficiaries. In the absence of specific instructions from the decedent

1. Rev. Proc. 2017-58.

as to how the estate tax will be paid, both state and federal laws will need to be examined. For example, in New York and Florida, tax is generally apportioned among the estate beneficiaries in proportion to the value of the estate property that each beneficiary has received.[1] Certain types of property (including marital deduction property) are specifically addressed at the federal level, and taxes relating to that property will be allocated to the person who received the property.[2]

In some cases, it can be beneficial for an individual to establish an irrevocable life insurance trust (see Q 9035) to provide liquidity to the estate in order to pay any anticipated estate taxes, rather than dividing liability for estate taxes between the heirs.

1. NY CLS EPTL §2-1.8; Fla. Stat. §733.817(2).
2. See IRC Secs. 2207A, 2058.

PART XXI: DIGITAL ASSET PLANNING

9037. What are digital assets?

Generally, an individual's digital property or digital assets include any information that exists in digital form (whether online or stored electronically on a device such as a USB drive or CD) that are either created by or about an individual. According to the Revised Uniform Fiduciary Access to Digital Assets Act (Uniform Act), now enacted in the majority of states, a digital asset is simply "an electronic record in which an individual has a right or interest," but not the "underlying asset or liability unless the asset or liability is itself an electronic record."[1]

In more practical terms, digital assets can be categorized as either (1) personal digital assets (with no monetary value, (2) personal digital assets with real monetary value or (3) digital assets related to a business.

These may be stored either on a physical device or media (such as a computer, hard drive, smartphone, memory stick, etc.) or electronically in the cloud (including email, social media, and other types of online accounts). Collectively, these make up a person's digital estate.

(a) Personal digital assets (without monetary value)

Many personal digital assets may have no monetary value, but hold a great deal of emotional value and preserve the memories, stories, interactions, and personal information of their owner. These include:

- Any personal electronic files, photos, videos, commercial programs or applications, and other information stored on physical devices, such as computers, smartphones, tablets, digital cameras, hard drives, flash drives, memory cards, memory sticks, CDs, DVDs, and other digital media and devices.
- Email and communications accounts, including Skype, iChat, FaceTime, WhatsApp, and other instant messenger (IM) programs, as well as related conversations, recordings, and other data.
- Electronic information stored in a smartphone or online on a mobile phone account, including downloaded applications (apps), photos, videos, contacts, text or SMS messages, call history, and voicemail messages.
- Social media accounts, such as Facebook, Twitter, LinkedIn, Tumblr, Pinterest, including content and interactions made through these accounts (*e.g.*, writing, posts, feeds, comments, chats, and recordings).
- Photo and video storage and sharing accounts, such as YouTube, Instagram, Flickr, Picasa, and PhotoBucket.

1. Uniform Law Commission (National Conference of Commissioners on Uniform State Laws), Fiduciary Access to Digital Assets Act, Revised (2015), at sec. 2(10), available at http://www.uniformlaws.org/shared/docs/Fiduciary%20Access%20to%20Digital%20Assets/2015_RUFADAA_Final%20Act_2016mar8.pdf (accessed June 28, 2017).

- Online storage accounts, such as Dropbox, Google Drive, and OneDrive.
- Online gaming accounts or applications (apps), including in-game purchases, virtual property, and avatars.
- Personal blogs, websites, and Internet domain names.
- Personal information, such as medical records and legal documents (whether stored on physical media or devices, on a website, or in the cloud).
- Any other personal online information or accounts.

(b) Personal digital assets with real monetary value

There are also many personal digital assets that have real monetary value, including:

- Money-management and financial accounts, such as online banking and investment accounts, PayPal, loyalty and rewards programs, and any other accounts with credit or value.
- Digital (also known as virtual) currencies, such as bitcoin.
- Intellectual property, such as copyrighted works, registered trademarks, and computer applications or programming code.
- Revenue-generating assets, including websites, blogs, certain social media accounts, Internet domain names (whether live/hosted or inactive), art, photos, music, eBooks, and other digital property.
- Assets related to personal online sales accounts, such as an eBay seller's account.

(c) Digital assets of a business

Digital assets related to a business—separate from personal digital assets with monetary value—may include:

- Online accounts (including financial accounts) associated with a business.
- Online businesses and sales accounts, such as an eBay, Etsy, or Amazon store, other commercial websites.
- Business email accounts, mailing lists, newsletter subscription lists, or email lists containing your company's clients.
- Contact information, customer history, and account information of business clients.

See Q 9038 for a discussion of the importance of estate planning for digital assets. Q 9039 to Q 9041 discuss the state and federal laws that now govern the disposition of digital assets.

9038. Why should digital assets be included in an estate plan?

Including digital assets in an estate plan serves the purpose of a traditional—but increasingly outdated—manila envelope, file folder, binder, locked cabinet, or safe deposit box containing the information needed to administer a decedent's estate.

Many people now manage their personal lives, finances, and business affairs online, but very few have organized or centralized information about those accounts. Estate planning for digital assets has an important, and growing, place in the future of estate planning generally. Here are some of the reasons to include digital assets in an estate plan:

- To preserve the inherent personal or emotional value of such items as family photos and videos, email accounts, and social media postings—thereby avoiding loss of an individual's personal story.
- To protect the financial value of such items as digital currencies, online seller accounts, and domain names—thereby preventing financial losses to an estate.
- To make administering the digital estate easier, in terms of trust or estate administration, of items such as legal and financial documents, contact lists, etc.—thereby enabling easier access for executors and family members.
- To ensure the security of the digital estate by preventing or minimizing the risks of identity theft, hacking of online accounts, 'ghost' or 'zombie' accounts of decedents, and the potential unwanted discovery of personal secrets.

The inclusion of digital assets in the estate planning process will also have the effect of preparing for an increasingly digital information-based society. Importantly, including digital assets as part of an estate plan also increases the likelihood that the disposition of an individual's digital assets will be carried out as actually intended by the owner.

9039. What uniform state laws are in place to safeguard digital assets after death? What is the Uniform Fiduciary Access to Digital Assets Act?

Until very recently, only a handful of states had enacted laws specifically to address issues surrounding digital assets. However, as people's digital and online presence has become more widespread, the legislative framework for digital asset protection has grown. As early as 2002, a few states began individually enacting legislation in an attempt to address certain discrete issues arising out of what would become the overarching category of digital assets—starting with email account access and termination—legislation began recognizing and addressing the need to cover additional forms of digital assets that were (and are) continually growing and changing.[1]

1. *See* Gerry W. Beyer, "Web Meets the Will: Estate Planning for Digital Assets," NAEPC Journal of Estate and Tax Planning, vol. 42, No. 3 (Mar. 2015), pp. 28–41, at pp. 39–40 (accessed June 28, 2017).

At the state level, a uniform system of dealing with digital assets has arisen relatively recently. In 2014, the National Conference of Commissioners on Uniform State Laws (Uniform Law Commission) completed drafting a proposed uniform law to address the issues surrounding digital assets. In 2015, the Conference approved and recommended for enactment its Revised Uniform Fiduciary Access to Digital Assets Act ("Uniform Act").[1] Essentially, the Uniform Act provides the legal authority for a fiduciary to manage a user's digital assets in accordance with the user's estate plan, while ensuring that the user's private electronic communications remain private, unless the user has consented to disclosure.

The number of states that have enacted the Uniform Act into law has grown very quickly since the Act's promulgation in 2015. As of June 2017, all but three states (Kentucky, Louisiana and Pennsylvania) have either adopted the Act or have legislation pending to adopt the Act.[2] Oklahoma still uses the statute it enacted in 2010 before promulgation of the Uniform Act.[3] Delaware has enacted a statute that is a substantial equivalent to the Uniform Act.[4] A detailed listing of each state's laws on digital assets can be found in Appendix C.

The Uniform Act provides the following legal authority for fiduciaries of a user and online service providers ("custodians" under the Act) of the user's digital assets:

- ***Fiduciaries*** and other designated persons are authorized to access and manage the digital assets and electronic communications of deceased users; and
- ***Custodians*** of digital assets and electronic communications are authorized to permit access or to disclose digital assets to a fiduciary or designated recipient of a user.

Although the Uniform Act addresses four different types of fiduciaries,[5] the most important for digital estate planning and administration are the executors or administrators of decedent's estate ("personal representatives" under the Act). Fiduciaries exercise authority over digital assets under the Uniform Act only on the user's behalf, which is distinct from other types of access to digital assets. Thus, unless family or friends of a decedent are also a user's fiduciary, they are not covered under the Uniform Act and are instead subject to any other applicable state or Federal laws (as discussed in Q 9041.)

9040. How can the Uniform Fiduciary Access to Digital Assets Act help an individual in planning for disposition of digital assets?

Section 4 of the Uniform Act provides a means for users to provide instructions for the disposition or deletion of their digital assets, and establishes a priority system when online

1. Uniform Law Commission, *Fiduciary Access to Digital Assets Act, Revised (2015)*.
2. *See* Uniform Law Commission, *Fiduciary Access to Digital Assets Act, Revised (2015) – Enactment Status Map* (accessed June 28, 2017).
3. Okla. Stat. § 58–269, http://webserver1.lsb.state.ok.us/OK_Statutes/CompleteTitles/os58.rtf (accessed June 28, 2017). Oklahoma failed to enact a bill introduced in 2016 to adopt the Uniform Act. See Appendix for details of the legislation.
4. Del. Code tit. 12, ch. 50, §§ 5001–5007, http://delcode.delaware.gov/title12/c050/, http://delcode.delaware.gov/title12/title12.pdf (accessed June 28, 2017).
5. These are: (1) personal representatives (executors or administrators) of the estates of deceased persons, (2) court-appointed conservators of the estates of protected (living) persons, (3) agents appointed by principals under powers of attorney, and (4) trustees acting on behalf of settlors (*i.e.*, trustors).

tools, legal documents, and terms of service conflict. Section 4 of the Uniform Act addresses the relationship of online tools, legal documents recording a user's intent, and terms-of-service agreements.

A user may use an online tool to authorize or deny disclosure of some or all of the user's digital assets, including the content of electronic communications. If the user's wishes have been expressed using an online tool from a provider, those instructions will override a contrary instruction in a legal document (will, trust, power of attorney, or other record) or in the provider's terms of service.

If the user has not provided instructions using an online tool from the provider, or if the provider does not have an online tool for that purpose, the user's instructions as expressed in a legal document will prevail, even if the provider's terms of service conflict with those instructions.

Finally, if the user provides no other direction, the service provider's terms of service will apply. If the terms of service do not address fiduciary access to users' digital assets, the default rules of the Uniform Act will apply.

The default rules contained in the Uniform Act provide that a fiduciary service provider must provide a "catalogue of electronic communications sent or received by the user" and digital assets of the user, but not the content of any electronic communications.[1] (The catalogue is a log with "information that identifies each person with which a user has had an electronic communication, the date and time of the communication, and the electronic address of the person."[2]) This section is intended to provide default access to the catalogue of electronic communications and to other digital assets not protected by Federal privacy law.

In each case, however, the fiduciary must provide a copy of the relevant document to the service provider when requesting access. A service provider may comply with requests for disclosure of a deceased user's digital assets by resetting the account's password and permitting the fiduciary access to the account. Alternatively, the provider may provide a copy of the digital assets to the fiduciary.[3]

Effect on Terms of Service Agreements

With respect to a service provider's terms of service agreement, the Uniform Act "does not change or impair a right of a custodian or a user under a terms-of-service agreement to access and use digital assets of the user."[4] In addition, "A fiduciary's … access to digital assets may be modified or eliminated by a user, by federal law, or by a terms-of-service agreement if the user has not provided direction under Section 4."[5]

1. Uniform Act § 8.
2. Uniform Act § 2(4).
3. Uniform Act § 6.
4. Uniform Act § 5(a).
5. Uniform Act § 5(c).

9041. What Federal laws are in place to safeguard digital assets?

Federal law regulates unauthorized access to digital assets and addresses the privacy of online communication. There are two significant Federal laws that users and their digital fiduciaries should take into consideration. These are the Computer Fraud and Abuse Act and the Stored Communications Act. These laws prohibit unauthorized access to digital assets and seek to ensure the privacy of a user's electronic communications, including email, social media, and website user accounts.

These two laws may pose potential problems for fiduciaries who seek to access a decedent's online digital assets, (as well as for online service providers asked to provide that access). In order to avoid running afoul of them, it is important to ensure that a user has provided specific legal authorization for the digital fiduciary to access the user's online accounts. However, if the online service provider's terms of services agreement prevents password sharing, such access, even with specific written authorization, may be considered "unauthorized," and therefore in (criminal) violation of the laws.

Computer Fraud and Abuse Act

The Computer Fraud and Abuse Act[1] prohibits unauthorized access to computers. This may give rise to problems if the online service provider's terms of service prohibit a user from granting others access to the account. If a user reveals his or her user name and password and another person uses that information to access an account, it could be in violation of these laws for being without "lawful consent". (Since the terms of service do not permit the user the authority to authorize access for someone else, the other person cannot be said to have sufficient lawful consent.)

Stored Communications Act

The Stored Communications Act[2] provides criminal penalties for anyone who "intentionally accesses without authorization" an online electronic communications account or "intentionally exceeds an authorization to access [the account]... and thereby obtains, alters, or prevents authorized access" to such an account.[3] The law also imposes civil penalties on service providers that for knowingly divulging the contents of an electronic communication, unless disclosure is made "with the lawful consent of the originator or an addressee or intended recipient of such communication, or the subscriber in the case of remote computing service."[4]

9042. How does an online provider's terms of service agreement impact the disposition of an individual's digital assets?

Each online service provider has its own terms of service agreement. Depending on the terms, there may be limitations or restrictions on what a user, or a digital fiduciary, can do with

1. 18 U.S.C. § 1030.
2. 18 U.S.C. §§ 2701–2712
3. 18 U.S.C. § 2701(a).
4. 18 U.S.C. § 2702.

respect to the user's account after death. They can also affect how the laws, particularly the Uniform Act (see Q 9039 to Q 9040) may be applied.

Even if the state's version of the Uniform Act authorizes service providers to disclose electronic communications and their contents, and the user authorizes the digital fiduciary to access those electronic communications, if the service provider's terms of service agreement with the user contains provisions that do not permit the user to authorize another party to access the user's data, it is the terms of service that will ultimately prevail.

This illustrates the importance of checking the terms of service—preferably while the user is alive—to ensure that the service provider's policies will permit the user's wishes regarding account to be carried out rather than thwart those wishes.

Planning Point: While the client's wishes may conflict with some companies' terms of service agreements, it is still valuable that the executor be made aware of those wishes. Companies frequently update their terms of service agreements, so the clients may be in line with the terms of service at some point in the future. *Jason Carr, M.S., M.Ed.*

9043. What steps should be taken to incorporate digital assets into an estate plan? How can an individual identify and secure his or her digital assets?

In order to ensure that a user's intentions regarding digital assets, the user should take measures to incorporate digital assets into a new or existing estate plan. Preparing a plan for digital assets can be organized in the following steps:

(1) Identify and secure the digital assets.

(2) Choose and authorize a digital fiduciary (Q 9044).

(3) Decide what to do with the digital assets after death (Q 9045).

Step 1: Identify and Secure the Digital Assets

Before a person can decide what to do with digital assets, the person must first determine what digital assets there are to plan for. Tools exist to help simplify this process so that all types of digital assets are accounted for. These tools include paper or electronic forms to fill out, checklists, and online guides.[1]

First and foremost, the individual should make a comprehensive inventory of digital assets, including electronic files, information, and accounts on all types of media, including (1) electronic files stored on personal hardware (computers, tablets, smartphones, hard drives, digital

1. *See*, e.g., Digital Estate Information Sample Form, in Gerry W. Beyer, "Web Meets the Will: Estate Planning for Digital Assets," NAEPC Journal of Estate and Tax Planning, vol. 42, No. 3 (Mar. 2015), pp. 28–41 (at pp. 34–37), http://www.naepc.org/journal/issue20p.pdf (accessed June 28, 2017); Everplans.com, "A Helpful Overview of All Your Digital Property and Digital Assets," https://www.everplans.com/articles/a-helpful-overview-of-all-your-digital-property-and-digital-assets (accessed June 28, 2017).
Everplans.com, "Digital Estate Planning: How to Organize All Your Digital Property and Assets," https://www.everplans.com/articles/digital-estate-planning-how-to-organize-all-your-digital-property-and-assets (accessed June 28, 2017).

cameras, flash drives, CDs or DVDs) and (2) personal online accounts (email, social media, cloud storage, file-sharing). Digital assets with monetary value or dealing with financial issues must also be accounted for. These assets include both personal (banking, investment accounts, utilities, online shopping, loyalty and reward programs) and business-related (electronic currency, online stores, websites, domain names) digital assets.

In order to provide access to digital assets, the individual should list login, password, PINs, and answers to any security questions. This sensitive information should be stored securely, with an attorney, a trusted family member or friend, a physical location (file cabinet, safety deposit box), or with an online storage or 'afterlife' service (see below).

Passwords and login information are constantly changing, so keeping up with those changes can be time-consuming, if done on paper, or even in a traditional electronic file. As a practical matter, a password manager program or service can be helpful in keeping track of these changes automatically. Making sure a designee can gain access to account information may require of sharing a 'master password' to permit sharing this information.

9044. What is a digital fiduciary and how can a digital fiduciary be useful in estate planning for digital assets?

A comprehensive estate plan covering digital assets should provide for the designation and authorization of a digital fiduciary, who has the right to access and manage digital assets and accounts on behalf of the decedent. It may be the same person named as executor of the estate or someone else authorized specifically to manage the estate's digital assets. Choosing a person familiar with modern technology can create a more efficient administration.

A digital fiduciary, once chosen, must be granted sufficient legal authorization to carry out necessary functions of estate administration, including accessing and managing the user's digital assets after the user dies.

The power of attorney, will, trust, or other legal instrument document appointing the digital fiduciary should grant specific authority to access and inspect any (1) online accounts (including electronic communications and the content of electronic communications), (2) electronic devices (including computers, hard drives, and smartphones), and (3) other tangible digital storage media. In States that have not adopted the Uniform Act, these authorizations may provide an alternative when State laws do not explicitly provide such authority to a fiduciary.

The authorizing document should also be cognizant of the provisions of the Computer Fraud and Abuse Act[1] and the Stored Communications Act[2] to avoid the fiduciary's liability and ensure the fiduciary's access to digital assets.

Finally, the effects of online service providers' varying terms of service should be considered, as those terms may override or effectively nullify the authorization.

1. 18 U.S.C. § 1030.
2. 18 U.S.C. §§ 2701-2712.

9045. What options does an individual have with respect to disposing of digital assets after death?

The next step in formulating a digital asset estate plan is to decide what to do with the assets after death. Because there are likely personal, individual financial, and business-related accounts and information, the preferred disposition of those assets will likely vary. The owner of the digital assets should specify how each type of asset should be handled after death.

Personal (Nonfinancial) Information and Accounts

Digital assets of a personal nature, without real monetary value, may nevertheless be priceless to family and friends. Alternatively, there may be information that an individual wants to ensure is not preserved or passed on to family or friends. Some of the ways that such personal assets can be disposed of are discussed below.

1. *Archive and save.* A person may want personal assets (such as photos, emails, contact or birthday lists, and any number of other types of information) to be saved and stored or archived for future use or reference (such as genealogical records) by others, or to preserve the individual's personal story of life. Some ways this may be done are the following:

    - Download online account information (when available to do so) to a home, business, or mobile computer, or other mobile device, or to tangible physical media, such as CDs, DVDs, external hard drives, flash drives, and even paper printouts.

    - Some online providers (such as Facebook and Google) allow users to download their account information (photos, posts, messages, comments, etc.).

    - There are also third-party apps and software to assist in downloading one's online account information, when the provider does not have an easy means of doing so.[1]

    - If already stored on a home, business, or mobile computer, or other mobile device, the information can be transferred, backed-up, or archived to tangible media.

2. *Transfer or make available to family members, friends, or others.* Whether they reside on personally owned hardware or tangible media, or is stored online in the cloud, a person may wish to transfer some personal digital assets to family, friends, business colleagues, alumni groups, or others. (Some formal and informal ways to do this are described in Step 3 below.)

    There are also ways of memorializing a decedent to make available the person's life story, as told through social media, photo-sharing accounts, or other personal accounts. These include Facebook's memorial profiles of deceased users and dedicated websites set up (usually posthumously) for a similar purpose.

1. For example, a service called Backupify, https://www.backupify.com/, can be used to help download content from Gmail, Facebook, Twitter, and other personal accounts. (Accessed June 28, 2017.)

3. *For some online accounts, specify disposition using available online tools*. Some online providers have developed online tools that a user may use to specify what should happen to the account in the event of the user's death or the extended inactivity on the account—for example, Google's Inactive Account Manager. (These tools are discussed in Q 9040 above.)

4. *Delete or erase*. Some personal digital assets and information serve no use after a person's death (such as an Amazon wish list, an eBay buyer's account, or smartphone apps) and may be deleted or erased.[1] There are also some personal digital assets and information that a person specifically wants *not* to be seen, read, saved, archived, or transferred to anyone else after the person's death. These may consist of anything from sensitive medical records to racy photos. (See Q 9046 for additional information about closed, deleted, and erased accounts.)

Assets with Real or Potential Monetary Value

For digital assets with real or potential monetary value, a person will probably want to provide for their transfer or handling in a specific way, and by specific parties, after the person's death. Here are some questions to ask when considering how to dispose of monetary digital assets:

1. *Assets with cash value*. For accounts with assets such as online digital currency and the like (other than ordinary banking, investment, or insurance accounts, which are typically covered under traditional estate planning):
   - Should the account be cashed out or remain (as an investment, for instance)?
   - Should the account be transferred to someone else, either as owner or fiduciary, to make decisions and receive or distribute any proceeds derived from the asset?

2. *Revenue-generating assets*. For revenue-generating assets, such as commercial websites, online stores, or registered domain names:
   - Should it be transferred to someone who will continue to manage the asset and collect or distribute the income?
   - Should it be closed after any remaining inventory is sold?
   - Should it be closed immediately?
   - If an asset continues to generating revenue, where, to whom, or for what purpose should the income go?

1. Deletion of an account may involve first closing the account—without retrieving, saving, or archiving the account information. Alternatively, many accounts will be disabled and eventually deleted after an extended period of inactivity. While a user could simply leave these types of accounts open, with the expectation that they will eventually be deleted, the more advisable course is to actively delete them in order to prevent their misuse or hijacking.

3. *Other assets*. For valuable digital assets that do not generate revenue, such as rewards, loyalty, frequent flyer, and similar programs:

- Should any credits, points, or available cash value be redeemed, and if so, by whom and for whose benefit? (The terms of each such account should be checked to ensure that the redemption value remains after the death of the account holder.)

9046. What measures should be taken to maintain security of digital assets before and after death?

When estate planning for digital assets, it is important to maintain the security of the assets while ensuring authorized access to the digital estate after the user's death. This may consist of asset or account information, passwords, encryption, and other security measures to maintain both security and access.

(a) General considerations

In order to balance these dual interests, the following general considerations should be kept in mind:

1. *Security of digital assets*. The digital assets themselves must be kept secure to ensure that they will be available—both to the user while alive and to whoever is authorized to deal with the assets after the user's death.

2. *Security of access information or credentials*. Typically, online digital accounts are secured by a password or other security features intended to ensure only the user, or someone authorized by the user, will have access to the asset and its management.

3. *Accessibility when needed after death*. While maintaining the security of digital assets during the user's lifetime is essential, that security is useless if no one can access the assets after the death of the user. Therefore, it is vital to make sure that someone (digital fiduciary, executor, or administrator, or other trusted person) will have the information needed to access the digital assets after death.

4. *Updating the information to keep it current*. Passwords and other security features typically need to be updated periodically to maintain the security of the associated account. Some software, app, and online service providers require a user to change or create a new password on a regular basis (e.g., every thirty, sixty, or ninety days). Because of the constantly changing nature of digital security measures, it is essential that the access information for a digital fiduciary be kept up to date at all times.

(b) Types of secure digital assets, access information, and digital security measures

1. **Types of digital assets**. The types of digital assets that may be protected by various types of security measures include the following:

Digital accounts, including any online accounts, operating systems, and profiles.

Software and apps installed on a personal electronic device.

Protected files and folders stored on a personal electronic device.

Encrypted hardware, including computers, smartphones tablets, and other physical storage media (such as external hard drives, flash drives, and CD- or DVD-ROMs). Protected hardware may require manually recording any passwords, PINs, or other information needed to access the device.

2. **Types of access information**. Some or all of the following types of access information (or credentials) may be needed to ensure security and access for a user's digital assets:

Identification information, such as the user's unique username, user ID, logon [login] name, or account number. This may be chosen by the user or assigned by the provider, and it often consists of the user's email address or phone number.

Security access information, which may consist of an identifying password, passcode, passphrase, PassMark, PIN (personal identification number), security questions, two-step verification, or biometric data—or some combination of them. (These are discussed below.)

Additional personal information, which may be the user's email or phone number (if it is not the same as the user's unique account ID) or other personally identifying information, such as the user's date of birth or social security number (or part of it).

Social media profiles, which are increasingly becoming an optional (and sometimes the only) way to create an account and access smartphone apps and websites that require registration.

3. **Types of digital security measures [and credentials]**. Security measures can range from simple passwords or PINs to biometric data that recognizes the user through unique physical characteristics. The main types of digital security measures are listed below:

Passwords. There are still the most common type of security feature, consisting of a string of characters (letters, numbers, and/or symbols), which often have specific requirements for validity (*e.g.*, eight-fourteen characters, with at least one capital letter, one lowercase letter, one number, and one symbol).

Passphrases. A passphrase is a type of password that consists of a series of random words, simple phrases, or sentences that are easy to remember, but hard to hack.

PassMarks. A PassMark is a type of enhanced security feature that typically consists of an image containing a phrase, as well as confidential challenge questions.

(PassMarks are increasingly used by financial institutions to prevent fraud and identity theft.)

Security or challenge questions. Confidential security or challenge questions are questions often chosen by a user from a list of questions (or even written by the user) that are unique and relate to personal information others would be unlikely to know. They are typically much more personalized than 'mother's maiden name' or 'city of birth.'

Two-step authentication. Two-step (or two-factor) verification or authentication (sometimes called 2FA) is a more secure solution that requires two different methods to authenticate a user. (For example, some online accounts now require a password as well as a code sent, at the time of logon, to a smartphone as a text message, or through an app installed on the user's phone.)

Biometric security. These are designed to use an individual's unique physical traits to confirm identity. They include fingerprints, facial recognition, iris scans, and voice recognition.

(c) Keeping track of passwords and other access information or credentials

Keeping track of multiple accounts with all the different security features and changing access to information can be a challenge. There are a number of ways to do this, though some methods are less secure and more difficult than others. The most common ways to keep track of accounts and access information are the following:

1. **Password management systems**. There are a number of password management systems and services (both free and commercial), which may consist of apps for smartphones or tablets, software for computers, and websites, that securely store usernames, passwords or credentials, and other sensitive information, and can automatically retrieve them and securely log into the user's online accounts.

   They encrypt login and password information, which is stored in a file (or vault) on the user's own device or online. The user has a master password to unlock or decrypt the data, making it easy to retrieve and update password information. Many also can create new strong passwords to better protect the user's accounts and have the ability to synchronize any updated information to all of the user's authorized devices.

   This makes it much easier to save and manage a large number of passwords and credentials than some of the other methods discussed below. Some popular password management systems and services are LastPass, Dashlane, True Key, Sticky Password, Keeper, RoboForm, OneLogin, and PasswordBox.)[1]

1. For reviews and comparisons of password managers, see ConsumerAffairs.com, "Compare Password Manager Reviews," https://www.consumeraffairs.com/internet/password-managers/# (accessed July 17, 2017).

2. **Other methods of storing passwords and login information.** There are other ways to store and keep track of account access information and credentials, though each have diminishing utility as the number of accounts and passwords a person needs seems to continue to increase. Each of the methods listed below must be manually updated whenever password or account information changes, which may not ensure that all the information is updated with current information in case of the user's death.

   Text file or spreadsheet, which lists accounts and corresponding access information. The user may want to save the list in a password-protected document.

   Checklist used for digital assets estate planning,[1] which will list the most important categories of accounts and their access information. This may be in either hard copy or electronic format.

   Sealed envelope or safe deposit box, with a hard copy list of account and access information. For added security, the information can be divided into two separate documents—one with usernames and the other with passwords. These would be kept separately, either in different locations or by different trusted individuals. This could also be used in conjunction with a password management system, to store the master password.

Planning Point: Clients should be advised to avoid keeping passwords in a will or formal estate planning document, as these documents may be subject to public inspection or otherwise be made available to third parties. Further, relying solely on memorizing passwords comes with the risk of forgetting the passwords and provides no means of passing that information on after }the user's death. Some service providers' terms of service (or federal or state law) may also prohibit sharing passwords with even a trusted third party. *Jason Carr, M.S., M.Ed.*

9047. What measures should be taken to ensure digital assets are preserved for administration of the digital estate after death?

A digital fiduciary should be prepared to take necessary steps to ensure that digital assets of the estate will continue to be in existence throughout the period of administration, probate, or other necessary time period. A digital fiduciary should have, or make, a comprehensive inventory of digital assets and take necessary measures to ensure that the assets are preserved and not deleted or otherwise destroyed except according to the decedent's wishes, or after they have been carried out. (*See* Q 9048) on ultimate disposition or disposal of digital assets.)

Digital assets can be divided into the following categories:

(a) Assets stored on electronic devices and tangible media (offline assets).

(b) Assets stored online, including email and other electronic communications and other online digital assets.

1. *See*, e.g., Digital Estate Information Sample Form, in Gerry W. Beyer, "Web Meets the Will: Estate Planning for Digital Assets," NAEPC Journal of Estate and Tax Planning, vol. 42, No. 3 (Mar. 2015), pp. 28–41 (at pp. 34–37), http://www.naepc.org/journal/issue20p.pdf (accessed July 17, 2017).

Each category of digital assets requires a different approach to preserving the assets after the death of the user, as discussed below. Digital assets stored on electronic devices require different measures than those stored in online accounts. Likewise, online electronic communications are subject to different rules than other online digital assets.

(a) Accessing offline digital assets

Some digital assets, particularly those stored on a person's own electronic hardware devices (computers, smartphones, tablets, digital cameras, etc.) and tangible media (such as external hard drives, flash drives, CD- and DVD-ROMs), are generally within the direct control of the owner or user. A digital fiduciary should take care in the use and handling of electronic devices. Some devices, such as smartphones, can be damaged or even wiped of data after too many unsuccessful login attempts. In addition, external hard drives can be damaged by mishandling and scratches on CDs and DVDs may render any data on them unreadable. To ensure that any digital assets on physical hardware and media is preserved after death, the original items should be stored carefully in protective cases and an appropriate environment (e.g., temperature or humidity controlled). In addition, the digital fiduciary should consider copying digital data from hardware to a separate backup that is kept separately in case of damage or loss of the original source. This is especially important for potentially valuable digital assets and information.

(b) Accessing online digital assets

Unlike digital information stored on physical devices and media, information in online accounts is often out of the direct control of the user and is subject to the particular terms of each online service provider's terms of service agreement. This means that a user must pay special attention to the terms of service and policies of the online service provider.

Some providers may delete a deceased user's account after a specified period of inactivity. In states that have adopted the Uniform Act, sections 7 and 8 set out a process for an executor or administrator of an estate to access the decedent's electronic communications and other digital assets. However, the terms of service may have an important impact on the ease and ability of an executor or administrator to access the deceased user's account. It is important to consult the service provider's policies on deletion of inactive accounts and any procedures the provider has in place to access a deceased user's account. (See also Q 9039 to Q 9040 above.)

1. **Online email and other electronic communications**. Email, social media, and other electronic communications are subject to the Uniform Act in states that have adopted it.

> The Uniform Act (§ 2(12)) defines an *electronic communication* by reference to Federal law, 18 U.S.C. § 2510(12), which defines the term very broadly as "any transfer of signs, signals, writing, images, sounds, data, or intelligence of any nature." This encompasses not only email, but also social media accounts, websites, and many other things. In states that have adopted the Uniform Act, section 7 covers the disclosure of the content of a deceased user's electronic communications.

2. **Online tools**. Online service providers are increasingly recognizing the need to provide tools and procedures to enable access to their account holders' accounts after they die. Under the Section 2(16) of the Uniform Act, these tools and procedures are encompassed within the term "online tool," which is defined as "an electronic service ... that allows the user, in an agreement distinct from the terms-of-service agreement..., to provide directions for disclosure or nondisclosure of digital assets to a third person."These tools are intended to be used by users while they are alive, to make decisions about the disposition of their accounts if the user dies (or in other cases of extended inactivity). An example of such a tool is Google's Inactive Account Manager,[1] which allows users to decide if and when a user's account is treated as inactive, what happens with the account's data, and who is notified.

    Section 4 of the Uniform Act sets out the procedure for use of an online tool to provide directions to the online service provider on disclosure of account information and content. The section also provides for substitution of authorization set out in a will, trust, or power of attorney when a user (the decedent) does not use an online tool or in the absence of an online tool.

3. **Programs for accessing deceased user's account**. Some online tools are created by online service providers to deal with issues surrounding decedents' (and others') accounts. These are covered under the Uniform Act and a user's instructions as expressed using an online tool will take precedence over provisions in a will, trust, or power of attorney.

    Other programs are designed to provide access to the accounts of deceased users. For example, Microsoft has a Next of Kin Process[2] to provide access to a decedent's account.

4. **Fiduciary access**. As discussed above, the fiduciary of a deceased user may access the user's electronic communications, including the content of such communications, and other digital assets, if and to the extent authorized by the user in an online tool, a legal document such as a will, trust, or power of attorney, and the service provider's terms of service.

    When complying with a request to disclose digital assets, a service provider may provide full access, partial access (sufficient to perform the tasks the fiduciary is charged with), or provide "a copy in a record of any digital asset that, on the date the custodian received the request for disclosure, the user could have accessed if the user were alive and had full capacity and access to the account."[3]

5. **Other online digital assets**. The fiduciary of a deceased user may obtain a copy of a catalogue of electronic communications, and the user's (noncommunication) digital assets. Section 8 of the Unified Act provides, "Unless the user prohibited disclosure of digital assets or the court directs otherwise, a custodian shall disclose to the personal representative of the estate of a deceased user a catalogue of electronic communications sent or received by

1. *See* https://support.google.com/mail/answer/14300?hl=en (accessed June 28, 2017).
2. *See* https://answers.microsoft.com/en-us/outlook_com/forum/oaccount-omyinfo/my-family-member-died-recently-is-in-coma-what-do/308cedce-5444–4185–82e8–0623ecc1d3d6 (accessed June 28, 2017).
3. Uniform Act § 6(a)(3).

the user and digital assets, other than the content of electronic communications, of the user, if the representative gives the custodian" [appropriate documentation].

(c) Importance of Terms of Service Agreements

From an estate planning perspective, some terms of service agreement provisions are important to consider, especially when planning for a user's incapacity or death. Each online service provider has its own terms of service and those terms change often. These terms often have restrictions on transferring the account to another person, letting another person use a password, as well as whether and how the account may be accessed after the death of the user.

Some online service providers have terms of service agreement provisions that specifically state that the account and its contents are not transferable to another person, even when of the user dies. (For example, Yahoo![1] and Apple[2] have such a provision, which means that a digital fiduciary administrator may only request the account's deletion. Note, however, that there may be exceptions.)[3]

These may also complicate important tasks, such as retrieving and paying a decedent's online bills and other important documents.

Here are several questions to consider in reviewing terms of service agreements:

1. May the user share the user's password or let others access the user's account?

2. May the user transfer the user's account?

3. Does the user's account terminate on the user's death?

4. What rights to the user's data are being assigned to the company?

9048. How are digital assets ultimately disposed of after death?

If a person has incorporated digital assets into estate planning, the disposition of the digital assets will be accomplished in accordance with the decedent's wishes. In the process of administering the digital estate, some digital assets, such as online accounts, would have been either closed and deleted or transferred to someone else designated by the decedent. The ultimate disposition of the digital assets will include the following:

Ownership or proceeds of assets distributed or transferred. Control of ownership of the assets, or the proceeds from their sale, goes to the designated beneficiaries.

1. *See* Yahoo.com, Help Pages, https://help.yahoo.com/kb/SLN9112.html?impressions=true (accessed July 17, 2017).
2. *See* Apple.com, Discussions, https://discussions.apple.com/thread/5934153 (accessed July 17, 2017).
3. While Yahoo's terms of service provide that "Neither the Yahoo account nor any of the content therein are transferable, even when the account owner is deceased," a Yahoo spokesman said, "While we do not allow access to a decedent's account, if an individual has lawful consent to the account's contents, we will provide the content." Rosalyn Retkwa, "Say you're dead – who gets access to your online accounts?" CBS News (Oct. 31, 2016), http://www.cbsnews.com/news/say-youre-dead-who-gets-access-to-your-online-accounts/ (accessed July 17, 2017).

Online accounts archived (offline), closed, and deleted for privacy reasons, because they are no longer needed, or pursuant to the wishes expressed in a digital assets estate plan.[1]

Data on storage devices securely deleted. Computers, external hard drives, flash drives, memory cards, and similar devices holding digital assets should be securely erased or 'wiped' (for privacy). This may require deleting and then overwriting the data several times to ensure that it cannot be recovered.

Hardware sold or recycled. After securely deleting any data, electronic devices memory storage items may be sold (as proceeds of the estate) or responsibly recycled.

Physical media destroyed and discarded. Physical media such as CD- and DVD-ROMs should be destroyed (*e.g.*, by shredding) and discarded.

Decedent's private or potentially embarrassing data should be discretely and completely deleted or destroyed, according to the decedent's instructions or wishes or merely for the decedent's privacy.

9049. How are digital assets valued for tax and estate planning purposes?

Although digital assets are a new category of asset for tax reporting and estate planning purposes, fiduciaries administering a decedent's digital estate will need to consider their value. Digital assets should be included on estate tax returns and probate inventories, and trust accountings.[2]

Like other assets, digital assets are valued under IRC Section 2031(a) and Treasury Regulation Section 20.2031-1(b), on the basis of fair market value (as defined as the price that would arise in an arm's-length transaction between a willing buyer and a willing seller).[3] Some examples of specific digital assets with likely monetary value include the following:

Money-management and financial accounts, such as online banking and investment accounts, PayPal, loyalty and rewards programs, and any other accounts with credit or value.

Digital currencies, such as bitcoin, which can be valued based on its exchange rate.

---

1. The terms of service for most online accounts prohibit transfer to other individuals. However, it is possible that future changes to those terms may occur, or a transfer mechanism could be created by the online service provider, by legislation, or by judicial action. In that case, the digital fiduciary would be able to transfer the accounts to beneficiaries.
2. *See generally* Elizabeth Ruth Carter, "Estate Planning for Digital Assets: Assigning Tax Basis and Value to Digital Assets" (Oct. 9, 2016). LSU 46th Annual Estate Planning Seminar, Oct. 27-28, 2016. Available at SSRN: https://ssrn.com/abstract=2850156 or http://dx.doi.org/10.2139/ssrn.2850156 (accessed July 20, 2017).

   See also Lauren G. Barron and Samantha L. Heaton, "Digital Assets in Estate Administration: Concerns and Considerations for Fiduciaries." Willamette Management Associates (http://www.willamette.com), *Insights* (Autumn 2014). Available at https://www.faegrebd.com/webfiles/Barron and Heaton Autumn 2014 Insights.pdf (accessed July 20, 2017).

   Many excellent resources for valuation of intangible assets, including digital assets specifically, are available through the website of Willamette Management Associates (http://www.willamette.com).
3. Nontransferable online accounts, licenses, or other digital assets, which effectively terminate after a person's death, should have very little or no value for Federal estate tax purposes. (For example, a decedent's Amazon Kindle library or digital music or videos purchased online, in which there are no transfer rights).

Online businesses and sales accounts, such as an eBay, Etsy, or Amazon store, other commercial websites.

Business customer information, such as client contact information, customer history, account information of business clients, newsletter subscription lists.

Domain names may be valuable and can be sold, often through brokers.

Intellectual property, such as copyrighted works, registered trademarks, and computer applications or programming code.

Other revenue-generating assets, including websites, blogs, certain social media accounts, Internet domain names (whether live/hosted or inactive), art, photos, music, eBooks, and other digital property. If there is ongoing revenue, cash flows from advertisements or royalties may be used to determine value.

9050. What other considerations exist regarding digital assets in estate planning?

Here are some additional tips and suggestions regarding digital assets in estate planning:

1. **Make as many decisions in advance at possible**. The more choices a person makes about digital assets, and incorporate them into digital estate planning, the better are the chances that those wishes will be carried out after death.

2. **Legislative developments**. Make sure to keep up with developments regarding state enactment of legislation regarding digital asset protection, particularly the (Revised) Uniform Fiduciary Access to Digital Assets Act.

3. **Online guides**. There are a number of online information sources, including guides, worksheets, checklists, and other helpful tools for planning the disposition of digital assets after death.

4. **Eliminating any 'skeletons' in the closet**.[1] Questionable browser history, racy photographs, and private health conditions are just a few posthumous scandals a client might want to avoid.

1. Everplans.com, "How to Eliminate All the Skeletons in Your Closet after You Die" (accessed July 20, 2017); *see also* Everplans.com, "Checklist: How to Identify Skeletons in Your Closet" (accessed July 20, 2017).

APPENDIX A

Income Tax Tables

(Tax Years Beginning in 2015 and beyond)

The American Taxpayer Relief Act of 2012 (ATRA) made the income tax brackets put into place under the Economic Growth and Tax Relief Reconciliation Act (EGTRRA) permanent and added a new top tax bracket for certain high income taxpayers. The permanence of the ATRA provisions eliminated much of the uncertainty faced by taxpayers in previous years.

Under ATRA, for tax years beginning after 2012, individual income tax rates are set at 10 percent, 15 percent, 25 percent, 28 percent, 33 percent, 35 percent and 39.6 percent.

Below are the 2017 and 2018 income tax rate brackets.

Individual 2018 Tax Rates

	Taxable Income			
Tax Rate	Single	Married Filing Jointly	Married Filing Separately	Head of Household
10%	$0 to $9,525	$0 to $19,050	$0 to $9,525	$0 to $13,600
15%	$9,525-$38,700	$19,050-$77,400	$9,525-$38,700	$13,600-$51,850
25%	$38,700-$93,700	$77,400-$156,150	$38,700-$78,075	$51,850-$133,850
28%	$93,700-$195,450	$156,150-$237,950	$78,075-$118,975	$133,850-$216,700
33%	$195,450-$424,950	$237,950-$424,950	$118,975-$212,475	$216,700-$424,950
35%	$424,950-$426,700	$424,950-$480,050	$212,475-$240,025	$424,950-$453,350
39.6%	Over $426,700	Over $480,050	Over $240,025	Over $453,350

Estates and Trusts 2018 Tax Rates

Tax Rate	Taxable Income
15%	$0 to $2,600
25%	$2,600-$6,100
28%	$6,100-$9,300
33%	$9,300-$12,700
39.6%	Over $12,700

Individual 2017 Tax Rates

Tax Rate	Single	Married Filing Jointly	Married Filing Separately	Head of Household
	Taxable Income			
10%	$0 to $9,325	$0 to $18,650	$0 to $9,325	$0 to $13,350
15%	$9,325-$37,950	$18,650-$75,900	$9,325-$37,950	$13,350-$50,800
25%	$37,950-$91,900	$75,900-$153,100	$37,950-$76,550	$50,800-$131,200
28%	$91,900-$191,650	$153,100-$233,350	$76,550-$116,675	$131,200-$212,500
33%	$191,650-$416,700	$233,350-$416,700	$116,675-$208,350	$212,500-$416,700
35%	$416,700-$418,400	$416,700-$470,700	$208,350-$235,350	$416,700-$444,550
39.6%	Over $418,400	Over $470,700	Over $235,350	Over $444,550

Estates and Trusts 2017 Tax Rates

Tax Rate	Taxable Income
15%	$0 to $2,550
25%	$2,550-$6,000
28%	$6,000-$9,150
33%	$9,150-$12,500
39.6%	Over $12,500

(2015 and 2016 Tax Years)

Below are the 2015 and 2016 income tax rate brackets.

Individual 2016 Tax Rates

Tax Rate	Single	Married Filing Jointly	Married Filing Separately	Head of Household
	Taxable Income			
10%	$0 to $9,275	$0 to $18,550	$0 to $9,275	$0 to $13,250
15%	$9,275-$37,650	$18,550-$75,300	$9,275-$37,650	$13,250-$50,400
25%	$37,650-$91,150	$75,300-$151,900	$37,650-$75,950	$50,400-$130,150
28%	$91,150-$190,150	$151,900-$231,450	$75,950-$115,725	$130,150-$210,800
33%	$190,150-$413,350	$231,450-$413,350	$115,725-$206,675	$210,800-$413,350
35%	$413,350-$415,050	$413,350-$466,950	$206,675-$233,475	$413,350-$441,000
39.6%	Over $415,050	Over $466,950	Over $233,475	Over $441,000

Individual 2015 Tax Rates

Tax Rate	Single	Married Filing Jointly	Married Filing Separately	Head of Household
		Taxable Income		
10%	$0 to $9,225	$0 to $18,450	$0 to $9,225	$0 to $13,150
15%	$9,925-$37,450	$18,450-$74,900	$9,225-$37,450	$13,150-$50,200
25%	$37,450-$90,750	$74,900-$151,200	$37,450-$75,600	$50,200-$129,600
28%	$90,750-$189,300	$151,200-$230,450	$75,600-$115,225	$129,600-$209,850
33%	$189,300-$411,500	$230,450-$411,500	$115,225-$205,750	$209,850-$411,500
35%	$411,500-$413,200	$411,500-$464,850	$205,750-$232,425	$411,500-$439,000
39.6%	Over $413,200	Over $464,850	Over $232,425	Over $439,000

Corporations†

(Tax Years Beginning in 2013[1])

From	To	The tax is:	Of the amount over:
Taxable Income			
$0	$50,000	15%	N/A
$50,001	$75,000	$7,500 + 25%	$50,000
$75,001	$100,000	$13,750 + 34%	$75,000
$100,001	$335,000	$22,250 + 39%	$100,000
$335,001	$10,000,000	$113,900 + 34%	$335,000
$10,000,001	$15,000,000	$3,400,000 + 35%	$10,000,000
$15,000,001	$18,333,333	$5,150,000 + 38%	$15,000,000
Over	$18,333,333	35%	

† Personal Service Corporations are taxed at a flat rate of 35%.

2018 Inflation Indexed Amounts

In April, 2017, the IRS announced, in Revenue Procedure 2017-37, these 2018 inflation indexed amounts:

Health Savings Accounts. An HDHP has annual deductible of not less than $1,350 for self-only coverage, $2,700 for family coverage, annual out-of-pocket expenses not exceeding $6,650 for self-only coverage, or $13,300 for family coverage. The maximum annual HSA contribution is $3,450 for self-only coverage and $6,900 for family coverage.

1. IRS Publication 542.

APPENDIX B

Transfer Tax Tables

Though the American Taxpayer Relief Act of 2012 made transfer tax rates permanent for tax years beginning after 2012, in an effort to keep you informed, we have inserted material throughout the text to explain the status of the information and changes that have occurred.

2010 Estate and Gift Tax Table

Taxable Gift/Estate		Tax on	Rate on
From	To	Col. 1	Excess
$0	$10,000	$0	18%
10,001	20,000	1,800	20%
20,001	40,000	3,800	22%
40,001	60,000	8,200	24%
60,001	80,000	13,000	26%
80,001	100,000	18,200	28%
100,001	150,000	23,800	30%
150,001	250,000	38,800	32%
250,001	500,000	70,800	34%
500,001	....	155,800	35%

2011-2012 Gift and Estate Tax Table

Taxable Gift/Estate		Tax on	Rate on
From	To	Col. 1	Excess
$0	$10,000	$0	18%
10,001	20,000	1,800	20%
20,001	40,000	3,800	22%
40,001	60,000	8,200	24%
60,001	80,000	13,000	26%
80,001	100,000	18,200	28%
100,001	150,000	23,800	30%
150,001	250,000	38,800	32%
250,001	500,000	70,800	34%
500,001	750,000	155,800	35%

IRC Secs. 2001(c), 2502(a), 2210, as amended by EGTRRA 2001.

2013-2018 Gift and Estate Tax Table

Taxable Gift/Estate From	Taxable Gift/Estate To	Tax on Col. 1	Rate on Excess
$0	$10,000	$0	18%
10,001	20,000	1,800	20%
20,001	40,000	3,800	22%
40,001	60,000	8,200	24%
60,001	80,000	13,000	26%
80,001	100,000	18,200	28%
100,001	150,000	23,800	30%
150,001	250,000	38,800	32%
250,001	500,000	70,800	34%
500,001	750,000	155,800	37%
750,000	1,000,000	248,300	39%
1,000,000		345,800	40%

IRC Secs. 2001(c), 2502(a), 2210, as amended by EGTRRA 2001 and ATRA.

2018 State Estate and Inheritance Tax Table

State	Estate Tax (Rate)	Inheritance Tax (Rate)	Exemption
Alabama	None	None	
Alaska	None	None	
Arizona	None	None	
Arkansas	None	None	
California	None	None	
Colorado	None	None	
Connecticut	7.2%-12%	None	$2 million
Delaware	0.8%-16%	None	$5.49 million
District of Columbia	0.8%-16%	None	$1 million
Florida	None	None	
Georgia	None	None	
Hawaii	0.8%-16%	None	$5.49 million
Idaho	None	None	
Illinois	0.8%-16%	None	$4 million
Indiana	None	None	
Iowa[1]	None	0%-15%	$25,000
Kansas	None	None	
Kentucky[2]	None	0%-16%	$1,000
Louisiana	None	None	
Maine	8%-12%	None	$5.49 million
Maryland[3]	0%-16%	0%-10%	$3 million (estate)
Massachusetts	0.8%-16%	None	$1 million

State	Estate Tax (Rate)	Inheritance Tax (Rate)	Exemption
Michigan	None	None	
Minnesota[4]	9%-16%	None	$1.6 million
Mississippi	None	None	
Missouri	None	None	
Montana	None	None	
Nebraska[5]	None	1%-18%	$40,000/$15,000/$10,000
Nevada	None	None	
New Hampshire	None	None	
New Jersey[6]	0.8%-16%	0%-16%	$675,000 (estate) $25,000 (inheritance for certain relatives only)
New Mexico	None	None	
New York[7]	5%-16%	None	$5.25 million
North Carolina	None	None	
North Dakota	None	None	
Ohio	None	None	
Oklahoma	None	None	
Oregon	0.8%-16%	None	$1 million
Pennsylvania[8]	None	0%-15%	
Rhode Island[9]	0.8%-16%	None	$1.5 million
South Carolina	None	None	
South Dakota	None	None	
Tennessee[10]	None	None	
Texas	None	None	
Utah	None	None	
Vermont	0.8%-16%	None	$2.75 million
Virginia	None	None	
Washington[11]	10%-20%	None	$2.129 million
West Virginia	None	None	
Wisconsin	None	None	
Wyoming	None	None	

[1] Most states that impose an inheritance tax distinguish the applicable tax rate or exemption based upon the person who inherits. In Iowa, a surviving spouse, parents, grandparents, children, grandchildren and certain charitable organizations are exempt from the inheritance tax regardless of the size of the estate. All others who inherit are entitled to the $25,000 exemption.

[2] In Kentucky, a surviving spouse, parents, children, grandchildren, brothers, and sisters are exempt from the state inheritance tax.

[3] Maryland passed a new law in 2014 that will gradually increase the estate tax exemption. The exemption will increase to $2 million (2016), $3 million (2017), $4 million (2018) and by 2019, the exemption will be equal to the federal exemption amount. Maryland's inheritance tax does not apply to surviving spouses, children, grandchildren, parents, grandparents, brothers or sisters of the decedent, among others.

[4] The Minnesota state estate tax exemption will rise by $200,000 each year until it reaches $2 million in 2018.

[5] A surviving spouse is exempt from the inheritance tax in Nebraska no matter how large the estate. The $40,000 exemption applies only to close family members, including parents, grandparents, children, and grandchildren. The $15,000 exemption applies to more distant relatives, including aunts, uncles, nieces, nephews, and the lineal descendants or spouses of these relatives. Any other heir receives the $10,000 exemption.

[6] Spouses, domestic partners, civil union partners, parents, grandparents, children (including stepchildren), grandchildren (but not step grandchildren) are exempt from the inheritance tax. The $25,000 inheritance tax exemption applies to brothers, sisters, spouses or civil union partners of the decedent's child, and surviving spouses or civil union partners of the decedent's child. There is no exemption for any other person who inherits.
[7] The New York exemption amount will increase by $1.0625 million on April 1 of each year until it reaches $5.25 million in 2017. On January 1, 2019, it will jump to the federal estate tax exemption amount.
[8] In Pennsylvania, the inheritance tax does not apply to surviving spouses, parents, stepparents (if the decedent was 21 or younger), charitable organizations and government entities that inherit. The Pennsylvania inheritance tax rates differ depending upon who inherits (children, grandchildren and spouses of children pay a 4.5% rate, while brothers and sisters pay a 12% rate, and all others pay a 15% rate).
[9] The Rhode Island exemption is indexed annually for inflation beginning in 2016.
[10] The Tennessee estate tax is scheduled to be eliminated for 2016 and beyond.
[11] The Washington exemption amount is indexed annually for inflation.

Estate Tax Unified Credit

Year	Exclusion Equivalent	Unified Credit
2000-2001	$675,000	$220,550
2002-2003	$1,000,000	$345,800
2004-2005	$1,500,000	$555,800
2006-2008	$2,000,000	$780,800
2009	$3,500,000	$1,455,800
2010	$5,000,000	$1,730,800
2011	$5,000,000	$1,730,800
2012	$5,120,000	$1,772,800
2013	$5,250,000	$2,045,800
2014	$5,340,000	$2,081,800
2015	$5,430,000	$2,117,800
2016	$5,450,000	$2,125,800
2017	$5,490,000	$2,141,800
2018	$5,600,000	$2,185,800

IRC Sec. 2010(c), as amended by EGTRRA 2001 and ATRA. Rev Proc. 2017-58.

Gift Tax Unified Credit

Year	Exclusion Equivalent	Unified Credit
1977 (1-1 to 6-30)	$30,000	$6,000
1977 (7-1 to 12-31)	120,667	30,000
1978	134,000	34,000
1979	147,333	38,000
1980	161,563	42,500
1981	175,625	47,000
1982	225,000	62,800
1983	275,000	79,300
1984	325,000	96,300
1985	400,000	121,800
1986	500,000	155,800
1987-1997	600,000	192,800

Year	Exclusion Equivalent	Unified Credit
1998	625,000	202,050
1999	650,000	211,300
2000-2001	675,000	220,550
2002-2009	1,000,000	345,800
2010	$5,000,000	$1,730,800
2011	$5,000,000	$1,730,800
2012	$5,120,000	$1,772,800
2013	$5,250,000	$2,045,800
2014	$5,340,000	$2,081,800
2015	$5,430,000	$2,117,800
2016	$5,450,000	$2,125,800
2017	$5,490,000	$2,141,800
2018	$5,600,000	$2,185,800

IRC Secs. 2505(a), 2010(c), as amended by EGTRRA 2001 and ATRA. Rev. Proc. 2017-58.

Maximum State Death Tax Credit (SDTC)

Adjusted Taxable Estate		Credit on	Rate on
From	To	Col. 1	Excess
$40,000	$90,000	$0	0.8%
90,001	140,000	400	1.6%
140,001	240,000	1,200	2.4%
240,001	440,000	3,600	3.2%
440,001	640,000	10,000	4.0%
640,001	840,000	18,000	4.8%
840,001	1,040,000	27,600	5.6%
1,040,001	1,540,000	38,800	6.4%
1,540,001	2,040,000	70,800	7.2%
2,040,001	2,540,000	106,800	8.0%
2,540,001	3,040,000	146,800	8.8%
3,040,001	3,540,000	190,800	9.6%
3,540,001	4,040,000	238,800	10.4%
4,040,001	5,040,000	290,800	11.2%
5,040,001	6,040,000	402,800	12.0%
6,040,001	7,040,000	522,800	12.8%
7,040,001	8,040,000	650,800	13.6%
8,040,001	9,040,000	786,800	14.4%
9,040,001	10,040,000	930,800	15.2%
10,040,001	....	1,082,800	16.0%

For this purpose, the term "adjusted taxable estate" means the taxable estate reduced by $60,000.

Reduction in Maximum SDTC

Year	Multiply Maximum SDTC Above By
2002	75%
2003	50%
2004	25%
2005-2009	NA *
2010	NA *
2011-2018	NA *

*deduction for state death taxes paid replaces credit

IRC Secs. 2011(b), 2011(g), 2058, as amended by EGTRRA 2001 and ATRA.

Qualified Family-Owned Business Deduction

Year	Deduction Limitation
1998-2003	$675,000
2004-2018	NA

IRC Secs. 2057(a)(2), 2057(j), as amended by EGTRRA 2001 and ATRA.

Estate Tax Deferral: Closely Held Business

Year	2% Interest Limitation
1998	$410,000
1999	$416,500
2000	$427,500
2001	$441,000
2002	$484,000
2003	$493,800
2004	$532,200
2005	$539,900
2006	$552,000
2007	$562,500
2008	$576,000
2009	$598,500
2010	($603,000)
2011	$601,600
2012	$486,500
2013	$572,000
2014	$580,000
2015	$588,000
2016	$592,000
2017	$596,000
2018	$608,000

Special Use Valuation Limitation

Year	Limitation
1997-1998	$750,000
1999	$760,000
2000	$770,000
2001	$800,000
2002	$820,000
2003	$840,000
2004	$850,000
2005	$870,000
2006	$900,000
2007	$940,000
2008	$960,000
2009	$1,000,000
2010	$1,000,000
2011	$1,020,000
2012	$1,040,000
2013	$1,070,000
2014	$1,090,000
2015	$1,100,000
2016	$1,110,000
2017	$1,120,000
2018	$1,140,000

IRC Sec. 2032A(a). As updated by Rev. Proc. 2017-58.

Qualified Conservation Easement Exclusion

Year	Exclusion Limitation
1998	$100,000
1999	$200,000
2000	$300,000
2001	$400,000
2002 and thereafter	$500,000

IRC Sec. 2031(c)(3).

Gift (and GST) Tax Annual Exclusion

Year	Annual Exclusion
1997-2001	$10,000
2002-2005	$11,000
2006-2008	$12,000
2009-2010	$13,000
2011-2012	$13,000
2013	$14,000
2014	$14,000
2015	$14,000
2016	$14,000
2017	$14,000
2018	$15,000

IRC Sec. 2503(b). As updated by Rev. Proc. 2017-58.

Gift Tax Annual Exclusion (Donee Spouse not U.S. Citizen)

Year	Annual Exclusion
1997-1998	$100,000
1999	$101,000
2000	$103,000
2001	$106,000
2002	$110,000
2003	$112,000
2004	$114,000
2005	$117,000
2006	$120,000
2007	$125,000
2008	$128,000
2009	$133,000
2010	$134,000
2011	$136,000
2012	$139,000
2013	$143,000
2014	$145,000
2015	$147,000
2016	$148,000
2017	$149,000
2018	$152,000

IRC Sec. 2523(i). As updated by Rev. Proc. 2017-58.

Generation-Skipping Transfer Tax Table

Year	Tax Rate
2001	55%
2002	50%
2003	49%
2004	48%
2005	47%
2006	46%
2007-2009	45%
2010	0%
2011-2012	35%
2013	40%
2014	40%
2015	40%
2016	40%
2017	40%
2018	40%

IRC Secs. 2641, 2001(c), 2664, as amended by EGTRRA 2001 and ATRA.

Generation-Skipping Transfer Tax Exemption

Year	GST Exemption
1997-1998	$1,000,000
1999	$1,010,000
2000	$1,030,000
2001	$1,060,000
2002	$1,100,000
2003	$1,120,000
2004-2005	$1,500,000
2006-2008	$2,000,000
2009	$3,500,000
2010-2011	$5,000,000
2012	$5,120,000
2013	$5,250,000
2014	$5,340,000
2015	$5,430,000
2016	$5,450,000
2017	$5,490,000
2018	$5,600,000

*Plus increases for indexing for inflation after 2012.

IRC Secs. 2631, 2010(c), as amended by EGTRRA 2001 and ATRA, Rev. Proc. 2017-58.

Indexed Amounts Source

Year	Rev. Proc.
1999	98-61, 1998-2 CB 811
2000	99-42, 1999-46 IRB 568
2001	2001-13, 2001-3 IRB 337
2002	2001-59, 2001-52 IRB 623
2003	2002-70, 2002-46 IRB 845
2004	2003-85, 2003-49 IRB 1184
2005	2004-71, 2004-50 IRB 970
2006	2005-70, 2005-47 IRB 979
2007	2006-53, 2006-48 IRB 996
2008	2007-66, 2007-45 IRB 970
2009	2008-66, 2008-45 IRB 1107
2010	2009-50, 2009-45 IRB 617
2011	2010-40, 2010-46 IRB 663
2012	2011-52, 2011-45 IRB 701
2013	2013-15, 2013-5 IRB 444
2014	2013-35, 2013 -47 IRB 537
2015	2014-61,2014-47 IRB 860
2016	2015-53, 2015-44 IRB 1
2017	2016-55, 2016-45 IRB 1
2018	2017-58, 2017-42 IRB 1

APPENDIX C

Summary and Status of State-Level Legislation on Digital Assets[1] as of November 3, 2017

State	Status of Legislation
Alabama	*Status:* Uniform Act adopted (2017). *Statute (codified):* Ala. Code §§ 19–1A-1 – 19–1A-18. *Enacting legislation:* Ala. Sess. Laws Act 2017–316. Ala. Sess. Laws Act 2017-316, enacting Ala. Code §§ 19–1A-1 – 19–1A-18. https://alisondb.legislature.state.al.us/ALISON/SearchableInstruments/2017RS/PrintFiles/HB138-enr.pdf (accessed June 16, 2017). *Effective date:* Jan. 1, 2018.
Alaska	*Status:* Uniform Act not (yet) adopted. 2017 legislation (pending): HB 108 (Alaska), 30th Legislature (2017-2018) (passed legislature Apr. 12, 2017, awaiting transmittal to Governor). http://www.akleg.gov/basis/Bill/Detail/30?Root=HB+108 (accessed June 28, 2017).
Arizona	*Status:* Uniform Act adopted (2016). *Statute (codified):* Ariz. Rev. Stat. § xx-xxxx. *Enacting legislation:* SB 1413 (Ariz. 2016) Revised Uniform Fiduciary Access to Digital Assets Act (approved by Governor and filed with Secretary of State, May 11, 2016). *Effective date:* ___________.
Arkansas	*Status:* Uniform Act adopted (2017). *Statute (codified):* Ark. Code §§ 28-75-101 – 28-75-118. *Enacting legislation:* Ark. Sess. Act 886 (approved Apr. 4, 2017). http://www.arkleg.state.ar.us/assembly/2017/2017R/Acts/Act886.pdf (accessed June 16, 2017). *Effective date:* ___________.
California	*Status:* Uniform Act adopted (2016). *Statute (codified):* Cal. Prob. Code §§ 870–884. *Enacting legislation:* AB-691 (Cal. 2016) Revised Uniform Fiduciary Access to Digital Assets Act (approved by Governor and filed with Secretary of State on Sept. 24, 2016). *Effective date:* ___________. *Previous statute:* Cal. Bus. & Prof. Code § 17538.35 (2010).

1. Source: https://legiscan.com/

State	Status of Legislation
Colorado	*Status:* Uniform Act adopted (2016). *Statute (codified):* Colo. Rev. Stat. § x-x-xxx. *Enacting legislation:* SB 16-088 (Colo. 2016) Revised Uniform Fiduciary Access to Digital Assets Act, (approved by Governor and filed with Secretary of State on April 7, 2016). *Effective date:* ___________.
Connecticut	*Status:* Uniform Act adopted (2016). *Statute (codified):* Conn. Gen. Stat. §§ 45a-334b – 45a-334s, Connecticut Revised Uniform Fiduciary Access to Digital Assets Act. https://www.cga.ct.gov/current/pub/chap_802b.htm#sec_45a-334b (accessed June 16, 2017). *Effective date:* Oct. 1, 2016. *Previous statute:* Conn. Gen. Stat. §§ 45a-334a (repealed 2016).
Delaware	*Status: Functional equivalent to the Uniform Act* (according to the Uniform Law Commission). *Statute (codified):* Del. Code tit. 12, ch. 50, §§ 5001–5007, the Fiduciary Access to Digital Assets and Digital Accounts Act, http://delcode.delaware.gov/title12/c050/, http://delcode.delaware.gov/title12/title12.pdf (accessed June 16, 2017). *Enacting legislation:* HB 345, Fiduciary Access to Digital Assets and Digital Accounts. *Effective date:* August 12, 2014. *Description:* "Recognizing that an increasing percentage of people's lives are being conducted online and that this has posed challenges after a person dies or becomes incapacitated, this Act specifically authorizes fiduciaries to access and control the digital assets and digital accounts of an incapacitated person, principal under a personal power of attorney, decedents or settlors, and beneficiaries of trusts." (From the original synopsis.)
District of Columbia	*Status:* Uniform Act legislation under review by the D.C. Council. 2017 Legislation (pending): B22-0199 (D.C. 2017), Uniform Fiduciary Access to Digital Assets Act of 2017, introduced Mar. 21, 2017; public hearing held June 1, 2017. http://lims.dccouncil.us/Legislation/B22-0199 (accessed June 28, 2017).
Florida	*Status:* Uniform Act adopted (2016). *Statute (codified):* Fla. Stat. § xxx.x-xxx. *Enacting legislation:* SB 494 (Fla. 2016), ch. 740, Florida Fiduciary Access to Digital Assets Act. *Effective date:* July 1, 2016.
Georgia	*Status:* Uniform Act legislation under consideration. *2017 legislation (pending):* SB 301, Revised Uniform Fiduciary Access to Digital Assets Act (Ga. 2017), introduced Mar. 28, 2017. http://www.legis.ga.gov/Legislation/en-US/display/20172018/SB/301 (accessed June 28, 2017).

State	Status of Legislation
Hawaii	*Status:* Uniform Act adopted (2016). *Statute (codified):* Haw. Rev. Stat. § xxx:x-x. *Enacting legislation:* SB 2298 (Haw. 2016), Revised Uniform Fiduciary Access to Digital Assets Act. *Effective date:* July 1, 2016.
Idaho	*Status:* Uniform Act adopted (2016). *Statute (codified):* Idaho Code Ann. § xx-x-xxx. *Enacting legislation:* SB 1303 (Idaho 2016), Revised Uniform Fiduciary Access to Digital Assets Act. *Effective date:* July 1, 2016.
Illinois	*Status:* Uniform Act adopted (2016). *Statute (codified):* xxx Ill. Comp. Stat. § x/x-xxx. *Enacting legislation:* HB 4648 (Ill. 2016) Revised Uniform Fiduciary Access to Digital Assets Act. *Effective date:* Aug. 12, 2016.
Indiana	*Status:* Uniform Act adopted (2016). *Statute (codified):* Ind. Code § xx-x-x-xxx. *Enacting legislation:* Ind. Session Laws, Pub. L. 137 (SB 253 (Ind. 2016), Revised Uniform Fiduciary Access to Digital Assets Act). *Effective date:* Mar. 23, 2016. *Previous statute:* Ind. Code § 19-1-13-1.1 (2007).
Iowa	*Status:* Uniform Act adopted (2017). *Statute (codified):* Iowa Code § xxx.xxxx. *Enacting legislation:* SF 333 (Iowa 2017). *Effective date:* ___________.
Kansas	*Status:* Uniform Act adopted (2017). *Statute (codified):* Kan. Stat. § xx-x-xxx. *Enacting legislation:* SB 63 (Kan. 2017). *Effective date:* ___________.
Kentucky	*Status:* State has NOT adopted Uniform Act. No Uniform Act legislation. [Ky. Rev. Stat. Ann. § xxx.x-xxx]
Louisiana	*Status:* State has NOT adopted Uniform Act. No Uniform Act legislation. *Current statute:* La. Rev. Stat. § 3191.
Maine	*Status:* Uniform Act legislation under consideration. *2017 legislation (pending):* LD 846 (Maine 2017), referred to committee (Mar. 7, 2017). *2016? legislation (NOT enacted):* LD 1177 (Maine 2016?) Maine Uniform Fiduciary Access to Digital Assets Act (died Mar. 10, 2016). [Me. Stat. tit. xx, § x-xxx.]

State	Status of Legislation
Maryland	*Status:* Uniform Act adopted (2016). *Statute (codified):* Md. Code, xxxxx Law § x-xxx. *Enacting legislation:* SB239 / HB507 (Md. 2016) Maryland Fiduciary Access to Digital Assets Act. *Effective date:* Oct. 1, 2016.
Massachusetts	*Status:* Uniform Act legislation under consideration. *2017 legislation (pending):* H 2083 / H 2208 (Mass. 2017), referred to committees. [Mass. Gen. Laws ch. xxx, § x-xxx].
Michigan	*Status:* Uniform Act adopted (2016). *Statute (codified):* Mich. Comp. Laws § xxx.xxxx. *Enacting legislation:* HB 5034 (Mich. 2016), Fiduciary Access to Digital Assets Act, http://www.legislature.mi.gov/documents/2015-2016/publicact/pdf/2016-PA-0059.pdf (accessed June 16, 2017). *Effective date:* June 27, 2016.
Minnesota	*Status:* Uniform Act adopted (2016). *Statute (codified):* Minn. Stat. § xxx.x-xxx. *Enacting legislation:* Minn. Stats., ch. 521A, Revised Uniform Fiduciary Access to Digital Assets Act. *Effective date:* Aug. 1, 2016.
Mississippi	*Status:* Uniform Act adopted (2017). *Statute (codified):* Miss. Code § xx-x-xxx. *Enacting legislation:* HB 849 (Ms. 2017). *Effective date:* ___________.
Missouri	*Status:* Uniform Act legislation under consideration. *2017 legislation (pending):* SB129/HB379 (Mo. 2017). [Mo. Rev. Stat. § xxx.x-xxx.]
Montana	*Status:* Uniform Act adopted (2017). *Statute (codified):* Mont. Code Ann. § xx-xx-xxx. *Enacting legislation:* SB 118 (Mont. 2017). *Effective date:* ___________.
Nebraska	*Status:* Uniform Act adopted (2016). *Statute (codified):* Neb. Rev. Stat. § x-xxx. *Enacting legislation:* LB 829 (Neb. 2016) Revised Uniform Fiduciary Access to Digital Assets Act. *Effective date:* Jan. 1, 2017.
Nevada	*Status:* Uniform Act adopted (2017). *Statute (codified):* Nev. Rev. Stat. §§ xxx.xxxx *Enacting legislation:* Nev. Sess. Laws ch. 38 (approved May 19, 2017). *Effective date:* Oct. 1, 2017.

State	Status of Legislation
New Hampshire	*Status:* Uniform Act legislation under consideration. *2017 legislation (pending):* SB 93 (N.H. 2017), motion to lay on table adopted (June 1, 2017). [N.H. Rev. Stat. § xxx-A: x-xxx.]
New Jersey	*Status:* Uniform Act legislation under consideration. *2017 legislation (pending):* AB 3433 (N.J. 2017), referred to committee (May 1, 2017). *2016 legislation (NOT enacted):* SB 2527 (N.J. 2016), Uniform Fiduciary Access to Digital Assets Act, introduced Sept. 12, 2016 (not enacted). (Would authorize executor or administrator to take control of online accounts of deceased person.) [N.J. Rev. Stat. § xxA:x-xx.]
New Mexico	*Status:* Uniform Act adopted (2017). *Statute (codified):* N.M. Stat. § xx-x-xxx. *Enacting legislation:* SB 60 (N.M. 2017). *Effective date:* ___________.
New York	*Status:* Uniform Act adopted (2016). *Statute:* N.Y. xxxxx Law § x-xxx (Consol.). *Enacting legislation:* AB A9910A (N.Y. 2016). *Effective date:* Sept. 29, 2016.
North Carolina	*Status:* Uniform Act adopted (2016). *Statute (codified):* N.C. Gen. Stat. § xx-x-xxx. *Enacting legislation:* SB 805 (N.C. 2016) Fiduciary Access to Digital Assets. *Effective date:* June 30, 2016.
North Dakota	*Status:* Uniform Act adopted (2017). *Statute (codified):* N.D. Cent. Code § xx-xx-x. *Enacting legislation:* HB 1214 (N.D. 2017). *Effective date:* ___________. *2013 legislation:* HB 1455 (N.D. 2013), introduced Jan. 21, 2013 (failed Apr. 9, 2013). (To create and enact a new chapter to title 34 of the North Dakota Century Code, relating to internet accounts and workplace privacy of social media accounts.)
Ohio	*Status:* Uniform Act adopted (2017). *Statute (codified):* Ohio Rev. Code § xxxx.xx. *Enacting legislation:* HB 432 (Ohio 2017). *Effective date:* ___________.

State	Status of Legislation
Oklahoma	*Status:* Uniform Act NOT adopted; no current legislation. *Current statute:* Okla. Stat. §58-269, http://webserver1.lsb.state.ok.us/OK_Statutes/CompleteTitles/os58.rtf (accessed June 16, 2017. *Effective date:* Nov. 1, 2010. *Full text:* § 58-269. Executor or administrator – Powers. The executor or administrator of an estate shall have the power, where otherwise authorized, to take control of, conduct, continue, or terminate any accounts of a deceased person on any social networking website, any microblogging or short message service website or any e-mail service websites. Added by Laws 2010, c. 181, § 1, eff. Nov. 1, 2010. *2016 legislation (NOT adopted):* SB 1107 (Okla. 2016), Uniform Fiduciary Access to Digital Assets (introduced Jan. 19, 2016; not enacted).
Oregon	*Status:* Uniform Act adopted (2016). *Statute (codified):* Or. Rev. Stat. § xx.xxxx. *Enacting legislation:* SB 1554 (Or. 2016) Revised Uniform Fiduciary Access to Digital Assets Act. *Effective date:* Jan. 1, 2017. [Oregon's Summary of Legislation, 2016] https://www.oregonlegislature.gov/citizen_engagement/Reports/2016SummaryOfLegislation.pdf
Pennsylvania	*Status:* Uniform Act NOT adopted; no current legislation. (State has no statute directly applicable to digital assets.) *2015 legislation (NOT enacted):* SB 518 (Pa. 2015), Revised Uniform Fiduciary Access to Digital Assets Act, Amending Title 20 (Decedents, Estates and Fiduciaries) (introduced Feb. 20, 2015; passed House Nov. 18, 2015; referred to Judiciary Cmte. Nov. 18, 2015; not enacted). [Status & Text | Full Text] *2012 Legislation (NOT enacted):* HB 2580 (Pa. 2012), introduced Aug. 23, 2012 (not enacted). (To amend Title 20 (Decedents, Estates and Fiduciaries) of the Pennsylvania Consolidated Statutes, to provide personal representatives power over decedent account on social networking website, micro-blogging or short message service website, or e-mail service website.) [Full Text <http://www.legis.state.pa.us/CFDOCS/Legis/PN/Public/btCheck.cfm?txtType=PDF&sessYr=2011&sessInd=0&billBody=H&billTyp=B&billNbr=2580&pn=3959>] [20 Pa. Cons. Stat. § xxxx]

State	Status of Legislation
Rhode Island	*Status:* Uniform Act legislation under consideration. *Current statute:* 33 R.I. Gen. Laws § 33-27-3 (Rhode Island Gen. Laws, tit. 33 (Probate Practice and Procedure), ch. 33-27 (Access to Decedents' Electronic Mail Accounts Act), § 33-27-3). *Effective date:* May 1, 2007. *Description:* (Executors may access email accounts. The state may require a death certificate and documentation of the executor's appointment before the estate's representative can see the deceased person's emails or social networking accounts.) *2017 legislation (pending):* HB 5443 (R.I. 2017). *2016 legislation (NOT enacted):* HB 8125 (R.I. 2016) Revised Uniform Fiduciary Access To Digital Assets Act, introduced April 29, 2016. (Appears to amend or replace current Access to Decedents' Electronic Mail Accounts Act.)
South Carolina	*Status:* Uniform Act adopted (2016). *Statute (codified):* S.C. Code Ann. § xx-x-xxx. *Enacting legislation:* SB 908 (S.C. 2016) South Carolina Uniform Fiduciary Access To Digital Assets Act. *Effective date:* June 3, 2016.
South Dakota	*Status:* Uniform Act adopted (2017). *Statute:* S.D. Codified Laws § xxx-x-xxx. *Enacting legislation:* HB1080 (S.D. 2017) Uniform Fiduciary Access to Digital Assets Act. *Effective date:* July 1, 2017.
Tennessee	*Status:* Uniform Act adopted (2016). *Statute (codified):* Tenn. Code § xx-x-xxx. *Enacting legislation:* SB 326 (Tenn. 2016) Uniform Fiduciary Access To Digital Assets Act. *Effective date:* July 1, 2016.
Texas	*Status:* Uniform Act adopted (2017). *Statute:* Tex. xxxxx Code § x.xxx. *Enacting legislation:* SB 1193 (Tex. 2017). *Effective date:* Sept. 1, 2017.
Utah	*Status:* Uniform Act adopted (2017). *Statute (codified):* Utah Code § xxA x-xxx. *Enacting legislation:* HB 13 (Utah 2017). *Effective date:* ___________. *2016 legislation (NOT enacted):* HB 383 (Utah 2016) Uniform Fiduciary Access to Digital Assets Act, introduced Feb. 18, 2016 (not enacted).
Vermont	*Status:* Uniform Act adopted (2017). *Statute (codified):* Vt. Stat. Ann. tit. xxA, § x-xxx. *Enacting legislation:* HB 152 (Vt. 2017). *Effective date:* ___________.

State	Status of Legislation
Virginia	*Status:* Uniform Act adopted (2017). *Statute (codified):* Va. Code § x.x-xxx. *Enacting legislation:* HB 1608 (Va. 2017). *Effective date:* ___________. *Previous statute:* Va. Code § 64.2-110. *2013 legislation:* SB 914 (Va. 2013), introduced Jan. 7, 2013.
Washington	*Status:* Uniform Act adopted (2016). *Statute (codified):* Wash. Rev. Code § xxA x-xxx. *Enacting legislation:* SB 5029 (Wash. 2016) Revised Uniform Fiduciary Access to Digital Assets Act. *Effective date:* June 9, 2016.
West Virginia	*Status:* Uniform Act legislation under consideration. *2017 legislation (pending):* SB 693 (W. Va. 2017), referred to committee (Mar. 30, 2017). [W. Va. Code § xx-x-xxx.]
Wisconsin	*Status:* Uniform Act adopted (2016). *Statute (codified):* Wis. Stat. § xxx.xxx. *Enacting legislation:* AB 695 (Wis. 2016) Revised Uniform Fiduciary Access to Digital Assets Act. *Effective date:* Apr. 1, 2016.
Wyoming	*Status:* Uniform Act adopted (2016). *Statute (codified):* Wyo. Stat. § xx.x-x-xxx. *Enacting legislation:* SF0034 (Wyo. 2016) Uniform Fiduciary Access to Digital Assets Act. *Effective date:* July 1, 2016.

2017 State Legislation on Digital Assets[1]

State	Bill	Status	Summary/Title	Last Action (Most Recent First)
AL	HB 138	Enroll	Fiduciaries, Revised Uniform Fiduciary Access to Digital Assets Act, adopted, fiduciaries, duties with regard to computer files, web domains, virtual currency and other digital assets, Secs. 19-1A-1 to 19-1A-18, inclusive, added [Detail][Text][Discuss]	2017-05-11 Delivered to Governor at 10:13 a.m. on May 11, 2017.
AK	HB 108	Enroll	An Act adopting and relating to the Revised Uniform Fiduciary Access to Digital Assets Act; and relating to a specific electronic communications power that a principal may select for an agent under the statutory form power of attorney. [Detail][Text][Discuss]	2017-04-21 (Passed Legislature, awaiting transmittal to Governor.)
AR	HB 2253	Pass	Revised Uniform Fiduciary Access To Digital Assets Act. [Detail][Text][Discuss]	2017-04-05 Notification that HB2253 is now Act 886
IA	SF 333	Pass	A bill for an act relating to a fiduciary's access to digital assets and including applicability provisions. (Formerly SSB 1086.) Effective 7-1-17. [Detail][Text][Discuss]	2017-04-20 Signed by Governor. S.J. 1113.
KS	SB 63	Pass	Enacting the revised uniform fiduciary access to digital assets act. [Detail][Text][Discuss]	2017-04-06 Senate Approved by Governor on Tuesday, April 4, 2017
MS	HB 849	Pass	An Act To Create The Revised Uniform Fiduciary Access To Digital Assets Act (2015); To Create Definitions For Terms Used In This Act; To Provide For Applicability; To Authorize User Direction For Disclosure Of Digital Assets; To Provide That The Act ... [Detail][Text][Discuss]	2017-04-12 Approved by Governor
MT	SB 118	Pass	Provide for uniform act regarding fiduciary access to digital assets [Detail][Text][Discuss]	2017-05-05 Chapter Number Assigned

1. Source: https://legiscan.com/
No current legislation: 6 States (Delaware, Kentucky, Louisiana, Massachusetts, Oklahoma, and Pennsylvania), plus Puerto Rico, Guam, and the U.S. Virgin Islands.

State	Bill	Status	Summary/Title	Last Action (Most Recent First)
ND	1214	Pass	AN ACT to create and enact a new chapter? 47-36 of the North Dakota Century Code, relating to a Uniform Fiduciary Access to Digital Assets Act. [Detail][Text][Discuss]	2017-03-31 Signed by Governor 03/30
NM	SB 60	Pass	Uniform Fiduciary Access To Digital Assets [Detail][Text][Discuss]	2017-02-19 [LD 34] Signed by the Governor - Chapter 72
NV	AB 239	Enroll	Enacts the Revised Uniform Fiduciary Access to Digital Assets Act. (BDR 59-687) [Detail][Text][Discuss]	2017-05-17 Enrolled and delivered to Governor.
SC	S 0415	Pass	Promote Uniformity Among The State's Forty-six Probate Courts, To Safeguard Adequate Due Process Protections For The State's Alleged Incapacitated Individuals, To Eliminate Over Reliance Upon Restrictive Full Or Plenary Guardianships, To Reduce The C... [Detail][Text][Discuss]	2017-05-09 Signed By Governor
UT	HB 0013	Pass	Uniform Fiduciary Access to Digital Assets Act [Detail][Text][Discuss]	2017-03-15 Governor Signed in Lieutenant Governor's office for filing
VA	SB 903	Pass	Uniform Fiduciary Access to Digital Assets Act. Creates the Uniform Fiduciary Access to Digital Assets Act. The bill allows fiduciaries to manage digital property such as computer files, web domains, and virtual currency, and restricts a fiduciary's ... [Detail][Text][Discuss]	2017-02-20 Governor: Acts of Assembly Chapter text (CHAP0080)
VA	HB 1608	Pass	Uniform Fiduciary Access to Digital Assets Act. Creates the Uniform Fiduciary Access to Digital Assets Act. The bill allows fiduciaries to manage digital property such as computer files, web domains, and virtual currency, and restricts a fiduciary's ... [Detail][Text][Discuss]	2017-02-17 Governor: Acts of Assembly Chapter text (CHAP0033)
VT	H 0152	Pass	An act relating to the Vermont Revised Uniform Fiduciary Access to Digital Assets Act [Detail][Text][Discuss]	2017-05-01 House message: Governor approved bill on 5/1/2017

TABLE OF CASES

(All references are to question numbers.)

TABLE OF IRC SECTIONS CITED

(All references are to question numbers.)

INDEX

References to question numbers.

A

B

C

D

E

I

J

K

L

M

N

Q

R

S

T